THE INDEX OF PSYCHOANALYTIC WRITINGS

ALEXANDER GRINSTEIN, M.D.

Preface by Ernest Jones, M.D.

INTERNATIONAL UNIVERSITIES PRESS, INC.

New York, N. Y.

THE INDEX OF PSYCHOANALYTIC WRITINGS

VOLUME XI

GAARDER—LYRA CHEBABI

73946—81838

INTERNATIONAL UNIVERSITIES PRESS, INC.

New York, N. Y.

Manufactured in the United States of America

CONTENTS

TABLE 1

LIST OF ABBREVIATIONS

Act NP Arg	Acta Neuropsiquíatrica Argentina
Acta psychother psychosom orthopaedag	Acta Psychotherapeutica, Psychosomatica et Orthopaedagogica
Acting Out	Abt, L. E. & Weissman, S. L. (Eds) *Acting Out: Theoretical and Clinical Aspects.* NY/London: Grune & Stratton 1965
Adolescents	Lorand, S. & Schneer, H. I. (Eds) *Adolescents: Psychoanalytic Approach to Problems and Therapy.* NY: Hoeber 1961
Adv ch Develop Behav	Lippsitt, L. P. & Spiker, C. C. (Eds) *Advances in Child Development and Behavior.* NY/London: Academic Pr, Vol 1, 1963; Vol 2, 1965; Vol 3, 1967
Adv PSM	Advances in Psychosomatic Medicine. Fortschritte der psychosomatischen Medizin. Progrès en Médecine Psychosomatique
AJP	American Journal of Psychology
Am Hbk Psychiat III	Arieti, S. (Ed) *American Handbook of Psychiatry.* NY: Basic Books 1966
Am Im	American Imago
Am Psych	American Psychologist
AMA ANP	A.M.A. Archives of Neurology and Psychiatry
An Surv Psa	Frosch, J. (Ed) *The Annual Survey of Psychoanalysis.* NY: IUP
Ann Np Psico-anal	Annali di Neuropsichiatria e Psicoanalisi
Ann Prog child Psychiat	Chess, S. & Thomas, A. (Eds) *Annual Progress in Child Psychiatry and Child Development.* NY: Brunner/Mazel
Arch crim Psychodyn	Archives of Criminal Psychodynamics
ASP	Journal of Abnormal and Social Psychology
Beh Sci	Behavioral Science
BMC	Bulletin of the Menninger Clinic
Bull Ass psa Fran	Bulletin de l'Association Psychanalytique de France
Bull Phila Ass Psa	Bulletin of the Philadelphia Association for Psychoanalysis
Ch Anal Wk	Geleerd, E. R. (Ed) *The Child Analyst at Work.* NY: IUP 1967
Chld Dth Pres	Wolfenstein, M. & Kliman, G. (Eds) *Children and the Death of a President: Multi-Disciplinary Studies.* Garden City, NY: Doubleday 1965
Clin Path	Journal of Clinical and Experimental Psychopathology
Clin Psych	Journal of Clinical Psychology
Compreh Txbk Psychiat	Freedman, A. M. & Kaplan, H. I. (Eds) *Comprehensive Textbook of Psychiatry.* Baltimore: Williams & Wilkins 1967

Contempo PT	Stein, M. I. (Ed) *Contemporary Psychotherapies*. Free Pr of Glencoe 1961
Crosscurrents in Ps & Psa	Gibson, R. W. (Ed) *Crosscurrents in Psychiatry & Psychoanalysis*. Phila/Toronto: J. B. Lippincott 1967
Cuad Psa	Cuadernos de Psicoanálisis. (Associatión Psicoanalítica Mexicana, México)
Curr psychiat Ther	Masserman, J. H. (Ed) *Current Psychiatric Therapies*. NY/London: Grune & Stratton 1961-69
Death & Identity	Fulton, R. (Ed) *Death and Identity*. NY/London/Sydney: John Wiley & Sons, Inc. 1965
Dev Mind	Lampl-de Groot, J. *The Development of the Mind. Psychoanalytic Papers on Clinical and Theoretical Problems*. NY: IUP 1965
Dr Af Beh 2	Schur, M. (Ed) *Drives, Affects, Behavior, Vol 2. Essays in Memory of Marie Bonaparte*. NY: IUP 1965
Dreams Contempo Psa	Adelson, E. T. (Ed) *Dreams in Contemporary Psychoanalysis*. NY: Soc Med Psa 1963
Encéph	Encéphale (et Hygiène Mentale)
Ency Ment Hlth	Deutsch, A. & Fishman, H. (Eds) *The Encyclopedia of Mental Health*. NY: Franklin Watts 1963, 1965
Ess Ego Psych	Hartmann, H. *Essays on Ego Psychology*. NY: IUP 1964
50 Yrs Psa	Wangh, M. (Ed) *Fruition of an Idea: Fifty Years of Psychoanalysis in New York*. NY: IUP 1962
Fortschr PSM	Fortschritte der psychosomatischen Medizin. Advances in Psychosomatic Medicine. Progrès en Médecine Psychosomatique
Fortschr Psa	Fortschritte der Psychoanalyse. Internationale Jahrbuch zur Weiterentwicklung der Psychoanalyse
GAP	Group for the Advancement of Psychiatry
Group PT	Group Psychotherapy
Hbh Kinderpsychother	Biermann, G. (Ed) *Handbuch der Kinderpsychotherapie*. Munich/Basel: Reinhardt 1969
Heirs Freud	Ruitenbeek, H. M. (Ed) *Heirs to Freud. Essays in Freudian Psychology*. NY: Grove Pr 1966
HPI	The Hogarth Press and the Institute of Psycho-Analysis
IJP	Indian Journal of Psychology
Int J grp PT	International Journal of Group Psychotherapy
Int J Np	International Journal of Neuropsychiatry
Int Psa Cong	International Psycho-Analytical Congress
Int Psychiat Clin	International Psychiatry Clinics. Boston: Little, Brown
Int Rec Med	International Record of Medicine
IPC	Imago Publishing Company
IUP	International Universities Press
J	International Journal of Psycho-Analysis
J Am Psa Ass	Journal of the American Psychoanalytic Association
J anal Psych	Journal of Analytical Psychology
J genet Psych	Journal of Genetic Psychology
J ind Psych	Journal of Individual Psychology
J Pers	Journal of Personality
J proj Tech	Journal of Projective Techniques and Personality Assessment

Table 1

viii

J Psa in Groups	The Journal of Psychoanalysis in Groups
J PSM	Journal of Psychosomatic Medicine
JAbP	Journal of Abnormal Psychology
JAMA	Journal of the American Medical Association
Jap J Psa	The Japanese Journal of Psycho-Analysis
Jb Psa	Dräger, K. et al (Eds) *Jahrbuch der Psychoanalyse. Beiträge zur Theorie und Praxis.* Bern: Huber
Jb Psychol Psychother	Jahrbuch für Psychologie und Psychotherapie
JMS	Journal of Mental Science
JNMD	Journal of Nervous and Mental Diseases
Lav Np	Lavoro Neuropsichiatrico
Learn Love	Ekstein, R. & Motto, R. L. (Eds) *From Learning for Love to Love of Learning. Essays on Psychoanalysis and Education.* NY: Brunner/Mazel Publ 1969
Lit & Psych	Literature and Psychology
M	British Journal of Medical Psychology
Marriage Relat	Rosenbaum, S. & Alger, I. (Eds) *The Marriage Relationship: Psychoanalyic Perspectives.* NY/London: Basic Books 1968
Menn Q	Menninger Quarterly
Meth Res PT	Gottschalk, L. & Auerbach, A. H. (Eds) *Methods of Research in Psychotherapy.* NY: Appleton-Century-Crofts 1966
MH	Mental Hygiene
MMW	Münchner medizinische Wochenschrift
Mod Con Psa	Salzman, L. & Masserman, J. H. (Eds) *Modern Concepts of Psychoanalysis.* NY: Philos Libr 1962
Mod Psa	Marmor, J. (Ed) *Modern Psychoanalysis: New Directions and Perspectives.* NY/London: Basic Books 1968
MPN	Monatsschrift für Psychiatrie und Neurologie
NPPA J	National Probation and Parole Association Journal
NTvG	Nederlandsch Tijdschrift voor Geneeskunde
NYSJM	New York State Journal of Medicine
Ops	American Journal of Orthopsychiatry
Ops Law	Levitt, M. & Rubenstein, B. (Eds) *Orthopsychiatry and the Law. A Symposium.* Detroit: Wayne Univ Pr 1968
Out Patient Schiz	Scher, S. C. & Davis, H. R. (Eds) *The Out-Patient Treatment of Schizophrenia.* NY/London: Grune & Stratton 1960
P	American Journal of Psychiatry
PPR	Psychoanalysis and the Psychoanalytic Review
Prax PT	Praxis der Psychotherapie
Problems in Psa	Raclot, M. et al: *Problèmes de Psychanalyse.* Paris: Fayard 1957. *Problems in Psychoanalysis.* A Symposium. Baltimore: Helicon Pr 1961
Proc III World Cong Psychiat 1961	Third World Congress of Psychiatry, Proceedings Montreal, Canada, 4-10 June 1961. Univ of Toronto Pr & McGill Univ Pr
Proc IV World Cong Psychiat 1966	Proceedings of the Fourth World Congress of Psychiatry. Amsterdam/NY/London: Excerpta Medica Foundation 1967-68

Proc RSM	Proceedings of the Royal Society of Medicine
Prog clin Psych	Riess, B. & Abt, L. E. (Eds) *Progress in Clinical Psychology*. NY: Grune & Stratton
Prog Neurol Psychiat	Spiegel, E. A. (Ed) *Progress in Neurology and Psychiatry*. NY: Grune & Stratton
Prog PT	Masserman, J. H. & Moreno, J. L. (Eds) *Progress in Psychotherapy*. NY: Grune & Stratton
Ps	Psychiatry
Psa	American Journal of Psychoanalysis
Psa Amer	Litman, R. E. (Ed) *Psychoanalysis in the Americas: Original Contributions from the First Pan-American Congress for Psychoanalysis*. NY: IUP 1966
Psa Clin Inter	Paul, L. (Ed) *Psychoanalytic Clinical Interpretation*. NY: The Free Pr of Glencoe 1963
Psa Curr Biol Thought	Greenfield, N. S. & Lewis, W. C. (Eds) *Psychoanalysis and Current Biological Thought*. Madison/Milwaukee: Univ Wisconsin Pr 1965
Psa Forum	The Psychoanalytic Forum
Psa–Gen Psychol	Loewenstein, R. M. et al (Eds) *Psychoanalysis—A General Psychology. Essays in Honor of Heinz Hartmann*. NY: IUP 1966
Psa Pioneers	Alexander, F. et al (Eds) *Psychoanalytic Pioneers*. NY/London: Basic Books 1966
Psa St C	Eissler, R. S. et al (Eds) *The Psychoanalytic Study of the Child*. NY: IUP
Psa St Soc	Muensterberger, W. & Axelrad, S. (Eds) *The Psychoanalytic Study of Society*. NY: IUP
Psa Stud Char 1969	Abraham, K. *Psychoanalytische Studien zur Charakterbildung und andere Schriften*. Frankfurt: Fisher 1969
Psa Tech	Wolman, B. B. (Ed) *Psychoanalytic Techniques: A Handbook for the Practicing Psychoanalyst*. NY: Basic Books 1967
PSM	Psychosomatic Medicine
Psych Issues	Psychological Issues
Psychiat Comm	Psychiatric Communications
Psychiat Q	Psychiatric Quarterly
Psychiat Res Rep	Psychiatric Research Reports
Psychodyn St Aging	Levin, S. & Kahana, R. J. (Eds) *Psychodynamic Studies on Aging: Creativity, Reminiscing, and Dying*. NY: IUP 1967
PT	American Journal of Psychotherapy
PT Pervers	Ruitenbeek, H. M. (Ed) *Psychotherapy of Perversions*. NY: Citadel Pr 1967
PUF	Presses Universitaires de France
Q	The Psychoanalytic Quarterly
R	The Psychoanalytic Review
R P PT	Nelson, M. C. (Ed) *Roles and Paradigms in Psychotherapy*. London/NY: Grune & Stratton 1968
Ra Pgc	Rassegna di Psicologia Generale e Clinica
Rass Np	Rassegna di Neuropsichiatria

Table 1

x

Recent Adv biol Psychiat	Wortis, J. (Ed) *Recent Advances in Biological Psychiatry*. NY: Plenum Pr 1960-68
Rev Psicoanál	Revista de Psicoanálisis, Buenos Aires
Rev Psiquiat Psicol	Revista de Psicquiatria y Psicología Médica de Europa y America Latinas
Rev urug Psa	Revista Uruguaya Psicoanálisis
RFPsa	Revue Française de Psychanalyse
Riv Pat nerv ment	Rivista di Patologie Nervosa e Mentale
Riv Psa	Rivista di Psicoanalisi
The Roots of Crime	Glover, E. *Selected Papers on Psycho-Analysis, Volume II. The Roots of Crime*. London: Imago Publishing Co.; NY: IUP 1960
Rv Np inf	Revue de Neuropsichiatrie infantile et d'Hygiène Mentale de l'Enfance
Schweiz ANP	Schweizer Archiv für Neurologie und Psychiatrie
Schweiz Z Psychol	Schweizerische Zeitschift für Psychologie und ihre Anwendungen. Revue Suisse de Psychologie Pure et Appliquée, Bern
Sci Psa	Masserman, J. H. (Ed) *Science and Psychoanalysis*. NY: Grune & Stratton
SE	Strachey, J. (Ed) *Standard Edition of the Complete Psychological Works of Sigmund Freud*. London: Hogarth Pr
Sel P EB	Bergler, E. *Selected Papers of Edmund Bergler, M.D. 1933-1961*. NY/London: Grune & Stratton 1969
Soc	American Journal of Sociology
Soc Casewk	Social Casework
Soc Psych	Journal of Social Psychology
Soc S R	Social Service Review
Teach Dyn Psychiat	Bibring, G. (Ed) *The Teaching of Dynamic Psychiatry*. NY: IUP 1968
Ther Nurs Schl	Furman, R. A. & Katan, A. (Eds) *The Therapeutic Nursery School: A Contribution to the Study and Treatment of Emotional Disturbances in Young Children*. NY: IUP 1969
Tokyo J Psa	Tokyo Journal of Psychoanalysis
WMW	Wiener medizinische Wochenschrift
Why Rep	Freeman, L. & Theodores, M. (Eds) *The Why Report*. NY: Arthur Bernhard 1964
Youth	Erikson, E. H. (Ed) *Youth: Change and Challenge*. NY/London: Basic Books 1963
Z Kinderpsychiat	Zeitschrift für Kinderpsychiatrie
Z PSM	Zeitschrift für psychosomatische Medizin and Psychoanalyse
Z Psychol	Zeitschrift für Psychologie

TABLE 2

ABBREVIATIONS USED
FOR NAMES OF ABSTRACTORS
REVIEWERS, AND TRANSLATORS

AaSt	Aaron Stein	EVN	Eugene V. Nininger
AEC	Alfred E. Coodley	EW	Emory Wells
AHM	Arnold H. Modell		
AJE	Alan J. Eisnitz	FB	Frank Berchenko
AL	Alfred Lilienfeld	FTL	Frank T. Lossy
AN	Alfredo Namnum		
ARK	Arthur R. Kravitz	GD	George Devereux
AS	Austin Silber	GLG	Gerald L. Goodstone
ASt	Alix Strachey	GPK	Geraldine Pederson-Krag
		GZ	Gregory Zilboorg
BB	Bernhard Berliner		
BEM	Burness E. Moore	HA	Herbert Aldendorff
BFM	Bennett F. Markel	HD	Hartvig Dahl
BL	Barbara Low	HFM	Henry F. Marasse
		HK	Hans Kleinschmidt
CBr	Charles Brenner	HL	Herbert Lehmann
CFH	Charles F. Hesselbach	HRB	H. Robert Blank
CG	Claude Girard	HS	Harry Slochower
CK	Curtis Kendrick	HW	Herbert Weiner
CR	Charles Rycroft		
		IBa	I. Barande
DB	Clement A. Douglas Bryan	ICFH	Ivan C. F. Heisler
DJM	David J. Myerson	IK	Irving Kaufman
DRu	David L. Rubinfine	IS	Irwin Solomon
DW	Daniel Weitzner		
		JA	Joseph Afterman
EBMH	Ethilde B. M. Herford	JAA	Jacob A. Arlow
EBu	Edith Buxbaum	JAL	John Arnold Lindon
ECM	E. Colburn Mayne	JB	J. Bernays
EDJ	Edward D. Joseph	JBa	Jose Barchilon
EFA	Edwin Frederick Alston	JBi	Joseph Biernoff
EG	Edward Glover	JC	Joseph Coltrera
EJ	Ernest Jones	JCS	J. Chasseguet-Smirgel
ELG	Eugene L. Goldberg	JFr	John Frosch
EMD	Edward M. Daniels	JKl	John Klauber
EMW	Edward M. Weinshell	JLan	Joseph Lander
ESt	Erwin Stengel	JLL	Jean-Louis Langlois

Table 2   xii

JLS	Jerome L. Saperstein	RCM	R. C. McWatters
JLSt	Julian L. Stamm	RdeS	Raymond de Saussure
JMa	J. Massoubre	RDT	Robert D. Towne
JO	Joel Ordaz	RHB	Ricardo H. Bisi
JPG	Joseph P. Gutstadt	RJA	Renato J. Almansi
JRiv	Joan Riviere	RLG	Renee L. Gelman
JS	James Strachey	RRG	Ralph R. Greenson
JTM	James T. McLaughlin	RSB	Richard S. Bralove
JWS	Joseph William Slap	RTh	Ruth Thomas
		RZ	Robert Zaitlin
KHG	Kenneth H. Gordon, Jr.		
KOS	Kurt O. Schlessinger	SAS	S. A. Shentoub
KR	Kenneth Rubin	SG	Sigmund Gabe
		SGo	Stanley Goodman
LCK	Lawrence C. Kolb	SL	Sidney Levin
LDr	L. Dreyfus	SLe	S. Lebovici
LRa	Leo Rangell	SLP	Sydney L. Pomer
		SO	Shelley Orgel
MBr	Marjorie Brierley	SRS	Stewart R. Smith
MG	Martin Grotjahn	STa	Sidney Tarachow
MGr	Milton Gray		
MK	Mark Kanzer	TC	Theodore Cherbuliez
		TFr	Thomas Freeman
NR	Norman Reider	TGS	Tom G. Stauffer
NRo	Nathaniel Ross		
NZ	Norman E. Zinberg	VC	Victor Calef
		Vega	Gabriel de la Vega
OS	Oscar Sachs		
		WAF	William A. Frosch
PB	P. Blos, Jr.	WAS	Walter A. Stewart
PCR	P. C. Racamier	WCW	William C. Wermuth
PLe	Pierre Levy	WH	Willi Hoffer
PS	Philip Spielman	WPK	William P. Kapuler

G

GAARDER, K.

73946 The internalized representation of the object in the presence and in the absence of the object. J 1965, 46:297-302

See Kafka, John S.

GABAY, J.

See Etchegoyen, Ricardo H.

GABBAY, F.

See Assael, M.; Winnik, Heinrich F.

GABE, SIGMUND

73947 Clinical studies. An Surv Psa 1957, 8:100-170
73948 (& Pomer, S. L.) Clinical studies. An Surv Psa 1958, 9:128-212
73949 Discussion of Kubie, L. S. "Reflections on training." Psa Forum 1966, 1:105-106
73950 (Reporter) The genetic determinants of obsessive-compulsive phenomena in character formation. (Panel: Am Psa Ass, Dec 1964) J Am Psa Ass 1965, 13:591-604
73951 History. An Surv Psa 1955, 6:3-14; 1956, 7:3-43

ABSTRACTS OF:
73952 Greenacre, P. Re-evaluation of the process of working through. An Surv Psa 1956, 7:315-316
73953 Hartmann, H. The development of the ego concept in Freud's work. An Surv Psa 1956, 7:81-82
73954 Kris, E. On some vicissitudes of insight in psychoanalysis. An Surv Psa 1956, 7:303-304
73955 Lampl-de Groot, J. The role of identification in psycho-analytic procedure. An Surv Psa 1956, 7:302-303
73956 Loewenstein, R. M. Some remarks on the role of speech in psychoanalytic technique. An Surv Psa 1956, 7:319-321
73957 Rycroft, C. The nature and function of the analyst's communication to the patient. An Surv Psa 1956, 7:321-322
73958 Tyson, A. & Strachey, J. A chronological hand-list of Freud's works. An Surv Psa 1956, 7:29

REVIEW OF:
73959 Alexander, F. et al (Eds): Psychoanalytic Pioneers. Am Im 1966,
       23:265-273

GABEL, JOSEPH S.

73960 Espace et sexualité. A propos d'un cas de réification sexuelle. [Space
       and sexuality. About an observation of sexual "reification." (Caruso)]
       Ann méd-psychol 1960, 118(2):267-284
73961 Ideologie und Schizophrenie. Formen der Entfremdung. [Ideology and
       Schizophrenia. Forms of Alienation.] (Foreword: Caruso, I. A.) Frank-
       furt a.M.:Fischer 1967
73962 Personalisation und das Unvollendetsein des Menschen. [Personaliza-
       tion and the Incompleteness of Man.] In Edelweiss, M. L. et al: Per-
       sonalisation, Vienna/Freiburg/Basel: Herder 1964, 18-27

GABRIEL, J.

73963 Children's moral development. Austral Psychol 1966, 1:86

GABRIELE, ANTHONY B.

73964 The principle of irrational loyalty. R 1966, 53:69-84
       Abs CG RFPsa 1968, 32:367

GABRIELSON, IRA W.

See Lewis, Melvin

GABURRI, E.

See Simone Gaburri, G. de

GABURRI, GILDA

TRANSLATION OF:
Dosuzkov, T. [71390]

ABSTRACTS OF:
73965 Lagache, D. La psicoanalisi come sublimazione. Riv Psa 1966, 12:
       325-327
73966 Perotti, N. Il contributo della psicoanalisi allo studio del linguaggio.
       Riv Psa 1966, 12:327

GADDINI, EUGENIO

73967 L'arte come espressione clinica. [Art as clinical expression.] Riv Psa
       1965, 11:227-233
73968 Contributo allo studio dell' "Effetto P.E.S." nella situazione analitica.
       [A contribution to the study of the effect of extra-sensory perception
       in the psychoanalytic situation.] Riv Psa 1965, 11:9-32; 12:89-92
73969 La controversia e l'eredità kleiniana. [Kleinian controversy and Klein-
       ian inheritance.] Foreword to Segal, H. Introduzione all'Opera di Mel-
       anie Klein, Florence: Martinelli 1968

73970 Discussion of Bak, R. C. "Sul rapporto oggettuale nella schizofrenia e nelle perversioni." Riv Psa 1967, 13:275

73971 Discussion of Ballanova, P. "Rapporti fra terapia ed espressione pittorica nel'analisi di un omosessuale." Riv Psa 1966, 12:95-97

73972 Discussion of Fajrajzen, S. "Alcune considerazione sull' aggressività controtransferenziale nel trattamento di pazienti psicotici." Riv Psa 1966, 12:106-107

73973 Discussion of Fajrajzen, S. "Reazioni depressive del paziente e dell'analista nella situazione analitica, e natura del processo terapeutico." Riv Psa 1967, 13:318

73974 Discussion of Forti, L. "Utilizzazione della tecnica psicoanalitica in situazioni diverse durante l'infanzia." Riv Psa 1966, 12:103

73975 Discussion of Limentani, A. "Problemi di ambivalenza riparazione e le situazione edipiche." Riv Psa 1967, 13:298-299

73976 Discussion of Matte Blanco, I. "Relazione tra i concetti di introiezione e proiezione e i concetti die spazio e tempo." Riv Psa 1967, 13:314

73977 Discussion of Muratori, A. M. T. "Rapporti oggettuali e struttura del l'io." Riv Psa 1966, 12:87-89

73978 Discussion of Muratori, A. M. "Sogni di progressi et sogni di regressi nella pratica psicoanalitica." Riv Psa 1963, 9:135

73979 Discussion of Muratori, A. M. "Vicissitudini della relazione simbiotica e angosce d'identità." Riv Psa 1967, 13:321-324

73980 Discussion of Servadio, E. "Considerazioni sulla Yoga." Riv Psa 1967, 13:289-290, 292-293

73981 Discussion of Turillazzi, M. S. M. "Evoluzione di alcuni condotte sessuali nel corso di un trattamento psicoanalitico." Riv Psa 1967, 13:307-308

73982 Oggettività e certezza. [Objectivity and certainty.] Riv Psa 1963, 9:135-136

73983 Psicoanalisi e fattori socio-culturali. [Psychoanalysis and socio-cultural factors.] Riv Psa 1963, 9:235-240

73984 Socio-cultural factors in psychoanalysis. Proc III World Cong Psychiat 1961, 121

73985 Sui fenomeni costitutivi del contro-transfert. [On the phenomena which constitute the counter-transference.] Riv Psa 1962, 8:97-118
Über Konstitutivphänomene der Gegenübertragung. Psyche 1964-65, 18:139-159

73986 Sullat imitazione. Riv Psa 1968, 14:77-110
. On imitation. J 1969, 50:475-484

See Benedetti, Reneta De

ABSTRACTS OF:

73987 Balint, M. The younger sister and Prince Charming. Riv Psa 1965, 11:184

73988 Barchilon, J. Analysis of a woman with incipient rheumatoid arthritis. Riv Psa 1965, 11:75

73989 Bonnard, A. Impediments of speech: a special psychosomatic instance. Riv Psa 1965, 11:74

73990 Fairbairn, W. R. D. Synopsis of an object-relations theory of the personality. Riv Psa 1965, 11:184

73991 Giovacchini, P. L. Somatic symptoms and the transference neurosis. Riv Psa 1965, 11:75
73992 Lewis, W. C. Some observations relevant to early defences and precursors. Riv Psa 1965, 11:73
73993 Weissman, P. The effects of preoedipal paternal attitudes on development and character. Riv Psa 1965, 11:72

GADDINI, R.

See Mussen, Paul Henry

GADPAILLE, WARREN J.

73994 The analyst as auxiliary ego in the treatment of action-inhibited patients. Sci Psa 1967, 11:161-181
73995 Discussion of Werkman, S. L. "Identity and creative surge in adolescence." Sci Psa 1966, 9:57-60
73996 Homosexual activity and homosexuality in adolescence. Sci Psa 1969, 15:60-70
73997 Homosexuality experience in adolescence. Med Asp hum Sexual 1968, 11(10):29-38
73998 Infertility and amenorrhea in the hysterical character. In *The Collected Award Papers*, NY: Gralnick Foundation 1966, 131-158

GAETE, S.

73998A [Consciousness as meaning.] (Sp) Actas Luso Esp Neurol Psiquiat 1969, 28:306-330

GAGNON, J. H.

73999 Insight and outlook. Partisan Rev 1967, 34:400-414

GAGNON, JOHN H.

74000 Sexuality and sexual learning in the child. Ps 1965, 28:212-228

GAIER, EUGENE L.

74001 (& Collier, M. J.) Adult reactions to preferred childhood stories: a Finnish-American comparison. Psa St Soc 1962, 2:263-279

See Collier, Mary Jeffrey; White, William F.

GAIR, DONALD S.

See Laufer, Maurice W.

GAIRINGER, LYDA ZACCARIA

74002 Discussion of Abadi, M. "Psicoterapia e psicodisleptici." Riv Psa 1967, 13:278
74003 Discussion of Muratori, A. M. "Sogni di progresso et sogni di regressi nella pratica psicoanalitica." Riv Psa 1963, 9:132

TRANSLATIONS OF:
Deutsch, H. [6777]. Kris, E. [18929]

REVIEW OF:
74004 Bak, R. C. Sul rapporto oggettuale nella schizofrenia e nelle perversioni. Riv Psa 1967, 13:275

GAITONDE, MANESH RAJARAM

74005 Hindu philosophy and analytic psychotherapy. Comprehen Psychiat
1961, 2:299-303

GALANTER, EUGENE H.

See Levine, Murray

74005A Effects of sexual arousal and guilt upon free associative sexual responses. J consult clin Psychol 1968, 32:707-711

GALBRAITH, GARY G.

74006 (& Hahn, K.; Leiberman, H.) Personality correlates of free-associative
sex responses to double-entendre words. J consult clin Psychol 1968,
32:193-197
74006A Reliability of free associative sexual responses. J consult clin Psychol
1968, 32:622

GALBRECHT, CHARLES R.

See Reese, William G.

GALDO, ANNA MARIA

74007 Gratificazione e frustrazione nella psicoterapia di un bambino psicotico.
[Gratification and frustration in psychotherapy of a psychotic child.]
Inf Anorm 1966, 67:3-27. Riv Psa 1966, 12:98

ABSTRACT OF:
74008 Held, R. Contribution à l'étude psychonalytique du phenonomènes
religieux. Riv Psa 1965, 11:76

GALDSTON, IAGO

74009 Discussion of Ackerman, N. W. "Psychotherapy with the family group."
Sci Psa 1961, 4:156-157
74010 Discussion of Niederland, W. G. "A contribution to the psychology of
gambling." Psa Forum 1967, 2:180-181
74011 Ethos, existentialism and psychotherapy. MH 1960, 33:529-534
74012 An existential clinical exposition of the ontogenic thrust. Psa 1964,
24:210-215
74013 Existential factors in psychotherapy. Existentialism and psychiatry: a
round table discussion. Psa 1963, 23:23-25
74014 Existentialism as a perennial philosophy of life and being. J existent
Psychiat 1960-61, 1:379-391

74015 (Ed) The Family: A Focal Point in Health Education. NY: IUP 1961, 216 p

S-46851 Freud's influence on contemporary culture.
Abs Falick, M. L. An Surv Psa 1956, 7:25-26

74016 The gambler and his love. P 1960, 117:553-555

74017 (Ed) Historic Derivations of Modern Psychiatry. NY: McGraw-Hill 1967, xiv + 241 p

74018 (Ed) Man's Image in Medicine and Anthropology. (Foreword: Fejos, P.) NY: IUP 1963, xvii + 525 p

74019 (Ed) Medicine and the Other Disciplines. New York Academy of Medicine. NY: IUP 1960

S-46853 A midcentury assessment of the residuum of Freud's psychoanalytic theory.
Abs RZ An Surv Psa 1957, 8:15-16

74020 On medical historiography—by way of introduction. In author's *Historic Derivations of Modern Psychiatry* 1-8

74021 Psyche and soul: psychiatry in the Middle Ages. In author's *Historic Derivations of Modern Psychiatry* 19-40

74022 Psychiatry and the maverick. Sci Psa 1968, 13:1-17

74023 (Ed) Psychoanalysis in Present-Day Psychiatry. NY: Brunner/Mazel 1969, xix + 69 p

74024 Psychoanalysis 1959. Bull NY Acad Med 1960, 36:702-713

74025 The psychopathology of paternal deprivation. Sci Psa 1969, 14:14-45

74026 Retrospect and prospect. In author's *Man's Image in Medicine and Anthropology* 521-525

GALDSTONE, A. I.

See Burnham, Donald L.

GALE, CONRAD

See Beres, David

GALEANO, J.

ABSTRACT OF:

74027 Grunberger, B. Essai sur la situation analytique et le processus de guérison. Rev urug Psa 1961-62, 4:378

GALEF, HAROLD R.

74028 A case of transvestism in a six year old boy. J Hillside Hosp 1965, 4:160-177

See Charatan, Fred B.

ABSTRACTS OF:

74029 Castaldo, V. & Holzman, P. S. The effects of hearing one's own voice on dream content: a replication. Q 1969, 38:671

74030 Haan, N. A tripartite model of ego functioning values and clinical and research applications. Q 1969, 38:671

74031 Raybin, J. B. Homosexual incest. Q 1969, 38:672

GALENSON, ELEANOR

74032 Comment on Dr. Call's paper, "Newborn approach behaviour and early ego development." J 1964, 45:294-295; RFPsa 1967, 31:481-483
      Abs EVN Q 1966, 35:460-461

74033 Comment on Mr. Khan's paper, "Ego distortion, cumulative trauma, and the role of reconstruction in the analytic situation." J 1964, 45:279
      Abs EVN Q 1966, 35:460

74034 (Reporter) Panel on prepuberty and child analysis. (Am Psa Ass, Dec 1963) J Am Psa Ass 1964, 12:600-609

GALIBERT, JACQUES

74035 Subnarcose amphétaminée et psychothérapie des états d'angoisse. [Subanaesthesia produced by amphetamine and psychotherapy in anxiety states.] Encéph 1960, 49:332-366

GALINSKY, MAEDA J.

See Sarri, Rosemary C.

GALINSKY, MORRIS D.

74036 (& Pressman, M. D.) Intellectualization and the intellectual resistances. (Read at Phila Ass Psa, 10 May 1963; Am Psa Ass, Dec 1963) Bull Phila Ass Psa 1963, 13:153-172
      Abs Cowitz, B. Bull Phila Ass Psa 1963, 13:202-203. EFA Q 1965, 34:134. PLe RFPsa 1967, 31:306

GALLAGHER, EUGENE B.

See Albert, Robert S.; Levinson, Daniel J.

GALLAGHER, JAMES ROSWELL

74037 Adolescents and their disorders. In Cooke, R. E. & Levin, S. *The Biologic Basis of Pediatric Practice*, NY/Toronto/London: McGraw-Hill 1968, 1670-1682

74038 (& Harris, H. I.) Emotional Problems of Adolescents. (Rev ed) London: Oxford Univ Pr 1958, 1964, x + 210 p

GALLAHORN, GEORGE

74039 (& Cushing, J.; Brody, E. B.) Anti-Negro prejudice before, during, and after an acute schizophrenic episode in a white woman. PT 1965, 19:650-652

GALLANT, D. M.

74040 Group staffing on an alcoholism treatment service. Int J grp PT 1964, 14:218-220

GALLART CAPDEVILA, JOSE M.

74041 La psychothérapie analytique dans les milieux socialistes: ses possibilités. [Analytic psychotherapy in socialist environments: its possibilities.] Psychother Psychosom 1967, 15:23

74042   La psychothérapie et la psychanalyse aux pays socialistes: ses possibilités. [Psychotherapy and psychoanalysis in socialist countries: its
possibilities.] Hum Context 1968, 1:93-98; 99-104

GALLI, T.

See Giannelli, A.

GALM, DIETER

74043   Die psychotherapeutische Behandlung eines neunjährigen einkotenden
Knaben. [The psychotherapeutic treatment of a nine-year-old boy
subject to encropresis.] Prax Kinderpsychol 1963, 12:284-288

GALOFRE, A. L.

74044   [The established scientific systems. History of a theory.] (Sp) Rev
Soc Odont Atlant 1967, 7:19-21

GALT, WILLIAM E.

° ° °   (Editor of) Burrow, T. *Preconscious Foundations of Human Experience.*

See Burrow, Trigant

GALTUNG, INGRID EIDE

74045   (& Galtung, J.) Some factors affecting local acceptance of a UN Force:
a pilot project report from Gaza. International Problems 1966, 4:1-25

GALTUNG, JOHAN

74046   Fengselssamfunnet, et Forsøk pa Analyse. [Prison Life, an Attempt to
Analyse.] Oslo: Universitetsforlaget 1959, 250 p
Dutch:The Hague: Bert Bakker
74047   A structural theory of aggression. J Peace Res 1964, 1:95-119. In
Zawodny, J. K. *Man and International Relations,* Vol. I, San Francisco:
Chandler Publ 1966, 545-566

See Galtung, Ingrid E.

GALVIN, JAMES A. V.

74048   (& Ludwig, A. M.) A case of witchcraft. JNMD 1961, 133:161-168

See MacDonald, John M.

GAMARD, R.

74049   Adieu à la médecine psychosomatique. [Farewell to psychosomatic
medicine.] Concours Méd 1961, 83:4375-4377

GAMBLE, KENNETH R.

74050   (& Kellner, H.) Creative functioning and cognitive regression. J Pers
soc Psychol 1968, 9:266-271

GAMBOR, C. GLENN

74051 Creative jazz musicians: a clinical study. Ps 1962, 25:1-15
74052 Emotional factors in hyperthyroidism. Arch gen Psychiat 1961, 4:160-165
74053 Psychotherapy of marital couples. Fam Proc 1963, 2:25-33

GAMM, STANFORD R.

See Basch, Michael F.

GANGER, ROSLYN

74054 (& Shugart, G.) Complementary pathology in families of male heroin addicts. Soc Casewk 1968, 49:356-361
74055 (& Shugart, G.) The heroin addict's pseudoassertive behavior and family dynamics. Soc Casewk 1966, 47:643-649

GANTER, GRACE

74056 (& Yeakel, M.; Polansky, N. A.) Intermediary group treatment of inaccessible children. Ops 1965, 35:739-746
       Abs JMa RFPsa 1967, 31:187
74057 (& Polansky, N. A.) Predicting the child's accessibility to individual treatment from diagnostic groups. Soc Wk 1964, 9(3):56-63

See Polansky, Norman A.

GANTHERET, FRANCOIS

74058 Bibliography of works of Paul Schilder. In Schilder, P. *L'Image du Corps*, Paris: Gallimard 1968

TRANSLATION OF:
(& Truffert, P.) Schilder, P. [29578]

GANTT, F. P.

See Lesse, Henry

GANTT, W. HORSLEY

74059 (& Newton, J. E. O.; Boyer, F. L.) [The mechanism and factors involved in the development of an experimental neurosis.] (Sp) Revista del Hospital Psiquiatrico de la Habana 1964, 5:528-536
       Abs Vega Q 1966, 35:165
74060 Neurophysiologic psychiatry: Descartes to Pavlov and after. In Galdston, I. *Historic Derivations of Modern Psychiatry*, NY: McGraw-Hill 1967, 139-157

GANZARAÍN CAJIAO, RAMÓN

74061 [Disturbances of male sexual functions.] (Sp) Bol Hosp S. Juan 1960, 7:89
74062 [Emotional factors in cardio-vascular disturbances.] (Sp) Bol Hosp S. Juan 1960, 7:89

74063 Die Forschungsarbeit in der Gruppentherapie. Ihre Probleme, Methoden und Aufgaben. [Research in group psychotherapy. Its problems, methods and results.] Psyche 1960, 14:524-537

74064 Human relations and the teaching-learning process in medical school. J med Educ 1966, 41:61

74065 [Psychosomatic aspects of headache.] (Sp) Bol Hosp S. Juan 1960, 7:169

74066 "Psychotic" anxieties in group analytic psychotherapy. Int ment Hlth N L 1960, 2(3 & 4):15

74067 (& Arensburg, B.) Relaciones entre psicoanalistas. [Relations between psychoanalysts.] Rev Psicoanál 1961, 18:26-55
Abs Vega Q 1962, 31:591-592

GANZER, V. J.

See Sarason, Irwin G.

GARAN, D. G.

74068 The Paradox of Pleasure and Relativity: The Psychological Causal Law. NY: Philos Libr 1963, vii + 499 p

GARATTINI, S.

74069 (& Sigg, E. B.) (Eds) Aggressive Behavior. (International Symposium on the Biology of Aggressive Behavior) NY/Amsterdam: Excerpta Medica Foundation 1969, 387 p

GARBARINO, HÉCTOR

74070 Algunos aspectos teóricos y técnicos de la agorafobia. Implicaciones derivadas de su relación con el "periodo umbilical." [Some theoretical and technical aspects of agoraphobia. Implications derived from its relation to the "umbilical period."] Rev urug Psa 1964, 6:99-125
Abs Vega Q 1965, 34:627

74071 Algunas consideraciones acerca del acting out en la enfermedad maniaco-depresiva. [Some considerations on acting out in manic-depressive illness.] Rev urug Psa 1966, 8:363-374
Abs Vega Q 1968, 37:633-634

74072 Contribution to symposium on acting out. (Read at Int Psa Cong, July 1967) J 1968, 49:193-194
Abs LHR Q 1969, 38:668

S-46887 El envejecimiento como un sintoma transitorio.
Abs Vega An Surv Psa 1958, 9:145-146

74073 (& Garbarino, M. F. de; Pizzolanti, G. M. de; Prego, V. M. de) Episodio maniáco en un grupo de niños. [A manic episode in a group of children.] Rev urug Psa 1966, 8:195-199

74074 Mecanismos confusionales en un paciente histérico. [Confusional mechanisms in a hysterical patient.] Rev Psicoanál 1962, 19:80-85

74075 (& Garbarino, M. F. de; Pizzolanti, G. M. de; Prego, V. M. de) El nacimiento y las vicisitudes del héroe. [Birth and vicissitudes of the hero.] Rev urug Psa 1967, 9:225-230

74076   Un núcleo confusional: el muerto vivo. [A confusional nucleus: living death.] Rev urug Psa 1965, 7:119-137

See Agorio, Rodolfo; Baranger, Willy; Garbarino, Mercedes F. de; Prego, Vida M. de

ABSTRACTS OF:
74077   Nacht, S. La névrose de transfert et son maniement technique. Rev urug Psa 1961-62, 4:373
74078   Nunberg, H. Transference and reality. Rev urug Psa 1961-62, 4:183
74079   Rosenfeld, H. Contribution to the discussion on variations in classical techniques. Rev urug Psa 1965, 7:389

GARBARINO, MERCEDES F. DE

74080   (& Garbarino, H.) [Adolescence.] (Sp) Rev urug Psa 1961-62, 4:453-464
        Abs Vega Q 1963, 32:459
74081   La ambiguedad y la identidad del psicoanalista. [Ambiguity and identity in the psychoanalyst.] Rev urug Psa 1965, 7:291-305
74082   El esquema corporal en la terapia de grupo. [The physical scheme in group therapy.] Rev urug Psa 1967, 9:231-235
74083   Estructura de los grupos terapéuticos. [The structure of therapeutic groups.] Rev urug Psa 1967, 9:201-216
74084   Estudio de la evolución del vinculo objetal entre perdida paranoide y perdida depresiva en el análisis de una niña fobica. [Study of the development of object links between paranoid and depressive traits in the analysis of a 4-year-old psychotic girl.] Rev urug Psa 1961-62, 4:621-646
74085   Grupos de niños. [Child groups.] Rev urug Psa 1967, 9:217-223
74086   (& Garbarino, H.) Grupos terapéuticos y grupos ideológicos. [Therapeutic groups and ideological groups.] Rev urug Psa 1961-62, 4:647-665
74087   La importancia de la fantasia del cuerpo en los análisis de niños. [The importance of fantasies about the body in child analysis.] Rev urug Psa 1966, 8:325-329
74088   El pie como medio de communicación en el análisis de una niña. [The foot as a means of communication in the analysis of a girl.] Rev Psicoanál 1961, 18:56-64

See Agorio, Rodolfo; Baranger, Madeleine; Garbarino, Héctor; Prego, Vida M. de

ABSTRACTS OF:
74089   Alvarez de Toledo, L. G. de: El análisis del "asociar" del "interpretar" y de las "palabras." Rev urug Psa 1961-62, 4:350
74090   Grinberg, R. Características de las relaciones de objeto en un claustrofobia. Rev urug Psa 1961-62, 4:546
74091   Mom, M. J. Aspectos teóricos y técnicos en las fobias y en las modalidades fóbricas. Rev urug Psa 1961-62, 4:546
74092   Riviere, J. Contribución al análisis de la reacción terapéutica negativa. Rev urug Psa 1961-62, 4:354

74093   Winnicott, D. W. Hate in the countertransference. Rev urug Psa 1961-62, 4:185

GARCIA, BLANCHE
See Sarvis, Mary A.

GARCÍA, H.
See Lizarazo, A.

GARCIA, ITALIA
74094   La personalidad. [The personality.] ADM 1967, 24:393-418
74095   La personalidad. Conclusión: concentración esquemática de algunas tipologías sobresalientes. [The personality. Schematic summary of some of the most important types.] ADM 1968, 25:75-84

GARCIA, JORGE S.
74096   Algunas consideraciones acerca de la agorafobia. [Some considerations on agoraphobia.] Rev Psicoanal Psiquiat Psicol 1966, 4:34-39

GARCIA, PEDRO F.
See Agoston, Tibor

GARCÍA, ROGER H.
74097   Algunas consideraciones sobre terminacion de análisis. [Some thoughts on termination of analysis.] Cuad Psa 1965, 1:349-354
74098   Angustia, separación y fases integrativas. [Anxiety, separation, and integrative phases.] Cuad Psa 1966, 2:1-18
74099   Transferencia, angustia de separación, angustia de reunión, y el "acting out." [Transference, separation anxiety, anxiety about reunion, and acting out.] Cuad Psa 1967, 3:227-234

GARCIA BADARACCO, J.
See Ajuriaguerra, Julien de

GARCIA-BARROSO, MANUEL
74100   Clinique psychanalytique chez les bègues. [Psychoanalytic clinic with stutterers.] Journée d'Études 1966, 19-21 May. Centre Claude-Bernard 1966, 126-136

GARCIA MONTENEGRO, JOSÉ
See Villalobos, J. Jesus

GARCIA REINOSO, DIEGO
S-46907 La interpretación en pacientes con trastornos de conversión. Abs RHB An Surv Psa 1957, 8:253-254
S-46908 Notas sobre la obesidad a través del estudio de Falstaff. Abs AN An Surv Psa 1956, 7:411

74101 Psicoterapiea en niños psicóticos. [Psychotherapy of psychotic chil-
       dren.] Acta psiquiat psicol Arg 1963, 9:242-249

GARCÍA VEGA, HORACIO

S-46932 Algunos aspectos del análisis de una psicosis paranoide.
       Abs AN An Surv Psa 1956, 7:185
S-46934 Conflictos emotionales y regresión oral-digestiva en un caso de obesi-
       dad neurótica.
       Abs Rodrigue, E. An Surv Psa 1956, 7:201-202

GARDE, M.

74102 (& Verbizier, J. de) Familles imaginaires à l'hôpital psychiatrique.
       [Imaginary families in the psychiatric hospital.] Ann méd-psychol
       1965, 123(2):511-515

GARDINER, MURIEL M.

74103 Discussion of Lubin, A. J. "The influence of the Russian Orthodox
       Church on Freud's Wolf-Man: a hypothesis." Psa Forum 1967, 2:163-
       165
S-46936 Feminine masochism and passivity.
       Abs An Surv Psa 1955, 6:201
74104 Introduction to Memoirs of the Wolf-Man, 1905-1908. Bull Phila Ass
       Psa 1964, 14:77-79
74105 Introduction to Memoirs of the Wolf-Man, 1908, Part I. Bull Phila Ass
       Psa 1967, 17:185
74106 Introduction to Memoirs of the Wolf-Man, 1914-1919. Bull Phila Ass
       Psa 1961, 11:1-5
       Abs Alston, E. F. Q 1962, 31:295-296
74107 The seven years of dearth. Bull Phila Ass Psa 1962, 12:168-170
       Abs PLe RFPsa 1967, 31:303
74108 A snowfall memory. Bull Phila Ass Psa 1963, 13:28-31
74109 The Wolf Man grows older. (Read at Am Psa Ass, May 1963) J Am
       Psa Ass 1964, 12:80-92

       See Augenfeld, Felix

       TRANSLATIONS OF:
       The Wolf-Man [95250, 95252]

GARDNER, A. H.

74110 The adolescent: history and theory. International Circulation Man-
       agers' Association Bulletin 1965, 61:1-3

GARDNER, CHARLES W., JR.

74111 (& Morris, G. O.) Ego changes in hypnosis: visual imagery in the
       trance. In Kline, M. V. Clinical Correlations of Experimental Hypnosis,
       Springfield, Ill: Thomas 1963, 25-42

       See Morris, Gary O.

GARDNER, ELMER A.

74112   (& Miles, H. C.; Bahn, A. K.; Romano, J.) All psychiatric experience in
        a community: a cumulative survey: report of the first year's experience.
        Arch gen Psychiat 1963, 9:369-378
74113   (& Miles, H. C.; Iker, H. P.; Romano, J.) A cumulative register of
        psychiatric services in a community. Amer J publ Hlth 1963, 53:1269-
        1277
74114   (& Babigian, H. M.) A longitudinal comparison of psychiatric services.
        Ops 1966, 36:818-828
            Abs JMa RFPsa 1968, 32:382
74115   (& Miles, H. C.; Iker, H. P.; Romano, J.) Monroe County card-codes
        psychiatric services. Publ Hlth Rep 1963, 78:137-138

        See Babigian, Haroutun M.; Miles, Harold C.; Retchler, R. J.

GARDNER, G. GAIL

° ° °   The facilitative relationship. See [74116]
74116   The psychotherapeutic relationship. Psychol Bull 1964, 61:426-437.
        With title: The facilitative relationship. In Berenson, B. G. & Carkhuff,
        R. R. Sources of Gain in Counseling and Psychotherapy, NY/Chicago/
        San Francisco: Holt, Rinehart & Winston 1967, 284-300
74117   The relationship between childhood neurotic symptomatology and later
        schizophrenia in males and females. JNMD 1967, 144:97-100

GARDNER, GEORGE E.

74118   Adjustment difficulties during adolescence. In Stuart, H. C. & Prugh,
        D. G. The Healthy Child: His Physical, Psychological and Social De-
        velopment, Cambridge, Mass: Harvard Univ Pr 1960, 329-339
74119   The American Child Psychiatry Clinics: internal and external present
        day influences and devolpments. Newsletter Am Ass Psychiat Clin
        Children 1964, 11(2):1-3
74120   The A. M. A. Council on mental health. Hampden Hippocrat 1964,
        20(5):1-4
74121   (& Sperry, B.) Basic word ambivalence and learning disabilities in
        childhood and adolescence. PT 1964, 18:377-392
74122   The child and the adolescent. In Kaufman, M. R. The Psychiatric Unit
        in a General Hospital: Its Current and Future Role, NY: IUP 1965,
        228-239; 284-304
74123   Child psychiatric principles in pediatric training. Med Clin N Amer
        1967, 51:1427-1438
74124   The child with school phobia. Postgrad Med 1963, 34:294-299
74125   (Contributor to) Bauer, W. W. Today's Health Guide, Chicago: AMA
        1965
74126   Discussant: "Physicians in the community." Teach Dyn Psychiat 180-
        185
74127   Discussion in "Observational research with emotionally disturbed chil-
        dren: session 11, Symposium 1958." Ops 1959, 29:590-591
74128   Discussion of Rexford, E. N. "A developmental concept of the prob-
        lems of acting out." J Amer Acad Child Psychiat 1963, 2:6-21. In

Rexford, E. N. *A Developmental Concept of the Problems of Acting Out*, NY: IUP 1966, 17-19

74129   Discussion of Rosenbaum, M. "The role of psychological factors in delayed growth in adolescence: a case report." Ops 1959, 29:762, 769

74130   Discussion of Schleifer, M. J. "The clinical process and research methodology." J Amer Acad Child Psychiat 1963, 2:72-98. In Rexford, E. N. *A Developmental Approach to Problems of Acting Out*, NY: IUP 1966, 97-98

74131   Education and training of physicians in the field of mental retardation. Clin Proc Child Hosp DC 1968, 24:1-12

74132   Foreword: The Treatment of choice. In "Training in child psychotherapy." Reiss-Davis Clin Bull 1966, 3(2):50-52

74133   Historic trends and persisting child care needs. MH 1966, 50:618-623

74134   Juvenile delinquency as a developmental task failure. Wash, DC: US Public Health Service 1959

74135   Mental retardation as part of the training program in child psychiatry. In Bowman, P. W. & Mautner, H. V. *Mental Retardation: Proceedings of the First International Medical Conference*, NY: Grune & Stratton 1960, 505-515

74136   The next decade: expectations from the social sciences and education. In *Mental Retardation: A Handbook for the Primary Physician*. JAMA 1965, 191:223-225

S-46944 (Reporter) Panel: affects, object relations, and gastric secretions.
            Abs KOS An Surv Psa 1956, 7:267

74137   Personality development and childhood behavioral disabilities. In Brill, N. Q. *Psychiatry in Medicine*, Berkeley/Los Angeles: Univ Calif Pr 1962, 161-195

S-46963 (Reporter) Problems of early infancy. (Panel)
            Abs An Surv Psa 1955, 6:253-257

74138   The psychiatric considerations underlying parental concern for handicapped children. Kemcol (International number) 1967, 40:17-24

S-46965 Psychiatric problems of adolescence.
            Abs Rascovsky, A. Rev Psicoanál 1966, 23:210

74139   Publicity and juvenile delinquents. Fed Probation 1959, 23(4):23-25. Juv Court Judges J 1964, 15(2):29-31

74140   The public's right to know (a symposium). J Nat Prob & Parole Assoc 1959, 5:431-442

S-46967 Separation of the parents and the emotional life of the child. In Crow, L. D. & Crow, A. *Readings in Child and Adolescent Psychology*, NY/London/Toronto: Longmans 1961, 545-554

S-46968 Training for the practice of child psychiatry in America. Crianca Port 1958, 17:197-208

See Krug, Othilda; Waldfogel, Samuel

GARDNER, M. ROBERT

ABSTRACTS OF:

74141   Swartz, J. Conformity and non-conformity: some psychoanalytic observations. Bull Phila Ass Psa 1962, 12:40-42

74142   Zetzel, E. R. Aggression and the theory of symptom formation. Bull Phila Ass Psa 1961, 11:88-89

GARDNER, MARTIN

74143   Freud's friend Wilhelm Fleiss and his theory of male and female life cycles. Sci Am 1966, 215(July):108-112

GARDNER, RICHARD ALAN

74144   The Child's Book About Brain Injury. NY: Assoc for Brain Injured Children 1966, 32 p
74145   The family; and the special child. Adams School Bull 1968, 3:1-2
74146   The game of checkers as a diagnostic and therapeutic tool in child psychotherapy. Acta paedopsychiat 1969, 36:142-152
74147   Guilt, Job, and J.B. Med Opin Rev 1969, 5:146-155
74148   The guilt reaction of parents of children with severe physical disease. P 1969, 126:636-644
74149   Mutual storytelling as a technique in child psychotherapy and psycho-analysis. (Read at Am Acad Psa, May 1968) Sci Psa 1969, 14:123-135
74150   The mutual storytelling technique: use in alleviating childhood Oedipal problems. Contempo Psa 1968, 4(2):161-177
74151   Psychogenic problems of brain-injured children and their parents. J Amer Acad Child Psychiat 1968, 7:471-491. In *Management of the Child with Learning Disabilities: An Interdisciplinary Challenge,* San Rafael, Calif: Academic Therapy Publ 1969, 266-271
74152   Sexual fantasies in childhood. Med. Asp hum Sexual 1969, 3:121-134

GARDNER, RILEY W.

74153   Cognitive controls of attention deployment as determinants of visual illusions. ASP 1961, 62:120-127
        Abs Rosen, I. C. Q 1962, 31:590
74154   (& Lohrenz, L. J.) Leveling—sharpening and serial reproduction of a story. BMC 1960, 24:295-304
        Abs HD Q 1961, 30:451-452
74155   Organismic equilibration and the energy-structure duality in psycho-analytic theory: an attempt at theoretical refinement. Closing comments. J Am Psa Ass 1969; 17:3-40; 65-67
74156   (& Moriarty, A.) Personality Development at Preadolescence: Explorations of Structure Formation. Seattle, Wash: Univ Wash Pr 1968, ix + 344 p
74157   (& Jackson, D. N.; Messick, S. J.) Personality Organization in Cognitive Controls and Intellectual Abilities. Psychol Issues Monograph No. 8, NY: IUP 1960, 149 p

        See Holzman, Philip S.; Mayman, Martin; Schlesinger, Herbert J.

GARDNER, WILLIAM

74158   The psychology of Plato. Canad Psychiat Ass J 1968, 13:463-464

GARETZ, FLOYD KENNETH

74159 A statistical study of treatment-oriented behavior. Arch gen Psychiat 1964, 10:306-309

GARFIELD, SOL L.

74160 Interpretation and the interpersonal interaction in psychotherapy. In Hammer, E. F. *Use of Interpretation in Treatment: Technique and Art*, NY: Grune & Stratton 1968, 59-61

GARFIELD, ZALMON

See Wolpe, Joseph

GARFINKEL, ELISA

74161 Técnicas psicotherápicas utilizadas en el tratamiento de las psicosis infantiles. [Psychotherapeutic techniques utilized in the treatment of infantile psychoses.] Act Np Arg 1961, 7(3):199-201

GARFINKEL, H.

See Stoller, Robert J.

GARFST, BETSY P.

74162 Horace Walpole and the unconscious: an experiment in Freudian analysis. Diss Abstr 1968, 29(5-A):1511-1512

GARLAND, JAMES A.

74163 (& Kolodny, R. L.; Waldfogel, S.) Social group work as adjunctive treatment for the emotionally disturbed adolescent: the experience of a specialized group work department. Ops 1962, 32:691-706

GARLAND, JOSEPH

74164 (& Stokes, J., III) (Eds) The Choice of a Medical Career; Essays on the Fields of Medicine. Phila: Lippincott 1961, x + 231 p; 1962 (2nd ed), x + 260 p

GARMA, ÁNGEL

74165 Actualización: investigaciones recientes sobre la sexualidad femenina. [Recent investigations on female sexuality.] Rev Psicoanál 1967, 24: 329-340
74166 Anotaciones psicoanaliticas acerca de Theodor Reik. [Psychoanalytical notes on Theodor Reik.] Rev Psicoanál 1964, 21:358-365
74167 Colour in dreams. J 1961, 42:556-559
Abs WPK Q 1962, 31:581-582
74168 (& Rascovsky, A.; Rascovsky, M.; Tomas, J.) Contribuciones al estudio de la mania. [Contributions to the study of mania.] Rev urug Psa 1966, 8:7-24
Abs Vega Q 1967, 36:476-477

74169 The curative factors in psycho-analysis. (Symposium) Contributions to discussion (ii). J 1962, 43:221-224
Abs RLG Q 1963, 32:598-599

74170 The deceiving superego and the masochistic ego in mania. (Read at Argentina Psa Ass, Nov 1964) Q 1968, 37:63-79

74171 Discussion of Alvarez de Toledo, L. G. et al: "Terminación del análisis didáctico." Rev psicoanál 1967, 24:288-291

74172 Discussion of Gitelson, M. "Le première phase de la psychanalyse." RFPsa 1963, 27:453-460

74173 Discussion of Litman, R. E. "Sigmund Freud on suicide." Psa Forum 1966, 1:214-215; 426-427

74174 Discussion of Greenacre and Winnicott: "The theory of the parent-infant relationship. Further remarks." Contributions to discussion (x). J 1962, 43:252-253

74175 Discussion of Sperling, M. "Migraine headaches, altered states of consciousness and accident proneness." Psa Forum 1969, 3:85-88

S-46980 El Dolor de Cabeza.
Les Maux de Tête. (Tr: Hawelka, E. R.) Paris: PUF 1962, 122 p
Rv Kestenberg, J. RFPsa 1964, 28:441-442

S-46981 Dynamik des Fetischismus.
Abs HFM An Surv Psa 1958, 9:180

74176 Early history of the Pan-American Psychoanalytic Congress. Psa Amer 3-8

74177 La evolución de las sintomas psicosomaticos. [The evolution of psychosomatic symptoms.] Rev Psicoanál 1969, 26

74178 Freud ante las disidencias y rivalidades de sus discípulos. (La correspondencia entre S. Freud y K. Abraham.) [Freud face to face with dissidents and rivals among his disciples.] Rev Psicoanál 1966, 23:438-449

74179 Les images inconscientes dans la genèse de l'ulcère peptique. [Unconscious images in the genesis of peptic ulcer. RFPsa 1961, 25:843-852

74180 La integración psicosomática en los tratamientos psicoanalíticos de los enfermos orgánicos. [Psychosomatic integration in the psychoanalytical treatment of organic diseases.] Rev Psicoanál 1964, 21:1-18
L'integration psychosomatique dans le traitement psychanalytique des maladies organiques. *XXIV Congrès des Psychanalystes des Langues Romanes,* Paris: PUF 1963. RFPsa 1964-65, 28(Suppl):5-45
Abs Vega Q 1965, 34:313

S-46994 Interpretaciones en sueños del psiquismo fetal. In Rascovsky, A. *El Psiquismo Fetal,* B. Aires: Paidos 1960
Abs RHB An Surv Psa 1957, 8:174-175

74181 Investigaciones recientes sobre el soñar y el dormir. [Recent investigation on dreaming and sleeping.] Rev Psicoanál 1966, 23:182-198
Abs Dupont M., M. A. Cuad Psa 1967, 3:246-247

S-46997 The meaning and genesis of fetishism.
Abs SLP An Surv Psa 1956, 7:213

S-46998 Obesidad y dos tipos de alimentación.
Abs AN An Surv Psa 1956, 7:202

74182 Obituary: Heinrich Racker, Rev Psicoanál 1961, 18:280-282

GASSERT, ROBERT G.

° ° ° (& Hall, B. H.) Mental Health and Religious Faith. See [74229]
74229 (& Hall, B. H.) Psychiatry and Religious Faith. (Foreword: Men-
       ninger, K.) NY: Viking Pr 1964, xx + 171 p. With title: Mental Health
       and Religious Faith, London: Darton, Longman & Todd 1966, xviii +
       171 p.
       Rv Hiltner, S. Am Im 1965, 22:202-203

GASSMAN, F.

See Sussex, James N.

GASSNER, JOHN

74230 Criticism: Far Country, by H. Denker. Educ Theatre J 1961, 13:214-
       217

GASSNER, SUZANNE

74231 (& Murray, E. J.) Dominance and conflict in the interactions between
       parents of normal and neurotic children. JAbP 1969, 74:33-41

GASTAGER, HEIMO

74232 Gruppenpsychotherapie im Rahmen einer psychotherapeutischen Am-
       bulanz. [Group psychotherapy within a psychotherapeutic outpatient
       clinic.] Z PSM 1963, 9:115-118
74233 Der Therapeutische Klub und seine Gruppendynamik. [The therapeu-
       tic club and its dynamics.] Z Psychother med Psychol 1962, 12:238-245
74234 (& Ringel, E.) Therapieversuche beim akuten exogenen Reaktionstyp.
       [Therapeutic trials in the acute exogenous reaction type.] In Hoff, H.
       Therapeutische Fortschritte in der Neurologie und Psychiatrie, Vienna:
       Verlag Urban & Schwarzenberg 1960, 289-294

See Arnold, O. H.

GASTON, W. R.

See Winokur, George

GATARSKI, J.

See Kepinski, A. I. T.

GATHERCOLE, C. E.

See Freeman, Thomas

GATTEGNO, C.

TRANSLATION OF:
(& Hodgson, F. M.) Piaget, J. [86524]

GAUGUE, D.

See Danon-Boileau, Henri

GAUTHIER, YVON

74235 (& Lebœuf, G.) Un cas d'anomalie sexuelle. [A case of sexual anomaly.] Laval Méd 1967, 38:108-112

74236 L'encoprésie en consultation psychiatrique. [Encopresis in a psychiatric consultation.] Canad Psychiat Ass J 1964, 9:57-62

74237 The mourning reaction of a ten-and-a-half-year-old boy. Psa St C 1965, 20:481-494

74238 The mourning reaction of a ten-year-old boy. Canad Psychiat Ass J 1966, 11(Suppl):S307-S308

S-47087 Observation on ego development: the birth of a sibling.
Abs EFA Q 1961, 30:600-601

74239 (& Drapeau, P.; Briones, L.; Leclaire, F.) Rapport preliminaire sur une étude des fonctions du moi chez les enfants encopretiques. [Preliminary report on a study of ego function in encopretic children.] Rv Np inf 1968, 16:727-737

See Bigras, Julien

GAUTNEY, D. B.

See Frede, M. C.

GAY, MICHAEL J.

74240 (& Tonge, W. L.) The late effects of loss of parents in childhood. Brit J Psychiat 1967, 113:753-759

GAY, MICHAEL L.

See Pierce, Chester M.

GAYLIN, WILLARD M.

74241 The homosexual act as a symptom. Psychiat Dig 1964, 25:25-30

74242 (Ed) The Meaning of Despair: Psychoanalytic Contributions to the Understanding of Depression. NY: Sci House 1968, 417 p
Abs J Am Psa Ass 1969, 17:277

74243 The prickly problems of pornography. Yale Law J 1968, 77:579-597

74244 Psychiatry and the law: partners in crime. Columbia Univ Forum 1965, 8(1):23-27

74245 Psychoanaliterature: the hazards of a hybrid. Columbia Univ Forum 1963, 6(2):11-16

See Daniels, George E.; Hendin, Herbert; Ovesey, Lionel

GAZDA, GEORGE MICHAEL

74246 (Ed) Basic Approaches to Group Psychotherapy and Group Counseling. Springfield, Ill: Thomas 1968, xiii x+ 323 p

74247 (Ed) Innovations to Group Psychotherapy. Springfield, Ill: Thomas 1968, xiii + 310 p

GEAHCHAN, DOMINIQUE J.

74248 Deuil et nostalgie. [Grief and nostalgia.] RFPsa 1968, 32:39-65
74249 Discussion of Kestemberg, E. & Kestemberg, J. "Contributions à la perspective génétique en psychanalyse." RFPsa 1966, 30:744-748

GEBHARD, PAUL H.

74250 Fetishism and sadomasochism. Sci Psa 1969, 15:71-80
74251 Homosexual socialization. Proc IV World Cong Psychiat 1966, 1028-1031
74252 Situational factors affecting human sexual behavior. In Beach, F. A. *Sex and Behavior,* NY: Wiley 1965

GEBHARDT, LINDA J.

See Hanawalt, Nelson G.

GEDO, JOHN E.

74253 Concepts for a classification of the psychotherapies. J 1964, 45:530-539
       Abs EVN Q 1966, 35:621-622
74254 Freud's self-analysis and his scientific ideas. (Read at Chic Inst Psa) Am Im 1968, 25:99-117
       Abs JWS Q 1969, 38:509
74255 The narcissistic neurosis. In "Traditional Subjects Reconsidered," Proc 2nd Regional Conf Chicago Psa Soc 1968
74256 Noch einmal der "gelehrte Säugling." [The wise baby reconsidered.] Psyche 1968, 22:301-319
74257 A note on non-payment of psychiatric fees. J 1963, 44:368-371
       Abs EVN Q 1965, 34:619
74258 On critical periods for corrective experience in the therapy of arrested development. M 1967, 40:79-83
74259 The psychotherapy of development arrest. M 1966, 39:25-33
74260 (& Pollock, G. H.) The question of research in psychoanalytic technique. Psa Tech 560-581
74261 (& Sabshin, M.; Sadow, L.; Schlessinger, N.) "Studies on hysteria," a methodological evaluation. J Am Psa Ass 1964, 12:734-751
       Abs JLSt Q 1967, 36:468
74262 Toward a developmental psychopathology. (Read at Chicago Psa Soc, 28 Nov 1967)
       Abs Siegel, S. B. Bull Phila Ass Psa 1968, 18:148-152
74263 Unmarried motherhood: a paradigmatic single case study. J 1965, 46:352-357

       See Gottschalk, Louis A.; Miller, Julian A.; Muslin, Hyman L.; Pollock, George H.; Sadow, Leo; Schlessinger, Nathan

GEEN, R. G.

74263A (& George, R.) Relationship of manifest aggressiveness to aggressive word associations. Psychol Rep 1969, 25:711-714

GEER, JAMES H.
See Bodin, Arthur M.

GEERAERTS, R.
74264 Quelques principes de psychotherapie de l'adolescent. [Some principles in psychotherapy of the adolescent.] Acta neurol psychiat Belg 1959, 59:1111-1115

GEERT-JØRGENSEN, EINAR
74265 Treatment of anxiety neuroses and psychosomatic syndromes by a new librium-metabolite: valium. Acta Psychiat Scand 1963, 39(Suppl No. 169):218-222
74266 Treatment of anxiety neuroses and psychosomatic syndromes using a new librium-metabolite, RO 4-5360. Acta Psychiat Scand 1963, 39 (Suppl No. 169):209-217

GEERTS, F.
74267 [Homosexuality.] (Dut) Belg T Geneesk 1964, 20:392-399

GEERTSMA, ROBERT H.
74268 (& Reivich, R. S.) Repetitive self-observation by videotape playback. JNMD 1965, 141:29-41

See MacAndrew, Craig; Stoller, Robert J.

GEHA, RICHARD, JR.
74269 Albert Camus: another will for death. R 1967, 54:662-678
74270 Richard Crashaw: (1613?-1650?). The ego's soft fall. Am Im 1966, 23:158-168

GEHL, RAYMOND H.
74271 Depression and claustrophobia. (Read at NY Psa Soc, 29 Jan 1963; at Int Psa Cong, July-Aug 1963) J 1964, 45:312-323
        Dépression et claustrophobie. RFPsa 1965, 29:233-255
        Abs Malev, M. Q 1963, 32:464-466. EVN Q 1966, 35:462
74272 Discussion of Weiss, E. "The psychodynamic formulation of agoraphobia." Psa Forum 1966, 1:387-389

GEHLEN, ARNOLD
74273 Ein anthropologisches Modell. An anthropological model. Un modèle anthropologique (sommaire). Hum Context 1968, 1:1-10; 11-20; 21-22

GEHRING, ANNEMARIE
See Blaser, Peter

GEIER, S.
See Soulairac, André

GEIGER, J.

See Suinn, Richard M.

GEIGER, THEODORE

74274 The Conflicted Relationship: The West and the Transformation of
Asia, Africa and Latin America. NY: McGraw-Hill 1967, xiv + 303 p
Rv Daly, R. W. R 1969, 56:481-482

GEIS, GILBERT

See Fulton, Robert

GEISMAR, MAXWELL DAVID

74275 Frank Norris: a gulf without bottom: excerpt from "Rebels and an-
cestors." In Malin, I. *Psychoanalysis and American Fiction*, NY: Dutton
1965, 187-198

GEISSER, SEYMOUR

See Scher, Jordan M.

GEISSMANN, PIERRE

74276 A propos d'un cas. [About a case.] Bull Ass psa Fran 1967, (3)
74277 Discussion du rapport de G. Darcourt. [Discussion of a report by G.
Darcourt.] Bull Ass psa Fran 1968, (4):61-62

GEIWITZ, P. JAMES

See Kimeldorf, Carol

GELB, LESTER A.

74278 Psychotherapy in a corrupt society. Sci Psa 1969, 14:215-227

See Ullman, Montague

GELDER, M. G.

74279 (& Marks, I. M.) Common ground behaviour therapy and psychodynamic methods. M 1966, 39:11-23
74280 Desensitization and psychotherapy research. M 1968, 41:39-46
74281 (& Marks, I. M.) Indications for three kinds of psychological treatment
for phobic states. Proc IV World Cong Psychiat 1966, 2836-2837

See Marks, Isaac M.

GELEERD, ELISABETH R.

74282 Adolescence and adaptive regression. BMC 1964, 28:302-308
Abs McGowan, L. Q 1966, 35:467-468
74283 The beginning of aggressiveness in children. Child Study 1957, 34(4):
3-7

S-47116 Borderline states in childhood and adolescence. In Weinreb, J. *Recent Developments in Psychoanalytic Child Therapy*, NY: IUP 1960, 154-170

> Borderline-Zustande in der Kindheit und Adoleszenz. Psyche 1966, 20:821-836
>
> Abs JA An Surv Psa 1958, 9:307-308

74284 Child analysis: research, treatment, and prophylaxis. J Am Psa Ass 1964, 12:242-258

74285 (Ed) The Child Analyst at Work. NY: IUP 1967, 310 p

> Abs J Am Psa Ass 1968, 16:180. Rv Settlage, C. F. Q 1969, 38:644-647

S-47117 Clinical contribution to the problem of the early mother-child relationship: some discussion of its influence on self-destructive tendencies of fugue states.

> Abs JA An Surv Psa 1956, 7:142-143

74286 Evaluation of Melanie Klein's "Narrative of a child analysis." (Read at Phila Ass Psa, 19 Oct 1962) J 1963, 44:493-506.

> Abs Cowitz, B. Bull Phila Ass Psa 1963, 13:39-41

74287 Intrapsychic conflicts as observed in child analysis. Ch Anal Wk 288-310

* * * Introduction. Ch Anal Wk 1-13

74288 Introduction to panel on child psychoanalysis. The separation-individuation phase: direct observations and reconstructions in analysis. (Read at Int Psa Cong 1969) J 1969, 50:91-94

74289 Some aspects of ego vicissitudes in adolescence. J Am Psa Ass 1961, 9:394-405

> Abs FB Q 1962, 31:416-417. SAS RFPsa 1962, 26:618

S-47118 Some aspects of psychoanalytic technique in adolescence.

> Abs Skolnick, A. An Surv Psa 1957, 8:239-241

74290 Symposium on child analysis. Contributions to discussion (i). (Read at Int Psa Cong, July-Aug 1961) J 1962, 43:338-341

> La psychanalyse infantile d'aujourd'hui. Contribution à la discussion. RFPsa 1964, 28:159-168
>
> Abs RLG Q 1963, 32:605-606

74291 Two kinds of denial: neurotic denial and denial in the service of the need to survive. Dr Af Beh 2:118-127

REVIEWS OF:

74292 Des Lauriers, A. M. The Experience of Reality in Childhood Schizophrenia. Q 1964, 33:110-113

74293 Lorand, R. L. Love, Sex and the Teenager. Q 1966, 35:608-609

74294 Winnicott, D. W. The Family and Individual Development. J 1967, 48:108-111

GELFAND, D.

See Levine, Murray

GELFMAN, MORRIS

74295 Narcissism. PT 1968, 22:296-303

74295A A post-Freudian comment on Sexuality. P 1969, 126:651-657

GELLER, EDWARD

See Eiduson, Bernice T.; Eiduson, Samuel

GELLER, JOSEPH J.

74296 Group psychotherapy in child guidance clinics. Curr psychiat Ther 1963, 3:219-228
74297 The use of group psychotherapy by the practicing psychoanalyst. Sci Psa 1965, 8:234-237
74298 Die Verwendung der Gruppenpsychotherapie für analytische Langzeitbehandlung. [Application of group psychotherapy for long term analytical treatment.] Z PSM 1969, 15:44-51

See Soble, D.

GELLER, MAX

See Blum, Lucille H.

GELLY, R.

See Arnoux, H.

GELMAN, RENÉE L.

74299 (Reporter) Current considerations of character neurosis and symptom neurosis. In "Traditional Subjects Reconsidered," Proc 2nd Regional Conf Chicago Psa Soc 1968

See Weiss, Samuel

ABSTRACTS OF:
74300 Bick, E. Symposium on child analysis. Q 1963, 32:605-606
74301 Bion, W. R. Symposium: the psycho-analytic study of thinking. Q 1963, 32:602-604
74302 Burks, H. L. & Harrison, S. I. Aggressive behavior as a means of avoiding depression. Q 1963, 32:137
74303 Cohen, S. The ontogenesis of prophetic behavior. Q 1963, 32:135
74304 De Monchaux, C. Symposium: the psycho-analytic study of thinking. Q 1963, 32:602-604
74305 Ekstein, R. Special training problems and psychotherapeutic work with psychotic and borderline children. Q 1963, 32:137
74306 Frankl, L. & Hellman, I. Symposium on child analysis. Q 1963, 32:605-606
74307 Garma, A. The curative factors in psycho-analysis. Q 1963, 32:598-599
74308 Geleerd, E. R. Symposium on child analysis. Q 1963, 32:605-606
74309 Gitelson, M. The curative factors in psycho-analysis. Q 1963, 32:598-599
74310 Harlow, H. F. Primary affectional patterns in primates. Q 1961, 30:303-304
74311 Heimann, P. The curative factors in psycho-analysis. Q 1963, 32:598-599
74312 Hellman, I. Symposium on child analysis. Q 1963, 32:605-606

74313 Hilgard, J. R. et al: Strength of adult following childhood bereavement. Q 1961, 30:304
74314 Kaplan, D. M. The emergence of projection in a series of dreams. Q 1963, 32:135
74315 King, P. The curative factors in psycho-analysis. Q 1963, 32:598-599
74316 Kuiper, P. The curative factors in psycho-analysis. Q 1963, 32:598-599
74317 Langer, M. Symposium: selection criteria for the training of psycho-analytic students. Q 1963, 32:601-602
74318 Loesch, J. G. & Greenberg, N. H. Some specific areas of conflict observed in pregnancy: a comparative study of married and unmarried pregnant women. Q 1963, 32:138
74319 Loewald, H. W. The superego and the ego-ideal. Q 1963, 32:599-601
74320 Nacht, S. The curative factors in psycho-analysis. Q 1963, 32:598-599
74321 Ramzy, I. Research in psycho-analysis. Q 1963, 32:602
74322 Rosenfeld, H. The superego and the ego-ideal. Q 1963, 32:599-601
74323 Sandler, J. Research in psycho-analysis. Q 1963, 32:602
74324 Scott, W. C. M. Symposium: a reclassification of psychopathological states. Q 1963, 32:606-607
74325 Segal, H. The curative factors in psycho-analysis. Q 1963, 32:598-599
74326 Shaskan, D. (Chairman): Symposium on combined and individual group psychoanalysis. Q 1961, 30:302-303
74327 Székely, L. Symposium: the psycho-analytic study of thinking. Q 1963, 32:602-604
74328 Toolan, J. M. Depression in children and adolescents. Q 1963, 32:136
74329 Ujamlalc, K. On the bullfight. Q 1963, 32:136
74330 Valenstein, A. F. The psycho-analytic situation. Q 1963, 32:604-605
74331 van der Leeuw, P. Symposium: selection criteria for the training of psycho-analytic students. Q 1963, 32:601-602
74332 Waelder, R. Symposium: selection criteria for the training of psycho-analytic students. Q 1963, 32:601-602
74333 Weigert, E. The superego and ego-ideal. Q 1963, 32:599-601
74334 Windholz, E. The psycho-analytic situation. Q 1963, 32:604-605
74335 Winick, C. & Holt, H. Differential recall of the dream as a function of audience perception. Q 1963, 32:135

GELPERIN, JULES

74336 Transference in the psychotherapy of adolescents; a panel. Bull Chicago soc Adol Psychiat 1968, 2(1)

GEMERT, W.

See Groen, Marten

GENDEL, EDWARD

74337 Chromosomes and sex. Sci Psa 1969, 15:1-11

GENDLIN, EUGENE T.

74338 Client-centered developments and work with schizophrenics. J consult Psychol 1962, 9:205-211. In Lindzey, G. & Hall, C. S. *Theories of Personality*, NY/London/Sydney: Wiley 1965, 1966, 1968, 484-490

74339 Client-centered: the experiential response. In Hammer, E. F. *Use of Interpretation in Treatment: Technique and Art*, NY: Grune & Stratton 1968, 208-227

74340 Existentialism and experimental psychotherapy. In Moustakas, C. *Existential Child Therapy*, NY: Basic Books 1966, 206-248

74341 Experiential explication and truth. J existent Psychiat 1965-66, 6:131-146

74342 Subverbal communication and therapist expressivity trends in client-centered therapy with schizophrenics. J existent Psychiat 1963-64, 4:105-120

See Rogers, Carl R.

GENDROT, J.-A.

74343 La formation psychologique des médecins. [Psychological training of doctors.] Évolut psychiat 1964, 29:559-581

74344 Introduction au colloque sur "Analyse terminée et analyse interminable" de Freud. [Introduction to the round table discussion on rereading in 1966 Freud's "Analysis, terminable and interminable."] RFPsa 1968, 32-215-225

See Kourilsky, R.

GENENDER, J.

See Weil, Jorge N.

GENERALI, I.

74345 (& Cocchi, A.; Caldarini, G.) [Infantile obesity. Psychodynamic aspects.] (It) Atti Accad Med Lombard 1966, 21(Suppl):239-244

See Cazzullo, A. Guareschi

GENERALI, LINE

See Paganoni, Anna Maria

GENEVARD, G.

74346 (& Schneider, P.-B; Jordi, P.; Delaloye, R.; Genton, M.; Gloor, C.; Villa, J. L.) Contribution de la psychothérapie de groupe a la compréhension de la névrose. [A contribution from group psychotherapy to understanding of neuroses.] Évolut psychiat 1961, 26:399-415

See Schneider, Pierre-Bernard

GENIS, ABRAHAM

74347 El concepto de grupo en psicoterápia. [The group concept in psychotherapy.] Rev Psiquiat Psicol 1966, 7:394-398

GENTILI, C.

74347A [The psychopathological aspects of consciousness of one's own personal identity.] (It) Riv Sper Freniat 1969, 93:7-20

GENTON, M.

See Genevard, G.; Schneider, Pierre-Bernard

GEOCARIS, KONSTANTIN

74348 Circumoral herpes simplex and separation experiences in psychotherapy. PSM 1961, 23:41-47
    Abs JPG Q 1961, 30:602

See Stuermann, W. E.

GEORGE, R.

See Geen, R. G.

GERARD, DONALD L.

74349 (& Saenger, G.; Wile, R.) The abstinent alcoholic. Arch gen Psychiat
1962, 6:83-95
74350 (& Saenger, G.) Out-Patient Treatment of Alcoholism. A Study of Outcome and Its Determinants. Toronto: Univ Toronto Pr 1966, 249 p
    Rv Savitt, R. A. Q 1968, 37:454

See Chein, Isidor

ABSTRACTS OF:
74351 Alexander, F. Unexplored areas in psychoanalytic theory and treatment. An Surv Psa 1958, 9:28-30
74352 Bose, B. The phenomenon of compulsion to repeat and its metapsychological significance. An Surv Psa 1958, 9:71-72
74353 Weisman, A. D. Reality sense and reality testing. An Surv Psa 1958,
9:106-108

GERARD, RALPH W.

74354 Neurons and neuroses. In Simon, A. et al: *The Physiology of Emotions*,
Springfield, Ill: Thomas 1961, 163-172
74355 Symbolic visualization—a method of psychosynthesis. Top Probl PT
1963, 4:70-80

See Margolin, Sydney G.

GERICKE, O. L.

74356 (& Lobb, L. G.) The critical role of defense mechanisms in the outcome
of chronic brain syndromes in the aged. J Amer Geriat Soc 1964, 12:
646-651

GERNAY, J. M.

See Bobon, J.

GERO, GEORGE

S-47155 (& Rubinfine, D. L.) On obsessive thoughts.
    Abs An Surv Psa 1955, 6:145-146

74357   Sadism, masochism, and aggression: their role in symptom-formation. (Read at Int Psa Cong, July-Aug 1957) Q 1962, 31:31-42
        Abs LDr RFPsa 1963, 27:358

        See Hoch, Paul H.

        REVIEWS OF:
74358   Abraham, K. On Character and Libido Development: Six Essays. Q 1968, 37:283-285
74359   Bremer, J. Asexualization. A Follow-up Study of 244 Cases. Q 1961, 30:587-589
74360   Hendin, H. Suicide in Scandinavia. A Psychoanalytic Study of Culture and Character. Q 1965, 34:111-113
74361   Mendelson, M. Psychoanalytic Concepts of Depression. Q 1962, 31:92-96

GERO-HEYMANN, ELIZABETH

S-47158 A short communication on a traumatic episode in a child of two years and seven months.
        Abs An Surv Psa 1955, 6:272-274

GERÖLY, STEFAN

74362   (Ed) Die Theorie des primären Anklammerungstriebes nach Imre Hermann. [The theory of the early clinging instinct according to Imre Hermann.] Greif Druck, Ujvary K. G. 1963, 84 p

GERSCOVICH, JOSÉ

74363   [The female castration complex and its relation to sexual dysfunctions in women.] (Por) Rev bras Med 1966, 23:322-326
74364   Psiquiatria de orientação analítica. [Analytically oriented psychiatry.] Rev bras Med 1962, 19:47-49
74365   Psiquiatria dinâmica e saúde mental. [Dynamic psychiatry and mental health.] Rev bras Med 1967, 24:24-27
74366   [Psychodynamic aspects of reactive depressions.] (Por) Rev bras Med 1963, 20:361-362

GERSHBERG, JACK M.

74367   The concept of empathy and the development of affect patterning. Psychiat Q 1967, 41:658-682
74368   The concept of father-fixation: an alternate hypothesis. Penn psychiat Q 1964, 4:3-11
74369   The use of dreams in reality testing. Comprehen Psychiat 1969, 10:391-397

GERSHMAN, HARRY

74370   The changing image of sex. Psa 1967, 27:24-33
74371   The evolution of gender identity. Bull NY Acad Med 1967, 43:1000-1018. Psa 1968, 28:80-90

74372 Homosexuality and some aspects of creativity. Psa 1964, 24:29-38
74373 Reflections on the nature of homosexuality. Psa 1966, 26:46-62

See Bieber, Irving

GERSHON, ELLIOT S.

74374 (& Cromer, M.; Klerman, G.) Hostility and depression. Ps 1968, 31:
224-235

GERSHWIN, BENJAMIN S.
See Kaye, Harvey E.

GERSHWIN, PATRICIA
See Kaye, Harvey E.

GERSTEL, GERDA

74375 A psychoanalytic view of artificial donor insemination. PT 1963, 17:
64-77

GERTY, FRANCIS J.
See Carmichael, Hugh T.; Chessick, Richard D.

GERVAIS LAURENT

74376 Bronchial asthma and identification with the aggressor. Canad Psychiat
Ass J 1966, 11:497-500
74377 La dynamique de groupe chez les residents en psychiatrie. [Group
dynamics in psychiatric residents.] Canad Psychiat Ass J 1968, 13:159-
162

GESSAIN, ROBERT

S-47170 "Vagina dentata" dans la clinique et la mythologie.
Abs RJA An Surv Psa 1957, 8:107-108

GETZELS, JACOB W.

74378 (& Jackson, P. W.) Creativity and Intelligence. Explorations with
Gifted Students. NY: Wiley 1962, 293 p
Rv Rosen, V. H. Q 1963, 32:423-425

GHENT, EMANUEL R.
See Shatan, Chaim F.

GHERARDI, DANILO

74379 Memoria e ipnosi. Contributo clinico-sperimentale. [Memory and hypnosis. Clinico-experimental contribution.] Riv Neurol 1964, 34:591-598
74380 Situation, the core of human behaviour. Proc IV World Cong Psychiat
1966, 1525-1527

GHOSAL, HIRONMOY

74381 Jean-Paul Sartre. Samiksa 1967, 21(4):169
74382 Science and psycho-analysis. Samiksa 1967, 21(1):40-53

GHOSAL, S. P.

74383 Hysterical ptosis. Indian J Pediat 1959, 26(139):295-298

GHYSBRECHT, PAUL FRANÇOIS ROSE MARIE

74384 Dieptepsychologie; Psychologie van het Zelfbedrog. [Depth Psychology.] Antwerp: Ontwikkeling 1960, 157 p

GIACANELLI, G.

See Priori, R.

GIACOMO, DONEGANI

74385 (& Grattarola, F. R.) Analisi clinica e psicopatologica delle melancolie. [Clinical and psychopathological analysis of melancholia.] Riv Pat nerv ment 1959, 80:653-672

GIANASCOL, ALFRED JOSEPH

74386 Psychiatry and the juvenile court: patterns of collaboration and the use of compulsory psychotherapy. In Szurek, S. A. & Berlin, I. N. *The Antisocial Child: His Family and His Community*, Palo Alto, Calif: Sci & Behav Books 1969, 149-159
74387 Psychodynamic approaches to childhood schizophrenia: a review. JNMD 1963, 137:336-348
        Abs BFM Q 1965, 34:137-138

GIANNELLI, A.

74387A (& Galli, T.; Vallillo, R.) [On structural interpretation of situational involutive depressions.] (It) Riv Sper Freniatr 1969, 93:21-57

GIBB, JACK R.

74388 Defensive communication. J Commun 1961, 11(Sept):141-148

GIBBINS, ROBERT J.

74389 (& Walters, R. H.) Three preliminary studies of a psychoanalytic theory of alcohol addiction. Quart J Stud Alcohol 1960, 21:618-641

GIBBONS, KATHRYN GIBBS

74390 Quentin's shadow. Lit & Psych 1962, 12:16-24

GIBBONS, M. J.

See Chapman, Arthur H.

GIBBS, JACK P.

74391   (Ed) Suicide. NY: Harper & Row 1968, 338 p

GIBBY, ROBERT G.

See Cooper, G. David

GIBELLO, B.

See Castets, Bruno

GIBERTI, F.

74392   (& Roccatagliata, G.; Rossi, R.) Pseudoneurotic schizophrenia. I. Critical review of the bibliography. Sist Nerv 1965, 17(3):121-148

See Roccatagliata, G.

GIBSON, GUADALUPE

See Ackerly, William C.

GIBSON, JAMES J.

74393   The concept of the stimulus in psychology. Am Psych 1960, 15:694-703

GIBSON, JOHN

See Jarvis, Jennifer M.

GIBSON, RALPH

See Fraiberg, Selma

GIBSON, ROBERT W.

74394   (Ed) Crosscurrents in Psychiatry and Psychoanalysis. Phila/Toronto: J. B. Lippincott 1967, 259 p
   Abs J Am Psa Ass 1969, 17:274. Rv Anderson, A. R. Q 1969, 38: 657-660. Mariner, A. S. R 1968-69, 55:703-706
74395   Discussion of Kubie, L. S. "The future of the private psychiatric hospitals." Crosscurrents in Ps & Psa 200-202
S-47179 The family background and early life experience of the manic-depressive patient. A comparison with the schizophrenic patient. In Palmer, J. O. & Goldstein, M. J. *Perspectives in Psychopathology*, NY: Oxford Univ Pr 1966, 42-62
   Abs WCW Qn Surv Psa 1958, 9:194-195
* * *   Foreword. Crosscurrents in Ps & Psa 5-6
74396   On the therapeutic handling of aggression in schizophrenia. Ops 1967, 37:926-931
74397   Psychotherapy of manic-depressive states. Psychiat Res Rep 1963, 17:91-102

See Burnham, Donald L.

GICKLHORN, JOSEF

S-47179A (& Gicklhorn, R.) Sigmund Freuds akademische Laufbahn im Lichte der Dokumente.
Rv MG Q 1962, 31:96-98

GICKLHORN (OVA), RENÉE

74398   Eine Episode aus S. Freuds Mittelschulzeit. [An episode from S. Freud's intermediate school days.] Unsere Heimat 1965, 36(1/3)
74399   The Freiberg period of the Freud family. J Hist Med 1969, 24:37-43
74400   (& Kalivoda, F.; Sajner, J.) Nové archívní nálezy o detství Sigmunda Freuda v Pribore (Freiberg). [New archive findings concerning Sigmund Freud's childhood in Pribor.] Cesk Psychiat 1967, 63:131-136
        Abs Wiedeman, G. H. Q 1969, 38:124-125

See Gicklhorn, Josef

GIDRO-FRANK, LOTHAR

See Stancer, H. C.

GIEL, R.

74401   (& Knox, R. S.; Carstairs, G. M.) A five-year follow-up of 100 neurotic out-patients. Brit med J 1964, (5402):160-163
74402   Freud and the devil in Ethiopian psychiatry. Psychiat Neurol Neurochir 1968, 71:177-183

GIFFEN, MARTIN B.

See Kahn, Theodore C.

GIFFIN, MARY E.

74403   The role of child psychiatry in learning disabilities. In Myklebust, H. R. *Progress in Learning Disabilities, Vol. 1*, NY/London: Grune & Stratton 1968, 75-97
74404   Value judgments in psychiatry and religion. J Relig Hlth 1965, 4:180-187

See Johnson, Adelaide M.; Litin, Edward M.

GIFFORD, SANFORD

74405   (& Murawski, B. J.; Pilot, M. L.) Anorexia nervosa in one of identical twins. In Rowland, C. V., Jr. *Anorexia and Obesity*, Boston: Little Brown 1969
74406   Death and forever: some fears of war and peace. Atlantic 1962, March: 88-92
74407   (& Murawski, B. J.; Brazelton, T. B.) Differences in individual development within a pair of identical twins. (Read at Int Psa Cong, July 1965) J 1966, 47:261-268
        Abs EVN Q 1968, 37:311-312

74408 Freud's theories of unconscious immortality and the death instinct: a reconstruction in the light of recent historical experience and modern biological knowledge. (Read at Boston Psa Soc, 29 May 1968)
    Abs Welpton, D. Bull Phila Ass Psa 1969, 19:100-102
74409 (& Murawski, B. J.) Minimal sleep deprivation alone and in small groups: effects on ego functioning and 24-hour body-temperature and adreno-cortical patterns. In *Symposium on Stress in the Military Climate,* Walter Reed Army Inst of Research, Wash DC: U.S. Govt Printing Office 1965
74410 (Reporter) Panel on repetition compulsion. (Am Psa Ass, Dec 1963)
    J Am Psa Ass 1964, 12:632-649
S-47189 Sleep, time, and the early ego.
    Abs JTM Q 1961, 30:593. SAS RFPsa 1962, 26:330
74410A Some psychoanalytic theories about death—a selective historical review.
    Ann NY Acad Sci 1969, 164:638-668
S-47190 Transient disturbances in perception: two psychoanalytic observations.
    Abs BEM An Surv Psa 1957, 8:164-165

    See Fox, Henry M.

GILBERT, ARNOLD L.

74411 The ecumenical movement and the treatment of nuns. (Read at Int Psa Cong, July 1967) J 1968, 49:481-483

GILBERT, BARBARA D.

    See Kanter, Stanley S.

GILBERT, JEFF

74412 Analytic first aid for a three-year-old. Ops 1960, 30:200-201

    See Globus, Gordon G.

GILBERT, JOHN P.

    See Colby, Kenneth M.

GILBERT, MARY A.

74413 Acting out behavior and its relationship to the delay function of the ego. Diss Abstr Int 1969, 30(4-B):1896

GILBERT, MICHAEL

    See Karpman, Benjamin

GILBERT-DREYFUS

* * * Preface to Held, R. R. *De la Psychanalyse à la Médecine Psychosomatique,* Paris: Payot 1968
S-47193 (& Held, R. R.) A propos des obésités.
    Abs HFM An Surv Psa 1958, 9:202-203

GILBORN, STEVEN N.

74414 The family plight in the plays of Emile Augier: a psychoanalytic study. Diss Abstr Int 1969, 30(3-A):1264

GILDEA, MARGARET C.-L.

74415 (& Glidewell, J. C.; Kantor, M. B.) Maternal attitudes and general adjustment in school children. In Glidewell, J. C. *Parental Attitudes and Child Behavior,* Springfield, Ill: Thomas 1961, 42-89

GILDER, RODMAN

ABSTRACT OF:
74416 Bergler, E. The Psychology of Gambling. An Surv Psa 1957, 8:142-144

REVIEW OF:
74417 Lippman, H. S. Treatment of the Child in Emotional Conflict. Q 1963, 32:123

GILKESON, ELIZABETH C.

See Lipton, Edgar L.

GILL, BENJAMIN F.

See Abram, Harry S.

ABSTRACT OF:
74418 Valenstein, A. F. Affects, emotional reliving and insight in the psychoanalytic process. Bull Phila Ass Psa 1962, 12:85-87

GILL, H.

REVIEW OF:
74419 Thomas, C. B. et al: An Index of Rorschach Responses. Studies on the Psychological Characteristics of Medical Students. J 1965, 46:399

GILL, HARWANT S.

See Sutherland, John D.

GILL, MERTON M.

74420 (& Rapaport, D.) Aportaciones a la Teoría de la Técnica Psicoanalítica. [Contributions to the Theory of Psychoanalytic Technique.] (Mexican Psychoanalytic Association's publication. Psychoanalytic Collection.) Mexico: Editorial Pax México 1962, 267 p
* * * Editor of *The Collected Papers of David Rapaport.*
74421 Obituary: David Rapaport 1911-1960. J Am Psa Ass 1961, 9:755-759. RFPsa 1964, 28:341-343
74422 The primary process. Psych Issues 1967, 5:260-298.
74423 (& Klein, G. S.) The structuring of drive and reality. David Rapaport's contributions to psycho-analysis and psychology. J 1964, 45:483-498
        Abs HW Q 1962, 31:300-302. Meza, C. Cuad Psa 1965, 1:209. EVN Q 1966, 35:621

74424 (& Simon, J.; Fink, G.; Endicott, N. A.; Paul, I. H.) Studies in audio-recorded psychoanalysis: I. General considerations. J Am Psa Ass 1968, 16:230-244

74425 Topography and Systems in Psychoanalytic Theory. (Psychological Issues. Monograph No. 10. Vol 3, No. 2) NY: IUP 1963, 180 p
    Rv Kaywin, L. R 1963, 50:688-689. Robbins, W. S. Q 1964, 33:580-581. NRo J 1965, 46:254-256

See Brenman, Margaret; Klein, Marjorie H.; Rapaport, David

REVIEWS OF:
74426 Meares, A. A System of Medical Hypnosis. Q 1962, 31:112
74427 Moodie, W. Hypnosis in Treatment. Q 1962, 31:112

GILL, R.
See Wijsenbeek, Henricus

GILLARD, B. J.
See Heilbrun, Alfred B., Jr.

GILLER, DONALD W.
See Blumberg, Stanley

GILLESPIE, JAMES F.
See Snortum, John R.

GILLESPIE, WILLIAM H.
74428 Concepts of vaginal orgasm. J 1969, 50:495-497
S-1170 A contribution to the study of fetishism. PT Pervers 234-251
74429 Dreams, psychopathology, and mental apparatus. Proc IV World Cong Psychiat 1966, 162-167
S-47205 Ernest Jones: Funeral Addresses
    Abs SLP An Surv Psa 1958, 9:6
S-47208 The general theory of sexual perversion.
    Abs SLP An Surv Psa 1956, 7:209
S-47209 Neurotic ego distortion.
    Abs GLG An Surv Psa 1958, 9:154-155
S-11711 Notes on the analysis of sexual perversions. PT Pervers 26-40
74430 Obituary: Maxwell Gitelson: 1902-1965. (Read at Brit Psa Soc, 17 Mar 1965) J 1965, 46:244
74431 Obituary: Willi Hoffer: 1897-1967. (Read at Brit Psa Soc, 16 Oct 1968) J 1969, 50:263-264
74432 Opening address at 21st International Psychoanalytic Congress (Copenhagen, 1959) RFPsa 1961, 25:443
74433 A psychoanalytic comment on mental health. M 1960, 33:255-257
    Abs RDT Q 1961, 30:459-460
74434 The psychoanalytic theory of child development. In Miller, E. *Foundations of Child Psychiatry,* Oxford, NY: Pergamon Pr 1968, 51-69

74435   The psychoanalytic theory of sexual deviation with special reference to fetishism. In Rosen, I. *The Pathology and Treatment of Sexual Deviation*, London: Oxford Univ Pr 1964, 123-145
74436   Some regressive phenomena in old age. M 1963, 36:203-209
74437   Symposium on homosexuality. (Read at Int Psa Cong, July-Aug 1963) J 1964, 45:203-209
          Homosexualité. RFPsa 1965, 29:323-336
          Abs EVN Q 1966, 35:456-457

REVIEWS OF:
74438   Hartmann, E. The Biology of Dreaming. J 1969, 50:413-414
74439   Menninger, K. et al: The Vital Balance: The Life Process in Mental Health and Illness. J 1965, 46:265-268
74440   Stoller, R. J. Sex and Gender. J 1969, 50:251-254
74441   Wangh, M. (Ed): Fruition of an Idea: Fifty Years of Psychoanalysis in New York. J 1963, 44:118

GILLETTE, NEDRA P.

74442   Changing methods in the treatment of psychosocial dysfunction. Amer J occup Ther 1967, 21:230-233

GILLETTE, PAUL J.

74443   Psychodynamics of Unconventional Sex Behavior and Unusual Practices. Los Angeles: Holloway House 1966, 317 p

GILLIAM, NAOMI R.

See Nehren, Jeanette

GILLIBERT, JEAN

74444   Deuil—Mort—Même. [Mourning—death—ego.] RFPsa 1967, 31:143-171
74445   Discussion of Barande, I. "Le vu et l'entendu dans la cure." RFPsa 1968, 32:88-93
74446   Discussion of Barande, R. "La pulsion de mort." RFPsa 1968, 32:496-497
74447   Discussion of Mendel, G. "La sublimation artistique." RFPsa 1964, 28:795-801
74448   Discussion of Rouart, J. "Investment and counter-investment." RFPsa 1967, 31:244
74449   Le meurtre de l'imago et le processus d'individuation. [The murder of the image and the processes of individuation.] RFPsa 1969, 33:375-414
74450   L'ontogenèse en psychopathologie. [Ontogenesis in psychopathology.] Évolut psychiat 1961, 26:477-510. In Ey, H. *Entrietiens Psychiatriques, No. 10*, Toulouse: Edoard Privat 1964
74451   La réminiscence et la cure. [Memory and cure.] RFPsa 1968, 32:385-418
74452   La situation oedipienne et la tragédie de la pensée. [The Oedipus situation and the tragedy of thought.] Évolut psychiat 1963, 28:243-252

REVIEWS OF:
74453 Dracoulidès, N. N. Psychanalyse d'Aristophane. RFPsa 1968, 32:625-627
74454 Freud, S. L'Interpretation des Rêves. RFPsa 1968, 32:788-790
74455 Freud, S. & Bullitt, W. C. Thomas Woodrow Wilson. RFPsa 1968, 32:787-788
74456 Jones, E. Hamlet and Oedipus. RFPsa 1968, 32:619-625

GILLIGAN, BERNARD B.
TRANSLATION OF:
Lepp, I. [80462]

GILLIS, SUE
See Dabritz, Linda

GILLMAN, ROBERT D.
74457 Brief psychotherapy: a psychoanalytic view. P 1965, 122:601-611
    Abs Loeb, L. Q 1967, 36:474
74458 The dreams of pregnant and maternal adaptation. Ops 1968, 38:688-692

GILMAN, LEONARD H.
74459 (Participant) On regression: a workshop. (Held at West Coast Psa Soc, 14-16 Oct 1966) Psa Forum 1967, 2:293-316

GILMORE J. BARNARD
74460 The role of anxiety and cognitive factors in children's play behavior. Child Develpm 1966, 37:397-416

GILTAY, H.
74461 Zur Psychologie der menschlichen Selbstentzweiung. [The psychology of the splitting of the human self.] Acta psychother psychosom 1960, 8:105-119

GINGRAS, G.
See Castro de la Mata, G.

GINOTT, HAIM G.
74462 (& Lebo, D.) Ecology of service. J consult Psychol 1963, 27:450-452
74463 Between Parent and Child: New Solutions to Old Problems. NY: Macmillan 1965, 223 p
74464 Between Parent and Teenager. NY: Macmillan 1969, 256 p
74465 Group Psychotherapy with Children. The Theory and Practice of Play Therapy. NY: McGraw-Hill 1961, xiv + 208 p
    Rv Piers, M. W. Q 1962, 31:266-267
74466 Innovations in group psychotherapy with preadolescents. In Gazda, G. M. Innovations to Group Psychotherapy, Springfield, Ill: Thomas 1968, 272-294

74467 Interpretations and child therapy. In Hammer, E. F. *Use of Interpretation in Treatment: Technique and Art,* NY: Grune & Stratton 1968, 291-299

74468 (& Harms, E.) Mental disorders in childhood. In Wolman, B. B. *Handbook of Clinical Psychology,* NY: McGraw-Hill 1965, 1094-1118

74469 (& Lebo, D.) Most and least used play therapy limits. J genet Psych 1963, 103:153-159

S-47222 Parent education groups in a child guidance clinic. In Crow, L. D. & Crow, A. *Readings in Child and Adolescent Psychology,* NY/London/Toronto: Longmans 1961, 535-541

74470 (& Lebo, D.) Play therapy limits and theoretical orientation. J consult Psychol 1961, 25:337-340

74471 Play therapy: the initial session. PT 1961, 15:73-88

74472 Problems in the playroom. In Haworth, M. R. *Child Psychotherapy,* NY/London: Basic Books 1964, 125-130

74473 A rationale for selecting toys in play therapy. J consult Psychol 1960, 24:243-246

74474 Research in play therapy. In Haworth, M. Child Psychotherapy, NY/London: Basic Books 1964, 431-435

74475 Die Spielzeugauswahl in der Kinderpsychotherapie. [The choice of play materials in child therapy.] Hbh Kinderpsychother 598-605

74476 Spielzimmer und Werkraum in der Kinderpsychotherapie. [Play room and work space in child therapy.] Hbh Kinderpsychother 605-617

74477 The theory and practice of "therapeutic intervention" in child treatment. In Haworth, M. R. Child Psychotherapy, NY/London: Basic Books 1964, 148-158

GINSBERG, M.

74478 The Psychology of Society. NY: Barnes & Noble 1964, 186 p

GINSBURG, BENSON E.

74479 Genotypic factors in the ontogeny of behavior. Sci Psa 1968, 12:12-17

GINSBURG, SOL W.

74480 A Psychiatrist's View on Social Issues. (Foreword: Menninger, K.) (Introd: Menninger, W. C.) NY: Columbia Univ Pr 1963, vii + 296 p

GINSPARG, SYLVIA

74481 (& Moriarty, A.; Murphy, L. B.) Young teen-agers' responses to the assassination of President Kennedy: relation to previous life experiences. Chld Dth Pres 1-29

GINZBERG, ELI

74482 Obituary: John L. Herma: in memoriam. (Read at Nat Psychol Ass Psa, 25 Sept 1966) R 1966, 53:673-676

74483 (Ed) Values and Ideals of American Youth. NY: Columbia Univ Pr 1961, xii + 338 p

GIOIA, TERENCIO
REVIEW OF:
74484 Jacobson, E. The Self and the Object World. Rev Psicoanál 1966, 23: 273

GIORGIO, A. DI
See Carloni, Glauco

GIOSCIA, VICTOR J.
74485 Patterns of relations: types of types. (Panel discussion: the classification of family types.) In Ackerman, N. W. et al: *Expanding Theory and Practice in Family Therapy*, NY: Fam Serv Ass Amer 1967, 69-76

GIOVACCHINI, PETER L.
74486 Aggression: adaptive and disruptive aspects. Bull Phila Ass Psa 1969, 19:76-86
74487 Aspectos voicos de la regressión. [Influential aspects in regression.] Rev Psicoanál 1968, 25:177-192
74488 Characterological aspects of marital interaction. Psa Forum 1967, 2: 8-14; 25-29; 282-283; 287-288
  Abs Cuad Psa 1967, 3:317
74489 Comment on Dr. Weissman's paper, "Psychological concomitants of ego functioning in creativity." (Read at Int Psa Cong, July 1967) J 1968, 49:469-470
74490 Compulsory happiness. Adolescent despair. Arch gen Psychiat 1968, 18:650-657. Bull Chicago Soc Adol Psychiat 1968, 2:1-8
74491 Discussion of Zetzel, E. R. "The analytic situation." Psa Amer 112-117
74492 Dream structure of the creative process. Bull Chicago Psa Soc 1965, 1:1-8
74493 Dreams and the creative process. M 1966, 39:105-115
74494 Ego adaptation and cultural variables. Arch gen Psychiat 1961, 5:37-45
  Abs KR Q 1962, 31:589
S-47244 The psychosomatic state: report of two cases.
  Abs LDr RFPsa 1962, 26:331
74495 (& Muslin, H.) Ego equilibrium and cancer of the breast. PSM 1965, 27:524-532
74496 Epilogue. In Boyer, L. B. & Giovacchini, P. L. *Psychoanalytic Treatment of Schizophrenic and Characterological Disorders*, NY: Sci House 1967, 306-335
74497 The frozen introject. (Read at Mich Ass Psa, 22 Jan 1966) J 1967, 48:61-67
  L'introjection "geleé." Méd et Hyg 1968, 26(833):839-840
  Abs EVN Q 1969, 38:158
74498 Frustration and externalization. (Read at Los Angeles Psa Soc, 21 Apr 1966) Q 1967, 36:571-583
  Abs Share, M. Bull Phila Ass Psa 1967, 17:39-40. Cuad Psa 1968, 4:43

74499 Further theoretical and clinical aspects. In Boyer, L. B. & Giovacchini, P. L. *Psychoanalytic Treatment of Schizophrenic and Characterological Disorders,* NY: Sci House 1967, 272-305

74500 The influence of interpretation upon schizophrenic patients. J 1969, 50:179-186

74501 Integrative aspects of object relationships. Q 1963, 32:396-407

74502 Letter to the editors [re Sandford, B. "A patient and her cats."] Psa Forum 1966, 1:324-325

74503 Maternal introjection and ego effects. (Read at Chicago Psa Soc, 26 Feb 1963) J Amer Acad Child Psychiat 1965, 4:279-292
　　　　Abs Kavka, J. Bull Phila Ass Psa 1964, 14:157-162

74504 Methodological aspects of psychoanalytic critique. Bull Phila Ass Psa 1967, 17:10-25

74505 (Participant) On regression: a workshop. (Held at West Coast Psa Soc, 14-16 Oct 1966) Psa Forum 1967, 2:293-316

S-47248 On scientific creativity.
　　　　Abs JTM Q 1962, 31:125-126. SAS RFPsa 1962, 26:331

74506 Panel on schizophrenia. Ill med Soc J 1968

* * * Preface to Boyer, L. B. & Giovacchini, P. L. *Psychoanalytic Treatment of Schizophrenic and Characterological Disorders,* NY: Sci House 1967, 11-15

74507 Psychoanalytic treatment of character disorders: introduction. In Boyer, L. B. & Giovacchini, P. L. *Psychoanalytic Treatment of Schizophrenic and Characterological Disorders,* NY: Sci House 1967, 208-234

74508 Psychopathologic aspects of the identity sense. Psychiat Dig 1965, 26:31-41

74509 Report of workshop on psychotherapy of adolescence. Bull Chicago Psa Soc Adol Psychiat 1967, 1

74510 (& Hilkevitch, A.) Report of workshop on structural theory. Bull Chicago Psa Soc 1966, 2

74511 Resistance and external object relations. J 1961, 42:246-254
　　　　Abs WPK Q 1962, 31:285

74512 Somatic symptoms and the transference neurosis. J 1963, 44:143-150
　　　　Abs Gaddini, E. Riv Psa 1965, 11:75. EVN Q 1965, 34:614

S-47249 Some affective meanings of dizziness.
　　　　Abs NZ An Surv Psa 1958, 9:147

74513 Some aspects of the development of the ego ideal of a creative scientist. Q 1965, 34:79-101

74514 Some elements of the therapeutic action in the treatment of character disorders. In Boyer, L. B. & Giovacchini, P. L. *Psychoanalytic Treatment of Schizophrenic and Characterological Disorders,* NY: Sci House 1967, 235-271

74515 Stress and psychic function—discussion. Forest Hosp Found Publ 1965, 3:17-31

74516 The submerged ego. J Amer Acad Child Psychiat 1964, 3:430-442

74517 Transference, incorporation and synthesis. J 1965, 46:287-296
　　　　Abs EVN Q 1967, 36:621

74518 El tratamiento psicoanalítico de los trastornos de carácter. [Psychoanalytic treatment of character disorders.] Cuad Psa 1968, 4:23-39

74519 Treatment of marital disharmonies: the classical approach. In Greene,

B. L. *The Psychotherapies of Marital Disharmony*, NY: Free Pr; London: Collier-Macmillan 1965, 39-82

74520　Treatment of schizophrenia—questions and answers. JAMA 1968, 200: 655

See Boyer, L. Bryce; Sklansky, Morris

REVIEW OF:

74521　Rossman, J. Industrial Creativity. The Psychology of the Inventor. Q 1964, 33:597-599

GIOVANARDI ROSSI, P.

74521A (& Frank, L.) [Disorders of time experience and depersonalization in adolescence.] G Psichiatr Neuropatol 1969, 97:655-690

GIRARD, CLAUDE

ABSTRACTS OF:

74522　Adatto, P. On the metamorphosis from adolescence into adulthood. RFPsa 1968, 32:356

74523　Applebaum, B. Some problems in contemporary ego psychology. RFPsa 1964, 28:457

74524　Barnett, M. C. Vaginal awareness in the infancy and childhood of girls. RFPsa 1968, 32:350

74525　Bibring, G. L. Some considerations regarding the ego ideal in the psychoanalytic process. RFPsa 1968, 32:175

74526　Bloch, D. Feelings that kill; the wish for infanticide in neurotic depression. RFPsa 1968, 32:170

74527　Clair, M. S. A note on the guilt of Oedipus. RFPsa 1963, 27:345

74528　Daniels, M. The dynamics of morbid envy in the etiology and treatment of chronic learning disability. RFPsa 1968, 32:167

74529　Davis, H. L. Short-term psychoanalytic therapy with hospitalized schizophrenics. RFPsa 1968, 32:365

74530　Deutsch, H. Some clinical considerations of the ego ideal. RFPsa 1968, 32:174

74531　Devereux, G. Mumbling: the relationship between a resistance and frustrated auditory curiosity in childhood. RFPsa 1968, 32:356

74532　Dickes, R. The defensive function of an altered state of consciousness: a hypnoid state. RFPsa 1968, 32:344

74533　Ekstein, R. Working through and termination of analysis. RFPsa 1968, 32:338

74534　Ferreira, A. J. On repetition compulsion. RFPsa 1968, 32:171

74535　Fine, R. Erotic feelings in the psychotherapeutic relationship. RFPsa 1968, 32:169

74536　Fischer, C. Psychoanalytic implications of recent research on sleep and dreaming. RFPsa 1968, 32:339-343

74537　Freeman, T. Some aspects of pathological narcissism. RFPsa 1968, 32:177

74538　Friedman, D. B. Toward a unitary theory on the passing of the Oedipus conflict. RFPsa 1968, 32:366

74539　Gabriele, A. B. The principle of irrational loyalty. RFPsa 1968, 32:367

74540 Hendrick, I. Narcissism and the prepuberty ego-ideal. RFPsa 1968, 32:175

74541 Hodges, D. C. Normal sadism and immoralism. RFPsa 1963, 27:346

74542 Honig, A. M. Negative transference in psychosis. RFPsa 1963, 27:343

74543 Jarvis, V. Loneliness and compulsion. RFPsa 1968, 32:338

74544 Jones, R. M. Dream interpretation and the psychology of dreaming. RFPsa 1968, 32:343

74545 Kanzer, M. Freud's uses of the term "autoeroticism" and narcissism. RFPsa 1968, 32:176

74546 Kaplan, E. Classical forms of neurosis in infancy and early childhood. RFPsa 1964, 28:458

74547 Kaywin, L. Notes on the psychoanalytic theory of affect. RFPsa 1968, 32:369

74548 Kernberg, O. Notes on countertransference. RFPsa 1968, 32:337

74549 Martin, P. A. A psychoanalytic study of the Marschallin theme in "Der Rosenkavalier." RFPsa 1968, 32:357

74550 Meerloo, J. A. M. The biology of laughter. RFPsa 1968, 32:368

74551 Miller, M. D. Music and tension. RFPsa 1968, 32:370-374

74552 Moriarty, D. M. Observations of the superego in a schizophrenic patient. RFPsa 1963, 27:346

74553 Murray, J. M. Narcissism and the ego ideal. RFPsa 1968, 32:173

74554 Novey, S. Principle of working through in psychoanalysis. RFPsa 1964, 28:460

74555 Novey, S. Why some patients conduct actual investigations of their biographies. RFPsa 1968, 32:354

74556 Palm, R. Identification and magical thinking. RFPsa 1963, 27:343

74557 Pfeffer, A. Z. The meaning of the analyst after analysis. RFPsa 1966, 30:514

74558 Rangell, L. On friendship. RFPsa 1966, 30:513

74559 Rosenthal, H. Emergency psychotherapy: a crucial need. RFPsa 1968, 32:362

74560 Ross, D. W. & Kapp, F. T. A technique for self-analysis of countertransference. Use of psychoanalyst's visual images in response to patient dreams. RFPsa 1964, 28:459

74561 Sandler, J. & Joffe, G. On skill and sublimation. RFPsa 1968, 32:352

74562 Searles, H. F. Schizophrenic communication. RFPsa 1963, 27:344

74563 Seidenberg, R. Sacrificing the first you see. RFPsa 1968, 32:366

74564 Shengold, L. The parent as Sphinx. RFPsa 1966, 30:516

74565 Sherfey, M. J. Evolution and nature of female sexuality in relation to psychoanalytic theory. RFPsa 1968, 32:347-350

74566 Siegman, A. J. Exhibitionism and fascination. RFPsa 1966, 30:327

74567 Simons, R. C. The clown as a father figure. RFPsa 1968, 32:172

74568 Stewart, W. A. An enquiry into the concept of working through. RFPsa 1966, 30:515

74569 Sullivan, C. T. On being loved; a contribution to the psychology of object relations. RFPsa 1968, 32:169

74570 Vitanza, A. A. Toward a theory of crying. RFPsa 1963, 27:343

74571 Woodbury, M. A. Altered body-ego experiences: a contribution to the study of regression, perceptive and early development. RFPsa 1968, 32:351

74572   Yasmajian, R. V. The testes and body-image formation in transvestism. RFPsa 1968, 32:352
74573   Yasmajian, R. V. Verbal and symbolic processes in slips of the tongue. RFPsa 1968, 32:354
74574   Zippin, D. Sex differences and the sense of humor. RFPsa 1968, 32:368

REVIEWS OF:
74575   Bremer, J. Asexualisation. RFPsa 1962, 26:136
74576   Lemay, M. Les Groupes de Jeune Inadaptés. Role du Jeune Meneur. RFPsa 1964, 28:283
74577   Michel, A. L'École Freudienne devant la Musique. RFPsa 1968, 32: 629

GIRARD, J. Y.
See Launay, C.

GIRARD, RENÉ
74578   Deceit, Desire, and the Novel; Self and Other in Literary Structure. (Tr: Freccero, Y.) Baltimore, Maryland: Johns Hopkins Pr 1965, 318 p
74579   Masochism and sadism. In author's Deceit, Desire, and the Novel, 176-192

GIRARD, V.
See Croco, Louis

GIRAUD, R.
74580   [A case of amenorrhoea with galactorrhoea of psychogenic origin.] (Fr) Bull Fed Gynec Obstet Franç 1960, 12:513-521

GITELSON, MAXWELL
74581   Analytic aphorisms. Q 1967, 36:260-270
74582   (Moderator) (& Kamm, B. A.; Kramer, P.; Robbins, F. P.) Analyzability: a panel discussion. (Read at Chicago Psa Soc, 23 Oct 1962)
        Abs Kavka, J. Bull Phila Ass Psa 1963, 13:36-39
74583   Bibliography of Maxwell Gitelson. J 1966, 47:444-445
74584   Communication from the president about the neoanalytic movement. J 1962, 43:373-375
74585   The curative factors in psycho-analysis. [Symposium] I. The first phase of psycho-analysis. (Read at Int Psa Cong, 31 July 1961) J 1962, 43: 194-205; 234
        La première phase de la psychanalyse. RFPsa 1963, 27:399-422; 478-481
        Abs RLG Q 1963, 32:598-599
74586   The curative importance of the first phase in psychoanalysis. (Read at Boston Psa Soc, 5 June 1961)
        Abs Cath, S. H. Bull Phila Ass Psa 1961, 11:132-135
74587   Discussant: "Psychiatric Residents." Teach Dyn Psychiat 116-118
74588   Heinz Hartmann. J 1965, 46:2-4
        Abs EVN Q 1967, 36:312

S-47252 On ego distortion.
Abs SLP An Surv Psa 1958, 9:153-154
74589 On the identity crisis in American psychoanalysis. (Read at Am Psa Ass, 3 May 1964) J Am Psa Ass 1964, 12:451-476
Abs JLSt Q 1967, 36:131
74590 On the problem of character neurosis. J Hillside Hosp 1963, 12:3-17
Abs JA Q 1967, 36:134
74591 The place of psychoanalysis in psychiatric training. BMC 1962, 26:57-72
Abs HD Q 1963, 32:134
S-47255 Psychoanalyst, U. S. A. 1955.
Abs RZ An Surv Psa 1956, 7:366-367
74592 Rapport du XXIIIe Congrès International de Psychanalyse. [Report of the 23rd International Congress of Psychoanalysis.] RFPsa 1963, 27:369-398
74593 A transference reaction in a sixty-six-year-old woman. In Berezin, M. A. & Cath, S. H. *Geriatric Psychiatry: Grief, Loss and Emotional Disorders in the Aging Process,* NY: IUP 1965, 160-186
74594 Zur gegenwärtigen wissenschaftlichen und sozialen Position der Psychoanalyse. [The present scientific and social position of psychoanalysis.] Psyche 1964, 18:1-14

REVIEW OF:
74595 Hartmann, H. Essays on Ego Psychology. Selected Problems in Psychoanalytic Theory. Q 1965, 34:268-273

GIUGANINO, PAOLO

74596 Contributo alla psicopatologia e alla psicodinámica del sentimento di colpa nella psicosi maniaco-depressiva. [Contribution to the psychopathology and psychodynamics of guilt feelings in manic-depressive psychosis.] Riv Psichiat 1967, 2:26-29
74597 Problemi di controtransfert e psicoterapie brevi. [Problems of countertransference and short-term psychotherapy.] Riv Psichiat 1967, 2:560-569

GLAD, DONALD DAVIDSON

74598 Alcoholism, a cultural and clinical integration. J Colo-Wyo Acad Sci 1949
74599 Attitudes and experiences of American-Jewish and American-Irish male youth as related to differences in adult rates of inebriety. Quart J Stud Alcohol 1947, 48(8):406-472
74600 (& Smith, W. L.; Glad, V. B.) Behavior factor reactions to leader emphases upon feelings or social expressions. Int J soc Psychiat 1957, 3:129-133
74601 (& Glad, V. B.; et al) The Emotional Projection Test. Plates and Manual, Psychological Test Specialists, Missoula, Montana 1956
74602 Grouping for development. Child Educ 1948-49, 25:354-356
74603 (& Woodcock, B.) An interest validation of the Rorschach and Thematic Apperception Tests. J Colo-Wyo Acad Sci 1950

74604 (& Glad, V. B.) Interpersonality Synopsis. NY: Libra 1963
74605 (& Raimey, R.) A method for quantifying social interaction in group therapy. J Colo-Wyo Acad Sci 1950
74606 "Mind" as an organismic integration. In Scher, J. *Theories of the Mind*, NY: Free Pr 1962, 529-534
74607 The network of psychiatric services. Int J grp PT 1965, 15:477-482
74608 (& Eddy, W. B.; et al) Organizational effects on training. Training and Devel J 1967, Feb:15-23
74609 Personality consequences of psychotherapy theories. In author's *Operational Values in Psychotherapy*, NY: Oxford 1959
74610 Psychology training and research in the mental health center. Univ Mo Med School 1967, 16 p
74611 (& Hayne, M. L.; Glad, V. B.; Ferguson, R. E.) Schizophrenic factor reactions to four group psychotherapy methods. Int J grp PT 1963, 13:196-210
74612 (& Glad, V. B.) Some styles and effects of leadership. In *Proceedings, Southern Association for Physical Education of College Women*, Duke Univ 1968, 4 (Abs)
74613 Theoretically systematic operations in group research. In author's *Operational Values in Psychotherapy*, NY: Oxford 1959
74614 (& Tiffany, D. W., Jr.; et al) Work Inhibition and Rehabilitation. Kansas City, Mo: Institute for Community Studies 1967, 121 p

See Smith, W. Lynn

GLAD, VIRGINIA B.

See Glad, Donald D.

GLADSTON, E.-R.

See Amado-Haguenauer, G.

GLADSTONE, ARTHUR I.

S-47265 The conception of the enemy. In Zawodny, J. K. *Man and International Relations, Vol. I*, San Francisco, Calif: Chandler Publ 1966, 537-543

See Burnham, Donald L.

GLADSTONE, HERMAN P.

74615 A study of techniques of psychotherapy with youthful offenders. Ps 1962, 25:147-159
       Abs HRB Q 1963, 32:139
74616 Youthful offenders in psychotherapy. Curr psychiat Ther 1964, 4:83-91

GLADWIN, THOMAS

74617 Latency and the equine subconscious. Amer Anthropologist 1962, 64:1292-1296

GLANZ, YOSEF

74618 [Piaget's studies on thinking.] (Heb) Megamot 1959-60, 10:15-39

GLASER, FREDERICK B.

74619 The case of Franz Kafka. R 1964, 51:99-121
       Abs SRS Q 1965, 34:310-311
74620 The dichotomy game; a further consideration of the writings of Dr.
       Thomas Szasz. P 1965, 121:1069-1074

GLASER, G. H.

See Schafer, Roy

GLASER, HELEN H.

See Bullard, Dexter M., Jr.

GLASER, KURT

74621 Attempted suicide in children and adolescents: psychodynamic ob-
       servations. PT 1965, 19:220-227
74622 Masked depression in children and adolescents. PT 1967, 21:565-574.
       Ann Prog child Psychiat 1968, 345-355
74623 Suicide in children and adolescents. Acting Out 87-99

GLASER, YOLANDE I. M.

74624 A unit for mothers and babies in a psychiatric hospital. J child Psychol
       Psychiat 1962, 3:53-60

GLASGOW, DOUGLAS

74625 (& Lurie, A.; Pinsky, S.) Milieu therapy program in a psychiatric hos-
       pital. Hospitals 1966, 40(May 16):79-90

GLASNER, SAUL

74626 Aberrant dependency. Psychiat Q 1967, 41:71-79

GLASS, ALBERT J.

See West, Louis J.

GLASS, DAVID C.

74627 (& Canavan, D.; Schiavo, S.) Achievement motivation, dissonance, and
       defensiveness. J Pers 1968, 36:474-492

GLASS, H.

See Levine, Murray

GLASS, JOHN F.

See Brill, Norman Q.

GLASSER, BETTY ANN

74628 (& Greenblatt, M.) The prevention of hospitalization. Curr psychiat
       Ther 1965, 5:178-185

See Hartmann, Ernest L.

GLASSER, LOIS N.

See Glasser, Paul H.

GLASSER, PAUL H.

74629 (& Glasser, L. N.) Adequate family functioning. Psychiat Res Rep 1966, 20:8-17
74630 Changes in family equilibrium during psychotherapy. Fam Proc 1963, 2:245-264. In Thomas, E. J. *Behavioral Science for Social Workers*, NY: Free Pr 1967, 156-169.
74631 Group methods in child welfare: review of preview. Child Welfare 1963, 42:213-220. In *Group Method and Services in Child Welfare*, NY: Child Welfare League of America, Inc., 1963, 5-11
74632 (& Glasser, L. N.) Role reversal and conflict between aged parents and their children. Marriage fam Liv 1962, 24:46-51. In Thomas, E. J. *Behavioral Science for Social Workers*, NY: Free Pr 1967, 78-85
74633 Social role, personality and group work practice. Soc Wk Practice 1962, 60-74

See Burns, Mary E.; Sarri, Rosemary C.

GLATZEL, J.

74633A [Thinking disorders in endogenous juvenile asthenic failure syndromes.] (Ger) Nervenarzt 1968, 39:393-398

GLATZER, HENRIETTE T.

74634 Aspects of transference in group psychotherapy. Int J grp PT 1965, 15:167-176
74635 Clinical aspects of interaction between group and leader in adult group psychotherapy. Topical Probl PT 1965, 5:197-204
74636 Combined individual and group analysis. Discussion. Ops 1960, 30: 243-246
74637 Concept of treatability. Transcript Scientific Program—Council of Psychoan Psychoth 1960, 10-15
74638 Handling narcissistic problems in group psychotherapy. Int J grp PT 1962, 12:448-455
74639 Neurotic factors of voyeurism and exhibitionism in group psychotherapy. Int J grp PT 1967, 17:3-9
       Abs GPK Q 1968, 37:630-631
74640 Selection of mothers for group therapy. Ops 1947, 17:477-483
74641 Working through in analytic group psychotherapy. Int J grp PT 1969, 19:292-306

See Durkin, Helen E.; Shaskan, Donald A.

GLAUBER, I. PETER

74642 Discussion of Weiss, E. "The psychodynamic formulation of agoraphobia." Psa Forum 1966, 1:393-395
74643 Dysautomatization: a disorder of preconscious ego functioning. (Read at Westchester Psa Soc, 8 May 1967) J 1968, 49:89-99
       Abs HRB Q 1968, 37:327-330. LHR Q 1969, 38:509

74644 Federn's annotation of Freud's theory of anxiety. J Am Psa Ass 1963, 11:84-96
   Abs JBi Q 1964, 33:135
S-47296 Freud's contributions on stuttering: their relation to some current insights.
   Abs WAS An Surv Psa 1958, 9:136-137
74645 Further contributions to the concept of stuttering. J Hillside Hosp 1962, 11:178-189
   Abs JA Q 1963, 32:291
S-47297 On the meaning of agoraphilia.
   Abs An Surv Psa 1955, 6:147-148
S-47301 The psychoanalysis of stuttering.
   Abs Auth An Surv Psa 1958, 9:137-140
S-47302 The rebirth motif in homosexuality and its teleological significance.
   Abs JAL An Surv Psa 1956, 7:215-216

REVIEWS OF:
74646 Murphy, A. T. & FitzSimons, R. M. Stuttering and Personality Dynamics. Play Therapy, Projective Therapy, and Counseling. Q 1961, 30:583-584
74647 Weiss, E. Agoraphobia in the Light of Ego Psychology. Q 1965, 34:276-281

GLAZ, A. ANDRÉ

74648 HAMLET, or the tragedy of Shakespeare. (Read at NY Psa Soc, 27 Sept 1955) Am Im 1961, 18:129-158
74649 Iago or moral sadism. Am Im 1962, 19:323-348

GLAZER, JEROME A.

See Nesbitt, Robert E. L., Jr.

GLAZER, NATHAN

See Riesman, David

GLEICHER, PEGGY

See Fried, Marc

GLEIZES, L.

See Becq, M.

GLEN, ROBERT S.

See Gordon, Ira J.

GLENN, JULES

S-47311 Circumcision and anti-semitism.
   Abs Sapochnik, L. Rev Psicoanál 1962, 19:280
74650 Opposite-sex twins. (Read at Long Island Psa Soc, June 1964; NY Psa Soc, 23 Mar 1965) J Am Psa Ass 1966, 14:736-759
   Abs Shorr, J. Q 1965, 34:636-638

74651   (Reporter) Panel on Melanie Klein. (NY Psa Soc, 25 May 1965) Q 1966, 35:320-322
74652   (& Glenn, S.) The psychology of twins. Dyn Psychiat 1968, (Suppl): 12-21
74653   The relation between child and adult analysis: technique. Bull NY Acad Med 1968, 44:576-580
74654   Sensory determinants of the symbol three. (Read at Am Psa Ass, Dec 1962) J Am Psa Ass 1965, 13:422-434
        Abs JLSt Q 1968, 37:471
74655   Testicular and scrotal masturbation. (Read at Am Psa Ass, Dec 1965; at Psa Ass NY, 15 Apr 1968) J 1969, 50:353-362
74656   (& Kaplan, E. H.) Types of orgasm in women: a critical review and redefinition. (Read at Long Island Psa Soc, 7 Mar 1967; at Am Psa Ass NY, 15 Dec 1967) J Am Psa Ass 1968, 16:549-564

REVIEW OF:
74657   Cohen, Y. A. The Transition from Childhood to Adolescence. Q 1965, 34:605-606

GLENN, MICHAEL L.

74658   (& Forrest, D. V.) Psychological criticism: essence or extract? Arch gen Psychiat 1969, 20:38-47
74659   Towards an "uncertainty principle" for psychology. R 1969, 56:215-224

GLENN, SYLVIA

See Glenn, Jules

GLESER, GOLDINE C.

74660   (& Gottschalk, L. A.; Springer, K. J.) An anxiety scale applicable to verbal samples. Arch gen Psychiat 1961, 5:593-605
74661   (& Ihilevich, D.) An objective instrument for measuring defense mechanisms. J consult Psychol 1969, 33:51-60
74662   (& Gottschalk, L. A.) Personality characteristics of chronic schizophrenics in relationship to sex and current functioning. Clin Psych 1967, 23:349-354

        See Gottlieb, Anthony A.; Gottschalk, Louis A.; Hirt, Michael; Kapp, Frederick T.; Kurtz, Richard; Pattison, E. Manuel

GLICK, BURTON STANLEY

74663   Conditioning therapy by an analytic therapist. Arch gen Psychiat 1967, 17:577-583
74664   Effect of altered clinic conditions on reported change in anxiety. J Neuropsychiat 1964, 5:291-296
74665   Freud, the problem of quality and the "secretory neuron." Q 1966, 35:84-97
74666   Freud's dream theory and modern dream research. PT 1967, 21:630-643

74667 Homosexual panic: clinical and theoretical considerations. JNMD 1959, 129:20-28

74668 A note on Freud's "empty" neuron. M 1967, 40:159-162

GLICK, IRA DAVID

74669 (& Singer, B.) Follow-up study of patients discharged from the rehabilitation service of a hospital for treatment of chronic disease. Arch phys Med Rehabil 1963, 44:29-36

74670 (& Graubert, D. N.) Kartagener's syndrome and schizophrenia: report of a case with chromosomal studies. P 1964, 121:603-605

74671 (& Levy, S. J.; et al) Living with Television. Chicago: Aldine Publ 1962, v + 262 p

74672 Mood and behavioral changes associated with the use of the oral contraceptive agents. A review of the literature. Psychopharmacologia 1967, 10:363-374

74673 (& Haley, J.) Psychiatry and the family, an annotated bibliography of articles published 1960-4. Monograph publ by Family Process, Palo Alto, Calif 1965

74674 (& Salerno, L. J.; Royce, J. R.) Psychophysiologic factors in etiology of preeclampsia. Arch gen Psychiat 1965, 12:260-266

74675 (& Setleis, H.; Woerner, M. G.; Pollack, M.) Schizophrenia in siblings reared apart: a case report. P 1967, 124:236-240

74676 The "sick" family and schizophrenia—cause and effect? Dis Nerv Sys, Suppl 1968, 23(5):129-132

See Greenberg, Irwin M.; Hauptman, Bruce

GLICKMAN, LEWIS

See Fink, Geraldine

GLICKSBERG, CHARLES IRVING

74677 Psychoanalysis and the tragic vision. In author's *The Tragic Vision in Twentieth-Century Literature,* Carbondale: Southern Ill Univ Pr 1963, 85-96

GLIDEWELL, JOHN C.

74678 On the analysis of social intervention. In author's *Parental Attitudes and Child Behavior,* Springfield, Ill: Thomas 1961, 215-239

See Brown, Martha M.; Gildea, Margaret C.-L.; Stringer, Lorene A.

GLITHERO, E.

See Slater, E. T.

GLOBUS, GORDON G.

74679 (& Gilbert, J.) A metapsychological approach to the architecture of Frank Lloyd Wright. R 1964, 51:285-297

74680 (& Pillard, R. C.) Tausk's *Influencing Machine* and Kafka's *In the Penal Colony.* (Read at Am Psa Ass, May 1965) Am Im 1966, 23:191-207 Abs Cuad Psa 1967, 3:244. JWS Q 1967, 36:629

See Heim, Edgar

GLOOR, C.

See Genevard, G.; Schneider, Pierre-Bernard

GLOOR, PIERRE-ANDRÉ

74681 Actualité de la sexologie. [Actuality of sexology.] Méd Hyg 1968, 26 (839):1-6
74682 Attitudes Féminines devant la Prévention des Naissances. [Women's Attitudes with Regard to Birth Control.] Paris: Doin-Deren 1968, 199 p
74683 Le médecin praticien et la sexologie. [The general practitioner and sexology.] Praxis 1968, 57(50):1770-1776
74684 Problèmes d'un groupe de praticiens selon Balint. Le point de vue d'un psychiatrie. [Problems of Balint's general practitioners group. The psychiatrist's point of view.] Praxis 1963, 52(41):1239-1242
74685 Quelques considérations psychosociologiques sur la prévention des naissances. [Some psychosociological considerations about the birth control problem.] Praxis 1965, 54(40):1166-1169

See Schneider, Pierre-Bernard

GLOTFELDTY, J.

See Zinberg, Norman E.

GLOVER, EDWARD

74686 Aggression and sado-masochism. In Rosen, I. *The Pathology and Treatment of Sexual Deviation,* London: Oxford Univ Pr 1964, 146-162
74687 The ambulant clinic. Brit J Delinq 1954, 4:223-224. Roots of Crime 369-370
74688 Bed-wetting and delinquency. Brit J Delinq 1952, 3:83-84. Roots of Crime 384-386
74689 Bibliography of Edward Glover. Q 1969, 38:532-548
74690 Biographical notice of Karl Abraham. NY: Psa Encycl 1968, 3-8
74691 The Birth of the Ego: A Nuclear Hypothesis. London: Allen & Unwin; NY: IUP 1968, 125 p
74692 Capital punishment. Brit J. Delinq 1958, 9. Roots of Crime 396-397
74693 The castration of sexual offenders. Brit J Delinq 1950, 1(5). Roots of Crime 390-393
74694 Classification. Brit J Delinq 1951, 1:239-240. Roots of Crime 377-378
74695 Clinical research: introduction. Roots of Crime 271
° ° ° The concept of "recidivism." See [47339]
74696 Co-ordination of research. Brit J Delinq 1954, 5:98. Roots of Crime 375-376
74697 Crime and modern science. Rationalist Annual 1961, 44-54
74698 Crime or perversion? Brit J Delinq 1956, 7:1-2. Roots of Crime 372-373

74699   The criminal psychopath. Roots of Crime 117-169
74700   Definition and classification. Brit J Delinq 1952, 2:194-195. Roots of Crime 378-380
74701   Delinquency: a special study. Brit J Delinq 1950, 1:3. Roots of Crime 363
74702   Depression and crime. Brit J Delinq 1957, 8:81-82. Roots of Crime 382-384
74703   Diagnosis and treatment of pathological delinquency. Roots of Crime 79-114
74704   Discussion of Eysenck, H. J. "The effects of psychotherapy." Int J Psychiat 1965, 1:158-160
74705   Efficacy of psychoanalysis. Brit med J 1960, 2:1162
S-47331 Ego-distortion.
            Abs JLS An Surv Psa 1958, 9:155-156
S-11864 Freud or Jung.
            Freud o Jung. (Foreword: Fachinelli, E.) Milan: Sugar 1967
74706   Freudian or neofreudian? Q 1964, 33:97-109
            Abs Dubcovsky, S. Rev Psicoanál 1964, 21:385
S-47332 The frontiers of psycho-analysis.
            Abs JA An Surv Psa 1956, 7:67-68
S-47333 The future development of psycho-analysis.
            Abs JA An Surv Psa 1956, 7:50
S-47334 The future of "dynamics" psychology.
            Abs CK An Surv Psa 1957, 8:23-24
74707   The government and the Wolfenden report on homosexuality and prostitution. Brit J Delinq 1959, 9:161-163. Roots of Crime 393-396
74708   Homosexuality. Brit J Delinq 1954, 5:2-3. Roots of Crime 388-389
74709   In honor of Lawrence Kubie. JNMD 1969, 149:5-18
74710   In praise of ourselves. J 1969, 50:499-502
74711   Institutional treatment. Brit J Delinq 1956, 7:2-3. **Roots of Crime 370-371**
* * *   Introduction to Freud, S. A *Psycho-Analytic Dialogue. The Letters of Sigmund Freud and Karl Abraham,* 1907-1926
74712   Is change progress? Listener, 1963, Dec 5
74713   Juvenile delinquency acts. Brit J Delinq 1950, 1:81. Roots of Crime 366
74714   Metapsychology or metaphysics. A psychoanalytic essay. Q 1966, 35:173-190
74715   Narcosis and court reports. Brit J Delinq 1951, 2:3-4. Roots of Crime 366-368
74716   Normal and abnormal behaviour. Brit J Delinq 1955, 6:4. Roots of Crime 363-364
S-11879 Notes on M'Naghten rules. Roots of Crime 339-346
S-11882 Outline of the investigation and treatment of delinquency in Great Britain, 1912-1948. Roots of Crime 27-59
74717   Outline of the investigation and treatment of delinquency in Great Britain, 1949-55. J crim Law Criminol Police Sci 1955, 46(2). Roots of Crime 60-67
74718   Outline of the investigation and treatment of delinquency in Great Britain, 1956-1959. Roots of Crime 68-76
* * *   Preface. The Roots of Crime ix-xiii

74719   The prevention of pathological crime. Roots of Crime 347-351
74720   The problem of male homosexuality. Roots of Crime 197-243
S-47339 Prognosis or prediction: a psychiatric examination of the concept of "recidivism." With title: The concept of "recidivism." Roots of Crime 327-338
S-47340 Psychiatric aspects of capital punishment. Roots of Crime 352-359
74721   Psychoanalysis and "controlled" research on delinquency. Brit J Delinq 1962-63, 3:63-67
S-47341 Psycho-analysis and criminology: a political survey. Roots of Crime 311-324
            Abs JAL An Surv Psa 1956, 7:404-406
74722   Psychoanalysis and psychotherapy. M 1960, 33:73-82; 225-230
            Abs IH Q 1961, 30:153
74723   Psychoanalysis in England. Psa Pioneers 534-545
74724   Psycho-analysis today. Yorkshire Post 1961, Aug 24
74725   The psychology of the psychotherapist. M 1962, 35:47-57
            Abs ICFH Q 1963, 32:141-142
S-11897 The psychopathology of prostitution. Roots of Crime 244-267
74726   Psychopathy. Brit J Delinq 1951, 2:77-78. Roots of Crime 380-381
74727   Psychopathy: classification and treatment. Brit J Delinq 1955, 6:1,2,4. Roots of Crime 381-382
74728   Psychotherapy by reciprocal inhibition: a comment on Dr. Wolpe's reply. M 1959, 32:236-238
74729   A question of responsibility. Psychiat soc Sci Rev 1968, 2:(Feb 2)
74730   Recent advances in the psycho-analytical study of delinquency. Roots of Crime 292-310
74731   Research in delinquency. Brit J Delinq 1951, 1:157-159. Roots of Crime 373-375
S-11901 Research methods in psycho-analysis. In Goldstein, A. P. & Dean S. J. The Investigation of Psychotherapy, NY: Wiley 1966, 13-20
74732   Research techniques in psychoanalysis and in general psychology: an essays in contrasts. In Cohen, J. Readings in Psychology, London: Allen & Unwin 1964, 354-360
74733   The roots of crime. Roots of Crime 3-24
74734   The Roots of Crime. Volume II of Selected Papers on Psycho-Analysis. London: Imago Publ Co; NY: IUP 1960, xiii + 422 p
            Abs J Am Psa Ass 1961, 9:169. Rv Gulotta, G. Riv Psa 1965, 11:178
74735   The roots of homosexuality. Brit J Delinq 1958, 9:5. Roots of Crime 389-390
74736   Sexual disorders and offences: introduction. Roots of Crime 173-174
74737   Sexual offences. Brit J Delinq 1952, 3:2-4. Roots of Crime 386-388
S-11904 The social and legal aspects of sexual abnormality. Roots of Crime 175-196
74738   Social defence or social aggression? Brit J Delinq 1954, 5:97. Roots of Crime 371-372
74739   Social psychiatry and the law. Brit J Delinq 1953, 4:79-80. Roots of Crime 364-366
74740   Some recent trends in psychoanalytic theory. Q 1961, 30:86-107
74741   Study of advanced cases. Brit J Delinq 1950, 1:4. Roots of Crime 376
S-47342 Team-research on delinquency. Roots of Crime 272-291

S-47344 Therapeutic criteria of psychoanalysis.
Criterios terapeúticos del psicoanálisis. Rev urug Psa 1961-62, 4:318-332
S-47345 The uses of Freudian theory in psychiatry.
Abs Frisch, A. J. An Surv Psa 1958, 9:51-52
74742 What I Believe (symposium contribution). London: Allen & Unwin 1966

See Eidelberg, Ludwig

REVIEWS OF:
74743 Bennett, I. Delinquent and Neurotic Children. J 1961, 42:291-292
74744 Fleiss, R. Ego and Body Ego: Contributions to Their Psychoanalytic Psychology. J 1963, 44:238-242
74745 Letters of Sigmund Freud 1873-1939. J 1962, 43:83-85

GLOVER, JAMES

74746 Divergent tendencies in psychotherapy. M 1962, 35:3-13
Abs ICFH Q 1962, 32:141-142

GLUCKSMAN, MYRON L.

74747 (& Hirsch, J.) The response of obese patients to weight reduction: a clinical evaluation of behavior. PSM 1968, 30:1-11
74748 (& Hirsch, J.; McCully, R. S.; Barron, B. A.; Knittle, J. L.) The response of obese patients to weight reduction. II. A quantitative evaluation of behavior. PSM 1968, 30:359-373
74749 (& Hirsch J.) The response of obese patients to weight reduction: III. The perception of body size. PSM 1969, 31:1-7

See McCully, Robert S.

GLUD, ARNE

74750 Filozofio Kaj Psikoanalizo. Prelego farita de la dua Internacia Konferenco de Esperantistaj Studentoj kaj Altlernejanjo (IKESA 2) en Ljubljana, Jugoslavujo, August 1953. [Philosophy and Psychoanalysis.] Copenhagen 1953

GLUECK, BERNARD C., JR.

74751 (& Stroebel, C. F.) The computer and the clinical decision process. II. P 1969, 125(Suppl 7):2-7
74752 Computers in psychiatry. P 1965, 122:325-326
74753 Current personality assessment research. Int Psychiat Clin 1966, 3(1): 205-222
74754 Pedophilia. In Slovenko, R. Sexual Behavior and the Law, Springfield, Ill: Thomas 1965, 539-562

See Azima, Hassan; Greenblatt, Milton; Solomon, Philip

GLUECK, BERNARD C., SR.

74755 Automation of patient behavioral observations. Proc IV World Cong Psychiat 1966, 1180

74756 (& Ackerman, N. W.) The reactions and behavior of schizophrenic patients treated with metrazol and camphor. JNMD 1939(3):310-332

74757 Sex offenses: a clinical approach. Law Contempo Probl 1960, 25:279-291

GLUECK, ELEANOR T.

74758 (& Glueck, S.) Identification of potential delinquents at 2-3 years of age. Int J soc Psychiat 1966, 12:5-16

GLUECK, SHELDON

74759 Discussion of Boorstein, S. "A psychoanalytic overview of the offender: implications for therapy." Psa Forum 1967, 2:260-261

74760 Law and Psychiatry. London: Tavistock 1963, 1967, 181 p

74761 (& Glueck, E. T.) Unraveling juvenile delinquency. In author's *Unraveling Juvenile Delinquency*, NY: Commonwealth Fund 1950, 192-197. In Lindzey, G. & Hall, C. S. *Theories of Personality*, NY: Wiley 1965, 1966, 1968, 340-343

74762 (& Glueck, E. T.) Ventures in Criminology. Selected Papers by Sheldon and Eleanor Glueck. London: Tavistock 1964, 363 p

See Glueck, Eleanor T.

GNEIST, J.

74762A [The religious character and religious behavior of the primary depressive personality.] (Ger) Confin Psychiat 1969, 12:164-184

GOBLE, A. J.

74763 Psychiatrists and psychoanalysis. Med J Aust 1964, (1):965

GÖDAN, HANS

74764 Der Traum als angebot für eine psychotherapeutische Zielsetzung. [The dream as an indicator for directed psychotherapy.] Z Psychother med Psychol 1966, 16:193-195

74765 Der Traum als Indikator für den therapeutischen Effekt. [The dream as an indicator of therapeutic effect.] Z Psychother med Psychol 1963, 13:54-56

GODENNE, GHISLAINE D.

74766 L'adolescence. [Adolescence.] In *Recipe*, Louvain, Belgium 1965, 383-386

74767 Aspect social des accidents du travail. [The social aspect of industrial accidents.] Brussels, Belgium 1946

74768 Dilemma and delinquency in teen-agers. Med Opin Rev 1966, 2:54-65

74769 Emotions and interpersonal relationships. In Schneiders, A. A. *Counseling the Adolescent*, San Francisco: Chandler Publ 1967, 182-187

74770 Emotions and interpersonal relationships in adolescence. In Schneiders, A. A. *The Teenager in American Culture*, Proceedings of the Workshop on the Teenager in American Culture, Mt. Saint Agnes College 1963, 107-112

74771 Les enfants inadaptes et delinquent aux Etats-Unis. (Conference) [Maladjusted and delinquent children in the United States.] Maroc Medical 1962, 41:879

74772 An experiment in teaching adolescence psychiatry. Adolescence 1967, 2(5):107-110

74773 Mental hygiene seminars for school personnel. Publ Hlth Rep 1966, 81: 348-350

74774 Outpatient adolescent group psychotherapy. I. Review of the literature on use of co-therapists, psychodrama, and parent group therapy. PT 1964, 18:584-593; 1965, 19:40-53

74775 A psychiatrist's techniques in treating adolescents. Children 1965, 12: 136-139

GODIN, ANDRÉ

74776 (Ed) Adult et Infant devant Dieu: Études de Psychologie Religieuse: Cahiers de Psychologie Religieuse. Brussels: Lumen Vitae Pr 1961, 182 p
      Child and Adult before God: Thought and Research: Lumen Vitae Studies in Religious Psychology. Brussels: Lumen Vitae Pr 1961, 151 p

74777 Freud et les préjugés religieux. [Freud and religious prejudices.] In *Journée Internationale Freud*, Brussels: International Organization for Preschool Children 1958, 21-30

74778 Guide pour Discerner les Troubles Mentaux. [Guide to Recognizing Mental Troubles.] Brussels: Tracts Publ 1968, (3rd ed) 40 p

74779 Mental health and Christian life. J Relig Hlth 1961, 1:41-54. In Belgum, D. *Religion and Medicine*, Ames, Iowa: Iowa State Univ Pr 1967, 144-159

74780 Psychotherapy and revelation. Continuum 1965, 2(4):672-679; 1966, 3(2):215-219

GOERTZEL, VICTOR

74781 (& May, P. R.; Salkin, J.; Schoop, T.) Body-ego technique: an approach to the schizophrenic patient. JNMD 1965, 141:53-60

GOETHALS, GEORGE W.

See Allinsmith, Wesley

GOFFIOUL, F.

See Bobon, J.

GOFFMAN, ERVING

74782 Normal deviants. In Greenblatt, M. et al: *The Patient and the Mental Hospital*, NY: Free Pr 1957, 507-510. In Scheff, T. J. *Mental Illness and Social Processes*, NY: Harper & Row 1967, 267-271

GOFORTH, EUGENE G.

74783 (& Mowatt, M. H.; Clarke, O. N. J.) Effect of the presence of an observer and a hidden observer on the defensive patterns of an ongoing group. Int J grp PT 1966, 16:338-343

74784   (& Tytus, J. S.; Oble, W.) Severe extrapyramidal signs associated with Trilafon therapy: a case report. Bull Mason Clin 1959, 13(1):9-13

ABSTRACTS OF:

74785   Dorpat, T. L. Regulatory mechanisms of the perceptual apparatus on involuntary physiological actions. Psa Forum 1966, 1:321-322

74786   Hilgard, E. R. The motivational relevance of hypnosis. Psa Forum 1966, 1:138

74787   Katz, A. et al: Cognitive regulation of autonimic responses. Psa Forum 1967, 2:88-89

74788   Reich, A. Masturbation and self esteem. Psa Forum 1966, 1:138

74789   Ross, N. The "as if" concept. Psa Forum 1967, 2:89-91

74790   Sinha, T. C. Psychoanalysis and the family life in India. Psa Forum 1966, 1:319-320

GOJA, HERMANN

S-12075 Das Zersingen der Volkslieder. Ein Beitrag zur Psychologie der Volksdichtung.
        The alteration of folk songs by frequent singing: a contribution to the psychology of folk poetry. Psa St Soc 1964, 3:111-170

GOLD, MILTON

74791   Freud's views on art. PPR 1961, 48(2):111-115

GOLDART, NATALIE

See Barbara, Dominick A.; Berk, Robert

GOLDBERG, ARNOLD I.

74792   (& Rubin, B.) Recovery of patients during periods of supposed neglect. M 1964, 37:265-272

See Offer, Daniel

GOLDBERG, BENJAMIN

74793   Family psychiatry and the retarded child. Canad Psychiat Ass J 1962, 7:140-146

GOLDBERG, EUGENE L.

See Kliman, Gilbert

ABSTRACTS OF:

74794   Archibald, H. C. et al: Bereavement in childhood and adult psychiatric disturbance. Q 1963, 32:608

74795   Blau, A. et al: The psychogenic etiology of premature births. Q 1964, 33:304

74796   Cassell, W. A. & Fisher, S. Body image boundaries and histamine flare reaction. Q 1964, 33:305-306

74797   Chertok, L. et al: Vomiting and the wish to have a child. Q 1964, 33:302-303

74798 Handlon, J. H. et al: Psychological factors lowering plasma 17-hydroxy-corticosteroid concentration. Q 1963, 32:610

74799 Kahana, R. J. A remission through crisis in ulcerative colitis. Q 1963, 32:610

74800 Lief, H. I. et al: Psychoendocrinologic studies in a male with cyclic changes in sexuality. Q 1963, 32:608-609

74801 McDonald, R. L. et al: Relations between maternal anxiety and obstetric complications. Q 1964, 33:306

74802 Pilot, M. L. et al: Duodenal ulcer in one of identical twins: a follow-up study. Q 1964, 33:305

74803 Poser, E. G. & Lee, S. G. Thematic content associated with two gastro-intestinal disorders. Q 1964, 33:303-304

74804 Renneker, R. E. et al: Psychoanalytical explorations of emotional correlates of cancer of the breast. Q 1964, 33:303

74805 Schoenberg, B. & Carr, A. C. An investigation of criteria for brief psychotherapy of neurodermatitis. Q 1964, 33:304-305

74806 Schonfeld, W. A. Gynecomastia in adolescence: effect on body image and personality adaptation. Q 1963, 32:609

74807 Shapiro, A. et al: Dream recall as a function of method of awakening. Q 1964, 33:304

74808 Stein, A. et al: Changes in hydrochloric acid secretion in a patient with a gastric fistula during intensive psychotherapy. Q 1963, 32:609

74809 Steinberg, R. Omnipotence, denial, and psychosomatic medicine. Q 1964, 33:303

74810 Weiner, H. et al: Cardiovascular responses and their psychological correlates. I. A study in healthy young adults and patients with peptic ulcer and hypertension. Q 1963, 32:609-610

GOLDBERG, F. H.

See Shaw, R.

GOLDBERG, I. A.

74811 (& McCarty, G. J.; Schwartz, E. K.; Wolf, A.) The absence of face to face contact in training in psychoanalysis in groups. In Proceedings of the 1st Congr Group Psychother, Milan, Italy, July 1963, 19:533-534

See McCarty, George J.; Wolf, Alexander

GOLDBERG, J.

See Danon-Boileau, Henri

GOLDBERG, JUNE

See Byrne, Donn E.

GOLDBERG, L.

REVIEW OF:
74812 Klein, M. The psychotherapy of the psychoses. Cuad Psa 1965, 1:387

GOLDBERG, MARTIN

74813 Psychiatric problems in marriage counseling. In Silverman, H. L. *Marital Counseling: Psychology, Ideology, Science,* Springfield, Ill: Thomas 1967, 91-99

74814 (& Mudd, E. H.) The effects of suicidal behavior on marriages and family. In Resnik, H. L. P. *Suicidal Behavior: Diagnosis and Management,* Boston: Little, Brown 1968, 348-356

GOLDBERG, PHILIP A.

74815 (& Milstein, J. T.) Perceptual investigation of psychoanalytic theory concerning latent homosexuality in women. Percept mot Skills 1965, 21:645-646

74816 (& Miller, S. J.) Structured personality tests and dissimulation. J proj Tech 1966, 30:452-455

GOLDBERGER, ALICE

See Burlingham, Dorothy T.

GOLDBERGER, LEO

74817 Discussion of Gorney, R. "Of divers things: preliminary note on the dynamics of scuba diving." Psa Forum 1966, 1:273-275

See Holt, Robert R.

GOLDBLATT, MICHAEL

74818 The effects of fantasy stimulation and inhibition of motor response on time estimation in the acting out adolescent. Diss Abstr 1967, 28(3-B): 969-970

GOLDBRUNNER, JOSEF

74819 Individuation: A Study of the Depth Psychology of Carl Gustav Jung. Notre Dame, Ind: Univ of Notre Dame Pr 1964, xii + 204 p

74820 The structure of the psyche and the personalist view of man: a critical study of the depth psychology of C. G. Jung. J psychol Res, Madras 1961, 5:97-102

GOLDEN, JOSHUA S.

74821 (& Wahl, C. W.) Psychosis in the hospitalized patient. Hosp Med 1967, 3(4):120-129

See Wahl, Charles W.

GOLDEN, JULES SAMLER

74822 (& Silver, R. J.; Marchionne, A. M.; Schwartz, E.) Process juvenile delinquents. Dis nerv Sys 1965, 27:383-388

GOLDEN, LESTER M.

74823 Freud's Oedipus: its mytho-dramatic basis. Am Im 1967, 24:271-282

GOLDEN, MORTON M.

74824 The acute attack of impotence. NYSJM 1961, 61:3787

74825 Education of the general practitioner by the psychiatrist in private practice. In *Monograph, Proceedings of the Fifth Amer Psychiat Assoc Colloquium for Postgraduate Teaching of Psychiatry,* Wash DC: Am Psychiat Ass 1966, 59-71

74826 Experience with small group seminars for psychiatric education of general practitioners. P 1965, 122:497-500

74827 The general practitioner—family physician and counsellor. Psychosomatics 1963, 4:263

74828 How are dental pain and pathology related to aggression, anger and hate? Why Rep 167-178

See Brody, Matthew

GOLDEN, RICHARD A.

74829 Hysterical personality and the psychiatric trainee. Virginia med Monthly 1968, 95:689-693

GOLDENBERG, GARY M.

74830 (& Auld, F., Jr.) Equivalence of silence to resistance. J consult Psychol 1964, 28:476

See Auld, Frank, Jr.

GOLDENBERG, HERBERT

See Bühler, Charlotte

GOLDENSON, ROBERT M.

See Hartley, Ruth E.

GOLDFARB, ALVIN IRVING

74831 Age and illness. In Lief, H. E. et al: *The Psychological Basis of Medical Practice,* NY/Evanston/London: Harper & Row 1963, 203-218

74832 The evaluation of geriatric patients following treatment. Proc Amer Psychopath Ass 1964, 52:271-308

74833 The geriatric group. In Kaufman, M. R. *The Psychiatric Unit in a General Hospital,* NY: IUP 1965, 240-268; 281-304

74834 Geriatric psychiatry. Compreh Txbk Psychiat 1564-1587

74835 Marital problems of older persons. Marriage Relat 105-119

74836 The mental health of the aged. Clinical perspectives. Psychiat Res Rep 1968, (23):170-178

74837 Patient-doctor relationship in treatment of aged persons. Geriatrics 1964, 19:18-23

74838 The search for aid. Psychiat Opin 1969, 6(6):12-15

74839 Social planning. Psychiat Res Rep 1968, (23):215-220

74840 What makes for successful retirement? Why Rep 471-484

See Altshuler, Kenneth Z.; Barad, Martin; Wolk, Robert L.

GOLDFARB, JACK HAROLD

74841 The concept of sexual identity in normals and transvestites: its relationship to the body-image, self-concept and parental identification. Diss Abstr 1964, 24:3385-3386

GOLDFARB, L.

See Rolo, A.

GOLDFARB, NATHAN

See Behrens, Marjorie L.; Goldfarb, William

GOLDFARB, S.

74841A (& Luminet, D.) [Illustration of the object-relationship in a case of corneal ulcer.] (Fr) Acta Neurol Belg 1969, 69:90-100

GOLDFARB, WILLIAM

74842 Anxiety and conflict in schizophrenic children. Sci Psa 1969, 14:151-162

74843 Child and adolescent services. In Ziskind, R. *Viewpoint on Mental Health*, NY: NYC Comm Ment Hlth Board 1967, 108-113

74844 Child psychosis. In Mussen, P. W. *Carmichael's Manual of Child Psychiatry, Vol. I.*, NY: Wiley 1969

74845 Childhood schizophrenia. J psychosom Res 1963, 7:65. Int Psychiat Clin 1964, 1:821-845

74846 Childhood Schizophrenia. Cambridge, Mass: Harvard Univ Pr 1962, vii + 216 p
Rv HRB Q 1963, 32:589-591

74847 (& Pollack, R. C.) The childhood schizophrenic's response to schooling in a residential treatment center. Proc Amer Psychopath Ass 1964, 52:221-246

74848 Corrective socialization: a rationale for the treatment of schizophrenic children. Canad Psychiat Ass J 1965, 10:481-496. J Hillside Hosp 1967, 16:53-72

74849 (& Goldfarb, N.) Evaluation of behavioral changes of schizophrenic children in residential treatment. PT 1965, 19:185-204

74850 Factors in the development of schizophrenic children: an approach to subclassification. In Romano, J. *The Origins of Schizophrenia*, Amsterdam/NY: Excerpta Medica Found 1967, 70-91

74851 Families of schizophrenic children. In Kolb, L. C. et al: *Mental Retardation*, Baltimore, Md: Williams & Wilkins 1962, 256-269

74852 An investigation of childhood schizophrenia: a retrospective view. Arch gen Psychiat 1964, 11:620-634

74853 (& Lorge, I.) A method for appraising children in inpatient psychiatric treatment: ranking for normality. J genet Psych 1959, 95:203-206

74854 The mutual impact of mother and child in childhood schizophrenia. Ops 1961, 31:738-747

74855 Pain reactions in a group of institutionalized schizophrenic children. Ops 1958, 28:777-785

74856 (& Mintz, I.) Schizophrenic child's reactions to time and space. Arch gen Psychiat 1961, 5:535-543

74857 Self-awareness in schizophrenic children. Arch gen Psychiat 1963, 8: 47-60
       Abs KR Q 1964, 33:300-301

74858 (& Goldfarb, N.; School, H. H.) The speech of mothers of schizophrenic children. P 1966, 122:1220-1227

74859 (& Braunstein, P.; Lorge, I.) A study of speech patterns in a group of schizophrenic children. Ops 1956, 26:544-555

74860 (& Mintz, I.; Stoock, K. W.) A Time to Heal: Corrective Socialization —A Treatment Approach to Childhood Schizophrenia. NY: IUP 1969, ix + 145 p

74861 (& Goldfarb, N.; Pollack, R. C.) Treatment of childhood schizophrenia. A three-year comparison of day and residential treatment. Arch gen Psychiat 1966, 14:119-128
       Abs PB Q 1969, 38:166

74862 (& Levy, D. M.; Meyers, D. I.) The verbal encounter between the schizophrenic child and his mother. In Goldman, G. S. & Shapiro, D. *Developments in Psychoanalysis at Columbia University*, NY: Hafner Publ 1966, 89-175

       See Behrens, Marjorie L.; Hoberman, Shirley E.; Levy, David M.; Meyers, Donald I.; Taft, L. T.

GOLDFRIED, MARVIN ROBERT

74863 The assessment of anxiety by means of the Rorschach. J proj Tech 1966, 30:364-380

74864 (& Ingling, J. H.) The connotative and symbolic meaning of the Bender Gestalt. J proj Tech 1964, 28:185-191

74865 A psychoanalytic interpretation of sensory deprivation. Psychol Rec 1960, 10:211-214

GOLDGAR, H.

74866 Square root of minus one: Freud and Robert Musil's Törless. Comp Lit 1965, 17:117-132

GOLDHIRSH, MARK ISADORE

74867 Manifest content of dreams of convicted sex offenders. ASP 1961, 63: 643-645

GOLDIN, PAUL CHANIN

74868 Experimental investigation of selective memory and the concept of repression and defense: a theoretical synthesis. ASP 1964, 69:365-380

74869 Repression and ego-defense: the effect of failure-stress on perceptual accuracy and self-concept. Diss Abstr 1963, 24:1697-1698

       See Fox, Ronald E.

GOLDING, STEPHEN L.

74870 (& Atwood, G. E.; Goodman, R. A.) Anxiety and two cognitive forms of resistance to the idea of death. Psychol Rep 1966, 18:359-364

GOLDINGS, CARMEN R.

74871 Some new trends in children's literature from the perspective of the child psychiatrist. J Amer Acad Child Psychiat 1968, 7:377-397

GOLDINGS, HERBERT J.

ABSTRACT OF:
74872 Van Amerongen, S. T. School problems of an adolescent patient. Bull Phila Ass Psa 1966, 16:92-95

GOLDMAN, ALFRED EMMANUEL

74873 (& Levine, M.) A developmental study of object sorting. Child Develpm 1963, 34:649-666
74874 Symbolic representation in schizophrenia. J Pers 1960, 28:293-316

GOLDMAN, ARNOLD

See Graff, Harold

GOLDMAN, BERNARD

REVIEW OF:
74875 Dorsey, J. M. Illness or Allness: Conversations of a Psychiatrist. Am Im 1965, 22:206-208

GOLDMAN, GEORGE D.

74876 The clinical psychologist as a therapist: training and practice. Prog clin Psych 1963, 5:178-188
74877 (& Milman, D. S.) (Eds) Modern Woman: Her Psychology and Sexuality. Springfield, Ill: Thomas 1969, xviii + 275 p
S-47461 Some applications of Harry Stack Sullivan's theories to group psychotherapy. In Rosenbaum, M. & Berger, M. *Group Psychotherapy and Group Function*, NY/London: Basic Books 1963, 188-194
74878 (& Shapiro, D.) (Eds) Developments in Psychoanalysis at Columbia University. NY: Hafner Publ 1966, xv + 357 p
       Rv Brandt, L. W. R 1969, 56:357-358
74879 Psychodynamics in schizophrenia. Int Psychiat Clin 1964, 1:711-734
S-47462 Reparative psychotherapy.
       Abs AaSt An Surv Psa 1956, 7:353-354

GOLDMAN, H.

See Rabin, Albert I.

GOLDMAN, IRVING B.

See Linn, Louis

GOLDMAN, MORRIS J.

74880 Beating fantasies; a critical review of an expaɪ ding concept. Bull Phila Ass Psa 1967, 17:63-74
74881 Popping and tonsillectomy. Bull Phila Ass Psa 1968, 18:83-87
74882 Some aspects of psychoanalytic understanding of symbolism. J Albert Einstein Med Center 1967, 15:151-156

See Fink, Paul J.; Levick, Myra

ABSTRACT OF:
74883 Weiner, N. D. On bibliomania. Bull Phila Ass Psa 1966, 16:101-103

GOLDSMITH, ETHEL

See Reding, Georges R.

GOLDSMITH, JEROME M.

74884 The Interprofessional Treatment of the Disturbed and Delinquent Adolescent. NY Acad Sci 1963
74885 The responsibility for mental health services to children. (Read at Amer Acad Psa, May 1968) Sci Psa 1969, 14:229-244

GOLDSTEIN, ARNOLD P.

74886 (& Dean, S. J.) (Eds) The Investigation of Psychotherapy: Commentaries and Readings. NY/London/Sydney: John Wiley & Sons 1966, xiv + 443 p
       Rv Beier, E. G. R 1967, 54:546-548. Simon, J. Q 1968, 37:452-454
74887 (& Shipman, W. G.) Patient expectancies, symptom reduction and aspects of the initial psychotherapeutic interview. Clin Psych 1961, 17:129-133. In author's The Investigation of Psychotherapy 307-311
74888 Patient's expectancies and nonspecific therapy as a basis for (un)spontaneous remission. Clin Psych 1960, 16:399-403. In author's The Investigation of Psychotherapy 202-206
74889 (& Heller, K.; Sechrest, L. B.) Psychotherapy and the Psychology of Behavior Change. NY: Wiley 1966, 472 p
       Rv Simon, J. Q 1968, 37:452-454
74890 Psychotherapy research and psychotherapy practice: independence or equivalence? In Lesse, S. An Evaluation of the Results of the Psychotherapies, Springfield, Ill: Thomas 1968, 5-17
74891 Psychotherapy research by extrapolation from social psychology. In author's The Investigation of Psychotherapy 36-42
74892 Therapist-Patient Expectancies in Psychotherapy. NY/Oxford: Pergamon Pr 1962, xvi + 141 p

GOLDSTEIN, FRED J.

See Kulka, Anna M.

GOLDSTEIN, IRIS BALSHAN

74893 (& Grinker, R. R., Sr.; Heath, H. A.; Oken, D.; Shipman, W. G.) Study in psychophysiology of muscle tension. I. Response specificity. Arch gen Psychiat 1964, 11:322-330

See Shipman, William G.

GOLDSTEIN, JACOB

See Friedman, Paul

GOLDSTEIN, JOSEPH

74894 (& Katz, J.) Abolish the "insanity defense"—why not? Yale Law J 1963, 72:853-876

74895 (& Katz, J.) Dangerousness and mental illness—some observations on the decision to release persons acquitted by reason of insanity. Yale Law J 1960, 70:225-239

74896 (& Katz, J.) The Family and the Law: Problems for Decision in the Family Law Process. NY: Free Pr; London: Collier-Macmillan 1965, xxxviii + 1229 p

Abs J Am Psa Ass 1967, 15:214. Rv Mulligan, W. G. Q 1967, 36: 127-129

74897 On the function of criminal law in riot control. (Read at Am Psa Ass, Dec 1968) Psa St C 1969, 24:463-487

74898 Psychoanalysis and jurisprudence: on the relevance of psychoanalytic theory to law. (Read at Hampstead Child-Therapy Clinic, 1965; at Am Psa Ass, May 1967; at Boston & Western New England Soc Psa, Oct 1967) Psa St C 1968, 23:459-479. Yale Law J 1968, 77:1053-1077

74899 (& Katz, J.) Why an "insanity defense." Daedalus 1963, 92:549-563

See Katz, Jay

GOLDSTEIN, KENNETH M.

See Blackman, Sheldon

GOLDSTEIN, KURT

74900 Human Nature in the Light of Psychopathology. NY: Schocken Books 1963, xiii + 258 p

S-12112B The Organism. A Holistic Approach to Biology Derived from Pathological Data in Man. Boston: Beacon Pr 1963, xx + 533 p. (Excerpt from) in Gardner, L. Theories of Personality, NY: Wiley 1965, 1966, 1968, 275-290

Rv Slochower, H Am Im 1964, 21:184

74901 La sonrisa del niño y el problema de la comprensión del "otro." [The child's smile and the problem of the comprehension of the "other."] Rev Psicoanal Psiquiat Psicol 1966, 30:69-82

GOLDSTEIN, LEO S.

See Deutsch, Martin

GOLDSTEIN, MELVIN

74902 Literature and Psychology, 1948-1968. (A commentary.) Lit & Psych 1967, 17:159-176

GOLDSTEIN, MICHAEL J.

74903 (& Jones, R. B.; Clemens, T. L.; Flagg, G. W.; Alexander, F. G.) Coping style as a factor in psychophysiological response to a tension-arousing film. J Pers soc Psychol 1965, 1:290-302

74904 (& Barthol, R. P.) Fantasy responses to subliminal stimuli. ASP 1960, 60:22-26
      Abs Appelbaum, S. A. Q 1961, 30:149-150

74905 (& Jones, R. B.; Kinder, M. I.) A method for the experimental analysis of psychological defenses through perception. J psychiat Res 1964, 2:135-146

74906 Perceptual reactions to threat under varying conditions of measurement. ASP 1964, 69:563-567

74907 Relationship between perceptual defense and exposure duration. J Pers soc Psychol 1966, 3:608-610

GOLDSTEIN, NESTOR

See Abuchaem, Jamil

GOLDSTEIN, NORMAN

See Parloff, Morris B.

GOLDSTEIN, ROBERT H.

See Salzman, Leonard F.

GOLEA, ANTOINE

74908 "Cosi fan tutte" im Lichte der Psychoanalyse. ["Cosi fan tutte" in the light of psychoanalysis.] Neue Z Musik 1960, 121:48-53

GOLIN, S.

See Teahan, John E.

GÖLLNITZ, G.

74909 Über das Phänomen der Angst in der Kinderpsychiatrie. [The phenomenon of anxiety in the psychiatry of children.] Psychiat Neurol med Psychol 1962, 14:121-128

GOLLOB, HARRY F.

74910 (& Levine, J.) Distraction as a factor in the enjoyment of aggressive humor. J Pers soc Psychol 1967, 5:368-372

74911 (& Dittes, J. E.) Effects of manipulated self-esteem on persuasibility depending on threat and complexity of communication. J Pers soc Psychol 1965, 2:195-201

GOLNER, JOSEPH

See Chafetz, Morris E.

GOLOSOW, NIKOLAS

74912 (& Weitzman, E. L.) Psychosexual and ego regression in the male transsexual. JNMD 1969, 149:328-336

GOLTZ, D.

74912A [Disease and speech.] (Ger) Sudhoffs Arch 1969, 53:225-269

GOMBOS, K.

74913 [Zoophobia in children.] (Hun) Gyermekgyogyaszat 1962, 13:124-128

GOMBRICH, ERNST H.

74914 Art and Illusion; A Study in the Psychology of Pictorial Representation. NY: Pantheon Books 1960, 466 p + 300 Illus
Rv Piers, M. W. Q 1962, 31:393-398
74915 The dream of reason: propaganda symbolism in the French Revolution. (Read at NY Psa Soc, 17 Dec 1962)
Abs Donadeo, J. Q 1963, 32:460-462
74916 Freud's aesthetics. Encounter 1966, 26(1):30-40
74917 Meditations on a Hobby Horse and Other Essays on the Theory of Art. Greenwich, Conn/London: Phaidon 1963, 184 p
74918 The use of art for the study of symbols. Am Psych 1965, 20:34-50

GOMES DE ARAUJO, H. A.

74919 Raison d'existence et psychotherapie. [The reason for existence and psychotherapy.] Ann méd-psychol 1960, 118(1):617-634

GOMEZ, EFRAIN

See Rabiner, Edwin L.

GOMEZ, JUAN

See Bobon, J.

GÓMEZ NEREA, J.

74920 Freud ao Ancance de Todos: a Higiene Sexual. [Freud within the Reach of All.] São Paulo: Musa 1966, 201 p
74921 Freud e Seu Processo de Curar. [Freud and His Method of Healing.] São Paulo: Editorial Sam Remo 1966, 156 p

GÓMEZ SOLER, SERGIO

74922 Teoria psicoanalitica de la hipnosis. [Psychoanalytical theory of hypnosis.] Rev dent Chile 1965, 55:170-173

GONDOR, LILY H.

74923 The fantasy of Utopia. PT 1963, 17:606-618
74924 Use of fantasy communications in child psychotherapy. In Haworth,
       M. R. *Child Psychotherapy*, NY/London: Basic Books 1964, 374-383

GONYEA, GEORGE C.

74925 The "ideal therapeutic relationship" and counseling outcome. Clin
       Psych 1963, 19:481-487

GONZÁLEZ, AVELINO

74926 Aspectos normales y patologicas del duelo. [Normal and abnormal
       aspects of mourning.] Cuad Psa 1965, 1:83-95
74927 Discussion of Bion, W. R. "Notes on memory and desire." Psa Forum
       1967, 2:275-277
74928 Editorial: Presentación. [Editorial—Introduction.] Cuad Psa 1965,
       1:3-5
74929 Obituary: Heinrich Racker. Rev Psicoanál 1961, 18:294-295
S-47488 Relaciones de objeto y oscilaciones en el ciclo depresión hipomanía.
       Abs RHB An Surv Psa 1957, 8:150-151
74930 (Reporter) Report of discussions of acting out—Spanish language sec-
       tion. J 1968, 49:227-228
       Abs LHR Q 1969, 38:668
74931 La urgencia de reunión como respuesta de la angustia de separacion.
       [The importance of reunion with respect to separation anxiety.] Cuad
       Psa 1967, 3:11-26

       See Aiza, Victor M.

       TRANSLATION OF:
       Levine, M. [20148]

GONZALEZ, JOHN R.

74932 Sexual aberration and problems of identity in schizophrenia. In Slo-
       venko, R. *Sexual Behavior and the Law*, Springfield, Ill: Thomas 1965,
       578-590

GONZÁLEZ, JOSÉ LUIS

74932A Esterilidad e infertilizacion. [Sterility and infertility.] Cuad Psa 1965,
       1:323-327
S-47495 Fantasías de retorno al seno materno e instintos de muerte.
       Abs An Surv Psa 1955, 6:174-175
74933 Los invulnerables. [The invulnerable.] Cuad Psa 1966, 2:31-38
S-47497 Psicosis paranoide transferencial.
       Abs An Surv Psa 1955, 6:348
74934 Repeticion obsesiva de una palabra compuesta y su significado edipíco.
       [Obsessive repetition of a made-up word and its oedipal significance.]
       Cuad Psa 1965, 1:175-178

GONZÁLEZ, MAURICIO
See Lizarazo, A.

TRANSLATION OF:
Menninger, K. A. [54010]

GONZÁLEZ DURO, E.
74935 Tratamiento de los delirios paranoides. [Treatment of paranoic delusions.] Actas Luso-esp Neurol Psiquiat 1968, 27:30-39

GONZÁLEZ MONCLÚS, E.
74936 Actitudes paranoides en la adolenscia. [Paranoid attitudes of adolescents.] Rev Psiquiat Psicol 1958, 3-5:381-394
Abs Vega An Surv Psa 1958, 9:312

GONZÁLEZ PINEDA, FRANCISCO
74937 Discussion of Cesarman, F. C. "Querer y deber." Cuad Psa 1967, 3: 151-155
74938 El Mexicano. Psicología de Su Destructividad. [The Mexican. Psychology of His Destructiveness.] Editorial Pax México (Monograph) Mex Psa Ass Publication
74939 El Mexicano. Su Dinámica Psicosocial. [The Mexican. His Psychosocial Dynamics.] Editorial Pax México. (Monograph) Mex Psa Ass Publication.

See Féder, Luis; Palacios López, Agustin

GOOD, JUNE A.
74940 Some relationships between hostility and fantasy production in children. Diss Abstr 1966, 26:6845-6846

See Burks, Henry L.

GOODE, BILL
74941 How little the Lady knew her Lord: a note on Macbeth. Am Im 1963, 20:349-356

GOODENOUGH, DONALD R.
74942 Discussion of Ephron, H. S. & Carrington, P. "Ego functioning in rapid eye movement sleep: implications for dream theory." Sci Psa 1967, 11:97-99
74943 The phenomena of dream recall. Prog clin Psych 1969, 8:136-153
74944 Some recent studies of dream recall. In Witkin, H. A. & Lewis, H. B. *Experimental Studies of Dreaming,* NY: Random House 1967, 127-147

See Karacan, Ismet; Lewis, Helen B.; Potter, Howard W.; Shapiro, A.; Witkin, Herman A.

GOODENOUGH, ERWIN R.

74945 The Psychology of Religious Experiences. NY/London: Basic Books
1965, 192 p
Rv Leavy, S. A. Q 1967, 36:292-293

GOODGLASS, HAROLD

See Deutsch, Felix; Pinderhughes, Charles A.

GOODHEART, EUGENE

74946 The Cult of the Ego. The Self in Modern Literature. Chicago/London:
Univ Chicago Pr 1968, x + 225 p
S-47510 Freud and Lawrence.
Abs EMW Q 1961, 30:458-459
74947 The Utopian Vision of D. H. Lawrence. Chicago: Univ Chicago Pr
1963, ix + 190 p

GOODMAN, HARVEY

74948 Passivity and psychotherapy. PT 1965, 19:616-621

GOODMAN, JEROME D.

74949 (& Silberstein, R. M.; Mandell, W.) Adopted children brought to child
psychiatric clinic. Arch gen Psychiat 1963, 9:451-456
74950 (& Sours, J. A.) The Child Mental Status Examination. NY: Basic
Books 1967, xii + 134 p

GOODMAN, JOHN T.

74951 Primary process thinking in children. Diss Abstr 1966, 26:4806

GOODMAN, LILLIAN R.

74952 Regression—some implications for nurses in large public psychiatric
hospitals. Nurs Outlook 1962, 10:265-267

GOODMAN, MORRIS

74953 (& Marks, M.) Oral regression as manifested and treated analytically
in group psychotherapy. Int J grp PT 1963, 13:3-9
74954 (& Marks, M.; Rockberger, H.) Resistance in group psychotherapy en-
hanced by the countertransference reactions of the therapist: a peer
group experience. Int J grp PT 1964, 13:332-343

GOODMAN, OSCAR B.

See Stetner, S. C. V.

GOODMAN, PAUL

74955 The freedom to be academic. The Cambridge Review 1956, (5):65-82.
In Stein, M. R. et al: *Identity and Anxiety*, Glencoe, Ill: Free Pr 1960,
351-366

74957 In search of community. Commentary 1960, 29:315-323

74958 A new deal for the arts. Commentary 1964, 37:68-71

74959 The psychological revolution and the writer's life-view. R 1963, 50: 367-374

      Abs SRS Q 1964, 33:605

74960 Utopian Essays and Practical Proposals. NY: Random House 1962, 289 p

GOODMAN, RICHARD A.

See Golding, Stephen L.

GOODMAN, STANLEY

74961 (Reporter) Current status of the theory of the superego. (Panel: Am Psa Ass, May 1964) J Am Psa Ass 1965, 13:172-180

74962 Discussion of Berliner, B. "Psychodynamics of the depressive character." Psa Forum 1966, 1:260-261

See Solnit, Albert J.

ABSTRACTS OF:

74963 Alpert, A. et al: Unusual variations in drive endowment. An Surv Psa 1956, 7:246-248

74964 Beres, D. Ego deviation and the concept of schizophrenia. An Surv Psa 1956, 7:279-282

74965 Boyer, L. B. On maternal overstimulation and ego defects. An Surv Psa 1956, 7:251-252

74966 Greenacre, P. Experiences of awe in childhood. An Surv Psa 1956, 7:255-256

74967 Hartmann, H. Notes on the reality principle. An Surv Psa 1956, 7: 110-113

74968 Kestenberg, J. S. On the development of maternal feelings in early childhood. Observations and reflexions. An Surv Psa 1956, 7:103-104

74969 Kris, E. The recovery of childhood memories in psychoanalysis. An Surv Psa 1956, 7:303-307

74970 Lustman, S. L. Rudiments of the ego. An Surv Psa 1956, 7:98-99

74971 Weil, A. P. Some evidences of deviational development in infancy and early childhood. An Surv Psa 1956, 7:285

74972 Zetzel, E. R. An approach to the relation between concept and content in psychoanalytic theory. An Surv Psa 1956, 7:68-71

GOODNOW, JACQUELINE J.

See Bruner, Jerome S.

GOODRICH, D. WELLS

74973 The aggression potential of two types of objects when used with aggressive children. Amer J occup Ther 1954, 8:165-170

74974 (& Bockhoven, J. S.; Hyde, R. W.) Behavioral characteristics of recovery from a psychosis. Occup Ther Rehabil 1951, 30:147-153

74975 Comment on Schleifer, M. J. "Methodology of clinical research studies of families of antisocial young children." J child Psychiat 1963, 2:72-98

74976   The developmental transaction, a basic unit for research on child mental health. In Proceedings of the Joint Meeting of the Japanese Society of Psychiatry and Neurology and the American Psychiatric Association, Suppl No. 7, Tokyo, Japan 1963

74977   Discussion of Schleifer, M. J. "The clinical process and research methodolgy." In Rexford, E. N. *A Developmental Approach to Problems of Acting Out*, NY: IUP 1966, 90-97

74978   (& Boomer, D. S.) Experimental assessment of marital modes of conflict resolution. Fam Proc 1963, 2:15-24

74979   (& Dittmann, A. T.) Observing interactional behavior in residential treatment. Arch gen Psychiat 1960, 2:421-428

74980   (& Ryder, R. G.; Raush, H. L.) Patterns of newlywed marriage. J Marriage & Fam 1968, 30:383-390

74981   Possibilities for preventive intervention during initial personality formation. In Caplan, G. *Prevention of Mental Disorders in Children*, NY: Basic Books 1961, 249-264

74982   Postgraduate education for clinical research. Ops 1968, 38:410-412

74983   Present status of research in occupational therapy. Amer J occup Ther 1954, 8:142-143; 183

74984   (& Fredman, S.; Ferguson, J.) A project in teaching scientific attitudes. Amer J occup Ther 1953, 7:125-127

74985   Psychological development and preventive psychiatry. J Nat Med Ass 1965, 57:199-202

74986   Quantification of the severity of overt psychotic symptoms. P 1953, 110:334-341

74987   Recent research in early family development and child personality. In Ojeman, R. H. *Recent Research Looking Toward Preventive Intervention*, Iowa: State Univ Iowa 1961, 41-87

74988   (& Swengel, E.; Saslow, G.) The social adjustment of 50 patients in a clinic for comprehensive medicine. JNMD 1954, 120:227-237

74989   (& Boomer, D. S.) Some concepts about therapeutic interventions with hyperaggressive children. Soc Casewk 1958, 39:207-213; 286-291

74990   (& Iflund, B.) Staff perceptions and reality in clinical behavior reporting. Hum Relat 1962, 15:351-363

74991   Toward a taxonomy of marriage. Mod Psa 407-423

See Boomer, Donald S.; Dittmann, Allen T.; Doniger, Joan; Kaplan, Donald M.; Raush, Harold L.; Ryder, Robert G.

GOODSITT, ALAN

74992   Anorexia nervosa. M 1969, 42:109-118

GOODSTEIN, L. D.

See Hunter, Clorinda G.

GOODSTONE, GERALD L.

74993   (& Wagner, P.; Rogawski, A.; Grotjahn, M.) Vocational hazards of psychoanalysis. A panel discussion. (Read at South Calif Psa Soc, 18 Mar 1963)
        Abs Peck, J. S. Bull Phila Ass Psa 1963, 13:148-150

ABSTRACTS OF:

74994 Baranger, W. The ego and the function of ideology. An Surv Psa 1958, 9:126-127

74995 Bell, A. I. Some thoughts on postpartum respiratory experiences and their relationship to pregenital mastery, particularly in asthmatics. An Surv Psa 1958, 9:205-206

74996 Bion, W. R. On arrogance. An Surv Psa 1958, 9:163-164

74997 Bion, W. R. On hallucination. An Surv Psa 1958, 9:184-185

74998 Bouvet, M. Technical variation and the concept of distance. An Surv Psa 1958, 9:345-347

74999 Gillespie, W. H. Neurotic ego distortion. An Surv Psa 1958, 9:154-155

75000 Greenson, R. R. Variations in classical psychoanalytic technique. An Surv Psa 1958, 9:343-344

75001 Inman, W. S. Clinical thought-reading. An Surv Psa 1958, 9:210-211

75002 Kemper, W. W. The manifold possibilities of therapeutic evaluation of dreams. An Surv Psa 1958, 9:214-215

75003 Leeuw, P. J. van der: On the pre-oedipal phase of the male. An Surv Psa 1958, 9:253-254

75004 Lorand, S. & Console, W. A. Therapeutic results in psychoanalytic treatment without fee (observation on therapeutic results). An Surv Psa 1958, 9:411-412

75005 Mahler, M. S. Autism and symbiosis, two extreme disturbances of identity. An Surv Psa 1958, 9:245-246

75006 Nacht, S. Causes and mechanisms of ego-distortion. An Surv Psa 1958, 9:158

75007 Payne, S. Dr. Ernest Jones. An Surv Psa 1958, 9:9

75008 Sperling, S. J. On denial and the essential nature of defence. An Surv Psa 1958, 9:120-123

75009 Wheelis, A. The Quest for Identity. An Surv Psa 1958, 9:454-460

GOODWIN, FREDERICK K.

See Hollender, Marc H.

GOODWIN, HILDA M.

75010 (& Mudd, E. H.) Concepts of marital diagnosis and therapy as developed at the Division of Family Study, Department of Psychiatry, School of Medicine, University of Pennsylvania. In Nash, E. M. et al: *Marriage Counseling in Medical Practice*, Chapel Hill: Univ North Carolina Pr 1964, 276-282

75011 A differential approach in marriage counseling with the disturbed client. In Silverman, H. L. *Marital Counseling: Psychology, Ideology, Science*, Springfield, Ill: Thomas 1967, 447-454

75012 (& Mudd, E. H.) Indications for marriage counseling, methods and goals. J comprehen Psychiat 1966, 7:450-462

75013 (& Dorfman, E.) Ministers evaluate their training in marriage counseling. J Relig Hlth 1965, 4:414-420

See Appel, Kenneth E.; Linden, Maurice E.; Mudd, Emily H.

GOODWIN, MARION S.

See Yarrow, Leon J.

GOOLKER, PAUL

75014   Affect communication in therapy. J Hillside Hosp 1961, 10:170-182
        Abs JA Q 1962, 31:585

REVIEWS OF:
75015   Abramson H. A. (Ed) Neuropharmacology. Transactions of the Fifth
        Conference, May 1959, Princeton, New Jersey. Q 1961, 30:449
75016   Abramson, H. A. (Ed) The Use of LSD in Psychotherapy. Trans-
        actions of a Conference on d-Lysergic Acid Diethylamide (LSD-25),
        April 1959, Princeton, New Jersey. Q 1961, 30:448-449
75017   Ostow, M. Drugs in Psychoanalysis and Psychotherapy. Q 1964, 33:
        285-286
75018   Stein, M. I. (Ed) Contemporary Psychotherapies. Q 1963, 32:117-119

GÖPPERT, HANS

75019   Klinische Psychotherapie der Neurosen im Rahmen der Psychiatrischen
        Klinik. [Clinical psychotherapy of the neuroses in the framework of the
        psychiatric hospital.] Nervenarzt 1962, 33:106-111
75020   Personale sexualpathologie. [Personal sexual pathology.] Jb Psychol
        Psychother med Anthropol 1960, 7:228-242
75021   Phänomenologie und Prognose der Zwangskrankheit. [Phenomenology
        and prognosis of obsessional disease.] Z PSM 1966, 12:111-118
75022   Psychotherapie der Angst. [Psychotherapy of anxiety.] Jb Psychol Psy-
        chother med Anthropol 1960, 7:214-217
75023   Sexual krisen bei Jugendlichen. [Sexual crises in adolescents.] Z Psy-
        chother med Psychol 1962, 12:112-122
75024   Zwang und Zwangsneurose. [Compulsion and compulsive neurosis.] Z
        Psychother med Psychol 1964, 14:87-95

GÖPPINGER, H.

75025   Die Bedeutung der Psychopathologie für die Kriminologie. [The im-
        portance of psychopathology for criminology.] In Kranz, H. Psycho-
        pathologie Heute, Stuttgart: Georg Thieme 1962, 316-321

GORDON, ANDREW

75026   "The Naked and the Dead": the triumph of impotence. Lit & Psych
        1969, 19(3-4):3-13

GORDON, BETTY N.

See Jensen, Gordon D.

GORDON, CAROL M.

75027   Some effects of information, situation, and personality on decision mak-
        ing in a clinical setting. J consult Psychol 1966, 30:219-224

See Spence, Donald P.

GORDON, DAVID

75028   The son and the father: patterns of response to conflict in Hemingway's fiction. Lit & Psych 1966, 16:122-138

GORDON, EDMUND W.

S-47527 (& Ullman, M.) Reactions of parents to problems of mental retardation in children. In Crow, L. D. & Crow, A. *Readings in Child and Adolescent Psychology*, NY/London/Toronto: Longmans 1961, 521-527

GORDON, EZRA

See Grinker, Roy R., Sr.

GORDON, IRA J.

75029   (& Regan, P. F.; Glen, R. S.; Jourard, S. M.) The first-year medical student: problems in the development of perceptiveness and self-awareness. Psychiat Res Rep 1961, (14):110-131

GORDON, JESSE E.

75030   (& Cohn, F.) Effect of fantasy arousal of affiliation drive on doll play aggression. ASP 1963, 66:301-307
75031   (Ed) Handbook of Clinical and Experimental Hypnosis. NY: Macmillan 1966, 1967, viii + 653 p
S-47534 Leading and following psychotherapeutic techniques with hypnotically induced repression and hostility. In Goldstein, A. P. & Dean, S. J. *The Investigation of Psychotherapy*, NY: Wiley 1966, 383-389
75032   (& Freston, M.) Role-playing and age regression in hypnotized and nonhypnotized subjects. J Pers 1964, 32:411-419

GORDON, KENNETH H., JR.

75033   An approach to childhood psychosis: simultaneous treatment of mother and child. J Amer Acad Child Psychiat 1963, 2:711-724
75034   Child with a defective stimulus barrier: ego development during treatment. Arch gen Psychiat 1961, 4:483-493
        Abs KR Q 1962, 31:428
75035   Psychotherapeutic technique. The application of psychoanalytic theory. J Amer Acad Child Psychiat 1968, 7:152-160
75036   Religious prejudice in an eight-year-old boy. (Read at Am Psa Ass, May 1963) Q 1965, 34:102-107
        Abs Hinojosa, J. R. Cuad Psa 1965, 1:300

GORDON, LILLIAN

S-47560 Incest as revenge against the pre-Oedipal mother.
        Abs An Surv Psa 1955, 6:154-155

GORDON, LOIS G.

75037   "Portnoy's Complaint": coming of age in Jersey City. Lit & Psych 1969, 19(3-4):57-60

GORDON, MICHAEL

See Green, Philip C.

GORDON, NORMA S.

75038 (& Bell, R. Q.) Activity in the human newborn. Psychol Rep 1961,
9:103-116

GORDON, ROSEMARY

75039 The concept of projective identification, an evaluation. J anal Psych
1965, 10:127-149
75040 The death instinct and its relation to the self. J anal Psych 1961, 6:119-
135
75041 Stereotype of Imagery and Belief as an Ego Defense: NY: Cambridge
Univ Pr 1962, vii + 96 p
75042 Symbols: content and process. J anal Psych 1967, 12:23-34
75043 Transference as a fulcrum of analysis. J anal Psych 1968, 13:109-117

GORDON, SOL

75044 A psychotherapeutic approach to adolescents with character disorders.
Ops 1960, 30:757-766

GORDON, W. W.

75045 A Pavlovian approach to psychiatry. Conditional Reflex 1966, 1:125-
136

GORER, GEOFFREY

75046 Ardrey on human nature. Animals, nations, imperatives. Encounter
1967, 28(6):66-71
75047 Chapter 3. In Rolph, C. H. *Does Pornography Matter?*, London: Routledge 1961, 27-40
75048 Death, Grief, and Mourning in Contemporary Britain. London: Cresset
Pr 1965, vii + 184 p
Rv Blauner, R. R 1968, 55:521-522
75049 The pornography of death. In Stein, M. R. et al: *Identity and Anxiety,*
Glencoe, Ill: Free Pr 1960, 402-407
75050 Psychoanalysis in the world. In Rycroft, C. *Psychoanalysis Observed,*
NY: Coward-McCann; London: Constable 1966

REVIEWS OF:
75051 Devereux, G. Mohave Ethnopsychiatry and Suicide: The Psychiatric
Knowledge and the Psychic Disturbances of an Indian Tribe. J 1963,
44:245-248
75052 Dicks, H. V. Marital Tensions: Clinical Studies Towards a Psychological Theory of Interaction. J 1968, 49:107-109
75053 Freud, S. & Bullitt, W. C. Thomas Woodrow Wilson: Twenty-Eighth
President of the United States—A Psychological Study. J 1967, 48:
468-470
75054 Hagen, E. E. On the Theory of Social Change. J 1965, 46:398-399

75055 Muensterberger, W. & Axelrad, S. (Eds) The Psychoanalytic Study of Society, Vol. 1. J 1962, 43:188-191

GORLOW, LEON

See Culbertson, Ellen

GORMAN, FRANK J.

See Freeman, Edith H.

GORMAN, WARREN F.

75056 Body words. R 1964, 51:15-28
   Abs Rosarios, H. Rev Psicoanál 1964, 21:188. SRS Q 1965, 34:309
75057 Flavor, Taste and the Psychology of Smell. Springfield, Ill: Thomas 1964, 106 p
   Rv Vega R 1965, 52(1):138-139
75058 (& Heller, L. G.) The psychological significance of words. R 1964, 51:5-14
   Abs SRS Q 1965, 34:308-309

REVIEWS OF:
75059 Barral, M. R. Merleau-Ponty: The Role of the Body-Subject in Interpersonal Relations. R 1968, 55:152-153
75060 Spitz, R. A. No and Yes. On the Genesis of Human Communication. R 1966, 53(1):145-148

GORNEY, RODERIC

75061 A case of schizophrenia with obsessive and paranoid features. J Hillside Hosp 1952, 1:166-189
75062 Of divers things: preliminary note on the dynamics of scuba diving. Psa Forum 1966, 1:266-269; 275-276
   Abs Cuad Psa 1967, 3:165
75063 Work and love revisited. Proc IV World Cong Psychiat 1966, 2542-2544

See Janowsky, D. S.

GÖRRES, ALBERT

75064 An den Grenzen der Psychoanalyse. [At the Boundaries of Psychoanalysis.] Munich: Kösel-Verlag 1968, 246 p
75065 (& Heiss, R.; Thomä, H.; Uexküll, T. von) Denkschrift zur Lage der Psychotherapie und der Medizinischen Psychosomatik. [The Position of Psychotherapy and Psychosomatic Medicine.] Franz Steiner Verlag 1964, 129 p
S-47567 Methode und Erfahrungen der Psychoanalyse.
   The Methods and Experience of Psychoanalysis. (Tr: Wharton, N.) (Foreword: Stern, K.) NY: Sheed and Ward 1962, 300 p
S-47569 Die Technik der Psychoanalyse. Zu Edward Glover: The Technique of Psycho-Analysis.
   Abs BB An Surv Psa 1956, 7:62

GORSUCH, RICHARD L.

75066   (& Spielberger, C. D.) Anxiety, threat, and awareness in verbal conditioning. J Pers 1966, 34:336-347
75067   The clarification of some superego factors. Diss Abstr 1965, 26:477-478
75068   The general factor in the test anxiety questionnaire. Psychol Rep 1966, 19:308

GOSHEN, CHARLES E.

75069   (Ed) Documentary History of Psychiatry; A Source Book on Historical Principles. NY: Philos Libr 1967, x + 904 p
75070   Mental retardation and neurotic maternal attitudes. A research report. Arch gen Psychiat 1963, 9:168-174
75071   Observations on the physiological and the psychiatric aspects of selected types of head injury. W Virginia med J 1966, 62:155-160
75072   The problem child. GP 1964, 30:78-84
75073   A systematic classification of the phenomenology of emotions. Psychiat Q 1967, 41:483-495
75074   Therapeutic implications of diagnosis. Curr psychiat Ther 1962, 2:8-18

GOSLINER, BERTRAM J.

See Mahler, Margaret S.

GOSLING, ROBERT H.

75075   Chapter 5. In Rolph, C. H. *Does Pornography Matter?* London: Routledge & Kegan 1961, 55-79
75076   The crisis of coming up. Cambridge Rev 1967, 89A(2155)
75077   (& Miller, D. H.; Woodhouse, D. L.; Turquet, P. M.) The Use of Small Groups in Training. London: Tavistock Inst of Medical Psychology, Codicote Pr 1967, 144 p
75078   What is transference? In Sutherland, J. D. *The Psychoanalytic Approach*, London: Baillière & Cassell 1968, 1-10

See Balint, Michael

GOSSELIN, JEAN-YVES

75079   (& Rouleau, Y.; Montgrain, N.-H.) Quelques aspects psychosomatiques du glaucôme. [Some psychosomatic aspects of glaucoma.] Canad Psychiat Ass J 1967, 12:559-562

GOSSETT, JOHN T.

75080   An experimental demonstration of Freudian repression proper. Diss Abstr 1964, 25:1332-1333

GOSTIGAN, GIOVANNI

75081   Sigmund Freud: A Short Biography. NY: Macmillan 1965, xiv + 206 p

GOTTESFELD, HARRY

See Fink, Geraldine; Waxenberg, Sheldon E.

GOTTHEIL, EDWARD

75082 Conceptions of orality and anality. JNMD 1965, 141:155-160
75082A (& Backup, C. E.; Cornelison. F. S., Jr.,) Denial and self-image confrontation in a case of anorexia nervosa. JNMD 1969, 148:238-250
75083 An empirical analysis of orality and anality. JNMD 1965, 141:308-317
75084 (& Stone, G. C.) Factor analytic study of orality and anality. JNMD 1968, 146:1-17
75085 (& Paredes, A.; Exline, R. V.) Parental schemata in emotionally disturbed women. JAbP 1968, 73:416-419

GOTTLIEB, ANTHONY A.

75086 (& Kramer, M.) Alternate-therapist group meetings: an approach to the severely ambivalent patient. Int J grp PT 1965, 15:187-197
75087 (& Pattison, E. M.) Married couples group psychotherapy. Arch gen Psychiat 1966, 14:143-152
75088 (& Gleser, G. C.; Gottschalk, L. A.) Verbal and physiological responses to hypnotic suggestion of attitudes. PSM 1967, 29:172-183

See Gottschalk, Louis A.

GOTTLIEB, J.

75089 (Contributor to) Discussion of Kanner, L. "Schizophrenia as a concept." Out-Patient Schiz 52-59
75090 (Contributor to) Discussion of Williams, G. E. "Crisis in the evaluation of the schizophrenic patient." Out-Patient Schiz 74-86

GOTTLIEB, JACQUES S.

75091 (& Tourney, G.) (Eds) Scientific Papers and Discussions. Divisional Meeting, Midwest Arena District Branches, American Psychiatric Association, Detroit, Michigan, October 29-31, 1959. Wash DC: Am Psychiat Ass 1960, 328 p

GOTTREICH, NORMAN S.

ABSTRACTS OF:
75092 Davidson, P. W., III: Depersonalization phenomena in 214 adult psychiatric inpatients. Q 1968, 37:476
75093 Frosch, J. The psychotic character: clinical psychiatric considerations. Q 1966, 35:312-313
75094 Goldberg, G. J. Obsessional paranoid syndromes. Q 1967, 36:321
75095 Jackel, M. M. Transference and psychotherapy. Q 1968, 37:475-476
75096 Maerov, A. S. Prostitution: a survey and review of twenty cases. Q 1967, 36:322
75097 Parkin, A. Neurosis and schizophrenia: I. Historical review. II. Modern perspectives. III. Clinical considerations. Q 1968, 37:476
75098 Purchard, P. R. "Neurodermatitis" with a case study. Q 1966, 35:313
75099 Roth, N. Psychogenic visual defect and the visual field. Q 1966, 35:312
75100 Sadoff, R. L. On the nature of crying and weeping. Q 1968, 37:476
75101 Schwartz, D. A. The paranoid-depressive existential continuum. Q 1966, 35:313

75102 Stancer, H. C. et al: Interpersonal psychodynamics of voluntary psychi-
       atric admissions. Q 1967, 36:321-322
75103 Zegans, L. S. Beyond the "wound and the bow." Q 1966, 35:313

GOTTSCHALK, LOUIS A.

75104 (& Gleser, G. C.) An analysis of the verbal content of suicide notes.
       M 1960, 33:195-204
75105 (& Stone, W. N.; Gleser, G. C.; Iacono, J. M.) Anxiety and plasma free
       fatty acids (FFA). Life Sci 1969, 8(2):61-68
75106 (& Stone, W. N.; Gleser, G. C.; Iacono, J. M.) Anxiety levels in
       dreams: relation to changes in plasma free fatty acids. Science 1966,
       153:654-657
75107 (Ed) Comparative Psycholinguistic Analysis of Two Psychotherapeutic
       Interviews. NY: IUP 1961, 221 p
          Rv Scheflen, A. E. Q 1963, 32:591-595
75108 Depressions—psychodynamic considerations. In Cole, L. O. & Witten-
       born, J. R. Pharmacotherapy of Depressions, Springfield, Ill: Thomas
       1966, 30-46
75109 (& Gleser, G. C.) Distinguishing characteristics of the verbal communi-
       cations of schizophrenic patients. Disorders of Communication A.R.N.
       M.D. 1964, 42:400-413
75110 (& Gleser, G. C.; Wylie, H. W., Jr.; Kaplan, S. M.) Effects of imi-
       pramine on anxiety and hostility levels. Psychopharmacologia 1965,
       7:303-310
75111 (& Gleser, G. C.; Springer, K. J.; Kaplan, S. M.; Shanon, J.; Ross,
       W. D.) Effects of perphenazine on verbal behavior patterns. Arch gen
       1960, 2:632-639
75112 (& Frank, E. C.) Estimating the magnitude of anxiety from speech.
       Behav Sci 1967, 12:289-295
75113 (& Springer, K. J.; Gleser, G. C.) Experiments with a method of assess-
       ing the variations in intensity of certain psychological states occurring
       during two psychotherapeutic interivews. In author's Comparative Psy-
       cholinguistic Analysis of Two Psychotherapeutic Interviews 115-138
75114 (& Gleser, G. C.; Magliocco, E. B.; D'Zmura, T. L.) Further studies on
       the speech pattern of schizophrenic patients. (Measuring inter-individ-
       ual differences in relative degree of personal disorganization and social
       alienation.) JNMD 1961, 132:101-113
75115 (& Auerbach, A. H.) Goals and problems in psychotherapy research.
       Meth Res PT 3-9
75116 Introspection and free-association as experimental approaches to assess-
       ing subjective and behavioral effects of psychoactive drugs. In Uhr,
       L. M. & Miller, J. G. Drugs and Behavior, NY: Wiley 1960, 587-590
75117 (& Winget, C. N.; Gleser, G. C.) Manual of Instructions for Using the
       Gottschalk-Gleser Content Analysis Scales: Anxiety, Hostility, and So-
       cial Alienation-Personal Disorganization. Berkeley, Calif: Univ Calif
       Pr 1969, vi + 176 p
75118 (& Winget, C. M.; Gleser, G. C.; Springer, K. J.) The measurement of
       emotional changes during a psychiatric interview: a working model
       toward quantifying the psychoanalytic concept of affect. Meth Res PT
       93-126

75119 The measurement of hostile aggression through the content analysis of speech: some biological and interpersonal aspects. In author's *The Measurement of Psychological States through the Content Analysis of Verbal Behavior.* In Garattini, S. & Sigg, E. B. *Aggressive Behavior,* NY/Amsterdam: Excerpta Medica Foundation 1969, 299-316

75120 (& Gleser, G. C.) The Measurement of Psychological States through the Content Analysis of Verbal Behavior. Berkeley, Calif: Univ Calif Pr 1969, xxi + 317 p

75121 Measuring individual responses to psychoactive drugs by an introspective method and a verbal behavior (or free-associative) method. In *Transactions of the 6th Annual Research Conference on Cooperative Chemotherapy Studies on Psychiatry and Broad Research Approaches to Mental Illness,* Veterans Administration 1961, 6:324-330

75122 (& Auerbach, A. H.) (Eds) Methods of Research in Psychotherapy. (Foreword: Brosin, H. W.) NY: Appleton-Century-Crofts 1966, xviii + 654 p

75123 The mild addictions to tobacco, alcohol, and the pills. Med Digest 1968, 14:39-54

75124 Phasic circulating biochemical reflections of transient mental content. In Mandell, A. & Mandell, M. *Methods and Theory in Psychochemical Research,* NY: Academic Pr 1968

75125 (& Mayerson, P.; Gottlieb, A. A.) The prediction and evaluation of outcome in an emergency brief psychotherapy clinic. JNMD 1967, 144:77-96

75126 (& Pattison, E. M.) Psychiatric perspectives on T-groups and the laboratory movement: an overview. P 1969, 126:823-839

75127 Psychiatric problems seen in the general practice of medicine. In Hofling, C. K. *Textbook of Psychiatry for Medical Practice,* Phila/Montreal: J. B. Lippincott 1963, 130-181

75128 Psychoanalytic notes on T-groups at the Human Relations Laboratory, Bethel, Maine. Comprehen Psychiat 1966, 7:472-487

75129 Psychologic factors in backache. Gen Practice 1966, 33:91-94. Lawyer's med J 1967, 13:73-87

75130 (& Titchener, J. L.; Piker, H. N.; Stewart, S. S.) Psychosocial factors associated with pregnancy in adolescent girls: a preliminary report. JNMD 1964, 138:524-534

S-47603 The relationship of psychologic state and epileptic activity. Psychoanalytic observations on an epileptic child.
        Abs JA An Surv Psa 1956, 7:275-279

75131 Some applications of the psychoanalytic concept of object relatedness: preliminary studies on a human relations content analysis scale applicable to verbal samples. (Read at Topeka Psa Soc, 20 Apr 1967) Comprehen Psychiat 1968, 9:608-620

75132 Some problems in the evaluation of psychoactive drugs, with and without psychotherapy, in the treatment of non-psychotic personality disorders. In Efron, D. *Psychopharmacology Research and Therapy,* Wash DC: US Govt Printing Office 1968, 255-269

75133 (& Gleser, G. C.; D'Zmura, T.; Hanenson, I. B.) Some psychophysiologic relations in hypertensive women, effect of hydrochlorothiazide on the relation of affect to blood pressure. PSM 1964, 26:610-617

75134 (& Whitman, R. M.) Some typical complications mobilized by the psycho-analytic procedure. (Read at Chicago Psa Soc, 24 May 1960) J 1962, 43:142-150
   Abs FTL Q 1963, 32:287

75135 (& Gleser, G. C.; Stone, W. N.; Kunkel, R. L.) Studies of psychoactive drugs effects on non-psychiatric patients. Measurement of affective and cognitive changes by content analysis of speech. In Evans, W. O. & Kline, N. S. *The Psychopharmacology of the Normal Human*, Springfield, Ill: Thomas 1968, 162-188

75136 (& Cleghorn, J. M.; Gleser, G. C.) Studies of relationships of emotions to plasma lipids. PSM 1965, 27:102-111

75137 Summary and critical comments. In author's *Comparative Psycholinguistic Analysis of Two Psychotherapeutic Interviews*, 202-221

75138 Theory and application of a verbal behavior method of measuring transient psychologic states. In Salzinger, K. & Salzinger, S. *Research in Verbal Behavior and Some Neurophysiological Implications*, NY: Academic Pr 1967, 299-325

75139 (& Gleser, G. C.; Springer, K. J.) Three hostility scales applicable to verbal samples. Arch gen Psychiat 1963, 9:254-279

75140 (& Kunkel, R. L.; Wohl, T.; Saenger, E.; Winget, C. N.) Total and half body irradiation: effect on cognitive and emotional processes. Arch gen Psychiat 1969, 21:574-580

75141 Training in psychosomatic research. Adv PSM 1967, 5:25-45

75142 The use of drugs in information-seeking interviews. In Uhr, L. M. & Miller, J. G. *Drugs and Behavior*, NY: Wiley 1960, 515-518

75143 The use of drugs in interrogation. In Biderman, A. D. & Zimmer, H. M. *The Manipulation of Human Behavior*, NY: Wiley 1961, 96-141

75144 (& Kaplan, S. M.; Gleser, G. C.; Winget, C. M.) Variations in magnitude of emotion: a method applied to anxiety and hostility during phases of the menstrual cycle. PSM 1962, 24:300-311

See Gleser, Goldine C.; Gottlieb, Anthony A.; Kaplan, Stanley M.; Kapp, Frederic T.; Kunkel, Robert L.; Pattison, E. Mansell

GOTTWALD, ADRIANE

TRANSLATION OF:
Beradt, C. [67107]

GOUDSMIT, H. R.

75145 [The father of the child of the unmarried mother.] (Dut) T Ziekenverpl 1966, 19:80-85

GOUDSMIT, W.

75146 Adolescenten en psychodysleptica. [Adolescents and psychodysleptica.] Maandbl voor Berechting en Reclassering 1968, 46:212-219

75147 De gestoorde delinkwent in de nazorg. [The mentally disturbed delinquent and aftercare.] In *Reclassering nu en Straks*, Alphen: N. Samsom 1967, 9-23

75148 Moord en ambivalentie. [Murder and ambivalence.] Ned Tijdschr Criminol 1966, 8:142-148

75149 On wil of onmacht. [Inability to act.] Ned Tijdschr Criminol 1960, 2:75-87

75150 Over psychotherapie. [On psychotherapy.] Maandblad voor Berechting en Reclassering 1962, 41:129-135

75151 Psychiatrie en Reclassering. [Psychiatry and Probation.] Boom: Meppel 1967, 336 p (summary in English)

75152 Psychotherapie bei delinquenten. [Psychotherapy of delinquents.] Psyche 1964, 17:664-684

75153 Über Abwehrmechanismen bei sogenannten Psychopathen. [Defense mechanisms in so-called psychopaths.] Psyche 1962, 16:512-520

75154 Zedendelicten: dader, slachtoffer en maatschappij. [Sex-offences: offender, victim and society.] T Ziekenverpleging 1963, 16:122-130

GOULD, ROBERT E.

75155 The delinquent adolescent. In Nichtern, S. *Mental Health Services for Adolescents, Proceedings of the Second Hillside Hospital Conference,* Frederick Praeger 1968, 186-220

75156 Discussion of Symonds, M. "The oppositional adolescent." Sci Psa 1966, 9:45-47

75157 Dr. Strangeclass or: how I stopped worrying about the theory and began treating the blue collar worker. Ops 1967, 37:78-86. J contemp PT 1968, 1:49-63

75158 The hippie scene. Med Times 1968, 96:449-510

75159 A psychiatrist views the beatnik. Med Times 1966, 94:1178-1188

75160 Suicide problems in children and adolescents. PT 1965, 19:228-246

See Martin, John M.; Sadock, Benjamin J.

GOULD, THOMAS

75161 Innocence of Oedipus and the nature of tragedy. Massachusetts Rev 1969, 10:281-300

75162 Platonic Love. NY: Free Pr Glencoe 1963, vii + 216 p

GOWDEY, C.

See Papageorgis, Demetrios

GOZZANO, M.

75163 (et al) Conferenza internazionale a tavola rotunda sugli aspetti psicosomatici dell'allergia. [International round table conference on the psychosomatic aspects of allergy.] Med psicosom 1960, 5:3-56

GOZZI, M. T.

See Carloni, Glauco

GRABER, GUSTAV HANS

75164 Abriss zur Geschichte der Traumdeutung. [Summary of the history of dream interpretation.] Psychol, Bern 1960, 12(7-8)

75165 Ambivalenz bei alten Völkern und Primitiven. [Ambivalence in old and in primitive people.] Psychol, Bern 1962, 14(12)

75166 Ambivalenz der Sexualität. [Ambivalence of sexuality.] Psychol, Bern 1962, 14(3)

75167 Artung und Entartung der weiblichen Liebe. [The formation and degeneration of womanly love.] In *Krisis und Zukunft der Frau*, Stuttgart: E. Klett-Verlag 1962. Psychol, Bern 1963, 15(11)

75168 Die Befreiung Der Frau. Entwicklung zum Weiblichen und Ewig-Weiblichen in Mädchen, Frau und Mutter. [The Liberation of Woman. The Development of Feminity and the Eternal Feminine in Young Girl, Wife, and Mother.] (2nd ed) Bern: Arjuna-Verlag 1960
L'Âme Feminine et son Devenir. L'Évolution vers la Féminité et l'Eternel Féminin chez la Jeune Fille, la Femme et la Mère. S.A. Geneve: Éditions du Mont-Blanc 1963

75169 Bücher über Psychologie, Kultur und Religion. [Books on psychology, culture, and religion.] Psychol, Bern 1963, 15(11)

75170 Charaktertypen und Schicksale in Tiefenpsychologischer Praxis und Sicht. [Character Types and Fate in Depth Psychological Theory and Practice.] Bern/Ratingen/Düsseldorf: Ardschuna-Verlag 1963

75171 Dr. Alphonse Maeder zum 80. Geburtstag. [Dr. Alphonse Maeder on his 80th birthday.] Psychol, Bern 1962, 14(10)

75172 Dozent Dr. Berthold Stokvis. [Dozent Dr. Berthold Stokvis.] Psychol, Bern 1963, 15(11)

75173 Das einzige Kind und seine Erziehung. [The only child and his upbringing.] Elternblatt 1968, (16)Feb.

75174 Erwachsene, Kinder und Puppen. Eine tiefenpsychologische Betrachtung. [Grown-ups, children and dolls. A depth psychological view.] Coop-Haushaltungsbuch 1967

75175 Das Familien-Dreieck. [The family triangle.] Eltern-Zeitschrift 1968, Oct. 10. Zürich: Verlag Orell-Füssli AG

75176 Flucht und Zuflucht. [Flight and refuge.] Der Bund, Bern 1967, 10(2)

75177 Frauliche Liebe und Sorge. [Womanly love and sorrow.] Psychol, Bern 1962, 14(7)

75178 Freud und Rank (Bilanz und Heutige Bilanz). [Freud and Rank (Evaluation and present day evaluation).] Psychol, Bern 1963, 15(8-9)

75179 Das Gehemmte Ich. [The secret ego.] Psychol, Bern 1960, 12(3-4)

75180 Grenzsituationen intrauterinen und Geburtstraumatischen verhaltens im psychotherapeutischen Heilungsverlauf. [Intrauterine and birth trauma situations in relation to the course of psychotherapeutic treatment.] In author's *Der Psychotherapeutische Heilungsverlauf und seine Grenzen*, Stuttgart: Klett-Verlag 1963. Psychol, Bern 1965

75181 Grossmutter—Einst und Jetzt. Zur Tiefenpsychologie ihres Gestaltwandels. [Grandmother—now and in the future. On the depth psychology of changes in her role.] Sonderdruck aus "Schweizer Haushaltungsbuch, Basel 1966

75182 Heinrich Meng zum 75. Geburtstag. [Heinrich Meng on his 75th birthday.] Psychol, Bern 1962, 14(7)

75183 Im Hexenhaus. Spätes Verstehen einer frühinfantil-fixierten Vorstellung. [In the witch's house. Late comprehension of an early infantile idee fixe.] Acta psychother psychosom 1963, 11:147-153

75184 Lebengeschichtliche Bilanz. Tagungsvorträge. [Life History Evaluation. Convention Lectures.] Bern/Ratingen/Düsseldorf: Ardschuna-Verlag 1963

75185 Leonardos Visionen vom Weltuntergang. [Leonardo's vision of world destruction.] Psychol, Bern 1961, 13(10)

75186 Märchengestalten bei Jugendlichen. [The character of fairy tales for young people.] In *Seelenspiegel des Kindes*, (2nd ed) Bern: Ardschuna-Verlag 1969. In *Märchenforschung und Tiefenpsychologie*. (Sammelband "Wissenschaftliche Buchgesellschaft, Darmstadt.) 1969

75187 Der Mensch und sein Hexenhaus. [Mankind and his house of magic.] Psychol, Bern 1964, 16(1)

75188 Menschliches Verhalten im Innenbaum und in der Aussenwelt. [Human behavior within and without.] Psychol, Bern (Jb) 1966

75189 Nachgeburtliche Lebensnot. [The difficulties of life after birth.] Psychol, Bern 1961, 13(8-9)

75190 Neuere Bücher der Psychologie und Menschenkunde. [New books on psychology and anthropology.] Psychol, Bern 1962, 14(10)

75191 Neuere Psychologische Bücher. [New psychological books.] Psychol, Bern 1960, 12(4-5)

75192 Der Neurotisch-Depressive Mensch. [The neurotic depressed person.] Psychol, Bern 1964, 16(5-6)

75193 Die Not des Lebens und ihre Überwindung. Zur Tiefenpsychologie des Geburtraumas und der nachgeburtlichen Lebensgestaltung. [The Difficulties of Life and Their Conquest. On the Depth Psychology of Birth Trauma and the Way of Life after Birth.] Bern/Ratingen/Düsseldorf: Ardschuna-Verlag 1966

75194 Nötige Erziehung zu Sinnvollen Lebensgewohnheiten. [Education necessary for significant life-long habits.] Wir Brückenbauer. Zürich 27 Jahrgang No. 7, 1967

75195 Phaidros—Der Dialog des Lebens. [Phaidros—the dialogue of life.] Psychol, Bern 1964, 16(3)

75196 Politik der Zukunft. [Politics of the future.] Psychol, Bern 1960, 12(2)

75197 (Ed) Probleme Moderner Psychotherapie. Sammlung von Beiträgen aus den Berner und Wiener Arbeitskreisen für Tiefenpsychologie. [Problems of Modern Psychotherapy.] Bern/Ratingen/Düsseldorf: Ardschuna-Verlag 1966

75198 Professor Charles Baudouin. Psychol, Bern 1963, 15(10)

S-47624 Zur Psychoanalyse eines Ekzem- und Asthmakranken.
Abs HA An Surv Psa 1957, 8:158

75199 Psychohygiene in der Politik. [Psychohygiene in politics.] Psychol, Bern 1960, 12(11)

75200 (Ed) Psychologe, Forscher und Mensch Gustav Hans Graber. Festschrift zu Seinem 70 Geburtstag. [Psychologist, Scholar and Human Being Gustav Hans Graber. Festschrift for his 70th Birthday.] Bern/Ratingen/Düsseldorf: Ardschuna-Verlag 1963

S-47625 Psychologie des Mannes. Neue Erkenntnisse über das männliche Triebleben. Munich: Goldmann 1965, 1966, 320 p
Psicologia del Hombre. Madrid/Mexico/Buenos Aires: Aguilar-Verlag 1962, 1965

75201 Psychologie und Lebenskonflikte des Mannes in der zweiten Lebenshälfte. [Psychology and life conflicts of man in the second half of life.] Psychol, Bern 1960, 12(1)

75202 (Ed) Der psychotherapeutische Heilungsverlauf und seine Grenzen. Tagungsvorträge. [The course of psychotherapeutic healing and its limits.] Bern/Ratingen/Düsseldorf: Ardschuna 1965

75203 (Ed) Psychotherapie als Selbstverwirklichung. Tagungsvorträge der Berner und Innsbrucker Arbeitskreise für Tiefenpsychologie. [Psychotherapy as loss of self.] Bern: Ardschuna-Verlag 1968

75204 Die Schöpferisch-Heilende Funktion im Traum. [The creative-healing function in dream.] Psychol, Bern 1960, 12(7-8)

75205 Seelische Leiden und Ihre Behandlung. [Mental Life and Its Treatment.] Bern/Ratingen/Düsseldorf: Ardschuna-Verlag 1962

75206 Die Sex-flut. [The flood tide of sex.] Wir Brückenbauer 1968, 24(5)

75207 Tiefenpsychologie der Frau. Die Entwicklung vom Mädchen zur Frau und Mutter. [Depth Psychology of Woman. The Development from Girl to Wife and Mother.] (3rd ed) Munich: Wilhelm Goldmann-Verlag 1966, 1967

75208 Über die Verschiedenen Einstellungen zum Leiden. [On various attitudes toward life.] Psychol, Bern 1962, 14(5-6)

75209 Über neuere Sexualpsychologische Bücher. [On new books on sexual psychology.] Psychol, Bern 1961, 13(7)

75210 Vater-Mutter-Sohn, Tiefenpsychologisches zum Geschlechterund Generation-problem. [Father-Mother-Son. Depth Psychology on Family and Generation Problems.] Coop-Hauschaltsbuch 1965

75211 Vom Ursprung zur Selbstverwirklichung. [On the origin of loss of self.] Psychol, Bern (Jb) 1968

75212 Widerstandsanalyse und Heilungsverlauf. [Resistance to analysis and the course of treatment.] Psychol, Bern 1962, 14(7)

75213 Wissenschaftliche Veröffentlichungen. [Scientific publications.] Psychol, Bern 1963, 15(5-6)

75214 Zeugungs- und Geburtsvorstellungen des Kindes—ihre Bedeutung in der Kinderpsychotherapie. [Children's introduction to procreation and birth.] Hbh Kinderpsychother 342-347

75215 Zur Analyse der Geburtstraumatisch und Totalregressiv Bedingten Urwiederstände. [Analysis of primary resistances of total regression, conditioned by the birth trauma.] Sonderdruck, Jahrbuch für Psychologie, Psychotherapie und medizinische Antrophologie, Freiburg/Munich: Verlag Karl Alber 1967
Del análisis de las resistencias primarias de regresión total, condicionadas por el trauma del nacimiento. Arch Estud psicoanal Psicol med 1967, 4:87-91

75216 Die Zweierlei Vorgänge der Identifizierung. [Two examples of identification.] Psychol, Bern 1962, 14(8-9)

75217 Zyklus und seelische Reaktionen der Frau. [Menstrual cycle and mental reactions in the female.] Acta psychother psychosom 1962, 10:280-285

GRABOWSKI, Z. A.

75218 Three great minds. Time and Tide 1960, 41:283-284

GRADOLPH, PHILIP C.

75219 (& Siegel, B.) Adolescent day treatment project. Ops 1967, 37:273-274

GRAETZ, H. R.

75220 The Symbolic Language of Vincent Van Gogh. NY: McGraw-Hill 1963, 315 p

GRAF, MAX

75221 From Beethoven to Shostakovich; The Psychology of the Composing Process. NY: Greenwood Pr 1969, 474 p

GRAFF, HAROLD

75222 (& Handford, A.) Celiac syndrome in the case histories of five schizo-phrenics. Psychiat Q 1961, 35:306-313

75223 Chronic wrist slashers. Hosp Topics 1967, 45:61

75224 Emotional aspects of weight loss in the cardiac patient. Penn Med 1967, 70(11):68

75225 Form of anxiety in obesity. Penn psychiat Q 1965, 5(3):51-53

75226 (& Stelar, E.) Hyperphagia, obesity and finickiness. J comp physiol Psychol 1962, 55:418-424

75227 Marihuana and scopolamine "high." P 1969, 125:1258-1259

75228 On a fantasy that the analyst is incompetent. Bull Phila Ass Psa 1967, 17:149-157

75229 Overweight and emotions in the obesity clinic. Psychosomatics 1965, 6:89-94

75230 Psychoanalysis and the philosophy of science. Bull Phila Ass Psa 1969, 19:28-44

75231 (& Hammett, van B. O.; Bash, N.; Fackler, W.; Goldman, A.) Results of four antismoking therapy methods. Penn med J 1966, 69:39-43

75232 (& Mallin, R.) The syndrome of the wrist cutter. P 1967, 124:36-42

75233 Thoughts on antismoking therapy. Med Tribune 1966, 7(5)

See Hammett, van Buren O.

ABSTRACTS OF:

75234 Harley, M. Fragments from the analysis of a dog phobia in a latency child. Bull Phila Ass Psa 1967, 17:127-129

75235 Sandler, J. Towards a basic psychoanalytic model. Bull Phila Ass Psa 1968, 18:154-156

REVIEW OF:

75236 Masserman, J. H. The Biodynamic Roots of Human Behavior. Bull Phila Ass Psa 1969, 19:95

GRAHAM, D.

TRANSLATIONS OF:
Chertok, L. [69905, 69913]

GRAHAM, FRANCIS W.

75237 A case treated by psychoanalysis and analytic group psychotherapy. Int J grp PT 1964, 14:267-290

75238 Obituary: Roy Coupland Winn 1890-1963. J 1964, 45:616-617

GRAHAM, STANLEY R.

75239 Effects of psychoanalytically oriented psychotherapy on levels of frequency and satisfaction in sexual activity. Clin Psych 1960, 16:94-95

GRAHAM, THOMAS FRANCIS

75240 Parallel Profiles; Pioneers in Mental Health. Chicago: Franciscan Herald Pr 1966, 245 p

GRAHAM, W. G. B.

See Heim, Edgar

GRALNICK, ALEXANDER

75241 Conjoint family therapy: its role in rehabilitation of the inpatient and family. JNMD 1963, 136:500-506

75242 Discussion of Masserman, J. H. "Sex and the singular psychiatrist." Sci Psa 1966, 9:125-128

75243 Family psychotherapy: general and specific considerations. Ops 1962, 32:515-526. In author's *The Psychiatric Hospital as a Therapeutic Instrument* 142-159

75244 (& Schween, P. H.) Family therapy. Psychiat Res Rep 1966, No. 20: 212-217. In author's *The Psychiatric Hospital as a Therapeutic Instrument* 178-185

75245 (& Yelin, G.) Family therapy in a private hospital setting. Curr psychiat Ther 1969, 9:179-181

75246 (& Yemez, R.; Turker, F.; Schween, P. H.; Greenhill, M.) Five-hundred case study in a private psychiatric hospital: further considerations in evaluation. Psychiat Q 1969, 43:46-71

75247 The future of the mental hospital: a perusal of the determinants. Ment Hosp 1962, 13:373-375. In author's *The Psychiatric Hospital as a Therapeutic Instrument* 247-251

S-47647 Inpatient psychoanalytic psychotherapy of schizophrenia: problem areas and perspectives. In author's *The Psychiatric Hospital as a Therapeutic Instrument* 30-44

75248 The private hospital: a promising facility for psychiatric education. Ment Hosp 1962, 13:478-481. In author's *The Psychiatric Hospital as a Therapeutic Instrument* 252-258

75249 (Ed) The Psychiatric Hospital as a Therapeutic Instrument; Collected Papers of High Point Hospital. NY: Brunner/Mazel 1969, xvi + 277 p

75250 Psychoanalysis and the treatment of adolescents in a private hospital. Sci Psa 1966, 9:102-108. In author's *The Psychiatric Hospital as a Therapeutic Instrument* 222-230
    Abs Kalina, E. & Rascovsky, A. Rev Psicoanál 1967, 24:217-218

75251 (& D'Elia, F. G.) A psychoanalytic hospital becomes a therapeutic community. Hosp Comm Psychiat 1969, 20:144-146

S-47648 (& Schacht, M.; Kempster, S. W.) Psychotherapy in a private mental hospital. In author's *The Psychiatric Hospital as a Therapeutic Instrument* 1-17

75252 (& D'Elia, F. G.) Role of the patient in the therapeutic community: patient participation. PT 1961, 15:63-72. In author's *The Psychiatric Hospital as a Therapeutic Instrument* 93-105

75253 Social forces and patient-progress in the psychotherapeutic community. Int J soc Psychiat 1968, 14:105-112

75254 The therapeutic community and its benefits. Dis nerv Sys 1961, 22:265-267

See Greenhill, Maurice H.; Lind, Alice; Rabiner, Edwin L.; Schween, Peter H.; Silverberg, J. William

GRAND, HENRY G.

75255 Discussion of Ziferstein, I. "The patient-therapist interaction in Soviet psychiatry." Sci Psa 1966, 9:156-159

75256 Psychoneurosis as pathological conditioning. Newsletter, Soc Med Psa 1965, 6(2):9-10

See Bieber, Irving

GRANEL, JULIO A.

75257 Consideraciones sobre la génesis y desarrollo de la interpretacion en la tratamiento psicoanalitico. [Thoughts concerning the genesis and development of interpretation in psychoanalytic treatment.] Rev urug Psa 1966, 8:239-246
      Abs Vega Q 1968, 37:162

75258 Obituary: Heinrich Racker. Rev Psicoanál 1961, 18:292-294

75259 (& Grimaldi, P.; Lumermann, S.; Rolla, E.; Schlossberg, N.) Sobre la hipótesis de la existencia de un aparato para pensar los pensamientos. [On the hypothesis of the existence of an apparatus for thinking thoughts.] Rev Psicoanál 1967, 24:125-130

ABSTRACT OF:

75260 Bion, W. R. A theory of thinking. Rev Psicoanál 1967, 24:393

GRANGE, KATHLEEN M.

75261 An eighteenth-century view of infantile sexuality in an engraving by William Hogarth (1697-1764). JNMD 1963, 137:417-419

75262 Samuel Johnson's accounts of certain psychoanalytic concepts. JNMD 1962, 135:93-98
      Abs Powelson, H. Q 1963, 32:454

GRANGER, CLIVE

See Craft, Michael

GRANGER, J. W.

See Sarason, Irwin G.

GRANIER, J.

See Charbonnier, Gabrielle

GRANLUND, ELNORE

75263 (& Knowles, L.) Child-parent identification and academic underachievement. J consult clin Psychol 1969, 33:495-496

GRANONE, FRANCO

75264 L'importance des rapports psycho-somatiques en thérapeutique hypnotique. [The importance of psychosomatic information in hypnotic therapy.] Proc IV World Cong Psychiat 1966, 2749-2751
75265 Stati di coscienza in ipnosi. [Conscious states in hypnosis.] Rass ital Ricerca psichica 1966, No. 1:35-40

GRANT, BRENDA

See Kalinowsky, Lothar B.

GRANT, EWAN C.

75266 An ethological description of non-verbal behaviour during interviews. M 1968, 41:177-184

GRANT, G.

75266A Adolescent problems and higher education. Proc Roy Soc Med 1969, 62:1261-1263

GRANT, NAOMI RAE

75267 Therapy . . . the Latency Age Child . . . the Casework. St. Louis: Family Service of Greater St. Louis 1966

GRANT, Q. A. F. R.

See Ackner, Brian

GRANT, VERNON W.

75268 Great Abnormals: The Pathological Genius of Kafka, van Gogh, Strindberg and Poe. NY: Hawthorne Books 1968, 248 p
S-47662 Paranoid dynamics: a case study.
       Abs RZ An Surv Psa 1956, 7:412-423
75269 This Is Mental Illness: How It Feels and What It Means. (Pref: Havens, L. L.) Boston: Beacon Pr 1963, 1966, viii + 210 p
       Abs Am Im 1964, 21(1-2):190

GRANVILLE-GROSSMAN, K. L.

75270 Early bereavement and schizophrenia. Brit J Psychiat 1966, 112:1027-1034

GRASSO, P. G. DI

75271 Gordon W. Allport e la psicologia della personalita. [Gordon W. Allport and the psychology of personality.] Orient pedag 1959, 6:605-631

GRATER, H. A.
See Mueller, William J.

GRATTAN, ROBERT T.
See Beckett, Peter G. S.

GRATTAROLA, FELICE RICCARDO
See Giacomo, Donegani

GRATTON, L.
75272 Essai d'une therapie psychoanalytique de groupe pour les enfants d'age
       préscolaire. [Psychoanalytical group therapy for preschool children.]
       Canad Psychiat Ass J 1962, 7:90-96
75273 (& Lafontaine, C.; Psy, B.; Guibeautt, J.) Group psychoanalytic work
       with children. Canad Psychiat Ass J 1966, 11:430-442

GRATWICK, MITCHELL
See Balser, Benjamin H.

GRAUBARD, PAUL
See Minuchin, Salvador

GRAUBARD, STEPHEN R.
75274 (Ed) Youth: change and challenge. Daedalus 1962, 91:1-239

GRAUBERT, DAVID N.
S-47668 (& Miller, J. S. A.) On ambivalence.
       Abs AaSt An Surv Psa 1957, 8:35
75275 (& Levine, A.) The concept of the representational world. J Hillside
       Hosp 1965, 14:227-233
       Abs JA Q 1967, 36:321

See Glick, Ira D.

GRAUER, DAVID
S-47669 Homosexuality and the paranoid psychoses as related to the concept
       of narcissism.
       Abs An Surv Psa 1955, 6:44-45; 190
S-47671 How autonomous is the ego?
       Abs CK An Surv Psa 1958, 9:114
S-47672 Some misconceptions of Federn's ego psychology.
       Abs KOS An Surv Psa 1957, 8:37-38

GRAUER, HARRY
75276 Psychodynamics of depression as seen in a geriatric out-patient clinic.
       Canad Psychiat Ass J 1966, 11(Suppl):S324-S328
75277 Psychodynamics of the survivor syndrome. Canad Psychiat Ass J 1969,
       14:617-622

GRAVES, ROBERT

75278   (& Patai, R.) Hebrew Myths, The Book of Genesis. Garden City, NY:
        Doubleday 1964, 311 p
           Rv Schupper, F. X. Am Im 1965, 22:155-156
75279   (& Patai, R.) Some Hebrew myths and legends. Encounter 1963, 20
        (2):3-18, 20(3):12-18

GRAY, BERNARD

See Cattell, Raymond B.; Toman, Walter

GRAY, ELIZABETH

See Switzer, Robert E.

GRAY, JAMES J.

75280   The effect of productivity on primary process and creativity. J proj
        Tech pers Assess 1969, 33:213-218

GRAY, PAUL

75281   (Reporter) Activity-passivity. (Panel: Am Psa Ass, Dec 1966) J Am
        Psa Ass 1967, 15:709-728
75282   (Reporter) Limitations of psychoanalysis. (Panel: Am Psa Ass, May
        1964) J Am Psa Ass 1965, 13:181-190
           Abs Kalina, E. Rev Psicoanál 1966, 23:357

See Ferber, Leon

GRAYDON, C.

See Bernstein, Stanley

GRAYSON, HENRY T., JR.

75283   Psychosexual conflict in adolescent girls who experienced early parental
        loss by death. Diss Abstr 1967, 28:2136

GRAYSON, ROBERT S.

ABSTRACTS OF:
75284   Rascovsky, A. & Rascovsky, M. On filicide and its meaning in the
        genesis of acting out and psychopathic behavior in Oedipus. Q 1969,
        38:345-346
75285   Wangh, M. The psychogenetic factor in the recurrence of war. Q
        1968, 37:481-483

GRAZIANO, ANTHONY

See Spivack, George

GREAVES, DONALD C.

75286   Discussion of Hamburg, D. A. "Evolution of emotional responses: evi-
        dence from recent research on nonhuman primates." Sci Psa 1968,
        12:52-54

75287   (& Green, P. E.; West, L. J.) Psychodynamic and psychophysiological aspects of pseudocyesis. PSM 1960, 22:24-31

GRECO, RAY S.

75288   (& Pittenger, R. A.) One Man's Practice. Effects of Developing Insight on Doctor-Patient Transactions. (Foreword: Balint, M.) London: Tavistock 1966, 123 p

75289   (& Pittenger, R. A.) Die "unorganisierte" Krankheit. [The "unorganized" disease.] Psyche 1968, 22:614-629

GREEN, ALFRED

75290   The mourning process in Thomas Wolfe's "Of Time and The River." Bull New Jersey Psa Soc 1968, 1:16-19

GREEN, ANDRÉ

75291   "Agir" et processus psychanalytique. [Acting (in-out) and the psychoanalytic process.] RFPsa 1968, 32:1071-1076

75292   Chimiothérapie et psychothérapie: problèmes posés par les comparisons des techniques chimiothérapeutiques et psychothérapeutiques et leur association en thérapeutique psychiatrique. [Drug therapies and psychotherapies: problems posed by comparisons of the techniques of drug therapy and psychotherapy and their association in psychiatric treatment.] Encéph 1961, 50:29-101

75293   Délire et imaginaire. [Delirium and imagination.] In Entretiens Psychiatriques 1955, 4:147-189

75294   (& Schmitz, B.) Le deuil maniaque (à propos d'un cas). [Manic mourning: a propos of a case.] Évolut psychiat 1958, 23:105-121

75295   La diachronie dans le freudisme. [Diachrony in Freudism.] Critique 1967, No. 238:359-385

75296   Discussion of Fornari, F. "La psychanalyse de la guerre." RFPsa 1966, 30:266-268

75297   Discussion of Schmitz, B. "Les états limites." RFPsa 1967, 31:261-262

75298   Discussion of Viderman, S. "Narcissisme et relation d'objet dans la situation analytique." RFPsa 1968, 32:123-124

75299   L'enjeu des options en présence sur la formation des psychiatres. [The stake of the choices involved in the making of psychiatrists.] Évolut psychiat 1967, 32:847-864

75300   Enseignement de la psychiatrie et formation du psychiatre. [Education in psychiatry and the formation of a psychiatrist.] In Livre Blanc de la Psychiatrie Française, I. (Évolut psychiat, suppl No. 3) 1965, 30:17-74

75301   Les fondements différenciateurs des images parentales. L'hallucination négative de la mère et l'identification primordiale au père. [The different foundations for parental images: the negative hallucination of the mother and the primordial identification with the father.] RFPsa 1967, 31:896-906

75302   L'inconscient et la psychopathologie. [The unconscious and psychopathology.] Inconscient 1966, 6:331-335

75303   L'inconscient freudien et la psychanalyse française contemporaine.

[The Freudian unconscious and contemporary French psychoanalysis.]
Temps modernes 1962, 18(195):365-379

75304 Mai 1968: le mouvement étudiant devant la psychiatrie. [May 1968:
the student movement as viewed by psychiatry.] Évolut psychiat 1968,
33:551-560

75305 Métapsychologie de la névrose obsessionelle. [Metapsychology of the
obsessional neurosis.] RFPsa 1967, 31:629-647

75306 Les méthodes en psychopathologie. [Methods in psychopathology.] In
Encyclopédie de Psychologie, I, Paris: Fernand Nathan 1962

75307 (& Delay, J.; Deniker, P.) Le milieu familial des schizophrènes. [The
family environment of schizophrenics.] Encéph 1962, 51:5-73

75308 Le narcissisme moral. [Moral narcissism.] RFPsa 1969, 33:341-374

75309 Le narcissisme primaire: structure ou état. [Primary narcissism: structure or state.] Inconscient 1967, No. 1:127-157; No. 2:89-116

75310 Névrose obsessionnelle et hysterie, leurs relations chez Freud et depuis.
[Obsessional neurosis and hysteria, their relation according to Freud,
and since.] RFPsa 1964, 28:679-716

75311 Note sur le corps imaginaire. [Note on the imaginary body.] RFPsa
1962, 26(Spec. No.):67-83

75312 L'objet (a) J. Lacan, sa logique et la théorie freudienne. [The object
of J. Lacan: its logic and Freudian theory.] Cah Analyse 1966, (3):
15-37

75313 Obsessions et psychonévrose obsessionelle. [Obsessions and obsessional
psychoneurosis.] In Encyclopédie Médico-Chirurgicale, Psychiatrie III,
37-370, 14 p., Bibliog.

75314 Oedipe: mythe et vérité. [Oedipus: myth and truth.] Arc 1968, No.
38:15-26

75315 Les portes de l'inconscient. [The gateway to the unconscious.] Inconscient 1966, 6:17-44

75316 Propos élémentaires sur l'inconscient. [Elementary remarks on the unconscious.] Évolut méd 1964, 431-438

75317 La psychanalyse devant l'opposition de l'histoire et de la structure.
[Psychoanalysis before the resistance of history and of form.] Critique
1963, (194):649-662

75318 Le psychanalyste, interprété. [The psychoanalyst interpreted.] Interprétation 1967, 1:8-20

75319 La psychopharmacologie: overture impasses, perspectives. [Psycho-
pharmacology: opening impasses, prospects.] Évolut psychiat 1966,
31:681-705

75320 Remarques méthodologiques sur l'interprétation des modes d'expression de certaines drogues psychotropes. [Methodological remarks on
the interpretation of the effects of certain psychotropic drugs.] In Lam-
bert, P. A. La Relation Médecin-Malade au Cours des Chimiothérapies
Psychiatriques, Masson 1965, 131-138

75321 Réponses au questionnaire: "Du thérapeute au médicament." [Answers
to the questionnaire: "From therapist to medicine."] Perspectives psychiat 1968, 21:35-44

75322 Le rôle: contribution à l'étude des mécanismes d'identification. [Role:
a contribution to the study of identification mechanisms.] Évolut psychiat 1961, 26:1-32

75323   Shakespeare, Freud et le parricide. [Shakespeare, Freud and parricide.] La Nef 1967, 31:64-82
75324   Die Situation der Psychoanalyse in Frankreich. [The situation of psychoanalysis in France.] Nervenarzt 1967, 38:398-399
75325   Sur la mère phallique. [On the phallic mother.] RFPsa 1968, 32:1-38
75326   [The training of general practitioners in psychotherapy. (Apropos of the experience of M. Balint at the Tavistock Clinic in London.)] (Fr) Sem Ther 1963, 39:341-343
75327   Une variante de la position phallique-narcissique. [A variant of phallic narcissism.] RFPsa 1963, 27:117-184
        Abs Donadeo, J. Q 1964, 33:613

   See Chasseguet-Smirgel, Janine

   REVIEW OF:
75328   Klein, M. Our Adult World and Other Essays. RFPsa 1964, 28:816-819

GREEN, ARTHUR H.

75329   Primitive concepts of death and rebirth in two adolescents. Psychiat Q Suppl 1964, 38:21-32
75330   Self-destructive behavior in physically abused schizophrenic children. Report of cases. Arch gen Psychiat 1968, 19:171-179
75331   Self-mutilation in schizophrenic children. Arch gen Psychiat 1967, 17:234-244
        Abs Bull Ass Psa Med 1967, 2:23-26

GREEN, BERNARD A.

75332   Character structure and its functions. R 1967, 54:329-354
        Abs SRS Q 1968, 37:473

   See Adelson, Joseph

GREEN, BERNARD L.
   See Solomon, Alfred P.

GREEN, GERALD ALLEN
   See Mendel, Werner M.

GREEN, HANNAH

75333   I Never Promised You a Rose Garden. NY: Holt, Rinehart & Winston 1964, 300 p
75334   "In praise of my doctor"—Frieda Fromm-Reichmann. Contempo Psa 1967, 4(1):73-77

GREEN, JAMES A.
   See Berkowitz, Leonard

GREEN, JOHN
   See Zacharis, James L.

GREEN, LOUISE

See Orr, William F.

GREEN, M.

75335 Discussion of Luquet, P. "Ouvertures sur l'artiste et le psychanalyste." RFPsa 1963, 27:615

GREEN, MARSHALL A.

75336 The stormy personality. PPR 1962, 49(4):55-67

GREEN, MAURICE R.

75337 (& Schecter, D. E.) Autistic and symbiotic disorders in three blind children. Psychiat Q 1957, 31:628-646
75338 The Challenge of Fear (on child development). (Pamphlet) Boston: Dept of Education, Unitarian-Universalist Assoc 1962
75339 Clara Thompson: a biographic note. Contempo Psa 1964, 1(1):80-82. In *Interpersonal Psychoanalysis, Selected Papers of Clara Thompson,* NY: Basic Books 1964
75340 Common problems in the treatment of schizophrenia in adolescents. Psychiat Q 1966, 40:294-307
75341 (Participant) Depression in adolescence. Panel discussion: the management of depression in children and adults. Contempo Psa 1965, 2(1): 42-47; 54-61
75342 Discussion of Einhorn, E. H. "Signal exchange patterns in the genesis of extra-marital affairs." Newsletter, Soc Med Psa 1967, 8
75343 Discussion of Erikson, E. "Eight ages of man." Int J Psychiat 1966, 2(3):302-303
75344 (& Ullman, M.; Tauber, E. S.) Dreaming and modern dream theory. Mod Psa 146-186
° ° ° Editor of Thompson, C. M. *Interpersonal Psychoanalysis.*
75345 Hospital ship neuropsychiatry care of the closed ward patient. Military Surgeon 1954, 114:460-462
75346 Interpersonal considerations of suicide. NY Med 1963, April 5
75347 Interpersonal situations. Int J Psychiat 1967, 4:74-76
75348 Martin Buber. Am Hbk Psychiat II: 1821-1826
75349 Prelogical experience in the thinking process. St art Educ 1961, 62, 3:66-74
75350 Prelogical processes and participant communication. Psychiat Q 1961, 35:726-740
75351 The problem of identity crisis. Sci Psa 1966, 9:69-79
75352 Psychological factors in genito-urinary diseases. In Kroger, W. S. *Psychosomatic Obstetrics, Gynecology and Endocrinology,* Springfield, Ill: Thomas 1962, 648-654
75353 The roots of Sullivan's concept of self. Psychiat Q 1962, 36:271-282
75354 (& Dean, A. L.) Some psychiatric aspects of symptoms of genito-urinary diseases. J Urology 1954, 72:742-747. Sexology 1956, June
75355 Suicide: the Sullivanian point of view. In Farberow, N. L. & Shneidman, E. S. *The Cry for Help,* NY/Toronto/London: McGraw-Hill 1961, 220-235

75356 (& Wiley, R.) The value of pediatric-psychiatric teamwork in the treatment of rheumatic fever. Report of a one-year project. Pediatrics 1956, 17:757-760

See Deutscher, Max; Tauber, Edward S.

GREEN, MORRIS

75357 (& Haggerty, R. J.) (Eds) Ambulatory Pediatrics. Phila/London/ Toronto: Saunders 1968, xxxi + 970 p
75358 Diagnosis and treatment: psychogenic, recurrent, abdominal pain. Pediatrics 1967, 40:84-89
75359 (& Durocher, M. A.) Improving parent care of handicapped children. Children 1965, 12:185-188
75360 (& Solnit, A. J.) Reactions to the threatened loss of a child: a vulnerable child syndrome. Pediatric management of the dying child, part III. Pediatrics 1964, 34:58-66

See Solnit, Albert J.

GREEN, P. C.

75361 (& Gordon, M.) Maternal deprivation: its influence on visual exploration in infant monkeys. Science 1964, 145:292-294

GREEN, P. E.

See Greaves, Donald C.

GREEN, R.

75362 Discussion of Pasche, F. Freud et l'orthodoxie judéo-chrétienne. RFPsa 1961, 25:84
75363 Discussion of Viderman, S. De l'instinct de mort. RFPsa 1961, 25: 121-123

GREEN, RALPH SAMUEL

75364 Fostering regression in patients. Ment Hosp 1964, 15:440-442

GREEN, RICHARD S.

75365 Childhood cross-gender identification. JNMD 1968, 147:500-509
75366 Introduction to panel II. [Conference on childhood schizophrenia.] J Hillside Hosp 1967, 16:73-74
75367 Sex reassignment surgery. P 1968, 124:997-998
75368 The significance of cross-gender behavior during childhood. Proc IV World Cong Psychiat 1966, 3043-3044
75369 Sissies and tomboys: a guide to diagnosis and management. In Wahl, C. W. *Sexual Problems,* NY: Free Pr; London: Collier-Macmillan 1967, 89-114
75370 (& Money, J.) (Eds) Transsexualism and Sex Reassignment. Baltimore: Johns Hopkins Univ Pr 1969, xxii + 512 p

See Steinberg, Harry R.

GREEN, SIDNEY L.

75371 The ego structure of the adolescent retardate; psychological principles for clinical application. Int Rec Med 1961, 174:205-211

75372 The pediatrician and the maternal-infant relationship. Psychosomatics 1964, 5:75-81

75373 Psychotherapy with adolescent girls. PT 1964, 18:393-404

S-47750 (& Schur, H.; Lipkowitz, M. H.) Study of a dwarf.
        Abs RTh J 1961, 42:472-473

See Kwalwasser, Simon

GREEN, WILLIAM

75374 Early object relations, somatic, affective, and personal. JNMD 1958, 126:225-253
        Abs DW An Surv Psa 1958, 9:235-238

GREENACRE, PHYLLIS

75375 Bertram David Lewin—an appreciation. Q 1966, 35:483-487

S-47753 Certain technical problems in the transference relationship.
        Abs JTM Q 1961, 30:139-140. Baranger, M. Rev urug Psa 1961-62, 4:198

S-47754 The childhood of the artist. Libidinal phase development and giftedness.
        Abs EMW An Surv Psa 1957, 8:325-326

S-47755 Considerations regarding the parent-infant relationship.
        Quelques considérations sur la relation parent-nourisson. RFPsa 1961, 25:27-53
        Abs JBi Q 1962, 31:123-124

75376 A critical digest of the literature on selection of candidates for psychoanalytic training. Q 1961, 30:28-55

75377 Discussion of Rosenfeld, H. A. "The need of patients to act out during analysis." Psa Forum 1966, 1:28

S-47756 Early physical determinants in the development of the sense of identity.
        Abs CFH An Surv Psa 1958, 9:244-245

S-47757 Experiences of awe in childhood.
        Abs SGo An Surv Psa 1956, 7:255-256

S-47758 The family romance of the artist.
        Abs Steinberg, S. An Surv Psa 1958, 9:487-488

75378 The fetish and the transitional object. Psa St C 1969, 24:144-164

S-47761 Further considerations regarding fetishism.
        Abs An Surv Psa 1955, 6:227-228

S-47763 The impostor.
        Abs NZ An Surv Psa 1958, 9:162-163

75379 Infantile trauma. (Read at NY Psa Soc, 9 June 1964)
        Abs Shanzer, H. Q 1965, 34:148-150

75380 The influence of infantile trauma on genetic patterns. In Furst, S. S. Psychic Trauma, NY: Basic Books 1967, 108-153

S-47765 "It's my own invention": a special screen memory of Lewis Carroll, its form and its history.
Abs An Surv Psa 1955, 6:446-449

S-47767 The mutual adventures of Jonathan Swift and Lemuel Gulliver. A study of pathography.
Abs An Surv Psa 1955, 6:444-446

75381 Obituary: Memorial tribute: Maxwell Gitelson. (Read at Int Cong Psa, July 1965) J 1966, 47:440-445

75382 On nonsense. Psa–Gen Psychol 655-677

75383 On the development and function of tears. Psa St C 1965, 20:209-219

75384 Perversions: general considerations regarding their genetic and dynamic background. (Read at NY Psa Soc, 27 Feb 1968) Psa St C 1968, 23:47-62

S-47771 Play in relation to creative imagination.
Abs RTh J 1961, 42:468-469

75385 Problems of acting out in the transference relationship. J Amer Acad Child Psychiat 1963, 2:144-160; 169-170. In Rexford, E. N. A Development Approach to Problems of Acting Out, NY: IUP 1966, 144-160

75386 Problems of overidealization of the analyst and of analysis: their manifestations in the transference and countertransference relationship. (Read at Pan-American Psa Cong, 2 Aug 1966; at NY Psa Soc, 11 Oct 1966) Psa St C 1966, 21:193-212
Probleme der Überidealisierung des Analytikers und der Analyse. Psyche 1969, 23:611-628
Abs Fine, B. D. Q 1967, 36:636-637

75387 Problems of training analysis. Q 1966, 35:540-567
Abs Cuad Psa 1967, 3:59

75388 The psychoanalytic process, transference, and acting out. (Read at Int Psa Cong, July 1967) J 1968, 49:211-218
Abs LHR Q 1969, 38:668

75389 The Quest for the Father. A Study of the Darwin-Butler Controversy, as a Contribution to the Understanding of the Creative Individual. (Read at NY Psa Soc, 22 May 1962) NY: IUP 1963, 128 p
Estudio Psicoanalítico Sobre la Actividad Creadora. Mexico: Editorial Pax México
Abs Auth Q 1963, 32:145-146. J Am Psa Ass 1964, 12:259. Rv LRa Q 1964, 33:575-578. Coltrera, J. T. J Am Psa Ass 1965, 13:634-703. Feldman, B. R 1968, 55:154-156

S-47775 Re-evaluation of the process of working through.
Abs SG An Surv Psa 1956, 7:315-316

S-47776 Regression and fixation: considerations concerning the development of the ego.
Abs JTM Q 1962, 31:133-134

S-47777 The relation of the impostor to the artist.
Abs Ford, E. S. C. An Surv Psa 1958, 9:161-162

75390 A study on the nature of inspiration. I. Some special considerations regarding the phallic phase. (Read at Am Psa Ass, Dec 1963) J Am Psa Ass 1964, 12:6-31
Abs JLSt Q 1966, 35:152

75391 Summary of discussion remarks on Dr. Löfgren's paper, "On weeping."
       (Read at Int Psa Cong, July 1965) J 1966, 47:381-383
S 47779 Swift and Carroll. A Psychoanalytic Study of Two Lives.
       Abs OS An Surv Psa 1955, 6:503-513
75392 The theory of parent-infant relationship. (Read at Phila Ass Psa, 17
       Feb 1961) J 1962, 43:235-237; 255-256
         French: RFPsa 1963, 27:484-487
         Abs Johnson, D. E. Bull Phila Ass Psa 1961, 11:97-99
S-47780 Toward an understanding of the physical nucleus of some defense
       reactions.
       Abs JLS An Surv Psa 1958, 9:251-253
75393 Treason and the traitor. Am Im 1969, 26:199-232
S-47781 Woman as artist.
       Abs Sapochnik, L. Rev Psicoanál 1961, 18:405. LDr RFPsa 1962,
       26:332

GREENBANK, RICHARD K.

75394 Allegedly prophetic dreams in psychotherapeutic treatment. Int J Para-
       psychol 1960, 2:81
75395 Are medical students learning psychiatry? Penn med J 1961, 65:989
75396 Can ESP be explained? Int J Neuropsychiat 1966, 2:532-538
75397 Christmas neurosis. Frontiers clin Psychiat 1967, 4(21):2
75398 For what crime? Penn psychiat Q 1965, 5:49
75399 How to find rational causes of irrational symptoms. Consultant 1966,
       6(10):16-18
         Comment decouvrir les causes rationnelles des symptomes irration-
       nels. Consultations 1967, 4(6):16
75400 The language without words. Frontiers clin Psychiat 1965, 2(21):5
75401 Management of sexual counter-transference. J Sex Res 1965, 1:233
75402 Mental health education for parents. Curr psychiat Ther 1969, 9:166-
       167
75403 Mental health for parents. MH 1968, 52:587
75404 Patients who talk without words. Psychosomatics 1965, 6:210-214
75405 A prophetic dream. Corrective Psychiat 1966, 12:213-218
75406 Psychotherapy using two therapists. PT 1964, 18:488-499
         Psychotherapie durch zwei Therapeuten ("Dual-Therapie"). Z Psy-
       chother med Psychol 1967, 17:117-125
75407 Special techniques in psychotherapy. Curr psychiat Ther 1966, 6:
       64-69
75408 The unnamed perversion. Corrective Psychiat 1965, 11:28-31

GREENBAUM, HENRY

75409 Discussion of Papanek, H. "Group psychotherapy with married
       couples." J Psa in Groups 1966-67, 2(1):42-44
75410 Evolution, moral values and psychoanalysis. Newsletter, Society of
       Medical Psychoanalysts 1967, 8(1):6-8
75411 A flexible psychoanalytic model of treatment. Newsletter, Society of
       Medical Psychoanalysts 1965, 6(4):5-7

75412 Imitation and identification in learning behavior. In Merin, J. H. & Nagler, S. H. *The Etiology of the Neuroses*, Palo Alto: Sci & Behav Books 1966, 69-79; 90-93

GREENBAUM, MARUIM

75413 The displaced child syndrome. J Child Psychol Psychiat 1962, 3:93-100

GREENBAUM, NATHAN

See Ekstein, Rudolf

GREENBAUM, RICHARD S.

75414 Treatment of school phobias, theory and practice. PT 1964, 18:616-634

GREENBERG, CAROL

See Wallach, Michael A.

GREENBERG, E. S.

See Werkman, Sidney L.

GREENBERG, HAROLD ABRAHAM

75415 Adverse behavior in a psychiatric research setting. Comprehen Psychiat 1967, 8:67-73

See Pieper, William J.

GREENBERG, HARVEY R.

75416 (& Blank, H. R.; Argrett, S.) The anatomy of elopement from an acute adolescent service: escape from engagement. Psychiat Q 1968, 42: 28-47
75417 Beyond Blauberman. A chronicle of disillusion. NYSJM 1967, 67:2232-2238
75418 Cutting them down to size. Psychiat Q Suppl 1967, 41:281-283
75419 Emergence of somnambulism during intensive psychotherapy. P 1964, 121:272-273
75420 (& Blank, H. R.; Greenson, D. P.) The jelly baby. Conception, immaculate and non-immaculate. Psychiat Q 1968, 42:211-216
75421 Notes on the parental exclusion phenomenon in twins. M 1966, 39: 61-63
75422 Psychiatric symptomatology in wives of military retirees. P 1966, 123: 488-490
75423 Pyromania in a woman. Q 1966, 35:256-262
      Abs LDr RFPsa 1967, 31:332
75424 (& Lustig, N.) Remission of malingered amnesia following a natural disaster. M 1967, 40:183-184
75425 (& Carrillo, C.) Thioridazine-induced inhibition of masturbatory ejaculation in an adolescent. P 1968, 124:991-993

75426 (& Sarner, C. A.) Trichotillomania: symptom and syndrome. Arch gen Psychiat 1965, 12:482-489
       Abs KR 1966, 35:474

See Abend, Sander M.; Blank, H. Robert

GREENBERG, IRWIN MORTON

75427 A comparison of the cross-cultural adaptive process with adolescence. Comprehen Psychiat 1961, 2:44-50
75428 Death and dying: attitudes of patient and doctor. IV. Studies on attitudes toward death. GAP Symp 1965, 5:623-631
75429 An exploratory study of reunion fantasies. J Hillside Hosp 1964, 13:49-59
       Abs JA Q 1967, 36:319
75430 (& Glick, I. D.; Mathch, S.; Riback, S. S.) Family therapy indications and rationale. Arch gen Psychiat 1964, 10:7-24

See Murphey, Elizabeth B.

GREENBERG, JUDITH W.

See Davidson, Helen H.

GREENBERG, L.

See Werkman, Sidney L.

GREENBERG, MILTON S.

75431 Role playing: an alternative to deception. J Pers soc Psychol 1967, 7:152-157
75432 Uterus = penis: a contribution to the female castration complex. Bull Phila Ass Psa 1967, 17:26-30

GREENBERG, NAHMAN H.

75433 Developmental effects of stimulation during early infancy: some conceptual and methodological considerations. Ann NY Acad Sci 1965, 118:831-859
75434 Origins of head-rolling (spasms nutans) during early infancy, clinical observations and theoretical implications. PSM 1964, 26:162-171
75435 Studies in psychosomatic differentiation during infancy. Arch gen Psychiat 1962, 7:389-406
       Abs KR Q 1964, 33:140-141
75436 (& Rosenwald, A. K.; Nielson, P. E.) A study in transsexualism. Psychiat Q 1960, 34:204-235
       Abs Engle, B. Q 1961, 30:301
S-47787 (& Rosenwald, A. K.) Transvestism and pruritus perinei.
       Abs RSB An Surv Psa 1958, 9:179-180

See Loesch, John G.

GREENBERG, R.

See Pinderhughes, Charles A.

GREENBERG, RAMON

75437 (& Pearlman, C.) Delirium tremens and dreaming. P 1967, 124:133-142
75438 Dream interruption insomnia. JNMD 1967, 144:18-21
75439 (& Leiderman, P. H.) Perceptions, the dream process and memory: an up-to-date version of notes on a mystic writing pad. Comprehen Psychiat 1966, 7:517-523

GREENBERG, RICHARD M.

ABSTRACTS OF:

75440 Guntrip, H. The schizoid compromise and psychotherapeutic stalemate. Q 1963, 32:457-458
75441 Khan, M. M. R. The role of polymorph-perverse body experiences and object relations in ego integration. Q 1963, 32:456-457
75442 Lomas, P. The origin of the need to be special. Q 1963, 32:458
75443 Markillie, R. E. D. Observations on early ego development. Q 1964, 33:310
75444 Miller, E. Individual and social approach to the study of adolescence. Q 1963, 32:455-456
75445 Novey, S. The meaning of history in psychiatry and psychoanalysis. Q 1963, 32:457
75446 Plesch, E. On the ontogenetic hierarchy of paternal identification systems: some normal and abnormal aspects. Q 1963, 32:458
75447 Sutherland, J. D. Object relations theory and the conceptual model of psychoanalysis. Q 1964, 33:309-310
75448 Volkan, V. Sleep. A bibliographical study. Q 1963, 32:456
75449 Wisdom, J. O. Fairbairn's contribution on object relationship, splitting, and ego structure. Q 1964, 33:310

GREENBERGER, ELLEN

75450 Fantasies of women confronting death. J consult Psychol 1965, 29:252-260
75451 "Flirting" with death: fantasies of a critically ill woman. J proj Tech 1966, 30:197-204

GREENBLATT, MILTON

75452 Beyond the therapeutic community. J Hillside Hosp 1963, 12:167-194
75453 (& Grosser, G. H.; Wechsler, H.) Choice of somatic therapies in depression. Curr psychiat Ther 1964, 4:134-142
75454 (& Solomon, M. H.; Evans, A. S.; Brooks, G. W.) (Eds) Drugs and Social Therapy in Chronic Schizophrenia. Springfield, Ill: Thomas 1965, xiii + 238 p
75455 (& Levinson, D. J.; Klerman, G. L.) (Eds) Mental Patients in Transition: Steps in Hospital-Community Rehabilitation. (Foreword: Ewalt, J. R.) Springfield, Ill: Thomas 1961, xxi + 378 p
75456 (& Emery, P. E.; Glueck, B. C., Jr.) (Eds) Poverty and Mental Health. Wash: Amer Psychiat Assoc 1967, 175 p
75457 (& Moore, R. F.; Albert, R. S.; Solomon, M. H.) The Prevention of Hospitalization. Treatment Without Admission for Psychiatric Patients. NY/London: Grune & Stratton 1963, xiv + 182 p

See Becker, Alvin; Cameron, D. Ewen; Freedman, Sanford J.; Glasser, Betty; Grosser, George H.; Grunebaum, Henry U.; Hartmann, Ernest L.; Schulberg, Herbert C.; Sharaf, Myron R.; West, Louis J.

GREENE, BERNARD L.

75458 Introduction: a multi-operational approach to marital problems. In author's *The Psychotherapies of Marital Disharmony*, 1-14
75459 Marital disharmony: concurrent analysis of husband and wife. Dis nerv Sys 1960, 21:1-6
75460 (& Solomon, A. P.) Marital disharmony: concurrent psychoanalytic therapy of husband and wife by the same psychiatrist. The triangular transference transactions. PT 1963, 17:443-456
75461 (Ed) The Psychotherapies of Marital Disharmony. NY: Free Pr; London: Collier-Macmillan 1965, xii + 191 p
75462 Sequential marriage: repetition or change? Marriage Relat 293-306
75463 (& Broadhurst, B. P.; Lustig, N.) Treatment of marital disharmony: the use of individual, concurrent, and conjoint sessions as a "combined approach." In author's *The Psychotherapies of Marital Disharmony* 135-151

See Solomon, Alfred P.

GREENE, JAMES C.

75464 A "madman's" searches for a less divided self. Contempo Psa 1969, 6:58-73
75465 Thought disorder. J 1967, 48:525-535

GREENE, LEE B.

See Marks, Morton

GREENE, MARSHALL A.

75466 (& Cushna, B.) Mental retardation and social class in an out-patient clinic population. Amer J ment Defic 1965, 70:114-119
75467 The stormy personality. PPR 1962, 49(4):55-67
        Abs Ekboir, J. G. de Rev Psicoanál 1964, 21:85

GREENE, R. J.

See Rabin, Albert I.

GREENFIELD, NORMAN S.

75468 (& Alexander, A. A.) The ego and bodily responses. Psa Curr Biol Thought 201-214
75469 (& Alexander, A. A.; Roessler, R.) Ego strength and physiological responsivity. II. The relationship of the Barron Ego Strength Scale to the temporal and recovery characteristics of skin resistance, finger blood volume, heart rate, and muscle potential responses to sound. Arch gen Psychiat 1963, 9:129-141
° ° ° (& Lewis, W. C.) Preface. Psa Curr Biol Thought vii-viii

75470 (& Lewis, W. C.) (Eds) Psychoanalysis and Current Biological
Thought. Madison/Milwaukee: Univ Wisconsin Pr 1965, x + 380 p

See Alexander, A. A.; Rice, David G.

GREENFIELD, PATRICIA M.

See Bruner, Jerome S.

GREENHILL, MAURICE H.

75471 (& Gralnick, A.; Duncan, R. H.; Yemez, R.; Turker, F.) Considerations
in evaluating the results of psychotherapy with 500 inpatients. PT
1966, 20:58-68. In Gralnick, A. *The Psychiatric Hospital as a Thera-*
peutic Instrument, NY: Brunner/Mazel 1969, 51-66
° ° ° Foreword to Gralnick, A. *The Psychiatric Hospital as a Therapeutic*
Instrument, NY: Brunner/Mazel 1969, ix-xi
75472 (& Gralnick, A.) The problem of primary change in psychotherapy and
psychoanalysis: repair vs. reconstruction. Proc IV World Cong Psychiat
1966, 758-764

See Gralnick, Alexander

GREENHOUSE, SAMUEL W.

See Birren, James E.

GREENING, THOMAS CARTWRIGHT

75473 Candide: an existential dream. J existent Psychiat 1965, 5:413-416

GREENLAND, CYRIL

75474 Ernest Jones in Toronto, 1908-1913. A fragment of biography. Publications by Ernest Jones, M. D. 1908-1913. Canad Psychiat Ass J
1961, 6:132-139; 1966, 11:512-513; 1967, 12:79-81

GREENLEAF, ERIC

75475 The Schreber case: remarks on psychoanalytic explanation. Psychotherapy 1969, 6:16-20

GREENSON, D. P.

See Blank, H. Robert; Greenberg, Harvey R.

GREENSON, JILL

See Drucker, Maureen N.

GREENSON, RALPH R.

75476 Comment on Dr. Limentani's paper, "A re-evaluation of acting out in
relation to working through." (Read at Int Psa Cong, July 1965) J
1966, 47:282-285

75477   Comment on Dr. Ritvo's paper, "Correlation of a childhood and adult
        neurosis: based on the adult analysis of a reported childhood case
        (summary)." (Read at Int Psa Cong, July 1965) J 1966, 47:149-150
            Commentaires sur l'article du Dr. Ritvo. RFPsa 1967, 31:565-567
75478   Discussion of Niederland, W. G. "A contribution to the psychology of
        gambling." Psa Forum 1967, 2:181-182
75479   Discussion of Parres, R. & Ramirez, S. "Termination of analysis." Psa
        Amer 263-266
75480   Discussion of Zetzel, E. R. "The analytic situation." Psa Amer 131-132
75481   Dis-identifying from mother: its special importance for the boy. (Read
        at Int Psa Cong, July 1967) J 1968, 49:370-374
            Abs LHR Q 1969, 38:670
S-47803 Empathy and its vicissitudes.
            L'empathie et ses phases diverses. RFPsa 1961, 25:801-814
            Zum Problem der Empathie. Psyche 1961, 15:142-154
            Abs JBi Q 1962, 31:119
75482   The enigma of modern woman. (Read at Phila Ass Psa, 20 May 1966)
        Bull Phila Ass Psa 1966, 16:173-185
            Abs EFA Q 1968, 37:159
S-47804 Forepleasure: its use for defensive purposes.
            Abs An Surv Psa 1955, 6:152-154
75483   Masculinity and femininity in our time. In Wahl, C. W. *Sexual Problems*, NY: Free Pr; London: Collier-Macmillan 1967, 39-52
75484   (& Wexler, M.) The non-transference relationship in the psychoanalytic
        situation. (Read at Int Psa Cong 1969) J 1969, 50:27-39
75485   On enthusiasm. (Read at Am Psa Ass, 11 Dec 1960; at Los Angeles Psa
        Soc, 20 Apr 1961) J Am Psa Ass 1962, 10:3-21
            Abs Hayman, M. Bull Phila Ass Psa 1961, 11:138-141. JBi Q 1963,
            32:130. IBa RFPsa 1964, 28:453
75486   On homosexuality and gender identity. (Read at Int Psa Cong, July-
        Aug 1963) J 1964, 45:217-219
            Homosexualité et identité. RFPsa 1965, 29:343-348
            Abs Garma, A. Rev Psicoanál 1964, 21:381. Guiard, F. Rev Psico-
            anál 1966, 23:208. EVN Q 1966, 35:456-457
S-47810 On screen defense, screen hunger and screen identity.
            Abs Margolis, N. M. An Surv Psa 1958, 9:170-172
75487   On sexual apathy in the male. Calif Med 1968, 108:275-279
75488   On the silence and sounds of the analytic hour. J Am Psa Ass 1961,
        9:79-84
            Abs Soifer, R. Rev Psicoanál 1961, 18:400. FB Q 1962, 31:289. SAS
            RFPsa 1962, 26:616
75489   The origin and fate of new ideas in psychoanalysis. (Read at Psa Ass
        NY, 19 May 1969) J 1969, 50:503-515
75490   Otto Fenichel 1898-1946. The encyclopedia of psychoanalysis. Psa
        Pioneers 439-449
S-47806 Phobia, anxiety, and depression.
            JTM Q 1961, 30:142-143. Prego, L. E. Rev urug Psa 1961-62,
            4:559. SAS RFPsa 1961, 25:158
75491   The problem of working through. Dr Af Beh 2:277-314

75492   (Reporter) The selection of candidates for psychoanalytic training. (Panel: Am Psa Ass, May 1960) J Am Psa Ass 1961, 9:135-145

75493   Special technical problems in handling transference during analysis. (Read at Los Angeles Psa Soc, 16 Nov 1961)
Abs Mayman, M. Bull Phila Ass Psa 1962, 12:47-49

75494   The Technique and Practice of Psychoanalysis: Volume I. NY: IUP; London: Hogarth 1967, xv + 452 p
Abs J Am Psa Ass 1968, 16:179. Rv Rawn, M. L. R 1968, 55:321-322. Waldhorn, H. F. Q 1969, 38:479-483. Zetzel, E. R. J 1969, 50: 411-412

75495   That "impossible" profession. (Read at Am Psa Ass, 2 May 1965) J Am Psa Ass 1966, 14:9-27
Abs Féder, L. Cuad Psa 1965, 1:387. JLSt Q 1969, 38:334

75496   A transvestite boy and a hypothesis. (Read at Int Psa Cong, July 1965) J 1966, 47:396-403
Abs EVN Q 1968, 37:315

S-47813 Variations in classical psychoanalytic technique.
Abs GLG An Surv Psa 1958, 9:343-344. Prego, V. M. de Rev urug Psa 1965, 7:387

75497   The working alliance and the transference neurosis. (Read at Cleveland Psa Soc, May 1964; at Los Angeles Psa Soc, May 1963) Q 1965, 34: 155-181
Das Arbeitsbündnis und die Übertragungsneurose. Psyche 1966, 20: 81-103
Abs LDr RFPsa 1966, 30(Spec no):325

GREENSPAN, JACK

75498   The original persecutor—a case study. Bull Phila Ass Psa 1964, 14:13-28
Abs EFA Q 1965, 34:135. PLe RFPsa 1967, 31:307

75499   (& Myers, J.) A review of the theoretical concepts of paranoid delusions with special reference to women. Penn psychiat Q 1961, 1:11-28

75500   Sex of the persecutor in female paranoid patients: a study based on the presentation of their delusional material. Arch gen Psychiat 1963, 9:217-223

75501   Sex of the persecutor in male paranoid patients: a clinical study of delusional material. Penn psychiat Q 1966, 6:3-16

GREENSTADT, WILLIAM M.

75502   An evaluation of types of drive and of ego strength variables in selected problem and non-problem elementary school boys. Diss Abstr 1964, 24:2610

GREENSTEIN, FRED I.

75503   Children and Politics. New Haven: Yale Univ Pr 1965, viii + 199 p

75504   Popular images of the president. P 1965, 122:523-529

75505   Private disorder and the public order: a proposal for collaboration between psychoanalysts and political scientists. (Read at Acad Psa and Am Polit Sci Ass, 29 Dec 1966) Q 1968, 37:261-281

75506   Young men and the death of a young president. Chld Dth Pres 172-192

GREENSTEIN, JULES MAURICE

75507 Father characteristics and sex typing. J Pers soc Psychol 1966, 3:271-277

GREENWALD, ALAN F.

See Bartemeier, Leo H.

GREENWALD, HAROLD

75508 (Ed) The Active Psychotherapy. NY: Atherton Pr 1967, xi + 384 p
75509 Failures in group psychotherapy. Top Probl PT 1965, 157-163
75510 Hypnosis and hallucinogenic drugs. J Long Island Consult Center 1966, 4(4)
75511 Introduction to Bayer, S. *Each Man Kills*, NY: Ballantine Books 1962
75512 Play and self-development. In Otto, H. A. & Mann, J. *Ways of Growth*, NY: Grossman Publ 1968, 15-23
75513 Play therapy in children over twenty-one. Psychotherapy 1967, 4:44-46
75514 (& Krich, A.) (Eds) The Prostitute in Literature. NY: Ballantine 1960
75515 Treatment of the psychopath. Voices 1967, 3:50-61
75516 Use of hypnosis to investigate resistance. PPR 1961, 48(3):116-120
75517 What is the meaning of perversion? Why Rep 205-214
75518 Why do so few people find their work satisfying? Why Rep 409-416

See Freeman, Lucy

REVIEW OF:
75519 Abrahamsen, D. The Psychology of Crime. PPR 1962, 49(4):139

GREENWOOD, EDWARD D.

75520 (& Menninger, R. W.) Schools and mental health. Part I: Year of challenge and discover. Menn Q 1965-66, 19(4):1-12

GREGG, GRACE S.

See Elmer, Elizabeth

GREGG, LUCIEN A.

See Earley, Leroy W.

GREGOR, A. J.

75521 Psychoanalytic disposition terms and reduction sentences. J Philos 1966, 63:737-745

GREGORIO, M.

See Fischetti, N. M.

GREGORY, HOOSAG K.

75522 Cowper's love of subhuman nature: a psychoanalytic approach. Philol Q 1967, 46:42-57

GREITHER, ALOYS

75523 (Ed) Tiefenpsychologie. Wesen und Deutung. [Depth Psychology. Reality and Interpretation.] Düsseldorf: Triltsch 1964, 88 p

GREMPEL, FRANZ

75524 Beitrag zur Ätiologie und Therapie des Schlafwandelns. [Contribution concerning the etiology and therapy of somnambulism.] Prax PT 1964, 9:108-117

GRENE, MARJORIE

75525 (Ed) Toward a Unity of Knowledge. (Psychological Issues Volume VI, No. 2) NY: IUP 1969, 302 p

GRESSOT, MICHEL

75526 Aspects fonctionnels de la vie onirique. [Functional aspects of the dream life.] RFPsa 1963, 27(Suppl):391-395
75527 Discussion of Alvim, F. Troubles de l'identification et image corporelle. RFPsa 1962, 26(Spec No):103-114
75528 Discussion of Flournoy, O. La sublimation. RFPsa 1967, 31:95-98
75529 Discussion of Kestemberg, E. & Kestemberg, J. Contribution à la perspective génétique en psychanalyse. RFPsa 1966, 30:729-731
75530 Discussion of Luquet, P. Les identifications précoces dans la structuration et la restructuration du moi. RFPsa 1962, 26(Spec No):283-285
75531 Discussion of Morgenthaler, F. & Parin, P. La genèse du moi chez les Dogons. RFPsa 1967, 31:47-58
75532 L'idée de composante psychotique dans les cas-limites accessibles à la psychothérapie. [The idea of psychotic component in the accessible limits to psychotherapy of a case.] Encéph 1960, 49:290-304
75533 Illusion et auto-erotisme. [Illusion and auto-eroticism.] RFPsa 1966, 30:732-734
75534 Les illusions gagnées. Reflexions sur le dualité functionnelle (structurante et defensive) des processes de rationalisation. [Gained illusions. Reflections on the structural and defensive functional duality of rationalization processes.] Évolut Psychiat 1965, 30:577-611
75535 L'interdit de l'inceste précurseur et noyan du surmoi oedipien organise la différenciation individuo-sociale en garantissant la dualité des sexes. [Prohibition against incest, precursor and nucleus of the Oedipal superego, organizes individual-social differentiation by guaranteeing the duality of the sexes.] RFPsa 1967, 31:1061-1068
75536 Problèmes cliniques et techniques du contre-transfert. [Clinical and technical problems of counter-transference.] RFPsa 1963, 27(Suppl): 195-199
S-47865 Psychanalyse et connaissance.
    Abs Noble, D. & Woodbury, M. A. An Surv Psa 1956, 7:116-125
75537 Psychanalyse et Psychothérapie, Leur Commensalisme; l'Esprit de la Psychanalyse est-il Compatible avec la Psychothérapie? [Psychoanalysis and Psychotherapy: Their Commensalism.] Paris: PUF 1963, 165 p. RFPsa 1964-65, 28(Suppl):47-223

75538 Réflexions sur la sélection des futurs analystes. [Thoughts on the selection of future analysts.] Bull Ass psa Fran 1966, (2). Bull schweiz Gscht Psa 1966, (4)
         Abs Garma, A. Rev Psicoanál 1967, 24:692

GREY, ALAN L.

75539 (Ed) Class and Personality in Society. NY: Atherton Pr 1969, 190 p
75540 Social class and the psychiatric patient: a study in composite character. Contempo Psa 1966, 2(2):87-121

REVIEW OF:
75541 Myers, J. K. et al: A Decade Later; A Follow-up of Social Class and Mental Illness. Contempo Psa 1969, 5(2):185-188

GREY, PAUL

See Ferber, Leon

GRIER, WILLIAM HENRY

75542 (& Cobbs, P. M.) Black Rage. NY: Basic Books 1968, viii + 213 p
75543 Some special effects of Negroness on the Oedipal conflict. J Nat Med Ass 1966, 58:416-418
75544 When the therapist is Negro: some effects on the treatment process. P 1967, 123:1587-1592

GRIESL, GOTTFRIED

75545 Zur Psychologie der Heilserwartung. [On the psychology of the expectation of holiness.] Jb Psychol Psychother med Anthropol 1961, 8:47-67

GRIESMER, ROBERT D.

See Helman, Robert D.

GRIFFIN, WILLIAM JAMES

75546 The use and abuse of psychoanalysis in the study of literature. In Manheim, L. F. & Manheim, E. B. *Hidden Patterns,* NY: Macmillan 1966, 19-36

GRIFFITH, B. C.

See Lipman, Ronald S.

GRIFFITH, RICHARD M.

See Baeyer, Walter von; Lee, Joan C.; Straus, Erwin W.

GRIFFITHS, RUTH

See Christ, Adolph E.

GRIGG, AUSTIN ERNEST

See Lucky, Arthur W.

GRIGG, KENNETH A.
See Levy, Joshua

GRIMALDI, PABLO
See Granel, Julio A.

ABSTRACTS OF:
75547 Bion, W. R. Attacks on linking. Rev Psicoanál 1967, 24:388-390
75548 Bion, W. R. Development of schizophrenic thought. Rev Psicoanál 1967, 24:382-383
75549 Bion, W. R. Notes on the theory of schizophrenia. Rev Psicoanál 1967, 24:377-379
75550 Bion, W. R. On hallucination. Rev Psicoanál 1967, 24:387-388

GRIMER, DAVID G.
See Wahl, Charles W.

GRIMM, ELAINE E.
75551 Women's attitudes and reactions to childbearing. In Goldman, G. D. & Milman, D. S. *Modern Woman*, Springfield, Ill: Thomas 1969, 129-151

GRIMSHAW, LINTON
75552 Anorexia nervosa—progress of a case. M 1963, 36:249-251

GRIMSON, WILBUR R.
See Usandivaras, Raúl J.

GRINBERG, LEÓN
S-47881 Sobra algunos mecanismos esquizoides en relación con el juego de ajedrez.
Abs An Surv Psa 1955, 6:165-166
S-47882 Sobre algunos problemas de técnica psicoanalítica determinados por la identificación y contraidentificación proyectivas.
Abs Vega An Surv Psa 1956, 7:337
S-47884 Aspectos mágicos en la transferencia y en la contratransferencia. Sus implicaciones técnicas.
Abs JO An Surv Psa 1958, 9:405
75553 Aspectos regresivos y evolutivos de los mecanismos obsesivos: el control omnipotente y el control adaptative. [Regressive and evolutionary aspects of obsessive mechanisms: omnipotent and adaptive control.] Rev Psicoanál 1967, 24:477-493
75554 Comment on Dr. Ritvo's paper, "Correlation of a childhood and adult neurosis: based on the adult analysis of a reported childhood case (summary)." (Read at Int Psa Cong, July 1965) J 1966, 47:145-148
Discussion du rapport du Dr. Ritvo. RFPsa 1967, 31:560-564
75555 Contribución al estudio de las modalidades de la identificación proyectiva. [Contribution to the study of modalities of projective identification.] Rev Psicoanál 1965, 21

75556 (et al) Cronología y resúmenes de la obra de Bion. [Chronology and résumés of the works of W. R. Bion.] Rev. Psicoanál 1967, 24:369-399

75557 Culpa y Depresion—Estudio Psicoanalitico. [Guilt and Depression. Psychoanalytic Study.] Buenas Aires: Editorial Paidos 1963, 247 p
Rv Urtubey, L. de Rev urug Psa 1964, 6:501-509. Vega Q 1964, 33:585; R 1964, 51:534. Rodrigue, E. J 1966, 47:583-585. Tomás, J. Rev Psicoanál 1966, 23:345

75558 Discussion of Berliner, B. "Psychodynamics of the depressive character." Psa Forum 1966, 1:256-258

75559 Discussion of Dorn, R. M. "Psychoanalysis and psychoanalytic education." Psa Forum 1969, 3:261-264

75560 (et al) Ecuación Fantástica. [Fantastic Equation.] Buenos Aires: Ed. Hormé 1966

75561 (& Langer, M.; Liberman, D.; Rodrigue, E.; Rodrigue, G. T. de) Elaboracion en el proceso analitico. [Elaboration in the analytic process.] Rev urug Psa 1966, 8:255-263

* * * Foreword to Bion, W. R. Aprendiendo de la Experiencia, Buenos Aires: Editorial Paidós 1965

* * * Foreword to Bion, W. R. Elementos del Psicoanálisis, Buenos Aires: Editorial Paidós 1966

* * * Foreword to French, T. & Alexander, F. Psicología y Asma Bronquial, Buenos Aires: Editorial Hormé 1966

* * * Foreword to Klein, M. Las Emociones Básicas del Hombre, Buenos Aires: Editorial Paidós

* * * Foreword to Knight, R. Psiquiatría Psicoanalítica, Buenos Aires: Editorial Hormé 1960

* * * Foreword to Meltzer, D. [The Psychoanalytic Process] (Sp) Buenos Aires: Editorial Hormé 1968

* * * Foreword to Segal, H. Introducción a la Obre de Melanie Klein, Buenos Aires: Editorial Paidós

75562 (& Campo, A.; Dellarossa, A.; Evelson, E.; Grinberg, R.; Luchina, A.; Serebriany, R.; Smolensky Dellarossa, G. de; Teper, E.; Wender, L.) Funciamento del yo en el duelo normal y patologico. [Ego function in normal and pathological grief.] Rev Psicoanál 1964, 21:129-137

75563 (et al) Función del soñar y clasificación clinica de los sueños en el proceso analítico. [The dream function and the clinical classification of dreams in the analytic process.] Rev Psicoanál 1967, 24:749-789

75564 (& Langer, M.; Rodrigué, E.) El Grupo Psicológico en la Terapéutica, Ensenanza e Investigación. [The Psychological Group in Therapy, Training and Research.] Buenos Aires: Ed. Nova 1960

75565 Historia y evolución de la psicología y psicoterapia de grupo en la Argentina. [History and evolution of group psychotherapy in Argentina.] Rev Psicol Psicoter Grupo 1961, 1

75566 El individuo frente a su identidad. [The individual confronted by his identity.] Rev Psicoanál 1961, 18:334-336

75567 Introducción a los últimos conceptos de Bion. [Introduction to Bion's latest ideas.] Rev Psicoanál 1967, 24:118-124

75568 (& Bleger, J.; Rascovsky, A.; Liberman, D.; Rascovsky, L.) Mesa redondo sobre "la teoría de los instintos." [Roundtable discussion on the theory of instincts.] Rev Psicoanál 1963, 20:147-149

S-47890 La negación en el comer compulsivo y en la obesidad.
  Abs AN An Surv Psa 1956, 7:201
75569 New ideas: conflict and evolution. J 1969, 50:517-528
75570 Nosotros . . . y la culpa. [We . . . and guilt.] Act Np Arg 1967, 7
75571 Obituary: H. Racker. Rev Psicoanál 1961, 18:277
75572 On a specific aspect of countertransference due to the patient's projective identification J 1962, 43:436-440
  Abs EVN Q 1965, 34:307-308
75573 On acting out and its role in the psychoanalytic process. (Read at Int
  Psa Cong, July 1967) J 1968, 49:171-178
  Sobre el acting en el process psicoanalítico. Rev Psicoanál 1968,
  25:681-713
  Abs LHR Q 1969, 38:668
S-47892 Perturbaciones en la interpretación por la contraidentificatión proyectiva.
  Abs RHB An Surv Psa 1957, 8:253
75574 Por qué negamos? [Why we deny.] Rev Psicoanál 1961, 18:118-130
  Abs Vega Q 1962, 31:434
75575 (& Langer, M.; Rodrigué, E.) Psicoanálisis de las Américas. [Psycho-
  analysis of the Americas.] Buenos Aires: Paidós 1968, 1969, 193 p
75576 Psicopatología de la identificación y contraidentificación proyectivas y
  de le contratransferencia. [Psychopathology of projective identification
  and counter-identification and of countertransference.] Rev Psicoanál
  1963, 20:112-123
  Abs Vega Q 1964,33:458
S-47893 (& Langer, M.; Rodrigué, E.) Psicoterapia del Grupo. Su Enfoque Psicoanalítica.
  Psycho-analytische Gruppentherapie. Stuttgart: Ernst Klett Verlag
  1960
  Rv Barande, R. RFPsa 1962, 26:138
75577 Psychoanalytic considerations on the Jewish Passover totemic sacrifice
  and meal. Am Im 1962, 19:391-424
75578 (& Langer, M.; Liberman, D.; Rodrigué, E. de; Rodrigué, G. T. de)
  The psycho-analytic process. (Read at Panamer Cong Psa, Aug 1966)
  J 1967, 48:496-503
  Abs LHR Q 1969, 38:507
75579 Relations between psycho-analysts. (Read at Latin-Amer Psa Cong,
  Jan 1960) J 1963, 44:362-367
  Abs EVN Q 1965, 34:619
75580 The relationship between obsessive mechanisms and a state of self
  disturbance: depersonalization. (Read at Int Psa Cong, July 1965) J
  1966, 47:177-183
  Rapports entre les mécanismes obsessionnels et certains troubles du
  soi: états de dépersonalisation. RFPsa 1967, 31:647-657
  Abs Auth Rev Psicoanál 1966, 23:260. Cuad Psa 1967, 3:162. EVN
  Q 1968, 37:310
75581 Reseña historica de la Asociación Psicoanalítica Argentina. [Recent
  history of the Argentine Psychoanalytic Association.] Rev Psicoanál
  1961, 18:299-303

S-47896 La rivalidad y los sueños legendarios de José.
Rivalry and envy between Joseph and his brothers. Samiksa 1963,
17(3):150-171

S-47897 Si Yo Fuera Usted: Contribución al estudio de la identificación proyectiva.
Abs RHB An Surv Psa 1957, 8:129

75582 Sintesis general de los relatos y correlatos sobre el tema "Mania." [A general synthesis of relations and correlations on the subject of mania.]
Rev urug Psa 1966, 8:183-192

75583 Sobre dos tipos de culpa. Su relación con los aspectos normales y patológicos del duelo. Rev Psicoanál 1963, 20:321-345
Two kinds of guilt—their relations with normal and pathological aspects of mourning. (Read at Int Psa Cong, July-Aug 1963) J 1964, 45:366-372
Deux sortes de culpabilité: leurs relations avec les aspects du deuil normal et pathologique. RFPsa 1965, 29:191-201
Abs Vega Q 1965, 34:142. EVN Q 1966, 35:464

75584 (& Grinberg, R. V. de) Los sueños del día lunes. [On Monday's dreams.] Rev Psicoanál 1960, 17:449-455
Abs Vega Q 1962, 31:298

75585 (et al) Yo y self. Su delimitación conceptual. [The ego and the self. Conceptual delimitations.] Rev Psicoanál 1966, 23:229-243
Abs Vega Q 1968, 37:162

See Alvarez de Toledo, Luisa G. de; Grinberg, Rebeca Vaisman de

GRINBERG, REBECA VAISMAN DE

75586 (& Grinberg, L.) La adquisición del sentimiento de identidad en el proceso analítico. [The acquisition of identity feeling in the analytic process.] Rev urug Psa 1966, 8:247-254
Abs Vega Q 1968, 37:162

S-47919 Características de las relaciones de objeto en una claustrofobia.
Abs Garbarino, M. F. de Rev urug Psa 1961-62, 4:546

75587 (& Faigen, D.; Soifer, R.) Conceptos actuales sobre el analisis de niños en el grupo argentino. [Present day concepts on child analysis in the Argentine group.] Rev Psicoanál 1968, 25:387-411

75588 El duelo en los niños. [Mourning in children.] Rev Psicoanál 1963, 20:377-388

75589 Interpretación psicoanalítica de "Las cabezas trocadas." Contribución al estudio de la patología de la identidad. [A psychoanalytic interpretation of "Die Betrogene" as a contribution to the study of pathology of identity.] Rev Psicoanál 1966, 23:161-181
Abs Barriguete, A. Cuad Psa 1967, 3:246. Vega Q 1967, 36:476

75590 Migración e identidad. [Migration and identity.] Biblioteca de la Asociación Psicoanálitica Argentina 1965

75591 (& Evelson, E.) El niño frente a la muerte. [The child confronted by death.] Rev Psicoanál 1962, 19(4)

75592 Sobre la curiosidad. [On curiosity.] Rev Psicoanál 1961, 18:321-336
Abs Vega Q 1962, 31:593

See Evelson, Elena; Grinberg, León

GRINKER, ROY RICHARD, JR.

75593 Complementary psychotherapy. Curr psychiat Ther 1968, 8:23-31
75594 Complementary psychotherapy: treatment of "associated" pairs. P 1966, 123:633-638
75595 Discussion of Giovacchini, P. L. "Characterological aspects of marital interaction." Psa Forum 1967, 2:20
75596 Ego, insight, and will power. Arch gen Psychiat 1961, 5:91-102
　　　　Abs KR Q 1962, 31:589
75597 Imposture as a form of mastery. Arch gen Psychiat 1961, 5:449-452
　　　　L'imposture, forme de domination. Méd et Hyg 1962, 20:608-609
75598 Self-esteem and adaptation. Arch gen Psychiat 1963, 9:414-418
　　　　Abs KR Q 1964, 33:610

　　　　See Grinker, Roy R., Sr.

GRINKER, ROY RICHARD, SR.

S-47930 Anxiety as a significant variable for a unified theory of human behavior.
　　　　Abs KR Q 1961, 30:148
75599 Bootlegged ecstacy. JAMA 1964, 187:192
75600 (& Werble, B.; Drye, R. C.) (Eds) The Borderline Syndrome: A Behavioral Study of Ego-Functions. NY/London: Basic Books 1968, xiv + 274 p
　　　　Abs J Am Psa Ass 1969, 17:278-279. WAS Q 1969, 38:652-654
75601 Clinical psychiatric studies. Reception of communications by patients in depressive states. Res Publ Ass Res Nerv Ment Dis 1964, 42:373-480
75602 Communications by patients in depressive states. Arch gen Psychiat 1964, 10:576-580
75603 Conceptual progress in psychoanalysis. Mod Psa 19-65
75604 Continuities in cultural evolution. Curr Anthropol 1966, 7:67
75605 A demonstration of the transactional model. Contempo PT 214-227
75606 Discussion of Alexander, F. "An experimental approach to study of physiological and psychological effects of emotional stress situations." In Tourlentes, T. T. et al: Research Approaches to Psychiatric Problems, NY/London: Grune & Stratton 1962, 204-208
75607 Discussion of papers of Drs. Millet and Ruesch. "The academy in perspective: past, present and future," & "The future of psychologically oriented psychiatry." Sci Psa 1966, 10:161-163
75608 Discussion of Silverberg, W. V. "An experimental theory of the process of psychoanalytic therapy." Sci Psa 1961, 4:167-171
75609 (& MacGregor, H.; Selan, K.; Klein, A.; Kohrman, J.) The early years of psychiatric social work. Soc S R 1961, 35:111-126
75610 Emerging concepts of mental illness and models of treatment: the medical point of view. P 1969, 125:865-869
75611 An essay on schizophrenia and science. Arch gen Psychiat 1969, 20: 1-24
° ° ° Foreword to Bailey, P. Sigmund the Unserene, Springfield, Ill: Thomas 1965
° ° ° Foreword to Offer, D. & Sabshin, M. Normality: Theoretical and Clinical Concepts of Mental Health, NY/London: Basic Books 1966

S-47949 Freud and medicine.
   Abs Richardson, G. A. An Surv Psa 1956, 7:27-28
S-47950 Growth, inertia and shame: their therapeutic implications and dangers.
   Abs An Surv Psa 1955, 6:357
75612 Homosexuality. Counseling 1962, 20(2)
75613 Identity or regression in American psychoanalysis. Arch gen Psychiat 1965, 12:113-125
75614 (& Werble, B.; Drye, R. C.; Wolpert, E. A.) Individual patients. In author's *The Borderline Syndrome* 98-112
75615 Introduction to symposium on psychoanalytic education. Sci Psa 1962, 5:1-5
75616 (& Grinker, R. R., Jr.; Timberlake, J.) Mentally healthy young males (Homoclites). Arch gen Psychiat 1962, 6:405-453
75617 Normality viewed as a system. Arch gen Psychiat 1967, 17:320-324
S-47952 On identification.
   Abs JAL An Surv Psa 1957, 8:81
75618 "Open-system" psychiatry. Psa 1966, 26:115-128
75619 The phenomena of depressions. Proc III World Cong Psychiat 1961, 161. In Katz, M. M. et al: *The Role and Methodology of Classification in Psychiatry and Psychopathology*, Chevy Chase, Md.: U. S. Dept of Health, Education, and Welfare 1968
75620 (& Miller, J.; Sabshin, M.; Nunnally, J. C.) The Phenomena of Depressions. NY: Paul B. Hoeber 1961, 249 p; 1963, 265 p
   Rv Jacobson, E. Q 1963, 32:252-255
75621 The physiology of emotions. In Simon, A. et al: *The Physiology of Emotions*, Springfield, Ill: Thomas 1961, 3-25
   Die Physiologie der Affekte. Psyche 1961, 15:38-58
75622 Presidential address: a dynamic study of the "homoclite." Sci Psa 1963, 6:115-134
75623 (& MacGregor, H.; Selan, K.; Klein, A.; Kohrman, J.) Psychiatric Social Work. A Transactional Case Book. NY: Basic Books 1961, xiv + 338 p
75624 Psychiatry rides madly in all directions. Arch gen Psychiat 1964, 10: 228-237
75625 Psychiatry: the field. In *International Encyclopedia of Social Sciences*, NY: Macmillan 1968
75626 The psychoanalysis of historical characters; an editorial. Arch gen Psychiat 1967, 16:389
75627 A psychoanalytic historical island in Chicago (1911-12). Arch gen Psychiat 1963, 8:392-394
75628 Psychoanalytic theory and psychosomatic research. In Marmorston, J. & Stainbrook, E. *Psychoanalysis and the Human Situation*, NY: Vantage 1964, 194-226
75629 The psychodynamics of suicide and attempted suicide. In Yochelson, L. *Symposium on Suicide*, Wash DC: George Wash Univ 1967, 60-70
75630 The psychosomatic aspects of anxiety. In Spielberger, C. D. *Anxiety and Behavior*, NY: Academic Pr 1966, 129-142
75631 Psychosomatic aspects of the cancer problem. In Bahnson, C. B. & Kissen, D. M. *Psychophysiological Aspects of Cancer*, Ann NY Acad Med 1966, 125:876-883

75632 Recent medical books: psychiatry. JAMA 1964, 188:266
75633 Research potentials of departments of psychiatry in general hospitals. In Kaufman, M. R. *The Psychiatric Unit in a General Hospital,* NY: IUP 1965, 405-422
75634 The sciences of psychiatry: fields, fences and riders. P 1965, 122:367-376
75635 (& Gordon, E.) The Simon Wexler Psychiatric Research and Clinic Pavilion. Ment Hosp 1963, 14:473-479
75636 The specificity of response to stress stimuli. Arch gen Psychiat 1966, 15:624
75637 A struggle for eclecticism. P 1964, 121:451-457
75638 Symbolism and general systems theory. In Gray, W. et al: *General Systems Theory and Psychiatry,* Boston: Little, Brown 1969, 135-140
75639 The testability of psychoanalytic hypotheses. In Abrams, A. et al: *Unfinished Tasks in the Behavioral Sciences,* Baltimore: Williams & Wilkins 1964, 231-235
75640 (Contributor) Timberline Conference on Psychophysiologic Aspects of Cardiovascular Disease. PSM 1964, 26:405
S-47987 A transactional model for psychotherapy. Contempo PT 190-213
       Um modelo transacional para a psicoterapia. Arqu Clin Pinel 1961, 1:101-122
75641 What do we do with it? Arch gen Psychiat 1966, 15:449
75642 Who does it to whom? Arch gen Psychiat 1966, 15:561

       See Goldstein, Iris B.; Oken, Donald; Rado, Sandor; Shipman, William G.

GRINSPOON, LESTER

75643 (& Menninger, R. W.) Introduction. [The range of human conflict: a symposium.] BMC 1966, 30:265-266
75644 (& Ewalt, J. R.; Shader, R.) Long-term treatment of chronic schizophrenia: preliminary report. Int J Psychiat 1967, 4:116-128; 140-141
75644A Marihuana. Sci Amer 1969, 221:17-25
75644B Psychosocial constraints on the important decision-maker. P 1969, 125:1074-1082
75645 (& Ewalt, J. R.; Shader, R. I.) A study of long-term treatment of chronic schizophrenia. Proc IV World Cong Psychiat 1966, 2992-2994

       See Cohen, Raquel E.; Messier, Michel

GRINSTEIN, ALEXANDER

75646 Discussion of Arlow, J. A. "Borderlines." *Newsletter,* Mich Soc Neurol Psychiat 1962, 4(5):72-74
S-47993 The dramatic device: a play within a play.
       Abs IS An Surv Psa 1956, 7:410
75647 Freud's dream of the botanical monograph. (Read at Mich Ass Psa, 11 Jan 1960; at Am Psa Ass, May 1960) J Am Psa Ass 1961, 9:480-503
       Abs FB Q 1962, 31:419
75648 Freud's dream of the open-air closet. (Read at Mich Ass Psa, 20 Nov 1965; Psa Ass NY, 7 Nov 1965)
       Abs Silverman, J. S. Q 1967, 36:325-327

75649   The Index of Psychoanalytic Writings, Vol 1-9. (Pref: Jones, E. L.)
NY: IUP 1956-1966
Abs JFr An Surv Psa 1957, 8:294-295; 1958, 9:437. J Am Psa Ass
1966, 14:230. Rv Bendix, L. Q 1967, 36:295-297
75650   James Beaumont Strachey: 1887-1967. Am Im 1967, 24:371-373
75651   On Sigmund Freud's Dreams. Detroit: Wayne State Univ Pr 1968,
475 p
75652   Profile of a "doll"—a female character type. (Read at Mich Ass Psa,
24 Oct 1961) R 1963, 50:321-334
75653   Some comments on breast envy in women. J Hillside Hosp 1962, 11:
171-177
Abs JA Q 1963, 32:291
S-47996 A specific defense met in psychoanalytic therapy: "Comes the knight
in shining armor."
Abs BEM An Surv Psa 1957, 8:250
S-47998 Vacations: a psychoanalytic study.
Abs An Surv Psa 1955, 6:166

REVIEWS OF:
75654   Frosch, J. & Ross, N. (Eds): The Annual Survey of Psychoanalysis,
Vol. VIII. Q 1967, 36:601-603
75655   Litman, R. E. (Ed): Psychoanalysis in the Americas. Original Contributions from the First Pan-American Congress for Psychoanalysis. Q
1968, 37:126-128

GRISELL, JAMES L.

See Beckett, Peter G. S.

GRISWOLD, B. B.

See Mendelsohn, Gerald A.

GROBSTEIN, R.

See Korner, Anneliese F.

GRODDECK, GEORG WALTER

75656   Medizinische und psychoanalytische Schriften. [Medical and psychoanalytic writings.] In author's *Psychoanalytische Schriften zur Psychosomatik* 389-394
75657   Psychoanalytische Schriften zur Literatur und Kunst. [Psychoanalytic
Writings about Literature and Art.] (Ed: Diersburg, E. R. von) Wiesbaden: Limes Publ 1964, 338 p
Extracts in: La Maladie, l'Art et le Symbole. [Illness, Art and Symbol.] (Tr: Lewinter, R.) (Pref: Lewinter, R.) Paris: Gallimard 1969,
331 p
Rv MG Q 1965, 34:298-299
75658   Psychoanalytische Schriften zur Psychosomatik. [Psychoanalytic Writings on Psychosomatics.] (Ed: Clauser, G.) Wiesbaden: Limes 1966
Extracts in: La Maladie, l'Art et le Symbole. [Illness, Art and Symbol.] (Tr: Lewinter, R.) (Pref: Lewinter, R.) Paris: Gallimard 1969,
331 p

GRODZICKI, W. D.

75659 Einige Bemerkungen zur Struktur masochistischen Verhaltens im Zusammenhang mit Übertragungs- und Gegenübertragungsvorgängen. [Some remarks on the structure of masochistic behavior in the connection between transference and counter-transference reactions.] Jb Psa 1967, 4:181-201

S-47999 Neue Wege in der Psychoanalyse?
Abs EW An Surv Psa 1956, 7:71-73

75660 Problems and difficulties in psychosomatic training. Adv Psm Med 195-200

GROEN, J. J.

75661 (& Welner, A.) The biological basis of psychosomatic medicine. Israel Ann Psychiat 1966, 4:136-147

75662 [The clinical-scientific examination technic in psychosomatic medicine.] (Ger) Verh Deutsch Ges inn Med 1967, 73:17-27

75663 (& Feldman-Toledano, Z.) Educative treatment of patients and parents in anorexia nervosa. Brit J Psychiat 1966, 112:671-681

75664 Possibilities of individual psychotherapy in schizophrenics. Psychiat Neurol Neurochir 1964, 67:130-136

75665 (et al) Psychosomatic Research. A Collection of Papers. NY: Macmillan 1964, 318 p
Rv Engel, G. L. Q 1966, 35:611-615. Wisdom, J. O. J 1966, 47: 585-588

GROEN, MARTEN

75666 (& Gemert, W.) Discriminant-analyse. [Discrimination-analysis.] Ned Tijdschr Psychol 1963, 18:467-480

GROLD, L. JAMES

75667 (& Jones, N. L.) Communicating the goals of activity therapy. J hosp comm Psychiat 1966, 17:200-201

75668 The community approach. Bull Med Staff, Westwood Hosp 1966, 3(2)

75669 Consistent treatment requires psychiatrist-nurse collaboration. J hosp comm Psychiat 1967, 18:340-342

75670 The continuous process of controlling milieu. J hosp comm Psychiat 1967, 18:182-183

75671 Drawing the family triangle: an adjunct to the psychiatric evaluation. BMC 1961, 25:69-77

75672 (& Hill, W. C.) Failure to keep appointments with the army psychiatrist: an indicator of conflict. P 1962, 119:446-450

75673 Medical director views his task. Bull Med Staff, Westwood Hosp 1966, 3(1):2

75674 Milieu therapy: its application in a private psychiatric hospital. Bull Med Staff, Westwood Hosp 1966, 3(3)

75675 Mother's Day. P 1968, 124:1456-1458

75676 The new role of the psychiatric nurse in a psychiatric hospital. Bull Med Staff, Westwood Hosp 1967, 4(1)

75677 (& Hill, W. C.) Predictions of ineffective performance in a combat
       ready division. Med Bull U.S. Army, Europe 1962, 19(9):180-182
75678 Resistance to changing a psychiatric ward. Ment Hosp 1960, 11:16-17
75679 (& Jones, N. L.) Work as therapy . . . in a private hospital. Ment Hosp
       1964, 15:694-695

GROLLMAN, EARL A.

75680 (Ed) Explaining Death to Children. Boston: Beacon Pr 1967, xv +
       296 p
75681 Judaism in Sigmund Freud's World. (Foreword: Ackerman, N. W.)
       NY: Bloch Publ Co 1966, xxv + 173 p
75682 Some sights and insights of history, psychology and psychoanalysis
       concerning the Father-god and Mother-goddess concepts of Judaism
       and Christianity. Am Im 1963, 20:187-209

GROMSKA, J.

75683 An attempt at an etiological qualification of encopresis in children.
       Pol med J 1968, 7:449-455

GRONLUND, NORMAN E.

75684 Sociometry in education: with special emphasis upon problems of ad-
       justment. Prog PT 1960, 5:191-194

GROOT, A. D. DE

75685 Thought and Choice in Chess. Hague: Mouton & Co 1965, xvi + 463 p

GROSS, MILTON M.

75686 Management of acute alcohol withdrawal states. Quart J Stud Alcohol
       1967, 28:655-666
75687 (& Halpert, E.; Sabot, L.) Some comment on Bleuler's concept of
       acute alcoholic hallucinosis. Quart J Study Alcohol 1963, 24:54-60

       See Kishner, Ira A.; Kissen, Benjamin

GROSS, RICHARD S.

       See Miller, Peter M.

GROSS, STEVEN J.

75688 (& Hirt, M.; Seeman, W.) Psychosexual conflicts in asthmatic children.
       J Psychosom Res 1968, 11:315-317

GROSSART, FRIEDRICH

75689 Gefühl und Strebung. [Emotion and Motivation.] Munich: Ernst Rein-
       hardt 1961, 196 p

GROSSBARD, HYMAN

75690 Ego deficiency in delinquents. Soc Casew 1962, 43:171-178

GROSSEN, JEAN-PIERRE

See Berman, Anne; Cambon, Fernand

GROSSER, GEORGE H.

75691 (& Paul, N. L.) Ethical issues in family group therapy. Ops 1964, 34: 875-884

75692 (& Wechsler, H.; Greenblatt, M.) (Eds) The Threat of Impending Disaster: Contributions to the Psychology of Stress. Cambridge: Institute of Technology 1964, xi + 335 p

See Greenblatt, Milton; Paul, Norman L.

GROSSMAN, CARL M.

75693 Transference, countertransference, and being in love. Q 1965, 34:249-256

75694 (& Grossman, S.) The Wild Analyst. The Life and Work of George Groddeck. NY: George Braziller 1965, 222 p
Abs J Am Psa Ass 1966, 14:237-238. Rv Am Im 1965, 22:220. Corbin, E. I. Q 1966, 35:290-292

GROSSMAN, DAVID

75695 Ego-activating approaches to psychotherapy. R 1964, 57:401-424
Abs SRS Q 1965, 34:623

GROSSMAN, SYLVIA

See Grossman, Carl M.

GROSSMAN, WILLIAM I.

75696 (& Simon, B.) Anthropomorphism: motive, meaning, and causality in psychoanalytic theory. Psa St C 1969, 24:78-111

75697 Reflections on the relationships of introspection and psychoanalysis. J 1967, 48:16-31
Abs EVN Q 1969, 38:157

ABSTRACT OF:

75698 Lampl-de Groot, J. An obstacle to cure in psychoanalysis: a discussion of Freud's "Analysis terminable and interminable." Q 1968, 37:479-481

GROSZ, H. J.

See Zimmerman, J.

GROTE, L. R.

S-12754 (& Meng, H.) Über interne und psychotherapeutische Behandlung der endogenen Magersucht.
Medical and psychotherapeutic treatment of endogenic *Magersucht* (anorexia). In Kaufman, M. R. & Heiman, M. *Evolution of Psychosomatic Concepts*, NY: IUP 1964, 167-180

GROTJAHN, MARTIN

75699 The academic lecture, merits of monogamy. Psychiat Spectator 1964, 2

75700 The aim and technique of psychiatric consultations. [Tape recording] Amer Acad Psychotherapists, AAP Tape Libr, Phila 19151

75701 The aim and technique of psychiatric family consultations. In Mendel, W. & Solomon, P. *The Psychiatric Consultation,* NY: Grune & Stratton 1968, 181-186

75702 The American family in crisis, lectures and discussions presented at the 1964-65 series. Forest Hosp Publ 1965, 3:34-40

75703 The Americanization of Martin Grotjahn. In Kosa, J. *The Home of the Learned Man, A Symposium on the Immigrant Scholar in America,* New Haven, Conn: Coll & Univ Pr 1968, 51-58

75704 An analyst's adjustment to America, Kosa Rep 1964

75705 Analytic group therapy with psychotherapists. Int J grp PT 1969, 19:326-333

S-48015 Analytic psychotherapy with the elderly.
    Abs An Surv Psa 1955, 6:374-375

75706 Das analytische Gruppenerlebnis im Rahmen der psychotherapeutischen Ausbildung. [The analytic group experiences in psychotherapeutic training.] Dyn Psychiat 1969, 2:2-11 Abs (Eng), 11-12

75707 The ancient Greek's awareness of their unconscious. (Read at South Calif Psa Soc, 16 Sept 1963)
    Abs Peck, J. S. Bull Phila Ass Psa 1964, 14:43-44

75708 Angoisse de mort et identité du moi. [The pangs of death and ego identity.] Extrait Psa 1961, 6

75709 (Ed) Apple Valley symposium, psychoanalysts view conjoint therapy. Psa Forum 1966, 1(2):147-167

75710 (& Wells, P. H.) Aspekte in der psychiatrischen Therapie die schizophrene Reaktion fördern und erhalten. [Schizophrenic trends in therapy.] Dyn Psychiat 1968, 1:31-33

75711 Beyond laughter, a summing up. In Corrigan, R. W. *Comedy: Meaning and Form,* San Francisco: Chandler Publ 1966, 270-276
    Au-delà du rire, résumé de l'ouvrage 1. Méd et Hyg 1961, (508):1-6

S-48016 Beyond Laughter. Humor and the Subconscious.
    Saper Ridere, Psicologia dell Umorismo. Milan: Dieci Illustrazioni Longanesi 1961, 315 p
    Abs AEC An Surv Psa 1957, 8:332-333

S-48017 On bullfighting and the future of tragedy.
    Tauromachie et avenir de la tragedie. Méd et Hyg 1961, (508)
    Abs PCR RFPsa 1961, 25:289

75712 Clinical illustrations from psychoanalytic family therapy. In Greene, B. L. *The Psychotherapies of Marital Disharmony.* NY: Free Pr; London: Collier-Macmillan 1965, 169-185

75713 Clinical observations about the dynamics of the family neurosis. Psychol Rep 1963, 13:830

75714 Consultation within the area of competency. Frontiers of clin Psychiat & Frontiers of Hosp Psychiat 1967, Nov

75715 The controversy in retrospect. Psychiat Opin 1968, 5(2):24-30

75716 Critical essay: Nunberg, H. & Federn, E. Minutes of the Vienna Psychoanalytic Society, Volume I, 1906-1908. Volume II: 1908-1910. J Hillside Hosp 1963, 12(1):50-53. J Otto Rank Ass 1967, 2(1):126-131; 1968, 3(1):79-84

S-48018 The defense against creative anxiety in the life and work of James Barrie. Commentary to John Skinner's research of "The Boy Who Wouldn't Grow Up."
Abs JC An Surv Psa 1957, 8:327-328

75717 Discussion of Friedman, L. J. "From Gradiva to the death instinct." Psa Forum 1966, 1:58-59

75718 Dynamics of growth and maturation in marriage and in psychoanalysis. Marriage Relat 341-356

75719 Ego identity and the fear of death and dying. J Hillside Hosp 1960, 9:147-155
Abs JA Q 1961, 30:450

75720 Franz Alexander: a pioneer of psychoanalysis. In Marmorston, J. & Stainbrook, E. *Psychoanalysis and the Human Situation,* NY: Vantage Pr 1964, 17-41

75721 Franz Alexander 1891-1964. The Western mind in transition. Psa Pioneers 384-398

75722 Franz Alexander, M.D.: teacher, student and pioneer of psychoanalysis. JNMD 1965, 140:319-322

75723 (Ed) Freud as a psychoanalytic consultant: from some unknown letters to Edoardo Weiss. Psa Forum 1966, 1:132-137

75724 Freud's tragic conflicts as presented in his dreams. Newsletter, South Calif Psa Soc & Inst 1967, Nov

75725 Georg Groddeck and the it. Voices 1965-66, 1(2):7-16

75726 Georg Groddeck 1866-1934. The untamed analyst. Psa Pioneers 308-320

75727 (& Wells, P. H.) "How motherly is a mother allowed to be, Dr. Rosen?" Voices 1967, 3(4):110-111

75728 How to consult with a general practitioner. Roche Rep 1965, 2(23): 5, 11

75729 Indications for psychoanalytic family therapy. Marriage Relat 283-291
 * * * Introduction to Weiss, E. *Sigmund Freud as a Consultant,* NY: Intercontinental Med Book Corp 1970, vii-xv

75730 Is there a hidden meaning in humor? Why Rep 141-152

75731 Jewish jokes and their relation to masochism. J Hillside Hosp 1961, 10:183-189
Abs JA Q 1962, 31:585

75732 Karl Abraham 1877-1925. The first German psychoanalyst. Psa Pioneers 1-13

75733 Laughter and sex. Human Sexuality 1969, 3(9):92-96

S-48021 A letter by Sigmund Freud with recollections of his adolescence.
Abs CFH An Surv Psa 1956, 7:31-32

75734 Letter to the editors [re "Conjoint therapy"]. Psa Forum 1966, 1:426

75735 Letter to the editor, re: *Psychoanalysis and the Family Neurosis.* Fam Proc 1964, 3:264

75736 My thanks to Theodor Reik. Am Im 1968, 25:27-31
Abs JWS Q 1969, 38:339

75737 The new technology and our ageless unconscious. Psa Forum 1966, 1:8-12; 18

75738 On being a sick physician. In Wahl, C. W. *New Dimensions of Psychosomatic Medicine*, Boston: Little, Brown 1964, 117-127

75739 On consultations: Southern California Psychiatric Society. Newsletter, South Calif Psychiat Soc 1968, 15(8):4-5

75740 "Open end" technique in psychoanalysis. Q 1964, 33:270-271

75741 Open letter to the editors. Voices 1967, 3(3):70

75742 Otto Rank on *Homer* and two unknown letters from Freud to Rank in 1916. J Otto Rank Ass 1969, 4(1):75-78

75743 Our ageless unconscious. In The Fund for the Republic, Center for the Stud of Democratic Institutions *Technology and Human Values*, 1966, 22-24

75744 (& Lindon, J. A.) Presenting the second issue. Psa Forum 1966, 1

S-48025 Problems and techniques of supervision.
        Abs An Surv Psa 1955, 6:385-386

75745 The process of awakening. In Sherman, M. H. *Psychoanalysis in America, Historical Perspectives*, Springfield, Ill: Thomas 1966, 150-170

75746 Profile of Edoardo Weiss. Psa Forum 1966, 1(1):132-134

75747 (& Treusch, J. V.) Psychiatric family consultations, the practical approach in family practice for the personal physician. Ann int Med 1967, 66:295-300

75748 Psychiatrist as a consultant: an outline of techniques. Psychiat News 1968, 3(2):5

75749 (& Treusch, J. V.) Psychiatrist sees patients in "medical" office, works jointly with clinician. Psychiat Prog 1966, 1(3):5

S-48026 Psycho-Analysis and the Family Neurosis.
        Abs J Am Psa Ass 1961, 9:169. Rv Berezin, M. A. Q 1961, 30:283-285. AEC J 1961, 42:475-477. Kaplan, D. PPR 1961, 48(1):117-122

75750 Psychoanalysis and the family neurosis. J Med Ass Georgia 1962, 51:459

75751 Psychoanalysis twenty-five years after the death of Sigmund Freud. Newsletter, South Calif Psa Soc 1964, No. 11, Nov. Psychol Rep 1965, 16:965-968

75752 A psychoanalyst looks up at Albert Schweitzer. In Roback, A. A. *Albert Schweitzer's Realms*, Cambridge, Mass: Sci-Art Publ 1962

75753 A psychoanalytic dialogue: the letters of Sigmund Freud and Karl Abraham, 1907-1926. Voices 1967, 3(3):85-89

S-12796 Psychoanalytic investigation of a seventy-one-year-old man with senile dementia. In Freeman, L. *The Mind: 12 Studies That Unlock the Secret of the Unconscious*, NY: Crowell Co 1967, 77-89

75754 (& Peck, J. S.; Becker, P.; Selesnick, S.; Ziferstein, I.) Psychoanalytic pioneers. (Read at South Calif Psa Soc, 15 Apr 1963)
        Abs Peck, J. S. Bull Phila Ass Psa 1963, 13:150-151

75755 "Psychoanalytic pioneers": a preliminary report on a research project. Percept mot Skills 1963, 17:640

S-48028 The recognition of the Oedipus complex in Greek antiquity. Two quotations from Aristophanes.
        Abs An Surv Psa 1955, 6:402-403

75756 Responsive action in psychoanalysis. Psa Tech 290-295

75757 (& Natterson, J. M.) Responsive action in psychotherapy. P 1965, 122: 140-143

75758 (& Wells, P. H.) Schizophrenogenic trends in therapy. Voices 1967, 3(2):14-17

75759 Sigmund Freud and the art of letter writing. JAMA 1967, 200:13-18

75760 (Ed) Sigmund Freud as a consultant and therapist: from Sigmund Freud's Letters to Edoardo Weiss. Psa Forum 1966, 1(2):223-231

75761 Sigmund Freud as dreamer, writer and friend. Voices 1969, 5(2):70-73

75762 Sigmund Freud—Woodrow Wilson controversy in retrospect. Psychiat Opin 1968, 5(2):24-30

75763 Sigmund Freud's insight into family dynamics, from an interview with Heinrich Meng about Sigmund Freud (1963). Psa Forum 1966, 1(4): 426

75764 Some dynamics of unconscious and symbolic communication in present-day television. Psa St Soc 1964, 3:356-369

75765 Some psychodynamics of unconscious and symbolic communication in present-day television. Psychol Rep 1963, 13:886

75766 (& Natterson, J. M.) Specific responsive action held important to psychotherapy. Roche Rep 1965, 2(20):3

75767 Supervision of analytic group psychotherapy. Group PT 1960, 13(3-4): 161-169

75768 The theatre of the absurd. Newsletter, South Calif Psychiat Soc 1966, 14(1):3-4. J Hillside Hosp 1968, 17(2-3)

75769 Trends in contemporary psychoanalytic literature. Bull South Calif Psa Soc & Inst 1968, (21):8-9

75770 Trends in contemporary psychotherapy and the future of mental health. M 1960, 33:263-267

75771 (& Natterson, J. M.) Value of responsive action in psychotherapy emphasized. Roche Rep 1965, 2(19):5-6

75772 (& Illing, H. A.) Victor Tausk 1877-1919. The influencing machine. Psa Pioneers 235-239

See Alexander, Franz; Goodstone, Gerald; Jackson, James; Rogawski, Alexander S.; Treusch, Jerome V.; Ziferstein, Isidore

TRANSLATIONS OF:
Friedemann, A. [73654, 73655]

REVIEWS OF:

75773 Alexander, F. The Western Mind in Transition: an Eyewitness Story. J 1961, 42:123-126

75774 Andreas-Salomé, L. The Freud Journal of Lou Andreas-Salomé. Q 1965, 34:274-276

75775 Cumming, E. & Henry, W. E. Growing Old. The Process of Disengagement. Q 1963, 32:125

75776 Edinger, D. Bertha Pappenheim: Leben und Schriften. Q 1964, 33:439

75777 Ehrenzweig, A. The Hidden Order in Art. A Study in the Psychology of Artistic Imagination. Q 1968, 37:608-612

75778 Freud, E. L. (Ed) Letters of Sigmund Freud. Q 1961, 30:265-271

75779 Freud, E. L. & Meng, H. (Eds) Sigmund Freud-Oskar Pfister: Briefe 1909-1939. Q 1963, 32:574-578

75780   Frosch, J. & Ross, N. (Eds) The Annual Survey of Psychoanalysis. Volume VI, 1955. Q 1962, 31:565

75781   Gicklhorn, J. & Gicklhorn, R. Sigmund Freuds akademische Laufbahn im Lichte der Dokumente. Q 1962, 31:96-98

75782   Groddeck, G. Psychoanalytische Schriften zur Literatur und Kunst. Q 1965, 34:298-299

75783   Grotjahn, M. et al (Eds) The Annual Survey of Psychoanalysis: A Comprehensive Survey of Current Psychoanalytic Theory and Practice. Vol. VII, 1956. J 1964, 45:607

75784   Krapf, E. E. Psychiatry, Volume I. Principles. Part 1, Personology; Part 2, General Psychiatry. Q 1963, 32:597

75785   Nunberg, H. & Federn, E. (Eds) Minutes of the Vienna Psychoanalytic Society. Volume II: 1908-1910. J 1968, 49:113-115

75786   Pfeiffer, E. (Ed) Sigmund Freud—Lou Andreas-Salomé Briefwechsel. Q 1967, 36:591-595

75787   Rapaport, D. The Structure of Psychoanalytic Theory: A Systematizing Attempt. Q 1961, 30:110-111

75788   Ruesch, J. Therapeutic Communication. Q 1963, 32:119-120

75789   Schaffner, B. (Ed) Group Processes, Transactions of the Fifth Conference, October 1958, Q 1961, 30:441-442

GROTSTEIN, JAMES S.

75790   Discussion of Rosenfeld, H. A. "The need of patients to act out during analysis." Psa Forum 1966, 1:26-27

See Malin, Arthur; Miller, Arthur A.

GROUNDS, VERNON CARL

75791   The concept of love in the psychology of Sigmund Freud. Diss Abstr 1961, 21:1995

GROUP FOR THE ADVANCEMENT OF PSYCHIATRY

75791A Death and Dying. Attitudes of Patient and Doctor. NY: GAP 1965, 75 p
          Rv Stern, M. M. Q 1967, 36:309-310

75791B Psychiatric Research and Assessment of Change. NY: GAP 1966, 357-478
          Rv Simon, J. Q 1968, 37:452-454

75791C Psychiatry and Public Affairs. Chicago: Aldine Publ 1966, 465 p
          Rv EDJ Q 1967, 36:612-613

75791D The Psychic Function of Religion in Mental Illness and Health. NY: GAP 1968, 653-730
          Rv Linn, L. Q 1969, 38:498-501

75791E Reports in Psychotherapy: Initial Interviews. NY: GAP 1961, 437-463

GROVE, DAVID L.

75792   Discussion of Krystal, H. "A psychoanalytic contribution to the theory of cyclicity of the financial economy." Psa Forum 1966, 1:368-371

GROVE, MARTA NIETO

75793 Algunas problemas del analista como investigador. [Some problems of the analyst as a researcher.] Rev urug Psa 1965, 7:5-27

75794 Comunicación extraverbal en el análisis de un niño de 9 años. [Nonverbal communication in the analysis of a 9-year-old boy.] Rev urug Psa 1961-62, 4:726-739

75795 De la histeria a la hipocondria. [On hysteria and hypochondria.] Rev urug Psa 1963, 5:367-389

75796 Fantasia de la cloaca y confusión. [Fantasy of a cloaca (sewer) and confusion.] Rev urug Psa 1964, 6:83-90

75797 Mecanismos obsesivos y defensa hipocondriaca. [Obsessive and defensive hypochrondriacal mechanisms.] Rev urug Psa 1964, 6:429-451

TRANSLATION OF:
(& Steiner, D.) Lewin, B. D. [52352]

GRUBER, HOWARD E.

75798 (& Terrell, G.; Wertheimer, M.) (Eds) Contemporary Approaches to Creative Thinking. NY: Atherton Pr 1963, xiv + 223 p
Rv Am Im 1965, 22:218

GRUEN, ARNO

75799 Autonomy and identification: the paradox of their opposition. J 1968, 49:648-655

75800 The couch?—or the man? R 1967, 54:72-80
Abs SRS Q 1968, 37:472

75801 The Oedipal experience and the development of the self. R 1969, 56: 265-270

GRUEN, WALTER

75802 Adult personality: an empirical study of Erikson's theory of ego development. In Neugarten, B. L. et al: *Personality in Middle and Late Life*, NY: Atherton Pr 1964, 1-14

75803 Rejection of false information about oneself as an indication of ego identity. J consult Psychol 1960, 24:231-233

See Zinberg, Norman E.

GRUENBERG, ERNEST M.

75804 (& Zusman, J.) The natural history of schizophrenia. Int Psychiat Clin 1964, 1:699-710

75805 Social organization of psychiatric services. In Hoch, P. H. & Zubin, J. *The Future of Psychiatry*, NY/London: Grune & Stratton 1962, 51-60

75806 (& Kolb, L. C.) The Washington Heights continuous care project. In Kolb, L. C. et al: *Urban Challenges to Psychiatry*, Boston: Little, Brown 1969, 269-292

75807 (& Kiev, A.; Stein, Z.; Wiehl, D.) Who are the Washington Heights psychiatric patients? In Kolb, L. C. et al: *Urban Challenges to Psychiatry*, Boston: Little, Brown 1969, 153-173

See Eisenberg, Leon

GRUENEWALD, DORIS

75808 Awareness vs. consciousness: a reply. Psychol Rep 1965, 16:758
75809 Notes toward a neuropsychological theory of dreams. Proc 73rd Annual
       Convention of the APA 1965, 217-218

GRUENEWALD, EDUARD

75810 De la higiene mental del psicoanalista. [Mental health of the psycho-
       analyst.] Arch Estud Psicoan Psicol Med 1967, 4:7-16

GRUENWALDT, G.

75811 Malerei psychischen Kranker. [Paintings of psychic patients.] Schweiz
       ANP 1967, 99:179-184

GRUNBERGER, BÉLA

75812 L'antisemite devant l'Oedipe. RFPsa 1962, 26:655-674
       The anti-semite and the Oedipal conflict. (Tr: Stewart, S.) (Read at
       Int Psa Cong, July-Aug 1963) J 1964, 45:380-385
       Der Antisemit und der Ödipuskomplex. Psyche 1962, 16:255-272
       L'antisemitismo e il conflitto edipico. Riv Psa 1963, 9:63-80
       Abs Auth Rev Psicoanál 1963, 20:192. EVN Q 1966, 35:464-465
75813 Considerazion sulla differenziazone del narcisismo dal processo di ma-
       turazione delle pulsazioni istintive. [Considerations on the differentia-
       tion between narcissism and the process of maturation.] Riv Psa 1961,
       7:9-26
       Considérations sur le clivage entre le narcissisme et la maturation
       pulsionnelle. RFPsa 1962, 26:179-209
       Abs Urtubey, L. de Rev urug Psa 1965, 7:107
75814 De l'image phallique. [On the phallic image.] RFPsa 1964, 28:217-234
       Über das Phallische. Psyche 1964, 17:604-620
       Abs Donadeo, J. Q 1966, 35:318-319
75815 Discussion of Barande, R. "Essai métapsychologique sur le silence: de
       l'objet total phallique dans le clinique du silence." RFPsa 1963, 27:99-
       103
75816 Discussion of Mendel, G. "La sublimation artistique." RFPsa 1964,
       28:780, 782-789
S-48096 Essai sur la situation analytique et le processus de guérison.
       Abs Woodbury, M. A. An Surv Psa 1957, 8:275-277. Galeano, J.
       Rev urug Psa 1961-62, 4:378
75817 Étude sur la dépression. [A study of depression.] RFPsa 1965, 29
       (Spec No):163-190
       Abs Ferretti, E. Riv Psa 1966, 12:328
S-48098 Étude sur la relation objectale anale.
       Abs RJA Q 1961, 30:155
75818 Étude sur le narcissisme. [Study on narcissism.] RFPsa 1965, 29:573-
       588
75819 L'oedipe et le narcissisme. [Oedipus complex and narcissism.] RFPsa
       1967, 31:825-839
S-48101 Préliminaires à une étude topique du narcissisme.
       Abs JLL An Surv Psa 1958, 9:70-71. Baranger, M. Rev urug Psa
       1965, 7:105

75820 Problèmes cliniques et techniques du contre-transfert. [Clinical and technical problems of counter-transference.] RFPsa 1963, 27(Suppl): 139-150

75821 Some reflections on the rat man. (Read at Int Psa Cong, July 1965) J 1966, 47:160-168
En marge de "l'homme aux rats." RFPsa 1967, 31:589-610
Einige Überlegungen zur Freud's "Rattenmann." Psyche 1967, 21: 576-591
Abs EVN Q 1968, 37:309-310

75822 Le suicide du mélancolique. [Suicide of melancholics.] RFPsa 1968, 32:574-594
Il suicidio del melanconico. Psiche 1965, 2(4):171-193

GRUNEBAUM, GUSTAVE EDMUND VON

75823 (& Caillois, R.) (Eds) The Dream and Human Societies. Berkeley/Los Angeles: Univ Calif Pr 1966, xiii + 457 p
Le Rêve et les Sociétés Humaines. Paris: Gallimard 1967
Los Sueños y las Sociedades Humanas. Buenos Aires: Editorial Sudamericana 1964

75824 Introduction: the cultural function of the dream as illustrated by classical Islam. In author's The Dream and Human Societies 3-21

GRUNEBAUM, HENRY U.

75825 (& Weiss, J. L.; Hirsch, L. L.; Barrett, J. E., Jr.) The baby on the ward. A mother-child admission to an adult psychiatric hospital. Ps 1963, 26:39-53
Abs HRB Q 1964, 33:143-144

75826 (& Christ, J.; Neiberg, N.) Diagnosis and treatment planning for couples. Int J grp PT 1969, 19:185-202

75827 Grief. Psychiat Opin 1968, 5(3):38-41

75828 Group psychotherapy of fathers: problems of technique. M 1962, 35: 147-154

75829 (& Christ, J.) Interpretation and the task of the therapist with couples and families. Int J grp PT 1968, 18:495-503

75830 (& Weiss, J. L.) Joint admission of mother and child: a context for inpatient therapy. Curr psychiat Ther 1965, 5:164-171

75831 (& Weiss, J. L.) Psychotic mothers and their children: joint admission to an adult psychiatric hospital. P 1963, 119:927-933

75832 (& Freedman, S. J.; Greenblatt, M.) Sensory deprivation and personality. P 1960, 116:878-882
Abs Leavitt, M. Q 1961, 30:145

75833 (& Strean, H. S.) Some considerations on the therapeutic neglect of fathers in child guidance. J child Psychol Psychiat 1964, 5:241-249

75834 (& Bryant, C. M.) The theory and practice of the family diagnostic. II. Theoretical aspects and resident education. Psychiat Res Rep 1966, No. 20:150-162

75835 (& Klerman, G. L.) Wrist slashing. P 1967, 124:527-534

See Bryant, Charles M.; Caplan, Gerald; Cohler, Bertram J.; DuPont, Robert L., Jr.; Freedman, Sanford J.; Roemele, V.; Van der Walde, Peter H.

GRUNEBAUM, MARGARET GALDSTON
See also FRANK, MARGARET G. (GRUNEBAUM)

75836 (& Hurwitz I.; Prentice, N. M.; Sperry, B. M.) Fathers of sons with primary neurotic learning inhibitions. Ops 1962, 32:462-472. In Kornrich, M. *Underachievement*, Glencoe, Ill: Free Pr 1965, 121-137
75837 A study of learning problems of children: casework implications. Soc Casewk 1961, 42:461-468

See Coolidge, John C.; Wallach, Michael A.; Zilbach, Joan J.

GRÜNEWALD, EDUARD (FRANZ-ALEXANDER)

75838 Heteronome Analyse und autonome Synthese personaler Existenz. [Heteronymous analysis and autonomous synthesis in personal existence.] In Edelweiss, M. L. et al: *Personalisation*, Vienna/Freiburg/Basel: Herder 1964, 28-39
75839 Lebensgeschichtliche Bilanz und Neurose. [Balance of life history and neurosis.] Z Psychosom Med 1965, 11:299-302

GRUNEWALD, LILIAN SIRACUSE

75840 Repudiating repression? Int J Psychiat 1968, 5:246-247

GRUSEC, JOAN

75841 Some antecedents of self-criticism. J Pers soc Psychol 1966, 4:244-252

See Bandura, Albert

GRUSHKA

See Moses, Rafael

GRÜTTER, EMIL

75842 Ein Rorschach-Blind-Gutachten. [A Rorschach false judgment.] Rorschachiana 1962, (3-4):3-12
75843 Triebstruktur von Pilotenanwärtern und bewährten Piloten. [Impulse structure in pilot candidates and established pilots.] In *Beiträge zur Diagnostik, Prognostik und Therapie des Schicksals*, Bern/Stuttgart: H. Huber 1962, 173-186
75844 Zur Theorie des Agierens. [On theories of acting out.] Psyche 1968, 22:582-603

GRYLER, R. B.

See Shapiro, A.

GRYNBAUM, BRUCE

See Diamond, M. David

GUARALDI, G. P.
See Zanocco, G.

GUARNER, ENRIQUE
75845 Psychodynamic aspects of drug experiences. M 1966, 39:157-162
REVIEWS OF:
75846 Bieber, I. Homosexuality. Cuad Psa 1965, 1:210
75847 Stone, L. The Psychoanalytic Situation. Cuad Psa 1965, 1:298

GUASCH, G.-P.
75848 (& Carenzo, M.-F.) La relation avec le médecin et sa representation dans le dessin de l'enfant. [The relations with the physician and its portrayal in the drawings of children.] Rev Np inf 1967, 15:669-688

GUBER, SELMA
75849 Sex role and the feminine personality. In author's dissertation: "A cross-cultural study of the perceived feminine role and self-concept of college women in the U.S. and Israel." In Goldman, G. D. & Milman, D. S. Modern Woman, Springfield, Ill: Thomas 1969, 75-91

GUERNEY, BERNARD
See Elbert, Shirley; Minuchin, Salvador

GUERNEY, BERNARD G., JR.
75850 Filial therapy: description and rationale. J consult Psychol 1964, 28:304-310
75851 (& Stover, L.; Demeritt, S.) A measurement of empathy in parent-child interaction. J genet Psych 1968, 112:49-55
75852 (Ed) Psychotherapeutic Agents: New Roles for Nonprofessionals, Parents, and Teachers. NY: Holt, Rinehart & Winston 1969, xii + 595 p
See Stollak, Garry E.

GUERRA, C. V.
75853 Regressão. [Regression.] Bol Inst Psicol Univ Brasil 1958, 8(7-8):35-43

GUIARD, FERNANDO E.
See Grinberg, León
ABSTRACTS OF:
75854 Apfelbaum, B. Some problems in contemporary ego psychology. Rev Psicoanál 1964, 21:76
75855 Bergman, M. The place of Paul Federn's ego psychology in psychoanalytic metapsychology. Rev Psicoanál 1966, 23:233
75856 Erikson, E. H. The problem of ego identity. Rev Psicoanál 1966, 23:244

75857 Greenson, R. R. Homosexualité et identité sexuelle. Rev Psicoanál 1966, 23:208
75858 Hartmann, H. Notes on the theory of sublimation. Rev Psicoanál 1966, 23:266
75859 Jacobson, E. Federn's contribution to ego psychology and the psychos. Rev Psicoanál 1966, 23:272
75860 Kanzer, M. Ego interest, egoism and narcissism. Rev Psicoanál 1966, 23:277
75861 Lichtenstein, H. The dilemma of human identity. Rev Psicoanál 1966, 23:278
75862 Miller, L. Confrontation, conflict and the body image. Rev Psicoanál 1966, 23:279
75863 Rosner, A. A. Mourning before the fact. Rev Psicoanál 1964, 21:78
75864 Silverman, S. Ego functions and bodily reactions. Rev Psicoanál 1964, 21:76
75865 Wiederman, G. Quelques remarques sur l'etiologie de homosexualité. Rev Psicoanál 1966, 23:207

GUIBEAUTT, J.

See Gratton, L.

GUIBOUT, D.

See Danon-Boileau, Henri

GUICHARNAUD, JEAN

TRANSLATION OF:
Delay, J. P. L. [70893]

GUIDO, S. M.

See Herron, William G.

GUILERA, NURIA

75866 Casework y psicoterápia. [Casework and psychotherapy.] Rev Psiquiat Psicol méd 1966, 7:399-406

GUILFORD, JOY PAUL

75867 Creativity and learning. In Brain Function, Vol 4, Berkeley: Univ Calif Pr 1963

GUILHOT, JEAN

75868 La science de la maturation et les voies nouvelles de la psychothérapie, de la psychanalyse et de la pédagogie contemporaines. [The science of maturation and new paths in contemporary psychotherapy, psychoanalysis and education.] Hum Context 1969, 1:231-242; 243-252

See Guilhot, M. A.

GUILHOT, M. A.

75869 (& Jost, J.; Garnier, P.; Guilhot, J.) Créativité symbolique et musi-cothérapie. [Symbolic creativity and music therapy.] Hyg Ment 1965, 54:229-234

GUILLAIN, GEORGES

75870 J.-M. Charcot, 1825-1893. His Life—His Work. (Ed & Tr: Bailey, P.) NY: Paul B. Hoeber 1959, 218 p
    Rv Lewin, B. D. Q 1961, 30:111-113

GUILLAUMIN, JEAN

75871 La Dynamique de l'Examen Psychologique: L'Analyse de l'Interaction dans une Situation de Face à Face. [Dynamics of the Psychological Examination: The Analysis of Interaction in a Face to Face Situation.] Paris: PUF 1965, 438 p

GUILLEMIN, J.

75871A [The fetishism of gloves in the last Bourbons.] (Fr) Sem Hop Paris 1969, 45:3411-3414

GUIORA, ALEXANDER Z.

75872 (& Schmale, H. T.) The continuous case seminar. Ps 1967, 30:44-59
75873 Daughter of a Don Juan—a syndrome. Psychiat Q 1966, 40:71-79
75874 Dysorexia: a psychopathological study of anorexia nervosa and bulimia. P 1967, 124:391-393

GUITON, MICHELINE

75875 (& Aubry, J.) L'enfant instable psycho-motor et la mère. [The child with psychomotor instability and the mother.] Rv Np inf 1967, 15:187-198

GULEVICH, GEORGE D.

75876 (& Dement, W. C.; Zarcone, V. P.) All-night sleep recordings of chronic schizophrenics in remission. Comprehen Psychiat 1967, 8:141-149
75877 (& Dement, W. C.; Johnson, L.) Psychiatric and EEG observations on a case of prolonged (264 hours) wakefulness. Arch gen Psychiat 1966, 15:29-35

GULL, WILLIAM W.

75878 The address on medicine. Lancet 1868, 2:171. In Kaufman, M. R. & Heiman, M. *Evolution of Psychosomatic Concepts*, NY: IUP 1964, 104-127
75879 Anorexia nervosa. Lancet 1888, 1:516. In Kaufman, M. R. & Heiman, M. *Evolution of Psychosomatic Concepts*, NY: IUP 1964, 139-140
75880 Anorexia nervosa (apepsia hysterica, anorexia hysterica). Trans Clin Soc London 1874, 7:22. In Kaufman, M. R. & Heiman, M. *Evolution of Psychosomatic Concepts*, NY: IUP 1964, 132-138

GULOTTA, G.

REVIEWS OF:
75881 Deutsch, H. Neuroses and Character Types. Riv Psa 1966, 12:220-221
75882 English, H. B. & English, A. C. A Comprehensive Dictionary of Psychology and Psychoanalytic Terms. Riv Psa 1965, 11:180
75883 Glover, E. The Roots of Crime. Riv Psa 1965, 11:178
75884 Michel, A. L'École Freudienne devant la Musique. Riv Psa 1966, 12: 221
75885 Zilboorg, G. The Psychology of the Criminal Act and Punishment. Riv Psa 1966, 12:222-224

GUMBEL, ERICH

75886 Discussion of Lehmann, H. "The lion in Freud's dreams." Psa Forum 1967, 2:237-239
75887 Obituary: Anna Smeliansky 1879-1961. J 1962, 43:360
75888 Psychiatric disturbances of holocaust survivors: symposium. (Abstract of discussion) Israel Ann Psychiat 1967, 5:98-99
75889 Psychoanalysis in Israel. Israel Ann Psychiat 1965, 3:89-98
       Die Psychoanalyse in Israel. Psyche 1966, 20:67-73
75890 Psychoanalytic training and its contribution to psychiatry education: symposium. Israel Ann Psychiat 1968, 6:93-95

GUMPERT, GARY

See Perlmutter, Morton S.

GUNDERSON, ELLSWORTH K.

75891 Emotional symptoms in extremely isolated groups. Arch gen Psychiat 1963, 9:362-368
75892 (& Johnson, L. C.) Past experience, self-evaluation, and present adjustment. Soc Psych 1965, 66:311-321

GUNDLACH, RALPH HARRELSON

75893 Childhood parental relationships and the establishment of gender roles of homosexuals. J consult clin Psychol 1969, 33:136-139
75894 Dreams: their meaning for therapy and mental organization. Prog clin Psych 1963, 5:112-136
75895 Group psychotherapy: new clinical and experimental approaches. Prog clin Psych 1960, 4:149-168

See Bieber, Irving; Riess, Bernard F.; Sager, Clifford J.

GUNN-SÉCHEHAYE, A.

75896 Suicide et tentative. [Suicide and attempted suicide.] Rev Med Suisse Rom 1968, 88:247-259

GÜNTHER, BITTNER

75897 Sublimierungstheorie und pädagogische Psychoanalyse. [Theory of sublimation and pedagogic psychoanalysis.] Psyche 1964, 18:292-304

GUNTHER, MEYER S.

75898   (& Blakeslee, C.; Susman, R. W.) Constructive use of psychiatric consultation in a rehabilitation program. MH 1965, 49:3-9
75899   Emotional aspects of spinal cord injuries. In Ruge, D. *Spinal Cord Injuries*, Springfield, Ill: Thomas 1969

See Barglow, Peter

GUNTRIP, HENRY JAMES SAMUEL (HARRY)

75900   The concept of psychodynamic science. J 1967, 48:32-43
75901   Discussion of Segal, H. "Melanie Klein's technique." Psa Forum 1967, 2:219-223
75902   Ego weakness and the hard core of the problem of psychotherapy. M 1960, 33:163-184
            Abs IH Q 1961, 30:608-609
75903   Healing the Sick Mind. (Foreword: Dicks, H. V.) London: Allen & Unwin 1964; NY: Appleton-Century 1965, 223 p
            Rv Leddy, K. J 1967, 48:471-472
75904   Klein, technique. Psa Forum 1967, 2:378
75905   The manic-depressive problem in the light of the schizoid process. J 1962, 43:98-112
            Abs FTL Q 1963, 32:286
75906   Object-relations theory and ego-theory. Mod Con Psa 173-188
75907   Personality Structure and Human Interaction; The Developing Synthesis of Psychodynamic Theory. London: HPI; NY: IUP 1961, 456 p
            Abs J Am Psa Ass 1962, 10:638-639. Rv MK J 1962, 43:355-357. CR J 1962, 43:352-355. DRu Q 1964, 33:279-281
75908   Psychodynamic theory and the problem of psychotherapy. M 1963, 36:161-172
            Abs JCS RFPsa 1967, 31:314
S-48142 Recent developments in psycho-analytical theory.
            Abs AJE An Surv Psa 1956, 7:73-75
75909   Religion in relation to personal integration. M 1969, 42:323-333
75910   The schizoid compromise and psychotherapeutic stalemate. M 1962, 35:273-286
            Abs Greenberg, R. M. Q 1963, 32:457-458. JCS RFPsa 1963, 27:332
75911   Schizoid Phenomena, Object-Relations, and the Self. NY: IUP 1968, 437 p
75912   The schizoid problem, regression, and the struggle to preserve an ego. M 1961, 34:223-244
            Abs ICFH Q 1962, 31:431

REVIEWS OF:
75913   Bion, W. R. Learning from Experience. J 1965, 46:381-385
75914   Segal, H. Introduction to the Work of Melanie Klein. J 1965, 46:258-261

GUPTA, S. C.

See Varma, R. M.

GURFIN, L.

See Kammerer, T.

GURLAND, BARRY J.

75915 (& Sharpe, L.) A cross-national view of DSM-II. Int J Psychiat 1969, 7:416-420

GURVITZ, MILTON S.

REVIEWS OF:
75916 Andrews, G. & Vinkenoog, S. (Eds): The Book of Grass: An Anthology of Indian Hemp. R 1969, 56:488
75917 Freud, S. & Bullitt, W. C. Thomas Woodrow Wilson: Twenty-Eighth President of the United States. A Psychological Study. R 1969, 56: 346-349
75918 Masters, R. E. L. Sexual Self-Stimulation. R 1969, 56:488

GUSDORF, CHARLES

75919 (& Markovitch, P.; Pinel, J. P.) La psychothérapie à la M.U.M.P. de Sceaux [Psychotherapy of the M.U.M.P. of Sceaux.] Perspectives psychiat 1965, 10

GUSTAFSON, DONALD F.

75920 (Ed) Essays in Philosophical Psychology. Garden City, NY: Doubleday 1964, 412 p

GUSTIN, JOHN C.

75921 The revolt of youth. PPR 1961, 48(2):78-90

GUTHEIL, EMIL A.

75922 The dream in the therapeutic process. Dreams Contempo Psa 212-221
75923 The exhibitionism of Jean Jacques Rousseau. An abstract of Stekel's analysis. PT 1962, 16:266-277
S-13205 The Handbook of Dream Analysis.
       Rv Edelheit, H. Q 1961, 30:118-119

See Lowy, Samuel

GUTHRIE, GEORGE M.

See Culbertson, Ellen

GUTIÉRREZ, JOSÉ

75924 El Método Psicoanalítico de Erich Fromm. [The Psychoanalytic Method of Erich Fromm.] Bogotá: Ediciones Tercer Mundo 1961, 196 p
75925 A note on juvenile delinquency: the gamin problem in Colombia. Contempo Psa 1967, 3(2):173-176
75926 El Sentido de Vivir. [The Experience of Being Alive.] (Foreword: Bernal, J. N.) Bogotá: Tercer Mundo 1966, 122 p

GUTSTADT, JOSEPH P.

ABSTRACTS OF:

75927 Abramson, J. H. Observations on the health of adolescent girls in relation to cultural change. Q 1961, 30:603

75928 Alexander, F. et al: Experimental studies of emotional stress: 1. Hyperthyroidism. Q 1961, 30:602

75929 Barber, T. X. Death by suggestion: a critical note. Q 1961, 30:603

75930 Brown, F. et al: The patient under study for cancer: a personality evaluation. Q 1961, 30:603-604

75931 Calden, G. et al: Psychosomatic factors in the rate of recovery from tuberculosis. Q 1961, 30:453

75932 Deutsch, F. Entering the mind through the sensory gateways in associative anamnesis. Q 1961, 30:454

75933 Engel, G. L. Is grief a disease? A challenge for medical research. Q 1961, 30:601-602

75934 Fleck, S. Family dynamics and origin of schizophrenia. Q 1961, 30: 452-453

75935 Geocaris, K. Circumoral herpes simplex and separation experiences in psychotherapy. Q 1961, 30:602

75936 Knight, J. A. False pregnancy in a male. Q 1961, 30:452

75937 Mendelson, M. & Meyer, E. Countertransference problems of the liaison psychiatrist. Q 1961, 30:602-603

75938 Natterson, J. M. & Knudsen, A. G., Jr. Observations concerning fear of death in fatally ill children and their mothers. Q 1961, 30:454

75939 Plesch, E. Rosacea and morbid reddening: some psychoanalytic aspects. Q 1961, 30:453-454

75940 Rainer, J. D. et al: Homosexuality and heterosexuality in identical twins. Q 1961, 30:452

75941 Wild, R. J. & Tupper, C. Personality, life situation, and communication: a study of habitual abortion. Q 1961, 30:454

GUTTMACHER, MANFRED S.

75942 Critique of views of Thomas Szasz on legal psychiatry. Arch gen Psychiat 1964, 10:238-245

75943 Discussion of Gaylin, W. M. "Psychiatry and the law." Columbia Univ Forum 1965, 8(2):44-45

75944 A historical outline of the criminal law's attitude toward mental disorder. Arch crim Psychodyn 1961, 4:647-670

75945 The "insanity" of George III. BMC 1964, 28:101-119

GUTTMAN, DANIEL A.

75946 Some aspects of scientific theory construction and psychoanalysis. J 1965, 46:129-136
Abs EVN Q 1967, 36:316

GUTTMAN, SAMUEL A.

S-48183 Bisexuality in symbolism.
Abs An Surv Psa 1955, 6:168-169

75947 The concept of structure. (Read at Phila Ass Psa, 30 Sept 1966)
       Abs Eisner, H. Bull Phila Ass Psa 1967, 17:125-127
S-48187 Dreams and affects.
       Abs An Surv Psa 1955, 6:234-236
75948 Indications and contraindications for psychoanalytic treatment. Intro-
       duction to the symposium. (Read at Int Psa Cong, July 1967) J 1968,
       49:254-255
       Abs LHR Q 1969, 38:669
75949 Obituary: Robert Waelder: 1900-1967. J 1969, 50:269-273
75950 (& Sloane, P.) Perception and its relation to thought. (Read at Phila
       Ass Psa, 17 Nov 1961)
       Abs Sloane, P. Bull Phila Ass Psa 1962, 12:91-93
75951 Some aspects of Robert Waelder. (Read at Phila Ass Psa 1968, 22
       Mar 1968) Bull Phila Ass Psa 1968, 18:27-39
75952 Some aspects of scientific theory construction and psychoanalysis.
       (Read at Phila Ass for Psa, 11 Mar 1964; at NY Psa Soc, NY, 9 Feb
       1965) J 1965, 46:129-136
       Abs Fine, B. D. Q 1965, 34:631-633

GUTTMANN, OSCAR

75953 The psychodynamics of a drug addict. A three-year study. PT 1965,
       19:653-665

See Krasner, Jack

GUYOTAT, J.

75954 [Attitude of the medical practitioner toward anxiety of the patient.]
       (It) Minerva Med 1965, 56:1689-1692
75955 [Attitude of the medical practitioner toward the anguish of his patient.
       (Fr) Europ Med, Paris 1965, 4:26-30

GUZE, HENRY

75956 Female body-image in personality and culture. In Goldman, G. D. &
       Milman, D. S. Modern Woman, Springfield, Ill: Thomas 1969, 103-117

See Bowers, Margaretta K.

GUZE, SAMUEL BARRY

See Winokur, George

GYARFAS, KALMAN

See Muslin, Hyman L.

GYARFAS, MARY GORMAN

75957 Ego Development, Ego Functioning and Family Stress in Boys with
       and without Learning Disability; a Dissertation. Chicago: Univ Chi-
       cago 1967, 206 p

GYNTHER, M. D.

See McDonald, Robert L.

GYOMROI, EDITH LUDOWYK

75958   The analysis of a young concentration camp victim. (Read at Brit Psa
Soc, 5 June 1963) Psa St C 1963, 18:484-510

GYÖRGY, PAUL

See Newton, Niles

GYÖRI, IWAN

75959   Symposium: psychiatric disturbances of holocaust ("shoa") survivors.
Israel Ann Psychiat 1967, 5(1)
Psychische Störungen bei Überlebenden der Verfolgung. Beobach-
tungen in einer Poliklinik in Israel. Psyche 1969, 23:517-531

H

HAAK, NILS

75959 Comment on Dr. Simenauer's paper "Notes on the psychoanalysis of aesthetic experience. With special reference to ethological considerations." J 1964, 45:436-437
   Abs EVN Q 1966, 35:466
S-48206 Comments on the analytical situation.
   Abs SLP An Surv Psa 1957, 8:258-259
75960 Norsk djuppsykologi i blickpunkten. [Norwegian depth psychology in focus.] Psykisk Hälsa 1965, 6:99-129
75961 Psykiska och nervösa sjukdomar. [Psychic and nervous diseases.] In Sjukvård i Hemmet, Stockholm: Tidens Förlag 1962, 160-174
75962 Psykoanalys. [Psychoanalysis.] In Människan i Focus, Almqvist och Wicksell 1961, 224-226
75963 Stödjande respektive insiktsbetonad psykoterapi. Terapeutisk flexibilitet. Psykofarmaka. [Concerning supportive insight psychotherapy. Therapeutic flexibility. Psychopharmacology.] Soc med Tidskr 1969, 46
75964 Utbilding i psykoterapi. [Training in psychotherapy.] Soc med Tidskr 1968, 45:167-171

HAAN, NORMA

75965 Coping and defense mechanisms related to personality inventories. J consult Psychol 1965, 29:373-378
75966 An investigation of the relationships of Rorschach scores, patterns, and behavior to coping and defense mechanisms. J proj Tech 1964, 28:429-441
75967 (& Smith, M. B.; Block, J.) Moral reasoning of young adults: political-social behavior, family background, and personality correlates. J Pers soc Psychol 1968, 10:183-201
75968 Proposed Model of Ego Functioning; Coping and Defense Mechanisms in Relationship to IQ Change. Psychol Monogr, 77(8) Wash DC: APA 1963, 23 p
75969 The relationship of ego functioning and intelligence to social status and social mobility. ASP 1964, 69:594-605
75970 A tripartite model of ego functioning values and clinical and research applications. JNMD 1969, 148:14-30
   Abs Galef, H. R. Q 1969, 38:671

HAAS, LADISLAV

75971 The effective factors in psychotherapy. Czech J Psychiat 1960, 56
75972 (& Dytrych, Z.) The problems of suicide. Czech Practit 1962, 43
75973 (& Wünchova, B.; Chodurova, A.) Psychosocial conception of suicide and delinquency. Czech J Psychiat 1964, 60
75974 The secondary defensive struggle against the symptom in sexual disturbances. (Read at Int Psa Cong, July 1967) J 1968, 49:402-407
75975 Symptom formation and character formation. J 1964, 45:161-163
Contribution à la discussion sur la formation des symptômes et la formation du caractère. RFPsa 1966, 30:254-258
Abs EVN Q 1966, 35:454-455
75976 Übertragung ausserhalb der analytischen Situation. Psyche 1965, 19:379-385
Transference outside the psycho-analytic situation. (Read at Int Psa Cong, July 1965) J 1966, 47:422-426
Abs Cuad Psa 1967, 3:164-165. EVN Q 1968, 37:316

HAASE, H.-J.

75977 Zum Verständnis paranoider und paranoid-halluzinatorischer Psychosen am Beispiel alleinstehender Frauen. [Understanding paranoid and paranoid-hallucinatory psychoses through the example of single women.] Nervenarzt 1963, 34:315-320

HABER, RALPH NORMAN

See Barclay, Andrew M.

HABERER, M. H.

See Nelson, Marven D.

HABERMAN, P. W.

75978 Factors related to increased sobriety in group psychotherapy with alcoholics. Clin Psych 1966, 22:229-235

HACKER, FREDERICK J.

75979 Creative possibilities for a consideration of creativity. In Anderson, H. H. Creativity in Childhood and Adolescence: A Diversity of Approaches, Palo Alto, Calif: Sci & Behav Books 1965, 35-45
75980 The discriminatory function of the ego. J 1962, 43:395-405
Abs EVN Q 1965, 34:306
75981 Discussion of Boorstein, S. "A psychoanalytic overview of the offender: implication for therapy." Psa Forum 1967, 2:257-260
S-48218 Freud, Marx, and Kierkegaard.
Abs AEC An Surv Psa 1956, 7:19-20
75982 (& Illing, H.; Bergreen, S. W.) Impact of different social settings on type and effectiveness of psychotherapy. R 1965, 52:38-44
Abs SRG Q 1966, 35:626
75983 (Participant) Individuelle und soziale Psychopathologie und ihre Wechselwirkungen. [Individual and social psychopathology and their effects.] Jb Psa 1968, 5:49-87

75984   The reality of myth. (Read at Int Psa Cong, July-Aug 1963) J 1964,
45:438-445
    Abs EVN Q 1966, 35:466-467
S-48222 Symbole und Psychoanalyse.
    Abs Nathan, W. An Surv Psa 1958, 9:101-104

See Bergreen, Stanley W.; Braverman, Malvin

HACKER, FRIEDRICH

75985   Die Zukunft einer Desillusion. [The future of a disillusion.] Wien Z
Nervenheilk 1964, 21:247-259

HACKETT, THOMAS P.

75986   (& Cassem, N. H.; Wishnie, H. A.) The coronary-care unit. An appraisal of its psychologic hazards. New Eng J Med 1968, 279:1365-
1370
75986A (& Weisman, A. D.) Denial as a factor in patients with heart disease
and cancer. Ann NY Acad Sci 1969, 164:802-817
75987   (& Weisman, A. D.) Psychiatric management of operative syndromes.
I. The therapeutic consultation and the effect of noninterpretive intervention. II. Psychodynamic factors in formulation and management.
PSM 1960, 22:267-282; 356-372
75988   (& Weisman, A. D.) The treatment of the dying. Curr psychiat Ther
1962, 2:121-126

See Sullivan, P. R.; Weisman, Avery D.

HACUK, P. A.

See Armstrong, Renate G.

HADDEN, SAMUEL B.

75989   The psychotherapy of homosexuality, 2: group psychotherapy in homosexuality. Psychiat Opin 1967, 4(2):9-12
75990   Treatment of male homosexuals in groups. Int J grp PT 1966, 16:13-21
    Abs GPK Q 1968, 37:477

HADDENBROCK, S.

75991   Die psychopathologische Diagnose und ihre normative Bewertung.
[Psychopathological diagnosis and its standard evaluation.] In Kranz,
H. Psychopathologie Heute, Stuttgart: Georg Thieme 1962, 278-287

HADDOX, V. G.

75992   (& Jacobson, M. D.) Comparison of conscious and unconscious affect.
Behav Sci 1968, 13:324-325

HADER, MARVIN

75993   Basic psychiatric gerontologic research. Psychoanalytic interpretation
in elderly brain-damaged patients. J Amer Geriat Soc 1965, 13:832-842

75994 The need for involvement of psychoanalysis with aged people. Gerontologist 1965, 5:259-260

75995 A study of aged "schizophrenogenic" parents. Dis nerv Sys 1965, 26: 443-445

75996 (& Schulman, P. M.) Value of fostering a parental image in aged psychotics. Geriatrics 1966, 21:226-230

HADFIELD, JAMES ARTHUR

75997 Introduction to Psychotherapy: Its History and Modern Schools. London: Allen & Unwin 1967, vi + 363 p

75998 The reliability of infantile memories. M 1962, 35:31-46
　　Abs ICFH Q 1963, 32:141-142

HADNI, J. C.

See Arnoux, H.

HAEBERLIN, U.

75999 Die Phantasie in Erziehung und Heilerziehung. [The Role of Fantasy in Education and Rehabilitation.] Bern: Huber 1969, 144 p

HAEFNER, DON P.

See Wolkon, George H.

HAENDEL, FRANK

76000 Discussant: "Medical Education." Teach Dyn Psychiat 78

HAER, JOHN L.

76001 Anger in relation to aggression in psychotherapy groups. Soc Psych 1968, 76:123-127

HAFFTER, CARL

76002 Deutung und Einsicht in der Kinderpsychotherapie. [Interpretation and insight in psychotherapy of children.] Schweiz ANP 1965, 96:97-108. Hbh Kinderpsychother 333-342

HÄFNER, HEINZ

76003 Daseinsanalytischen Gewissenspsychopathologie. [Psychopathology of conscience according to existential analysis.] Psyche 1960, 13:667-685

76004 Psychopathen; daseinsanalytische Untersuchungen zur Struktur und Verlaufsgestalt von Psychopathien. [Psychopaths: Existential Analytic Investigations on the Structure and Pattern of Development of Psychopathies.] (Foreword: Binswanger, L.) Berlin: Spinger 1961, iv + 230 p

HAGEN, J.

See Levine, Murray

HAGGARD, ERNEST A.

76005 (& Isaacs, K. S.) Micromomentary facial expressions as indicators of ego mechanisms in psychotherapy. Meth Res PT 154-165

76006 (& Hiken, J. R.; Isaacs, K. S.) Some effects of recording and filming on the psychotherapeutic process. Ps 1965, 28:169-191

See Hamburg, David A.; Isaacs, Kenneth S.; Miller, Arthur A.; Sklansky, Morris A.

HAGGERTY, ROBERT J.

See Green, Morris

HAGNER, SAMUEL B.

76007 Patient outcome in a comprehensive medicine clinic: its retrospective assessment and related variables. Med Care 1968, 6(2):144-156

See Fischer, H. Keith

HAGOPIAN, JOHN V.

S-48245 A psychological approach to Shelley's poetry.
Abs An Surv Psa 1955, 6:454

76008 Symbol and metaphor in the transformation of reality into art. Comp Lit 1968, 20(Winter):45-54

HAHN, H.

See Rayner, Eric H.

HAHN, KENNETH

See Galbraith, Gary G.

HAIGH, BASIL

TRANSLATION OF:
Uznadze, D. N. [93536]

HAIGH, GERARD V.

76009 Alternative strategies in psychotherapy supervision. Psychotherapy 1965, 2:42-43

HAIM, A.

76010 (& Caquant-Didier, E.; Cohen, S.; Kipman, D.; Salinger, R.) Psychanalyse et assistance. Psychothérapie en hôpital de jour. [Psychoanalysis and assistance. Psychotherapy in the day hospital.] Rv Np inf 1967, 15:883-891

HAIMOWITZ, MORRIS

76011 (& Haimowitz, N. R.) (Eds) Human Development: Selected Readings. NY: Thomas Y. Crowell 1960, xiv + 799 p

HAIMOWITZ, NATALIE R.

See Haimowitz, Morris

HAIN, J. D.

See Stevenson, Ian

HAINES, JAMES R.

See Santos, John F.

HALDEMAN, R. B.

See Wolkon, G. H.

HALDER, ARUNA

76012 The Buddhist conception of personality as based on Abhidharmakosa of Vasubandhu. Samiksa 1967, 21(2):55-66

HALE, FRANK A.

76013 Discussion of Kuhns, R. F. "Modernity and death: *The Leopard* by Giuseppe di Lampedusa." Contempo Psa 1969, 5(2):126-128

HALE, M. L.

76014 (& Abram, H. S.) Patients' attitudes toward psychiatric consultations in the general hospital. Virginia Med Monthly 1967, 94:342-347

HALEY, JAY

76015 The art of being a failure as a therapist. Ops 1969, 39:691-695
76016 Control in brief psychotherapy. Arch gen Psychiat 1961, 4:139-153
       Abs KR Q 1962, 31:297
76017 The doctor as part of the schizophrenic interchange. Int J Psychiat 1967, 4:534-542
76018 Editor of *Selected Papers of Milton H. Erickson, M.D. Volume I. Advanced Techniques of Hypnosis and Therapy.*
76019 Strategies of Psychotherapy. NY/London: Grune & Stratton 1963, x + 204 p
76020 (& Hoffman, L.) Techniques of Family Therapy. NY: Basic Books 1968, x + 480 p

See Glick, Ira D.; Jackson, Don D.

REVIEWS OF:
76021 Berne, E. Games People Play: The Psychology of Human Relationships. R 1965, 52:489-492
76022 London, P. The Modes and Morals of Psychotherapy. R 1965, 52:489-492
76023 Weiss, E. Agoraphobia in the Light of Ego Psychology. R 1965, 52:489-492

HALL, BERNARD H.

76024   (& Rhodes, R.) Editors of Menninger, W. C. *Living in a Troubled World.*

76025   (& Wallerstein, R. S.) Operational problems of psychotherapy research: II. Termination studies. BMC 1960, 24:190-216
        Abs HD Q 1961, 30:147-148

S-48262 (Ed) A Psychiatrist's World: The Selected Papers of Karl Menninger, M.D.
        Japanese: Vols 1 & 2, Tokyo: Nippon Kyobun Sha 1962

        See Gassert, Robert G.; Wallerstein, Robert S.

HALL, C. L.

        See Heilbrun, Alfred B., Jr.

HALL, CALVIN SPRINGER

76026   (& Domhoff, B.) Aggression in dreams. Int J soc Psychiat 1963, 9:259-267

76027   Are prenatal and birth experiences represented in dreams? R 1967, 54:157-174

76028   Attitudes toward life and death in poetry. R 1965, 52:67-83
        Abs SRS Q 1966, 35:470

76029   Caveat Lector! [Special book review: Hartmann, E. *The Biology of Dreaming.*] R 1967, 54:655-661

76030   A comparison of the dreams of four groups of hospitalized mental patients with each other and with a normal population. JNMD 1966, 143:135-139

76031   (& van de Castle, R. L.) The Content Analysis of Dreams. NY: Appleton-Century-Crofts 1966, xiv + 320 p
        Abs J Am Psa Ass 1967, 15:224-225

76032   Dreams of American College Students. Lawrence: Univ of Kansas 1963, 217 p

76033   (& Domhoff, B.) The dreams of Freud and Jung. Psychol Today 1968, 2:42-45

76034   (& van de Castle, R. L.) An empirical investigation of the castration complex in dreams. J Pers 1965, 33:20-29. In Lindzey, G. & Hall, C. S. *Theories of Personality*, NY/London/Sydney: Wiley 1965, 1966, 1968, 28-33

76035   Freud subverted. Gawein 1961, 9:137-144

76036   (& Domhoff, B.) Friendliness in dreams. Soc Psych 1964, 62:309-314

76037   A Manual for Classifying Activities in Dreams. Miami, Fla: Institute Dream Research 1962, 7 p

76038   A Manual for Classifyying Aggressions, Misfortunes, Friendly Acts, and Good Fortune in Dreams. Miami, Fla: Institute Dream Research 1962, 17 p

76039   A Manual for Classifying Characters in Dreams. Miami, Fla: Institute Dream Research 1962, 10 p

76040   A Manual for Classifying Emotions in Dreams. Miami, Fla: Institute Dream Research 1962, 3 p

76041 A Manual for Classifying Fears and Anxieties in Dreams. Miami, Fla:
       Institute Dream Research 1962, 7 p
76042 A Manual for Classifying Settings and Objects in Dreams. Miami, Fla:
       Institute Dreams Research 1962, 16 p
76043 The Meaning of Dreams. NY: McGraw-Hill 1966, xxv + 244 p
76044 A modest confirmation of Freud's theory of a distinction between the
       superego of men and women. ASP 1964, 69:440-442
76045 Out of a dream came the faucet. PPR 1962, 49(4):113-116
           Abs HL Q 1963, 32:612. Ekboir, J. G. de Rev Psicoanál 1964, 21:86
76046 (& Lindzey, G.) The relevance of Freudian psychology and related
       viewpoints for the social sciences. In Lindzey, G. & Aronson, E. *The
       Handbook of Social Psychology*, Reading, Mass: Addison-Wesley Publ
       Co 1968
76047 Representation of the laboratory setting in dreams, JNMD 1967, 198-
       206
76048 Slang and dream symbols. R 1964, 51:38-48
           Abs SRS Q 1965, 34:309
76049 Strangers in dreams: an empirical confirmation of the Oedipus complex.
       J Pers 1963, 31:336-345
76050 (& Domhoff, B.) A ubiquitous sex difference in dreams. ASP 1963, 66:
       278-280
           Abs Rosen, I. C. Q 1964, 33:308-309

       See Domhoff, Bill; Lindzey, Gardner; Smith, Madorah E.

HALL, D. D.
       See Rinsley, Donald B.

HALL, DEE M.
76051 Capacity for understanding children through adaptive ego regression
       and authoritarian attitudes of foster mothers who differ in mothering
       skill. Diss Abstr 1969, 29(8-B):3086

HALL, EDWARD T.
76052 Proxemics: the study of man's spatial relations. In Galdston, I. *Man's
       Image in Medicine and Anthropology*, NY: IUP 1963, 422-445

HALL, LAURENCE B.
       REVIEW OF:
76053 Sarnoff, I. Society with Tears. Q 1968, 37:153-154

HALL, M.
       See Laughlin, Henry P.

HALL, MARY H.
76054 An interview with "Mr. Humanist": Rollo May. Psychol Today 1967,
       24-29, 72-73
76055 An interview with "Mr. Psychology": Edwin G. Boring. Psychol Today
       1967, 16-19, 65-67

HALL, ROBERT ARNOLD

76056 (& Closson, W. G., Jr.) An experimental study of the couch. JNMD 1964, 138:474-480

HALL, VERNON, JR.

76057 Freudianism and literature. In author's A Short History of Literary Criticism, NY: NY Univ Pr 1963, xii + 184 p

HALLE, LOUIS J.

76058 Collective guilt. Encounter 1965, 24(4):61-62

HALLECK, SEYMOUR L.

76059 American psychiatry and the criminal: a historical review. Curr psychiat Ther 1965, 5:26-32
76060 The criminal's problem with psychiatry. Ps 1960, 23:409-412
76061 Hysterical personality traits. Psychological, social, and iatrogenic determinants. Arch gen Psychiat 1967, 16:750-757
76062 (& Bromberg, W.) Psychiatric Aspects of Criminology. Springfield, Ill: Thomas 1968, 82 p
76063 Psychiatric treatment of the alienated college student. P 1967, 124:642-650
76064 Psychiatry and the Dilemmas of Crime: A Study of Causes, Punishment and Treatment. (Foreword: Menninger, K.) NY: Harper & Row 1967, xiv + 382 p
76065 Psychopathy, freedom and criminal behavior. BMC 1966, 30:127-140

See Pacht, Asher R.

HALLENBECK, PHYLLIS NEWTON

76066 (& Lundstedt, S.) Some relations between dogmatism, denial, and depression. Soc Psych 1966, 70:53-58

HALLMAN, G. L.

See Abram, Harry S.

HALLMAN, RALPH

76067 The archetypes in Peter Pan. J anal Psych 1969, 14:65-73
76068 Psychology of Literature. A Study of Alienation and Tragedy. NY: Philos Libr 1961, 262 p
         Rv Wangh, M. Q 1963, 32:441-442

HALLOWELL, A. IRVING

76069 The role of dreams in Ojibwa culture. In Grunebaum, G. E. von & Caillois, R. The Dream and Human Societies, Berkeley/Los Angeles: Univ Calif Pr 1966, 267-292

HALMOS, PAUL

76070   The Faith of the Counsellors. A Study in Theory and Practice of Social Case Work and Psychotherapy. London: Constable 1965; NY: Schocken 1966, 220 p

HALPER, IRA STEPHEN

76071   An occult conversion reaction superimposed on a facial nerve lesion. Psychosomatics 1966, 7:311-314

HALPERIN, ALEXANDER

See Schaffer, Leslie

HALPERN, B.

See Assael, M.

HALPERN, FLORENCE

76072   Diagnostic methods in childhood disorders. In Wolman, B. B. *Handbook of Clinical Psychology*, NY: McGraw-Hill 1965, 621-638
76073   The Rorschach Test with children. In Rabin, A. I. & Haworth, M. R. *Projective Techniques with Children*, NY/London: Grune & Stratton 1960, 14-28

See Fish, Barbara

HALPERN, HOWARD M.

76074   Alienation from parenthood in the Kibbutz and in America. Marriage fam Liv 1962, 24
76075   An essential ingredient in successful psychotherapy. Psychotherapy 1965, 2(4)
76076   (& Halpern, T.) Four perspectives on anti-achievement. R 1966, 53: 83-93
        Abs SRS Q 1967, 36:631
76077   A Parent's Guide to Child Psychotherapy. NY: A.S. Barnes & Co 1963, 178 p
        Rv Woltmann, A. G. R 1964, 51:334
76078   Psychodynamic and cultural determinants of work inhibition in children and adolescents. R 1964, 51:173-189
        Abs SRS Q 1965, 34:468-469
76079   Psychodynamic correlates of underachievement. In Gottsegen, M. G. & Gottsegen, G. B. *Professional School Psychology: III*, NY: Grune & Stratton 1969, 318-337
76080   Therapy with the anti-achiever. Voices 1966, 2(4)
76081   Transitional phenomena: constructive or pathological? Voices 1968, 4

HALPERN, L.

S-48303 (et al) [Freud's Festival.] (Heb)
        Abs An Surv Psa 1956, 7:17

HALPERN, SIDNEY

76082 Body-image symbols of repression. Int J clin exp Hypn 1965, 13:83-91
76083 A classical error in Freud's *The Interpretation of Dreams.* Q 1964, 33: 350-356
      Abs Rosarios, H. Rev Psicoanál 1964, 21:263
76084 Free association in 423 B.C.: Socrates in "The Clouds" of Aristophanes. R 1963, 50:419-436
      Abs SRS Q 1964, 33:606
76085 Hypnointrospection—a contribution to the practice and theory of hypnotherapy: II. Studies in the therapeutic effects of immobilization. J Psychol 1964, 57:329-376
76086 The man who forgot he crucified Jesus: an exegesis of Anatole France's "Procurator of Judea." R 1964-65, 51:597-611
76087 The mother-killer. R 1965, 52:215-218
76088 Nelson's farewell kiss. PPR 1961, 48(4):119-125
76089 Thanatopsis: life's last stand. Am Im 1964, 21(3-4):23-36
      Abs JWS Q 1965, 34:621

HALPERN, THELMA

See Halpern, Howard M.

HALPERT, EUGENE

See Gross, Milton M.

ABSTRACTS OF:
76090 Jackel, M. M. The common cold and depression. Q 1969, 38:347-348
76091 Schur, M. (Moderator) Workshop on Dr. Edith Jacobson's book *The Self and the Object World.* Q 1968, 37:324-325
76092 Shengold, L. Once doesn't count. Q 1969, 38:347

HALS, HÅKON

See Askevold, Finn

HALSTEAD, HERBERT

76093 Group psychotherapy for the middle-aged. M 1968, 41:139-148

HALVERSON, JOHN

76094 Prufrock, Freud, and others. Sewanee Rev 1968, 76(Autumn):571-588

HAM, GEORGE C.

76095 Discussion of Levy, N. A. "An investigation into the nature of psychoanalytical process: a preliminary report." Sci Psa 1961, 4:140-144
76096 Genes and the psyche. In Millon, T. *Approaches to Personality,* NY/Toronto/London: Pitman Publ 1968, 133-142
76097 Psychoanalysis and medical education. Curr psychiat Ther 1961, 1:125-130
76098 Reintegration of psychoanalysis into teaching. P 1961, 117:877-882

HAMBIDGE, GOVE, JR.

S-48313   On the ontogenesis of repression.
          Abs CFH An Surv Psa 1956, 7:134

HAMBURG, DAVID A.

76099   Evolution of emotional responses: evidence from recent research on
        nonhuman primates. Sci Psa 1968, 12:39-52
76100   Observations of mother-infant interactions in primate field studies. In
        Foss, B. M. *Determinants of Infant Behaviour IV*, London: Methuen
        1969, 3-14
76101   (& Adams, J. E.) A perspective on coping behavior: seeking and utiliz-
        ing information in major transitions. Arch gen Psychiat 1967, 17:277-
        284
76102   Recent advances in biological sciences pertinent to the study of human
        behavior. Sci Psa 1962, 5:37-53
76103   (& Bibring, G. L.; Fisher, C.; Stanton, A. H.; Wallerstein, R. S.; Wein-
        stock, H. I.; Haggard, E.) Report of ad hoc committee on central fact-
        gathering data of the American Psychoanalytic Association. J Am Psa
        Ass 1967, 15:841-861
76104   Sex hormones in the development of sex differences in human behavior.
        In Maccoby, E. E. *The Development of Sex Differences*, Stanford,
        Calif: Stanford Univ Pr 1966, 1-24

        See Bunney, William E.; Coelho, George V.; Friedman, Stanford B.;
        Murphey, Elizabeth B.; Silber, Earle; Yalom, Irvin D.

HAMBURGER, ERNEST

76105   Tattooing as a psychic defence mechanism. Int J soc Psychiat 1966,
        12:60-62

HAMBURGER, WALTER W.

S-48320 The occurrence and meaning of dreams of food and eating: I. Typical
        food and eating dreams of four patients in analysis.
        Abs RSB An Surv Psa 1958, 9:221

HAMBURGER, WERNER

S-48322 A clinical observation on emotion and childbirth.
        Abs DJM An Surv Psa 1957, 8:168-169
S-48323 Legal guilt and the unconscious.
        Abs IK An Surv Psa 1957, 8:131-132

HAMID, PAUL N.

        See Boshier, Roger

HAMILTON, E. G.

76106   Frigidity in the female. Missouri Med 1961, 58:1040-1051

HAMILTON, JAMES W.

76107 Object loss, dreaming, and creativity: the poetry of John Keats. Psa St C 1969, 24:488-531
76108 The rear-end collision; a specific form of acting out. J Hillside Hosp 1967, 16:187-204
76109 Some comments about Ingmar Bergman's "The Silence" and its socio-cultural implications. J Amer Acad Child Psychiat 1969, 8:367-373
76110 Some dynamics of anti-Negro prejudice. R 1966, 53:5-15
       Abs SRS Q 1967, 36:138

HAMILTON, MARIAN W.

76111 Psychopathology from a social and cultural aspect. In Kranz, H. *Psychopathologie Heute*, Stuttgart: Georg Thieme 1962, 345-354

See Hoenig, J.

HAMILTON, MARSHALL L.

See Byrne, Donn E.

HAMILTON, VERNON

76112 Theories of anxiety and hysteria—a rejoinder to Hans Eysenck. Brit J Psychol 1959, 50:276-280

HAMILTON, W. J.

76113 Countertransference and the psychiatrist. Comprehen Psychiat 1966, 7:264-277

HAMM, MARY

76114 Some aspects of difficult therapeutic (working) alliance. Ch Anal Wk 185-205

HAMMER, EMANUEL F.

76115 Acting out and its prediction by projective drawing assessment. Acting Out 288-319
76116 Creativity. An Exploratory Investigation of the Personalities of Gifted Adolescent Artists. NY: Random House 1961, x + 150 p
76117 Creativity and feminine ingredients in young male artists. Percept mot Skills 1964, 19:414
76118 Emotional instability and creativity. Percept mot Skills 1961, 12:102
76119 Exhibitionism. In Blank, L. *Nudity and Nudism: Studies in Voyeurism and Exhibitionism*, Chicago: Aldine Publ 1966
76120 An exploratory study of the personalities of creative adolescent artists. Stud art Educ 1960, 1:42-68
76121 Insight and personality expansion. Professional Digest 1967, 3(2):2-6
76122 Interpretation as interpersonal structuring. In author's *Use of Interpretation in Treatment: Technique and Art* 62-66
76123 Interpretations in treatment: their place, role, timing, and art. R 1966, 53:139-144
       Abs SRS Q 1967, 36:632

76124 Interpretation: science or art? In author's *Use of Interpretation in Treatment: Technique and Art* 372-374
76125 Interpretation: what is it? In author's *Use of Interpretation in Treatment: Technique and Art* 1-4
76126 Interpretations: where and when. In author's *Use of Interpretation in Treatment: Technique and Art* 22-26
76127 Interpretive technique: a primer. In author's *Use of Interpretation in Treatment: Technique and Art* 31-42
76128 Masculine character posturing. In Buck, J. N. *The House-Tree-Person Technique*, Calif: Western Psych Services 1966, 198-209
76129 Personality Dimensions of Creativity. NY: Lincoln Institute of Psychotherapy 1962, 65 p
76130 Personality patterns in young creative artists. Adolescence 1966, 1:327-350
76131 The role of interpretation in therapy. In author's *Use of Interpretation in Treatment: Technique and Art* 5-12
76132 Symptoms of sexual deviation: dynamics and etiology. R 1968, 55:5-27
         Abs SRS Q 1969, 38:340
76133 Use of imagery in interpretative communication. J Long Island Consult Center 1967, 5:3-12. In author's *Use of Interpretation in Treatment: Technique and Art* 148-155
76134 (Ed) Use of Interpretation in Treatment: Technique and Art. NY/London: Grune & Stratton 1968, xii + 379 p
76135 Varying technique in treatment. In author's *Use of Interpretation in Treatment: Technique and Art* 156-168
76136 What is human creativity? Psychiat Opin 1967, 4(2):16-20

REVIEWS OF:
76137 Barron, F. Creativity and Psychological Health: Origins of Personal Vitality and Creative Freedom. R 1967, 54:382-384
76138 Levine, M. & Spivack, G. The Rorschach Index of Repressive Style. Am Im 1965, 22:158-159
76139 Wallach, M. A. & Kogan, N. Modes of Thinking in Young Children: A Study of the Creativity-Intelligence Distinction. R 1966, 53:317-321

HAMMER, LEON I.

76140 Discussion of Schaefer, L. C. "Frigidity." In Goldman, G. D. & Milman, D. S. *Modern Woman*, Springfield, Ill: Thomas 1969, 180-184
76141 Family therapy with multiple therapists. Curr psychiat Ther 1967, 7:103-111

HAMMER, MAX

76142 The concepts of loss and gain in an anal personality. Psychotherapy 1964, 1:129-131
76143 Homosexuality in a women's reformatory. Corrective Psychiat J soc Ther 1965, 11:168-169
76144 (& Kaplan, A. M.) (Eds) The Practice of Psychotherapy with Children. Homewood, Ill: Dorsey Pr 1967, xiii + 294 p

HAMMERMAN, STEVEN

76145 Conceptions of superego development. J Am Psa Ass 1965, 13:320-355
          Abs JLSt Q 1968, 37:470
76146 Ego defect and depression. Q 1963, 32:155-164
76147 Masturbation and character. J Am Psa Ass 1961, 9: 287-311
          Abs FB Q 1962, 31:292-311. Auth Rev Psicoanál 1963, 20:90

REVIEW OF: ˙
76148 The Psychoanalytic Study of the Child, Vol. XX. Q 1967, 36:101-105

HAMMERTON, MAX

76149 Freud: the status of an illusion. The Listener 1968, 29 Aug

HAMMETT, VAN BUREN O.

76150 A consideration of psychoanalysis in relation to psychiatry generally,
          circa 1965, P 1965, 122:42-54
          Abs Loeb, L. Q 1967, 36:473
76151 Correspondence with Martin H. Stein. P 1966, 122:830
76152 Delusional transference. PT 1961, 15:574-581
76153 Discussion of Stoller, R. J. "Gender identity and a biological force."
          Psa Forum 1967, 2:326-327
76154 Obituary: Morris J. Goldman, M.D. Bull Phila Ass Psa 1968, 18:89-90
76155 Psychological changes with physical fitness training. Canad Med Ass J
          1967, 96:764-769
76156 (& Graff, H.) Therapy of smoking. Curr psychiat Ther 1966, 6:70-75

See Graff, Harold

HAMMOND, GUYTON B.

76157 Man in Estrangement: A Comparison of the Thought of Paul Tillich
          and Erich Fromm. Nashville, Tenn: Vanderbilt Univ Pr 1965,
          xii + 194 p
          Rv Loomis, E. A., Jr. Q 1968, 37:455-456

HAMMOND, HAROLD

See Usandivaras, Raúl J

HAMMOND, JOHN W.

See Mayer, Joseph

HAMPE, WARREN W., JR.

76158 (& Bacon, C. L.) Treatment of psychosis. Int Psychiat Clin 1964,
          1:443-459

See English, O. Spurgeon

HAMPSHIRE, STUART

76159 Disposition and memory. (Read at Brit Psa Soc, 15 June 1960) J 1962,
          43:59-68
          Abs FTL Q 1963, 32:284-285

HAMPTON, PETER J.

76160 Group psychotherapy with parents. Ops 1962, 32:918-926

HANAWALT, NELSON GILBERT

76161 (& Gebhardt, L. J.) Childhood memories of single and recurrent incidents. J genet Psych 1965, 107:85-89

HAND, MORTON H.

76162 (& Meisel, A. M.) Dynamic aspects of suicide. NYSJM 1966, 66:3009-3016

See Kurian, Milton; Meisel, Arthur M.

HANDEL, GERALD

76163 Psychological study of whole families. Psychol Bull 1965, 63:19-41
76164 (Ed) The Psychosocial Interior of the Family: A Sourcebook for the Study of Whole Families. Chicago: Aldine Publ 1967, xi + 560 p

HANDELMAN, N. S.

See Lachman, Frank M.

HANDELSMAN, IRVING

76165 The effects of early object relationships on sexual development. Autistic and symbiotic modes of adaptation. Psa St C 1965, 20:367-383

HANDERSON, A. S.

See Preswick, G.

HANDFORD, ALLEN

See Graff, Harold

HANDLER, JOEL STANLEY

76166 Commitment to ideals and volunteer service. PT 1968, 22:637-644
76167 Psychotherapy and medical responsibility. Arch gen Psychiat 1959, 1:464-468

ABSTRACTS OF:
76168 Basch, M. F. Perception, subliminal perception and Freud's "project." Bull Phila Ass Psa 1969, 19:238-242
76169 Engel, G. Ego development following severe trauma in infancy. Bull Phila Ass Psa 1969, 19:234-236

HANDLER, LEONARD

See Frisch, Giora R.

HANDLON, J. H.

See Parloff, Morris B.

HANDLON, M. W.

See Wenar, Charles

HANENSON, IRWIN B.

See Gottschalk, Louis A.

HANFMANN, EUGENIA

76170 (& Jones, R. M.) Editors of Angyal, A. *Neurosis and Treatment.*
76171 Holistic theories of neurosis. Sci Psa 1965, 8:49-58
76172 (& Jones, R. M.; Baker, E.; Kovar, L.) Psychological Counseling in a
       Small College. (Introd: Frank, L. K.) Cambridge, Mass: Schenkman
       1963, xi + 131 p
         Rv Woltmann, A. G. R 1964, 51:681-683

HANKOFF, LEON DUDLEY

76173 (& Engelhardt, D. M.; Freedman, N.; Mann, D.; Margolis, R.) Denial
       of illness in relation to differential drug response. JNMD 1963, 137:29-
       41
76174 (& Engelhardt, D. M.; Freedman, N.; Mann, D.; Margolis, R.) The
       doctor-patient relationship in a psychopharmacological treatment
       setting. JNMD 1960, 131:540-546

HANNA, WILLIAM JOHN

76175 Political recruitment and participation: some suggested areas for re-
       search. R 1965-66, 52:67-80
76176 Splitting: the case of the Soviet delegates in the United Nations Se-
       curity Council. Am Im 1963, 20:175-185

HANNEMANN, E.

76177 [What do we mean by the symptom of narcissism.] (Ger) Deutsch
       Zbl Krankenpfl 1968, 12:615-616

HANNETT, FRANCES

76178 Discussion of Little, R. B. "Transference, counter-transference and
       survival reactions following an analyst's heart attack." Psa Forum
       1967, 2:115-116
76179 The haunting lyric. The personal and social significance of American
       popular songs. Q 1964, 33:226-269

REVIEW OF:
76180 Pitcher, E. G. & Prelinger, E. Children Tell Stories. An Analysis of
       Fantasy. J 1965, 46:278

HANNON, JOHN E.

See Eisenman, Russell

HANSEL, C. E. M.

76181 ESP: A Scientific Evaluation. NY: Charles Scribner's Sons 1966
         Rv Löfgren, L. B. J Am Psa Ass 1968, 16:146-178

HANSEN, B.

See Spanheimer, L.

HANSEN, DANIELS

76182 Physical symptoms that may reveal sexual conflict. In Wahl, C. W. *Sexual Problems*, NY: Free Pr; London: Collier-Macmillan 1967, 28-38

HANSEN, ERIK BJERG

76183 Die hypochondrische Paranoia. [Hypochondriacal paranoia.] In Retterstøl, N. & Magnussen, F. *Report on the Fifteenth Congress of Scandinavian Psychiatrists,* Acta psychiat Scand, Suppl No. 203, Copenhagen 1968, 33
76184 Probleme bei der paranoiden Symptombildung. [Problems related to paranoid symptom formation.] Psyche 1963, 17:146-163

HANSEN, ERNST

See Seay, Bill

HANSEN, HOWARD

See Friedman, David B.

HANSEN, T. J.

See Tjossem, T. D.

HARARI, CARMI

76185 (& Chwast, J.) The antisocial crisis in psychotherapy with delinquents. Corrective Psychiat 1964, 10:301-314
76186 (& Chwast, J.) Class bias in psychodiagnosis of delinquents. Crime Delinq 1964, 10:145-151

See Chwast, Jacob

HARBAUER, H.

76187 Die Neuropathie des Kindes und ihre Abgrenzung. [Neuropathy of children and its demarcation.] In Kranz, H. *Psychopathologie Heute,* Stuttgart: Georg Thieme 1962, 370-378

HÁRDI, ISTVÁN

76188 Verlaufsaspekte dynamischer Zeichungsuntersuchungen bei Psychosen. [Clinical aspects of dynamic drawing investigations in psychoses.] Arch Psychiat Nervenkr 1967, 210:174-181

HARDING, D. W.

76189 Freudianism and the traditional virtues. New Statesm 1966, 71(April 22):578

HARDING, GÖSTA

76190 Comment on Dr. Lidz's paper "August Strindberg: a study of the relationship between his creativity and schizophrenia." (Read at Int Psa Cong, July-Aug 1963) J 1964, 45:406-410
Abs Q 1966, 35:465

HARDING, MARY ESTHER

76191 The "I" and the "Not-I": A Study in the Development of Consciousness. NY: Pantheon Books 1965, x + 244 p
76192 Obituary notice: Frances G. Wickes. J anal Psych 1968, 13:67-69
76193 The Parental Image: Its Injury and Reconstruction. (Foreword: Riklin, F.) NY: Putnam; London: Stuart 1965, xviii + 238 p
76194 The reality of the psyche. In Wheelwright, J. B. *The Reality of the Psyche,* NY: Putnam 1968, 1-13

See Jackson, Murray

HARE, E. H.

76195 Masturbatory insanity: the history of an idea. JMS 1962, 108:1-25
Abs HR Q 1962, 31:591

HARE, MARY L.

See Balint, Michael

HARGADON, B. K.

76196 Transference: a student-teacher interaction. Sch R 1966, 74:446-452

HARITON, N.

76197 The kinetic test of hostility as an indicator of unconscious rejection. Canad Psychiat Ass J 1962, 7:174-177

HARKAVY, EDWARD E.

76198 Discussion of Niederland, W. G. "A contribution to the psychology of gambling." Psa Forum 1967, 2:182-183

REVIEWS OF:
76199 Hoch, P. H. & Zubin, J. (Eds) Current Approaches to Psychoanalysis. Q 1961, 30:568-571
76200 Masserman, J. H. (Ed) Science and Psychoanalysis, Vol. IV. Psychoanalysis and Social Process. Q 1962, 31:257-259

HARKINS, ELIZABETH B.

See Polansky, Norman A.

HARLEY, MARJORIE

76201 Fragments from the analysis of a dog phobia in a latency child. (Read at Phila Ass Psa, 18 Nov 1966)
Abs Graff, H. Bull Phila Ass Psa 1967, 17:127-129

76202 Masturbation conflicts. Adolescents 51-57
76203 (Reporter) Resistances in child analysis. (Panel: Am Psa Ass, Dec 1960) J Am Psa Ass 1961, 9:548-561
76204 The role of the dream in the analysis of a latency child. (Read at Am Psa Ass, 4 Dec 1959) J Am Psa Ass 1962, 10:271-288
    Abs JBi Q 1963, 32:131-132. IBa RFPsa 1964, 28:455
76205 A secret in prepuberty (its bisexual aspects). (Read at NY Psa Soc, 26 Mar 1963)
    Abs Fine, B. D. Q 1963, 32:616-617
76206 Some observations on the relationship between genitality and structural development at adolescence. (Read at Am Psa Ass, 5 Dec 1958) J Am Psa Ass 1961, 9:434-460
    Abs FB Q 1962, 31:418. SAS RFPsa 1962, 26:618
76207 Transference developments in a five-year-old child. Ch Anal Wk 115-141

REVIEW OF:
76208 Fraiberg, S. H. The Magic Years. Understanding and Handling the Problems of Early Childhood. Q 1961, 30:127-129

HARLOW, HARRY F.

76209 (& Seay, B.) Affectional systems in Rhesus monkeys. J Arkansas Med Soc 1964, 61:107-110
76210 Behavioral approaches to psychiatric theory. Sci Psa 1964, 7:93-113
76211 (& Harlow, M. K.) The effect of rearing conditions on behavior. BMC 1962, 26:213-224. In Rosenblith, J. F. & Allinsmith, W. The Causes of Behavior, Boston: Allyn & Bacon 1966, 134-139
    Abs HD Q 1964, 33:142-143
76212 The heterosexual affectional system in monkeys. Am Psych 1962, 17:1-9
76213 (& Harlow, M. K.) Learning to love. Amer Sci 1966, 54:244-272
76214 Love in infant monkeys. Sci Am 1959, 200(6):68-74
76215 Primary affectional patterns in primates. Ops 1960, 30:676-684. In Dulany, D. E., Jr. et al: Contributions to Modern Psychology, NY: Oxford Univ Pr 1964, 274-284
    Abs RLG Q 1961, 30:303-304. JMa RFPsa 1962, 26:319
76216 Sexual behavior in the Rhesus monkey. In Beach, F. A. Sex and Behavior, NY: Wiley 1965
76217 (& Harlow, M. K.) The young monkeys. Psychol Today 1967, 1:40-47

See Seay, Bill

HARLOW, MARGARET KUENNE
See Harlow, Harry F.

HARLOW, MINNIE
See Konopka, Gisela

HARLOW, ROBERT G.
See Ford, E. S. C.; Prugh, Dane G.

HARMATZ, J.
See Shader, Richard I.

HARMATZ, M. G.
See Sarason, Irwin G.

HARMELING, JAMES D.
See Schwab, John J.

HARMS, ERNEST

76218 Die amerikanische "self"-Psychologie. [The American self psychology.] Psyche 1964, 17:645-648
76219 (Ed) Drug Addiction in Youth. Oxford/NY: Pergamon Pr 1965, xi + 210 p
Rv Savitt, R. A. Q 1936, 35:609-610
76220 (& Schreiber, P.) (Eds) Handbook of Counseling Techniques. Oxford: Pergamon; NY: Macmillan 1963, 506 p
Rv Hayward, S. T. J 1965, 46:399
76221 Obituary: Carl Gustav Jung. P 1962, 118:728-732
76222 Origins of Modern Psychiatry. (Foreword: Braceland, F. J.) Springfield, Ill: Thomas 1967, xiv + 256 p
76223 (Ed) Pathogenesis of Nervous and Mental Diseases in Children. NY: Libra Publ 1968, 293 p
76224 (Ed) Problems of Sleep and Dream in Children. NY: Macmillan 1964, v + 147 p
Rv Furer, M. Q 1965, 34:120-121. Spotnitz, H. R 1966, 53:148-149
76225 A socio-genetic concept of family therapy. Acta psychother psychosom 1964, 12:53-60
76226 (Ed) Somatic and Psychiatric Aspects of Childhood Allergies. (Introd: Abramson, H. A.) Oxford: Pergamon; NY: Macmillan 1963, x + 292 p
Rv Freedman, D. A. Q 1964, 33:593-594
76227 Specific forms of interpretation in psychotherapy with adolescents. In Hammer, E. F. *Use of Interpretation in Treatment: Technique and Art*, NY: Grune & Stratton 1968, 321-331
76228 Zur Entstehung und Entwicklung religiösen Symbolerlebens bei Kindern. [The origin and development of experiences of religious symbols in children.] Psyche 1960, 14:552-560

See Friedman, Arnold P.; Ginott, Haim G.

HARNACK, G. A. VON

76229 Die Bedeutung der Mutter für die seelische Entwicklung des Kindes. Zur Problematik der "maternal deprivation." [The significance of the mother in the psychologic development of the child. On the problem of "maternal deprivation."] Dtsch med Wschr 1965, 90:1221-1222

HARPER, ROBERT ALLAN

76230 Critique and overview. In author's *Psychoanalysis and Psychotherapy*, Englewood Cliffs, N.J. Prentice Hall 1959. With title: Some common effects of diverse approaches. In Berenson, B. G. & Carkhuff, R. R. *Sources of Gain in Counseling and Psychotherapy,* NY/Chicago/San Francisco: Holt, Rinehart & Winston 1967, 86-98

° ° ° Some common effects of diverse approaches. See [76230]

See Ellis, Albert

HARRELL, S. N.

See Heilbrun, Alfred B., Jr.

HARRINGTON, M.

76231 The management of regression in the treatment of emotionally disturbed children. J Child Psychol Psychiat 1960, 1:228-237

HARRIS, DALE B.

76232 Early deprivation and enrichment, and later development: an introduction to a symposium. Child Develpm 1965, 36:839-842

See Rafferty, Janet E.

HARRIS, DEAN VERNON

76233 The effects of inhibition and tension on fantasy. Diss Abstr 1963, 24(4): 1686

HARRIS, H.

See Beisser, Arnold R.

HARRIS, HERBERT I.

76234 Discussion of Niederland, W. G. "A contribution to the psychology of gambling." Psa Forum 1967, 2:183-184
76235 Drop-out and negative institutional transference. PT 1966, 20:664-668
76236 Gambling addiction in an adolescent male. Q 1964, 33:513-525
76237 Methods of treating everyday emotional problems in adolescents. Med Clin N Amer 1965, 49:371-386
S-48433 Telephone anxiety.
Abs KOS An Surv Psa 1957, 8:101

See Gallagher, J. Roswell

HARRIS, IRVING D.

76238 Birth order and creative styles. Sci Psa 1965, 8:74-85
76239 Birth order and responsibility. J Marriage Fam 1968, 30:427-432
S-48445 The dream of the object endangered.
Abs JA An Surv Psa 1957, 8:177
76240 Dreams about the analyst. J 1962, 43:151-158
Abs FTL Q 1963, 32:287-288
76241 Emotional Blocks of Learning: A Study of the Reasons for Failure in School. NY: Free Pr 1961, 1965, 1966, x + 210 p
76242 Normal Children and Mothers: Their Emotional Opportunities and Obstacles. Glencoe, Ill: Free Pr 1959, x + 287 p

76243 The Promised Seed. A Comparative Study of Eminent First and Later
      Sons. NY/London: Free Pr of Glencoe 1964, ix + 339 p
          Abs J Am Psa Ass 1966, 14:232
S-48447 Typical anxiety dreams and object relations.
          Abs JBi Q 1962, 31:124
S-48448 Unconscious factors common to parents and analysts.
          Abs JBi Q 1961, 30:298. Bianchedi, E. T. de Rev Psicoanál 1961,
      18:177. PCR RFPsa 1964, 28:295

HARRIS, RAMÓN

76244 Thomas Jefferson: female identification. Am Im 1968, 25:371-383

HARRIS, ROBERT E.

See Burton, Arthur

HARRIS, SARA

See Freeman, Lucy

HARRISON, ADA M.

See Lifschutz, Joseph E.

HARRISON, IRVING B.

S-48458 A clinical note on a dream followed by elation.
          Abs JTM Q 1961, 30-597-598
76245 Follow-up note on a patient who experienced hypomania following a
      dream. J Am Psa Ass 1967, 15:366-369
76246 A reconsideration of Freud's "A disturbance of memory on the Acropo-
      lis" in relation to identity disturbance. J Am Psa Ass 1966, 14:518-527
          Abs Cuad Psa 1967, 3:57. JLSt Q 1969, 38:338

ABSTRACTS OF:
76247 Beres, D. Superego and depression. Q 1967, 36:635-636
76248 Bergler, E. Homosexuality: Disease or Way of Life? An Surv Psa 1956,
      7:212-213, 433-436
76249 Brody, S. & Axelrad, S. Anxiety, socialization, and ego formation in
      infancy. Q 1967, 36:480-481
76250 Jacobson, E. Guilt, shame, and identity. Q 1963, 32:475-477

HARRISON, ROBERT H.

See Mendelson, Jack H.; Stein, Steven H.

HARRISON, SAUL I.

76251 (& Cain, A.; Benedek, E.) The childhood of a transsexual. Arch gen
      Psychiat, 1968, 19:28-37
76252 (& Davenport, C. W.; McDermott, J. F.) Children's reactions to be-
      reavement: adult confusions and misperceptions. Arch gen Psychiat
      1967, 17:593-597
76253 Communicating with children in psychotherapy. Int Psychiat Clin
      1964, 1:39-51

S-48460 Direct supervision of the psychotherapist as a teaching method. Ops 1960, 30:71-78

76254 Discussion of McDermott, J. F. "Residential treatment of children. The utilization of transference behavior." J Amer Acad Child Psychiat 1968, 7:169-192

76255 A girl reared as a boy. J Amer Acad Child Psychiat 1965, 4:53-76

76256 (& Carek, D. J.) A Guide to Psychotherapy. Boston: Little, Brown; London: J. & A. Churchill 1966, xiii + 263 p
Rv Dewald, P. A. Q 1968, 37:306-307

76257 Individual psychotherapy. Compreh Txbk Psychiat 1453-1463

76258 (& Hess, J.; Zrull, J. P.) Paranoid reactions in children. J Amer Acad Child Psychiat 1963, 2:677-692

76259 (& Klapman, H. J.) Relationships between social forces and homosexual behavior observed in a children's psychiatric hospital. J Amer Acad Child Psychiat 1966, 5:105-110

76260 (& McDermott, J. F.; Chethik, M.) Residential treatment of children: the psychotherapist-administrator. J Amer Acad Child Psychiat 1969, 8:385-410

76261 (& McDermott, J. F.; Wilson, P. T.; Schrager, J.) Social class and mental illness in children. Arch gen Psychiat 1965, 13:411-417
Abs PB Q 1968, 37:319-320

76262 (& Burks, H. L.) Some aspects of grouping in a children's psychiatric hospital. Ops 1964, 34:148-152

76263 Some considerations in dealing with emotionally disturbed children. Med Times 1961, 89-1216-1220

76264 Some problems in the treatment of emotionally disturbed children. J Mich Med Soc 1960, 59:1395-1398

76265 (& Carek, D. J.) What is psychotherapy? Postgrad Med 1965, 38:16-22

76266 Youthful defensiveness, not senile rigidity. Int J Psychiat 1968, 6:314

See Brody, Morris W.; Burks, Henry L.; Kemph, John P.; Mathews, W. Mason; McDermott, John F., Jr.; Schneider, Stanley F.

HARROW, MARTIN

76267 (& Schulberg, H. C.) Implications from psychological testing for theoretical formulations of *folie à deux*. ASP 1963, 67:166-172
Abs Rosen, I. C. Q 1964, 33:460

76268 (& Astrachan, B. M.; Becker, R. E.) An investigation into the nature of the patient-family therapy group. Ops 1967, 37:888-890

HARROWER, MOLLY RACHEL

76269 Clinical psychologists at work. In Wolman, B. B. *Handbook of Clinical Psychology*, NY/Toronto/London: McGraw-Hill 1965, 1443-1458

76270 The contribution of the projective techniques to the problem of diagnosis. Prog PT 1960, 5:105-111

76271 (et al) Creative Variations in the Projective Techniques. (Foreword: Klopfer, B.) Springfield, Ill: Thomas 1960, 138 p
Rv Kurth, G. M. Q 1962, 31:570-573

76272 Differential diagnosis. In Wolman, B. B. *Handbook of Clinical Psychology*, NY/Toronto/London: McGraw-Hill 1965, 381-402

76273 The Practice of Clinical Psychology. Springfield, Ill: Thomas 1961, xiv + 321 p
76274 Psychodiagnostic Testing: An Empirical Approach Based on a Follow-up of 2000 Cases. (Foreword: Kubie, L. S.) Springfield, Ill: Thomas 1965, xii + 90 p

HART, BERNARD

76275 The conception of dissociation. M 1962, 35:15-29
       Abs ICFH Q 1963, 32:141-142

HART, EDWARD L.

76276 "Christopher must slay the dragon." (A note on Smart's satire.) Lit & Psych 1967, 17:115-119

HART, HENRY HARPER

76277 Displacement, guilt and pain. In Sherman, M. H. *Psychoanalysis in America: Historical Perspectives*, Springfield, Ill: Thomas 1966, 438-453
76278 Fear of homosexuality in college students. In Wedge, B. M. *Psychosocial Problems of College Men*, New Haven: Yale Univ Pr 1958, 200-213
S-48487 Maternal narcissism and the Oedipus complex.
       Abs JLS An Surv Psa 1958, 9:128-129
S-48489 The meaning of passivity.
       Abs An Surv Psa 1955, 6:201-203
76279 A review of the psychoanalytic literature on passivity. Psychiat Q 1961, 35:331-352
       Abs Engle, B. Q 1962, 31:587
S-48493 A scarcely recognized factor in the Oedipus complex.
       Abs AS An Surv Psa 1956, 7:150

HART, JUANITA T.

76280 (& Kraft, I. A.; Williams, S. G.; Blair, M.) Interview group psychotherapy of boys and girls of latency age: a preliminary study. J Psa in Groups 1968, 2(2):9-14
76281 (& Kraft, I. A.; Miller, M.; Williams, S. G.) A preliminary descriptive study of interview group psychotherapy of mixed sex latency age children. J Psa in Groups 1969

HART DE RUYTER, THEODOOR

76282 Behandelingsmogelijkheden van jeugdige delinkwenten. [Possibilities for treatment of juvenile delinquents.] Maanblad voor Berechting en Reclassering 1961, 40(11)
76283 Bemerkungen zum Problem einer Systematik der psychogenen Störungen aus psychoanalytischer Sicht. [Remarks on the problem of a taxonomy of psychogenic disturbances from a psychoanalytic viewpoint.] In *Systematik der psychogenen Störungen*, Bern: Huber 1968, 9-24
76284 (Ed) Capita Selecta uit de Kinderpsychiatrie. [Selections from Child Psychiatry.] Zeist: E. de Haan 1963

76285 Constanten en varianten in de betekenis van de gezinseleden. [Constants in variations in the meaning of family life.] Tijdschr Maatschappelijk Werk 1964, 18(1-2)

76286 Debilitas Mentis, zwakbegaafdheid en vertraagde ontwikkeling. [Mental Retardation: The Result of Retarded Development.] Groningen: J. B. Wolters 1961, 92 p

76287 De emotionele relatie als basis voor het opvoedkundig en didactisch werk. [Emotional relation as the basis for pedagogy in didactic work.] Pedag-didakt Bull 1967, 1:14-20

76288 Enkele gedachten over de verhouding tussen orthopedagogiek en psychotherapie in een opvoedkundig behandelingstehuis en in een kinderpsychiatrische behandelingskliniek. [Some thoughts on the ratio between orthopedagogy and psychotherapy in a pedagogic treatment residence and a child psychiatric treatment clinic.] In *Doorgangshuis 1865-de Helper Haven-1965*, Groningen: J. B. Wolters 1965

76289 Enkele opmerkingen over psychogene leerstoornissen. [Some remarks on psychogenic learning disturbances.] In *Hoofdstukken uit de Hedendaagse Psychoanalyse*, Arnheim: Slaterus 1967, 162-180

76290 (& Hubertus, E.) Gesinsverpleging. [Nursing the injured.] (Brochure, uitgegeven door het Nationaal Bureau voor Kinderbescherming, Den Haag, Nat Fed. v. K. N., Ned. Bond Moederschapszorg en kinderhygiëne en de Stichting voor het kind, Amsterdam 1962)

76291 De gezagsverhouding in het maatschappelijk werk en de verijheid van het individu. [The ratio of authority in social work and the frustration of the individual.] The Hague: Nationale Raad v. Maatschappelijk Werk 1962, Brochure no. 29

76292 Kurzer Auszug einer Einleitung zum Thema: Psychotherapie und Strafvollzug bei jugendlicher Kriminalität. [A short extract of a preface on the subject: psychotherapy and punishment for youthful criminals.] In *Concilium Paedopsychiatricum*, Basel 1968, 434 p

76293 (& Noome, H. B.) In memoriam Dr. P. H. C. Tibout. In Mededelingenblad no. 10 (Dec 1968) van de Ned. Ver. v. Psychiatrie en Neurologie, 3-5

76294 The notion of prevention in the evolution of child psychiatry. Acta paedopsychiat 1962, 29(7-8):199-222

Der Gedanke der Prävention in der Entwicklung der Kinderpsychiatrie. In *Kinderpsychiatrie und Prävention*, Bern: Huber 1964, 64-76

76295 Orthopedagogische Preventie in de Kleuterleeftijd. [Orthopedagogic preventive measures for toddlers.] Schoolblad 1967, 2(5 & 6). Maandbl geest Volksgezondh 1967, 22(10)

76296 De orthopedagoog en het emotioneel gehandicapte kind. [Orthopedagogy of the emotionally handicapped child.] Tijdschr Orthopedag 1962, 1(1)

76297 Over gezinsverpleging. [On family care.] Koepel 1964, 18(10):246-490

76298 Over ontstaan en behandeling van de zogenaamde ontwikkelingspsychopathie. [On the origin and treatment of so-called developmental psychopathology.] In *Capita Selecta uit de Kinder- en Jeugdpsychiatrie*, IV, Zeist: W. de Haan 1963, 72-132

76299 De plaats van het M.O.B. in het kader van de geestelijke gezondheids-
       zorg [On the place of M.O.B. in the framework of mental health care.]
       Maandbl geest Volksgezondh 1965, 20(9)
76300 De psychische ontwikkeling van kinderen met lichte hersenbeschadig-
       ing. Klinische Les. [On the psychic development of children with slight
       brain damage.] Ned Tijdschr Geneeskunde 1961, 105(16)
76301 Psychopathiform gedrag fij kinderen. [Psychopathic behavior in chil-
       dren.] Hfst. 2. Het oligofrene gedrag. Hfst 4. In *Ned. Handboek der
       Psychiatrie, III,* Arnhem: Slaterus 1965
76302 Psychopathologie van puberteit en adolescentie. [Psychopathology of
       puberty and adolescence.] In *Capita Selecta uit de Kinder- en Jeugd-
       psychiatrie,* Zeist: W. de Haan 1963, 132-172
76303 Psychosen in de puberteit. [Psychoses in puberty.] Tijdschr Med
       Anal 1968, 23(3):104-112
76304 Stoorissen van puberteit en adolescentie. [Disturbances of puberty and
       adolescence.] In Planting, G. J. *Leerboek voor Moederschapszorg en
       Kinderhygiëne,* 1962, 327-345
76305 De taak van de huisarts bij de herkenning van het bedreigde kind.
       [The task of the family doctor in the recognition of the deceitful child.]
       Medisch Contact 1964, 19(43). Huisarts en Wetenschap 1965, 8(10)
76306 De therapeutische gezinsverpleging als fase in het behandelingsplan
       van het onaangepaste gedrag. [Therapeutic hospital nursing as a part
       of the treatment plan for unacceptable behavior.] Maandbl geest Volks-
       gezondh 1967, 22(2):44-54
76307 Wisselwerkingen—een vergeten aspect in de voorlichting. [Interaction
       —one forgotten aspect in public enlightenment.] In *Maatschappelijk
       Werk, deel II. Terreinen b. Maatsch. Werk,* Assen: Van Gorcum 1965
76308 Zijn wij met het Medisch Opvoedkundig Bureau op de goede weg?
       [Can we favor the M.O.B. as a good way?] Amersfoort: Ned Federatie
       v. M.O.B.'s 1964
76309 De zorg voor de psychische gezondheid van het kind. [Care for the
       mental health of the child.] In *Jeugd en Samenleving,* II, The Hague:
       Nijgh en Van Ditmar 1965, 83-99
76310 Zur Psychotherapie der Dissozialität im Jugendalter. [The psycho-
       therapy of antisocial behavior in youth.] Jb Jugendpsychiat & ihre
       Grenzgebiete 1967, 6:79-108

       See Boeke, Pieter E.

HARTLAND, J.

76311 Hypnosis in the development of modern psychological medicine. J
       Amer Soc Psychosom Dent Med 1968, 15:4-17
76312 The value of "ego-strengthening" procedures prior to direct symptom-
       removal under hypnosis. Amer J clin Hyp 1965, 8:89-93

HARTLEY, EUGENE

76313 (& Rosenbaum, M.) Criteria used by group psychotherapists for judg-
       ing improvement in patients. Int J grp PT 1963, 13:80-83

       See Peatman, John G.; Rosenbaum, Max

HARTLEY, RUTH E.

76314 (& Frank, L. K.; Goldenson, R. M.) The benefits of water play. In Haworth, M. R. *Child Psychotherapy*, NY/London: Basic Books 1964, 364-368

HARTMAN, RICHARD H.

76315 Letter to the editors [re Alger, I. "Analyst's responses."] Psa Forum 1967, 2:104

HARTMAN, V.

76316 Notes on group psychotherapy with pedophiles. Canad Psychiat Ass J 1965, 10:283-289

See Markson, Elliott R.

HARTMANN, DORA

76317 A study of drug-taking adolescents. (Read at Am Psa Ass 1969) Psa St C 1969, 24:384-398

See Esman, Aaron

HARTMANN, ERNEST L.

76318 (& Glasser, B. A.; Greenblatt, M.; Solomon, M. H.; Levinson, D. J.) Adolescents in a Mental Hospital. NY/London: Grune & Stratton 1968, ix + 197 p
76319 The Biology of Dreaming. Springfield, Ill: Thomas 1967, 206 p
        Rv Hall, C. S. R 1967, 54:655-661. Fisher, C. K 1969, 38:135-138. Gillespie, W. H. J 1969, 50:413-414
76320 Dauerschlaf; a polygraphic study. Arch gen Psychiat 1968, 18:99-111
76321 Dreaming sleep (the D-state) and the menstrual cycle. JNMD 1966, 143:406-416
76322 The D-state: a review and discussion of studies on the physiologic state concomitant with dreaming. Int J Psychiat 1966, 2(1):11-30. (Concl) New Eng J Med 1965, 273
76323 Longitudinal studies of sleep and dream patterns in manic-depressive patients. Arch gen Psychiat 1968, 19:312-329
76324 (& Verdone, P.; Snyder, F.) Longitudinal studies of sleep and dreaming patterns in psychiatric patients. JNMD 1966, 142:117-126
76325 The 90-minute sleep-dream cycle. Arch gen Psychiat 1968, 18:280-286
76326 On the pharmacology of dreaming sleep (The D state) JNMD 1968, 146:165-173
76327 The psychophysiology of free will: an example of vertical research. Psa—Gen Psychol 521-536
76328 Reserpine: its effect on the sleep-dream cycle. Psychoparacologia 1966, 9:242-247

REVIEW OF:
76329 Witkin, H. A. & Lewis, H. B. (Eds) Experimental Studies of Dreaming. Q 1969, 38:650-652

HARTMANN, HEINZ

S-13636 The applications of psychoanalytic concepts to social science. Ess Ego Psych 90-98

Die Anwendung psychoanalytischer Bergriffe auf die Sozialwissenschaft. Psyche 1964, 18:367-374

76330 Bibliography. Psa—Gen Psychol 679-685

S-13640 (& Kris, E.; Loewenstein, R. M.) Comments on the formation of the psychic structure.

Abs Raimondi, R. S. Rev Psicoanál 1966, 23:267

S-13641 Comments on the psychoanalytic theory of the ego. Ess Ego Psych 113-141

Commentaires sur la théorie psychanalytique du moi. RFPsa 1967, 31:339-378

Bemerkungen zur psychoanalytischen Theorie des Ichs. Psyche 1964, 18:330-354

Abs Perrotta, A. Rev Psicoanál 1966, 23:266

S-13642 Comments on the psychoanalytic theory of instinctual drives. Ess Ego Psych 69-89

S-48515 Comments on the scientific aspects of psychoanalysis. Ess Ego Psych 297-317

Abs Steinberg, S. An Surv Psa 1958, 9:18-20

76331 Concept formation in psychoanalysis. Psa St C 1964, 19:11-47

S-48516 Contribution to the metapsychology of schizophrenia. Ess Ego Psych 182-206

Ein Beitrag zur Metapsychologie der Schizophrenie. Psyche 1964, 18:375-396

S-48517 The development of the ego concept in Freud's work. Ess Ego Psych 268-296

Die Entwicklung des Ich-Begriffes bei Freud. Psyche 1964, 18:420-444

Abs SG An Surv Psa 1956, 7:81-82

76332 Essays on Ego Psychology. Selected Problems in Psychoanalytic Theory. NY: IUP 1964, xv + 492 p

Abs J Am Psa Ass 1966, 14:622-623. Rv Gitelson, M. Q 1965, 34: 268-273. HS Am Im 1965, 22:159-160. Shuren, I. R 1968, 55:147-150

S-13644 An experimental contribution to the psychology of obsessive-compulsive neurosis: on remembering completed and uncompleted tasks. Ess Ego Psych 404-418

76333 From the International Psycho-Analytic Association. 50 Yrs Psa 55-56

S-13648 (& Betlheim, S.) Über Fehlreaktionen bei der Korsakowschen Psychose.

On parapraxes in the Korsakoff psychosis. Ess Ego Psych 353-368

76334 Gesamtverzeichnis der Veröffentlichungen Heinz Hartmanns. [Complete listing of the publications of Heinz Hartmann.] Psyche 1964, 18: 475-481

S-13658 Ich-Psychologie und Anpassung. Psyche 1960, 14:81-164

La Psychologie du Moi et la Problème de l'Adaption. Paris: PUF 1968, 104 p

Psicologie dell'Io e Problema dell'Adattamento. (Tr: Low-Beer, M.) Turin: Boringhiere 1966

[Japanese] Tokyo: Seishin Shobo 1966(?)
La Psicología del Yo y el Problema de la Adaptación. Mexico: Cesarman 1960; Editorial Pax-México 1961, 162 p
Abs Simon, J. An Surv Psa 1958, 9:59-69. Rv Wender, L. Rev Psicoanál 1961, 18:376. Rev Psicoanál 1966, 23:262

76335 Introduction. Ess Ego Psych ix-xv

76336 Introductory comments on "menschen Kenntnis." J 1969, 50:529-531

S-13665 The mutual influences in the development of ego and id. Ess Ego Psych 155-181
Les influences réciproques du Moi et du Ça dans le développement. RFPsa 1967, 31:379-401

S-48521 Notes on the reality principle. Ess Ego Psych 241-267
Notes sur le principe de réalité. RFPsa 1967, 31:403-428
Bemerkungen zum Realitätsproblem. Psyche 1964, 18:397-419
Abs SGo An Surv Psa 1956, 7:110-113

76337 (& Loewenstein, R. M.) Notes on the superego. (Read at Cong Int Psa, 2 Aug 1961) Psa St C 1962, 17:42-81. Psychol Issues 1964, 14:144-181
Notes sur le surmoi. RFPsa 1964, 28:639-678

S-48522 Notes on the theory of sublimation. Ess Ego Psych 215-240
Abs An Surv Psa 1955, 6:120-123. Guiard, F. Rev Psicoanál 1966, 23:266

76338 (& Kris, E.; Loewenstein, R. M.) Papers on Psychoanalytic Psychology. (Psychol Issues Monogr No. 14) NY: IUP 1964, 206 p

76339 Preface. Ess Ego Psych vii

S-48524 Problems of infantile neurosis. Ess Ego Psych 207-214

S-13668 Psychiatrische Zwillingsprobleme.
Psychiatric studies of twins. (Tr: Brandt, L. W.) Ess Ego Psych 419-445

S-13674 Psychoanalysis and the concept of health. Ess Ego Psych 3-18. Heirs Freud 144-163

S-13675 Psychoanalysis and developmental psychology. Ess Ego Psych 99-112
Psychoanalyse und Entwicklungspsychologie. Psyche 1964, 18:354-366

S-48525 Psychoanalysis and Moral Values.
Psicoanálisis y Valores Morales. Mexican Psa Ass Monogr. Mexico: Editorial Pax-México
Abs J Am Psa Ass 1961, 9:168-169. Rv van der Waals, H. G. Q 1961, 30:426-431. MBr J 1962, 43:351-352

76340 (Chm) Psychoanalysis and moral values. (Panel discussion, NY Psa Soc, 17 Jan 1961)
Abs WAS Q 1961, 30:469-472

S-13676 Psychoanalysis and sociology. Ess Ego Psych 19-36

S-48526 Psychoanalysis as a scientific theory. Ess Ego Psych 318-350
Die Psychoanalyse als wissenschaftliche Theorie. Psyche 1964, 18:445-474

S-13680 On rational and irrational action. Ess Ego Psych 37-68

S-13685 Technical implications of ego psychology. Ess Ego Psych 142-154
Implications techniques de la psychologie du Moi. RFPsa 1967, 31:367-378

76341 Toward a concept of mental health. M 1960, 33:243-248
       Abs RDT Q 1961, 30:459
76342 Verstehen und Erklären. In author's *Die Grundlagen der Psychanalyse*
       36-61
       Understanding and explanation. Ess Ego Psych 369-403

REVIEW OF:
76343 Freud, A. Normality and Pathology in Childhood. Assessments of De-
       velopment. J 1967, 48:97-101

HARTMANN, KLAUS

76344 Über die Entbehrung des Vaters und ihr Bedeuting für die männliche
       Jugendverwahrlosung. [Concerning paternal deprivation and its signifi-
       cance in male juvenile delinquency.] Prax Kinderpsychol 1961, 10(7):
       249-254
76345 Über psychoanalytische "Funktionstheorien" des Spiels. [On the psy-
       choanalytic "theory of function" of play.] Jb Psa 1961-62, 2:143-157
76346 Zur Problematik des kindlichen Autismus und der psychiatrischen No-
       sologie. [On the problems of infantile autism and psychiatric nosology.]
       Prax Kinderpsychol 1964, 13:91-95

HARTMANN, LAWRENCE

76347 For the seventieth birthday of my father: November 4, 1964. Psa—
       Gen Psychol xiii-xiv

HARTMANN, R.

76348 (& Witter, H.) Le concept de "Antrieb" en psychiatrie Allemande. [The
       concept of "Antrieb" in German psychiatry.] Évolut psychiat 1966,
       31:25-31

HARTOCOLLIS, PETER

76349 Denial of illness in alcoholism. BMC 1968, 32:47-53
76350 A dynamic view of alcoholism: drinking in the service of denial. Dyn
       Psychiat 1969, 2:173-180; Abs (Ger), 180-182
76351 Hospital romances: some vicissitudes of transference. BMC 1964, 28:
       62-71
       Abs McGowan, L. Q 1965, 34:468

HARTOGS, RENATUS

76352 Application of Hartmann's ego psychology to the Schreber case. R
       1964-65, 51:562-568
76353 (& Fantel, H.) Four-letter Word Games; The Psychology of Obscenity.
       NY: M. Evans 1967, 186 p
76354 (& Freeman, L.) The Two Assassins. NY: Thomas Y. Crowell 1965,
       xv + 264 p

REVIEWS OF:
76355 Desmonde, W. H. Magic, Myth and Money: The Origin of Money
       in Religious Ritual. PPR 1962, 49(4):124

76356 Dry, A. M. The Psychology of Jung (A Critical Interpretation). R 1963, 50:693
76357 Meerloo, J. A. M. Suicide and Mass Suicide. PPR 1962, 49(4):124
76358 Meerloo, J. A. M. Unobtrusive Communication: Essays in Psycholinguistics. R 1965, 52:491

HARTUP, WILLARD W.

76359 (& Zook, E. A.) Sex-role preferences in three- and four-year-old children. J consult Psychol 1960, 24:420-426

HARTZELL, JOHN P.

76360 A preliminary study of nurturant and/or aggressive therapists' responsiveness to expressions of dependency and hostility in the initial phase of psychotherapy. Diss Abstr 1967, 28:1195-1196

HARWAY, NORMAN I.

76361 (& Iker, H. P.) Content analysis and psychotherapy. Psychotherapy 1969, 6:97-104
76362 (& Dittmann, A. T.; Raush, H. L.; Bordin, E. S.; Rigler, D.) The measurement of depth of interpretation. J consult Psychol 1955, 19:247-253. In Goldstein, A. P. & Dean, S. J. *The Investigation of Psychotherapy*, NY: Wiley 1966, 120-126

See Salzman, Leonard F.

HASELHOFF, OTTO W.

76363 Zur Soziologie psychoanalytischen Wissens. [On the sociology of psychoanalytical knowledge.] Köl Z Soziol Soz-psychol 1962, 14:40-58

HASKELL, D.

76363A (& Pugatch, D.; McNair, D. M.) Time-limited psychotherapy for whom. Arch gen Psychiat 1969, 21:546-552

HASKEL, MARTIN R.

76364 Socioanalysis and psychoanalysis. Group PT 1962, 15:105-113

HASKELL, R. E.

76365 The analogic and psychoanalytic theory. R 1968-69, 55:662-680

HASSEL, L.

See Eisenbud, Jule

HASSENFELD, IRWIN N.

See Hollender, Marc H.

HASTIE, E. L.

See Chafetz, Morris E.

HASTINGS, DONALD WILSON

76366 The clinical management of depression. Curr psychiat Ther 1961, 1: 112-116

76367 A Doctor Speaks on Sexual Expression in Marriage. Boston: Little, Brown 1966, xvii + 613 p

76368 Impotence and Frigidity. Boston: Little, Brown & Co 1963; NY: Dell Publ 1966, ix + 144 p

HATFIELD, JOHN S.

76369 (& Ferguson, L. R.; Alpert, R.) Mother-child interaction and the socialization process. Child Devel 1967, 38:365-414

HATTERER, LAWRENCE J.

76370 The Artist in Society. Problems and Treatment of the Creative Personality. NY: Grove Pr 1965, 188 p
Rv Weissman, P. Q 1967, 36:310-311

76371 Psychiatric treatment of creative work block. Psychiat Q 1960, 34:634-647

76372 A psychotherapeutic dimension: creative identity. Curr psychiat Ther 1965, 5:112-118

76373 Work identity: a psychotherapeutic dimension. P 1966, 122:1284-1286

HAU, EGON C.

76374 Familienneurose und Familientherapie. Besprechung neuer psychoanalytischer Ergebnisse von W. Grotjahn. Teil II: Behandlungstechnische Aspekte der psychoanalytischen Familientherapie. [Family neurosis and family therapy. Discussion of new psychoanalytic results of W. Grotjahn. Part II: Technical aspect of treatment in psychoanalytic family therapy.] Z PSM 1964, 10:145-152; 221-227

HAU, ELISABETH M.

76375 Psychologische Aspekte zum Übergang von der Grundschule zur Oberschule. [Psychological aspects concerning the passage from elementary school to high school.] Prax Kinderpsychol 1965, 14:117-122

76376 Das Schmuckbedürfnis des Menschen: Ethnologische, psychologische und psychoanalytische Aspekte. [Man's need for adornment: ethnological, psychological and psychoanalytic aspects.] Z PSM 1968, 14:211-221

76377 Die soziologische Theorie David Riesmans und ihre Beziehung zur Psychoanalyse. [David Riesman's sociological theory and its relation to psychoanalysis.] Prax Kinderpsychol 1964, 13:311-316

HAU, THEODOR F.

76378 Entwicklung und Weiterentwicklung der analytischen Ich-Psychologie. [Development and further development of the analytical ego psychology.] Z PSM 1962, 8:54-63

76379 Ermüdungserscheinungen in der psychoanalytischen Behandlungssituation. [Symptoms of fatigue during the pyschoanalytic treatment situation.] Psychother Psychosom 1966, 14:323-328

76380 Frühkindliches Schicksal und Neurose. Schizoide und depressive Neurose-Erkrankungen als Folge frühkindlicher Erlebnisschäden in der Kriegszeit. [Destiny and Neurosis in Early Childhood. Schizoid and Neurotic-Depressive Illnesses as a Result of Destructive Experiences in Early Childhood in Wartime.] Göttingen: Verlag für Medizinische Psychologie 1968, 153 p

76381 Eine grundlegend pathogenetische Motivation bei Patienten mit Angina pectoris vasomotorica. [A fundamental pathogenetical motivation in patients with angina pectoris vasomotorica.] Z PSM 1967, 13:234-236

76382 Ich-Organisation und die Struktur des Erlebens. [The organization of the ego and the structure of the inner experience.] Z PSM 1965, 11: 119-128

76383 Die Ich-Psychologie im Sinne der Psychoanalyse Schultz-Henckes. [Ego-psychology in the psychoanalytical perspective of Schultz-Hencke.] Prax Kinderpsychol 1961, 10:288-292

76384 Indikation und Prognose in der Psychotherapie. [Indication and prognosis in psychotherapy.] Psychol Rsch 1964, 15:220-224

76385 Neurotische Abwehr und Symptomatik. [Neurotic defense and symptomatology.] Z Psychother med Psychol 1964, 14:148-152

76386 Psychoanalytische Behandlungstechnik. [Psychoanalytic treatment technique.] Z PSM 1959-60, 6:109-110

76387 (& Rüppell, A.) Psychodynamik bei Koronarerkrankungen. [Psychodynamics in coronary diseases.] Med Klin 1966, 61:369-371

76388 Psychodynamische Faktoren bei Angina pectoris. [Psychodynamic factors in angina pectoris.] Z PSM 1964, 10:26-36

76389 Psychosomatische und psychotherapeutische Gesichtsspunkte bei Schlafstörungen. [Psychosomatic and psychotherapeutic comments on sleep disturbances.] Z PSM 1967, 13:190-195

76390 Die spezifischen Widerstände in der Behandling einer Zwangsneurose. [Specific resistance in the treatment of an obsessional neurosis.] Z PSM 1966, 12:119-128

76391 Stationäre Psychotherapie: ihre Indikationen und ihre Anforderungen an die psychoanalytische Technik. [Stationary psychotherapy: indications and requirements on the psychoanalytic technic.] Z PSM 1968, 14:116-125

76392 Strukturwandel de Neurosen Jugendlicher nach dem Kriege. [Structural changes in neuroses of young people after the war.] Z Psychother med Psychol 1965, 15:208-210

76393 Über die Einstellung der russischen Psychologie zur Psychoanalyse. [On the attiture of Russian psychology towards psychoanalysis.] Z PSM 1960, 7:37-44

HAUBEN, ROBERT

76394 Hans Van Meegeren: a study of forgery. BMC 1967, 31:164-175

HAUCK, PAUL ANTHONY

See Armstrong, Renate G.

HAUG, ELSIE
See Koff, Robert H.

HAUGK, EDNA
See Simmons, James E.

HAUPTMAN, BRUCE
76395 (& Glick, I. D.) Auditory hallucinations with imipramine. J Hillside Hosp 1968, 17:32-34

HAUSER, ANDRÉE
S-48545 La doctrine d'Adler.
        The doctrine of Adler. Problems in Psa 69-87

See Raclot, Marcel

HAUSER, E. WILLIAM
76396 Process problems in community psychiatry. P 1969, 126:112-116

HAUSMAN, C. R.
76397 Creativity and self-deception. J existent Psychiat 1967, 7:295-308

HAUTMANN, GIOVANNI
76398 Discussion of Fornari, F. "La psychanalyse de la guerre." RFPsa 1966, 30:289
76399 Discussion of Muratori, A. M. "Sogni di progresso et sogni di regresso nella pratica psicoanalitica." Riv Psa 1963, 9:127

HAVEL, JOAN
See Holt, Robert R.

HAVELKA, JAROSLAV
76400 The Nature of the Creative Process. A Psychological Study. The Hague: Martinus Nijhoff 1968, xiii + 230 p
        Rv Slochower, H. Am Im 1969, 26:86-87

HAVENS, LESTON L.
76401 Charcot and hysteria. JNMD 1965, 141:505-516
76402 Karl Jaspers and American psychiatry. P 1967, 124:66-70
76403 Main currents of psychiatric development. Int J Psychiat 1968, 5:288-327
76404 Pierre Janet. JNMD 1966, 143:383-398
76405 The placement and movement of hallucinations in space: phenomenology and theory. J 1962, 43:426-435
        Abs EVN Q 1965, 34:307

76406   Preface to Grant, V. W. *This is Mental Illness*, Boston: Beacon Pr 1963, 1966

See Bullard, Dexter M., Jr.

HAVIGHURST, ROBERT J.
See Peck, Robert F.

HAVLICEK, Z.

76407   [Authenticity and role of regressive experiences during analytical LSD psychotherapy.] (Cz) Ceskoslov Psychiat 1964, 236-240

76408   [Contribution to the dynamics of "lucid" dreams.] Ceskoslov Psychiat 1966, 62:309-315

HAWARD, LIONEL R. C.

76409   Some psychological aspects of pregnancy. Midwives Chron 1968, 81: 112-113; 274-275; 320; 350-351; 394-395; 418; 1969, 82:336-337

76410   The subjective meaning of stress. M 1960, 33:185-194

HAWELKA, ELZA RIBEIRO

76411   Discussion [Changement individuel et processus analytique.] Bull Ass psa Fran 1967, No. 3

TRANSLATIONS OF:
Garma, A. [46980]. Heiman, P. [48629]. Segal H. [90262].

HAWKINS, DAVID R.

76412   The gap between the psychiatrist and other physicians. PSM 1962, 24: 94

76413   (& Monroe, J. T., Jr.; Clarke, M. G.; Vernon, C. R.) Group psychotherapy as a method for the study of affects. In *The International Handbook of Group Psychotherapy*, Phil Libr & Int Council of Group Psychotherapy 1966

76414   Implications for psychoanalytic theory of psychophysiologic sleep research. (abs) Med psicosom 1967, 12:290

76415   (& Mora, G.; Vernon, C. R.; Monroe, J. T., Jr.; Sandifer, M. G.) An integrated teaching program between the department of psychiatry and the basic sciences. J med Educ 1958, 33:483

76416   (& Sandifer, M. G.; Vernon, C. R.; Monroe, J. T.) Psychological and physiological responses to continuous epinephrine infusion—an approach to the study of the affect, anxiety. In West, L. J. & Greenblatt, M. *Psychiatric Research Reports* of the American Psychiatric Association, Explorations in Physiology of Emotions 1960

76417   (& Mendels, J.) The psychophysiological investigation of sleep in patients with depression. Proc IV World Cong Psychiat 1966, 1893-1897

76418   A review of psychoanalytic dream theory in the light of recent psychophysiological studies of sleep and dreaming. M 1966, 39:85-104

Abs JCS RFPsa 1967, 31:326

See Mendels, Joe

HAWORTH, MARY R.

76419 The CAT: Facts about Fantasy. NY: Grune & Stratton, 1966, xii +
322 p
76420 (Ed) Child Psychotherapy. Practice and Theory. Forty-Five Specialists
Discuss the Major Theoretical and Methodological Approaches. NY/
London: Basic Books 1964, vii + 459 p
Psicoterapia Infantile. Rome: Armando Editore 1967, 580 p
Rv Bussel, L. R. Q 1965, 34:453-456. Hood, J. J 1965, 46:396
76421 The children's apperception test: its use in developmental assessments
of normal children. J proj Tech 1968, 32:405
76422 Parental loss in children as reflected in projective responses. J proj
Tech 1964, 28:31-45
76423 (& Menolascino, F. J.) Some aspects of psychotic behavior in young
children. Arch gen Psychiat 1968, 18:355-359
76424 (& Keller, M. J.) The use of food in the diagnosis and therapy of emotionally disturbed children. J Amer Acad Child Psychiat 1962, 1:548-
563
76425 (& Keller, M. J.) The use of food in therapy. In author's *Child Psychotherapy* 330-338
Über das Essen in der Therapiestunde. Hbh Kinderpsychother 510-
517

See Rabin, Albert I.

HAYCOX, JAMES A.

76426 Discussion of Christ, J. "Psychoanalytical treatment of a dissociative
state with hallucinations." Int Psychiat Clin 1968, 5(1):60-64

HAYES, RICHARD

76427 Marital interaction. Psa Forum 1967, 2:282

HAYES, ROBERT C.

See Nesbitt, Robert E. L., Jr.

HAYLETT, CLARICE H.

76428 (& Rapoport, L.) Mental health consultation. In Bellak, L. *Handbook
in Community Psychiatry*, NY: Grune & Stratton 1963, 319-339

See Estes, Hubert R.

HAYLEY, T. T. S.

76429 The Anatomy of Lango Religion and Groups. Cambridge: Univ Pr
1947, 207 p

HAYMAN, ANNE

76430 Psychoanalyst sub-poenaed. Lancet 1965, (Oct 6):785-786
76431 Some aspects of regression in non-psychotic puerperal breakdown. M
1962, 35:135-145
Abs JCS RFPsa 1964, 28:309

76432 Verbalization and identity. (Read at Israel Psa Soc, 9 Jan 1965) J 1965, 46:455-466

Abs EVN Q 1967, 36:625

76433 What do we mean by "id?" J Am Psa Ass 1969, 17:353-380

REVIEW OF:

76434 Schon, D. A. Invention and the Evolution of Ideas. J 1968, 49:112-113

HAYMAN, MAX

76435 Alcoholism: Mechanism and Management. Springfield, Ill: Thomas 1966, xv + 315 p

Japanese: Tokyo: Bunkodo Publ 1968

76436 Classification and spectrum of therapy of alcoholics. Postgrad Med 1966, 40:161-170

76437 Drugs—and the psychoanalyst. PT 1967, 21:644-654

76438 The effects of librium in psychiatric disorders. JNMD 1961, 22 (Suppl):60

76439 Failure of drugs in chronic alcoholism. Int J Psychiat 1967, 3:248-266

76440 The general practitioner and the alcoholic. Mind 1963, 1:198-202. Modern Med 1963, 31:186

76441 (& Ditman, K. S.) Influence of age and orientation of psychiatrists on their use of drugs. Comprehen Psychiat 1966, 7:152-165

76442 Medical, fellowship and religious resources for alcoholics. In *Proceedings of the Pacific Southwest Regional Conferences on Court Processing of Alcoholic Offenders*, Los Angeles 1965

76443 The medical practitioner, alcoholism and motivation. Calif Med 1966, 104:345-351

76444 The medical practitioner, alcoholism, and the law. J Forensic Sci 1966, 2:111-123

76445 Methods of therapy in alcoholism. Calif Med 1966, 105:117-123

76446 The myth of social drinking. P 1967, 124:585-594

76447 (& Peskin, R.) The needs of the research-oriented psychiatrist for information retrieval. Dis nerv Sys 1967, 28:798-803

76448 Science, mysticism and psychopharmacology. Calif Med 1964, 101: 266-271

S-48559 Traumatic elements in the analysis of a borderline case.

Abs SLP An Surv Psa 1957, 8:152-153

76449 The treatment of alcoholics in private practice with an antabuse-oriented program. Quart J Stud Alcohol 1965, 26:460-467

See Ditman, Keith S.

ABSTRACTS OF:

76450 Greenson, R. R. On enthusiasm. Bull Phila Ass Psa 1961, 11:138-141

76451 Greenson, R. R. Special technical problems in handling transference during analysis. Bull Phila Ass Psa 1962, 12:47-49

76452 Walsh, M. N. Notes on the neurosis of Leonardo da Vinci. Bull Phila Ass Psa 1961, 11:95-97

76453 Walsh, M. N. Psychoanalytic studies on war. Bull Phila Ass Psa 1962, 12:129-131

HAYNAL, ANDRÉ

76454 Contributions à l'étude de la notion de "force du moi." [Contributions to the study of the notion of "ego-strength."] Évolut psychiat 1967, 32: 617-638
76455 Le syndrome de couvade. (Et contribution à la psychologie et psychopathologie de l'homme en face de la reproduction.) [Couvade syndrome (and a contribution to the psychology and psychopathology of men in relation to reproduction.)] Ann méd-psychol 1968, 126(1): 539-571

HAYNE, MELVIN L.

See Glad, Donald D.

HAYS, CAROLYN A.

76456 Clinical aspects of homosexuality. (Read at Los Angeles Psa Soc, 18 Nov 1965)
Abs Shane, M. Bull Phila Ass Psa 1966, 16:99-101

HAYS, DAVID SIMON

76457 Problems involved in organizing and operating a group therapy program in the New York State parole setting. Psychiat Q 1960, 34:623-633

HAYWARD, MALCOLM L.

76458 Psychotherapy based on the primary process. PT 1961, 15:419-430

HAYWARD, S. T.

REVIEW OF:
76459 Harms, E. & Schreiber, P. (Eds) Handbook of Counseling Techniques. J 1965, 46:399

HAYWOOD, T. J.

See Knight, James A.

HAZAMA, H.

76460 [Written language of schizophrenic patients.] (Jap) Jap J Psa 1963, 10(1):6-10

HAZARI, ANANDI

See Sandler, Joseph

HAZELTON, J. E.

See Kanter, Victor B.

HEADLEY, E. B.

See Pattison, E. Manuel

HEAGARTY, MARGARET C.

See Bullard, Dexter M., Jr.

HEALY, MARY TENNEY

See Healy, William

HEALY, WILLIAM

76461 (& Healy, M. T.) Pathological Lying, Accusation, and Swindling: A Study in Forensic Psychology. Montclair, N. J.: Patterson Smith 1969, x + 286 p

HEARST, ELIOT

76462 Psychology across the chessboard. Psychol Today 1967, 1:28-37

HEATH, EDGAR SHELDON

76463 (& Haoken, P. C. S.; Sainz, A. A.) Hypnotizability in state-hospitalized schizophrenics. Psychiat Q 1960, 34:65-68
76464 (& McKerracher, D. G.) Impressions of a common psychiatric entity. Canad Med Ass J 1959, 80:896-897
76465 (& Bacal, H. A.) A method of group psychotherapy at the Tavistock Clinic. Int J grp PT 1968, 18:21-30
76466 The minister as a mental health worker. Canad Psychiat Ass J 1967, 12:607-610
76467 (& Adams, A.; Wakeling, P. L. G.) Short courses of E.C.T. and simulated E.C.T. in chronic schizophenia. Brit J Psychiat 1964, 111(469): 800-807
76468 Uses and misuses of psychiatric occupational therapy: occupational therapy as a haven. Amer J occup Ther 1968, 22:19-22

See Hebb, D. O.; Malan, David H.

HEATH, HELEN A.

76469 (& Oken, D.; Korchin, S. J.; Towne, J. C.) A factor analytic study of multivariate psychosomatic changes over time. Arch gen Psychiat 1960, 3:467-477
76470 (& Oken, D.; Shipman, W. G.) Muscle tension and personality. A serious second look. Arch gen Psychiat 1967, 16:720-726

See Goldstein, Iris B.; Oken, Donald; Shipman, William G.

HEATH, ROBERT G.

76471 (& Monroe, R. R.; Lief, H. I.) The integration of psychiatric and psychoanalytic training at Tulane: a ten year overview; 1950-60. J med Educ 1961, 36:857-874
76472 (& Monroe, R. R.; Lief, H. I.) The integration of psychiatric and psychoanalytic training at Tulane: the psychoanalyst as teacher and administrator. Sci Psa 1962, 5:216-227
76473 (& Monroe, R. R.; Lief, H. I.) An international survey of the teaching

of psychiatry and mental health. WHO Public Health Pap 1961, 9:123-158

76474   (& Shelton, W. H.) The psychoanalyst's role in community mental health centers. Sci Psa 1968, 12:262-264

76475   Psychoanalytic training and community psychiatry. Sci Psa 1965, 8:268-277

See Lief, Harold I.

HEBB, D. O.

76476   Concerning imagery. Psychol Rev 1968, 75:466-477

76477   (& Heath, E. S.; Stuart, E. A.) Experimental deafness. Canad J Psychol 1954, 8:152-156

76478   The social significance of animal studies. In Lindzey, G. & Aronson, E. *The Handbook of Social Psychology*, Reading, Mass: Addison-Wesley Publ Co 1968, 729-774

HECHLER, JACOB

76479   *Accent on Form* and other works by Lancelot Law Whyte. J Otto Rank Ass 1968, 3(2):98-111

76480   Man the player. J Otto Rank Ass 1967, 2(2):97-106

HECK, E. MARJORIE

See Kronenberger, Earl J.

HEDENBERG, SVEN

76481   Strindberg's fear of dogs. Acta Psychiat Scand 1964, 40(Suppl 180): 111-113

HEDGSON, R. C.

See Zaleznik, Abraham

HEDLUND, J. L.

See Morgan, David W.

HEDRI, A.

76482   Eine Indikationserweiterung der Psychotherapie: die Unfallbereitschaft. [Extension of psychotherapeutic indication: accident proneness.] Fortschr PSM 1963, 3:154-159

HEERSEMA, PHILIP HENRY

76483   (& Fry, W. F., Jr.) Conjoint family therapy. A new dimension in psychotherapy. Top Probl PT 1963, 4:147-153

76484   Homosexuality and the physician. JAMA 1965, 195:815-817

HEGETHORN, BRITTA

76485   An elementary developmental stage and its significance for the etiology of psychoses. Acta Psychiat Scand 1968, 44(Suppl 203):189-194

HEIDER, FRITZ

76486 The Gestalt theory of motivation. In Jones, M. R. *Nebraska Symposium on Motivation, Vol. III*, Lincoln, Neb: Univ Neb Pr 1960

S-48595 On Perception and Event Structure, and the Psychological Environment.
Rv Holzman, P. S. Q 1962, 31:392-393

76487 The Psychology of Interpersonal Relations. NY: John Wiley & Sons 1967, ix + 322 p

HEIDER, GRACE MOORE

76488 The mark of the beast. J Hist behav Sci 1969, 5:266-267

76489 Vulnerabilities, sources of strength, and capacity to cope in the "normal" child. Proc XIV Int Cong Appl Psychol, Copenhagen: Munksgaard 1961, 79-94

76490 Vulnerability in infants. BMC 1960, 24:104-115

76491 Vulnerability in infants and young children. A pilot study. Genet Psychol Monogr 1966, 73:1-216

76492 What makes a good parent? Children 1960, 7:207-213

See Escalona, Sibylle K.

HEIDRICH, R.

76493 [On some experiences with autogenous training and hypnosis in teaching and practices.] (Ger) Ger Deutsch Gesundh 1959, 14:902-906

HEIDTKE, P.

76493A [Don Quixotism—an aspect of the male neglect.] (Ger) Prax Kinderpsychol 1969, 18:66-71

HEIGL, FRANZ S.

76494 Die analytische Gruppenpsychotherapie im Heim: Indikation und Prognose. [Analytical group psychotherapy in the institution: indication and prognosis.] Prax Kinderpsychol 1963, 12:115-122; 1964, 13: 113-116; 1965, 14:46-51

76495 Factores de eficacia en la terapia psicoanalítica. [Efficiency factors in psychoanalytic therapy.] Rev Psicoanál Psiquiat Psicol 1967, 7:67-80

76496 Franz Alexander. In Memoriam. Z PSM 1965, 11:1

76497 Die Gegenübertragungsangst und ihre Bedeutung. [Counter-transference anxiety and its meaning.] Z PSM 1959-60, 6:29-35

S-48599 Die Handhabung der Gegenübertragung in der analytischer Psychotherapie.
Abs Spiegel, N. An Surv Psa 1958, 9:401-402

76498 Die humanistische Psychoanalyse Erich Fromms. [The humanistic psychoanalysis of Erich Fromm.] Z PSM 1961, 7:77-84; 153-161; 235-249

76499 Persönlichkeitsstruktur und Prognose. Z PSM 1964, 10:102-114
Personality structure and prognosis in psychoanalytic treatment. Contempo Psa 1966, 2(2):151-167

76500 Ein prognostisch entscheidender Charakterzug bei verwahrlosten Jugendlichen. [A prognostically significant character trait in neglected adolescents.] Prax Kinderpsychol 1962, 11:197-201

76501 Prognostische Kriterien in der Psychotherapie. [Prognostic criteria in psychotherapy.] Z PSM 1966, 12:196-203

76502 Psychosomatische Medizin und psychoanalytische Behandlungsmethoden. Bericht über die Internationale Arbeitstagung der Deutschen Psychoanalytischen Gesellschaft des Internationalen Forums für Psychoanalyse vom 29. August bis 1. September 1968 in Göttingen. [Psychosomatic medicine and psychoanalytic methods of therapy. Report on the International Workshop of the German Psychoanalytic Society of the International Forum for Psychoanalysis August 29 to September 1, 1968 in Göttengen.] Z PSM 1969, 15:62-69

76503 Über Bedeutung and Behandlung der Gegenübertragung. Literaturübersicht und grundsätzliche Gesichtspunkte. [The importance and treatment of countertransference. A review of the literature and basic points of view.] Z PSM 1960, 6:110-123

76504 Über eine spezielle Gegenübertragungsreaktion in der psychoanalytischen Behandlung. [On a special countertransference reaction in psychoanalytic treatment.] Z PSM 1963, 9:41-50

76505 Was ist wirksam in der psychoanalytischen Therapie? [What is effective in psychoanalytic therapy?] Z PSM 1966, 12:282-292

76506 Zur Handhabung der Gegenübertragung. [On the management of countertransference.] Fortschr Psa 1966, 2:124-139

76507 Zur Psychodynamik der Lernstörungen. [On the psychodynamics of learning difficulties.] Z PSM 1969, 15:239-251

76508 Zur Toleranzgrenze. [On the limitations of tolerance.] Z PSM 1965, 11:64-66

HEIGL-EVERS, ANNELIESE

76509 Aggressivität als Abwehrmechanismus. Die Identifizierung mit dem Angreifer. [Aggression as a defense mechanism. The identification with the aggressor.] Z PSM 1965, 11:91-104

76510 (& Laux, G.) Angst und Aggression in der Gruppe. [Fear and aggression in the group.] Z PSM 1968, 14:137-147

76511 Die "dienende Magd"—ein Charaktertyp. Struktur und psychoanalytische Therapie einer Charakterneurose. [The "maidservant"—a character type. Structure and psychoanalytic therapy of a character neurosis.] Z PSM 1965, 11:281-295
La "mujer servil"—un tipo de carácter: extructura y terapia psicoanalítica de un carácter neurótico. Rev. Psicoanál Psiquiat Psicol 1967, 5:34-54

76512 Einige psychogenetische und psychodynamische Zusammenhänge beim Krankheitsbild des endogenen Ekzems. [Some psychogenetic and psychodynamic connections in the clinical picture of endogenous eczema.] Z PSM 1966, 12:163-178

76513 Einige technische Prinzipien der analytischen Gruppenpsychotherapie. [A few technical principles of analytic group psychotherapy.] Z PSM 1968, 14:282-291

76514 Gruppendynamik und die Position des Therapeuten. [Group dynamics and the position of the therapist.] Z PSM 1967, 13:31-38

76515 Die Rolle der Kränkung bei Ehekonflikten und daraus resultierende Beratungsprobleme. Beitrag zur Eheberatung in tiefenpsychologischer Sicht. [The role of grievance in marital conflicts and the counseling problems that it raises. Depth psychology in marriage counseling.] Prax Kinderpsychol 1967, 16:33-41

76516 Trauminterpretation in der analytischen Behandlung. [Dream interpretation in the analytic treatment.] Z PSM 1960, 7:193-204

76517 Die Übertragungsinterpretation des Traumes. Die Frage der Indikation, überprüft an kasuistischem Material. [The transference interpretation of the dream. The problem of indication, examined from case material.] Z PSM 1962, 8:195-205

76518 Zum sozialen Effekt klinischer analytischer Gruppenpsychotherapie. [The social effect of clinical analytic group psychotherapy.] Psychother Psychosom 1969, 17:50-62

76519 Zur Behandlungstechnik in der analytischen Gruppentherapie. [Therapeutic technique in analytical group therapy.] Z PSM 1967, 13:266-276

76520 Zur Frage der hysterischen Abwehrmechanismen, dargestellt an kasuistischem Material. [On the problem of the hysterical defense mechanisms presented on case reports.] Z PSM 1967, 13:116-130

HEIJNINGEN, H. KITS VAN

76521 (& Treuerniet, N.) Psychodynamic factors in myocardial infarction. (Read at Int Psa Cong, July 1965) J 1966, 47:370-374
Abs Garma, A. Rev Psicoanál 1967, 24:219

HEILBRUN, ALFRED B., JR.

76522 Cognitive sensitivity to aversive maternal stimulation in late-adolescent males. J consult clin Psychol 1968, 32:326-332

76523 Conformity to masculinity-feminity stereotypes and ego identity in adolescents. Psychol Rep 1964, 14:351-357

76524 (& Orr, H. K.) Maternal childbearing control history and subsequent cognitive and personality functioning of the offspring. Psychol Rep 1965, 17:259-272

76525 The measurement of identification. Child Develpm 1965, 36:112-127

76526 (& Fromme, D. K.) Parental identification of late adolescents and level of adjustment: the importance of parent-model attributes, ordinal position, and sex of the child. J genet Psych 1965, 107:49-59

76527 Parental model attributes, nurturant reinforcement, and consistency of behavior in adolescents. Child Develpm 1964, 35:151-167

76528 Perceived maternal attitudes, masculinity-femininity of the maternal model, and identification as related to incipient psychopathology in adolescent girls. J gen Psychol 1964, 70:33-40

76529 (& Orr, H. K.) Perceived maternal childbearing history and subsequent motivational effects of failure. J genet Psych 1966, 109:75-89

76530 (& Harrell, S. N.; Gillard, B. J.) Perceived maternal child-rearing patterns and the effects of social non-reaction upon achievement motivation. Child Develpm 1967, 38:267-281

76531 (& Gillard, B. J.; Harrell, S. N.) Perceived maternal rejection and cognitive interference. J child Psychol Psychiat 1965, 6:233-242

76532 (& Hall, C. L.) Resource mediation in childhood and identification. J child Psychol Psychiat 1964, 5:139-149
76533 Sex differences in identification learning. J genet Psych 1965, 106:185-193
76534 Sex role, instrumental-expressive behavior and psychopathology in females. JAbP 1968, 73:131-136
76535 Social value: social behavior consistency, parental identification, and aggression in late adolescence. J genet Psych 1964, 104:135-146

HEILBRUN, E.

76536 (Reporter) Reports of discussions of acting out—German language section. J 1968, 49:228
       Abs LHR Q 1969, 38:668

HEILBRUNN, GERT

76537 Advances in psychoanalytic therapy. Curr psychiat Ther 1962, 2:19-29
76538 Balance. J sch Health 1968, 38:18-26
S-48605 The basic fear.
       Abs An Surv Psa 1955, 6:86-88
S-48606 Comments on a common form of acting out.
       Abs ARK An Surv Psa 1958, 9:408-409
76539 Comments on adolescent drug users. N West Med 1967, May:457-460
76540 How "cool" is the beatnik? Psa Forum 1967, 2:32-39; 52-54; 379-380
       Abs Cuad Psa 1967, 3:318
76541 Letter to the editors [re Devereux's "Cannibalistic Impulses"]. Psa Forum 1966, 1:233-234
76542 The neurobiologic aspect of three psychoanalytic concepts. Comprehen Psychiat 1961, 2:261-268
76543 Objectivity in psychiatry. Comprehen psychiat 1964, 5:219-231
76544 On sharing. PT 1967, 21:750-756
S-48610 On weeping.
       Abs Surv Psa 1955, 6:160-162
76545 Psychoanalysis of yesterday, today, and tomorrow. Arch gen Psychiat 1961, 4:321-330
       Abs KR Q 1962, 31:428
76546 Results with psychoanalytic therapy and professional commitment. PT 1966, 20:89-99
76547 Results with psychoanalytic therapy (report of 241 cases). PT 1963, 17:427-435

HEILIG, S. M.

See Farberow, Norman L.; Litman, Robert E.

HEILIZER, F.

76548 An exploration of the relationship between hypnotizability and anxiety and/or neuroticism. J consult Psychol 1960, 24:432-436

HEILMEYER, L.

* * * Foreword to Clauser, G. Psychotherapie-Fibel, Stuttgart: Thieme 1963

HEIM, EDGAR

76549 (& Constantine, H.; Knapp, P. H.; Graham, W. G. B.; Globus, G. G.; Vachon, L.; Nemetz, S. J.) Airways resistance and emotional state in bronchial asthma. PSM 1967, 29:450-467

76550 (& Knapp, P. H.; Vachon, L.; Globus, G. G.) Emotion, breathing and speech. J psychosom Res 1968, 12:261-274

76551 (& Vachon, L.; Knapp, P. H.) Emotional influence on breathing during speech. Proc IV World Cong Psychiat 1966, 2718-2720

HEIMAN, MARCEL

76552 Comment on Dr. Stoller's paper, "A further contribution to the study of gender identity." (Read at Int Psa Cong, July 1967) J 1968, 49:368-369

76553 Discussion of Sherfey's paper on female sexuality. J Am Psa Ass 1968, 16:406-416

76554 Female sexuality: introduction. (Read at Am Psa Ass, 6 May 1967) J Am Psa Ass 1968, 16:565-568

76555 (& Kleegman, S. J.) Insemination: a psychoanalytic and infertility study. Fertility & Sterility 1966, 17:117-125

76556 Obituary: Laci Fessler: 1897-1965. Q 1965, 34:629

76557 (& Moore, B. F.; Joseph, E. D.) A pre-examination of the significance of clitoral versus vaginal orgasm. (Read at NY Psa Soc, 12 Mar 1968) Abs Ennis, J. Q 1969, 38:517

S-48617 The problem of family diagnosis. Abs CK An Surv Psa 1956, 7:155-156

76558 Psychoanalytic observations on the relationship of pet and man. Vet Med 1965, 60:713-718

76559 Psychoanalytic view of pregnancy. In Rovinsky, J. J. & Guttmacher, A. F. *Medical, Surgical, and Gynecologic Complications of Pregnancy*, Baltimore: Williams & Wilkins 1960, 1965, 473-511

S-48621 The relationship between man and dog. Abs SO An Surv Psa 1956, 7:162-164

76560 (& Levitt, E. G.) The role of separation and depression in out-of-wedlock pregnancy. Ops 1960, 30:166-174

76561 Sexual response in women: a correlation of physiological findings with psychoanalytic concepts. (Read at Am Psa Ass, Dec 1960; at NY Psa Soc, 11 Apr 1961) J Am Psa Ass 1963, 11:360-385 Abs RGS Q 1961, 30:615-616. JBi Q 1964, 33:138-139

See Kaufman, M. Ralph

TRANSLATIONS OF:
Grote, L. R. & Meng, H. [12754]; Weizäcker, V. von [34432]

REVIEWS OF:

76562 Kronhausen, P. & Kronhausen, E. The Sexually Responsive Woman. Q 1966, 35:305-307

76563 Rheingold, J. C. The Fear of Being a Woman: A Theory of Maternal Destructiveness. Q 1968, 37:617-620

HEIMAN, NANETTE

76564 (& Cooper, S.) An experiment in clinical integration. J Hillside Hosp 1959, 8:290-297
76565 Oedipus at Colonus. A study of old age and death. Am Im 1962, 19:91-98

HEIMANN, PAULA

76566 Bemerkungen zum Arbeitsbegriff in der Psychoanalyse. [Comments on the concept of "work" in psychoanalysis.] Psyche 1966, 20:321-361
76567 Comment on Dr. Katan's and Dr. Meltzer's papers. "Fetishism, splitting of the ego, and denial" and "The differentiation of somatic delusions from hypochondria" respectively. (Read at Int Psa Cong, July-Aug 1963) J 1964, 45:251-253
     Abs EVN Q 1966, 35:458-459
76568 Comment on Dr. Kernberg's paper. (Read at Int Psa Cong, July 1965) J 1966, 47:254-260
76569 Counter-transference. M 1960, 33:9-15
     Bemerkungen zur Gegenübertragung. Psyche 1962, 16:483-493
     Acerca de la contratransferencia. Rev urug Psa 1961-62, 4:129-136; 137-149
     Abs IH Q 1961, 30:151-152
76570 The curative factors in psycho-analysis. J 1962, 43:228-231
     Abs RLG Q 1963, 32:598-599
76571 Discussion of Gitelson, M. "La première phase de la psychanalyse." RFPsa 1963, 27:467-475
S-48629 Dynamics of transference interpretation.
     Dynamique des interprétations de transfert. (Tr: Hawelka, E. R.) Bull Ass psa Fran 1969, No. 5:159-178
     Abs SLP An Surv Psa 1956, 7:335-336
76572 Entwicklungssprünge und das Auftreten der Grausamkeit. [Breaks in development and the appearance of cruelty.] In Mitscherlich, A. Bis Hierher und nicht weiter, Munich: R. Piper 1969, 104-118
76573 The evaluation of applicants for psychoanalytic training. J 1968, 49:527-539
76574 Gedanken zum Erkenntnisprozess des Psychoanalytikers. [Reflections on the cognitive process of the psychoanalyst.] Psyche 1969, 23:2-24
     Abs J 1969, 50:401
76575 Notes on the anal stage. J 1962, 43:406-414
     Bemerkungen zur analen Phase. Psyche 1962, 16:420-439
     Notas sobre la etapa anal. Rev Psicoanál 1969, 26:181-200
     Abs EVN Q 1965, 34:307
76576 Obituary: Joan Riviere 1883-1962. (Read at Brit Psa Soc, 3 Oct 1962) J 1963, 44:230-233

REVIEW OF:
76577 Parker, B. My Language is Me. Psychotherapy With a Disturbed Adolescent. J 1964, 45:593-597

HEIMS, LORA W.

See Kaufman, Irving

HEINE, RALPH W.

76578 (& Trosman, H.) Initial expectations of the doctor-patient interaction as a factor in continuance in psychotherapy. Ps 1960, 23:275-278
    Abs HRB Q 1961, 30:300
76579 (Ed) The Student Physician as Psychotherapist. Chicago: Univ Chicago Pr 1962, 241 p

See Wepman, Joseph M.

HEINICKE, CHRISTOPH M.

76580 (& Westheimer, I. J.) Brief Separations. (Foreword: Bowlby, J.) NY: IUP; London: Longmans 1965, xi + 355 p
    Abs J Am Psa Ass 1967, 15:220-221. Rv Stone, F. J 1967, 48:330-331. McDevitt, J. B. Q 1968, 37:297-298
76581 Frequency of psychotherapeutic session as a factor affecting outcome: analysis of clinical ratings and test results. JAbP 1969, 74:533-560
76582 (& Afterman, J.; Bradley, M.; Kaplan, L.; Korner, A. F.; Moore, J.) Frequency of psychotherapeutic session as a factor affecting the child's developmental status. Psa St C 1965, 20:42-98
76583 Notes on the strategy of a child psychotherapy project. Reiss-Davis Clin Bull 1965, 2:80-86

HEINRICH, J.-P.

See Lanter, R.

HEINRICH, JEROME F.

See Seward, Georgene H.

HEINSTEIN, MARTIN I.

76584 Behavioural correlates of breast-bottle regimes under varying parent-infant relationships. Lafayette, Indiana: Child Development Publ, Purdue Univ 1963, 61 p
76585 Influence of breast feeding on children's behavior. Children 1963, 10(March): 93-97

HEINZE, SHIRLEY J.

See Offer, Daniel; Stein, Morris I.

HEISER, KARL F.

76586 (& Wolman, B. B.) Mental deficiencies. In Wolman, B. B. *Handbook of Clinical Psychology*, NY: McGraw-Hill 1965, 838-854

HEISLER, IVAN C. F.

ABSTRACTS OF:
76587 Culpin, M. The conception of nervous disorder. Q 1963, 32:141-142
76588 Eder, M. D. The myth of progress. Q 1963, 32:141-142
76589 Fordham, M. Countertransference. Q 1961, 30:151
76590 Freeman, T. Clinical and theoretical notes on chronic schizophrenia. Q 1961, 30:152-153

76591   Glover, E. Psychoanalysis and psychotherapy. Q 1961, 30:153
76592   Glover, E. The psychology of the psychotherapist. Q 1963, 32:141-142
76593   Glover, J. Divergent tendencies in psychotherapy. Q 1963, 32:141-142
76594   Guntrip, H. Ego weakness and the hard core of the problem of psychotherapy. Q 1961, 30:608-609
76595   Guntrip, H. The schizoid problem, regression, and the struggle to preserve an ego. Q 1962, 31:431
76596   Hadfield, J. A. The reliability of infantile memoires. Q 1963, 32:141-142
76597   Hart, B. The concept of dissociation. Q 1963, 32:141-142
76598   Heimann, P. Countertransference. Q 1961, 30:151-152
76599   Hinkle, L. E. Ecological observations of the relation of physical illness, mental illness, and the social environment. Q 1962, 31:427
76600   Inman, W. S. Can a blow cause cancer? Q 1962, 31:431-432
76601   Ittelson, W. H. et al: Some perceptual differences in somatizing and nonsomatizing neuropsychiatric patients. Q 1962, 31:426
76602   Leveton, A. F. Reproach: the art of shamesmanship. Q 1963, 32:142
76603   Little, M. Countertransference. Q 1961, 30:152
76604   McGhie, A. A comparative study of the mother-child relationship in schizophrenia. I. The interview. II. Psychological testing. Q 1962, 31:431
76605   Meyer, B. C. et al: A clinical study of psychiatric and psychological aspects of mitral surgery. Q 1962, 31:425-426
76606   Money-Kryle, R. E. On prejudice: a psychoanalytical approach. Q 1961, 30:609
76607   Ross, T. A. Some difficulties in analytical theory and practice. Q 1963, 32:141-142
76608   Ruesch, J. Psychosomatic medicine and the behavioral sciences. Q 1962, 31:426
76609   Sandler, J. Psychology and psychoanalysis. Q 1963, 32:142
76610   Searles, H. F. Phases of the patient-therapist interaction in the psychotherapy of chronic schizophrenia. Q 1962, 31:430-431
76611   Strauss, R. Countertransference. Q 1961, 30:152
76612   Weisman, A. D. & Hackett, T. P. Predilection to death. Q 1962, 31:426
76613   Winnicott, D. W. Countertransference. Q 1961, 30:152

HEISS, H. W.

76613A [Accident prevention as the task of preventive medicine.] (Ger) Psychother Psychosom 1968, 16:256-260

HEISS, R.

See Görres, Albert

HEKIMIAN, LEON J.

See Alpert, Murray; Frosch, William A.

HEKMAT, H.

See Phelan, Joseph G.

HELD, RENÉ R.

76614 Contribution à l'étude psychanalytique du phénomène religieux [Contribution to the psychoanalytic study of the religious phenomenon.] RFPsa 1962, 26:211-266
    Abs Galdo, A. M. Riv Psa 1965, 11:76
S-48650 Les critères de la fin du traitement psychanalytique.
    Abs An Surv Psa 1955, 6:351-352

76615 De la Psychanalyse à la Medecine Psychosomatique. [From Psychoanalysis to Psychosomatic Medicine.] (Pref: Gilbert-Dreyfus) Paris: Payot 1968

76616 De la singularité de structure obsessionnelle aux nécessités techniques impliquées par cette singularité. [The peculiarity of the obsessional pattern: technical requirements and necessities.] RFPsa 1961, 25:319-332
    Abs Auth Rev Psicoanál 1962, 19:284. RJA Q 1962, 31:432-433

76617 Discussion of Alvim, F. "Troubles de l'identification et image corporelle." RFPsa 1962, 26(Spec. No.):85-101

76618 Discussion of Kestemberg, J. "A propos de la relation érotomanique." RFPsa 1962, 26:590

76619 Discussion of Lebovici, S. "Colloque sur les interprétations en thérapeutique psychanalytique." RFPsa 1962, 26:53

76620 Discussion of Pasche, F. "Freud et l'orthodoxie judéochrétienne." RFPsa 1961, 25:82-84

76621 Discussion of Pasche, F. "On depression." RFPsa 1963, 27:216-220

76622 Discussion of Racamier, P. C. "Propos sur la réalité dans la théorie psychanalytique." RFPsa 1962, 26:709-710

76623 Discussion of Rouart, J. "La temporisation comme maitrise et comme défense." RFPsa 1962, 26:418

76624 Discussion of Viderman, S. "De l'instinct de mort." RFPsa 1961, 25:115-117

76625 [Emergency psychotherapy of "passionate amorous crises."] (Fr) Sem Ther 1961, 37:728-732

76626 Hypnotisme, hystérie, relaxation: mythes et réalités. [Hypnotism, hysteria, relaxation: myths and realities.] In Lassner, J. *Hypnosis and Psychosomatic Medicine*, Berlin/Heidelberg/NY: Springer 1967, 135-142

76627 L'insomnie névrotique [Neurotic insomnia.] Évolut psychiat 1960, 25:1-61

76628 [Minor medicopsychosomatic clinical information.] (Fr) Rev Méd psychosom 1967, 9:203-215

76629 Obituary: Odette Laurent-Lucas-Championnère. RFPsa 1964, 28:637-638
S-48662 Psychanalyse et médicine.
    Abs WAF An Surv Psa 1956, 7:196-197

76630 [Psychopharmacology and psychotherapy in psychosomatic medicine.] Rev Méd psychosom 1961, 3(3):29-35
    Abs RJA Q 1962, 31:436

76631 Psychothérapie et Psychanalyse. [Psychotherapy and psychoanalysis.] Paris: Payot 1968, 316 p

76632 [Psychotherapy of preoperative anxiety.] (Fr) Sem Ther 1961, 37:623-626

76633 [Psychotherapy of psychoanalytic orientation and maintenance psycho-
       therapy.] (Fr) Sem Ther 1963, 39:198-202
76634 Rapport Clinique sur les Psychothérapies d'Inspiration Psychanalytique
       Freudienne. [Clinical Report on Psychotherapies of the Freudian Psy-
       choanalytic Inspiration.] Paris: PUF 1963, 163 p. RFPsa 1964-65,
       28(Suppl):225-460
76635 Training in psychosomatic research. PSM 1967, 5:126-137

       See Gilbert-Dreyfus; Nacht, Sacha

HELD, TILO

76636 Das analytische Psychodrama. [Analytic psychodrama.] Z PSM 1969,
       15:287-295

HELDT, THOMAS J.

76637 Responsibility of psychiatry in alcoholism. Dis nerv Sys 1965, 26:446-
       461

HELLER, JUDITH BERNAYS

76638 Freud's mother and father: a memoir. Commentary 1956, 21(5):May

HELLER, KENNETH

76639 Ambiguity in the interview interaction. In Shlien, J. M. et al: *Research
       in Psychotherapy*, Vol. III, Wash DC: APA 1968, 242-259
76640 (& Myers, R. A.; Kline, L. V.) Interviewer behavior as a function of
       standardized client roles. J consult Psychol 1963, 27:117-122. In Gold-
       stein, A. P. & Dean, S. J. *The Investigation of Psychotherapy*, NY:
       Wiley 1966, 398-403

       See Goldstein, Arnold P.

HELLER, LOUIS G.

       See Burton, Arthur; Gorman, Warren F.

HELLER, MELVIN S.

76641 The influence of law on the psychotherapist. Int Psychiat Clin 1964,
       1:403-415

HELLERSBERG, ELISABETH F.

76642 Child's growth in play therapy. In Haworth, M. R. *Child Psychotherapy*,
       NY/London: Basic Books 1964, 168-176

HELLMAN, DANIEL STEELE

76643 (& Blackman, N.) Enuresis, firesetting and cruelty to animals: a triad
       predictive of adult crime, P 1966, 122:1431-1435

HELLMAN, ILSE

76644 Assessment of analysability illustrated by the case of an adolescent pa-
       tient. (Read at Cleveland Psa Soc, 10 Apr 1964)
       Abs McDonald, M. Bull Phila Ass Psa 1964, 14:234-237

76645 Hampstead Nursery follow-up studies: I. Sudden separation and its effect followed over twenty years. Psa St C 1962, 17:159-174
    Abs SLe RFPsa 1964, 28:812

76646 (& Frankl, L.) Neurotic learning disturbances and subsequent maladjustment as work. Acta paedopsychiat 1966, 33:6-7, 209

76647 Observations on adolescents in psycho-analytic treatment. Brit J Psychiat 1964, 110:406-410
    Abs JWS Q 1965, 34:625

S-48675 (& Friedman, O.; Shepheard, E.) Simultaneous analysis of mother and child. In Lomas, P. The Predicament of the Family, London: HIP 1967, 90-106
    Analyse simultanée de la mère et de son enfant. RFPsa 1963, 27: 619-636
    Simultanalyse von Mutter und Kind. Jb Psa 1961-62, 2:259-275

76648 Symposium on child analysis. Contributions to discussion. J 1962, 43: 342-343
    Abs RLG Q 1963, 32:605-606

    See Frankl, Liselotte

REVIEW OF:
76649 Lorand, S. & Schneer, H. E. (Eds) Adolescents: Psychoanalytic Approach to Problems and Therapy. J 1963, 44:514

HELM, JOHANNES

76650 [Theory of cognition problems and empirical results on the problem of "consciousness and the unconscious."] (Ger) Z Psychol 1968, 175:1-28

HELSINGER, FRANKLIN S.

76651 A study of aggression in acting out and non acting out boys. Diss Abstr 1967, 28(3-B):1196

HEMMENDINGER, LAURENCE

76652 Developmental theory and the Rorschach method. In Rickers-Ovsiankina, M. A. Rorschach Psychology, NY/London: Wiley 1960, 58-79

HEMMI, T.

76653 A psychiatric study on epileptics among habitual offenders. Bull Osaka Med Sch Suppl 1967, 12:379 +

HENDERSON, DAVID

76654 (& Batchelor, I. R. C.) Henderson and Gillespie's Textbook of Psychiatry. Ninth Edition. London/NY: Oxford Univ Pr 1962 (Rev), 578 p
    Rv HRB Q 1964, 33:288-289

HENDERSON, J. G.

76655 Denial and repression as factors in the delay of patients with cancer presenting themselves to the physician. Ann NY Acad Sci 1966, 125: 856-864

HENDERSON, JOSEPH L.

76656 Ancient myths and modern man. In Jung, C. G. et al: *Man and His Symbols*, NY: Doubleday 1964, 104-157
76657 Thresholds of Initiation. Middletown, Conn: Wesleyan Univ Pr 1967, 260 p
76658 (& Oakes, M.) The Wisdom of the Serpent: The Myths of Death, Rebirth, and Resurrection. NY: George Braziller 1963, xxiv + 262 p

HENDERSON, NORMAN B.

76659 Married group therapy: a setting for reducing resistances. Psychol Rep 1965, 16:347-352

HENDIN, HELEN C.

See Lennard, Henry L.

HENDIN, HERBERT

76660 Black suicide. Arch gen Psychiat 1969, 21:407-422
76661 Black Suicide. NY: Basic Books 1969, ix + 176 p
76662 (& Gaylin, W.; Carr, A.) Psychoanalysis and Social Research. The Psychoanalytic Study of the Nonpatient. Garden City, NY: Doubleday 1965; Anchor 1966, 106 p
       Abs J Am Psa Ass 1966, 14:236-237. Rv Muensterberger, W. Q 1966, 35:436-437
76663 The psychodynamics of suicide. JNMD 1963, 136:236-244
76664 Suicide. Compreh Txbk Psychiat 1170-1179
76665 Suicide in Scandinavia. A Psychoanalytic Study of Culture and Character. NY/London: Grune & Stratton 1964, xii + 153 p; Garden City, NY: Doubleday 1965, xiii + 177 p
       Abs J Am Psa Ass 1966, 14:230-231. Rv Gero, G. Q 1965, 34:111-113
76666 Suicide in Sweden. Psychiat Q 1962, 36:1-28
       Abs Engle, B. S. Q 1963, 32:292
76667 Suicide: psychoanalytic point of view. In Farberow, N. L. & Schneidman, E. S. *The Cry for Help*, NY/Toronto/London: McGraw-Hill 1961, 181-192

See Ovesey, Lionel

HENDRICK, IVES

76668 Author's response [to reviews of *Psychiatric Education Today*]. Psa Forum 1966, 1:310-312
76669 The birth of an institute. In author's *The Birth of an Institute* 1-94
76670 (& Lewin, B. D.; Menninger, K.; Murray, J. M.) The Birth of an Institute. Papers Presented at the Twenty-Fifth Anniversary of the Boston Psychoanalytic Institute. Freeport, Maine: Bond Wheelwright Co 1961, xiv + 164 p
       Abs J Am Psa Ass 1962, 10:640. Rv Bookhammer, R. S. Q 1962, 31:560-562

76671 Discussion of Kubie, L. S. "Reflections on training." Psa Forum 1966, 1:103-104

S-48690 Dream resistance and schizophrenia.
Abs Solomon, R. G. An Surv Psa 1958, 9:187-188

76672 Narcissism and the prepuberty ego ideal. (Read at Boston Psa Soc, 27 Mar 1963) J Am Psa Ass 1964, 12:522-528
Abs Rev urug Psa 1965, 7:101. JLSt Q 1967, 36:132. CG RFPsa 1968, 32:175

76673 Our generation of psychiatrists: changes in our words and changes in our thinking. Crosscurrents in Ps & Psa 23-35

S-48693 Presidential Address: Professional standards of the American Psycho-analytic Association.
Abs An Surv Psa 1955, 6:380-384

76674 Psychiatry Education Today. NY: IUP; London: Bailey Bros 1965, vii + 110 p
Rv Enelow, A. J. Psa Forum 1966, 1:304-305. Brill, N. Q. Psa Forum 1966, 1:306-308. Abrahamson, S. Psa Forum 1966, 1:308-309. IK Q 1966, 35:444-448

HENDRICKSON, WILLARD J.

76675 Communicating with adolescent patients. Int Psychiat Clin 1964, 1:73-87

76676 (& Holmes, D. J.) Institutional psychotherapy of the delinquent. Prog PT 1960, 5:169-176

76677 Tradition versus the space age. P 1968, 124:995-996

HENDRIX, VERNON L.

See Robinson, Sandra A.

HÉNIN-ROBERT, N.

See Appaix, A.

HENKIN, R.

76678 (& Buchsbaum, M.; Welpton, D. F.; Zahn, T.; Scott, W.; Wynne, L.; Silverman, J.) Physiological and psychological effects of LSD in chronic users. Clin Res 1967, 15(4):484

HENLEY, ARTHUR

76679 Psychoanalysis as a creative act. Long Island Consult Center 1967, 5:52-54

HENNIG, WILFRIED

76680 Der projektive Test als Mittel zum Einstieg in die Psychotherapie. [The projective test as a means of approach to psychotherapy.] Z Psychother med Psychol 1968, 18:184-189

HENNINGER, JAMES F.

76681 A candid look at the M'Naghten and Durham rules. Penn psychiat Q 1965, 5:9-13

HENNINGSEN, HARALD

76682   Die Entwicklung der analytischen Kinderpsychotherapie. [The development of psychoanalytic child psychotherapy.] Psyche 1964, 18:59-80

HENNY, R.

76683   Colloque de psychanalyse d'enfants. [Round table on child psychoanalysis.] RFPsa 1967, 31:1105-1109

76684   Considérations sur les psychoses précoces. [Considerations on early psychoses.] In Müller, C. & Benedetti, G. *Psychotherapy of Schizophrenia (3rd Int Symp 1964)*, Basel/NY: Karger 1965, 97-107

76685   De quelques aspects structuraux et psychothérapiques de l'adolescence. [Some structural and psychotherapeutic aspects of adolescence.] RFPsa 1961, 25:379-404
            Abs Auth Rev Psicoanál 1962, 19:285. RJA Q 1962, 31:433

76686   Discussion of Schneider, P.-B. "La psychanalyse et la médecine psychosomatique." RFPsa 1968, 32:677

76687   Similitudes et différences entre psychanalyse d'enfant et d'adulte dans la relation thérapeutique. [Similarities and differences in the psychoanalysis of children and adults in the therapeutic relation.] Schweiz ANP 1966, 97:387-412

HENRIQUEZ, ENRIQUE C.

76688   [Convulsive and ecstatic crisis in fanatics and ignorant people.] (Sp) Rev Arch Neurol Psiquiat, Cuba 1961, 2:16-22
            Abs Vega Q 1963, 32:144

76689   [The mystical and fanatic static convulsive crisis in voodoo (The Saint Came Down).] (Sp) Rev Arch Neurol Psiquiat, Cuba 1961, 11:16-23
            Abs Vega Q 1962, 31:437

HENRIQUEZ, F.

76690   La Sexualité Sauvage. [Savage Sexuality.] (Pref: Devereux, G.) Paris 1965

HENRY, GEORGE W.

S-48706 All the Sexes. With title: Masculinity and Feminity. NY: Collier Books 1964, 320 p

* * *   Foreword in Caprio, F. S. *Variations in Sexual Behavior*, NY: Grove Pr 1962

76691   Freud's pathography and psychoanalysis. Ann NY Acad Sci 1962, 96:823-830

* * *   Masculinity and Femininity. See [48706]

76692   Society and the Sex Variant. NY: Macmillan 1965, 382 p

HENRY, JULES

76693   Culture Against Man. NY: Random House 1963; London: Tavistock 1966, xiv + 495 p
            Rv Padel, J. H. J 1967, 48:609-610

76694 Discussion of Erikson, E. "Eight ages of man." Int J Psychiat 1966, 2: 304-305
76695 The study of families by naturalistic observation. Psychiat Res Rep 1966, (20):95-106

HENRY, P.

See Bourgeois, M.

HENRY, WILLIAM EARL

76696 Psychodynamics of the executive role. In Warner, W. L. & Martin, N. H. *Industrial Man*, NY: Harper 1959, 24-34
76697 Some observations on the lives of healers. Hum Develpm 1966, 9:47-56

See Carr, Arthur C.; Cumming, Elaine

HENSELER, HEINZ

76698 Fünf oft übersehene Formen neurotischer Persönlichkeitsentwicklung. [Five patterns of neurotic personality development frequently overlooked.] Hippokrates 1968, 39:484-489
76699 Neurose—eingebildete Krankheit? [Neurosis—an imaginary disease?] Med Klin 1968, 63:424-428
76700 Über den Umgang mit schwierigen Kranken. [On dealing with problem patients.] Dtsch Zbl Krankenpflege 1968, 12:3-6
76701 Zum gegenwärtigen Stand der Beurteilung erlebnisbedingter Spätschäden nach Verfolgung. [The current psychiatric view concerning late emotional sequelae of persecution. A review of the literature concerning clinical picture etiology and legal aspects.] Nervenarzt 1965, 36:333-338
76702 Zum Verständnis psychogener Lähmungen. [Towards better understanding of psychogenic paralyses.] Krankengymnastik 1967, 19:234-238
76703 Zur Psychodynamik der Pseudologie. [On psychodynamics of pseudologia.] Nervenarzt 1968, 39:106-114

HENYER, GEORGES

76704 Propos sur la psychoanalyse. [Remarks on psychoanalysis.] Rev Paris 1962, 69:95-116

HEPBURN, JAMES G.

76705 Deeper chaos and larger order: psychoanalysis confronting art. Lit & Psych 1961, 11:101-111
76706 A dream that hath no bottom. Comment on N. Holland's paper. Lit & Psych 1964, 14:3-6

HEPPS, ROBERT

76707 (& Dorfman, E.) Interfaith marriage and social participation. J Relig Hlth 1966, 5:324-333

HERBERG, WILL

S-48719 Freud, the revisionists, and the social reality.
Abs AEC An Surv Psa 1956, 7:20

HERBERT

TRANSLATION OF:
Freud, S. [10415]

HERBERT, CHARLES C.

76708 (& Mead, N. E.) Life-influencing interactions. In Simon, A. et al:
The Physiology of Emotions, Springfield, Ill: Thomas 1961, 187-208

See Simon, Alexander

HERKIMER, JESSIE K.

See Meerloo, Joost A. M.

HERMA, JOHN L.

76709 The therapeutic act. In Hammer, E. F. *Use of Interpretation in Treatment: Technique and Art*, NY: Grune & Stratton 1968, 121-128

HERMAN, DAVID

76710 Federico Fellini. Am Im 1969, 26:251-268

HERMAN, MELVIN

See Schreiber, Flora R.

HERMAN, M. N.

76711 (& Sandok, B. A.) Conversion symptoms in a case of multiple sclerosis.
Milit Med 1967, 132:816-818

HERMAN, WILLIAM

REVIEW OF:
76712 Weissman, P. Creativity in the Theatre: A Psychoanalytic Study. R
1967, 55:550-551

HERMANN, IMRE

76713 Beobachtungen über die Zwangsneurose. [Observations on compulsion
neurosis.] Acta psychother psychosom 1960, 8:82-88
76713A G. Th. Fechner betegsége. [The disease of G. Th. Fechner.] Orvosi
Hetilap 1969, 110:2832
76713B A kiválasztásos gondolkodás pszichológiája és pszichopathólogiája. [The
psychology and psychopathology of selective thinking.] Pszichológiai
Tanulmányok 1959, 2:345-353
76713C Az ösztönök és az érzelmek térvonatkozása. [Space relation of instincts
and emotions.] Pszichológiai Tanulmányok 1965, 7:255-263

76713D A parafrénia orvosi lélektanának néhány szempontje. [Some aspects of the medical psychology of paraphrenia.] Pszichológiai Tanulmányok 1963, 4:349-363

76714 Die Psychoanalyse als Methode. [Psychoanalysis as a Method.] Cologne/Opladen: Westdeutscher Verlag 1963 (2nd rev ed), 139 p
Rv Rosenfeld, E. M. J 1965, 46:275-276

76714A (& Fonagy, I.) [The self-regulation of loudness under usual and unusual circumstances.] (Ger) Z Phonetik, Sprachwissenschaft und Kommunikationsforschung 1964, 17:209-214

76715 Tanulmányok a lélektan történetéhez. [Studies from the history of psychology.] Pszichológiai Tanulmányok 1966, 9:681-697

76716 Die Theorie des primaren Anklammerungstriebes. [The Theory of Primary Clinging Instinct.] Munich: Stefan Geroly 1963

76717 Tudat. Tudattalan. [Consciousness and the unconscious.] Magyar Pszichol Szle 1960, 17:415-425

76717A Ujabb adatok a lélektan történetéchez. Álom és álommagyrarázat a régi magyar irodalomban. [Dream in the old Hungarian literature.] Magyar Pszichológiai Szemle 1969, 24:459-461

76717B Warum verliess Gauguin seine Familie? [Why did Gauguin leave his family?] Der Psychologe 1964, 16:1-6

76717C Zur Dynamik der Perversionen. [On the dynamics of perversion.] Der Psychologe 1962, 14:47-51

76718 Zur Frage des Bettnässens. [The problem of enuresis.] Acta paedopsychiat 1961, 28:308-311

HERMANN, P.

See Schneider, Pierre-Bernard

HERNALSTEEN, L.

See Eyck, M. van

HERNBERG, RAE SHIFRIN

76719 (& Chapman, J.; Shakow, D.) Psychotherapy research and the problem of intrusions of privacy. Ps 1958, 21:195-203
Abs WCW An Surv Psa 1958, 9:412-413

HERNDON, C. N.

See Nash, Ethel M.

HERNER, TORSTEN

76720 Significance of the body image in schizophrenic thinking. PT 1965, 19:455-466
Abs Auth Rev Psicoanál 1966, 23:72

76721 Theoretische Erwägungen über das Körperbild, gewonnen in der Psychotherapie eines Falles von chronischer Schizophrenie. [Theoretical considerations on body build in psychotherapy of a case of chronic schizophrenia.] In Benedetti, G. & Müller, C. Psychotherapy of Schizophrenia (2nd Int Symp 1959), Basel/NY: Karger 1960, 140-155

HERON, MICHAEL

TRANSLATION OF:
De Becker, R. [70851]

HERRERA, JÚLIO JOSE

76722 (& Espinosa, N. A.) Encuentro y abandono: a propósito de una feno-
menología de la actitud corporal en la relación médico-enfermo, en psiquiatría. [Encounter and abandonment: concerning a phenomenology
of the corporal attitude in the doctor-patient relationship in psychiatry.] Rev Psiquiat Psicol méd 1965, 7:229-242

HERRICK, GEORGE W.

See Cappadonia, Anthony C.

HERRICK, JOAN

See Kaufman, Irving

HERRON, WILLIAM G.

76723 The assessment of ego strength. J psychol St 1962, 13:73-203
76724 The evidence for the unconscious. PPR 1962, 49(1):70-92
76725 The IES "experiment." Percept mot Skills 1966, 23:279-290
76726 (& Guido, S. M.; Kantor, R. E.) Relationships among ego strength measures. Clin Psych 1965, 21:403-404

HERSCH, CHARLES

76727 The cognitive functioning of the creative person: a developmental analysis. J proj Tech 1962, 26:193-200
76728 The discontent explosion in mental health. Am Psych 1968, 23:497-
506
76729 The process of collaboration: a case study: Comm ment Hlth J 1967,
3:254-258

HERSEN, MICHEL

See Feldman, Marvin J.

HERSHENSON, DAVID B.

76730 Life-stage vocational development system. J counsel Psychol 1968, 15:
23-30
76731 "Proofreader's syndrome" and scientific method. J Hist behav Sci 1968,
5:263-265
76732 Sense of identity, occupational fit, and enculturation in adolescence.
J counsel Psychol 1967, 14:319-324

HERSHER, LEONARD

See Caldwell, Bettye M.

HERSKO, MARVIN

76733 Group psychotherapy with delinquent adolescent girls. Ops 1962, 32: 169-175

HERSKOVITZ, HERBERT H.

76734 (& Levine, M.; Spivack, G.) Anti-social behavior of adolescents from higher socio-economic groups. JNMD 1959, 129:467-476

76735 Discussion of Bion, W. R. "Notes on memory and desire." Psa Forum 1967, 2:278-279

76736 A psychodynamic view of sexual promiscuity. In Pollak, O. & Friedman, A. S. *Family Dynamics and Female Sexual Delinquency*, Palo Alto, Calif: Sci & Behav Books 1969, 89-98

HERSKOWITZ, M. S.

76737 The mechanistic distortion in treatment of infants and children. J Amer Coll Neuropsych 1964, 3:13-18

HERSOV, L.

76738 Emotional factors in cerebral palsy. Develpm Med Child Neurol 1963, 5:504-511

HERTER, C. A.

TRANSLATION OF:
Bernheim, H. [67452]

HERTRICH, O.

76739 Beitrag zur Diagnostik und Differentialdiagnostik der leichteren depressiven Zustandsbilder. [The diagnosis and differential diagnosis of mild depressive states.] Fortsch Neurol Psychiat 1962, 30:237-272

HERTZ, MARGUERITE R.

76740 Detection of suicidal risks with the Rorschach. Acting Out 257-270

HERTZ, MARY ANN

See Kurtz, Richard

HERTZIG, MARGARET E.

See Chess, Stella; Thomas, Alexander

HERTZMAN, MAX

REVIEW OF:
76741 Meerloo, J. A. M. & Nelson, M. C. Transference and Trial Adaptation. R 1967, 54(1):177-179

HERWEGEN, J. VAN

76742 Einige beschouwingen over de dynamiek van een speltherapie aan de hand van een concreet geval. [Some considerations of the dynamics of play therapy as based on a concrete case.] Acta neurol Psychiat Belg 1962, 62:1038-1050

HERZ, MARVIN I.

See Korchin, Sheldon J.; Oken, Donald

HERZOG, EDGAR

76743 Psyche and Death: Archaic Myths and Modern Dreams in Analytical Psychology: NY: Putnam 1967, 224 p

HERZOG-DÜRCK, JOHANNA

76744 Menschsein als Wagnis: Neurose und Heilung im Sinne einer personalen Psychotherapie. [The Challenge of Being Human; Neurosis and Cure in the Sense of an Anthropological Psychotherapy.] Stuttgart: Klett 1960, 500 p
76745 Probleme menschlicher Reifung. Person und Identität in der personalen Psychotherapie. [Problems of Human Maturation. Role and Identity in Anthropological Psychotherapy.] Stuttgart: Klett 1969, 330 p

HES, J. P.

76745A [Treatment of obsessive and phobic states.] (Heb) Dapim Refuiim 1968, 27:311-313

HESNARD, ANGELO LOUIS MARIE

76746 Ce qu'il faut penser de la P. O. P. (Psychothérapie d'inspiration psychanalytique). [What to think of the P. O. P. (Psychotherapy on psychoanalytical inspiration).] Sud Med Chir 1961, 97(2468):9226-9230
76747 Le destin du complexe d'Oedipe, de l'enfance à l'état adulte. [The destiny of the Oedipus complex, from childhood to adult age.] Inform psychol 1964, 13:51-74
76748 Freud dans la Société d'après Guerre [Freud in Post-War Society.] Geneva: Mont-Blanc 1946, 170 p
76749 Les Phobies et la Névrose Phobique; des États Nerveux d'Angoisse aux Phobies Systematiques. [Phobias and Phobic Neurosis. From Anxiety States to Systematic Phobias.] (Pref: Lagache, D.) Paris: Payot 1961, 477 p

HESS, J. B.

See Kern, Howard M., Jr.

HESS, JOHN H.

See Finch, Stuart M.; Harrison, Saul I.

HESS, ROBERT D.

76750 (& Bear, R. M.) (Eds) Early Education: Current Theory, Research and Practice. Chicago: Aldine 1968, x + 272 p
76751 (& Shipman, V. C.) Early experience and the socialization of cognitive modes in children. Child Develpm 1965, 36:869-886

HESS, RUDOLPH

See Bleuler, Eugen

HESSE, HERMANN

76752 Artist and psychoanalyst. (Tr: Reik, M. M.) R 1963, 50:355-360
       Abs SRS Q 1964, 33:605

HESSELBACH, CHARLES F.

76753 A note on the feeling of confusion in analysis. Q 1962, 31:252-253
76754 Superego regression in paranoia. Q 1962, 31:341-350
       Abs LDr RFPsa 1963, 27:358

ABSTRACTS OF:
76755 Bonnard, A. Pre-body ego types of (pathological) mental functioning.
       An Surv Psa 1958, 9:246-249
76756 Greenacre, P. Early physical determinants in the development of the
       sense of identity. An Surv Psa 1958, 9:244-245
76757 Grotjahn, M. A letter by Sigmund Freud with recollections of his ado-
       lescence. An Surv Psa 1956, 7:31-32
76758 Hambidge, G., Jr. On the ontogenesis of repression. An Surv Psa 1956,
       7:134
76759 Jones, E. Our attitudes toward greatness. An Surv Psa 1956, 7:5-6
76760 Kestenberg, J. S. Vivissitudes of female sexuality. An Surv Psa 1956,
       7:100-103
76761 Kligerman, C. A psychoanalytic study of the confessions of St. Augus-
       tine. An Surv Psa 1957, 8:301-303
76762 Kris, E. The personal myth: a problem in psychoanalytic technique. An
       Surv Psa 1956, 7:316-319
76763 Menninger, K. A. Freud and American psychiatry. An Surv Psa 1956,
       7:7
76764 Posinsky, S. H. The death of Maui. An Surv Psa 1957, 8:306-307
76765 Watters, T. A. Forms of the family romance. An Surv Psa 1956, 7:157-
       158
76766 Weissman, P. Conscious and unconscious autobiographical dramas of
       Eugene O'Neill. An Surv Psa 1957, 8:328-331

HESSEN, J. S. VAN

See Musaph, Herman

HETHERINGTON, EILEEN MAVIS

76767 A developmental study of the effects of sex of the dominant parent on
       sex-role preference, identification, and imitation in children. J Pers soc
       Psychol 1965, 2:188-194
76768 (& Frankie, G.) Effects of parental dominance, warmth, and conflict
       on imitation in children. J Pers soc Psychol 1967, 6:119-125
76769 Effects of paternal absence on sex-typed behaviors in Negro and white
       preadolescent males. J Pers soc Psychol 1966, 4:87-91
76770 (& Brackbill, Y.) Etiology and covariation of obstinacy, orderliness, and
       parsimony in young children. Child Develpm 1963, 34:919-943

HEUSCHER, JULIUS E.

76771 Cinderella, eros and psyche. Dis nerv Sys 1963, 24:286-292
76772 Clinical application of the concept "world-design": a procedure. J existent Psychiat 1965, 5:371-388
76773 Death in the fairy-tale. Dis nerv Sys 1967, 28:462-468
76773A The existential dimension in a dream. Compr Psychiat 1969, 10:302-313
76774 J. W. Goethe's contribution to the phenomenology of thinking: based on Goethe's fairy tale. Dis nerv Sys 1965, 26:422-427
76775 Lucifer and Eros. (A commentary to the psychiatric study of fairy tales). Confin psychiat 1964, 7:151-159
76776 The meaning of fairy tales and myths. Confin psychiat 1968, 11:90-105
76777 A Psychiatric Study of Fairy Tales. Springfield, Ill: Thomas 1963, x + 224 p
76778 Spontaneity versus technique. A study of the applicability of existentialist concepts in psychotherapy. Psa 1967, 27:61-74
76778A The use of existential-philosophic concepts in psychotherapy. Psa 1969, 29:170-185
76779 What is existential psychotherapy? Rev existent Psychol Psychiat 1964, 4:158-167

HEUYER, G.

76779A [On psychiatry.] (Fr) Ann Med Psychol 1969 (1):625-639
76780 Pour la psychiatrie infantile. [Child psychiatry.] Acta Paedopsychiat 1969, 36:235-248

HEWITT, CHARLES CHRISTIAN

76781 On the meaning of effeminacy in homosexual men. PT 1961, 15:592-602

HEYDER, D. W.

76782 School phobia: a case abstract with analytic interpretations. Virginia med Monthly 1960, 87:453-455
76783 (& Wambach, H. S.) Sexuality and affect in frogmen. An investigation of personality factors in resistance to prolonged stress. Arch gen Psychiat 1964, 11:286-289

HEYER, GUSTAV RICHARD

76784 [Depth psychology as a marginal science.] (Ger) Landarzt 1967, 43:1575-1581
76785 [Instructive mistakes.] (Ger) Landarzt 1964, 40:860-865
76786 [New data in the field of psychotherapy and depth psychology.] (Ger) Landarzt 1960, 36:1093-1097; 1961, 37:1342-1346; 1965, 41:462-465

HEYMANS, C.

See Hiddema, F.

HEYWOOD, ROSALIND

76787 Attitudes to death in the light of dreams and other "out-of-the-body" experience. In Toynbee, A. et al: *Man's Concern with Death*, NY: McGraw-Hill 1968, 1969, 185-218

76788 Beyond the Reach of Sense: An Inquiry into Extra-Sensory Perception. NY: Dutton 1961, 224 p

HIATT, HAROLD

76789 The problem of termination of psychotherapy. PT 1965, 19:607-615

HIATT, L. R.

76790 Nabokov's *Lolita*; a "Freudian" cryptic crossword. Am Im 1967, 24: 360-370
Abs JWS Q 1969, 38:166

HIDDEMA, F.

76791 Acute temporary depersonalisation syndrome as a result of a defense process. Psychiat Neurol Neurochir 1966, 69:197-204

76792 Climacteric depression. Psychiat Neurol Neurochir 1964, 67:385-393

76793 (& Heymans, C.) Masochism, a case report. Psychiat Neurol Neurochir 1961, 64:434-438

76794 Neurotische factoren bij endogene depressies. [Neurotic factors in endogenous depressions.] Ned Tijdschr Geneeskunde 1962, 106:651-653

76795 Psychoanalytic considerations regarding the character structure, vocational choice and disorders of adaptation in patients employed as travelling salesmen. Folia Psychiat Neerl 1959, 62:1-7

HIFT, E.

76796 (& Hift, S.; Spiel, W.) Ergebnisse der Schockbehandlungen bei kindlichen Schizophrenien. [Results of shock treatment in infantile schizophrenia.] Arch Neurol Psychiat 1960, 86:256-272

See Spiel, Walter

HIFT, S.

See Arnold, O. H.; Hift, E.

HIGASHIMACHI, WILFRED H.

76797 The construct validity of the Progressive Matrices as a measure of superego strength in juvenile delinquents. J consult Psychol 1963, 27:415-419

HIGBIE, IMOGENE SMITH

See Perlmutter, Morton S.

HIGGINBOTHAM, ELIZABETH S.

See Burks, Henry L.

HIGGINS, B. A.

See Cramond, W. A.

HIGGINS, JERRY

76798 Effects of child rearing by schizophrenic mothers. J psychiat Res 1966, 4:153-167

HIGGINS, JOHN W.

76799 Discussion of Krystal, H. "A psychoanalytic contribution to the theory of cyclicity of the financial economy." Psa Forum 1966, 1:367-368
76800 Some considerations of psychoanalytic theory preliminary to a philosophical inquiry. Proc Amer Cath Phil Ass 1961, 32:21-44

HIGGINS, MARY

76801 (& Raphael, C. M.) Editors of *Reich Speaks of Freud: Wilhelm Reich Discusses His Work and His Relationship with Sigmund Freud.*

HIKEN, JULIA R.

See Haggard, Ernest A.

HILDEBRAND, H. P.

76802 "We rob banks." Mental Health 1967, 26:15-17

HILDEBRAND, PETER

See Balint, Michael

HILGARD, ERNEST ROPIEQUET

76803 Classical and instrumental conditioning: do single-process or two-process theories exhaust the alternatives? In *Brain Function: Vol. 4,* Berkeley: Univ Calif Pr 1963
76804 (& Marquis, D. G.) Conditioning and Learning. London: Methuen 1961, 590 p
76805 Foreword to Zawdony, J. K. *Man and International Relations,* San Francisco, Calif: Chandler Publ 1966, xvii-xviii
S-48799 Freud and experimental psychology.
        Abs JLan An Surv Psa 1957, 8:7
76806 Hypnotic Susceptibility. NY: Harcourt, Brace & World 1965, xiii + 434 p
76807 A methodological study of Freudian theory. Is revision to come from inside or outside psychoanalysis? Int J Psychiat 1966, 2:549-550
76808 Motivation in learning theory. In Koch, S. *Psychology: A Study of a Science, Vol. 5,* NY: McGraw-Hill 1963, 253-283
76809 The motivational relevance of hypnosis. (Read at Seattle Psa Soc 12 Oct 1965) Nebraska Symposium on Motivation 1964, 12.
        Abs Goforth, E. Psa Forum 1966, 1:138
76810 (& Hilgard, J. R.) The personality background of susceptibility to hypnosis. In Lassner, J. *Hypnosis and Psychosomatic Medicine,* Berlin/Heidelberg/NY: Springer 1967, 143-150

76811   Psychology: its present interests. In Berelson, B. *The Behavioral Sciences Today*, NY: Basic Books 1963, 38-51
76812   (& Bower, G. H.) Theories of Learning. NY: Appleton-Century-Crofts 1966 (3rd ed), vii + 661 p
76813   (& Copper, L. M.; Lenox, J.; Morgan, A. H.; Volvodsky, J.) The use of pain-state reports in the study of hypnotic analgesia to the pain of ice water. JNMD 1967, 506-513

See Hilgard, Josephine R.

HILGARD, JOSEPHINE R.

76813A (& Moore, U. S.) Affiliative therapy with young adolescents. J Amer Acad Child Psychiat 1969, 8:577-605
76814   Depressive and psychotic states as anniversaries to sibling death in childhood. Int Psychiat Clin 1969, 6(2):197-211
76815   (& Hilgard, E. R.) Developmental-interactive aspects of hypnosis: some illustrative cases. Genet Psychol Monogr 1962, 66:143-178
76816   (& Fisk, F.) Disruption of adult ego identity as related to childhood loss of a mother through hospitalization for psychosis. JNMD 1960, 131:47-57
76817   (& Newman, M. F.) Early parental deprivation in schizophrenia and alcoholism. Ops 1963, 33:409-420
76818   (& Newman, M. F.) Evidence for functional genesis in mental illness: schizophrenia, depressive psychoses and psychoneuroses. JNMD 1961, 132:3-16
76819   (& Newman, M. F.) Parental loss by death as an etiological factor among schizophrenic and alcoholic patients compared with a non-patient community sample. JNMD 1963, 137:14-28
         Abs BFM Q 1965, 34:136
76820   Personality and hypnotizability: influences from case studies. In Hilgard, E. R. *Hypnotic Susceptibility*, NY: Harcourt 1965, 343-374
76821   (& Hilgard, E. R.; Newman, M. F.) Sequelae to hypnotic induction with special reference to earlier chemical anesthesia. JNMD 1961, 133:461-478
         Abs Powelson, H. Q 1963, 32:294
76822   (& Newman, M. F.; Fisk, F.) Strength of adult ego following childhood bereavement. Ops 1960, 30:788-798. Death and Identity 259-272
         Abs RLG Q 1961, 30:304. JMa RFPsa 1962, 26:321

See Hilgard, Ernest R.

HILKEVITCH, A.

See Giovacchini, Peter L.

HILL, BRIAN

76823   (Ed) Gates of Horn and Ivory: An Anthology of Dreams. NY: Taplinger Publ 1968, xix + 216 p
76824   (Ed) Such Stuff as Dreams. London: Hart-Davis 1967, xxiv + 214 p

HILL, DENIS
See Stafford-Clark, David

HILL, GERALD
See Barr, Richard H.

ABSTRACT OF:
76825 Jackson, M. Jung's "archetype": clarity or confusion? Q 1961, 30:153-154

HILL, H.
See Svinn, Richard M.

HILL, J. C.
76826 Further thoughts on the unconscious mind in teaching. Reiss-Davis Clin Bull 1967, 4:34-50
76827 The unconscious mind in teaching. Reiss-Davis Clin Bull 1966, 3:18-35. Learn Love 79-94

HILL, J. M. M.
76828 (& Trist, E. L.) Industrial accidents, sickness and other absences. Tavistock Pamphlet No. 4, Tavistock Publ 1962, 58 p

HILL, K. T.
See Sarason, Seymour B.

HILL, L. K.
See Worell, Leonard

HILL, MARJORIE J.
See Blane, Howard T.

HILL, REUBEN
See Aldous, Joan

HILL, WILLARD M.
76829 An evaluation of two research instruments for the measurment of certain ego defensive mechanisms. Diss Abstr 1967, 27:3287

HILL, WILLIAM C.
See Grold, L. James

HILLEL. J.-M.
76830 (& Fortin, J.-N.; Bordeleau, J.-M.; Tetreault, L.) Traitement d'un groupe de couples: approche méthodologique. [Treatment of a group of couples: methodological approach.] Laval Méd 1967, 38:47-57

HILLENBRAND, D.

See Arnds, H. G.

HILLER, J.

76831 (& Müller-Gegemann, D.; Wendt, H.) Experimentelle Untersuchungen über den Einfluss des autogenen Trainings auf die Erholung. [Experimental research on the influence of autogenous training on rest.] Psychiat Neurol med Psychol 1960, 12:417-420

HILLES, LINDA

76832 Changing trends in the application of psychoanalytic principles to a psychiatric hospital. BMC 1968, 32:203-218
76833 Problems in the hospital treatment of a disturbed criminal. BMC 1966, 30:141-149
76834 The reliability of anamnestic data. BMC 1967, 31:219-228

HILLIX, WILLIAM A.

See Marx, Melvin H.

HILLMAN, JAMES

76835 Emotion: A Comprehensive Phenomenology of Theories and Their Meanings for Therapy. Evanston, Ill: Northwestern Univ Pr 1961, 318 p
Rv Keisman, I. B. PPR 1962, 49(4):135-136
76836 Suicide and the Soul. NY: Harper & Row 1964, 191 p
Selbstmord und seelische Wandlung. (Tr: Binswanger, H.) Zurich/ Stuttgart: Rascher 1966

See Donoghue, A. K.

HILLMER, M. L., JR.

See Stotland, Ezra

HILTMANN, HILDEGARD

76837 (& Clauser, G.) Psychodiagnostik und aktiv-analytische Psychotherapie Jugendlicher, dargestellt an der Pubertätsmagersucht. [Psychodiagnosis and active analytical psychotherapy in adolescents, with references to anorexia nervosa in puberty.] Prax PT 1961, 6:168-178

HILTNER, SEWARD

76838 Alcohol prevention and reality. Quart J Stud Alcohol 1967, 29:348-349
76839 An appraisal of pastoral psychology today. Pastoral Psychol 1957, 8(77):9-10; 66
76840 An appraisal of religion and psychiatry since 1954. J Relig Hlth 1965, 4:217-226
76841 Bibliography of Seward Hiltner. Pastoral Psychol 1968, 19(180):6-22
76842 Carl Gustav Jung. Pastoral Psychol 1961, 12(119):7-9

76843 Carl Gustav Jung: an editorial. Pastoral Psychol 1956, 6(60):78-81
76844 Case-work technique and the therapeutic use of religion. In Tippy,
       W. M. *Spiritual Factors in Social Work*, Federal Council of the
       Churches of Christ in America 1936, 67-70
76845 Christian faith and psychotherapy. Religion in Life 1952, 21(4):492-
       501
76846 Christmas and suicide. Pastoral Psychol 1953, 4(39):7-8; 66
76847 (& Ziegler, J. H.) Clinical pastoral education and the schools. J pastoral
       Care 1961, 15(Fall):129-143
76848 Clinical psychology and religion. Prog clin Psych 1966, 7:129-150
76849 (& Menninger, K.) (Eds) Constructive Aspects of Anxiety. NY: Abing-
       don 1963, 173 p
76850 A contemporary Christian view of sex. In author's *Sex Ethics and
       Kinsey Reports.* Pastoral Psychol 1953, 4(38):43-51
76851 The contribution of religion to mental health. MH 1940, 24(34):366-
       377
76852 Control of human behavior. Pastoral Psychol 1962, 13(128):7-11
76853 Convictions in counseling. Pastoral Psychol 1950, 1(8):31-36.
76854 Counseling by the old professions. Pastoral Psychol 1967, 18(179):45-
       50
76855 Darwin and pastoral psychology. Pastoral Psychol 1960, 10(100):7-10
76856 Darwin and religious development. J Relig 1960, 40(4):282-295
76857 The death of God: a psychological perspective. Pastoral Psychol 1966,
       17(167):5-9
76858 The dialogue on man's nature. In Doniger, S. *The Nature of Man,*
       NY: Harper 1962, 237-261
76859 Discussion. [Conference volume] *Research in Religion and Health,*
       Academy of Religion and Mental Health, NY: Fordham Univ Pr 1963
76860 Discussion of Dorn, R. M. "Psychoanalysis and psychoanalytic educa-
       tion." Psa Forum 1969, 3:259-261
76861 Divorced ministers. Pastoral Psychol 1958, 9(87):18-24. In Oates,
       W. E. *The Minister's Own Mental Health,* Great Neck: Channel Pr
       1961, 188-198
76862 (Contributor to) "The doctor's dilemma in a world of changing morals."
       Chicago: Amer Med Assoc 1967, 24-29
76863 Empathy in counseling. Pastoral Psychol 1951, 1(10):25-30.
76864 Erich Fromm and pastoral psychology. Pastoral Psychol 1955, 6(56):
       11-12
76865 The fate of the will in modern theology. In Lapsley, J. N. *The Con-
       cept of Willing,* Nashville: Abingdon Pr 1967, 102-115
76866 (& Rogers, W. R.) General considerations on method in research. J
       scient Stud Relig 1963, 2:204-208
76867 Homosexuality. Pastoral Psychol 1955, 6(56):44-49
76868 Hostility in counseling. Pastoral Psychol 1950, 1(1):35-42
76869 How far can the pastor go in counseling? Crozer Quart 1948, 25(2):
       97-108
76870 The influence of Adolf Meyer. Pastoral Psychol 1956, 7(66):11-12
76871 Interpersonal relationships. Forum of the AOS of the YMCA 1963,
       July-Aug, 52-56
76872 Karen Horney. Pastoral Psychol 1950, 1(6):11-12

76873 Karl Menninger. Pastoral Psychol 1958, 9(88):6; 66
76874 Karl Menninger as author. Pastoral Psychol 1963, 14(139):5-9
76875 Kinsey on religious influences. In author's *Sex Ethics and the Kinsey Reports*. In Himelhoch, J. & Faya, S. F. *Sexual Behavior in American Society*, NY: Norton 1955, 212-225
76878 Men and women. In author's *Sex Ethics and the Kinsey Reports*. In Himelhoch, J. & Faya, S. F. *Sexual Behavior in American Society*, NY: Norton 1955, 132-144
76877 The Menninger School of Psychiatry: an appraisal. BMC 1958, 22(5): 173-179
76878 New roles of the clergyman in promoting mental health. Prevention and Community mental Health 1965, 33-46
76879 The past and the present. In author's *Sex Ethics and the Kinsey Reports*. In Himelhoch, J. & Faya, S. F. *Sexual Behavior in American Society*, NY: Norton 1955, 312-325
76880 (& Elliott, R. E.; McDill, T. H.; Schultz, R.; Shaffer, J. T.; Wennerstrom, C. E.; Willis, J. S.) Pastoral symposium: a case of adultery. Pastoral Psychol 1955, 6(54):23-24; 6(55):11-24
76881 Pastoral theology and psychology. In Nash, A. S. *Protestant Thought in the Twentieth Century*, NY: Macmillan 1951, 181-199
76882 (& Dicks, R. L.) The pastor's loan shelf. The Pastor 1946, July
76883 Paul Tillich and pastoral psychology. Pastoral Psychol 1965, 16(159): 5-10
76884 The place of the clergyman in the community mental health team. In *The Fourth Health Conference for Public Officials*, Ann Arbor, Mich: School of Public Health, Continuing Education Series, 66, 1957, 23-31
76885 A program in religion and psychiatry. BMC 1959, 23:217-225. Pastoral Psychol 1960, 11(104):12-18
76886 The psyche and modern theology. Christendom 1941, 6(2):234-245
76887 Psychiatric understandings of man: a theological appraisal. In Rian, E. H. *Christianity and World Revolution*, NY: Harper & Row 1963, 87-105
76888 The psychiatrist and mental health. Pastoral Psychol 1957, 8(74):9-10
76889 Psychiatry and Christian hope. Pastoral Psychol 1960, 11(103):7-9
76890 Psychiatry and religion. Pastoral Psychol 1954, 5(49):8-9
76891 Psychoanalysis. In Macquarrie, J. *Dictionary of Christian Ethics*, Phila: Westminster Pr 1967, 281-282
76892 Psychoanalytic education: a critique. Q 1961, 30:385-403
76893 Psychoanalytic education in the United States. Pastoral Psychol 1961, Dec:22-26
76894 Psychological briefs. Pastoral Psychol 1950, 1(6):12
76895 Psychology and ethics. In Macquarrie, J. *Dictionary of Christian Ethics*, Phila: Westminster Pr 1967, 282
76896 Psychology and morality. University: A Princeton Magazine 1964, (22)Fall:3-6. Princeton Alumni Weekly 1964, 65(1):15-18
76897 Psychology and shelters. Pastoral Psychol 1962, 13(124):7-11. This Day 1963, 14(10)
76898 Psychology and the resurrection. Pastoral Psychol 1965, 16(153):5-7
76899 The psychology of pastoral economics. Pastoral Psychol 1965, 16(152): 14-22. The Princeton Seminary Bull 1965, 58(3):11-19

76900 Psychotherapy and counseling in professions other than the ministry. Pastoral Psychol 1956, 7(62):8-14

76901 Report on mental illness. Pastoral Psychol 1961, 12(114):49-52

76902 (& Schultz, H. P.) Report on the clergy-physician relationship in Protestant hospitals. (Pamphlet) American Protestant Hospital Association 1942, 28 p

76903 Research in pastoral psychology: a new proposal. Pastoral Psychol 1956, 6(60):84-86

76904 (& Rogers, W. R.) Research on religion and personality dynamics. Religious Education 1962, 57(Suppl)(4):S128-S140

76905 Sex and violence. Pastoral Psychol 1965, 16(151):5-8; 65

76906 Sex Ethics and the Kinsey Reports. NY: Association Pr 1953, xi + 238 p

76907 Sex: sin or salvation? Pastoral Psychol 1952, 3(26):27-33. In Doniger, S. *Sex and Religion Today*, NY: Association Pr 1953, 3-16

76908 A theologian's monthly date with psychiatry. Princeton Seminary Bull 1962, 55(2):19-25. Menn Q 1962, 16(2):22-29

76909 Tillich and pastoral psychology. Pastoral Psychol 1952, 3(29):9-10; 66

76910 Timing in counseling. Pastoral Psychol 1950, 1(7):20-24

76911 Toward a theology of conversion in the light of psychology. Pastoral Psychol 1966, 17(166):35-42

76912 Who is qualified to treat the alcoholic? Comment on the Krystal-Moore discussion. Quart J Stud Alcohol 1964, 25:354-357

76913 William C. Menninger, M. D. Pastoral Psychol 1966, 17(168):5-7

76914 Writing by the clinician. BMC 1965, 29(5):264-274

REVIEWS OF:

76915 Braceland, F. J. & Stock, M. Modern Psychiatry: A Handbook for Believers. Am Im 1965, 22:202-203

76916 Gassert, R. G. & Hall, B. H. Psychiatry and Religious Faith. Am Im 1965, 22:202-203

HIMELSTEIN, P.

76917 Una alternativa a la terapia psicoanalítica. [An alternative to psychoanalytic therapy.] Rev mex Psicol 1966, 2:758-762

HINE, FREDERICK R.

76918 Discussion of White, R. W. "Competence and the growth of personality." Sci Psa 1967, 11:54-58

76919 (& Feather, B. W.) Psychiatry and philosophy of science. II. Some approaches to conceptual problems. JNMD 1961, 133:25-35

HINKLE, LAWRENCE, E.

76920 Ecological observations of the relation of physical illness, mental illness, and the social environment. PSM 1961, 23:289-297
          Abs ICFH Q 1962, 31:427

See Stafford-Clark, David

HINOJOSA, ARMANDO

76921 Lógica y semántica en psicoanálisis. [Logic and semantics in psycho-analysis.] Rev Psicoanál Psiquiat Psicol 1967, 6:29-40

76922 [Psychoanalytic study of the character structure of university students.] (Sp) Rev Psicoanál Psiquiat Psicol 1965, 1:20-37
Abs Vega Q 1966, 35:629

HINOJOSA, JOSÉ RUBÉN

See Arizmendi Ch., Fernando

ABSTRACT OF:

76923 Gordon, K. T., Jr. Religious prejudice in an 8-year-old boy. Cuad Psa 1965, 1:300

HINSIE, LELAND E.

76924 The Person in the Body: An Introduction to Psychosomatic Medicine. NY: Norton 1962, 262 p

HINSLEY, D. B.

76925 A contribution to the theory of ego and self. Psychiat Q 1962, 36:96-120

HIPPLER, ARTHUR E.

76926 Popular art styles in Mariachi Festivals. Am Im 1969, 26:167-181

HIRE, A. WILLIAM

See Chase, Louis S.; Mathews, W. Mason

HIRSCH, C. L.

76927 (& Dana, R. H.) Repression-sensitization and psychological defenses. Percept mot Skills 1968, 27:32

HIRSCH, ERNEST A.

76928 Basic mistrust and defensive omnipotence in a severely disorganized child. J Amer Acad Child Psychiat 1966, 5:243-254

HIRSCH, HERMAN

76929 [Psychogenic sterility.] (Heb) Harefuah 1966, 71:311-313

HIRSCH, JULES

See Glucksman, Myron L.; McCully, Robert S.

HIRSCH, LINDA L.

See Grunebaum, Henry U.

HIRSCH, STEVEN J.

76930   Left, right, and identity. Arch gen Psychiat 1966, 14:84-88
          Abs PB Q 1968, 37:630

        See Hollender, Marc H.

HIRSCH, STEVEN R.

76931   Need for redefining the role of psychoanalysis. P 1968, 124:1468-1469

HIRSCHBERG, J. COTTER

76932   (& Mandelbaum, A.) The adolescent and his parents: ego development
          and differentiation. Forest Hosp Publ 1964, 2:25-35
76933   The basic functions of a child psychiatrist in *any* setting. J Am Acad
          Child Psychiat 1966, 5:360-366
76934   (& Noshpitz, J.) Comments on sociopsychological aspects of juvenile
          delinquency. Amer J Dis Children 1955, 89:361-367
76935   Dreaming, drawing and the dream screen in the psychoanalysis of a
          two-and-a-half-year-old boy. P 1966, 122(Suppl):37-45
76936   Foreword: the diagnostic process in child psychiatry. Reiss-Davis Clin
          Bull 1967, 4:62-65
76937   Military psychiatry, a summary of some of the literature. Amer J Med
          Sci 1943, 206:112
S-48842 Parental anxieties accompanying sleep disturbance in young children.
          Abs Deutsch, L. An Surv Psa 1957, 8:210-212
76938   Play therapy. Tokyo J Psa 1968, 26:19-22
76939   (& Mandelbaum, A.) Problems of administration and supervision in an
          inpatient treatment center for children. BMC 1957, 21:208-219
76940   Residential school services for the exceptional child. In *Services for
          Exceptional Children*, Langhorne, Pa: The Woods School 1956, 45-71
76941   Some comments on religion and childhood. BMC 1955, 19:227-228
76942   (& Rogers, L.; Stubblefield, R. L.; Thaler, M.; Princi, F.; Coleman,
          J. V.) A study of miners in relation to the accident problem. I. Psychi-
          atric evaluation. Ops 1950, 20:552-559
76943   (& Kass, W.; Wheeler, M. E.) Survey of State Residential Child Care
          and Treatment Institutions in Kansas. (Summary report to the State
          Dept of Social Welfare and the Director of Institutions, Sept 1955)
          Topeka, Kan: State Printer 1956

        See Bryant, Keith N.; Krug, Othilda; Margolin, Sydney G.; Murphy,
        Lois B.; Switzer, Robert E.

HIRSCHHORN, THEODORA

        See Sher, Elizabeth

HIRSCHI, TRAVIS

76944   (& Selvin, H. C.) Delinquency Research. An Appraisal of Analytic
          Methods. NY: Free Pr 1967, xiv + 280 p

HIRSH, HERMAN

76945 The family physician as a role player. Postgrad Med 1964, 35:159-164
76946 Psychologic clues in the medical history. GP 1964, 29:106-112

ABSTRACTS OF:
76947 Alexander, J. M. & Isaacs, K. S. The function of affect. Q 1965, 34:472
76948 Bram, F. M. The gift of Anna O. Q 1966, 35:317
76949 Fairbairn, W. R. D. A note on the origin of male homosexuality. Q 1965, 34:142
76950 Hofling, C. K. Percival Lowell and the canals of Mars. Q 1965, 34:142
76951 Honig, A. M. Pathological identifications. Q 1964, 33:612
76952 Janis, I. L. Group identification under conditions of external danger. Q 1964, 33:611-612
76953 Lichtenberg, J. D. Untreating—its necessity in the therapy of certain schizophrenic patients. Q 1964, 33:612
76954 Liebermann, L. P. Case history of a borderline personality. Q 1966, 35:316
76955 Miller, A. A. et al: The nature of the observing function of the ego. Q 1966, 35:318
76956 Novey, S. The significance of the actual historical event in psychiatry and psychoanalysis. Q 1966, 35:316
76957 Ostow, M. The libido plethora syndrome: a clinical study. Q 1965, 34:472
76958 Sachs, L. J. & Stern, B. H. Bernard Shaw and his women. Q 1966, 35:316-317
76959 Sym, J. C. B. The mathematical thought process with reference to a single case. Q 1966, 35:318
76960 Thomae, H. Some psychoanalytic observations on anorexia nervosa. Q 1964, 33:612
76961 Weblin, J. E. Psychogenesis in asthma. Q 1964, 33:611
76962 Wisdom, J. O. A methodological approach to the problem of obsessional neurosis. Q 1965, 34:472
76963 Yorke, C. Some metapsychological aspects of interpretation. Q 1966, 35:317

HIRT, MICHAEL

76964 (& Ross, W. D.; Kurtz, R.; Gleser, G. C.) Attitudes to body products among normal subjects. JAbP 1969, 74:486-489
76965 (Ed) Psychological and Allergic Aspects of Asthma. Springfield, Ill: Thomas 1965

See Gross, Steven J.; Kurtz, Richard; Ross, William Donald

HISAMATSU, SHIN-ICHI
See Jung, Carl G.

HISHER, S.
See Nesbitt, Robert E. L., Jr.

HITCHCOCK, JOHN

76966 (& Mooney, W. E.) Mental health consultation: a psychoanalytic formulation. Arch gen Psychiat 1969, 21:353-358

HITSCHMANN, EDWARD (EDUARD)

S-14566A Letter to Freud, May 6, 1916.
   Abs AHM An Surv Psa 1956, 7:10-11
S-14601A Some psycho-analytic aspects of biography.
   Abs JAL An Surv Psa 1956, 7:411
S-14603 Das Strafen aus analerotischen Motiven. In Bittner, G. & Rehm, W. *Psychoanalyse und Erziehung*, Bern/Stuttgart: Hans Huber 1964
S-14606 Telepathy and psychoanalysis. Heirs Freud 101-120

HJORTZBERG-NORDLUND, H.

76967 [Obesity in 50-year-old men: genetic, social and psychic aspects.] (Sw) Lakartidningen 1966, 63:526-530

HOAKEN, P. C. S.

See Heath, E. Sheldon

HOBBS, DAVID B.

76968 (& Osman, M. P.) From prison to the community: a case study. Crime Dlinq 1967, 13:317-322

HOBBS, NICHOLAS

76969 Ethics in clinical psychology. In Wolman, B. B. *Handbook of Clinical Psychology*, NY/Toronto: McGraw-Hill 1965, 1507-1514
* * * A new cosmology. See [76970]
76970 Sources of gain in psychotherapy. Am Psych 1962, 17:18-34. In Hammer, E. F. *Uses of Interpretation in Treatment: Technique and Art*, NY: Grune & Stratton 1968, 13-21. With title: A new cosmology. In Berenson, B. G. & Carkhuff, R. R. *Sources of Gain in Counseling and Psychotherapy*, NY/Chicago/San Francisco: Holt, Rinehart & Winston 1967, 114-125

HOBERMAN, SHIRLEY E.

76971 (& Goldfarb, W.) Speech reception thresholds in schizophrenic children. J speech hear Res 1963, 6:101-106

HOBSON, R. F.

76972 Psychological aspects of circumcision. J anal Psych 1961, 6:3-33

HOCH, ERNA M.

76973 Biochemical individuality: a psychiatrist's point of view. Transactions of All-India Institute of Mental Health 1965, 5:125-137
76974 A pattern of neurosis in India. Psa 1960, 20:8-25
76975 Psychotische Episoden bei Asthmatikern. [Psychotic episodes in asthmatics.] Z PSM 1965, 11:22-36; 83-91

HOCH, PAUL H.

76976 Biological bases of psychiatry: the viewpoint of the clinician. Recent Adv biol Psychiat 1965, 7:125-133

76977 The combination of psychotherapy with drug therapy. Sci Psa 1963, 6:269-277

76978 (& Zubin, J.) (Eds) Comparative Epidemiology of the Mental Disorders. NY: Grune & Stratton 1961, xvi + 290 p

76979 Concepts of schizophrenia. Out-Patient Schiz 1-16

76980 (& Cattell, J. P.; Strahl, M. O.; Pennes, H. H.) The course and outcome of pseudoneurotic schizophrenia. J 1962, 119:106-115
　　　Abs Loeb, L. Q 1963, 32:608

S-48856 (& Zubin, J.) (Eds) Current Approaches to Psychoanalysis
　　　Rv Harkavy, E. E. Q 1961, 30:568-571

76981 Current approaches to psychoanalysis. JNMD 1962, 288-291

76982 Discussion of Appel, K. E. "Some perspectives in psychoanalysis." In author's The Future of Psychiatry 137-141

76983 (Contributor to) Discussion of Arieti, S. "Etiological considerations of schizophrenia." Out-Patient Schiz 30-32

76984 Discussion of Kalinowsky, L. B. "Evaluation of somatic therapies." Proc Amer Psychopath Ass 1964, 52:52-57

76985 Discussion of Kanner, L. "Schizophrenia as a concept." Out-Patient Schiz 52-59; 154-155

76986 (Contributor to) Discussion of Rado, S. "Theory and therapy." Out-Patient Schiz 102-113

76987 (Contributor to) Discussion of Williams, G. E. "Crisis in the evaluation of the schizophrenic patient." Out-Patient Schiz 74-86

76988 Drugs and psychotherapy. Prog PT 1960, 5:46-50

76989 (& Zubin, J.) (Eds) The Evaluation of Psychiatric Treatment. NY: Grune & Stratton 1964, 326 p
　　　Rv Robbins, L. L. Q 1966, 35:443-444

76990 (& Zubin, J.) (Eds) The Future of Psychiatry. NY/London: Grune & Stratton 1962, xii + 271 p
　　　Rv VC Q 1964, 33:115-119

76991 (& Rado, S.) A graduate school for psychiatric education of physicians in mental hospital service. P 1961, 117:883-886

76992 Methods and analysis of drug-induced abnormal mental states in man. Comprehen Psychiat 1960, 1(5):265-272
　　　Abs Saucier, J.-L. RFPsa 1962, 26:605

76993 Preface to Brussel, J. A. The Layman's Guide to Psychiatry, NY: Barnes & Noble 1961, vii-viii

76994 (& Gero, G.; Rado, S.; Will, O. A., Jr.) Problems in the psychoanalytic treatment of depressions: panel discussion. Bull Ass Psa Med 1963, 2(3):35-40

76995 Psychodynamics and psychotherapy of depressions. Canad Psychiat Ass J 1959, 4(Suppl):24-31

76996 (& Zubin, J.) (Eds) Psychopathology of Perception. NY/London: Grune & Stratton 1965, xii + 336 p

76997 (& Zubin, J.) (Eds) Psychopathology of Schizophrenia. NY/London: Grune & Stratton 1966, xii + 582 p
　　　Rv Richter, P. Q 1968, 37:615-616

76998 Research: ongoing and needed: Out-Patient Schiz 203-211
76999 The responsibility of psychoanalysts in community mental health programs. Sci Psa 1965, 8:262-267
77000 Schizophrenia. Proc Amer Psychopath Ass 1966, 54:283-301
77001 The somatotherapies and psychopharmacology. In Kaufman, M. R. *The Psychiatric Unit in a General Hospital,* NY: IUP 1965, 193-198; 281-304

See Horowitz, William A.; Kalinowsky, Lothar B.; Lesse, Stanley; Lewis, Nolan D. C.

HOCH, S.

See Alston, Edwin F.

HOCHHEIMER, WOLFGANG

77002 Probleme einer politischen Psychologie. [Problems of a political psychology.] Psyche 1962, 16:1-33
    Abs IBa RFPsa 1964, 28:462
77003 Die Psychotherapie von C. G. Jung. Bern/Stuttgart: Huber 1966, 87 p
    The Psychotherapy of C. G. Jung. (Tr: Nagel, H.) NY: Barrie & Rockliff; Putnam 1969, 160 p
77004 Vorurteilsminderung in der Erziehung und die Prophylaxe des Antisemitismus. [Decrease of prejudices in education and the prevention of anti-Semitism.] Psyche 1962, 16:285-311
77005 Zur Rolle von Autorität und Sexualität im Generationskonflikt. [On the role of authority and sexuality in the conflict of the generations.] Psyche 1966, 20:493-519

HOCKETT, CHARLES F.

See Pittenger, Robert E.

HODGE, JAMES R.

77005A (& Wagner, E. E.) The effect of trance depth on Rorschach responses. Amer J clin Hypn 1969, 11:234-238
77005B (& Wagner, E. E.) An exploration of psychodynamics with hypnosis. Amer J clin Hypn 1969, 12:91-94

See Wagner, Edwin E.

HODGE, MARSHALL BRYANT

77006 Your Fear of Love. Garden City, NY: Doubleday 1967, x + 270 p

HODGES, DONALD CLARK

77007 Normal sadism and immoralism. PPR 1961, 48(2):33-40
    Abs CG RFPsa 1963, 27:346
77008 Psychopathy: a philosophical approach. Arch Crim Psychodyn 1961, (Spec No):489-501

HODGSON, F. M.

See Gattegno, C.

HODGSON, R. J.

See Rachman, Stanley

HODIN, JOSEF PAUL

77009 Cultural psychology of Sigmund Freud. In author's *Dilemma of Being Modern,* London: Routledge 1956, 193-219

HOEDEMAKER, EDWARD D.

77010 Discussion of Kubie, L. S. "Reflections on training." Psa Forum 1966, 1:108-110
77011 Intensive psychotherapy of schizophrenia. Canad Psychiat Ass J 1967, 12:253-261
S-48909 Preanalytic preparation for the therapeutic process in schizophrenia. Abs WCW An Surv Psa 1958, 9:364-365
S-48910 Psychoanalytic technique and ego modifications. Abs PCR RFPsa 1964, 28:293-294
77012 The psychotic identifications in schizophrenia: the technical problem. In Boyer, L. B. & Giovacchini, P. L. *Psychoanalytic Treatment of Schizophrenic and Characterological Disorders,* NY: Sci House 1967, 189-207
S-48911 The therapeutic process in the treatment of schizophrenia. Abs An Surv Psa 1955, 6:370-372

HOEDEMAKER, F. S.

See Kales, Anthony

HOEHN-SARIC, RUDOLF

77013 (& Frank, J. D.; Imber, S. D.; Nash, E. H.; Stone, A. R.; Battle, C. C.) Systematic preparation of patients for psychotherapy: I. Effects on therapy behavior and outcome. J psychiat Res 1964, 2:267-281

See Imber, Stanley D.; Nash, Earl H.; Stone, Anthony R.; Truax, Charles D.

HOEK, ASHER

77014 (& Moses, R.; Terraspolsky, L.) Emotional disorders in an Israeli immigrant community. Israel Ann Psychiat 1965, 3:213-228
77015 (& Moses, R.; Terraspolsky, L.) Recognized emotional disorders in an Israeli immigrant community. Med Care 1965, 3:230-239

See Moses, Rafael; Wollstein, Shlomoh

HOEK, SHELOMIT

77016 [Some problems of mothers of handicapped children.] (Heb) Megamot 1962, 12:146-153

See Moses, Rafael

HOEKSTRA, MARTHA
See Burks, Henry L.

HOENIG, J.

77017 The clinical usefulness of the phenomenology of delusions. Int J Psychiat 1968, 6:41-45

TRANSLATIONS OF:
(& Hamilton, M. W.) Jaspers, K. [15744, 77739]

HOFF, HANS

77018 Bergrüssungsworte und Hinweis auf die Tradition der Wiener Psychiatrischen Klinik. [A word of greeting and a reference to the tradition of the Wiener Psychiatrische Klinik.] WMW 1960, 110:712-713
77019 (& Kraus, H.) Die chirurgische Behandlung des Schmerzes. [The surgical treatment of pain.] In author's *Therapeutische Fortschritte in der Neurologie und Psychiatrie* 144-159
77020 Discussion of Bleuler, M. "Conception of schizophrenia within the last fifty years and today." Int J Psychiat 1965, 1(4):521-523
77021 Die Einheit der Schizophrenie. [The uniformity of schizophrenia.] Wien Z Nervenheilk 1968, 26:1-12
77022 Eröffnungsvortrag. [Proceedings of the 5th International Congress of Psychotherapy. Introductory lecture.] Acta psychother psychosom 1962, 10:89-98
77023 (& Pateisky, K.; Tschabitscher, H.) Die funktionsmässigen und neurophysiologischen Grundlagen der modernen Neurologie. [The functional and neurophysiological principles of modern neurology.] In author's *Therapeutische Fortschritte in der Neurologie und Psychiatrie* 3-21
77024 Gegenwärtige Problematik der Prüfungsneurosen in Wien. [Present problems of examination neuroses in Vienna.] Wien klin Wschr 1967, 79:153-155
77025 In Memoriam. Univ.-Professor Dr. Erwin Stransky. [In memoriam: Professor Erwin Stransky.] WMW 1962, 112:181-182
77026 (& Ringel, E.) A modern psychosomatic view of the theory of organ inferiority by Alfred Adler. Adv PSM 1960, 1:120-127
77027 (& Strotzka, H.) [Modern trends in psychotherapy.] (Ger) Mat med Nordmark 1962, 14:347-356
77028 The multifactorial approach in psychiatry. J Neuropsychiat 1960, 1:173-181
77029 [On anxiety.] (Ger) Ther Gegenw 1965, 104:287-292
77030 (et al) Phase-specific therapy of psychic disturbances: biologic, psychotherapeutic and sociodynamic aspects. Psychiat Dig 1968, 29:11-14
77031 Die Problematik der organischen Demenz. [On the problem of organic dementia.] WMW 1966, 116:259-261
77032 [The psychological roots of social behavior.] (Ger) Landarzt 1961, 37:1289-1294
77033 Schizophrener Defekt oder Residualzustand. [Schizophrenic defect or residual state.] Wien Z Nervenheilk 1966, 24:82-84

77034 Social factors in the symptomatology of schizophrenia. Int J Psychiat 1967, 4:131
77035 (Ed) Therapeutische Fortschritte in der Neurologie und Psychiatrie. [Therapeutic Progress in Neurology and Psychiatry.] Vienna/Innsbruck: Verlag Urban & Schwarzenberg 1960, viii + 510 p
77036 (& Pateisky, K.; Strotzka, H.) Die Therapie der Epilepsie. [Treatment of epilepsy.] In author's *Therapeutische Fortschritte in der Neurologie und Psychiatrie* 203-227
77037 (& Pateisky, K.; Strotzka, H.) Die Therapie der kindlichen Epilepsie. [Treatment of childhood epilepsy.] In author's *Therapeutische Fortschritte in der Neurologie und Psychiatrie* 228-233
77038 Les troubles de la conscience dans les lésions temporales. [Disorders of consciousness in temporal lesions.] Riv sper Freniat 1965, 89:1583-1587
77039 War die Errichtung einer kinderpsychiatrisch-neurologischen Abteilung nötig? [Was the erection of a child psychiatric-neurological department necessary?] Wien Z Nervenheilk 1962, 19:101-104

See Arnold, O. H.

HOFFBERG, CAROLINE

77040 (& Fast, I.) Ego-id relationships and professional identity. J proj Tech 1966, 30:488-498

HOFFER, WILLI

77041 Bemerkungen zur Abwehrlehre. In van der Leeuw, P. J. et al: *Hoofdstukken uit de Hedendaagse Psychoanalyse,* Arnheim: Van Loghum Slaterus 1967, 20-30
Notes on the theory of defense. Psa St C 1968, 23:178-188
S-14911 Bericht über die Einleitung einer Kinderanalyse. In Bittner, G. & Rehm, W. *Psychoanalyse und Erziehung,* Bern/Stuttgart: Hans Huber 1964
77042 Bibliography of Willi Hoffer. Psa St C 1968, 23:9-11
S-14912 Deceiving the deceiver.
Der getauschte Hochstapler. In Bolterauer, L. *Aus der Werkstatt des Erziehungsberaters,* Vienna: Verlag f. Jugend und Volk 1960, 207-213
S-14913 Development of the body ego.
Abs Raimondi, R. S. Rev Psicoanál 1966, 23:270
77043 Discussion of Lubin, A. J. "The influence of the Russian Orthodox Church on Freud's Wolf-man: a hypothesis." Psa Forum 1967, 2:163
77044 Geleitworte. [Preface.] Jb Psa 1960, 1:viii-ix
S-14920 Mouth, the hand and ego integration.
Mund, Hand und Ich-Integration. Psyche 1964, 18:81-88
Abs Raimondi, R. S. Rev Psicoanál 1966, 23:269
77045 Obituary: Melanie Klein. (Read at Brit Psa Soc, 5 Oct 1960) J 1961, 42:1-3
S-48653 Psychoanalysis: Practical and Research Aspects.
Abs WAS An Surv Psa 1955, 6:514-519
77046 Siegfried Bernfeld and "Ferubbaal." An episode in the Jewish youth movement. Year Book X of the Leo Baeck Institute, London 1965, 150-167

77047   Eine therapeutische Illusion. [A therapeutic illusion.] Jb Psa 1961-62, 2:245-258
S-14926 Three psychological criteria for the termination of treatment.
           Abs Baranger, M. Rev urug Psa 1961-62, 4:363
S-48955 Transference and transference neurosis.
           Abs JAL An Surv Psa 1956, 7:332-333. Prego, V. M. de Rev urug Psa 1961-62, 4:205
77048   Über die sozialen und wissenschlaftlichen Verpflictungen des Psychoanalytikers. [On the social and scientific obligations of psychoanalysis.] Jb Psa 1961-62, 2:279-293

REVIEW OF:
77049   Nunberg, H. & Federn, E. (Eds) Minutes of the Vienna Psychoanalytic Society, Vol. I: 1906-1908. (Read at Brit Psa Soc, 17 June 1964) J 1965, 46:375-381

HOFFMAN, BARBARA R.

See Bullard, Dexter M., Jr.

HOFFMAN, CAROL A.

See Burks, Henry L.

HOFFMAN, FRANCIS H.

77050   A pattern of teaching psychotherapy. Int Psychiat Clin 1964, 1:283-292
S-48982 (& Brody, M. W.) The symptom, fear of death.
           Abs CK An Surv Psa 1957, 8:101
77051   (Ed) Teaching of Psychotherapy. (International Psychiatry Clinics 1964, Vol. 1, [2].) Boston: Little, Brown 1964, xx + 271-497

See Devereux, George; Jaffe, Beryl

HOFFMAN, FREDERICK JOHN

77052   Literary form and psychic tension. In Manheim, L. & Manheim, E. *Hidden Patterns*, NY: Macmillan 1966, 50-65
77053   The Mortal No; Death and the Modern Imagination. Princeton, N.J.: Princeton Univ Pr 1964, xv + 507 p

HOFFMAN, LOIS WLADIS

77054   (& Hoffman, M. L.) (Eds) Review of Child Development Research. Vol. II. NY: Russell Sage Foundation 1966, xi + 598 p

HOFFMAN, LYNN

See Haley, Jay

HOFFMAN, MARTIN

77055   Drug addiction and "hypersexuality": related modes of mastery. Comprehen Psychiat 1964, 5:262-270

77056 The Gay World. Male Homosexuality and the Social Creation of Evil. NY: Basic Books 1968, x + 212 p
77057 The idea of freedom in psycho-analysis. (Read at Am Psa Ass, May 1964) J 1964, 45:579-583
77058 A note on the origins of ego psychology. PT 1962, 16:230-234
77059 On the concept of genital primacy. JNMD 1963, 137:552-556
77060 On the relationship between psychoanalysis and the philosophy of mind. Q 1962, 31:62-72
77061 Psychiatry, nature and science. P 1960, 117:205-210

HOFFMAN, MARTIN L.

77062 (& Saltzstein, H. D.) Parent discipline and the child's moral development. J Pers soc Psychol 1967, 5:45-57
77063 Personality, family structure, and social class as antecedents of parental power assertion. Child Develpm 1963, 34:869-884

See Hoffman, Lois Wladis

HOFFMAN, MICHAEL B.

See Reding, Georges R.

HOFFMANN, GERHARD

77064 Angustia existential y perspectiva de integracion. [Existential anxiety and integration span.] Revista de Psichiatria ye Psicologia Médica de Europa y Américas Latinas, 4 Congreso Internacional de Psicoterapia 1959-60, 282-287
S-48991 Die Beziehungen zwischen Aktualneurosen, Psychoneurosen und Realitätsprinzip. Abs HK An Surv Psa 1958, 9:52-53
77065 Hochschulpsychiatrie. [College psychiatry.] Dyn Psychiat 1969, 2(1-2):96-103. Abs (Eng) 103-104
77066 Hochschulpsychiatrie: Sozialer Aufsteig und Störungen bei Studenten. [College psychiatry: social and psychological disturbances in students.] Dyn Psychiat 1969, 2:183-186. Abs (Eng) 187

HOFFMANN, S. O.

77067 Ist es nützlich, die Psychoanalyse als "historische" Wissenschaft zu betrachten? [Is it useful to treat psychoanalysis as a "historical" science?] Psyche 1969, 23:838-841
77068 (& Perrez, M.; Rosenkötter, L.) Über den logischen Status der psychoanalytischen Theorie. [On the logical status of psychoanalytic theory.] Psyche 1969, 23:838-853

HOFFNUNG, R. J.

77068A Conditioning and transfer of affective self-references in a role-played counseling interview. J consult clin Psychol 1969, 33:527-531

HOFFS, JOSHUA A.

77069 Anthropophagy (cannibalism): its relation to the oral stage of development. R 1963, 50:187-214
77070 Comments on psychoanalytic biography with special reference to Freud's interest in Woodrow Wilson. R 1969, 56:402-414

HOFLING, CHARLES K.

77071 (& Leininger, M.) Basic Psychiatric Concepts in Nursing. (Foreword: Levine, M.) (Introd: Redmond, M. H.) Phila: Lippincott 1960, 540 p
77072 Dynamic psychology and creative writing. BMC 1963, 27:219-226
77073 (& Pierce, C. M. et al) An experimental study in physician-nurse relationships. JNMD 1966, 143:171-180
77074 General Custer and the battle of the Little Big Horn. R 1967, 54:303-328
        Abs SRS Q 1968, 37:473
77075 Hemingway's *The Old Man and the Sea* and the male reader. Am Im 1963, 20:161-173
77076 The Hyde effect. Medical Opinion & Review 1969, 5(6):152-155
77077 Linkages between psychiatric and non-psychiatric insights. Ment Hosp 1964, 15(2):101-107
77078 Notes on Shakespeare's *Cymbeline*. In Barroll, J. L. *Shakespeare Studies, Vol. I*, Cincinnati: Univ of Cincinnati 1965
77079 Percival Lowell and the canals of Mars. M 1964, 37:33-42
        Abs Hirsch, H. Q 1965, 34:142
77080 The place of great literature in the teaching of psychiatry. BMC 1966, 30:368-373
77081 Psychological aspects of creative writing. McGraw-Hill Sound Seminars 1969
77082 Some psychological aspects of malingering. GP 1965, 21:115
77083 (et al) (Eds) Textbook of Psychiatry for Medical Practice. Phila/ Montreal: Lippincott 1963, 1968, xv + 558 p
        Spanish: 1965
77084 Thomas Hardy and *The Mayor of Casterbridge*. Comprehen Psychiat 1968, 9:428-439

See Ornstein, Paul H.

HOFMANN, G.

See Arnold, O. H.; Hoff, Hans

HOFMANN, H.

77085 Children's dreams; their expression and interpretation. Childh Educ 1963, 40(Nov):143-146

HOFSTÄTTER, PETER R.

77086 Die Diktatur der Vernunft. Der 23. September: Sigmund Freuds fünfundzwangzigster Todestag. [The dictatorship of reason. September 23rd: the 25th anniversary of Sigmund Freud's death.] Die Zeit 1964, 19(39):19-23

HOFSTEIN, SAUL
77087 Inner choice and outer reality. J Otto Rank Ass 1968, 3(1):54-65

HOGAN, PETER
See Alger, Ian

HOGENRAAD, R.
See Wilmars, Charles Mertens de

ABSTRACT OF:
77088 Wilmars, C. M. de & Hogenraad, R. Essai d'analyse du contexte linguistique chez une prépsychotique. RFPsa 1967, 31:183

HÖGLUND, BENGT
77089 (& Ulrich, J. W.) (Eds) Conflict Control and Conflict Resolution. (Interdisciplinary Studies from the Scandinavian Summer University.) Scan Univ Books 1968

HOHLEN, A.
See Richter, Horst-Eberhard

HOIRISCH, ADOLFO
See Manhaes, Maria P.

HØJER-PEDERSEN, WILLY
77090 The dysphoric syndrome, with special reference to dysphoric neurosis as an independent depressive mental disturbance. Acta Psychiat Scand 1963, 39(Suppl 1969):382-392
77091 États névrotiques chez les malades atteints d'un ulcère du duodenum. [Neurotic states in patients with duodenal ulcer.] RFPsa 1961, 25:875-879
77092 The hysterical personality type. Its relation to other neurotic characters and hysteriform syndromes. Acta Psychiat Scand 1965, 41:122-128
77092A [Psychoanalysis and freedom.] (Dan) Nord Psykiat T 1969, 23:59-66
77093 [Social consultation, social casework, psychotherapy and psychoanalysis.] (Dan) Ugeskr Laeg 1963, 125:1370-1374
S-49011 Symposium on disturbances of the digestive tract.
Abs JBi Q 1962, 31:120-121

HOJMAN, RAQUEL K. DE
ABSTRACTS OF:
77094 Bergler, E. The clinical importance of "Rumpelstiltskin" as anti-male manifesto. Rev Psicoanál 1961, 18:390
77095 Feldman, A. A. The Davidic dynasty and the Davidic messiah. Rev Psicoanál 1961, 18:388
77096 Skinner, J. Ritual matricide: a study of the origins of sacrifice. Rev Psicoanál 1961, 18:390
77097 Veszy-Wagner, L. Mistress Pokai—a contribution of the theory of obsessive doubts. Rev Psicoanál 1961, 18:387

HOKANSON, JACK E.

77098 Effects of guilt arousal and severity of discipline on adult aggressive behavior. Clin Psych 1961, 17:29-32

See Caldon, George

HOLBROOK, DAVID

77099 Enlightenment or demoralization. 20th Cent 1966, 175(Aug):33-37
77100 R. D. Laing & the death circuit. Encounter 1968, 31(2):35-45
77101 Society and our instincts; phantom authorities for the new moral revolution. Univ Q 1966, 21(Dec):52-65

HOLDEN, H. M.

77102 Psychiatry and the law. Brit med J 1963, Part 2 (5366):1201
77103 Psychotherapy of a shared syndrome in identical twins. Brit J Psychiat 1965, 111:859-864

See Chandler, E.

HOLDEN, MARJORIE A.

See Scheidlinger, Saul

HOLDER, ALEX

77104 Theoretical and clinical notes on the interaction of some relevant variables in the production of neurotic disturbances. Psa St C 1968, 23:63-85

See Sandler, Joseph

HOLEMON, E.

See Winokur, George

HOLFELD, H.

77104A (& Leuner, H.) ["Patricide" as the central conflict of a psychogenic psychosis.] (Ger) Nervenarzt 1969, 40:203-209

HOLLAND, B.

See Spence, Donald P.

HOLLAND, BERNARD

See Earley, Leroy W.

HOLLAND, GLEN A.

77105 Fundamentals of Psychotherapy. NY: Holt, Rinehart & Winston 1965, xi + 308 p
       Rv Rawn, M. L. R 1966, 53:159-162
77106 The three self images of the patient in psychotherapy. J ind Psych 1966, 22:94-99

HOLLAND, NORMAN NORWOOD

77107   Caliban's dream. (Read at Boston Psa Soc & Inst, Spring 1966) Q 1968, 37:114-125

77108   Clinical, yes. Healthy, no. Lit & Psych 1964, 14:121-125

77109   Comment on "The death of Zenocrate." Lit & Psych 1966, 16:25-26

77110   The Dynamics of Literary Response. NY: Oxford Univ Pr 1968, xviii + 378 p; 1969, 341 p
Rv Burgum, E. B. Am Im 1969, 26:79-82. Weiner, N. D. Bull Phila Ass Psa 1969, 19:91-94

77111   Freud and form: fact about fiction. Vict Stud 1966, 10:76-82

77112   Freud and H. D. J 1969, 50:309-315

77113   Freud and the poet's eye. Lit & Psych 1961, 11:36-45. In Manheim, L. & Manheim, E. *Hidden Patterns*, NY: Macmillan 1966, 151-170

77114   Freud on Shakespeare. PMLA 1960, 75:163-173. M. I. T. Humanities Series, No. 47. Show 196?, 4(2 Feb):86, 108

77115   Hobbling with Horatio; or, The uses of literature. Hudson Rev 1959-60, 12:549-557

77116   A literary critic's view of Heinz Hartmann's concept of adaptation. (Read at Boston Psa Inst, Spring 1964) Bull Phila Ass Psa 1965, 15:4-9
Abs EFA Q 1966, 35:154

77117   Literary value: psychoanalytic approach. Lit & Psych 1964, 14:43-55

77118   Literature, the irrational, and the Professor Shumaker. Lit & Psych 1962, 12:51-54

77119   Macbeth as hibernal giant. Lit & Psych 1960, 10:37-38

77120   Meaning as transformation: the Wife of Bath's tale. College English 1967, 28:279-290

77121   Prose and minds: a psychoanalytic approach to non-fiction. In Levine, G. & Madden, W. *The Art of Victorian Prose*, NY: Oxford Univ Pr 1968, 314-317

77122   Psychoanalysis and Shakespeare. NY/Toronto/London: McGraw-Hill 1966, xi + 412 p
Abs J Am Psa Ass 1967, 15:220. Rv Feldman, A. B. R 1966, 53:312-317. HS Am Im 1966, 23:283. Weiner, N. D. Bull Phila Ass Psa 1967, 17:169-172

77123   Psychoanalytic criticism and perceptual psychology. An article-review. Lit & Psych 1966, 16:81-92

77124   Psychological depths and Dover Beach. Vict Stud 1965, 9(Suppl):5-28

77125   Psychology on Shakespeare, 1897-2064. Shakespeare Newsletter 1964, 14(April-May), Quadricentennial Issue, 27

77126   Puzzling movies: three analyses and a guess at their appeal. J soc Issues 1964, 20:71-96

77127   Realism and the psychological critic; or, how many complexes had Lady Macbeth? Lit & Psych 1960, 10:5-8

77128   Romeo's dream and the paradox of literary realism. (Read at Boston Psa Inst, May 1962) Lit & Psych 1963, 13:97-104

77129   Shakespearean tragedy and the three ways of psychoanalytic criticism. Hudson Rev 1962, 15:217-227. In Ruitenbeek, H. *Psychoanalysis and Literature*, NY: Dutton & Co 1964

77130   Toward a psychoanalysis of poetic form: some mixed metaphors un-mixed. Lit & Psych 1965, 15:79-91

HOLLANDER, E. P.

77130A (Julian, J. W.) Contemporary trends in the analysis of leadership processes. Psychol Bull 1969, 71:387-397

HOLLANDER, FRANKLIN

See Stein, Aaron

HOLLANDER, LEONARD

See Shakow, David

REVIEW OF:
77131 Kolburne, L. L. Effective Education for the Mentally Retarded Child.
What to Teach, How to Teach, and Why. Q 1967, 36:454-455

HOLLANDER, R.

77132 Compulsive cursing. An approach to factors in its genesis, development,
and pathology. Psychiat Q 1960, 34:599-622
    Abs Engle, B. Q 1961, 30:302

HOLLENBERG, CLEMENTINA KUHLMAN

See Berger, Ellen T.

HOLLENDER, MARC H.

77133 (& Luborsky, L.; Scaramella, T. J.) Body contact and sexual enticement.
Arch gen Psychiat 1969, 20:188-191
77134 (& Kaplan, E. A.) (Eds) Clinical Conferences: Topical and Diagnostic.
(International Psychiatry Clin 1965, Vol 2, [3].) Boston: Little, Brown
1965, xii + 537-714
77135 (& Goodwin, F. K.; Fleiss, A. N.; Butz, J. L.; Mariner, A. S.; Kaplan,
E. A.; Hunt, W. L.; Pearl, N. H.) The compensation problem. Int
Psychiat Clin 1965, 2:583-602
77136 (& Pearl, N. H.; Pittenger, R. E.; Diamond, S.; Orgel, S.; Leifer, R.;
Rosner, B. L.; Hassenfeld, I. N.; Rubert, S. L.; Steckler, P. P.; Carmen,
L. M.; Seidenberg, R.; Appalaraju, D.) Cross-cultural psychiatry. Int
Psychiat Clin 1965, 2:537-560
77137 (& Duffy, P. E.; Feldman, H. A.; Steckler, P. P.; Kaplan, E. A.; Fager,
R. E. Fleiss, A. N.) Encephalitis or schizophrenia? Int Psychiat Clin
1965, 2:691-709
77138 (& Hirsch, S. J.) Hysterical psychosis. P 1964, 120:1066-1074
77139 Is the wish to sleep a universal motive for dreaming? J Am Psa Ass
1962, 10:323-328
77140 Marital problems: the selection of therapy. Current trends in psychiatry. Forest Hosp Publ 1968
77141 Marriage and divorce. Arch gen Psychiat 1959, 1:657-661
77142 (& Malev, J. S.; Robinson, D. B.; Streeten, D. H. P; Pearl, N. H.)
Myxedema and psychosis. Int Psychiat Clin 1965, 2:641-664
S-49019 (& Szasz, T. S.) Normality, neurosis, and psychosis: some observations
on the concepts of mental health and mental illness.
    Abs RZ An Surv Psa 1957, 8:154-155

77143 Perfectionism. Comprehen Psychiat 1965, 6:94-103
77144 The Practice of Psychoanalytic Psychotherapy. NY/London: Grune & Stratton 1965, x + 156 p
       Abs J Am Psa Ass 1967, 15:221. Rv Dewald, P. A. Q 1967, 36:455-456. Sternbach, O. R 1967, 54(1):180-182
77145 Privileged communication and confidentiality. Dis nerv Sys 1965, 26:169-175
77146 The prostitute's two identities. Med Asp hum Sexual 1968, 2:45
77147 Prostitution, the body, and human relatedness. J 1961, 42:404-413
       Abs WPK Q 1962, 31:578. PCR RFPsa 1964, 28:301-302
77148 Psychiatric problems in office practice. In Hollender, A. R. *Office Practice of Otolaryngology*, Phila: F. A. Davis Co 1965
77149 (& Mann, W. A.; Danehy, J. J.) The psychiatric resident and the family of the hospitalized patient. Arch gen Psychiat 1960, 2:125-130
77150 The psychiatrist and the release of patient information. P 1960, 116:828-833
       Abs Leavitt, M. Q 1961, 30:145
77151 Psychiatry as part of a mixed internship. A novel program which claims certain unique advantages. JAMA 1961, 175:489-490
77152 (& Kaplan, E. A.) Psychiatry as part of a mixed internship; a report based on five years of experience. Arch gen Psychiat 1965, 12:18-22
77153 Psychoanalysis and behavior therapy—similarities and dissimilarities. Int J Psychiat 1969, 7:508-510
77154 Psychological factors during the postoperative period. In Artz, C. P. & Hardy, J. D. *Complications in Surgery and Their Management*, Phila: Saunders 1960, 363-375
77155 Psychology of office practice. In Hollender, A. R. *Office Practice of Otolaryngology*, Phila: F. A. Davis Co 1965
77156 (& Hirsch, S. J.; Goodwin, F. K.; Kaplan, E. A.; Rubert, S. L.; Watkins, E. S.; Walker, L.; Steckler, P. P.; Albaugh, J. K.; Ripich, L. J.) Schizophrenia or temporal lobe disorder? Int Psychiat Clin 1965, 2:667-689
S-49028 The seeking of sympathy or pity.
       Abs DW An Surv Psa 1958, 9:165-166
77157 Selection of patients for definitive forms of psychotherapy. Arch gen Psychiat 1964, 10:361-369
       Abs KR Q 1965, 34:312
77158 A study of patients admitted to a psychiatric hospital after pelvic opera-tions. Am J Obst Gyn 1960, 79:498-503
77159 Women's fantasies during sexual intercourse. Arch gen Psychiat 1963, 8:86-90
       Abs KR Q 1964, 33:301

       See Malev, Jonathan S.; Nesbitt, Robert E. L., Jr.; Rubert, Shirley L.

HOLLINGSHEAD, AUGUST B.

S-49030 (& Redlich, F. C.) Social Class and Mental Illness.
       Classi Sociali e Malattie Mentali. Turin: Einaudi 1965
       Rv Ravasini, C. Riv Psa 1965, 11:181

HOLLINGSWORTH, IRENE
See Ekstein, Rudolf

HOLLIS, FLORENCE
77160   Casework: A Psychosocial Therapy. NY: Random House 1964, xx +
300 p

HOLLISTER, LEO E.
See Overall, John E.

HOLLISTER, WILLIAM G.
See Bower, Eli M.

HOLLITSCHER, WALTER
* * * Psychoanalysis and Civilization: An Introduction to Sigmund Freud.
See [14988]
S-14988 Sigmund Freud: An Introduction. With title: Psychoanalysis and Civi-
lization: An Introduction to Sigmund Freud. NY: Grove 1963, viii +
119 p

HOLLON, THOMAS H.
77161   Ego psychology and the supportive therapy of borderline states. Psychotherapy 1966, 3:135-138
77162   A rationale for supportive psychotherapy of depressed patients. PT
1962, 16:655-664
77163   (& Zolik, E. S.) Self-esteem and symptomatic complaints in the initial
phase of psychoanalytically oriented psychotherapy. PT 1962, 16:83-93

HOLLOWAY, BETTE
See Singer, Paul

HOLLOWAY, HARRY
See Vogel, William

HOLMES, DAVID S.
77163A (& Tyler, J. D.) Direct versus projective measurement of achievement
motivation. J consult clin Psychol 1968, 32:712-717
77164   (& Watson, R. I.) Early recollections and vocational choice. J consult
Psychol 1965, 29:486-488

HOLMES, DONALD J.
77165   The Adolescent in Psychotherapy. (Foreword: Waggoner, R. W.) Boston: Little, Brown 1964, xviii + 337 p
Rv Strean, H. S. R 1964, 51:679-681
77166   Expressive function of the face. Int Psychiat Clin 1964, 1:19-37

See Hendrickson, Willard J.

HOLMES, DOUGLAS SCOTT

77167 A contribution to a psychoanalytic theory of work. Psa St C 1965, 20: 384-393
77168 An experimental study of catharsis and guilt in aggressive behavior. Diss Abstr 1963, 24(6):2557
77169 Male-female differences in MMPI ego strength: an artifact. J consult Psychol 1967, 31:408-410

HOLMES, ROGER

77170 Freud and social class. Brit J Sociol 1965, 16:48-67

HOLMES, THOMAS H.

See Dorpat, Theodore L.; Dudley, Donald L.; Kogan, W. S.

HOLMSTROM, R.

77171 [On indications for psychoanalysis.] (Fin) Suom Laak 1966, 21:1870-1876

HOLROYD, MICHAEL

77172 Lytton Strachey: A Critical Biography. Vol. I, The Unknown Years. Vol. II, The Years of Achievement. NY: Holt, Rinehart & Winston 1967; 1968, xxii + 479 p; xii + 754 p
    Rv Sherman, M. H. R 1969-70, 56:597-608

HOLSTIJN, A. J.

77173 Verschiedene Definitionen und Auffassungen von "Angst." [Various definitions and interpretations of "anxiety."] Fortschr Psa 1966, 2:174-188

HOLSTIJN, A. J. WESTERMAN

77174 [Remarks on the development of psychoanalytic technic.] (Dut) Belg T Geneesk 1964, 20:1-15
77175 Zwijgende patiënten in de psychoanalyse. [Silent patients in psychoanalysis.] Ned Tijdschr Geneeskunde 1961, 105:2489-2493

HOLT, EDWIN B.

S-15068 The Freudian Wish and Its Place in Ethics.
    Rv J. S. RFPsa 1968, 32:331

HOLT, HERBERT

77176 The case of Father M. A segment of an existential analysis. J existent Psychiat 1966, 6:369-395
77177 (& Winick, C.) The consention approach to dreams. J existent Psychiat 1960-61, 1:219-232
77178 Existential analysis and pastoral counseling. J existent Psychiat 1964-65, 5:233-242

77179 Existential analysis, Freud, and Adler. J existent Psychiat 1967, 8:203-222

77180 The existential conflict between psychiatrists and ministers. MH 1966, 50:186-193

77181 (& Winick, C.) Group psychotherapy with obese women. Arch gen Psychiat 1961, 5:156-168

77182 The hidden roots of aggression in American society. J existent Psychiat 1965-66, 6:225-234

77183 Ludwig Binswanger (1881-1966): a tribute. J existent Psychiat 1966, 6:93-96

77184 The problem of interpretation from the point of view of existential psychoanalysis. In Hammer, E. F. *Use of Interpretation in Treatment: Technique and Art*, NY: Grune & Stratton 1968, 240-252

77185 (& Winick, C.) Psychiatry, religion, and self. Pastoral Psychol 1968, 19(183):35-38

77186 (& Winick, C.) Some psychodynamics in divorce and separation. MH 1965, 49:443-452

See Winick, Charles

REVIEWS OF:

77187 Boyer, B. L. & Giovacchini, P. L. Psychoanalytic Treatment of Characterological and Schizophrenic Disorders. R 1969, 56:150-154

77188 Kelman, H. (Ed) New Perspectives in Psychoanalysis: Contributions to Karen Horney's Holistic Approach. R 1966, 53(1):154-158

HOLT, ROBERT R.

77189 Beyond vitalism and mechanism: Freud's concept of psychic energy. (Read at NY Psa Soc, 22 Sept 1965) Sci Psa 1967, 11:1-41
  Abs Brauer, P. H. Q 1966, 35:476-477

77190 Brave beginning to an enormous task. Int J Psychiat 1966, 2:545-548

77191 Clinical judgment as a disciplined inquiry. JNMD 1961, 133:369-382

77192 A critical examination of Freud's concept of bound vs. free cathexis. (Read at San Francisco Psa Soc, 11 Apr 1960) J Am Psa Ass 1962, 10:475-525
  Abs JBi Q 1963, 32:446. Schlossberg, N. Rev Psicoanál 1963, 20:289

77193 David Rapaport: a memoir. (September 30, 1911—December 14, 1960). Psych Issues 1967, 5:7-17. In author's *Motives and Thought* 7-17

77194 The development of the primary process: a structural view. Psych Issues 1967, 5:345-383. In author's *Motives and Thought* 344-383

77195 Diagnostic testing: present status and future prospects. JNMD 1967, 144:444-465

77196 Ego autonomy re-evaluated. (Read at NY Psa Soc, 26 Oct 1965) J 1965, 46:151-167. Int J Psychiat 1967, 3:481-536
  Abs Fine, B. D. Q 1966, 35:479-481. EVN Q 1967, 36:316-317

77197 The emergence of cognitive psychology. J Am Psa Ass 1964, 12:650-665

77198 Experimental methods in clinical psychology. In Wolman, B. B. *Handbook of Clinical Psychology*, NY/Toronto/London: McGraw-Hill 1965, 40-77

77199 Forcible indoctrination and personality change. In Worchel, P. & Byrne, D. *Personality Change*, NY: Wiley 1964

77200 Freud's cognitive style. Am Im 1965, 22:163-179
Abs JWS Q 1966, 35:474

77200A (Chairman) Ideal training programme for psychoanalysts. (Report on a conference on an ideal programme for psychoanalysts, NY Univ, NY, 21-24 Mar 1963) J 1964, 45:141-142

77201 Imagery: the return of the ostracized. Am Psych 1964, 19:254-264

77202 Individuality and generalization in the psychology of personality. J Pers 1962, 30:377-404

77202A Is the unconscious necessary? The lasting value of the unconscious, or Rabkin fails to Peirce Freud. Int J Psychiat 1969, 8:585-589

77203 Kubie's dream and its impact upon reality. Psychotherapy as an autonomous profession. JNMD 1969, 149:186-207

77204 Measuring libidinal and aggressive motives and their controls by means of the Rorschach test. Nebraska Symposium on Motivation 1966, 14:1-47

77205 (& Havel, J.) A method for assessing primary and secondary process in the Rorschach. In Rickers-Ovsiankina, M. A. *Rorschach Psychology*, NY/London: John Wiley 1960, 263-315

77206 (Ed) Motives and Thought: Psychoanalytic Essays in Honor of David Rapaport. (Psychological Issues, Vol. 5 [2-3] Monograph 18/19) NY: IUP 1967, vi + 413 p
Abs J Am Psa Ass 1968, 16:182. Rv Salzman, L. Am Im 1967, 24:377-379. DRu Q 1968, 37:440-446

77207 New directions in the training of psychotherapists: editorial. JNMD 1963, 137:413-416

77208 On freedom, autonomy, and the redirection of psychoanalytic theory: a rejoinder. Int J Psychiat 1967, 3:524-536

77209 (& Goldberger, L.) Personological correlates of reactions to perceptual isolation. USAF Wright Air Development Center Technical Report 1959, 59-737:1-46

77210 Recent developments in psychoanalytic ego psychology and their implications for diagnostic testing. J proj Tech 1960, 24:254-266

77211 A review of some of Freud's biological assumptions and their influence on his theories. Psa Curr Biol Thought 93-124

S-49048 (& Luborsky, L. B.) The selection of candidates for psychoanalytic training: on the use of interviews and psychological tests.
Abs An Surv Psa 1955, 6:384-385

77212 Two influences on Freud's scientific thought: a fragment of intellectual biography. In White, R. W. *The Study of Lives*, NY: Atherton Pr 1966, 364-387

See Janis, Irving L.; Pine, Fred

HOLT, WILLIAM E.

77213 The concept of motivation for treatment. P 1967, 123:1388-1394

See Stein, Marvin

HOLTZER, F. P. TH. H.

77214 Stoornissen in de vroegste relaties als wortel van eenzaamheidsprob-
lematiek. [Disorders in early relations as the root of the problem of
loneliness.] Ned Tijdschr Psychol 1963, 18:325-335

HOLTZMAN, WAYNE H.

77215 Inkblot perception and personality. The meaning of inkblot variables.
BMC 1963, 27:84-95. In Megargee, E. I. *Research in Clinical Assessment*, NY/London: Harper & Row 1966, 541-552

See Sargent, Helen D.; Sutherland, Robert L.

HOLZBERG, JULES D.

See Farina, Amerigo

HOLZER, CHARLES E.

See Schwab, John J.

HOLZMAN, PHILIP S.

77216 (& Gardner, R. W.) Leveling-sharpening and memory organization. ASP
1960, 60:176-180
Abs Applebaum, S. A. Q 1961, 30:309
77217 (& Rousey, C.; Snyder, C.) On listening to one's own voice: effects on
psychophysiological responses and free associations. J Pers soc Psychol
1966, 4:432-441
77218 On procrastinating. (Read at Topeka Psa Soc, 20 Dec 1962) J 1964,
45:98-109
Abs EVN Q 1966, 35:312
77219 Process in the supervision of psychotherapy, BMC 1965, 29:125-130
77220 Psychoanalysis and Psychopathology. NY: McGraw-Hill 1969, xvi +
204 p
77221 Repression and cognitive style. BMC 1962, 26:273-282
Abs HD Q 1964, 33:602
77222 (& Rousey, C.) The voice as a percept. J Pers soc Psychol 1966, 4:79-
86
77223 (& Berger, A.; Rousey, C.) Voice confrontation: a bilingual study. J
Pers soc Psychol 1967, 7:423-428

See Castaldo, Vincenzo; Schlesinger, Herbert J.; Wallerstein, Robert S.

REVIEWS OF:
77224 Heider, F. On Perception and Event Structure, and the Psychological
Environment. Q 1962, 31:392-393
77225 Wolman, B. B. Contemporary Theories and Systems in Psychology. Q
1962, 31:106-108

HOMANS, P.

77226 Transference and transcendence: Freud and Tillich on the nature of
personal relatedness. J Relig 1966, 46(2):148-164

HOME, H. J. H.

77227 The concept of mind. (Revised version of paper read at Brit Psa Soc, Apr 1964) J 1966, 47:42-49
El concepto de la mente. Rev Psicoanal 1969, 26:141-157
Abs EVN Q 1968, 37:156

REVIEW OF:
77228 Abercrombie, M. L. J. The Anatomy of Judgment. J 1961, 42:127-128

HONIG, ALBERT M.

S-49083 Negative transference in psychosis.
Abs CG RFPsa 1963, 27:343
77229 Pathological identifications. A contribution to direct analysis. M 1963, 36:331-339
Abs Hirsh, H. Q 1964, 33:612. JCS RFPsa 1967, 31:318
77230 Subnormal mental functioning in mental illness. R 1966, 53:112-133
Abs SRS Q 1967, 36:140

HONIGMANN, JOHN JOSEPH

77231 Discussion of Saul, L. J. & Pulver, S. E. "The concept of emotional maturity." Int J Psychiat 1966, 2:446-469
77232 The interpretation of dreams in anthropological field work: a case study. In Kaplan, B. *Studying Personality Cross-Culturally*, NY/Evanston/London: Harper & Row 1961, 579-585
77233 Personality in Culture. NY: Harper & Row 1967, xii + 495 p

HONORTON, C.

77233A Some current perspectives on the hypnotic dream. J Amer Soc Psychosom Dent Med 1969, 16:88-92

HOOD, JAMES ROBERTSON

77234 On therapeutic intervention in the child guidance setting: a case of refusal to stay in school. Brit J child PT 1964, 1

REVIEWS OF:
77235 Bennett, E. A. What Jung Really Said. J 1967, 48:472
77236 Haworth, M. R. (Ed) Child Psychotherapy. J 1965, 46:396

HOOK, SIDNEY

77237 (Ed) New York University Institute of Philosophy. Dimensions of Mind; a Symposium. NY: NY Univ Pr 1960, xiii + 281 p
S-49087 (Ed) Psychoanalysis, Scientific Method, and Philosophy.
Rv Waelder, R. J Am Psa Ass 1962, 10:617-637

HOOKER, EVELYN

77238 The case of E: a biography. J proj Tech 1961, 25:252-267
77239 An empirical study of some relations between sexual patterns and

gender identity. In Money, J. *Sex Research, New Developments,* NY: Rinehart & Winston 1965, 24-52

See Carr, Arthur C.

HOOVER, KENNETH H.

77240 Relationship of psychological theory of instructional practices. Educ Res 1963, 5:132-136

HOPE, K.

See Caine, Thomas M.

HOPKINSON, G.

77241 (& Reed, G. F.) Bereavement in childhood and depressive psychosis. Brit J Psychiat 1966, 112:459-463

77242 The prodromal phase of the depressive psychosis. Psychiat Neurol, Basel 1965, 149:1-6

See Sedman, G.

HOPPE, KLAUS D.

77243 Concentration camp. Psa Forum 1967, 2:186-187

77244 (& Molnar, J.; Newell, J. E.; Land, A.) Diagnostic and developmental classification of adolescent offenders. Comprehen Psychiat 1967, 7:277-283

77245 Discussion in "Symposium: Psychological problems after severe mental stress." Proc IV World Cong Psychiat 1966, 937-938

77246 The emotional reactions of psychiatrists when confronting survivors of persecution. Psa Forum 1969, 3:187-196; 210-211

77247 The existential approach—the existential situation in neurotic and psychotic patients, illuminated by their self-portraits. Med Times 1960, 88:343-352

77248 (& Molnar, J.; Newell, J. E.) Love- and hate-addiction in delinquent male adolescents. Psychother Psychosom 1965, 13:271-277. Proc VI Int Cong PT, Part II, 23-29

77249 Persecution and conscience. R 1965, 52:106-116
   Abs SRS Q 1966, 35:471

77250 Persecution, depression and aggression. BMC 1962, 26:195-203
   Verfolgung, Aggression und Depression. Psyche 1963, 16:521-537

77251 Psychoanalytic remarks on Schnitzler's "Fraulein Else." J Int Arthur Schnitzler Res Ass 1964, 3(1):4-8

77252 The psychodynamics of concentration camp victims. Psa Forum 1966, 1:76-80; 85

77253 Psychosomatic reactions and disorders in victims of persecution. Proc IV World Cong Psychiat 1966, 2734-2737
   Psychosomatische reaktionene und Erkrankungen bei überlebenden schwerer Verfolgung. Psyche 1968, 22:464-477

77254 Psychotherapie bei Konzentrationslageropfern. Psyche 1965, 19:290-319

Psychotherapy with survivors of concentration camps. In Krystal, H. *Massive Psychic Trauma*, Detroit: Wayne Univ Pr 1968

77255 Relaxation through concentration—concentration through relaxation: autogenic training with neurotic and psychotic patients. Med Times 1961, 89:254-263

77256 Re-somatization of affects in survivors of persecution. [Symposium: psychic traumatization through social catastrophe.] (Read at Int Psa Cong, July 1967) J 1968, 49:324-326
   Abs LHR Q 1969, 38:669

77257 Über den Einfluss der Übergangsobjekte und Phänomene auf die Behandlungssituation. [The influence of transitional objects and phenomena on psychotherapy.] Jb Psa 1967, 4:63-81

77258 Über den Einfluss der Übergangsobjekte und Phänomene auf die Symptombildung. [The influence of transitional objects and phenomena on symptom formation.] Jb Psa 1964, 3:86-115

77259 Verfolgung und Gewissen. [Persecution and conscience.] Psyche 1964, 18:305-313

77260 Zum gegenwärtigen Stand der Beurteilung erlebnisbedingter Spätschäden nach Verfolgung. [On the present evaluation of emotional effects after persecution.] Nervenarzt 1966, 37:124

HORA, J.

See Renneker, Richard E.

HORDER, J. P.

77261 Teaching psychosomatic medicine to young general practitioners. J psychosom Res 1967, 11:101-106

HORKHEIMER, MAX

77262 Die Beziehungen zwischen der Soziologie und der Psychoanalyse aus der Sicht der Soziologie. [The relationship between sociology and psychoanalysis from the point of view of sociology.] Jb Psa 1968, 5:9-19

77263 (Participant in symposium) Individuelle und soziale Psychopathologie und ihre Wechselwirkungen. [Individual and social psychopathology and their effects.] Jb Psa 1968, 5:49-87

HÖRMANN, HANS

77264 Psychologie der Sprache. [Psychology of Speech.] Berlin/Heidelberg/NY: Springer 1967, xi + 395 p

HORMIA, A.

77265 Das Kind als Identifikationsobjekt seiner Eltern. [The child as object of identification of its parents.] Acta psychother psychosom 1960, 8:44-52

HORN, EDWARD N.

77266 Surgery, a child and a toy gun. Bull Phila Ass Psa 1961, 11:124-126
   Abs PLe RFPsa 1963, 27:338

HORN, K.

See Berndt, Heide

HORN, KLAUS

77267 Dressur oder Erziehung, Schlagerituale und ihre gesellschaftliche Funktion. [Breaking-In or Education, Beating Rituals and Their Social Function.] Frankfurt: Suhrkamp, Schriften zur Psychologie und Soziologie 1967, 127 p
Rv Veszy-Wagner, L. J 1967, 48:610-611
77268 Fragen einer psychoanalytischen Sozialpsychologie. [Issues of psychoanalytic social psychology.] Psyche 1968, 22:896-911
Abs J 1969, 50:401

See Marcuse, Herbert; Mitscherlich, Alexander

HORNE, B.

See Aslan, Carlos M.

HORNE, BERNADINO C.

See Bellagamba, Hugo F.

HORNER, ALTHEA J.

77269 To touch—or not to touch. Voices 1968, 4(2):26-28

See Bühler, Charlotte

HORNEY, KAREN

77270 Collected Works. NY: W. W. Norton 1963, 2 Vols.
S-15184 Culture and neurosis. In Lindzey, G. & Hall, C. S. *Theories of Personality*, NY/London/Sydney: Wiley 1965, 1966, 1968, 131-136
S-15185 The denial of the vagina: a contribution to the problem of the genital anxieties specific to women. In the author's *Feminine Psychology*, 147-161
S-15188 The dread of women: observations on a specific difference in the dread felt by men and by women respectively for the opposite sex. In author's *Feminine Psychology* 133-146
77271 Feminine Psychology. (Ed: Kelman, H.) London: Routledge; NY: W. W. Norton 1967, 269 p
Abs J Am Psa Ass 1968, 16:180
S-15192 The flight from womanhood: the masculinity complex in women as viewed by men and by women. In author's *Feminine Psychology* 54-70
S-15194 Gehemmte Weiblichkeit. Psychoanalytischer Beitrag zum Problem der Frigidität.
Inhibited feminity: psychoanalytical contributions to the problem of frigidity. In author's *Feminine Psychology* 71-83
S-15195 Zur Genese des weiblichen Kastrationskomplexes.
On the genesis of the castration complex in women. In author's *Feminine Psychology* 37-53

77272 Der Kampf in der Kultur: Einige Gedanken und Bedenken zu Freuds Todestrieb und Destruktionstrieb. [Culture and aggression: some considerations and objections to Freud's theory of instinctual drives toward death and destruction.] (Tr: Van Bark, B. S.) Psa 1960, 20:130-138

S-15199 Maternal conflicts. In author's *Feminine Psychology* 175-181

S-15202 Das Misstrauen zwischen den Geschlechtern.
The distrust between the sexes. In author's *Feminine Psychology* 107-118

S-15208 Das neurotische Liebesbedürfnis.
The neurotic need for love. In author's *Feminine Psychology* 245-258

S-15211 The overvaluation of love. A study of a common present-day feminine type. In author's *Feminine Psychology* 182-213

S-15212 Personality changes in female adolescents. In author's *Feminine Psychology* 234-244

S-15213 Die prämenstruellen Verstimmungen.
Premenstrual tension. In author's *Feminine Psychology* 99-106

S-15215 The problem of feminine masochism. PT Pervers 137-157. In author's *Feminine Psychology* 214-233

S-15218 The problem of the monogamous ideal. In author's *Feminine Psychology* 84-98

S-15220 Zur Problematik der Ehe.
Problems of marriage. In author's *Feminine Psychology* 119-132

S-15222 Psychogenic factors in functional female disorders. In author's *Feminine Psychology* 162-174

S-15233 Die Technik der psychoanalytischen Therapie.
The technique of psychoanalytic therapy. Psa 1968, 28:3-12

See Kelman, Harold

HORNICK, EDWARD J.

77273 Healthy responses, developmental disturbances and stress or reactive disorders. II: Adolescence. Compreh Txbk Psychiat 1366-1369

HORNSTRA, L.

77274 De actualiteit van Marx en de vervreemding. [The current interest of Marx and alienation.] De Nieuwe Stem 1965, 20(Nov)

77275 The antecedents of the negative Oedipus complex. J 1966, 47:531-538 Abs EVN Q 1968, 37:465

77276 Blauwe en rode jeugd. [Youth in revolt]. De Nieuwe Stem 1964, 19(Aug)

77277 Dachau-spel: geen exces. [Ragging students before admission.] Nieuwe Rotterdamse Courant 1962, 25 Oct

77278 Dialoog met het Oosten. [Dialogue with the East.] Nieuwe Rotterdamse Courant 1963, 7 April

77279 Distrust and aggression: an interpersonal-international analogy. J Conflict Resolut 1968, 12:69-81

77280 Een existentiële, psychoanalytische visie op Ingmar Bergman. [An existential and psychoanalytical vision on the films of Ingmar Bergman.] Nieuwe Rotterdamse Courant 1965, 2 April

77281 De Groentijd. [Ragging of students.] De Nieuwe Stem 1963, 18
77282 Homosexuality. J 1967, 48:394-402
        Abs Fernandez, A. A. Rev urug Psa 1967, 9:248-254. LHR Q 1969,
        38:505
77283 Homosexuelen. [Homosexuals.] De Nieuwe Linie 1968, 6 Jan
77284 De humanisten en de geestelijke verzorging. [The humanists and
        spiritual affairs.] Nieuwe Rotterdamse Courant 1962, 8 Jan
77285 Jews and the unconscious. Jerusalem Post 1966, 15 March
77286 Lustmoordenaars. [Murderers for lust?] Nieuwe Rotterdamse Courant
        1967, 30 Aug
77287 Martha Graham: teveel boodschap. [Martha Graham: too much mes-
        sage.] Ballet en Theater 1963, 1(1)
77288 "De meiden" van Jean Genet. ["The maid-servants" of Jean Genet.]
        De Nieuwe Stem 1967, 22(12). Inval 1968, 1(1)
77289 De niet-aangepaste militair. [The non-adjusted soldier.] Nieuwe Rotter-
        damse Courant 1963, 21 Nov
77290 Om de zin van het bestaan. [On the sense of being.] Nieuwe Rotter-
        damse Courant 1963, 28 Sept
77291 Over "Die Ermüding." (in English) [On Fatigue.] Psychiat Neurol
        Neurochir 1967, (70)
77292 Het psychologisch aspect van de kunst. [The psychological aspect of
        art.] Studium Generale, University of Leyden 1964, 27 Oct
77293 Recht op schijn. [Right to discretion.] De Nieuwe Stem 1965, 20(Sept)
77294 Le Sacre du Printemps. [The "Sacre du Printemps."] Residentie-
        Orkest 1963, 1(1)
77295 De socialistische markt (en de aliënatie). [The socialistic market (and
        alienation).] De Nieuwe Stem 1966, 21(Jan)
77296 Tagore en de positie van de vrouw. [Tagore and the status of woman.]
        Nieuwe Rotterdamse Courant 1961, 29 May
77297 Wilhelm Reich en de sexualiteit. [Wilhelm Reich and sexuality.] De
        Nieuwe Stem 1967, 22(Aug/Oct)

HOROVITZ, M.

See Winnik, Heinrich Z.

HOROWITZ, FRANCES DEGEN

77298 (& Lovell, L. L.) Attitudes of mothers of female schizophrenics. Child
        Develpm 1960, 31:299-305

HOROWITZ, I. A.

77299 (& Rothenberg, P. L.) The Personality of Chess. NY: Macmillan 1963,
        xii + 372 p

HOROWITZ, MARDI J.

77300 Art therapy media and techniques. Bull Art Ther 1965, 4:70-73
77301 (& Duff, D. F.; Stratton, L. O.) Body-buffer zone, exploration of per-
        sonal space. Arch gen Psychiat 1964, 11:651-656
77302 Body image. Arch gen Psychiat 1966, 14:456-460
        Abs PB Q 1969, 38:341

77303 Depersonalization in spacemen and submarines. Milit Med 1964, 129: 1058-1060
77304 (& Adams, J. E.; Rutkin, B.) Dream scintillations. PSM 1967, 29:284-292
77305 Drugs, images, and post-graduate education. Bull Drug React 1965, 1:47-48
77306 (& Cohen, F. M.) The effects of temporal lobectomy on the psychosocial functioning of psychomotor epileptics. Epilepsia 1968, 9:23-41
77307 Graphic communication: a study of interaction painting with schizophrenics. PT 1963, 17:230-239
77308 Graphic communication in psychiatric treatment. National Society for the study of Communications, Communication Spectrum '7, 83-91
77309 Group therapy of psychosis. Curr psychiat Ther 1966, 6:204-210
77310 The homosexual's image of himself. MH 1964, 48:197-201
77311 Human spatial behavior. PT 1965, 19:20-28
77312 The imagery of visual hallucinations. JNMD 1964, 138:513-521
         Abs BFM Q 1966, 35:156
77313 (& Horowitz, N. F.) Psychologic effects of education for childbirth. Psychosomatics 1967, 8:196-202
77314 Some psychodynamic aspects of respiration. In Lowry, T. Hyperventilation, Springfield, Ill: Thomas 1967
77315 Spatial behavior and psychopathology. JNMD 1968, 146:24-35
77316 (& Weisberg, P. S.) Techniques for the group psychotherapy of acute psychosis. Int J grp PT 1966, 16:42-50
77317 Visual imagery: a study of pictorial cognition using the dot-image sequence. JNMD 1965, 141:615-622
77318 Visual imagery and cognitive organization. P 1967, 123:938-946
77319 Visual thought images in psychotherapy. PT 1968, 22:55-59.

See Meyer, Mortimer M.

HOROWITZ, MILTON J.

77320 (& Motto, R. L.; Meyer, M. M.) Training in child psychotherapy. Reiss-Davis Clin Bull 1966, 3:53-61

HOROWITZ, N. F.

See Horowitz, Mardi J.

HOROWITZ, WILLIAM A.

77321 (& Polatin, P.; Kolb, L. C.; Hoch, P. H.) Study of cases of schizophrenia treated by "direct analysis." P 1958, 114:780-783
         Abs Shepard, M. An Surv Psa 1958, 9:25

See Kestenbaum, Clarice J.

HOROWITZ, WILLIAM S.

77322 Discussion of Dorn, R. M. "Psychoanalysis and psychoanalytic education." Psa Forum 1969, 3:267-270

77323 Toward a unifying conception of narcissism. (Read at Los Angeles Psa Soc, 17 Dec 1964)
Abs RZ Bull Phila Ass Psa 1965, 15:180-183

HORST-OOSTERHUIS, C. J. VAN DER

77324 Quelques idées relatives à la structure du monde des psychotiques. [Some ideas concerning the structure of the world of psychotics.] Évolut psychiat 1961, 26:511-522

77325 Realisation of the body from inner experience. Fortschr PSM 1963, 3:110-117

HORTON, DAVID L.

See Baxter, James C.; Becker, James C.

HORVAI, I.

See Vondráček, V.

HORWITZ, LEONARD

77326 Group psychotherapy training for psychiatric residents. Curr psychiat Ther 1968, 8:223-232

77327 Training groups for psychiatric residents. Int J grp PT 1967, 7:421-435

77328 Transference in training groups and therapy groups. Int J grp PT 1964, 14:202-213

See Sargent, Helen D.

HORWOOD, CARLA

See Plank, Emma N.; Wolff, Ernst

HOSKEN, B.

See Kagan, Jerome

HOSLEY, ELEANOR

See Archer, Lois

HOSTA, GEOFFREY

See Money, John

HOSTIE, R.

77329 Du Mythe à la Religion dans la Psychologie Analytique de C. G. Jung. [From Myth to Religion in the Analytic Psychology of C. G. Jung.] Paris: Desclée de Brouwer 1968, 325 p

HOTT, LOUIS R.

77330 The changing role of psychoanalysis in the clinic. Psa 1967, 27:50-60

77331 Discussion of the article by Dr. Harry Gershman "The evolution of gender identity." Bull NY Acad Med 1967, 43:1028-1033

HOUBEN, ANTON
See Thomä, Helmut

HOUBEN, M. E.
See Pierloot, Roland-Alphonse

HOUCK, JOHN H.
77332 Discussion: We need to record these pioneer efforts. P 1969, 125(Suppl 7):32-34

HOUGHTON, DONALD E.
77333 Attitude and illness in James's "Daisy Miller." Lit & Psych 1969, 19:51-60

HOUGHTON, G.
77334 A systems-mathematical interpretation of psychoanalytic theory. Bull Math Biophys 1968, 30:61-86

HOUK, R. L.
77335 (& Thomas, M. A.; Ripley, H. S.) Some determinants of the ideology of mental hospital attendants. Amer Psychiat Assoc Summaries 1962, 4-5

See Thomas, N. F.

HOUSTON, MARIETTA
See Menninger, Karl A.

HOUWINK, R. H.
TRANSLATION OF:
Bally, G. [66342]

HOVEY, RICHARD B.
77336 Hemingway's "Now I Lay Me": a psychological interpretation. Lit & Psych 1965, 15:70-78

HOVLAND, CARL I.
77337 (& Janis, I. L.; Kelley, H. O.) Communication and Persuasion: Psychological Studies of Opinion Change. New Haven: Yale Univ Pr 1953, 1963, xii + 315 p

HOWARD, A.
See McCord, Joan

HOWARD, H. S.
77338 Incest—the revenge motive. Delaware St med J 1959, 31:223-225

HOWARD, KENNETH I.

77339 (& Orlinsky, D. E.) Effects of suggested time perspective and order of presentation on responses to questions about dreaming. Percept mot Skills 1965, 20:223-227

See Orlinsky, David E.

HOWARD, RICHARD

TRANSLATION OF:
Foucault, M. [73158]

HOWARD, ROBERT

77340 Discussion of Gorney, R. "Of divers things: preliminary note on the dynamics of scuba diving." Psa Forum 1966, 1:272-273

HOWARD, S. M.

77341 (& Kubis, J. F.) Ego identity and some aspects of personal adjustment. J Psychol 1964, 58:459-466

HOWARD, W. MARCUS

77342 (& Bowers, M. K.) Hypnosis and schizophrenia in the dental situation, a case report. Int J clin exp Hyp 1961, 9:47

HOWARTH, EDGAR

77343 Extroversion and dream symbolism: an empirical study. Psychol Rep 1962, 10:211-214

See Cattell, Raymond B.

HOWE, LOUISA P.

S-49141 Some sociological aspects of identification. Abs An Surv Psa 1955, 6:132

HOWELL, R. J.

77344 A verified childhood memory elicited during hypnosis. Amer J clin Hyp 1966, 8:141-142

HOWELLS, JOHN G.

77345 (Ed) Modern Perspectives in Child Psychiatry. Springfield, Ill: Thomas 1965, xvi + 595 p

HOXTER, S.

77346 The experience of puberty and some implications for psychotherapy. Psychother Psychosom 1965, 13:278-284

HOYLE, JAMES F.

77347 "Kubla Khan" as an elated experience. Lit & Psych 1966, 16:27-39
77348 Sylvia Plath: a poetry of suicidal mania. Lit & Psych 1968, 18:187-203

HSU, FRANCIS L. K.

77349 (Ed) Psychological Anthropology. Approaches to Culture and Personality. Homewood, Ill: The Dorsey Pr 1961, 520 p
Rv Axelrad, S. Q 1963, 32:278-280

HSU, J.

77349A (& Tseng, W. S.) Chinese culture, personality formation and mental illness. Int J soc Psychiat 1969, 16:5-14

HUANTE, HÉCTOR PRADO

77350 Un caso de fobia de la desfloración como expresion de la fantasia de cautiverio. [A case of phobia of defloration as an expression of fantasy of captivity.] Cuad Psa 1967, 3:235-240

HUBBACK, JUDITH

77351 VII. Sermones ad mortuos. J anal Psych 1966, 11:95-112
77352 The symbolic attitude in psychotherapy. J anal Psych 1969, 14:36-47

HUBBARD, BETTY L.

77353 An attempt to identify, by psychometric and peer rating techniques, three oral character types described in psychoanalytic literature. Diss Abstr 1968, 28:4757

HUBER, G.

77354 Das Problem der Schuldfähigkeit in der Sicht des psychiatrischen Sachverständigen. [The problem of criminality as seen by psychiatric experts.] Fortschr Neurol Psychiat 1968, 36:454-473
77355 Typen und Korrelate psychoorganischer Abbau-Syndrome. [Types and correlations of psycho-organic syndromes of disintegration.] In Kranz, H. Psychopathologie Heute, Stuttgart: Georg Thieme 1962, 234-242

HUBER, WINFRED

77356 (& Piron, H.; Vergote, A.) La Psychanalyse, Science de l'Homme. [Psychoanalysis, Science of Man.] Brussels: Dessart 1964, 305 p

HUBERTUS, E.

See Hart de Ruyter, Theodoor

HÜBSCH, HEIKE

See Tausch, Anne-Marie

HUCKEL, HELEN

S-49148 The tragic guilt of Prometheus.
Abs An Surv Psa 1955, 6:411-412

HUDOLIN, VLADIMIR

77357 (& Muačević, V.) Die Möglichkeit der Psychotherapie in grosser
Gruppe bei Alkoholikern. [The possibility of psychotherapy with alcoholics in larger groups.] Psychother Psychosom 1967, 15:31

See Muačević, Vasco

HUDON, EUGÈNE

TRANSLATION OF:
Ancona, L. [65795]

HUDSON, LIAM

77358 Contrary Imaginations: A Psychological Study of the Young Student.
NY: Schocken Books 1966, 181 p

HUELS, MARY A.

See Chessick, Richard D.

HUEY, WILLIAM F.

See Adams, Paul L.

HUFFER, VIRGINIA

77359 Fee problems in supervised analysis. (Read at Baltimore Psa Soc,
Oct 1961) Bull Phila Ass Psa 1963, 13:66-83
      Abs EFA Q 1964, 33:300
77360 (& Middleton, E.) Patients and their obstetricians. Psychosomatics
1963, 4:142-149
77361 (& Scott, W.; Connor, T. B.) Psychological studies of adult male patients with sexual infantilism before and after androgen therapy. Ann
intern Med 1964, 61:255-268

HUFNER, H.

See Baeyer, Walter von

HÜGEL, KATE

See Boor, Clemens de

TRANSLATION OF:
Leavy, S. A. [80215]

HUG-HELLMUTH, HERMINE VON

77362 The child's concept of death. (Tr: Kris, A. O.) Q 1965, 34:499-516

HUGHES, CONSTANCE

See Kanter, Stanley S.

HUGHES, HELLEN M.

See Grinker, Roy R., Sr.

HUGHES, JOHN E.

77363 Passivity: interpretative and theoretical aspects in psychoanalytic treat-
       ment. (Read at NY Psa Soc, 31 Oct 1961)
       Abs Furer, M. Q 1962, 31:149-150

HUGHES, R. E.

77364 The five fools in *A Tale of a Tub*. Lit & Psych 1961, 11:20-22

HUGUET, P.

See Daumézon, G.

HUIGE, FRIDA F. L.

77365 Nerval's "Aurélia": schizophrenia and art. Am Im 1965, 22:255-274

HUIZINGA, JOHAN

77366 Homo Ludens, A Study of the Play Elements in Culture. Boston:
       Beacon Pr 1955

HULBECK, CHARLES R.

77367 The existential mood in American psychiatry. Psa 1964, 24:82-88
77368 Psychoanalytical notes on modern art. Psa 1960, 20:164-173
77369 Three creative phases in psychoanalysis: the encounter, the dialogue
       and the process of articulation. Psa 1963, 23:157-163. In Ruitenbeek,
       H. M. *The Creative Imagination*, Chicago: Quadrangle Books 1965,
       313-323

HULL, R. F. C.

TRANSLATIONS OF:
Jung, C. G. [17468, 77946, 77959]. Neumann, E. [85084, 85085A]

HULSE, WILFRED C.

77370 Applications and modifications of group psychotherapy in contempo-
       rary psychiatric and mental health practice. J Hillside Hosp 1963,
       12:140-144
77371 Do parents have mixed feelings about children? If so, to what extent
       are these feelings sexual? Why Rep 351-363
77372 Das heilende Element in der Gruppenpsychotherapie. [The healing
       element in group psychotherapy.] Top Probl PT 1963, 4:133-146
77373 Multiple transferences or group neurosis? A preliminary communica-
       tion on changing thinking models in group psychotherapy. Acta psycho-
       ther psychosom 1961, 9:348-357
77374 (Ed) Topical Problems of Psychotherapy. Vol. II. Sources of Conflict
       in Contemporary Group Psychotherapy. Basel: S. Karger, Acta psy-
       chother psychosom 1960, 7, Suppl No. 2, vi + 197 p
77375 (& Franzblau, A. N.; Kleinschmidt, H. J.) What can we learn from
       existential psychotherapists? J Mount Sinai Hosp 1962, 29:137-146

77376 What is mental health? Why Rep 491-492
77377 What is psychotherapy? Why Rep 545-556

See Cohn, Isadore H.; Durkin, Helen E.; Freeman, Lucy; La Vietes, Ruth L.; Mathews, W. Mason

HUME, PORTIA BELL

77378 Community psychiatry, social psychiatry and community mental health work: some inter-professional relationships in psychiatry and social work. P 1964, 121:340-343
77379 General principles of community psychiatry. Am Hbk Psychiat III: 418-441
77380 Principles and practice of community psychiatry: the role and training of the specialist in community psychiatry. In Bellak, L. *Handbook of Community Psychiatry*, NY: Grune & Stratton 1964, 56-81
77381 (& Rudin, E.) Psychiatric inpatient services in general hospitals. Calif Med 1960, 93:200-207
77382 (& Bondurant, J. V.) The significance of unasked questions in the study of conflict. Inquiry 1964, 7:318-327
77383 Social psychiatry as prevention and rehabilitation: some critical points in evaluation. In Zubin, J. & Fritz, A. F. *Social Psychiatry*, NY: Grune & Stratton 1968, 300-311

HUMMEL, R.

See Whiteley, John M.

HUNDLEBY, JOHN DENNIS

77384 (& Cattell, R. B.) Personality structure in middle childhood and the prediction of school achievement and adjustment. Monogr Soc Res Child Develop 1968, 33:1-61

HUNEEUS, M. EUGENIA

77385 Dynamic approach to marital problems. Soc Casewk 1963, 44:142-148

HUNNYBUN, NOEL K.

See Ferard, Margaret L.

HUNSDAHL, JØRGEN B.

77386 Concerning Einfühlung (empathy): a concept analysis of its origin and early development. J Hist behav Sci 1967, 3:180-191

HUNT, HOWARD F.

77386A Prospects and possibilities in the development of behaviour therapy. Int Psychiat Clin 1969, 6:246-273

See Zubin, Joseph

HUNT, MORTON M.

77387   (& Corman, R.; Ormont, L. R.) The Talking Cure. (Introd: Bellak, L.)
        NY: Harper & Row 1963, xii + 171 p
        Rv Strean, H. S. R 1964, 51:328-329
77388   The Thinking Animal. Boston: Little, Brown 1964

HUNT, RAYMOND G.

77389   Social class and mental illness. P 1960, 116:1065-1069
        Abs Leavitt, M. Q 1961, 30:456
77390   (& Winokur, G.) Some generalities concerning parental attitudes with
        special reference to changing them. In Glidewell, J. C. *Parental Atti-
        tudes and Child Behavior*, Springfield, Ill: Thomas 1961, 174-182

        See Brown, Martha M.

HUNT, ROBERT L.

S-49254 Aspects of a case of neurotic acting out.
        Abs An Surv Psa 1955, 6:195, 338-339
77391   The ego ideal and male homosexuality. Bull Phila Ass Psa 1967, 17:
        217-244

HUNT, WILLIAM ALVIN

77392   (& Jones, N. F.) The experimental investigation of clinical judgment.
        In Bachrach, A. J. *Experimental Foundations of Clinical Psychology*,
        NY: Basic Books 1962
77393   (& Blumberg, S.) Manifest anxiety and clinical judgment. Clin Psych
        1961, 17:8-11
77394   (& Walker, R. E.) Manifest anxiety and clinical judgment—a re-
        examination. Clin Psych 1963, 19:494-497

HUNT, WILSON L.

        See Hollender, Marc H.

HUNTER, CLORINDA GOLTRA

77395   (& Goodstein, L. D.) Ego strength and types of defensive and coping
        behavior. J consult Psychol 1967, 31:432

HUNTER, D.

77396   Training in child psychotherapy at the Tavistock Clinic. J child Psychol
        Psychiat 1960, 1:87-93

HUNTER, DORIS M.

77397   (& Babcock, C. G.) Some aspects of the intrapsychic structure of cer-
        tain American Negroes as viewed in the inter-cultural dynamic. (Read
        at Pittsburgh Psa Soc, 23 Nov 1964; at Am Psa Ass, 1 May 1965) Psa
        St Soc 1967, 4:124-169

Einige Aspekte der psychischen Struktur amerikanischer Neger
unter dem Blickwinkel der interkulturellen Dynamik. Psyche 1968,
22:1-49

REVIEW OF:
77398   Parker, S. & Kleiner, R. J. Mental Illness in the Urban Negro Community. Q 1967, 36:613-615

HUNTER, RICHARD A.

* * *   (& Macalpine, I.) Introduction to Battie, W. *A Treatise on Madness.*
77399   (& Macalpine, I.) Introduction to Conolly, J. *The Construction and
Government of Lunatic Asylums,* London: Dawson 1968
77400   (& Macalpine, I.) Introduction to Conolly, J. *An Inquiry Concerning
the Indications of Insanity (1830),* London: Dawson 1964
77401   (& Macalpine, I.) John Haslam: his will and his daughter. Med Hist
1962, 6:22-26
77402   (& Blackwood, W.; Bull, J.) Three cases of frontal meningiomas presenting psychiatrically. Brit med J 1963(3):9-16
77403   (& Macalpine, I.) Three Hundred Years of Psychiatry 1535-1860. A
History Presented in Selected English Texts. London: Oxford Univ Pr
1963, 1107 p
Rv Niederland, W. G. Q 1964, 33:586-587

See Macalpine, Ida

HUNTER, ROBIN C. A.

77404   The analysis of episodes of depersonalization in a borderline patient.
J 1966, 47:32-41
Abs Cuad Psa 1966, 2:120. EVN Q 1968, 37:155-156
77405   (& Lohrenz, J. G.; Schwartzman, A. E.) Nosophobia and hypochondriasis in medical students. JNMD 1964, 139:147-152
Abs BFM Q 1966, 35:158
77406   On the experience of nearly dying. P 1967, 124:84-88

HUNTINGTON, DOROTHY S.

See Bibring, Grete L.

HUNTLEY, JOHN F.

77407   Body sickness and social sickness in Milton's figure of Satan. Lit &
Psych 1968, 18:101-108

HUNZIKER-FROMM, G.

77408   Beziehungen zwischen Kinderpsychotherapeuten und Eltern. [The
relationships between child-psychotherapists and parents.] Schweiz Z
Psychol 1967, 26:125-137

HURLEY, JOHN R.

See Rabin, Albert I.

HURLEY, PETER
See Bahn, Anita K.

HURN, HAL T.
77409 Synergic relations between the processes of fatherhood and psycho-analysis. J Am Psa Ass 1969, 17:437-451

HURTEAU, PHYLLIS
See Robinson, Alice M.

HURVICH, MARVIN S.
77410 (& Bellak, L.) Ego function patterns in schizophrenics. Psychol Rep 1968, 22:299-308

See Bellak, Leopold

HURVITZ, MARTIN
77411 The treatment of a septuagenarian. J Hillside Hosp 1963, 12:99-105
       Abs JA Q 1967, 36:136

HURWITT, ELLIOTT S.
See Baudry, Francis (Frank)

HURWITZ, IRVING
See Grunebaum, Margaret G.; Sjostedt, Elsie M.

HURWITZ, L. J.
See Allison, R. S.

HURWITZ, MERVIN H.
77412 Termination of a symptom following interpretation of a dream. Q 1966, 35:122-124

ABSTRACT OF:
77413 Keiser, S. Disturbances of ego functions of speech and abstract think-ing. Q 1961, 30:622-623

HURZELER, MARC
See Kallman, Franz J.

HUSQUINET, ALBERT
77414 La Relation entre la Mère and l'Enfant à l'Age Préscolaire. [The Rela-tionship Between the Mother and the Pre-School Child.] Paris: Société d'Edition: Les Belles Lettres 1963, 450 p

HUSS, HERMANN

77415 (& Schröder, A.) (Eds) Antisemitismus. [Antisemitism.] Frankfurt/
Main: Europäische Verlagsanstalt 1965

HUSSEIN TUMA, A.

See May, Philip R. A.

HUSTON, ALETHA C.

See Bandura, Albert

HUTT, MAX L.

77416 Psychological assessment methods. Prog Neurol Psychiat 1968, 23:532-
547
77417 (& Isaacson, R. L.; Blum, M. L.) Psychology: The Science of Interpersonal Behavior. NY: Harper & Row 1966, xii + 430 p
77418 Psychopathology, assessment, and psychotherapy. In Rabin, A. I. *Projective Techniques in Personality Assessment,* NY: Springer 1969, 64-
84

See Carr, Arthur C.

HUTTEN, ERNEST H.

77419 An interpretation of the mind-body problem. Am Im 1961, 18:269-277
77420 The Origins of Science: An Enquiry into the Foundations of Western
Thought. London: Allen & Unwin 1962, 241 p
    Rv Meltzer, D. J 1963, 44:382-383

HUXLEY, SIR JULIAN

77421 A discussion on ritualization of behavior in animals and man. Royal
Society of London: Philosophical Transaction Series B. Biological Sciences No. 772, 1966, Vol. 251:247-526

HYDE, R. W.

See Goodrich, D. Wells

HYLAND, H. H.

See Farquharson, R. F.

HYMAN, GEORGE A.

See Kutscher, Austin H.

HYMAN, MARVIN

77422 (& Ruzumna, R. A.) Women "on the fringe." R 1967, 54:21-30

HYMAN, MAX

ABSTRACT OF:
77423 Greenson, R. R. On enthusiasm. Bull Phila Ass Psa 1961, 11:138-141

HYMAN, STANLEY EDGAR

77424 After the great metaphors. Amer Scholar 1962, 31:236-258
77425 A critical look at psychology. Amer Scholar 1960, 29:21-29
S-49282 Psychoanalysis and the climate of tragedy. In author's *The Promised End*, Cleveland: World Publ 1963, 103-120
      Abs AEC An Surv Psa 1956, 7:25
77426 The ritual view of myth and mythic. In Vickery, J. B. *Myth and Literature; Contemporary Theory and Practice*, Univ Neb Pr 1966, 47-58
77427 The Tangled Bank; Darwin, Marx, Frazer and Freud as Imaginative Writers. NY: Atheneum 1962, xii + 492 p

I

IACONO, JAMES M.
See Gottschalk, Louis A.

IANDELLI, CARLO L.

77428 (& Colonna, M. T.; Coghi, I.) Aspetti psicodinamici della personalità in menopausa: uno studio introduttivo. [Psychodynamic aspects of personality in menopause: an introductory study.] Med Psicosomática 1966, 11:141-212. Studi e Ricerche di Psicologia 1967, 10

77429 Introduzione al simbolica del serpente: uno studio psicologico-analitico e storico-religioso. [Introduction to the symbolism of the serpent: a psychological-analytic and historical-religious study.] Rass Stud Psichiat 1966, 55:103-139. Studi e Ricerche di Psicologia 1967, 10

77430 The serpent symbol. In Wheelwright, J. B. *The Reality of the Psyche,* NY: G. P. Putnam's Sons 1968, 98-113

IBERALL, A. S.

77431 (& Cardon, S. Z.) Analysis of the dynamic systems response of some internal human systems. NASA CR-141. US NASA 1965, 1-109

77432 Study of the general dynamics of the physical-chemical systems in mammals. NASA CR-129. US NASA 1964, 1-115

ICHHEISER, G.

77433 On Freud's blind spots concerning some obvious facts. J ind Psych 1960, 16:45-55

IERODIAKONOU, C. S.

77434 [Depressive states in childhood.] (Gr) Enképhalos 1963, 1:230-239

77435 Problems of technique in the psychotherapy of the anxiety neurotic. Psychother Psychosom 1967, 15:31

IFLUND, BORIS
See Goodrich, D. Wells; Parloff, Morris B.

IGERT, M.

77436 Regard sur les indications actuelles de la thérapeutique psychanalytique. [A study of the present indications for psychoanalytic therapy.] Ann méd-psychol 1968, 126(2):759-760

IHILEVICH, DAVID

77437 The relationship of defense mechanisms to field dependence-independence. Diss Abstr 1968, 29(5-B):1843-1844

See Gleser, Goldine C.

IKEDA, YOSHIKO

77438 [Problems of the co-therapist in group psychotherapy reviewed through dream interpretation.] (Jap) Eng Summary. J ment Hlth 1968, (16): 29-36, 133-135

IKEMI, Y.

77439 Training in psychosomatic research. Adv PSM 1967, 5:111-118

IKER, HOWARD P.

See Gardner, Elmer A.; Harway, Norman I.; Schmale, Arthur H., Jr.

ILAN, ELIEZER R.

77440 (& Alexander, E.) Eyelash and eyebrow pulling. (Trichotillomania) Treatment of two adolescent girls. Israel Ann Psychiat 1965, 3:267-281

77441 The problem of motivation in the educator's vocational choice. (Read at Israel Psa Soc, Jan 1961) Psa St C 1963, 18:266-285

ILES, RALPH

See Klingsporn, M. J.

ILLING, HANS A.

77442 C. G. Jung on the present trends in group psychotherapy. Hum Relat 1957, 10:77-83. In Rosenbaum, M. & Berger, M. *Group Psychotherapy and Group Functions,* NY: Basic Books 1963, 180-187

77443 Central themes of delusional productions in group psychotherapy with schizophrenic patients. Acta psychother psychosom 1961, 9:1-9

77444 Critique on group psychotherapy. Bull Am Coll Neuropsychiat 1957, 11:6-7

77445 (& Brownfield, B.) Delusions of schizophrenic patients in group psychotherapy. J soc Ther 1960, 6:32-36

77446 Eighty years of Carl Jung. Guide to Psychiatric & Psychological Literature 1956, 2:6-8

77447 Entwicklung und Stand der amerikanischen Musiktherapie. [The development and condition of American music therapy.] In Teirich, H. R. *Musik in der Medizin,* Stuttgart: Gustav Fischer Verlag 1959

77448 Environment and aging. J Amer Geriat Soc 1958, 16:405-410

77449 Die Ethik der Gruppenpsychotherapeuten. [The ethics of group psychotherapists.] Heilkunst 1956, 70

S-49316 Freud and Wagner-Jauregg. A contribution to Freudiana. Abs DJM An Surv Psa 1958, 9:12-13

77450 Group psychotherapy and group work in authoritarian settings. J crim Law Criminol 1958, 48:387-393

77451 Idee und Praxis der Gruppenpsychotherapie. [Concept and practice of group psychotherapy.] Psychol, Bern 1957, 9:465-470

77452 Jung and the Jews. Chicago Jewish Forum 1957, 14:200-202

77453 Jung and die moderne Tendenz in der Gruppenpsychotherapie. [Jung and the modern trend in group psychotherapy.] Heilkunst 1956, 68: 77-80

77454 Klinische Erfahrungen mit Ehepaaren in der Gruppenpsychotherapie. [Practical clinical experience with married couples in group psychotherapy.] Psychol, Bern 1958, 10:149-154

77455 Mental hygiene in German criminology. Arch crim psychodyn 1960, 4:154-158

77456 Music as a medium of group therapy with adolescent girls. J child psychiat 1952, 2:350-359

77456A (& Miles, J. E.) Outpatient group psychotherapy with sex offenders. Int J soc Psychiat 1969, 15:258-263

77457 The prisoner in his group. Int J grp PT 1951, 1:264-277

77458 Psychoanalytische Gruppenpsychotherapie. [Psychoanalytic group psychotherapy.] Das Psychoanalytische Volksbuch 1964, 2

77459 Psychotherapeutische Behandlung von Ehepaaren. [Psychotherapeutic treatment of married couples.] Heilkunst 1960, 73:259-261

77460 Die Rückkehr in die Gruppe: Zur Dynamik der vorzeitigen Beendigung der Gruppen-psychotherapie. [Returning to the group: dynamics of pseudo-termination in group therapy.] Dyn Psychiat 1969, 2:164-171. Abs (Eng), 171-172

77461 Short-contact group psychotherapy. Int J grp PT 1952, 2:377-382

77462 Sociometry and group psychotherapy. Group PT 1957, 10:85-94

77463 Some aspects of authority over groups of military offenders. Calif Youth Authority Q 1956, 9:27-30

77464 Some aspects of the C. Y. A. "special treatment program." J crim Law Criminol 1959, 49:423-425

77465 Some aspects of treatment in the case of a drug-addict. J crim Law Criminol Police Sci 1959, 50:277-279

77466 Some historical notes on psychotherapy. Freud and Wagner-Jauregg: a contribution to Freudiana. Top Prob PT 1960, 1:44-50

77467 A theory of the group according to C. G. Jung. Acta psychother psychosom 1958, 6:137-144

77468 The therapist and the group evaluate. MH 1957, 41:512-516

77469 Training in group counseling of group psychotherapy. PPR 1962, 49 (4):74-99

77470 Transference and countertransference in analytical group counseling. Acta psychother psychosom 1962, 10:13-25

See Bergreen, Stanley W.; Grotjahn, Martin; Hacker, Frederick J.; Welch, E. Parl

REVIEWS OF:

77471 Eissler, K. R. Goethe. A Psychoanalytic Study. 1775-1786. J 1964, 45:126-128

77472 Ferenczi, S. Bausteine zur Psychoanalyse. Q 1966, 35:136-137

77473 Freud, E. L. (Ed) Sigmund Freud—Arnold Zweig Breifwechsel Q
       1969, 38:643-644
77474 Freud, S. Briefe 1873-1939. Q 1969, 38:126-127

IMBASCIATI, A.

77475 Il concetto di proiezione. [The concept of projection.] Arch Psicol Neu-
       rol Psichiat 1967, 28:169-182

IMBER, STANLEY D.

77476 (& Nash, E. H.; Hoehn-Saric, R.; Stone, A. R.; Frank, J. D.) A ten-year
       follow-up study of treated psychiatric outpatients. In Lesse, S. *An
       Evaluation of the Results of the Psychotherapies,* Springfield, Ill:
       Thomas 1968, 70-81

       See Frank, Jerome D.; Hoehn-Saric, Rudolf; Nash, Earl H.; Stone,
       Anthony R.; Truax, Charles D.

IMBODEN, JOHN B.

See Ziegler, Frederick J.

IMIELINSKI, K.

77477 [A few remarks on sexual neuroses.] (Pol) Neurol Neurochir Psychiat
       Pol 1964, 14:699-703
77478 Sexuelle Abstinenz, Neurosen und Perversion. [Sexual abstinence, neu-
       roses and perversion.] Psychiat Neurol med Psychol 1965, 17:148-151
77479 Über den nächtlichen Orgasmus bei Frauen. [Nocturnal orgasm in
       women.] Psychiat Neurol med Psychol 1961, 13:390-392

IMMERGLUCK, LUDWIG

77480 Determinism-freedom in contemporary psychology: an ancient prob-
       lem revisited. Am Psych 1964, 19:270-281

IMURA, TSUNEO

77481 [On the Amae theory: symposium on the Amae theory.] (Jap) Jap
       J Psa 1968, 14(3):2

INDERMILL, R. R.

See Sours, John A.

INFANTE, JOSÉ A.

77482 Algunas reflexiones acerca de la relación analitica. [Some thoughts on
       the analytic relation.] Rev Psicoanál 1968, 25:3-4
77483 Discussion of Aull, G. & Strean, H. S. "The analyst's silence." Psa
       Forum 1967, 2:84-85
77484 (& Whiting, C.) Transferencia y contratransferencia. Discussion. [Trans-
       ference and countertransference. Discussion.] In *Psicoanálisis en las
       Américas,* Buenos Aires: Paidós 1968

       See Whiting, Carlos

INGALLS, A.
See Sobel, Raymond

INGE, G. P., III
See Rinsley, Donald B.

INGHAM, JOHN
77485   The bullfighter: a study of sexual dialectic. Am Im 1964, 21:95-102
        Abs JWS Q 1965, 34:621

INGLING, J. H.
See Goldfried, Marvin R.

INGLIS, BRIAN
77486   The psychopath. Encounter 1960, 15(3):3-14
77487   Road past Freud. Spectator 1961, 207:954

INGLIS, JAMES
77488   Sensory deprivation and cognitive disorder. Brit J Psychiat 1965, 111:
        309-315

INGRAHAM, B.
See Rafferty, Frank T.

INGRAHAM, MERLE RAYMOND
77489   (& Moriarty, D. M.) A contribution to the understanding of the Ganser
        syndrome. Comprehen Psychiat 1967, 8:35-44

INGRAM, I. M.
77490   Obsessional personality and anal-erotic character. JMS 1961, 107:1035-
        1042

INHELDER, BÄRBEL
77491   (& Piaget, J.) The Early Growth of Logic in the Child. Classification
        and Seriation. (Tr: Lunzer, E. A. & Papert, D.) NY: Norton 1969,
        xxv + 302 p
77492   Operational thought and symbolic imagery. Monogr Soc Res Child
        Develop 1965, 30:4-18
77493   (Ed) "Psychologie et Epistemologie Genetique," Hommage à Jean
        Piaget. ["Psychology and Genetic Epistemology," Tribute to Jean Pia-
        get.] Paris: Dunod 1966
77494   Some aspects of Piaget's genetic approach to cognition. In Cohen, J.
        Readings in Psychology, London: Allen & Unwin 1964, 85-103

See Piaget, Jean

INKELES, ALEX

77495 Freudian theory and sociological research. Int J Psychiat 1966, 2:550-555

INMAN, OLIVE B.

77496 Development of two different types of cancer in a patient undergoing psychoanalytic treatment. In Kissen, D. M. & LeShan, L. L. *Psychosomatic Aspects of Neoplastic Disease,* London: Pitman Med Publ; Phila/ Montreal: Lippincott 1964, 105-108

INMAN, WILLIAM S.

77497 Can a blow cause cancer? M 1961, 34:271-275
       Abs ICFH Q 1962, 31:431-432
77498 (& Dillon, F.) Cat phobia. Brit med J 1960, 2:804
S-49336 Clinical thought-reading.
       Abs GLG An Surv Psa 1958, 9:210-211
77499 Emotion and rodent ulcer. In Kissen, D. M. & LeShan, L. L. *Psychosomatic Aspects of Neoplastic Disease,* London: Pitman Med Publ; Phila/Montreal: Lippincott 1964, 95-104
77500 Emotion, cancer and time: coincidence or determinism? M 1967, 40:225-231
77501 Emotional factors in diseases of the cornea. M 1965, 38:277-287
77502 Ophthalmic adventure: a story of frustration and organic disease. M 1962, 35:299-309

INOUYE, EIJI

77503 Similar and dissimilar manifestations of obsessive-compulsive neuroses in monozygotic twins. P 1965, 121:1171-1175

INSTITUT FÜR PSYCHOTHERAPIE UND TIEFENPSYCHOLOGIE

77504 Felix Schottlaender zum Gedächtnis. [In Memory of Felix Schottlaender.] Stuttgart: Klett 1959, 186 p
77505 Neurose: Ein psychosoziales Problem. [Neurosis: A Psychological Problem.] Stuttgart: Klett 1960, 231 p

INTERNATIONALE FORSCHUNGSGEMEINSCHAFT FÜR SCHICKSALPSYCHOLOGIE

77506 Kriminalität, Erziehung und Ethik. [Criminality, Education and Ethics.] Zurich: Huber 1967, 354 p

INUI, TAKASHI

77507 [Psychology of the Unconscious—Psychoanalysis and Its Later Development.] (Jap) Tokyo 1948

INWOOD, E. R.

77508 (& Anderson, M. M.) Suicide and the family physician. GP 1964, 30:130-133

IONESCO, EUGÈNE

77509 Journal. Encounter 1966, 26(2):3-20

IRÁNYI, C.

See Nyirö, J.

IRELAND, E.

77510 The social worker's contribution to training in child psychiatry. J child Psychol Psychiat 1967, 8:99-104

IRISH, DONALD P.

77511 Sibling interaction: a neglected aspect in family life research. Social Forces 1964, 42:279-288

IRLE, G.

77512 Wann ist das körperliche Fixieren eines Kranken nötig und erlaubt? [When is physical restraint of a patient necessary or permissible?] Dtsch med Wschr 1962, 87:2019-2022

IRONSIDE, WALLACE

77513 The psychopathology of suicide and the individual patient. New Zeal Med J 1964, 63:763-767

IRWIN, HELEN

See Silberstein, Richard M.

IRWIN, M. G.

77514 Doctor Johnson's troubled mind. Lit & Psych 1963, 13:6-11

IRWIN, R. C.

See Weston, Donald L.

ISAAC-EDERSHEIM, E.

See Frijling-Schreuder, Elisabeth C. M.

ISAACS, KENNETH S.

77515 (& Alexander, J. M.; Haggard, E. A.) Faith, trust and gullibility. J 1963, 44:461-469
       Abs EVN Q 1966, 35:309
77516 (& Haggard, E. A.) Some methods used in the study of affect in psychotherapy. Meth Res PT 226-239

See Alexander, James M.; Haggard, Ernest A.; Miller, Arthur A.; Sklansky, Morris A.

ISAACS, NEIL D.

77517   The autoerotic metaphor in Joyce, Sterne, Lawrence, Stevens, and Whitman. Lit & Psych 1965, 15:92-106

ISAACS, SUSAN SUTHERLAND (FAIRHURST)

S-15504 Intellectual Growth in Young Children. NY: Schocken Books 1966, xi + 295 p

ISAACS, SUSANNA

77518   A glimpse of child psychiatry. St. Mary's Hosp Gazette 1965
77519   Intellectual and emotional mobility in adolescence. Case Conf 1966-67, 13:435-437
77520   Obituary: Melanie Klein, 1882-1960. J child Psychol Psychiat 1961, 2:1-4
77521   Physical ill-treatment of children. Lancet 1968, 1:37-39
77522   Psycho-analysis of a psychotic child. Proceedings of Int Congress of Child Psychiat 1965

REVIEW OF:
77523   Robertson, J. Young Children in Hospital. J 1961, 42:127

ISAACSON, ROBERT L.

See Hutt, Max L.

ISCOE, IRA

77524   (& Stevenson, H. W.) (Eds) Personality Development in Children. Austin, Texas: Univ Texas Pr 1960, viii + 171 p

ISENBERG, MORRIS

77525   Morality and the neurotic patient. PT 1966, 20:477-488

ISHAM, A. CHAPMAN

S-49355 The ego and identification.
        Abs An Surv Psa 1955, 6:36-37, 131-132
S-49356 The ego, consciousness, motor processes, and thought.
        Abs An Surv Psa 1955, 6:37, 118-119

ISHIBASHI, YASUKO

77526   (& Okonogi, K.) [Misuse of pseudo-psychoanalytic knowledge by the confused child-rearing attitudes.] (Jap) (Read at Jap Psa Ass, Oct 1963) Jap J Psa 1965, 11(6):25-26

ISHIDA, Y.

77526a [Psychoanalysis. 2. Analysis of a dream: expression of the subconscious.] (Jap) Jap J Nurs 1969, 33:62-63

ISRAEL, G.
See Israël, L.

ISRAEL, HYMAN A.
See Kubie, Lawrence S.

ISRAËL, L.
77527 (& Couadau, A.) [Consideration on the object relation apropos of a case of eczema.] (Fr) Rev Méd psychosom 1966, 8:377-393
77528 (& Israel, G.) [Playing doctor and physician-patient relationship.] (Fr) Rv Np inf 1961, 9:363-379
77529 La victime de l'hystérique. [The victim of hysteria.] Évolut psychiat 1967, 32:517-546

ISRAEL, MOSHE
77530 [Brother and sister as motive and first symbol in literature.] (Heb) Ofakim 1960, 14:226-236

ISRAEL, PATRICK
See Becker, George S.

ISSACHAROFF, AMMON
77531 Hippolytus as an alternative to Oedipus: a study in triangular relationships. Psychother Psychosom 1967, 15:32

ISSAHAROFF, EDUARDO
See Usandivaras, Raúl J.

IVERSON, M. A.
See Schwab, John R.

IVEY, M. E.
77532 (& Bardwick, J. M.) Patterns of affective fluctuation in the menstrual cycle. PSM 1968, 30:336-345

IWASAKI, TETSUYA
77533 [Schreber case: Symposium.] (Jap) Jap J Psa 1968, 14(2):9-11. Discussion 32-34

See Kitami, Yoshio; Yamamoto, J.

IZARD, CARROLL E.
77534 (& Tomkins, S. S.) Affect and behavior: anxiety as a negative affect. In Spielberger, C. D. Anxiety and Behavior, NY/London: Academic Pr 1966, 81-125

See Tomkins, Silvan S.

J

JAARSMA, RICHARD J.

77535 The tragedy of Banquo. Lit & Psych 1967, 17:87-94

JABLENSKI, ASSEN

See Dimitrov, Christo T.

JACKEL, MERL M.

77536 Clients with character disorders. Soc Casewk 1963, 44:315-322
77537 The common cold and depression. (Read at Psa Ass NY, 18 Dec 1967) J Hillside Hosp 1968, 17:165-177
    Abs Halpert, E. Q 1969, 38:347-348
77538 Interruptions during psychoanalytic treatment and the wish for a child. J Am Psa Ass 1966, 14:730-735
77539 Transference and psychotherapy. Psychiat Q 1966, 40:43-58
    Abs Gottreich, N. S. Q 1968, 37:475-476

ABSTRACT OF:
77540 Beres, D. Perception, imagination, and reality. Q 1961, 30:160-162

JACKSON, B.

77541 Observations sur la phase terminable de la psychotherapie chez les enfants. [Observations on the terminal phase of psychotherapy in children.] Rv Np inf 1968, 16:425-433

JACKSON, BASIL

77542 Reflections on DSM-II. Int J Psychiat 1969, 7:385-392

JACKSON, CHARLES WESLEY, JR.

77543 (& Pollard, J. C.; Kansky, E. W.) The application of findings from experimental sensory deprivation to cases of clinical sensory deprivation. Amer J Med Sci 1962, 243:558-563

JACKSON, DON D.

77544 (& Watzlawick, P.) The acute psychosis as a manifestation of growth experience. Psychiat Res Rep 1963, 16:83-94
77545 Aspects of conjoint family therapy. In Zuk, G. H. & Boszormenyi-Nagy, I. *Family Therapy and Disturbed Families*, Palo Alto, Calif: Sci & Behav Books 1967, 28-40.

77546 (& Yalom, I.) Conjoint family therapy as an aid to intensive psycho-
       therapy. In Burton, A. *Modern Psychotherapeutic Practice*, Palo Alto,
       Calif: Sci & Behav Books 1965, 81-97
77547 Critique of twin studies of schizophrenia. In author's *The Etiology of
       Schizophrenia* 57-71. In Palmer, J. O. & Goldstein, M. J. *Perspectives
       in Psychopathology*, NY: Oxford Univ Pr 1966, 265-277
77548 Differences between "normal" and "abnormal" families. (Panel discus-
       sion: communication within the family.) In Ackerman, N. W. et al:
       Expanding Theory and Practice in Family Therapy, NY: Fam Serv Ass
       Amer 1967, 99-102
77549 Discussion of J. Jaffe's "Electronic computers in psychoanalytic re-
       search." Sci Psa 1963, 6:170-172
77550 Discussion of Rogawsky, A. S. (Moderator) "Symposium on psycho-
       analysts view conjoint therapy." Psa Forum 1966, 1:163-164
S-49380 (Ed) The Etiology of Schizophrenia.
            Rv Rosen, J. N. Q 1961, 30:276-283. TFr J 1962, 43:182-184
77551 (& Yalom, I.) Family homeostasis and patient change. Curr psychiat
       Ther 1964, 4:155-165
77552 (& Yalom, I.) Family research on the problem of ulcerative colitis.
       Arch gen Psychiat 1966, 15:410-418
            Abs PB Q 1969, 38:514
77553 Family therapy in the family of the schizophrenic. Contempo PT 272-
       287
77554 Filming of psychotherapeutic sessions as a personal experience. Meth
       Res PT 64-65
77555 Interactional psychotherapy. Contempo PT 256-271
77556 (& Riskin, J.; Satir, V.) A method of analysis of a family interview. Arch
       gen Psychiat 1961, 5:321-339
77557 The monad, the dyad, and the family therapy of schizophrenics. In
       Burton, A. *Psychotherapy of the Psychoses*, NY: Basic Books 1961, 318-
       328
77558 Myths of Madness: New Facts for Old Fallacies. NY: Macmillan 1964,
       178 p
77559 (& Bodin, A. M.) Paradoxical communication and the marital paradox.
       Marriage Relat 3-20
77560 Psychoanalytic education in the communication processes. Sci Psa
       1962, 5:129-145
77561 Schizophrenia the nosological nexus. In Romano, J. *The Origins of
       Schizophrenia*, Amsterdam/NY: Excerpta Medica Found 1967, 111-
       120
77562 The study of the family. Fam Proc 1965, 4:1-20
77563 The transactional viewpoint. Int J Psychiat 1967, 4:543-544
77564 (& Haley, J.) Transference revisited. JNMD 1963, 137:363-371
            Abs BFM Q 1965, 34:138

       See Block, Jeanne; Glover, Edward

                          JACKSON, DONALD D. Q.
       See Lederer, William J.

JACKSON, DOUGLAS N.
See Gardner, Riley W.

JACKSON, EDGAR N.
77565 Grief and guilt. Pastoral Counselor 1963, 1:34-38

See Bowers, Margaretta K.

JACKSON, HARRY W.
See Silverman, Martin A.

JACKSON, JAMES
77566 Consensus and conflict in treatment organizations. Hosp Comm Psychiat 1968, 19:161-167
77567 (& Grotjahn, M.) The efficacy of group therapy in a case of marriage neurosis. Int J grp PT 1959, 9:420-428
S-49409 (& Grotjahn, M.) The treatment of oral defenses by combined individual and group psychotherapy.
Abs RSB An Surv Psa 1958, 9:428-429

JACKSON, JAY M.
77568 Reference group processes in a formal organization. In Cartwright, D. & Zander, A. *Group Dynamics,* Evanston, Ill: Row, Peterson 1960, 120-140

JACKSON, JOAN K.
See Dorpat, Theodore L.

JACKSON, LYDIA
77569 Anxiety in adolescents in relation to school refusal. J child Psychol Psychiat 1964, 5:59-73
77570 (& Todd, K. M.) Changes in meaning of play. In Haworth, M. R. *Child Psychotherapy,* NY/London: Basic Books 1964, 369-371
77571 (& Todd, K. M.) Play as expression of conflict. In Haworth, M. R. *Child Psychotherapy,* NY/London: Basic Books 1964, 314-321
77572 A study of 200 school children by means of the test of family attitudes. Brit J Psychol 1964, 55:333-354
77573 Unsuccessful adoptions: a study of 40 cases who attended a child. M 1968, 41:389-398
77574 (& Todd, K. M.) Work with the parents. In Haworth, M. R. *Child Psychotherapy,* NY/London: Basic Books 1964, 76-80

JACKSON, M. P.
77575 Suggestions for a controlled experiment to test precognition in dreams. J Amer Soc psychical Res 1967, 61:346-353

JACKSON, MURRAY

77576 Chair, couch and countertransference. J anal Psych 1961, 6:35-43
77577 The importance of depression emerging in a therapeutic group. J anal
       Psych 1964, 9:51-59
77578 Jung's "archetype": clarity or confusion? M 1960, 33:83-94
          Abs Hill, G. Q 1961, 30:153-154
77579 Jung's "archetypes" and psychiatry. JMS 1960, 106:1518-1526
77580 Jung's later work. The archetype. M 1962, 35:199-204
          Abs JCS RFPsa 1964, 28:310-311
77581 (& Harding, E.) Symbol formation and the delusional transference. A
       critical appreciation. J anal Psych 1963, 8:145-159. Archetype, Basel
       1964, 30-47
77582 Technique and procedure in analytic practice with special reference to
       schizoid states. J anal Psych 1963, 8:51-63

JACKSON, PAUL R.

77583 Henry Miller's literary pregnancies. Lit & Psych 1969, 19:35-49

JACKSON, PHILIP W.

See Getzels, Jacob W.

JACKSON, STANLEY W.

77584 (Reporter) Aspects of culture in psychoanalytic theory and practice.
       (Panel: Am Psa Ass, Dec 1967) J Am Psa Ass 1968, 16:651-670
77585 The history of Freud's concepts of regression. J Am Psa Ass 1969, 17:
       743-784

JACOB, CAROL GRETA

77586 The value of the family interview in the diagnosis and treatment of
       schizophrenia. Ps 1967, 30:162-172

JACOB, ELIZABETH

See Seitz, Philip F. D.

JACOB, MAURICE

TRANSLATION OF:
(& Dibon, P.) Mitscherlich, A. [84011]

JACOB, W.

77587 [On the history of psychotherapy and the science of neuroses.] (Ger)
       Landarzt 1968, 44:1-6
77588 Psychosomatische und psychotherapeutische Strömungen in der Medizin
       unserer Zeit. Konzepte und kritische reflexion. 13. Anthropologische
       Grundlagen der Psychoanalyse. [Psychosomatic and psychotherapeutic
       trends in today's medicine. Concepts and critical reflections. 13. An-
       thropological bases of psychoanalysis.] Hippokrates 1969, 40:63-68

JACOBI, JOLANDE (SZÉKÁCS)

77589 Bilderreich der Seele. [Images of the Psyche.] Freiburg: Walter 1969,
       280 p
77590 Freud y Jung: encuentro y separación. [Freud and Jung: meeting and
       separation.] Rev Psicol gen apl Madrid 1958, 13:723-738
77591 Symbols in an individual analysis. In Jung, C. G. et al: *Man and His
       Symbols*, NY: Doubleday 1964, 272-303
S-49420 Versuch einer Abgrenzung der wichtigsten Konzeptionen C. G. Jungs
       von denen S. Freuds.
       Abs An Surv Psa 1955, 6:20-22

JACOBS, D.

77592 [Defense mechanisms.] (Dut) T Ziekenverpl 1967, 20:82-85

JACOBS, DAVID

       See Bellak, Leopold

JACOBS, HANS

77593 Western Psychotherapy and Hindu-Sâdhanâ. A Contribution to Com-
       parative Studies. NY: IUP; London: Allen & Unwin 1961, 232 p

JACOBS, J.

       See Teicher, Joseph O.

JACOBS, LEON I.

77594 The primal crime. R 1965-66, 52:116-144
       Abs SRS Q 1966, 35:629

JACOBS, M.

77594A The treatment of homosexuality. S Afr med J 1969, 43:1123-1126

JACOBS, MARTIN ALLEN

77595 (& Muller, J. J.; Eisman, H. D.) The assessment of change in distress
       level and styles of adaption as a function of psychotherapy. JNMD
       1967, 145:392-404
77596 (& Pugatch, D.; Spilken, A.) Ego strength and ego weakness. Compari-
       son of psychiatric patients and functioning normals. JNMD 1968, 147:
       297-307
77597 Fantasies of mother-child interaction in hay fever sufferers. Diss Abstr
       1963, 24(4):1698-1699
77598 (& Anderson, L. S.; Champagne, E.; Karush, N.; Richman, S. J.; Knapp,
       P. H.) Orality, impulsivity and cigarette smoking in men: further find-
       ings in support of a theory. JNMD 1966, 143:207-219
77599 (& Knapp, P. H.; Anderson, L. S.) Relationship of oral frustration fac-
       tors with heavy cigarette smoking in males. JNMD 1965, 141:161-171
77600 Studies of mood. Int Psychiat Clin 1966, 3:223-236
77601 The use of projective techniques in research design: the family inter-
       action test. Int Psychiat Clin 1966, 3:237-264

JACOBS, ROBERT LOUIS

77602   A Freudian view of "The Ring." Music Rev 1965, 26:201-219

JACOBS, THEODORE

77603   Discussant: "Medical Education." Teach Dyn Psychiat 78-80

JACOBS, THEODORE J.

See Rosenbaum, Milton

JACOBSEN, ERLING

77604   Psychoneuroses. Danish med Bull 1967, 14:119-123
77605   De Psykiske Grundprocessor. [Fundamental Psychic Process.] Copen-
        hagen: Berlingske 1968, 148 p

JACOBSON, ALLAN

See Kales, Anthony

JACOBSON, EDITH

77606   Adolescent moods and the remodeling of psychic structures in adoles-
        cence. (Read at NY Psa Soc & Inst, 7 Mar 1961) Psa St C 1961, 16:
        164-183
        Abs WAS Q 1961, 30:612-613
S-15661 Beitrag zur Entwicklung des weiblichen Kindwunsches.
        On the development of the girl's wish for a child. (Tr: Kessler, E.)
        Q 1968, 37:523-538
S-49431 Denial and repression.
        Abs Solomon, R. G. An Surv Psa 1957, 8:96-98
S-49432 Depersonalization.
        Abs JTM Q 1961, 30:140-141. SAS RFPsa 1961, 25:158
77607   Discussion of Hoppe, K. D. "The psychodynamics of concentration
        camp victims." Psa Forum 1966, 1:84
S-49433 "The exceptions." An elaboration of Freud's character study.
        Abs RTh J 1961, 42:470-471
S-49434 Federn's contribution to ego psychology and psychoses.
        Abs Guiard, F. Rev Psicoanál 1966, 23:272
77608   Ein Fall von Sterilität. [A case of sterility.] Z PSM 1964, 10:83-94
77609   Guilt, shame, and identity. (Read at Westchester Psa Soc, 1 Apr 1963)
        Abs Harrison, I. Q 1963, 32:475-477
S-49435 Interaction between psychotic partners. I. Manic-depressive partners.
        Abs Shevin, F. F. An Surv Psa 1956, 7:179-181
77610   Introjection in mourning. Int J Psychiat 1967, 3:433-435
77611   Das Lachen des Kindes. [Laughter of the child.] Prax Kinderpsychol
        1961, 10:33-43
77612   Negación y repressión. [Negation and repression.] Rev Psicoanál 1967,
        24:545-578
S-49436 Normal and pathological moods: their nature and functions.
        Abs EMW An Surv Psa 1957, 8:68-73

77613 Problems in the differentiation between schizophrenic and melancholic states of depression. Psa—Gen Psychol 499-518

77614 Psychotic Conflict and Reality. (Read at NY Psa Soc, 11 May 1965) NY: IUP; London: HPI 1967, 80 p
   Abs J Am Psa Ass 1969, 17:272. Rv Jucovy, M. E. Q 1966, 35:167-169. Freudenberger, H. J. R 1969, 56:349. Rosenfeld, H. J 1969, 50:405-408

77615 The return of the lost parent. Canad Psychiat Ass J 1966, 11(Suppl): S259-S266. Dr Af Beh 2:193-211

77616 The Self and the Object World. NY: IUP 1964; London: Hogarth 1965, xiii + 250 p
   Rv Anderson, A. R. Q 1965, 34:584-589. Fordham, M. J 1965, 46:525-529. Searles, H. F. J 1965, 46:529-532. Gioia, T. Rev Psicoanál 1966, 23:273. Walker, H. I. Bull Phila Ass Psa 1966, 16:147-152

REVIEW OF:
77617 Grinker, R. R., Sr. et al: The Phenomena of Depressions. Q 1963, 32:252-255

JACOBSON, G.

77617A (& Ryder, R. G.) Parental loss and some characteristics of the early marriage relationship. Ops 1969, 39:779-787

JACOBSON, GEORGE

77618 The briefest psychiatric encounter. Acute effects of evaluation. Arch gen Psychiat 1968, 18:718-724

77619 National Institute for the study of conflict resolution suggested. P 1968, 125:116-117

JACOBSON, GERALD F.

77620 Crisis theory and treatment strategy: some sociocultural and psychodynamic considerations. JNMD 1965, 141:209-218

77621 (& Strickler, M.; Morley, W. E.) Generic and individual approaches to crisis intervention. Amer J Publ Hlth 1968, 58:338-343

77622 A note on Shakespeare's "Midsummer Night's Dream." Am Im 1962, 19:21-26

77623 (& Wilner, D. M.; Morley, W. E.; Schneider, S. F.; Strickler, M.; Sommer, G.) The scope and practice of an early access brief treatment psychiatric center. P 1965, 121:1176-1182

77624 Some psychoanalytic considerations regarding crisis therapy. (Read at Am Psa Ass, 30 Apr 1965) R 1967, 54:649-654
   Abs SRS Q 1969, 38:164

See Strickler, Martin

JACOBSON, JEROME E.

See Ziskind, Eugene

JACOBSON, M. D.

See Haddox, V. G.

JACOBSON, WAYNE E.

See Meyer, Eugene

JACOBY, A.

See Zucker, Howard D.

JACOBY, M.

77624A A contribution to the phenomenon of transference. J anal Psych 1969, 14:133-142

JACQUELIN, CLAIRE

77625 Ophthalmologie et psychiatrie, psychopathologie du voir. [Ophthalmology and psychiatry: psychopathology of vision.] Évolut psychiat 1963, 28:555-576

JACQUES, HENRI-PAUL

77626 Mythologie et Psychanalyse. Le Châtiment des Danaides. [Mythology and Psychoanalysis. The Punishment of the Danaides.] Montreal: Les Éditions Lemeac 1969

JAEGER, JACOB O. S.

S-49444 Mechanisms in depression.
Abs An Surv Psa 1955, 6:150-151

JAFFÉ, ANIELA

77627 Apparitions and Precognition. A Study from the Point of View of C. G. Jung's Analytic Psychology. (Foreword: Jung, C. G.) New Hyde Park, NY: Univ Books 1963, viii + 214 p
* * * (Editor of) Jung, C. G. *Memories, Dreams, Reflections.*
77628 Aus Leben und Werkstatt von C. G. Jung. [Life and Workshop of C. G. Jung.] Zürich: Rascher, 160 p
77629 Symbolism in the visual arts. In Jung, C. G. et al: *Man and His Symbols,* NY: Doubleday 1964, 230-271

JAFFE, BERYL

77630 (& Hoffman, F. H.) The function of personal analysis. Int Psychiat Clin 1964, 1:367-375

JAFFE, DANIEL S.

S-49446 Analysis of a repetitive dream with painful content.
Abs IK An Surv Psa 1957, 8:177-178
77631 Fatigue states—asthenic reactions. In Cantor, P. D. *Traumatic Medicine and Surgery for the Attorney, Part XII. Psychiatry,* Wash/London: Butterworths 1961, 22-34
77632 The masculine envy of woman's procreative function. (Read at Am Psa Ass, 6 May 1966) J Am Psa Ass 1968, 16:521-548
77633 The mechanism of projection: its dual role in object relations. (Read at Am Psa Ass, May 1961) J 1968, 49:662-677

JAFFE, JOSEPH

77634 Computer assessment of dyadic interaction rules from chronographic data. In Shlien, J. M. et al: *Research in Psychotherapy, Vol. III*, Wash DC: APA 1968, 260-276

77635 Discussion of Feldstein, S. "Vocal patterning of emotional expression." Sci Psa 1964, 7:208-210

77636 Dyadic analysis of two psychotherapeutic interviews. In Gottschalk, L. A. *Comparative Psycholinguistic Analysis of Two Psychotherapeutic Interviews*, NY: IUP 1961, 73-90

77637 Electronic computers in psychoanalytic research. Sci Psa 1963, 6:160-170

77638 (& Dahlberg, C. C.; Feldstein, S.) Practical aspects of systematic research in psychoanalytic office settings: report of the committee on research. Sci Psa 1967, 11:202-226

77639 Social factors in the doctor-patient relationship. Sci Psa 1961, 4:81-88

See Feldstein, Stanley

JAFFE, RUTH

77640 Dissociative phenomena in former concentration camp inmates. (Read at Int Psa Cong, July 1967) J 1968, 49:310-312
Abs LHR Q 1969, 38:669

77641 Group activity as a defense method in concentration camps. Israel Ann Psychiat 1963, 1:235-243

77642 Moshe Woolf b. 1878. Pioneering in Russia and Israel. Psa Pioneers 200-209

77642A Psychiatric classification and theories. Israel Ann Psychiat 1969, 7:145-157

77643 Psychopathological investigation of a case of periodic hypersomnia and bulimia (Kleine-Levin syndrome). Israel Ann Psychiat 1967, 5:43-52

JAFFIN, DAVID

77644 The methodology of the historian and psychoanalysis. Int J Offender Therapy 1968, 12(2):85-89

JAHODA, GUSTAV

77645 The Psychology of Superstition. London: Penguin 1969, 158 p

JAHODA, MARIE

77646 Notes on work. Psa—Gen Psychol 622-633

77647 Race relations and mental health. In *Race and Science*, United Nations Educational, Scientific and Cultural Organization, NY: Columbia Univ Pr 1961

77648 Some notes on the influence of psychoanalytic ideas on American psychology. Hum Relat 1963, 16:111-129

JAKOVLJEVIC, V.

77649 Kulturna sredina i neuroze. [Cultural environment and neurosis.] Med Glas 1961, 15(2-2a):50-54

JAMES, B.

77650 Learning theory and homosexuality. New Zeal Med J 1967, 66:748-751

JAMES, MARTIN

77651 The application of discussion in the treatment group. In *Discussion Method*, London: The Bureau of Current Affairs 1950, 67-71

77652 Children in hospital: preparation and aftercare. Royal Society for the Promotion of Health Journal 1959, 79:567-573

77653 Comment on the paper by Drs. Axelrad and Brody. (Read at Int Psa Cong, July 1965) J 1966, 47:230-235

77654 Discussion of Greenacre, P. & Winnicott, D. W. "The theory of the parent-infant relationship. Further remarks." Contributions to discussion (IV). J 1962, 43:247-248

* * * Editor of Lebovici, S. & McDougall, J. *Dialogue with Sammy: A Psycho-Analytical Contribution to the Understanding of Child Psychosis.*

77655 Infantile narcissistic trauma. Observations on Winnicott's work in infant care and child development. J 1962, 43:69-79
Abs FTL Q 1963, 32:285

77656 Interpretation and management in the treatment of preadolescents: the handling of pre-Oedipal and Oedipal material in child development and psycho-analysis. J 1964, 45:499-511

S-49462 Premature ego development. Some observations upon disturbances in the first three months of life.
Le développement prématuré du moi. Quelques observations sur les troubles des trois premiers mois de la vie. RFPsa 1961, 25:577-590
Spanish: Acta Neuropsychiatrica Argent 1960, 41:288-294
Abs Bianchedi, E. T. de Rev Psicoanál 1961, 18:395-396. JBi Q 1962, 31:116

77657 Psychoanalysis and childhood 1967. In Sutherland, J. D. *The Psychoanalytic Approach*, London: Baillière & Cassell 1968, 11-30

77658 Some notes on group therapy. Brit med Students' J 1950, Spring: 1-6

REVIEWS OF:
77659 Shields, R. W. A Cure of Delinquents. The Treatment of Maladjustment. J 1965, 46:270-275

77660 Spitz, R. A. The First Year of Life. J 1967, 48:118-121

JAMES, PATRICIA

See Dickoff, James

JAMESON, JEAN

* * * (& Klein, H.) Editors of Rado, S. *Adaptional Psychodynamics.*

See Ovesey, Lionel

JAMESON, MICHAEL H.

77661 The mysteries of Eleusis. (Read at Phila Ass Psa, 16 May 1969) Bull Phila Ass Psa 1969, 19:114-132

JAMET, F.
See Bergeron, Marcel

JANCHILL, M. P.
77662 Systems concepts in casework theory and practice. Soc Casewk 1969, 50:74-82

JANET, PIERRE
77663 Excerpts from *The Major Symptoms of Hysteria*. In Kaufman, M. R. & Heiman, M. *Evolution of Psychosomatic Concepts*, NY: IUP 1964, 156-159

JANEWAY, CHARLES A.
77664 Discussion of Olden, C. "Work with teachers." In Weinreb, J. *Recent Developments in Psychoanalytic Child Therapy*, NY: IUP 1960, 64-69

JANI, NATWAR M.
77665 Random thoughts on isolation. Int J Psychiat 1961, 3:217-223

JANIS, IRVING LESTER
77666 (& Mann, L.) Effectiveness of emotional role-playing in modifying smoking habits and attitudes. J exp Res Pers 1965, 1:84-90
77667 (& Terwilliger, R. F.) An experimental study of psychological resistances to fear arousing communications. ASP 1962, 65:403-410
77668 Group identification under conditions of external danger. M 1963, 36:227-238
         Abs Hirsh, H. Q 1964, 33:611-612
77669 (& Mahl, G. F.; Kagan, J.; Holt, R. R.) (Eds) Personality: Dynamics, Development, and Assessment. NY/Chicago/San Francisco: Harcourt, Brace & World 1969, xxxii + 895 p
77670 (& Leventhal, H.) Psychological aspects of physical illness and hospital care. In Wolman, B. B. *Handbook of Clinical Psychology*, NY: McGraw-Hill 1965, 1360-1377
77671 (& Katz, D.) The reduction of intergroup hostility: research problems and hypotheses. J Conflict Resolut 1959, 3:85-100. In Zawdony, J. K. *Man and International Relations, Vol. II*, San Francisco: Chandler Publ 1966, 644-657
77672 Some implications of recent research on the dynamics of fear and stress tolerance. In Redlich, F. C. *Social Psychiatry*, Baltimore: Williams & Wilkins 1969, 86-100

See Hovland, Carl I.

JANIS, MARJORIE G.
77673 A Two-Year-Old Goes to Nursery School. A Case Study of Separation Reactions. London: Tavistock 1964, 156 p

JANKOWITZ, ABRAHAM
See Nichtern, Sol

JANNONE, D.

See Zacco, M.

JANOTA, O.

77674 [Psychosomatic medicine and clinical psychiatry.] (Cz) Ceskoslov
Psychiat 1968, 64:6-12

JANOWITZ, HENRY D.

See Stein, Aaron

JANOWITZ, MORRIS

See Bettelheim, Bruno

JANOWSKY, D. S.

77675 (& Gorney, R.; Kelley, B.) The curse—vicissitudes and variations of
the female fertility cycle. Part I. Psychiatric aspects. Psychosomatics
1966, 7:242-247

JANSE DE JONGE, ADRIAAN L.

77676 Psychopathologie van de kraamheer. [Psychopathology of the father
to be.] Ned Tijdschr Psychol 1960, 15:1-10

JANSEN, ELBERT

77677 Psychoanalytische behandeling van een lijder aan schizofrenie. [Psy-
choanalytic treatment of a schizophrenic.] NTvG 1960, 104:600-603

JANSSEN, DIRK

77678 Zur Psychosomatik eines urologischen Syndroms. [On the psychosomatic nature of a urological syndrome.] Z PSM 1964, 10:77-83

JANSSEN, J.

77679 (& Pierloot, R.) Renforcement du moi par la sociotherapie. [Ego-
strengthening by sociotherapy.] In IV Int Cong of Group-Psycho-
therapy, Vienna: Verlag der Wiener Medizinish Akademie 1968

JANSSON, BENGT

77680 [Behavior therapy—a psychiatric alternative.] (Sw) Lakartidningen
1968, 65:2364-2366

JANSZEN, H. H.

See West, Louis J.

JANZ, D.

77681 Differentialtypologie der idiopathischen Epilepsien. [Differential typ-
ology of idiopathic epilepsies.] In Kranz, H. Psychopathologie Heute,
Stuttgart: Georg Thieme 1962, 176-184

JANZ, HANS-WERNER

77682 Zur Problematik der Hoffnung in der Psychotherapie. [On the problematic of hope in psychotherapy.] Z Psychother med Psychol 1968, 18:121-133

JANZARIK, WERNER

77683 Die Erinnerungen alter Schizophrener und der mnestische Aspekt sellischer Struktur. [Memories of old schizophrenics and the mnemic aspect of the structure of the soul.] In Kranz, H. *Psychopathologie Heute*, Stuttgart: Georg Thieme 1962, 94-107

77684 Der Wahn in strukturdynamischer Sicht. [Delusions from the structural and dynamic viewpoint.] Stud Gen 1967, 20:628-638

77685 Zur Sexualität und sexuellen Thematik chronisch schizophrener Kranker. [On sexuality and sexual thematic of chronic schizophrenics.] Arch Psychiat Nervenkr 1965, 207:280-295

JAPPE, GEMMA

77686 (& John, G.; Vogel, H.) Die Testuntersuchung als spezifisches Übertragungsfeld. Überlegungen zur analytischen Fundierung der Testdiagnostik. [The test situation as a specific transference situation. Considerations on the analytical foundations of test diagnosis. Psyche 1965, 19:40-67

JAQUES, ELLIOTT

77687 (& Brown, W.) The business school syllabus—a systematic approach. Manager 1964, April. With title: Management teaching. In author's *Glacier Project Papers*

77688 Collaborative group methods in a wage negotiation situation. Hum Relat 1950, 3(3)

77689 Death and the mid-life crisis. J 1965, 46:502-514. In Ruitenbeek, H. M. *Death: Interpretations*, NY: Dell Publ 1969, 140-165
La muerte y la crisis de la mitad de la vida. Rev Psicoanál 1966, 23:402-423
Abs EVN Q 1967, 36:626

77690 Discussion of Rosenfeld, H. A. "The need of patients to act out during analysis." Psa Forum 1966, 1:27-28

S-49505 Disturbances in the capacity to work.
Les troubles de la faculté de travail. RFPsa 1961, 25:711-731
Abs Bianchedi, E. T. de Rev Psicoanál 1961, 18:391

77691 Economic justice—by law? Twentieth Century 1964, Spring. In author's *Glacier Project Papers*

77692 Equitable Payment: A General Theory of Work, Differential Payment, and Individual Progress. London: Heinemann; NY: John Wiley & Sons 1961, 336 p. Penguin Edition 1967
French: Neuilly-sur-Seine: Editions Hommes et Techniques 1963
Rv Money-Kyrle, R. E. J 1961, 42:562-563

77693 Executive organisation and individual adjustment. J psychosom Res 1966, 10

77694 Field theory and industrial psychology. Occupational Psychol 1948, July

77695 (& Brown, W.) Glacier Project Papers. London: Heinemann Educational Books; NY: Basic Books 1965

77696 Guilt, conscience and social behavior. In Sutherland, J. D. *The Psychoanalytic Approach,* London: Baillière & Cassell 1968, 31-43

77697 The impact of the production engineer upon the structure of work and payment in industry. Inst Production Engineers J 1957, May

77698 Interpretive group discussion as a method of facilitating social change. Hum Relat 1948, 1(4)

77699 Leadership and group behavior. Discussion (Bureau of Current Affairs) 1948, No. 6(Sept)

* * * Management teaching. See [77687]

S-49508 Measurement of Responsibility: A Study of Work, Payment and Individual Capacity.
La Valutazione delle Responsabilita. Turin: Isper Edizioni 1966

77700 Miscomprehensions of parents concerning child health and behavior. Ops 1942, 12(2)

77702 National wage and salary policy in Britain. Nature 1957, 180:525-526

77703 Note on the etymology of work. In author's *Glacier Project Papers*

77704 An objective approach to pay differentials. New Scientist 1958, 4(85)

77705 Objective measures for pay differentials. Harv bus Rev 1962, Jan-Feb

77706 On children's film appraisal. Documentary News Letter 1947, Aug-Sept

77707 (& Brown, W.) Product Analysis Pricing. London: Heinemann Educational Books 1964

77708 Progression Handbook: How to Use Earnings Progression Data Sheets for Assessing Individual Capacity, for Progression, and for Manpower Planning and Development. London: Heinemann Educational Books; Carbondale: Southern Ill Univ Pr 1968, vii + 72 p

77709 Psychology and organisation. In author's *Glacier Project Papers*

77710 The resolution of disputes over pay differentials. J Inst of Personnel Management 1957, March

77711 The science of society. Hum Relat 1966, 19(2)

77712 (& Rice, A. K.; Hill, J. M. M.) The social and psychological impact of a change in method of wage payment. Hum Relat 1951, 4(4)

77713 Social-analysis and the Glacier Project. Hum Relat 1964, 17(4). In author's *Glacier Project Papers*

77714 A system for income equity. New Society 1963, 12 Dec. With title: "National incomes policy." In author's *Glacier Project Papers*

77715 Time-Span Handbook. London: Heinemann Educational Books 1964; NY: Basic Books 1965
Manuel d'Evaluation des Fonctions. Paris: Editions Hommes et Techniques 1965

77716 The time span *is* an accurate yardstick. Personnel Management and Welfare 1957, June

77717 Too many management levels. Calif Management Rev 1965

77718 Two contributions to a general theory of organisation and management. Scient Business 1964, Aug. In author's *Glacier Project Papers*

77719 Work, payment and capacity. Trans Ass of industrial med Officers 1957, 7(1)

JARAST, ELÍAS

77720 La fantasia contratransferencial como "señal de alarma." [Countertransference fantasy as "alarm-signal."] Rev Psicoanál 1965, 22:45-68

See Rascovsky, Arnaldo

REVIEW OF:
77721 Salerno, E. V. Ginecologia psicosomática. Rev Psicoanál 1964, 21:378

JARAST, SARA G. DE

S-49519 El duelo en relación con el aprendizaje.
Abs JO An Surv Psa 1958, 9:301-302
77722 Evolución en el tratamiento de un niño de cinco anos por un cambio de enfoque en la interpretación. [Development in the treatment of a five-year-old boy by changing the focus of interpretation.] Rev Psicoanál 1962, 19:86-92
77723 Urgencia quirúrgica y psicoanálisis. [Surgical emergency and psychoanalysis.] Rev Psicoanál 1964, 21:220-226

JARDIM, ANNE

See Zaleznik, Abraham

JARDIN, F.

77724 (& Flavigny, H.) [The role of the father in children's running away.] Rv Np inf 1965, 13:744-765

JAROSCH, K.

77725 [On the psychopathology of arsonists.] (Ger) Z Ges Gerichtl Med 1959, 49:64-65

JAROSZ, MAREK

77726 [Neurosis tristitiosa.] (Cz) Ceskoslov Psychiat 1963, 59:415-418
77727 Przegląd i krytyka podstawowych pojęc psychoanalizy oraz psychoanalitycznej teorii nerwic. [A review and critique of basic concepts of psychoanalysis and psychoanalytic theory of neuroses.] Przeglad Psychologiczny 1962, 5:149-182

JARREAU, R.

77728 (& Klotz, R.) Relaxation analytique et langage. [Analytic relaxation and language.] Rev Méd psychosom 1968, 10:439-443

JARUS, ARIE

77729 Treatment of adolescents as seen from the Mental Health Centre. Proc IV World Cong Psychiat 1966, 1205-1206

5759

Jaspers

JARVIK, LISSY

See Kestenbaum, Clarice J.

JARVIS, JENNIFER M.

77730   (& Gibson, J.) Psychology of Nurses. Springfield, Ill: Thomas 1962, 131 p

JARVIS, VIVIAN

S-49521 Clinical observations on the visual problem in reading disability.
Klinische Beobachtungen über das visuelle Problem bei Lesestörungen. Psyche 1960, 14:204-220
Abs JA An Surv Psa 1958, 9:302-304
77731   Countertransference in the management of school phobia. Q 1964, 33: 411-419
Abs Rosarios, H. Rev Psicoanál 1964, 21:2635
77732   Learning disability and its relationship to normal fantasy formation. (Read at Council of Psa Psychotherapists, 27 Feb 1967) R 1969, 65: 288-298
77733   Loneliness and compulsion. J Am Psa Ass 1965, 13:122-158
Abs CG RFPsa 1968, 32:338. JLSt Q 1968, 37:468
77734   A note on "the pill" and emotional conflict. Q 1969, 38:639-642

JARVIS, WILBUR

77735   Some effects of pregnancy and childbirth on men. J Am Psa Ass 1962, 10:689-700
Abs JBi Q 1963, 32:448
S-49522 "When I grow big and you grow little."
Abs NZ An Surv Psa 1958, 9:297

JASPERS, KARL

77736   The axial age of human history. Commentary 1948, 6:430-435. In Stein, M. R. et al: *Identity and Anxiety*, Glencoe, Ill: Free Pr 1960, 597-605
77737   Delusion and awareness of reality. Int J Psychiat 1968, 6:25-38
77738   Gesammelte Schriften zur Psychopathologie. [Collected Writings on Psychopathology.] Berlin: Springer 1963, viii + 421 p
77739   The Nature of Psychotherapy; A Critical Appraisal. (Tr: Hoenig, J. & Hamilton, M. W.) Chicago: Univ Chicago Pr 1965, xi + 52 p
77740   Our German trouble. Some critical (and self-critical) remarks of a German philosopher. Encounter 1961, 17(3):21-24
77741   The phenomenological approach in psychopathology. Brit J Psychiat 1968, 114:1313-1323
S-15744 Psychopathologie Generale.
General Psychopathology. (Tr: Hoenig, J. & Hamilton, M. W.) Chicago: Univ Chicago Pr; Manchester: Manchester Univ Pr 1963, 922 p
Rv Laing, R. D. J 1964, 45:590-593. Niederland, W. G. Q 1966, 35: 130-135

JAVAL, I.
See Klotz, H. P.

JAY, M.
77742 Les traitements de la schizophrenie infantile. [The treatments of child-hood schizophrenia.] Rv Np inf 1960, 8:134-138

JEANGUYOT, M.
See Douadi, D.

JEANNEAU, AUGUSTIN
77743 Initiation à la psychanalyse. [Introduction to Psychoanalysis.] Paris: Beauchesne 1965, 189 p

JEANNEQUIN, L.
77744 Action non-directive de l'educateur. [Nondirective action by the educa-tor.] Rv Np inf 1969, 17:11-25

JEANNIERE, ABEL
77745 The Anthropology of Sex. (Tr: Kerman, J.) (Foreword: Sullivan, D.) NY: Harper & Row 1967, 188 p

JEANS, R. F.
See Garner, Harry H.

JEDLICKI, WITOLD
77746 Co Sądzić o Freudyzmie i Psychoanalizie. [What One Is to Say (or Judge) about Freudianism and Psychoanalysis.] Warsaw: Wiedza Powszechna 1961, 138 p

JEFFERS, FRANCES C.
77747 (& Nichols, C. R.; Eisdorfer, C.) Attitudes of older persons toward death: a preliminary study. J Gerontol 1961, 16:53-56. Death & Iden-tity 142-146

JEFFREY, LLOYD N.
77748 A Freudian reading of Keats's "Ode to Psyche." R 1968, 55:289-306

JEGARD, SUZANNE
77749 (& Walters, R. H.) A study of some determinants of aggression in young children. Child Develpm 1960, 31:739-747

JEKEL, J.
See Tapia, Fernando

JEKELS, LUDWIG

S-15793 (& Bergler, E.) Instinct dualism in dreams. Sel P EB 22-37
S-15794 (& Bergler, E.) Transference and love. Sel P EB 2-21

JELLINEK, E. M.

See Shakow, David

JENKINS, JOHN S.

77750 (& Watters, T. A.) The pastor learns the art of counseling. Pastoral
Psychol 1967, 18(171):22

JENKINS, RICHARD LEOS

77751 Diagnoses, dynamics, and treatment in child psychiatry. Psychiat Res
Rep 1964, (18):91-138
77752 (& Cole, J. O.) (Eds) Diagnostic Classification in Child Psychiatry.
(Psychiat Res Report No. 18) Wash: Amer Psychiat Assoc 1964, 152 p
77752A (& Boyer, A.) Effects of inadequate mothering and inadequate fathering on children. Int J soc Psychiat 1969, 16:72-78
77753 Psychiatric syndromes in children and their relation to family background. Ops 1966, 36:450-457
77754 The varieties of children's behavioral problems and family dynamics.
P 1968, 124:1440-1445

JENKINS, W. O.

See Pascal, Gerald R.

JENNINGS, EUGENE E.

77755 An Anatomy of Leadership: Princes, Heroes, and Supermen. NY:
Harper & Brothers 1960, xvi + 256 p

JENNINGS, HELEN H.

See Moreno, Jacob L.

JENNINGS, R. M.

See Krinsky, L. W.

JENSEN, ARTHUR R.

See Deutsch, Martin; Symonds, Percival M.

JENSEN, ELLEN

77756 Anna O: Ihre späteres Schicksal. [Anna O: her later fate.] Acta psychiat neurol Scand Kbh 1961, 36:119-131

JENSEN, GORDON D.

77757 Discussion of Shainess, N. "Mother-child relationships: an overview."
Sci Psa 1969, 14:85-88

77758 (& Robbitt, R. A.) Implications of primate research for understanding infant development. In Hellmuth, J. *The Exceptional Infant, Vol. I,* Seattle, Wash: Special Child Publ 1967. Sci Psa 1968, 12:55-81

77759 (& Bobbitt, R. A.) Monkeying with the mother myth. Psychol Today 1968, 1:41-43, 68-69

77760 (& Bobbitt, R. A.; Gordon, B. N.) Sex differences in social interaction between infant monkeys and their mothers. Recent Adv biol Psychiat 1966, 9:283-293

JENSEN, JOSEPH S.

77761 (& Kirschbaum, R. A.) Occupational therapy in the treatment of borderline psychiatric patients. Amer J occup Ther 1961, 15:19-21

JENSEN, LEO

77762 Anorexia nervosa. Acta Psychiat Scand 1968, 44(Suppl 203):113-116

JENSEN, VERN A.

77763 Failure and capability in love: an integrative study of the psychology of Erich Fromm and the theology of Emil Brunner. Diss Abstr 1967, 27:2602

JENSEN, VIGGO W.

S-49536 (& Petty, T. A.) The fantasy of being rescued in suicide. Abs EMD An Surv Psa 1958, 9:174-175

JENTZSCH, MAIELIES

77764 Über psychoanalytische Berträge zum Erleben des Säuglings. [On psychoanalytic contributions to the experiences of infants. A comparative study.] Prax Kinderpsychol 1964, 13:204-212; 284-296

JEPPSON, JANET

REVIEW OF:

77765 Platt, J. R. The Step to Man. Contempo Psa 1967, 4(1):78-82

JERNBERG, ANN

See Margolis, Philip M.

JEROTIC, V.

See Klajn, V.

JERVIS, GEORGE A.

See Zubin, Joseph

JESSNER, LUCIE

77766 The development of identity and self-awareness in the child. Pan Amer Med Assoc 1960, 102

77767 Dynamic psychopathology in childhood. Psychiat Neurol Neurochirur 1962, 65:214-215

S-49545 (& Lamont, J. H.; Long, R. T.; Rollins, N.; Whipple, B.; Prentice, N. M.) Emotional impact of nearness and separation for the asthmatic child and his mother.
Abs An Surv Psa 1955, 6:274-277

77768 The genesis of a compulsive neurosis. J Hillside Hosp 1963, 12:81-95
Abs JA Q 1967, 36:136

77769 On becoming a mother. In Von Bayer, W. & Griffith, R. M. *Conditio Humana*, NY/Heidelberg: Springer 1966, 102-114

77770 Pregnancy as a stress in marriage. In Nash, E. M. et al: *Marriage Counseling in Medical Practice*, Chapel Hill: Univ North Carolina Pr 1964, 136-142

77771 The psychoanalysis of an eight-year-old boy with asthma. In Schneer, H. I. *The Asthmatic Child*, NY: Harper & Row 1963, 118-137

77772 (& Abse, D. W.) The psychodynamic aspects of leadership. Daedalus 1961, 90:693-710. In Graubard, S. R. & Holten, G. *Excellence and Leadership in a Democracy*, NY: Columbia Univ Pr 1962, 76-94

77773 Psychotherapy in psychosomatic disorders of childhood. In Hammer, M. & Kaplan, A. M. *The Practice of Psychotherapy with Children*, Homewood, Ill: Dorsey Pr 1967

77774 (& Abse, D. W.) Regressive forces in anorexia nervosa. M 1960, 33: 301-311
Abs RDT Q 1961, 30:460

77775 The role of the mother in the family. In Liebman, S. *Emotional Forces in the Family*, Phila/Montreal: Lippincott 1959, 19-36

S-49547 Some observations on children hospitalized during latency.
Beobachtungen an Kindern im Krankenhaus in der Latenzphase.
Hbh Kinderpsychother 849-859

77776 Training of a child psychiatrist. J Amer Acad Child Psychiat 1963, 2: 746-755

See LaBarre, Maurine B.; Nash, Ethel M.

REVIEW OF:
77777 Mahler, M. S. & Furer, M. On Human Symbiosis and the Vicissitudes of Individuation: Vol. I, Infantile Psychoses. Q 1969, 38:316-318

JESSOR, RICHARD

77778 (& Feshbach, S.) (Eds) Cognition, Personality, and Clinical Psychology: A Symposium Held at the University of Colorado. San Francisco: Jossey-Bass 1967, xv + 222 p

JIMENEZ GARCIA, J. L.

77779 [Impact of psychoanalysis on modern psychiatry.] (Sp) Hisp Med 1960, 17:535-538

JINDAL, R. C.

See Varma, R. M.

JOADWINE, MARION M.

See Kramer, Charles H.

JOËL, C. A.

77780 (& Sulman, F. G.) Einführung in die allgemeine Endokrinologie. [Introduction to general endocrinology]. In Meng, H. *Psyche und Hormon,* Bern/Stuttgart: Hans Huber 1960, 139-289

JOFEN, JEAN B.

77781 Two mad heroines. A study of the mental disorders of Ophelia in *Hamlet* and Margarete in *Faust.* Lit & Psych 1961, 11:70-77

JOFFE, WALTER G.

77782 (& Sandler, J.) Comments on the psychoanalytic psychology of adaptation, with special reference to the role of affects and the representational world. (Read at Int Psa Cong, July 1967) J 1968, 49:445-456
Kommentare zur psychoanalytischen Anpassungspsychologie, mit besonderem Bezug zur Rolle der Affekte und der Repräsentanzenwelt. Psyche 1967, 21:728-744
77783 A critical review of the status of the envy concept. J 1969, 50:533-545
77784 (& Sandler, J.) Notes on pain, depression, and individuation. Psa St C 1965, 20:394-424
Remarques sur la souffrance, la dépression et l'individuation. Psychiat Enfant 1967, 10:123-154
77785 (& Sandler, J.) On the concept of pain, with special reference to depression and psychogenic pain. J psychsom Res 1967, 11:69-75
77786 (& Sandler, J.) Psychoanalytic psychology and learning theory. Ciba Foundation Symposium, Role of Learning in Psychotherapy, Churchill, London 1968
77787 (& Sandler, J.) Some conceptual problems involved in the consideration of disorders of narcissism. J child PT 1967, 2:56-66
Über einige begriffliche Probleme im Zusammenhang mit dem Studium narzisstischer Storungen. Psyche 1967, 21:152-165
77788 (Ed) What is Psycho-Analysis? London: Institute of Psycho-Analysis 1968

See Sandler, Joseph

REVIEW OF:
77789 French, T. M. & Fromm, E. Dream Interpretation: A New Approach. J 1965, 46:532-533

JOHANNET, PIERRE

ABSTRACTS OF:
77790 Nodet, C.-H. Quelques réflexions sur les valeurs engagés dans la cure analytique. An Surv Psa 1958, 9:324-325
77791 Schneider, J. & Fain, M. Une observation de gastro-entérologie. An Surv Psa 1958, 9:197-198

JOHANSON, EVA

77792 Mild paranoia. Description and analysis of fifty-two in-patients from an open department for mental diseases. Acta Psychiat Scand 1964, 40(Suppl 177):1-100

JOHANSSON, A.

77793 Wandlungen einer paranoiden Patientin dürch psychoanalytische Behandlung. [Changes in a female paranoiac achieved through psychoanalytic therapy.] Psyche 1963, 17:218-236

JOHN, GISELA

77794 Zum Problem der Nachuntersuchung von Patienten durch Retests. [Follow-up studies by means of retests.] Psyche 1968, 22:792-801
       Abs J 1969, 50:399

See Jappe, Gemma

JOHN, VERA P.

See Deutsch, Martin

JOHNS, ETHEL

* * * Editor of Odlum, D. M. *Mental Health, the Nurse and the Patient.*

JOHNSEN, G.

77794A Family treatment in psychiatric hospitals. Psychother Psychosom 1968, 16:333-338

JOHNSEN, GORDON

77795 Three years' experience with use of LSD as an aid in psychotherapy. Acta Psychiat Scand 1964, 40(Suppl 80):383-388

JOHNSGARD, KEITH W.

77796 (& Muench, G. A.) Group therapy with normal college students. PT 1965, 2:114-116

JOHNSON, A.

See Barglow, Peter

JOHNSON, ADELAIDE MARGARET

77797 Experience, Affect, and Behavior; Psychoanalytic Explorations of Dr. Adelaide McFadyen Johnson. (Ed: Robinson, D. B.) (Foreword: Szurek, S.) Chicago: Univ Chicago Pr 1969, xx + 511 p
S-49561 (& Giffin, M. E.; Watson, E. J.; Beckett, P. G. S.) Studies in schizophrenia at the Mayo Clinic. II. Observations on ego functions in schizophrenia.
       Abs JA An Surv Psa 1956, 7:182

See Barry, Maurice J., Jr.; Beckett Peter G. S.; Estes, Hubert R.; Kolb, Lawrence C.; Litin, Edward M.

JOHNSON, B. S.

77798 The blotting paper syndrome, a counter-transference phenomenon. Perspect Psychiat Care 1967, 5:288-230

JOHNSON, COURTNEY

77799 Henry James' "The Jolly Corner." Am Im 1967, 344-359

JOHNSON, DEAN

77800 Marriage Counseling: Theory and Practice. Englewood Cliffs, N. J.:
       Prentice-Hall 1961, x + 246 p

JOHNSON, DON E.

S-49576 The neurotic character of a gentleman.
       Abs IK An Surv Psa 1957, 8:115-116

ABSTRACTS OF:

77801 Greenacre, P. The theory of parent-infant relationship. Bull Phila Ass
       Psa 1961, 11:97-99
77802 Marcovitz, E. Bemoaning the lost dream: Coleridge's "Kubla Khan"
       and addiction. Bull Phila Ass Psa 1962, 12:49-50
77803 Neubauer, P. B. The one parent child and his Oedipal development.
       Bull Phila Ass Psa 1961, 11:141-142

JOHNSON, FRANK A.

77804 Discussion. [Symposium: the psychoanalyst as mediator and double
       agent.] (Read at Scientific Conf on Psa, Council of Psychoanalytic
       Psychotherapists, 14 Feb 1965) R 1965, 52:400-404

REVIEW OF:

77806 Seeley, J. R. The Americanization of the Unconscious. R 1969, 56:353-
       355

JOHNSON, G. J.

See Papageorgis, Demetrios

JOHNSON, GRANVILLE B.

77806 Penis-envy? or pencil-needing? Psychol Rep 1966, 19:758

JOHNSON, HAROLD

77807 (& Eriksen, C. W.) Preconscious perception: a re-examination of the
       Pötzel phenomenon. ASP 1961, 62:497-503
       Abs Rosen, I. C. Q 1962, 31:591

JOHNSON, JAMES A., JR.

77808 Group Therapy: A Practical Approach. NY: McGraw-Hill 1963, xi +
       467 p

JOHNSON, L. C.

See Gunderson, Ellsworth K.

JOHNSON, LAVERNE
See Gulevich, George D.

JOHNSON, M.
See Overall, John E.

JOHNSON, M. H.
77809 (& Fordyce, W. E.; Masuda, M.; Dorpat, T. L.) The Abood and Aker-feldt tests: assessment of their reliability, predictive efficiency, and relationship to the MMPI. J Neuropsychiat 1960, 2:24-30
77810 (& Meadow, A.) Parental identification among male schizophrenics. J Pers 1966, 34:300-309

JOHNSON, MARGUERITE F.
See McNerney, Thomas P.

JOHNSON, MARTIN
77811 Dream reports and percept-genetic defensive organization in the DMT. Psychol Res Bull 1967, 7(12):1-17

JOHNSON, MIRIAM M.
77812 Sex role learning in the nuclear family. Child Develpm 1963, 34:319-333

JOHNSON, P. E.
77813 Religion and psychotherapy. Prog PT 1960, 5:201-206

JOHNSON, R. C.
77814 (& Suzuki, N. S.; Olds, W. K.) Phonetic symbolism in an artificial language. ASP 1964, 69:233-236
77815 (& Ackerman, J. M.; Frank, H.) Resistance to temptation, guilt following yielding, and psychopathology. J consult clin Psychol 1968, 32:169-175

JOHNSON, TRINIDAD C. M.
See Eiduson, Bernice T.

JOHNSON, VIRGINIA E.
See Masters, William H.

JOHNSON, W. R.
77816 Hypnotic analysis of aggression-blockage in baseball pitching. Amer J clin Hyp 1961, 4:102-105

JOHNSTON, GRACE F.
See Kramer, Charles H.

JOHNSTON, MC CLAIN

77817 European psychoanalytic training: current status. Samiska 1963, 17(2): 97-107

77818 Features of orality in an hysterical character. R 1963, 50:663-681
Abs SRS Q 1964, 33:609

JOHNSTON, THOMAS E.

77819 Freud and Political Thought. NY: Citadel Pr 1965, 160 p

JOHNSTONE, JOHN W. C.

See Coleman, James S.

JOHNSTONE, R. E.

See Claman, Lawrence

JOKIPALTIO, LEENA MAIJA

77820 Ablehnung der Weiblichkeit bei einem 6-jährigen Mädchen. [Rejection of femininity in a 6-year-old girl.] Schweiz Z Psychol 1966, 25:322-335

JONASSOHN, KURT

See Coleman, James S.

JONCKHEERE, P.

77821 Considerations sur la psychothérapie: A propos de 72 névroses. [Considerations on psychotherapy: with regard to 72 neurotics.] Acta neurol psychiat Belg 1965, 65:667-684

JONES, A.

See Deutsch, Felix

JONES, AUSTIN

77822 (& Lepson, D. S.) Mediated and primary stimulus-generalization bases of sexual symbolism. J consult Psychol 1967, 31:79-82

77823 Sexual symbolic response in prepubescent and pubescent children. J consult Psychol 1961, 25:383-387

JONES, C. DAVID

See Elson, Abraham

JONES, D. STANLEY

77824 The structure of emotion. II: The physical basis of anxiety. JNMD 1957, 125:247-258
Abs RZ An Surv Psa 1957, 8:73-74

77825 The structure of emotion. III: The physiology of the Oedipus complex. JNMD 1957, 125:259-272
Abs RZ An Surv Psa 1957, 8:74-76

JONES, DOROTHEA
See Kaufman, Irving

JONES, E. A.
77826 The use of speech as a security operation. Perspect Psychiat Care 1965,
3:18-21

JONES, ERNEST
S-16500B The birth and death of Moses.
Abs SLP An Surv Psa 1958, 9:443-444
* * * Editor of *Collected Papers of Sigmund Freud*. NY: Basic Books 1959,
5 Volumes
S-16532A Free Associations. Memoirs of a Psychoanalyst.
Rv Niederland, W. G. J Am Psa Ass 1964, 12:223-241
* * * Hamlet and Oedipus. See [16594]
S-16549A The inception of "Totem and Taboo."
Abs SLP An Surv Psa 1956, 7:30
S-16560A The Life and Work of Sigmund Freud. (Ed: Trilling, L.; Marcus,
S.) NY: Basic Books 1961, xxvi + 541 p; Doubleday 1963, xxiv + 532
p (abr)
Vita e Opere do Freud. (Pref: Servadio, E.)
Japanese: (Tr: Taketomo, Y. & Fujii, H.) Tokyo: Kinokuniya Book-
store 1964
Abs An Surv Psa 1955, 6:3-4. SLP An Surv Psa 1957, 8:3-6. J Am
Psa Ass 1962, 10:638. Rv Niederland, W. G. J Am Psa Ass 1964, 12:
223-241
S-16574A The nature of genius. (Read at NY Psa Soc & Inst, 23 Apr 1956) In
author's *Sigmund Freud: Four Centenary Addresses* 3-34
Abs AEC An Surv Psa 1956, 7:4-5
S-16594 The Oedipus Complex as an explanation of Hamlet's mystery: a study
in motive.
Hamlet et Oedipe, connaissance de l'inconscient.
Rv Gillibert, J. RFPsa 1968, 32:619-625
77827 On "dying together" and an unusual case of "dying together." In
author's *Essays in Applied Psychoanalysis* 9-21. In Ruitenbeek, H. M.
Death: Interpretations, NY: Dell Publ 1969 50-60
S-16596 The origin and structure of the superego. Heirs Freud 33-46
S-16596A Our attitude toward greatness. (Read at Am Psa Ass, 28 Apr, 1956)
In author's *Sigmund Freud: Four Centenary Addresses* 37-64
Abs CFH An Surv Psa 1956, 7:5-6
S-16597A Pain.
Abs SLP An Surv Psa 1957, 8:156
77828 Psychiatry before and after Freud. (Read at Am Psa Ass, 30 Apr 1956)
In author's *Sigmund Freud: Four Centenary Addresses* 67-93
Abs AEC An Surv Psa 1956, 7:6
77828 Sigmund Freud: the man and his achievements. In author's *Sigmund
Freud: Four Centenary Addresses* 97-150
Abs AEC An Surv Psa 1956, 7:3-4

JONES, G. SEABORN

77830 Treatment or Torture: The Philosophy, Techniques and Future of Psychodynamics. London: Tavistock 1958, viii + 324 p

JONES, IVOR H.

77831 Subincision among Australian western desert aborigines. M 1969, 42: 183-190

JONES, JACK

77832 Otto Rank: a forgotten heresy. Commentary 1960, 30:219-229

JONES, KATHERINE

77833 In an Outworn Tradition. Poems by Katherine Jones. Brookside Pr 1963
77834 A note on Milton's "Lycidas." Am Im 1962, 19:141-155

REVIEW OF:
77835 Robert, M. The Psychoanalytic Revolution. Sigmund Freud's Life and Achievement. J 1967, 48:471

JONES, MARSHALL R.

77836 (Ed) Human Motivation: A Symposium. Lincoln, Nebraska: Univ Nebraska Pr 1965, viii + 87 p
77837 (Ed) Miami Symposium on the Prediction of Behavior, 1967: Aversive Stimulation. Coral Gables, Fla: Univ Miami Pr 1968
77838 (Ed) Nebraska Symposium on Motivation. Vol. III. Lincoln, Nebraska: Univ Neb Pr 1960, xi + 268 p
77839 (Ed) Nebraska Symposium on Motivation, 1961. Lincoln, Nebraska: Univ Neb Pr 1962 ix + 210 p

JONES, MAXWELL

77840 Beyond the Therapeutic Community; Social Learning and Social Psychiatry. New Haven/London: Yale Univ Pr 1968, xxii + 150 p

JONES, MERVYN

S-49622 Ernest Jones: Funeral Addresses.
         Abs SLP An Surv Psa 1958, 9:5

JONES, NANCY L.

See Grold, L. James

JONES, NELSON FREDERICK

77841 (& Kahn, M. W.) Dimensions and consistency of clinical judgment as related to the judges' level of training. JNMD 1966, 142:19-24

See Hunt, William A.; Kahn, Marvin W.

JONES, RICHARD MATHEW

S-49623 An Application of Psychoanalysis to Education.
Abs J Am Psa Ass 1961, 9:167. Rv Piers, M. W. Q 1961, 30:439-441.
Woltmann, A. G. R 1964, 51:333-334. Semrad, E. V. & Day, M. J.
J Am Psa Ass 1966, 14:591-618
77842 (Ed) Contemporary Educational Psychology: Selected Essays. NY:
Harper & Row 1967, vi + 275 p
77843 Dream interpretation and the psychology of dreaming. J Am Psa Ass
1965, 13:304-319
Abs CG RFPsa 1968, 32:343. JLSt Q 1968, 37:469-470
77844 Ego Synthesis in Dreams. Cambridge, Mass: Schenkman Publ 1962,
100 p
Rv Kaywin, L. Q 1963, 32:257-258. Spotnitz, H. R 1963, 50:152-155
77845 Fantasy and Feeling in Education. NY: NY Univ Pr 1968, 240 p
S-49626 A model of transitional thought: organization.
Abs NZ An Surv Psa 1958, 9:100-101
77846 On the metaphor of the dream censor. Percept mot Skills 1962, 15:45-
46
77847 The problem of "depth" in the psychology of dreaming. JNMD 1964,
139:507-515
Abs BFM Q 1967, 36:141
77848 The psychoanalytic theory of dreaming—1968. JNMD 1968, 147:587-
604
77849 Psychosexuality in speech development. Percept mot Skills 1964,
19:390
77850 Role of self-knowledge in the educative process. Harv educ Rev 1962,
32:200-209
77851 Sexual symbols in dreams. Percept mot Skills 1964, 19:118

See Friedman, Neil; Hanfmann, Eugenia

JONES, ROBERT B.

See Feifel, Herman; Goldstein, Michael J.

JONES, ROGER W.

77852 Differential effects of verbal approval and psychoanalytically derived
interpretations as vicarious reinforcers with schizophrenics, normals,
and sociopaths. Diss Abstr 1969, 29(9-B):3486-3487

JONES, WARREN L.

77853 The A-B-C method of crisis management. MH 1968, 52:87-89
77854 The villain and the victim: group therapy for married couples. P 1967,
124:351-354

See Tabachnick, Norman

JONES, WENDELL E.

See Kramer, Charles H.

JORDAN, S. J.
See Koegler, Ronald R.

JORDAN, SIDNEY
77855 D. H. Lawrence's concept of the unconscious and existential thinking. Rev existential Psychol Psychiat 1965, 5:34-43

JORDI, P.
See Genevard, G.; Schneider, Pierre B.

JORES, ARTHUR
77856 (& Freyberger, H.) (Eds) Advances in Psychosomatic Medicine. Symposium of Fourth European Conference on Psychosomatic Research. (Int J Psychother & Psychosom Supplement, Basel: Karger 1960.) NY: Brunner 1961, 334 p
77857 (& Krekjarto, M. von) Der Asthmatiker. [The Asthmatic.] Bern/ Stuttgart: Hans Huber 1967, 194 p
  Rv Woltmann, A. G. R 1968, 55:325-326
77858 Bemerkungen zur Arbeit W. W. Kemper: Neue Beiträge aus der Phylogenese zur Bio-Psychologie der Frau. [Notes on the work of W. W. Kemper: New contributions to phylogenesis in the bio-psychology of women.] Z PSM 1965, 11:221-222
77859 Dialogische Psychotherapie. [Dialogue psychotherapy.] Z PSM 1969, 15:108-112
77860 Der iatrogene Kranke. (Die Induzierung und Chronifizierung einer Neurose durch den Arzt.) [Iatrogenic illness. A neurosis induced and made chronic by the physician.] Psychother Psychosom 1967, 15:142-152. In Dynamics in Psychiatry, Basel/NY: Karger 1968, 58-68
77861 Leidenszustände bei gewandelten soziokulturellen Bedingungen. [Diseases in changed socio-cultural conditions.] Med Klin 1968, 63:1960-1962
77862 [Obesity, with special reference to its psychosomatic aspects.] (Ger) Aesthet Med, Berlin 1965, 14:306-313
77863 The original sin of mankind: an attempt at a psychological interpretation. In Belgum, D. Religion and Medicine, Ames, Iowa: Iowa State Univ Pr 1967, 135-143
77864 Psychologische Behandlungsmethoden psychosomatischer Krankheiten. [Psychological treatment methods in psychosomatic diseases.] Fortschr PSM 1963, 3:57-67
77865 Über die erfolgreiche Behandlung eines Falles von Herzphobie. [On the successful treatment of heart phobia cases.] Z PSM 1960, 7:249-254

See Deutsch, Felix; Reichsman, F.

JÖRGENSEN, CARL
77866 Needs and affects in the structure of personality. Acta Psychiat Scand 1964, 40(Suppl 180):277-282

JORSTAD, JARL

77867 Clay forming in psychotherapy: a possible remedy to communication and insight. Acta Psychiat Scand 1965, 41:491-526

JORSWIECK, EDUARD

77868 Ein Beitrag zur statistischen Contentanalyse manifesten Traummaterials. [A contribution on the statistical content analysis of manifest dream material.] Z PSM 1966, 12:254-264
77869 (& Katwan, J.) Neurotische Symptome—eine Statistik über Art und Auftreten in den Jahren 1947, 1956 und 1965. [Neurotic symptoms—statistics on type and incidence in the years 1947, 1956 and 1965] Z PSM 1967, 13:12-24
77870 Zur Problematik psychoanalytische orientierter Langstreckenbehandlung; dargestellt an acht kasuistischen Beispielen. [On the problems of psychoanalytically oriented long term therapy demonstrated in 8 cases.] Z PSM 1969, 15:77-90

See Dührssen, Annemarie

JOSEPH, BETTY

77871 Discussion of Aull, G. & Strean, H. S. "The analyst's silence." Psa Forum 1967, 2:83-84
77872 Obituary: Sonny S. Davidson 1911-1961. J 1961, 42:560-561
77873 Persecutory anxiety in a four-year-old boy. (Read at Int Psa Cong, July 1965) J 1966, 47:184-188
       Angoisse persécutoire chez un garçon de quatre ans. RFPsa 1967, 31:659-668
       Abs Cuad Psa 1967, 3:162. EVN Q 1968, 37:310
S-49631 Some characteristics of the psychopathic personality.
       Quelques caractéristiques de la personalité psychopathique. RFPsa 1961, 25:969-978
       Über einige Persönlichkeitsmerkale des Psychopathen. Psyche 1961, 15:132-141
       Abs Perrotta, A. Rev Psicoanál 1961, 40:396

JOSEPH, EDWARD D.

77874 (Ed) Beating Fantasies and Regressive Ego Phenomena in Psychoanalysis. NY: IUP 1965, 103 p
       Rv Anderson, A. R. Q 1966, 35:599-600
S-49633 Cremation, fire and oral aggression.
       Abs Auth Rev Psicoanál 1961, 18:191
77875 Identity and Joseph Conrad. (Read at Westchester Psa Soc, Dec 1961; at NY Psa Soc, 28 Feb 1962; at Am Psa Ass, May 1962) Q 1963, 32:549-572
       Abs RGS Q 1962, 31:440-441
77876 (Ed) Indications for Psychoanalysis: The Place of the Dream in Psychoanalysis. NY: IUP 1967, 106 p
       Abs J Am Psa Ass 1967, 15:733-734

77877 Memory and conflict. (Read at Am Psa Ass 1962; at Mich Psa Soc, 1963; at Westchester Psa Soc, 1963) Q 1966, 35:1-17
77878 (Reporter) The psychology of twins. (Panel: Am Psa Ass, May 1960) J Am Psa Ass 1961, 9:158-166
77879 (& Tabor, J. H.) The simultaneous analysis of a pair of identical twins and the twinning reaction. (Read at Am Psa Ass, 7 May 1960; at Canadian Psa Ass, 16 Feb 1961; at NY Psa Soc, 31 Jan 1961) Psa St C 1961, 16:275-299
　　Abs WAS Q 1961, 30:319-321

See Fine, Bernard D.; Heiman, Marcel

ABSTRACTS OF:
77880 Beres, D. Communication in psychoanalysis and in the creative process: a parallel. An Surv Psa 1957, 8:78-80
77881 Blos, P. Preadolescent drive organization. An Surv Psa 1958, 9:273-274
77882 Bychowski, G. Escapades: a contribution to the study of dissociation of ego identity. Q 1961, 30:613-614
77883 Koff, R. H. The therapeutic man Friday. An Surv Psa 1957, 8:335-336
77884 Kohut, H. Observations on the psychological functions of music. An Surv Psa 1957, 8:336-337
77885 Kramer, P. Note on one of the preoedipal roots of the superego. An Surv Psa 1958, 9:269-270
77886 Lewis, H. The effect of shedding the first deciduous tooth upon the passing of the Oedipus complex of the male. An Surv Psa 1958, 9:249-251
77887 Peller, L. Reading and day dreams in latency, boy-girl differences. An Surv Psa 1958, 9:270-271
77888 Róheim, G. Magic and Schizophrenia. An Surv Psa 1955, 6:188-189, 564-575
77889 Trevett, L. D. Origin of the creation myth: a hypothesis. An Surv Psa 1957, 8:299-300

REVIEWS OF:
77890 Choisy, M. Sigmund Freud: A New Appraisal. Q 1964, 33:439-440
77891 Maynard, B. The Nature of Ego. A study. Q 1964, 33:127-128
77892 Meyer, B. C. Joseph Conrad: A Psychoanalytic Biography. Q 1968, 37:293-296
77893 Novey, S. The Second Look. The Reconstruction of Personal History in Psychiatry and Psychoanalysis. Q 1969, 38:326-327
77894 Paul, L. (Ed) Psychoanalytic Clinical Interpretation. Q 1964, 33:274-276
77895 Pitcher, E. G. & Frelinger, E. Children Tell Stories. An Analysis of Fantasy. Q 1965, 34:593-594
77896 Psychiatry and Public Affairs. Reports and Symposia of the Group for the Advancement of Psychiatry. Q 1967, 36:612-613
77897 Szekely, E. Basic Analysis of Inner Psychological Functions. Q 1967, 36:290-291
77898 Wittenberg, R. Common Sense About Psychoanalysis. Q 1963, 32:425-426

JOSEPH, FLORENCE

77899   Transference and countertransference in the case of a dying patient.
PPR 1962, 39(4):21-34
Abs HL Q 1963, 32:611. Ekboir, J. G. de Rev Psicoanál 1964, 21:83

JOSEPH, HARRY

77900   Treatment and management of acting out in the suicidal patient. Acting
Out 198-207

JOSEPH, ROBERT J.

77901   John Ruskin: radical and psychotic genius. R 1969, 56:425-441
77902   Letter to the editors [re "Office treatment."] Psa Forum 1967, 2:189-
190

JOSEPHSON, ERIC

REVIEW OF:
77903   (& Josephson, M.) Ruitenbeek, H. M. The Individual and the Crowd.
A Study of Identity in America. Am Im 1965, 22:210-211

JOSEPHSON, MARY

See Josephson, Eric

JOSHI, MEERA

77904   Freud's place in the history of science. Madhya Bharati 1960, 9:56-60

JOŚĪ, MĪRĀ

See Jośī, Mohana Candra

JOŚĪ, MOHANA CANDRA

77905   (& Jośī, Mīrā) [Freudism.] (Hindi) Sagar, Sathi Publ 1963, 315 p

JOSSELYN, IRENE MILLIKEN

77906   The acting out in adolescence. Acting Out 68-75
77907   Adolescence. Joint Commission on Mental Health of Children, Task
Force III, Washington, D. C. 1968
77908   Adolescence and orthodontia. In Horowitz, S. & Hixon, E. The Nature
of Orthodontic Diagnosis, St. Louis: C. V. Mosby Co 1960, 217-227
S-17239 The Adolescent and His World.
L'Adolescente e Il Suo Mondo. [The Adolescent and His World.]
Florence: Editrice Universitaria 1964
El Adolescente y Su Mundo. Buenos Aires, Argentina: Editorial
Psique 1966, 189 p
77909   The adolescent today. Smith Coll stud soc Wk 1967, 38:1-15
77910   Adolescents: everyone's special concern. Int J Psychiat 1968, 5:478-482
77911   Child psychiatric clinics—Quo vademus? J Amer Acad Child Psychiat
1964, 3:721-734

77912 The child psychiatrist and the juvenile delinquent. Arizona Med 1965, 22:397-399

77913 Community psychiatry and the adolescent. Quart Camarillo 1966, 2:3-12

77914 Concepts related to child development: (1) The oral stage. (2) Weaning. J Amer Acad Child Psychiat 1962, 1:209-224; 1963, 2:357-369

77915 Discussion of Devereux, G. "The cannibalistic impulses of parents." Psa Forum 1966, 1:125-127

77916 Discussion of Esman, A. H. "Drug use by adolescents: some valuative and technical implications." Psa Forum 1967, 2:350-351

77917 Discussion of Saul, L. J. & Pulver, S. E. "The concept of emotional maturity." Int J Psychiat 1966, 2:446-469

77918 The emotionally disturbed child. In Gellis, S. & Kagan, B. *Current Pediatric Therapy*, Phila: Saunders 1964, 17-21

S-49644 The family as a psychological unit. In Kasius, C. *Social Casework in the Fifties*, NY: Fam Serv Ass Amer 1962, 106-118

77919 How many basic drives? Smith Coll Stud soc Wk 1968, 39:1-19

77920 Observations concerning child development and psychological terminology. (Read at Chicago Psa Soc, 23 May 1961)
    Abs Seitz, P. F. D. Bull Phila Ass Psa 1961, 11:136-138

77921 The older adolescent. In Ginzberg, E. *Values and Ideals of American Youth*, NY: Columbia Univ Pr 1961, 27-35

77922 Passivity. J Amer Acad Child Psychiat 1968, 7:569-588. Ann Prog child Psychiat 1969, 468-484

77923 The problem of school dropouts. Children 1962, 9:194-196

77924 (& Littner, N.; Spurlock, J.) Psychological aspects of ulcerative colitis in children. J Amer Med Wom Ass 1966, 21:303-306

77925 Psychological changes in adolescence. Children 1959, 6:43-47

77926 Psychological effect of menarche. In Kroger, W. S. *Psychosomatic Obstetrics, Gynecology and Endocrinology*, Springfield, Ill: Thomas 1962, 84-91

S-17248 The Psychosocial Development of Children.
    Dessarrolo Psicosocial del Niño. Buenos Aires: Editorial Psique, 175 p
    Lo Sviluppo Psico-sociale del Fanciullo. Florence: Editrice Universitaria 1965

77927 Psychosomatic diseases. Arizona Med 1965, 22:609-613, 695-699

77928 Some psychological aspects of adoption. In Kroger, W. S. *Psychosomatic Obstretrics, Gynecology and Endocrinology*, Springfield, Ill: Thomas 1962, 638-644

77929 Sources of adolescent identity in earlier childhood. Smith Coll Stud soc Wk 1964, 34:89-106

77930 The sources of sexual identity. National Elementary Principal 1966, 46(2):25-29

77931 Treatment of the adolescent: some psychological aspects. Amer J occup Ther 1960, 14:191-195

77932 The unmarried mother. In Slovenko, R. *Sexual Behavior and the Law*, Springfield, Ill: Thomas 1965, 356-378

See Mohr, George J.

REVIEWS OF:
77933 Murphy, L. B. et al: The Widening World of Childhood. Paths toward
       Mastery. Q 1964, 33:114-115
77934 Ruben, Margarete et al: Parent Guidance in the Nursery School. Q
       1961, 30:438-439

JOST, J.

See Guilhot, M. A.

JOURARD, SIDNEY M.

See Gordon, Ira J.

JOVANOVIĆ, UROŠ J.

77935 [Effect of the first examination night on erections during sleep.] (Ger)
       Psychother Psychosom 1969, 17:295-308
77936 Einige Charakteristik des Traumbeginns. [Some characteristics of the
       beginning of dreams.] Psychol Forsch 1967, 30:281-306
77937 [Most recent exploration of dreams.] (Ger) Verh Deutsch Ges inn Med
       1967, 73:666-682
77937A [The present status of physiological dream research.] (Ger) Hippok-
       rates 1969, 40:121-132

JOYEUX, J.

77938 (& Joyeux-Quercy, D.) Caractérologie et psychanalyse. [Characterology
       and psychoanalysis.] Ann med-psychol 1959, 117(2):278-283

JOYEUX-QUERCY, D.

See Joyeux, J.

JUCOVY, MILTON E.

ABSTRACTS OF:
77939 Jacobson, E. Psychotic conflict and reality. Q 1966, 35:167-169
77940 Lewin, B. D. Knowledge and dreams. Q 1964, 33:148-151
77941 Pacella, B. L. The dream process. Q 1962, 31:597-600
77942 Schur, M. The problem of death in Freud's writings and life. Q 1965,
       34:144-147

JUDSON, ABE J.

77943 Love and death in the short stories of W. Somerset Maugham: a psy-
       chological analysis. Psychiat Q Suppl 1963, 37:250-262

JUDSON, P.

77944 (& Meyer, R.) School phobia and the countertransference. Int J soc
       Psychiat 1964, 10:282-291

JUEL-NIELSEN, NIELS

77945 Individual and environment. A psychiatric-psychological investigation
       of monozygotic twins reared apart. Acta Psychiat Scand 1964, 40(Suppl
       183):1-158

JULIA, H.

See Sander, Louis W.

JULIAN, J. W.

See Hollander, E. P.

JUMEL, L.

TRANSLATION OF:
Freud, S. [73592]

JUNG, CARL GUSTAV

S-17290 Aion: Untersuchungen zur Symbolgeschichte.
      Aion. The Collected Works of C. G. Jung, Vol. 9, Part 2. London:
      Routledge & Kegan Paul; NY: Pantheon 1959
77946 Alchemical Studies. The Collected Works of C. G. Jung, Vol. 13 (Tr:
      Hull, R. C. F.) Princeton, N.J.: Princeton Univ Pr; London: Routledge
      & Kegan Paul 1967, xiv + 453 p
77947 Allgemeine Gesichtspunke zur Psychologie des Traumes. In author's
      Über psychische Energetik und das Wessen der Träume, Zurich:
      Rascher 1948
      General aspects of dream psychology. In author's *The Structure and
      Dynamics of the Psyche* 237-280
77948 Allgemeines zur Komplextheorie. In author's *Über psychische Energetik
      und das Wesen der Träume*, Zurich: Rascher 1948
      A review of the complex theory. In author's *The Structure and Dy-
      namics of the Psyche* 92-106
77949 L'Ame et la Vie. [Spirit and Life.] (Ed: Jacobi, J.; Tr from German:
      Cahen, R. & Le Lay, Y.) Paris: Buchet-Chastel 1965, 534 p
S-17294 L'analyse des rêves.
      The analysis of dreams. In author's *Freud and Psychoanalysis* 25-34
S-17296 Analytische Psychologie und Erziehung.
      Analytical psychology and education. In author's *Contributions to Ana-
      lytical Psychology* 313-382; in author's *The Development of Person-
      ality* 63-132
77950 Analytische Psychologie und Weltanschauung. In author's *Seelen-
      probleme der Gegenwart*, Zurich: Rascher 1931
      Analytical psychology and *Weltanschauung*. In author's *Contribu-
      tions to Analytical Psychology* 141-163; in author's *The Structure
      and Dynamics of the Psyche* 358-381
77951 Antwort auf Hiob. Zurich: Rascher 1952
      Answer to Job. In author's *Psychology and Religion: West and East*
      355-473
77952 Approaching the unconscious. In author's *Man and His Symbols* 18:
      1-3
S-17297 Der archaische Mensch. In author's *Seelenprobleme der Gegenwart*,
      Zurich: Rascher 1931
      Archaic man. In author's *Civilization in Transition* 50-73
S-17298 Über die Archetypen des kollektiven Unbewussten. In author's *Von den
      Wurzeln des Bewusstseins*, Zurich: Rascher 1954

Archtypes of the collective unconscious. In author's *The Archtypes and the Collective Unconscious* 3-41

S-49663 The Archetypes and the Collective Unconscious. The Collected Works of C. G. Jung, Vol 9, Part I. London: Routledge & Kegan Paul; NY: Pantheon 1959

S-17299 Über den Archetypus mit besonderer Berücksichtigung des Animabegriffes. In author's *Von den Wurzeln des Bewusstseins*, Zurich: Rascher 1954

Concerning the archetypes, with special reference to the anima concept. In author's *The Archetypes and the Collective Unconscious* 54-74

S-17299A Ärztliches Gutachten über einen Fall von simulierter geistiger Störung.

A medical opinion on a case of simulated insanity. In author's *Psychiatric Studies* 188-208

77953 Der Aufgang neuen Welt. Neue Zürcher Zeitung, Zurich 1930

The rise of a new world. In author's *Civilization in Transition* 489-495

77954 Die Bedeutung der Psychologie für die Gegenwart. In author's *Wirklichkeit der Seele*, Zurich: Rascher 1934

The meaning of psychology for modern man. In author's *Civilization in Transition* 134-156

77955 Die Bedeutung der schweizerische Linie im Spektrum Europas. Neue Schweizer Rundschau, Zurich 1928, 24

The Swiss line in the European spectrum. In the author's *Civilization in Transition* 479-488

S-17308 Die Bedeutung von Vererbung und Konstitution für die Psychologie.

The significance of constitution and heredity in psychology. In author's *The Structure and Dynamics of the Psyche* 107-113

S-17308A De Begabte.

The gifted child. In author's *The Development of Personality* 133-148

S-17309 Ein Beitrag zur Kenntnis des Zahlentraumes.

On the significance of number dreams. In author's *Freud and Psychoanalysis* 48-55

S-17310 Ein Beitrag zur Psychologie des Gerüchtes.

A contribution to the psychology of rumour. In author's *Freud and Psychoanalysis* 35-47

S-17314 Bewusstsein, Unbewusstes und Individuation.

Conscious, unconscious, and individuation. (Revised version of "The meaning of individuation" [17383]) In author's *The Archetypes and the Collective Unconscious* 275-289

S-17315 Über die Beziehungen der analytischen Psychologie zum dichterischen Kunstwerk. In author's *Seelenprobleme der Gegenwart*, Zurich: Rascher 1931

On the relation of analytical psychology to poetry. In author's *The Spirit in Man, Art, and Literature* 65-83

S-17316 Die Beziehungen der Psychotherapie zur Seelsorge.

Psychotherapists or the clergy. In author's *Psychology and Religion: West and East* 327-347

S-17317 Die Beziehungen zwischen dem Ich und dem Unbewussten.
        The relations between the ego and the unconscious. In author's *Two Essays on Analytical Psychology* 123-244
77956 Brother Klaus. Neue Schweizer Rundschau, Zurich 1933, 1 (n.s.)
        English: In author's *Psychology and Religion: West and East* 316-326
77957 Child development and education. (Tr from unpublished German original) In author's *The Development of Personality* 47-62
77958 [Circular letter.] Zentralblatt 1934, 7
        English: In author's *Civilization in Transition* 545-546
77959 Civilization in Transition. The Collected Works of C. G. Jung, Vol 10. (Tr: Hull, R. F. C.) London: Routledge & Kegan Paul; NY: Pantheon 1964, xi + 618 p
        Rv HS Am Im 1965, 22:220-221
* * * The complications of American psychology. See [78017]
S-17323 The concept of the collective unconscious. In author's *The Archetype and the Collective Unconscious* 42-53
S-17326 The content of the psychoses. See [17371]
S-17329 Contributions to Analytical Psychology (Tr: Baynes, H. G. & Baynes, C. F.) London: Routledge & Kegan Paul 1928, xi + 410 p
77960 The Development of Personality. The Collected Works of C. G. Jung, Vol. 17. NY: Pantheon; London: Routledge & Kegan Paul 1954
77961 Dialectique du moi et de l'inconscient. [Dialectic of the ego and the unconscious.] (Tr from German: Cahen, R.) Paris: Gallimard 1964
77962 Die Dynamik des Unbewussten. [Dynamics of the Unconscious.] Zurich/Stuttgart: Rascher 1967, xii + 671 p
77963 [Editorial note] Zentralblatt 1935, 8
        English: In author's *Civilization in Transition* 552-553
77964 [Editorial] Zentralblatt 1933, 6; 1935, 8
        English: In author's *Civilization in Transition* 533-534, 547-551
S-17334 Die Ehe als psychologische Beziehung.
        Marriage as a psychological relationship. In author's *The Development of Personality* 187-204. In author's *Contributions to Analytical Psychology* 189-203
S-17337 Zur Empirie des Individuationsprozesses.
        A study in the process of individuation. In author's *The Archetypes and the Collective Unconscious* 290-354
S-17338 Über die Energetik der Seele.
        On psychic energy. In author's *The Structure and Dynamics of the Psyche* 3-66. In author's *Contributions to Analytical Psychology* 1-76
77965 Erinnerungen, Träume, Gedanken. Zurich/Stuttgart: Rascher 1967, 423 p
        Memories, Dreams, Reflections. (Ed. Jaffe, A.) (Tr: Winston, R. & Winston, C.) NY: Pantheon; London: Collins & Routledge 1963, xviii + 393 p
        Abs Am Im 1964, 21:187. Rv Winnicott, D. W. J 1964 45:450-455
S-17346 Ein Fall von hysterischem Stupor bei einer Untersuchungsgefangenen.
        A case of hysterical stupor in a prisoner in detention. In author's *Psychiatric Studies* 137-158

77966   The fight with the shadow. The Listener, London 1946, 36. In author's
        Civilization in Transition 218-226

* * *   Foreword to *The I Ching, or Book of Changes,* NY: Pantheon; London:
        Routledge & Kegan Paul 1950. In author's *Psychology and Religion:
        West and East* 589-608

* * *   Foreword to Werblowsky, R. J. Z. *Lucifer and Prometheus,* London:
        Routledge & Kegan Paul 1952. In author's *Psychology and Religion:
        West and East* 311-315

* * *   Foreword to White, V. *God and the Unconscious,* London: Harvill
        1952; Chicago: H. Regnery 1953. In author's *Psychology and Religion:
        West and East* 299-310

S-17348 Die Frau in Europa.
        Woman in Europe. In author's *Contributions to Analytical Psychol-
        ogy* 164-188. In author's *Civilization in Transition* 113-133

77967   Freud and Psychoanalysis. The Collected Works of C. G. Jung, Vol. 4.
        London: Routledge & Kegan Paul; NY: Pantheon 1961, xii + 376 p
        Freud und die Psychoanalyse. Zurich: Rascher 1969, 433 p

S-17349 Die Freud'sche Hysterietheorie.
        The Freudian theory of hysteria. In author's *Freud and Psychoan-
        alysis* 10-24

77968   Gegenwart und Zukunft. Zurich: Rascher 1957
        The undiscovered self (present and future). In author's *Civilization
        in Transition* 245-306

S-17352 Zur Gegenwärtigen Lage der Psychotherapie.
        The state of psychotherapy today. In author's *Civilization in Transi-
        tion* 157-173

S-17353 [Europäischer Kommentar] to *Das Geheimnis der goldenen Blüte:
        Ein chinesisches Lebensbuch* (5th ed) Zurich: Rascher 1957
        Commentary on "The Secret of the Golden Flower." In author's *Al-
        chemical Studies* 1-56

S-17353A Geist und Leben.
        Spirit and life. In author's *The Structure and Dynamics of the
        Psyche* 319-337. In author's *Contributions to Analytical Psychology*
        77-98

S-17354 Der Geist Mercurius. In author's *Symbolik des Geistes,* Zurich: Rascher
        1948
        The spirit Mercurius. In author's *Alchemical Studies* 191-250

S-17358 Geleitwort und psychologischer Kommentar zur Bardo Thödol. In
        Das Tibetanische Totenbuch (5th ed) Zurich: Rascher 1953
        Psychological commentary on *The Tibetan Book of the Dead.* In
        author's *Psychology and Religion: West and East* 509-528

S-17359 Geleitwort zu Suzuki, D. S. *Die Grosse Befreiung: Einführung in den
        Zen-Buddhism.*
        Foreword to Suzuki's *Introduction to Zen Buddhism.* In author's
        Psychology and Religion: West and East 538-557

77969   Das Gewissen in psychologischer Sicht. In *Das Gewissen* (Studien aus
        dem C. G. Jung-Institut, VII) Zurich: Rascher 1958
        A psychological view of conscience. In author's *Civilization in Tran-
        sition* 437-455

S-17364 Grundfragen der Psychotherapie.
> Fundamental questions of psychotherapy. In author's *The Practice of Psychotherapy* 111-128

77970 Das Grundproblem der gegenwärtigen Psychologie. In author's *Wirklichkeit der Seele*, Zurich: Rascher 1934
> Basic postulates of analytical psychology. In author's *The Structure and Dynamics of the Psyche* 338-357. See [17305]

S-17365 Grundsätzliches zur praktischen Psychotherapie.
> Principles of practical psychotherapy. In author's *The Practice of Psychotherapy* 3-20

77971 Gut und Böse in der analytischen Psychologie. In Bitter, W. *Gut und Böse in der Psychotherapie*, Stuttgart: "Arzt und Seelsorger" 1958
> Good and evil in analytical psychology. In author's *Civilization in Transition* 456-466

77972 Heilbare Geisteskranke? Berliner Tageblatt 1928
> Mental disease and the psyche. In author's *The Psychogenesis of Mental Disease* 226-232

S-17366 Die Hysterielehre Freuds: Eine Erwiderung auf die Aschaffenburgsche Kritik.
> Freud's theory of hysteria: a reply to Aschaffenburg. In author's *Freud and Psychoanalysis* 3-9

S-17367 Über hysterisches Verlesen.
> On hysterical misreading. In author's *Psychiatric Studies* 89-94

S-17368 On the importance of the unconscious in psychotherapy. In author's *The Psychogenesis of Mental Disease* 203-210

S-17371 Der Inhalt der Psychose in Freuds Schriften zur angewandten Seelenkunde.
> The content of the psychoses. In author's *The Psychogenesis of Mental Disease* 153-178. See [17326]

S-17372 Instinct and the unconscious. See [Instinkt und Unbewusstes]

77973 Instinkt und Unbewusstes. In author's *Über psychische Energetik und das Wesen der Träume*, Zurich: Rascher 1948
> Instinct and the unconscious. In author's *Contributions to Analytical Psychology* 270-281. In author's *The Structure and Dynamics of the Psyche* 129-138. See [17372]

S-17375 Introduction to Wickes's *Analyse der Kinderseele*. Stuttgart: Hoffman 1931
> English: In author's *The Development of Personality* 37-46

77974 Introduction to Zimmer, H. *Der Weg zum Selbst*. Zurich: Rascher 1944
> The holy men of India. In author's *Psychology and Religion: West and East* 576-588

S-17377 Über Konflikte der kindlichen Seele.
> Psychic conflicts in a child. In author's *The Development of Personality* 1-36

S-17378 Kritik über E. Bleuler: Zur Theorie des schizophrenen Negativismus.
> A criticism of Bleuler's Theory of Schizophrenic Negativism. In author's *The Psychogenesis of Mental Disease* 197-202

S-17379 Zur Kritik über Psychoanalyse.
> On the criticism of psychoanalysis. In author's *Freud and Psychoanalysis* 74-77

S-17380 Kryptomnesie.
      Cryptomnesia. In author's *Psychiatric Studies* 95-108
° ° ° Die Lebenswende. See [17448A]
77975 The love problem of a student. (1922?) In author's *Civilization in Transition* 97-112
77976 (& Franz, Marie L. von) (Eds) Man and His Symbols. Garden City, NY: Doubleday 1964, 320 p
      Der Mensch und seine Symbole. (Tr: Thiele-Dohrmann, K.) Olten/Freiburg: Walter 1968, 320 p
77977 Mandalas. Du, Zurich 1955, 14 (4:Apr)
      Mandalas. In author's *The Archetypes and the Collective Unconscious* 385-390
S-17381 Über Mandalsymbolik.
      Concerning Mandala symbolism. In author's *The Archetypes and the Collective Unconscious* 355-384
S-17382 Über manische Verstimmung.
      On manic mood disorder. In author's *Psychiatric Studies* 109-136
S-17383 The meaning of individuation. See [S-17314]
S-17383A Medizin und Psychotherapie.
      Medicine and psychotherapy. In author's *The Practice of Psychotherapy* 84-93
77978 Ein moderner Mythus: Von Dingen, die am Himmel gesehen werden. Zurich/Stuttgart: Rascher 1958
      Flying Saucers: A Modern Myth of Things Seen in the Skies. In author's *Civilization in Transition* 307-436
S-17384 Morton Prince: "The Mechanism and Interpretation of Dreams": a critical review. In author's *Freud and Psychoanalysis* 56-73
77979 Mysterium Coniunctionis: Untersuchung über die Trennung und Zusammensetzung der seelischen Gegensätze in der Alchemie, Parts I and II. Zurich: Rascher 1955, 1956, 1968, 821 p
      Mysterium Coniunctionis: An Inquiry into the Separation and Synthesis of Psychic Opposites in Alchemy. The Collected Works of C. G. Jung, Vol. 14. NY: Bollingen Found; London: Routledge & Kegan Paul 1963 xix + 704 p
S-17375A Nach der Katastrophe.
      After the catastrophe. In author's *Civilization in Transition* 194-217
77980 Nachruf für Richard Wilhelm. In *Das Geheimnis der goldenen Blüte: Ein chinesisches Lebensbuch* (5th ed) Zurich: Rascher 1957
      Richard Wilhelm: in memoriam. In author's *The Spirit in Man, Art, and Literature* 53-64
° ° ° Nachwort to Aufsätze sur Zeitgeschichte [17304]
      Epilogue to *Essays on Contemporary Events*. In author's *Civilization in Transition* 227-243
S-17387 Neue Bahnen der Psychologie.
      New paths in psychology. In author's *Two Essays in Analytical Psychology* 245-268
77981 Ein neues Buch von Keyserling. Basler Nachrichten 1934, 28
      English: La Revolution Mondiale. In author's *Civilization in Transition* 496-501

S-17389 Obergutachten über zwei widersprechende psychiatrische Gutachten.
A third and final opinion on two contradictory psychiatric diagnoses.
In author's *Psychiatric Studies* 209-218

S-17393 Paracelsus. In author's *Wirklichkeit der Seele*. Zurich: Rascher 1934
Paracelsus. In author's *The Spirit in Man, Art, and Literature* 3-12

S-17394 Paracelsus als Arzt.
Paracelsus the physician. In author's *The Spirit in Man, Art, and Literature* 13-32

77982 Paracelsus als geistige Erscheinung. In author's *Paracelsus: Zwei Vorlesungen über den Arzt und Philosophen Theophrastus,* Zurich: Rascher 1942
Paracelsus as a spiritual phenomenon. In author's *Alchemical Studies* 109-190

77983 Zur Phänomenologie des Geistes im Märchen. In author's *Symbolik des Geites,* Zurich: Rascher 1948
The phenomenology of the spirit in fairytales. In author's *The Archetypes and the Collective Unconscious* 207-254

77984 Das philosophische Baum. In author's *Von den Wurzeln des Bewusstseins,* Zurich: Rascher 1954
The philosophical tree. In author's *Alchemical Studies* 251-350

77985 Picasso. In author's *Wirklichkeit der Seele,* Zurich: Rascher 1934
English: In author's *The Spirit in Man, Art, and Literature* 135-142

77986 The Practice of Psychotherapy. The Collected Works of C. G. Jung, Vol. 16. NY: Pantheon; London: Routledge & Kegan Paul 1954

S-17395 Die Praktische Verwendbarkeit der Traumanalyse. In author's *Wirklichkeit der Seele,* Zurich: Rascher 1934
The practical use of dream-analysis. In author's *The Practice of Psychotherapy* 139-162

77987 Preface to Custance, J. *Wisdom, Madness, and Folly,* NY: Pellegrini & Cudahy 1952

77988 Presidential address to the 8th General Medical Congress for Psychotherapy, Bad Nauheim, 1935. (Tr from unpublished MS) In author's *Civilization in Transition* 554-556

77989 Presidential address to the 9th International Medical Congress for Psychotherapy, Copenhagen, 1937. (Tr from unpublished MS) In author's *Civilization in Transition* 561-563

77990 Presidential address to the 10th International Medical Congress for Psychotherapy, Oxford, 1938. In author's *Civilization in Transition* 564-568

S-17397 On the problem of psychogenesis in mental disease. In author's *The Psychogenesis of Mental Disease* 211-225

77991 Psychiatric Studies. The Collected Works of C. G. Jung, Vol. 1. London: Routledge & Kegan Paul; NY: Pantheon 1957

S-17403 Zur Psychoanalyse.
Concerning psychoanalysis. In author's *Freud and Psychoanalysis* 78-81

S-17406 Psychoanalyse und Seelsorge.
Psychoanalysis and the cure of souls. In author's *Psychology and Religion: West and East* 348-354

77992 The Psychogenesis of Mental Disease. The Collected Works of C. G.

Jung, Vol. 3. London: Routledge & Kegan Paul; NY: Pantheon 1960, 312 p

S-17410 On the psychogenesis of schizophrenia. In author's *The Psychogenesis of Mental Disease* 233-249

77993 Psychological commentary on *The Tibetan Book of the Great Liberation*. In *The Tibetan Book of the Great Liberation*, London/NY: Oxford Univ Pr 1954. In author's *Psychology and Religion: West and East* 475-508

S-17412 Psychological factors determining human behaviour. In author's *The Structure and Dynamics of the Psyche* 114-128

S-17413 The psychological foundations of belief in spirits. (Tr: Baynes, H. G. & Baynes, C. F.) In author's *Contributions to Analytical Psychology* 250-269

S-17414 On psychological understanding. In author's *The Psychogenesis of Mental Disease* 179-196

S-17416 Psychologie und Alchemie.
Psychology and Alchemy. The Collected Works of C. G. Jung, Vol. 12. London: Routledge & Kegan Paul; NY: Pantheon 1953

S-17418 Über die Psychologie der dementia praecox: Ein Versuch.
The psychology of Dementia praecox. In author's *The Psychogenesis of Mental Disease* 1-152

77994 Zur Psychologie des Kind-Archetypus. In author's *Einführung in das Wesen der Mythologie* (4th ed), Zurich: Rhein-Verlag 1951
The psychology of the child archetype. In author's *The Archetypes and the Collective Unconscious* 151-181

S-17419 Psychologie und Dichtung.
Psychology and literature. In author's *The Spirit in Man, Art, and Literature* 84-108

S-17420 Zur Psychologie östlicher Meditation. In author's *Symbolik des Geistes*, Zurich: Rascher 1948
The psychology of Eastern meditation. In author's *Psychology and Religion: West and East* 558-575

S-17421 Zur Psychologie und Pathologie sogenannter okkulter Phänomene.
On the psychology and pathology of so-called occult phenomena. In author's *Psychiatric Studies* 3-88

S-17423 Die Psychologie der Übertragung.
Psychologie of the transference. In author's *The Practice of Psychotherapy* 163-322

S-17424 Die Psychologie der unbewusste Prozesse.
On the psychology of the unconscious. In author's *Two Essays on Analytical Psychology* 3-122

S-17428 Psychologische Typen.
Psychological types. (Tr: Baynes, H. G. & Baynes, C. F.) In *Problems of Personality*, London: Kegan Paul; NY: Harcourt Brace. In author's *Contributions to Analytical Psychology* 295-312

S-17429 Psychologische Typen.
Psychological Types. The Collected Works of C. G. Jung, Vol. 6. London: Routledge & Kegan Paul; NY: Pantheon

77995 Zum psychologischen Aspekt der Kore-Figur. In author's *Einführung in das Wesen der Mythologie* (4th ed), Zurich: Rhein-Verlag 1951

The psychological aspects of the Kore. In author's *The Archetypes and the Collective Unconscious* 182-206

S-17431 Die psychologischen Aspekte des Mutter-Archetypus. In author's *Von den Wurzeln des Bewusstseins*, Zurich: Rascher 1954

Psychological aspects of the mother archetype. In author's *The Archetypes and the Collective Unconscious* 75-112

* * * Die psychologischen Grundlagen des Geisterglaubens.

The psychological foundations of belief in spirits. In author's *The Structure and Dynamics of the Psyche* 301-318. See [17413]

S-17432 Zur psychologischen Tatbestandsdiagnostik.

On the psychological diagnosis of facts. In author's *Psychiatric Studies* 219-224

S-17434 Psychology and religion. In author's *Psychology and Religion: West and East* 3-106

77996 Psychology and Religion: West and East. The Collected Works of C. G. Jung, Vol 11. London: Routledge & Kegan Paul; NY: Pantheon 1958

77997 On the psychology of the trickster-figure. (Tr from part 5 of Radin, P. *Der Göttliche Schelm*, with commentaries by Jung, C. G. & Kerenyi, K., Zurich: Rhein-Verlag 1954). In author's *The Archetypes and the Collective Unconscious* 255-274

S-17439 Die Psychotherapie in der Gegenwart. In author's *Aufsätze zur Zeitgeschichte*, Zurich: Rascher 1946

Psychotherapy today. In author's *The Practice of Psychotherapy* 94-110

S-17440 Psychotherapie und Weltanschauung.

Psychotherapy and a philosophy of life. In author's *The Practice of Psychotherapy* 76-83

S-17441 The question of the therapeutic value of "abreaction." Revised with title: The therapeutic value of abreaction. In author's *The Practice of Psychotherapy* 129-138. In author's *Contributions to Analytical Psychology* 282-294

77998 Recent thought on schizophrenia (1956). In author's *The Psychogenesis of Mental Disease* 250-255

77999 [A rejoinder to Dr. Bally.] Neue Zürcher Zeitung 1934, 155

English: In author's *Civilization in Transition* 535-544

S-49682 On the relation of analytical psychology to poetic art. Brit J Psychol 1923, 5(3). In Keyserling, H. *Ehebuch*, Heidelberg: Niels Kampmann 1925; NY: Harcourt Brace; London: Jonathan Cape

78000 Die Schizophrenie. Schweizer Archiv für Neurol Psychiat, Zurich 1958, 81

Schizophrenia. In author's *The Psychogenesis of Mental Disease* 256-274

78001 Seele und Erde. In Keyserling, *Mensch und Erde*, Darmstadt: Otto Riechl 1927. In author's *Seelenprobleme der Gegenwart*, Zurich: Rascher 1931

Mind and earth. In author's *Contributions to Analytical Psychology* 99-140. In author's *Civilization in Transition* 29-49

S-17446A Seele und Tod.

The soul and death. In author's *The Structure and Dynamics of the Psyche* 404-416

S-17447 Das Seelenproblem des modernen Menschen. In author's *Seelenprobleme der Gegenwart*, Zurich: Rascher 1931
      The spiritual problem of modern man. In author's *Civilization in Transition* 74-94

S-17448A Die seelischen Probleme der menschlichen Altersstufen.
      The stages of life. In author's *The Structure and Dynamics of the Psyche* 387-403

S-17450 Sigmund Freud als kulturhistorische Erscheinung.
      Sigmund Freud in his historical setting. In author's *The Spirit in Man, Art, and Literature* 33-40

78002 Sigmund Freud: Ein Nachruf. Sonntagsblatt der Basler Nachrichten 1939, 33
      In memory of Sigmund Freud. In author's *The Spirit in Man, Art, and Literature* 41-52

78003 The significance of the unconscious in individual education. (Tr from unpublished German original) In author's *The Development of Personality* 149-164. In author's *Contributions to Analytical Psychology* 383-402

S-17452 Über Simulation von Geistesstörung.
      On simulated insanity. In author's *Psychiatric Studies* 159-187

S-17452A Some aspects of modern psychotherapy. In author's *The Practice of Psychotherapy* 29-35

78004 The Spirit in Man, Art, and Literature. The Collected Works of C. G. Jung, Vol. 15. NY: Bollingen Foundation; London: Routledge & Kegan Paul 1966

78005 The Structure and Dynamics of the Psyche. The Collected Works of C. G. Jung, Vol. 8. London: Routledge & Kegan Paul; NY: Pantheon 1960

S-17455 La structure de l'inconscient.
      The structure of the unconscious. In author's *Two Essays in Analytical Psychology* 269-304

78006 Die Struktur der Seele. In author's *Seelenprobleme der Gegenwart*, Zurich: Rascher 1931
      The structure of the psyche. In author's *The Structure and Dynamics of the Psyche* 139-158

° ° ° Symbole der Wandlung. See [17468]

78007 Über Synchronizität. *Eranos Jahrbuch 1951*, Zurich: Rhein-Verlag 1952
      On synchronicity. In author's *The Structure and Dynamics of the Psyche* 520-532

S-17457 Synchronizität als ein Prinzip akausaler Zusammenhänge.
      Synchronicity: an acausal connecting principle. In author's *The Structure and Dynamics of the Psyche* 417-519

78008 Theoretische Überlegungen zum Wesen des Psychischen. In author's *Von den Wurzeln des Bewusstseins*, Zurich: Rascher 1954
      On the nature of the psyche. In author's *The Structure and Dynamics of the Psyche* 159-236

° ° ° The therapeutic value of abreaction. See [17441]

78009 Die Transzendente Funktion (1916). In *Geist und Werk*, Zurich: Rhein-Verlag 1958
      The transcendent function. In author's *The Structure and Dynamics of the Psyche* 67-91

S-17459 Two Essays on Analytical Psychology. The Collected Works of C. G.
Jung, Vol. 7. London: Routledge & Kegan Paul; NY: Pantheon 1953,
1966
    Zwei Schriften über analytische Psychologie. Zurich: Rascher 1964,
    x + 371 p
S-17460 Ulysses. In author's *Wirklichkeit der Seele,* Zurich: Rascher 1934
    Ulysses: a monologue. In author's *The Spirit in Man, Art, and Litera-
    ture* 109-134. In Manheim, L. F. & Manheim, E. B. *Hidden Patterns,*
    NY: Macmillan 1966, 192-219
S-17461 Über das Unbewusste. Schweizerland, Zurich 1918, 4
    The role of the unconscious. In author's *Civilization in Transition*
    3-28
78010 (& Hisamnatsu, Shin-ichi) On the unconscious, the self and the therapy:
    a dialogue. Psychologia: An International J of Psychology in the Orient
    1968, 11(1-2):25-32
78011 Versuch zu einer psychologischen Deutung des Trinitätsdogmas. In
    author's *Symbolik des Geistes,* Zurich: Rascher 1948
    A psychological approach to the dogma of the trinity. In author's
    Psychology and Religion: West and East 107-200
78012 Die Visionen des Zosimos. In author's *Von den Wurzeln des Bewusst-
    seins,* Zurich: Rascher 1954
    The visions of Zosimos. In author's *Alchemical Studies* 57-108
° ° °   Vorrede to Wolff, *Studien zu C. G. Jung's Psychologie,* Zurich: Rhein
    1959
    Introduction to Toni Wolff's *Studies in Jungian Psychology.* In
    author's *Civilization in Transition* 467-478
° ° °   Vorwort to author's *Aufsätze zur Zeitgeschichte* [17304].
    Preface to *Essays on Contemporary Events.* In author's *Civilization
    in Transition* 177-178
78013 Votum C. G. Jung Schweizerische Aerztezeitung für Standesfragen,
    Bern 1935, 16
    Contribution to a discussion on psychotherapy. In author's *Civiliza-
    tion* 557-560
S-17468 Wandlungen und Symbole der Libido. Rewritten with title: Symbole
    der Wandlung, Zurich: Rascher 1952
    Symbols of Transformation. London: Routledge & Kegan Paul; NY:
    Pantheon 1956. With title: Symbols of Transformation: An Analysis of
    the Prelude to a Case of Schizophrenia. (Tr: Hull, R. F. C.) 2 vols. NY:
    Harper 1962, xxix + 273 p, ix + 274-557 p
S-17469 Das Wandlungssymbol in der Messe. In author's *Von den Wurzeln
    des Bewusstseins,* Zurich: Rascher 1954
    Transformation symbolism in the mass. In author's *Psychology and
    Religion: West and East* 201-298
S-17469A Was ist die Psychotherapie?
    What is psychotherapy. In author's *The Practice of Psychotherapy*
    21-28
S-17470A Vom Werden der Persönlichkeit.
    The development of personality. In author's *The Development of
    Personality* 165-186

S-17470B Vom Wesen der Träume.
     On the nature of dreams. In author's *The Structure and Dynamics of the Psyche* 281-300
78014 What India can teach us. Asia, New York 1939, 39. In author's *Civilization in Transition* 525-532
S-17471 Über Wiedergeburt.
     Concerning rebirth. In author's *The Archtypes and the Collective Unconscious* 113-150
S-17473 Wirklichkeit und Überwirklichkeit.
     The real and the surreal. In author's *The Structure and Dynamics of the Psyche* 382-386
S-17474 Wotan.
     English: In author's *Civilization in Transition* 179-193
78015 Yoga and the West. (Tr from MS) Prabuddha Bharata, Calcutta 1936, Feb. In author's *Psychology and Religion: West and East* 529-537
78016 Yoga, Zen and Koestler. [Letter to the editors.] Encounter 1961, 16(2):56-58
78017 Your Negroid and Indian behavior. Forum, NY 1930, 83. With title: The complications of American psychology. In author's *Civilization in Transition* 502-514
S-17496 Über die Ziele der Psychotherapie.
     The aims of psychotherapy. In author's *The Practice of Psychotherapy* 36-52

C. G. JUNG INSTITUT

78018 Die Angst. [Anxiety] Zurich: Rascher 1959, 253 p
78019 Evil. Evanston, Ill: Northwestern Univ Pr 1967, xiii + 265 p

JUNGRIES, JEROME E.

See Friedman, Alfred S.

JUNKINS, DONALD

78020 Hawthorne's *House of Seven Gables:* a prototype of the human mind. Lit & Psych 1967, 17:192-210

JUNOD, L.

See Schneider, Pierre-Bernard

JURGEN, JOHAN

78021 Analyse van Een Leven. Persoonsbeschrijving Vanuit een Psychoanalyse. [Analysis of a life. Personal writings from a psychoanalysis.] (Foreword: Meerloo, J. A. M.) Amsterdam: Van Ditmar 1966, 184 p

JUS, ANDRZEJ

78022 (& Jus, K.) Étude neurophysiologique de l'inconscient. [Neurophysiological study of the unconscious.] In Lassner, J. *Hypnosis and Psychosomatic Medicine*, Berlin/Heidelberg/NY: Springer 1967, 172-179

See Jus, Karolina

JUS, KAROLINA

78023 (& Jus, A.) Próba neurofizjologicznego podejścia do zagadnień nieświadomości. Analogie kliniczno-doświadczalne. [An attempt to approach the problem of unconsciousness by the neurophysiological method. Clinico-experimental analogies.] Neurol Neurochir Psychiat Pol 1963, 13:887-893

78024 (& Jus, A.) Pecepcja i percepcja a poziom świadomości. [Reception and perception and the level of consciousness.] Psychiat Pol 1967, 1:661-666

See Jus, Andrzej

K

KACHALSKY, HYMAN D.

See Abend, Sander M.

KADINSKY, D.

78025 Der Mythos der Maschine. [The Myth of the Machine.] Bern: Huber 1969, 232 p

KADIS, ASYA L.

78026 (& Winick, C.) (Eds) Group Psychotherapy Today. Selected Papers Presented at the Scientific Meetings of the Eastern Group Psychotherapy Society, 1960-1963. Basel/NY: Karger 1965, 256 p

78027 A new approach to marital therapy. Int J soc Psychiat 1964, 10:261-265

78028 (& Krasner, J. D.; Winick, C.; Foulkes, S. H.) A Practicum of Group Psychotherapy. NY: Harper & Row 1963, vii + 195 p
Abs J 1964, 45:610. Rv Ormont, L. R. R 1964, 51:330-333. Semrad, E. V. & Day, M. J Am Psa Ass 1966, 14:591-618

78029 (& Markowitz, M.) The therapeutic impact of co-therapist interaction in a couple's group. In Moreno, J. L. *Inter-National Handbook of Psychotherapy,* NY: Philos Libr 1966, 446-455

See Durkin, Helen E.; Markowitz, Max

KADUSHIN, ALFRED

78030 Research in psychotherapy of significance to social casework: the "good" client, the "good" therapist, the "good" relationship. J Hillside Hosp 1964, 13:221-243

KADUSHIN, C.

78031 Friends and supporters of psychotherapy: on social circles in urban life. Amer sociol Rev 1966, 31:786-802

KAEL, HOWARD C.

See Noblin, Charles D.

KAFFMAN, MORDECAI

78032 Children of the kibbutz: clinical observations. Curr psychiat Ther 1963, 3:171-179

78033   (& Cohen, N. J.) Children raised on the kibbutz in Israel: a critical evaluation. Clin Ped 1968, 7:141-148

78034   A comparison of psychopathology: Israeli children from kibbutz and from urban surroundings. Ops 1965, 35:509-520
         Abs JMa RFPsa 1966, 30:526

KAFKA, ERNEST

78035   (& Reiser, M. F.) Defensive and adaptive ego processes. Their relationship to GSR activity in free imagery experiments. Arch gen Psychiat 1967, 16:34-40

ABSTRACTS OF:

78036   Roiphe, H. On an early genital phase, with an addendum on genesis. Q 1969, 38:169-170

78037   Spiegel, N. T. An infantile fetish and its persistence into young womanhood. Q 1968, 37:635-636

KAFKA, J.

78038   "Le verdict" de Franz Kafka envisage au point de vue psychopathologique. ["The verdict" of Franz Kafka from the point of view of psychopathology.] Enceph 1969, 58:481-485

KAFKA, JOHN S.

78039   Art therapy and psychotherapy. Bull Art Ther 1961, 1:21

78040   The body as transitional object: a psychoanalytic study of a self-mutilating patient. M 1969, 42:207-212

78041   (& McDonald, J. W.) The latent family in the intensive treatment of the hospitalized schizophrenic patient. Curr psychiat Ther 1965, 5:172-177

78042   (& Gaarder, K.) Some effects of the therapist's LSD experience on his therapeutic work. PT 1964, 18:236-243

78043   Technical applications of a concept of multiple reality. J 1964, 45:575-578
         Abs EVN Q 1966, 35:623

KAGAN, IRVING N.

See Masserman, Jules H.

KAGAN, JEROME

78044   American longitudinal research on psychological development. Child Develpm 1964, 35:1-32

78045   (& Moss, H. A.) Availability of conflictful ideas: a neglected parameter in assessing projective test responses. J Pers 1961, 29:217-234

78046   The child's sex role classification of school objects. Child Develpm 1964, 35:1051-1056

78047   (& Hosken, B.; Watson, S.) Child's symbolic conceptualization of parents. Child Develpm 1961, 32:625-636

78048 (& Lesser, G.) (Eds) Contemporary Issues in Thematic Apperceptive Methods. Springfield, Ill: Thomas 1961, xiv + 328 p
78049 Creativity and learning. Personality and the learning process. Daedalus 1965, Summer:527-734
78050 (& Moss, H. A.) Personality and social development: family and peer influences; process of identification. Rev educ Res 1961, 31:469

See Janis, Irving L.; Moss, Howard A.; Mussen, Paul H.

KAHANA, RALPH J.

78051 Common psychiatric problems in aged patients admitted to the general hospital. Hosp Med 1967, 3:104-109
78052 Discussion of Berezin, M. A. and Fern, D. J. "Persistence of early emotional problems in a seventy-year-old woman." J geriat Psychiat 1967, 1:73-74
78053 Longevity and adaptation. Gerontologist 1964, 4:41-43
78054 Management of various personality types. Hosp Med 1966, 2:42-44
78055 Medical management, psychotherapy and aging. J geriat Psychiat 1967, 1:78-89
78056 (& Bibring, G. L.) Personality types in medical management. In Zinberg, N. E. *Psychiatry and Medical Practice in a General Hospital*, NY: IUP 1964, 108-123
78057 Psychiatric education: notes on psychiatric careers. Comprehen Psychiat 1968, 9:275-282
78058 Psychotherapy: models of the essential skill. Teach Dyn Psychiat 87-103; 135-136
78059 A remission through crisis in ulcerative colitis. PSM 1962, 24:499-506 Abs ELG Q 1963, 32:610
78060 Teaching medical psychology through psychiatric consultation. J med Educ 1959, 34:1003-1009. In Zinberg, N.E. *Psychiatry and Medical Practice in a General Hospital*, NY: IUP 1964, 98-107

See Bibring, Grete L.; Levin, Sidney

ABSTRACT OF:
78061 Marmor, J. Psychoanalytic therapy as an educational process: common denominators in the therapeutic approaches of different psychoanalytic "schools." Bull Phila Ass Psa 1962, 12:122-125

KAHLER, ERICH

78062 The Meaning of History. NY: George Braziller 1964, vii + 224 p
78063 The nature of the symbol. In May, R. *Symbolism in Religion and Literature*, NY: Braziller 1960, 50-74
78064 Out of the Labyrinth: Essays in Clarification. NY: Braziller 1967, xi + 241 p

KAHN, EDWIN

78065 (& Dement, W. C.; Fisher, C.; Barmack, J. E.) Incidence of color in immediately recalled dreams. Science 1962, 137:1054-1055

See Dement, William C.

KAHN, ERNEST

78066 Coltrera, J. T. The gifts of Daedalus: an adaptive aspect of the super-ego in the maintenance of psychic structure. Bull Phila Ass Psa 1963, 13:145-147

KAHN, EUGEN

78067 On experiencing. P 1963, 120:131-134
78068 On incest and Freud's Oedipus complex. Confin psychiat 1965, 8:89-101
78069 Self-pity. P 1965, 122:447-451
78070 Über Angst und traurige Verstimmung. [On anxiety and melancholia.] Psychiat Neurol, Basel 1964, 148:321-332
78071 Whence now. P 1964, 121:442-445

KAHN, HERMAN

78072 (& Fromm, E.; Maccoby, M.) The question of civil defense—a debate. Commentary 1962, 33:1-23

KAHN, J. H.

78073 School phobia. (Correspondence) Brit med J 1960, 2:1015-1016
78074 School Phobia. Acta paedopsychiat 1968, 35:4-10
78075 (& Nursten, J. P.) School refusal: a comprehensive view of school phobia and other failures of school attendance. Ops 1962, 32:707-718

KAHN, MARVIN W.

78076 (& Kirk, W. E.) The concepts of aggression: a review and reformulation. Psychol Rec 1968, 18:559-573
78077 Correlates of Rorschach reality adherence in the assessment of murderers who plead insanity. J proj Tech 1967, 31:44-47
78078 A factor analytic study of personality, intelligence and history characteristics of murderers. Proc APA 1965
78079 (& Jones, N. F.) Human figure drawings as predictors of admission to a psychiatric hospital. J proj Tech 1965, 29:319-322
78080 Implications for a theory of adult personality from developments in psychoanalytic theory. Comprehen Psychiat 1965, 6:85-93
78081 Superior performance IQ of murderers as a function of overt act or diagnosis. Soc Psych 1968, 76:113-116

See Jones, Nelson F.

KAHN, SAMUEL

78082 The Psychology of Love. NY: Philos Libr 1968, 101 p

KAHN, THEODORE CHARLES

78083 (& Giffen, M. B.) Psychological Techniques in Diagnosis and Evaluation. Oxford, NY: Pergamon Pr 1960, 164 p

KAHNE, MERTON J.

78084 Bureaucratic structure and impersonal experience in mental hospitals. Ps 1959, 22:363-375. In Weinberg, S. K. *The Sociology of Mental Disorders,* Chicago: Aldine 1968

78085 On the persistence of transitional phenomena into adult life. J 1967, 48:247-258
       Abs EVN Q 1969, 38:159

78086 Rehabilitation of chronic mental patients. Psychiat Q 1963, 37:704-709

78087 Rehabilitation of prisoner patients. In Stone, B. *A Critical Review of Treatment Progress in a State Hospital Reorganized toward the Communities Served,* Pueblo, Colorado: Pueblo Assoc for Mental Health 1963, 130-136

78088 Rehabilitation, reform and social structure. In Stone, B. *A Critical Review of Treatment Progress in a State Hospital Reorganized toward the Communities Served,* Pueblo, Colorado: Pueblo Assoc for Mental Health 1963, 192-199

78089 The relation of mental hospital personnel organization to patient suicide. In *Year Book of the American Philosophical Society,* 1964, 277-280

78090 Some implications of the concept of position for the study of mental hospital organization. Ps 1962, 25:227-243

78091 Suicide research: a critical review of strategies and potentialities in mental hospitals. Int J soc Psychiat 1966, 12:120-129; 177-186

78092 Suicides in mental hospitals: a survey of the psychiatrists who conducted their therapy. Ps 1968, 31:32-43

See Behymer, Alice F.

KAI, T.

See Erikson, Erik H.

KAIJ, L.

78093 (& Malmquist, A.; Nilsson, A.) Psychiatric aspects of spontaneous abortion. II. The importance of bereavement, attachment and neurosis in early life. J psychosom Res 1969, 13:53-59

KAIMAN, BERNARD DAVID

See Desroches, Harry F.

KAIRYS, DAVID

78094 Discussion of Dorn, R. M. "Psychoanalysis and psychoanalytic education." Psa Forum 1969, 3:264-267

78095 The training analysis, a critical review of the literature and a controversial proposal. Q 1964, 33:485-512

KAISER, EBERHARD

See Molinski, Hans

KAISER, G.

78096 (& Schindler, R.; Tschabitscher, H.) Fortschritte in der Betrachtung und Behandlung der senilen Erkrankungen. [Advances in the consideration and treatment of senile diseases.] In Hoff, H. *Therapeutische Fortschritte in der Neurologie und Psychiatrie*, Vienna: Verlag Urban & Schwarzenberg 1960, 251-262

KALES, ANTHONY

78097 (& Hoedemaker, F. S.; Jacobson, A.) Dream deprivation: an experimental reappraisal. Nature 1964, 204:1337-1338
78098 (& Malmstrom, E. J.; Tan, T-L.) Drugs and dreaming. Prog clin Psych 1969, 8:154-167
78099 (& Jacobson, A.; Paulson, M. J.; Kales, J. D.; Walter, R. D.) Somnambulism: psychophysiological correlates. I. All night EEG studies. II. Psychiatric interviews, psychological testing and discussion. Arch gen Psychiat 1966, 14:586-594; 595-604
    Abs PB Q 1969, 38:342

KALES, JOYCE D.

See Kales, Anthony

KALINA, EDUARDO

78100 Aborte y parasitesis. [Abortion and parasitosis.] Rev Psicoanál 1968, 25:211-217. In *Aborte, Estudio Psicoanalítico*, Buenos Aires: Hormé 1968, 295-300
78101 Contribución al estudio del encuadre en el análisis de adolescentes. [Contribution to the study of the setting in the analysis of adolescents.] Rev Psicoanál 1967, 24:311-327
78102 Elaboración del proceso puberal en un paciente de 11 años. [Improvement of the pubertal process in an 11-year-old patient.] Rev Psicoanál 1966, 23:57-67
78103 Psicoanálisis de adolescentes. [Psychoanalysis of adolescents.] Rev Asoc Méd Arg 1964, 78:636-638
78104 Psicoterapia psicoanalítica de la pareja. Su enfoque como psicoterapia breve. [Psychoanalytic psychotherapy of the couple considered as a brief therapy.] Acta psiquiát psicol Amér Latina 1968, 14:311-318
78105 Relación entre el habite do fumar y la manía. [The relation between the smoking habit and mental illness.] Rev Asoc Méd Arg 1965, 79:386-391
    Abs Auth Rev Psicoanál 1966, 23:208
78106 Sobre la naturaleza maníaca del chisme. [On the manic nature of gossip.] In *Psicoanalisis de la Manía y la Psicopatía*, Buenos Aires: Paidós 1966, 386-393
78107 Tratamiento psicoanalítico de un adolescente a través del dibujo. [Psychoanalytic treatment of an adolescent boy by means of drawing.] Acta psiquiát psicol Arg 1962, 8:218-226

See Aray, Julio

ABSTRACTS OF:

78108   Becker, T. E. Panel reports on latency. Rev Psicoanál 1966, 23:199-204

78109   Casuso, G. La relación entre el análisis de niños y la teoria y práctica del psicoanálisis. Rev Psicoanál 1966, 23:348

78110   (& Rascovsky, A.) Ekstein, R. The opening gambit in psychotherapeutic work with psychotic adolescents. Rev Psicoanál 1967, 24:441-444

78111   (& Rascovsky, A.) Ekstein, R. The Orpheus and Euridice theme in psychotherapy. Rev Psicoanál 1967, 24:446-448

78112   (& Rascovsky, A.) Ekstein, R. Puppet play of a psychotic adolescent girl in the psychotherapeutic process. Rev Psicoanál 1967, 24:445-446

78113   (& Rascovsky, A.) Ekstein, R. & Caruth, E. To sleep but not to dream. On the use of electric tape recording in clinical research. Rev Psicoanál 1967, 24:448-449

78114   (& Rascovsky, A.) Gralnick, A. Psychoanalysis and the treatment of adolescents in a private hospital. Rev Psicoanál 1967, 24:217-218

78115   Gray, P. Limitaciones del psicoanálisis. Rev Psicoanál 1966, 23:357

78116   (& Rascovsky, A.) Loeb, L. The clinical course of anorexia. Rev Psicoanál 1966, 23:502

78117   Miller, A. et al: On the nature of the observing function of the ego. Rev Psicoanál 1966, 23:77

78118   Neubauer, P. B. Contribuciones psicoanalíticos a la nosología de los trastornos psiquicos infantiles. Rev Psicoanál 1966, 23:485

78119   Prego Silva, L. E. Notas sobre el tratamiento de la psicopatía. Rev. Psicoanál 1966, 23:503

78120   (& Simoes, G.) Rosenbaum, J. B. Some misuses and abuses of our private language. Rev Psicoanál 1966, 23:364

78121   Savitt, R. Extramural psychoanalytic treatment of a case of narcotic addiction. Rev Psicoanál 1966, 23:209

78122   Schmale, H. T. Working through. Rev Psicoanál 1966, 23:492

78123   Spotnitz, H. Adolescence and schizophenia. Problems in differentiation. Rev Psicoanál 1966, 23:210

78124   Teruel, G. Considerations for a diagnostic in marital psychotherapy. Rev Psicoanál 1967, 24:215

78125   Teruel, G. Recent trends in the diagnosis and treatment of marital conflict. Rev. Psicoanál 1967, 24:217

78126   Zimmerman, D. Aspectos psicologicos de sintoma del robo en adolescentes. Rev Psicoanál 1966, 23:76

REVIEWS OF:

78127   Niederland, W. G. Memory and repression. Rev Psicoanál 1967, 24:677-691

78128   Solnit, A. J. The vicissitudes of ego development in adolescence. Rev Psicoanál 1967, 24:427-440

78129   Waldhorn, H. F. The silent patient (Round table). Rev Psicoanál 1967, 24:941-952

78130   Zimmermann, D. et al: Contribution to the study of sociotherapy. Rev Psicoanál 1967, 24:957-959

KALINOWSKY, LOTHAR B.

78131 (& Hoch, P. H.; Grant, B.) Somatic Treatments in Psychiatry; Pharmacotherapy; Convulsive, Insulin, Surgical, Other Methods. NY: Grune & Stratton 1961, 413 p

KALISH, HARRY I.

78132 Behavior therapy. In Wolman, B. B. *Handbook of Clinical Psychology,* NY: McGraw-Hill 1965, 1230-1253

REVIEW OF:
78133 Mowrer, H. O. Leanring Theory and Behavior. PPR 1961, 48(2):121-124

KALISH, RICHARD A.

78134 Some variables in death attitudes. Soc Psych 1963, 59:137-145. Death & Identity 170-177

KALIVODA, F.

See Gicklhorn, Renée

KALLEJIAN, VERNE

See Wayne, George J.

KALLIAPHAS, SPYRIDŌN MICHAĒL

78135 [Psychology of Bathos: Carl Jung, Sigmund Freud, Alfred Adler.] Athens: Ethotikos Oikos P. Demetrahou 1950, 238 p

KALLICH, MARTIN

S-49744 Psychoanalysis, sexuality, and Lytton Strachey's theory of biography. Abs DJM An Surv Psa 1958, 9:476-477

KALLJN, V.

78136 (& Jerotic, V.; Volf, N. et al) [Modern medical and social aspects of homosexuality.] (Ser) Med Glas 1968, 22:428-436

KALLMANN, FRANZ J.

78137 (& Rainer, J. D.) The genetic approach to schizophrenia: clinical, demographic, and family guidance problems. Int Psychiat Clin 1964, 1:799-820

See Kolb, Lawrence C.; Rainer, John D.

KALMAN, GEORGE J.

See Baak, W. W.

KALMANOVITCH, JEANNINE
TRANSLATIONS OF:
Frankl, L. & Hellman, I. [73333]. Lampl de Groot, J. [79945].
Nagera (Perez), H. [84883]. Spitz, R. A. [60063, 91994]. Winnicott,
D. W. [62561]. (& Massoubre) Winnicott, D. W. [62572].

REVIEW OF:
78138 Bentz, H. Freud in translation. RFPsa 1967, 31:298-299

KALMANSON, DENISE
S-49746 Psychanalyse d'une névrose obsessionnelle chez un enfant de 11 ans.
Abs Yacoubian, J. An Surv Psa 1957, 8:235-237

KALMAR, JACQUES M.
78139 Anti-pensée et Monde des Conflits. [Anti-thought and World of Conflicts.] Neuchâtel: Delachaux & Niestlé 1967, 158 p

KALOGERAKIS, MICHAEL GEORGE
78140 The role of olfaction in sexual development. PSM 1963, 25:420-432

KALOUTSĒS, ANDREAS A.
78141 [Psychoanalysis and psychology, Early Beginnings of Analytic Psy-
chology]. Athens 1955, 142 p

KALTHOFF, ROBERT J.
See Ornstein, Paul H.

KALZ, F.
See Wittkower, Eric D.

KAMAL, A.
78142 Folie à cinq: a clinical study. Brit J Psychiat 1965, Ill: 583-586

KAMANO, DENNIS K.
78143 Relationship of ego disjunction and manifest anxiety to conflict resolution. ASP 1963, 66:281-284

KAMBLEY, ARNOLD HERMAN
78144 Milieu control: an aid in the psychiatric treatment of adolescent under-
achievers. Confin psychiat 1968, 11:34-42

KAMIYA, MIYEKO
78145 Virginia Woolf. An outline of a study on her personality, illness and
work. Confin psychiat 1965, 8:189-205

KAMM, BERNARD A.

78146 Confidentiality in psychoanalysis. Samisksa 1960, 14:24-27
78147 (& Segenreich, H.; Serota, H.; Tower, L. E.) Confidentiality in psycho-analysis. A panel discussion. (Read at Chicago Psa Soc, 22 Nov 1960) Abs Seitz, P. F. D. Bull Phila Ass Psa 1961, 11:41-43
78148 Limits of analyzability. Samiksa 1964, 18:53-61
78149 Some thoughts on the qualification of training and supervising analyst. Samiksa 1963, 17:1-4.

See Gitelson, Maxwell

KAMMERER, T.

78150 [Addiction in epilepsy. Photogenic epilepsy with self-induced seizures.] (Ger) Dtsch Z Nervenheilk 1963, 185:319-330
78151 [Applications of Schultz's relaxation method in neuropsychiatry.] (Fr) Vie Med 1963, 44:53-57
78152 (& Gurfin, L.; Durand de Bousingen, R.) [Autogenic training and the structure of hysteria. Clinical study. Remarks on the psychopathology. (Apropos of 20 cases treated at the Strasbourg Psychiatric Clinic.)] (Fr) Rev Méd psychosom 1967, 9:117-126
78153 (& Singer, L.; Michel, D.) Les incendiaires. Étude criminologique, clinique et psychologique de 72 cas. [The incendiary. Criminologic, clinical and psychological study of 72 cases.] Ann méd-psychol 1967, 125(1):687-716
78154 [Reflections on psychic trauma.] (Fr) Évolut psychiat 1967, 32:65-87
78155 (& Ebtinger, R.; Pierron, G.) Représentation artistique d'un délire de bisexualité chez un schizophrène. [Artistic representation of a delusion of bisexuality in a schizophrenic.] Ann méd-psychol 1968, 126(2):41-56

KAMOUH, M. C.

78156 (& Laplanche, J.) Quelques caractéristiques structurales de phrases interprétées par un schizophrène. [Some structural characteristics of phrases interpreted by a schizophrenic.] Encéph 1966, 55:7-14. In Psychopathologie de l'Expression, Paris 1966, 7-14

KANDABASHI, JOJI

78157 [On the psychodynamic structure of the "borderline cases" as revealed by drug-psychotherapy.] (Jap) Kyushu Neuropsychiat 1966, 12:190-221
78158 [Reinterpretation of the Schreber case (S. Freud): Symposium.] (Jap) Jap J Psa 1968, 14(2):20-22; Discussion 32-34
78159 (& Nishizono, M.) [Transference psychosis.] (Jap) Jap J Psa 1964, 11(3):1-4

KANDEL, DENISE

See Lesser, Gerald

KANDELIN, ALBERT

78160 California's first psychoanalytic society. BMC 1966, 30:351-357

KANE, RUTH POWELL

See Browne, William F.

KANEDA, F.

See Okonogi, Keigo

KANFER, FREDERICK H.

78161 (& Phillips, J. S.) Behavior therapy. Arch gen Psychiat 1966, 15:114-128
   Abs PB Q 1969, 38:511

See Phillips, Jeanne S.

KANNER, LEO

78162 Autistic disturbances of affective contact. Acta paedopsychiat 1968, 35:100-136
78163 (Contributor to) Discussion of Hoch, P. H. "Concepts of schizophrenia." Out-Patient Schiz 17-23; 174-177; 194-202
78164 (Contributor to) Discussion of Rado, S. "Theory and therapy." Out-Patient Schiz 102-113
78165 (Contributor to) Discussion of Williams, G. E. "Crisis in the evaluation of the schizophrenic patient." Out-Patient Schiz 74-86
78166 Early infantile autism. J Pediat 1944, 211-217
78167 Early infantile autism revisited. Psychiat Dig 1968, 29:17-28
78168 A History of the Care and Study of the Mentally Retarded. Springfield, Ill: Thomas 1964, x + 150 p
78169 Schizophrenia as a concept. Out-Patient Schiz 46-59

KANNAS, S.

See Bornstein, S.

KANSKY, E. W.

See Jackson, Charles W., Jr.

KANT, FRITZ

78170 Frigidity; Dynamics and Treatment. Springfield, Ill: Thomas 1969, ix + 61 p

KANTER, STANLEY S.

78171 (& Burack, J.; Castagnola, R. L.; Gilbert, B. D.; Den Hartog, G.; Hughes, C.; Kruger, S. I.) A comparison of oral and genital aspects in group psychotherapy. Int J grp PT 1964, 14:158-165
   Abs GPK Q 1965, 34:471
78172 (& DiMascio, A.) Description of the patient—the setting of the therapy and summary comments by the therapists. In Gottschalk, L. A. *Comparative Psycholinguistic Analysis of Two Psychotherapeutic Interviews*, NY: IUP 1961, 15-58

See Levin, Sidney

KANTER, VICTOR B.

78173 (& Hazelton, J. E.) An attempt to measure some aspects of personality in young men with duodenal ulcer by means of questionnaires and a projective test. J psychosom Res 1964, 8:297-309
78174 Background and methods. (Symposium held by the Medical Section 28 Feb 1962. "A controlled clinical trial of imipramine ("Tofranil") on depressives in an outpatient setting.) Bull Brit Psychol Soc 1962, 15
78175 A comparison by means of psychological tests: young men with duodenal ulcer and controls. In Goldberg, E. M. *Family Influences and Psychosomatic Illness,* London: Tavistock Publ 1958, 227-261
78176 Freud's reading of Shakespeare. Bull Brit Psychol Soc 1969, 22(76): 225-226
78177 Training in psychosomatic research. Adv PSM 1967, 5:138-147

See Abraham, Hilda C.

KANTOR, D.
See Sharaf, Myron R.

KANTOR, I.
See Bernstein, Stanley

KANTOR, J. ROBERT
78178 The Scientific Evolution of Psychology. Vol. I. Illinois: Principia Pr 1963, 387 p

KANTOR, MARTIN
See Weinberger, Jerome L.

KANTOR, MILDRED B.
See Gildea, Margaret C.-L.; Rae-Grant, Quentin A. F.

KANTOR, ROBERT E.
78179 Art, ambiguity and schizophrenia. Art J 1965, 24:234-239

See Herron, William G.

KANZER, MARK
S-49771 Acting out and its relation to impulse disorders.
        Abs CK An Surv Psa 1957, 8:138-140. Mendilaharsu, S. A. de Rev urug Psa 1966, 8:409
S-49772 Acting out, sublimation and reality testing.
        Abs OS An Surv Psa 1957, 8:122-123. Agorio, R. Rev urug Psa 1966, 8:412-413
S-49773 Anality in inspiration and insight.
        Abs An Surv Psa 1955, 6:453-454

78180 Andre Gide: acting out and the creative imagination. Acting Out 30-39

78181 Applied psychoanalysis. III. Literature, arts, aest etics. An Surv Psa 1956, 7:408-418; 1957, 8:324-348

78182 (& Blum, H. P.) Classical psychoanalysis since 1939. Psa Tech 93-144

S-49777 The communicative function of the dream.
      Abs An Surv Psa 1955, 6:236-237

78183 Discussion of Engel, G. L. "Some obstacles to the development of research in psychoanalysis." J Am Psa Ass 1968, 16:211-214

78184 Discussion of Rosenfeld, H. A. "The need of patients to act out during analysis." Psa Forum 1966, 1:25-26

78185 Discussion of Veszy-Wagner, L. "Little Red Riding Hood on the couch." Psa Forum 1966, 1:410

78186 Ego alteration and acting out. (Read at Int Psa Cong, July 1967) J 1968, 49:431-437

78187 Freud and the demon. J Hillside Hosp 1961, 10:190-202
      Abs JA Q 1962, 31:585

78188 Freud's uses of the terms "autoerotism" and "narcissism." (Read at Am Psa Ass, Fall 1961) J Am Psa Ass 1964, 12:529-539
      Abs JLSt Q 1967, 36:133. CG RFPsa 1968, 32:176

S-49782 Gogol—a study on wit and paranoia.
      Abs An Surv Psa 1955, 6:190, 461-463

S-49783 Image formation during free association.
      Abs EMD An Surv Psa 1958, 9:104-106

78189 Imagery in King Lear. Am Im 1965, 22:3-13
      Abs Cuad Psa 1966, 2:126. JWS Q 1966, 35:163

78190 Inappropriate framework; a critical evaluation of "A methodological study of Freudian theory," by Kardiner, Karush, and Ovesey. Int J Psychiat 1966, 2:555-557

78191 The motor sphere of the transference. Q 1966, 35:522-539
      Abs Cuad Psa 1967, 3:57-58. LDr RFPsa 1968, 32:360

S-17651 The Oedipus trilogy. In Manheim, L. & Manheim, E. *Hidden Patterns*, NY: Macmillan 1966, 66-78

78192 On interpreting the Oedipus plays. [Panel on mythology and ego psychology.] (Read at Psa Assoc of NY, 21 May 1962) Psa St Soc 1964, 3:26-38

78193 Psychic determinism: Freud's specific propositions. Freud Anniversary Lecture. (Read at Psa Ass NY, 15 May 1967)
      Abs Scharfman, M. Q 1968, 37:485-486

S-49788 The reality-testing of the scientist.
      Abs An Surv Psa 1955, 6:130-131

78194 Sigmund and Alexander Freud on the Acropolis. (Read at Michigan Psa Soc, 11 Apr 1969) Am Im 1969, 26:324-354

S-49779 (& Eidelberg, L.) The structural description of pleasure.
      Description structurale du plaisir. RFPsa 1961, 25:733-739

78195 Verbal and nonverbal aspects of free association. (Read at Psa Ass NY, 21 Nov 1960) Q 1961, 30:327-350
      Abs Kolker, J. Q 1961, 30:167-169. LDr RFPsa 1962, 26:627

See Almansi, Renato J.; Blos, Peter

ABSTRACTS OF:

78196 Bieber, T. B. The emphasis on the individual in psychoanalytic group therapy. An Surv Psa 1957, 8:279

78197 Pearson, G. H. J. Some notes on masochism. An Surv Psa 1956, 7:186-187

REVIEWS OF:

78198 Desmonde, W. H. Magic, Myth and Money: The Origin of Money in Religious Ritual. Q 1963, 32:122-123

78199 Eissler, K. R. Leonardo da Vinci: Psycho-Analytic Notes on the Enigma. Q 1962, 31:269-271

78200 Guntrip, H. Personality Structure and Human Interaction. J 1962, 43:355-357

78201 King, C. D. The States of Human Consciousness. Q 1964, 33:597

78202 Milner, M. On Not Being Able to Paint (2nd ed). J 1962, 43:357-358

78203 Sartre, J.-P. Essays in Aesthetics. Q 1964, 33:599-600

78204 Stone, L. The Psychoanalytic Situation. J 1963, 44:108-110

78205 Waelder, R. Psychoanalytic Avenues to Art. Q 1966, 35:428-430

78206 Whyte, L. L. The Unconscious Before Freud. Q 1961, 30:292-293

KAPAMADZIJA, B.

78207 [Pathological stealing.] (Ser) Med Pregl 1965, 18:29-33

KAPLAN, ABRAHAM

78208 The Conduct of Inquiry. Methodology for Behavioral Science. San Francisco: Chandler Publ Co 1964, xix + 428 p

S-49929 Freud and modern philosophy. In author's The New World of Philosophy, NY: Random House 1961, 129-159
Freud et la philosophie moderne. Études Philos 1964, 19:361-373
Abs AEC An Surv Psa 1956, 7:21

78209 Maturity in religion. (Read at Phila Ass Psa, 24 May 1963) Bull Phila Ass Psa 1963, 13:101-119
Abs EFA Q 1965, 34:133. PLe RFPsa 1967, 31:305

KAPLAN, ALBERT J.

78210 The meaning of REM sleep—a hypothesis. Bull Phila Ass Psa 1965, 15:236-239

S-49936 An oral transference resistance.
Abs EFA Q 1961, 30:601

78211 Preventive psychiatry in the public schools. A clinical report. Med Times 1962, 90:1045-1054

78212 The psychoanalyst in the public schools. Penn Med 1961, 64:1582-1585

REVIEW OF:

78213 Eissler, K. R. Medical Orthodoxy and the Future of Psychoanalysis. Q 1966, 35:597-599

KAPLAN, ALEX H.

78214 Joint parent-adolescent interviews as a parameter in the psychoanalysis of the younger adolescent. JNMD 1969, 148:550-558

78215 Joint parent-adolescent interviews in the psychotherapy of the younger adolescent. In Caplan, G. & Lebovici, S. *Adolescence*, NY: Basic Books 1968, 315-321

78216 Problems of psychotherapy in the adolescent. In Hammer, M. & Kaplan, A. M. *The Practice of Psychotherapy with Children*, Homewood, Ill: Dorsey Pr 1967

78217 (& Milder, B.) Psychologic aspects of ophthalmologic practice. I. Psychodynamics of looking; ocular neurosis. Amer J Ophthal 1961, 52: 515-520

78218 Psychological disorders in summer residential camps. In Goldring, D. *Camp Physician's Manual*, Springfield, Ill: Thomas 1967

See Milder, Benjamin; Rothman, David

KAPLAN, ARTHUR M.

See Hammer, Max

KAPLAN, BERNARD

78219 Meditations on genesis. (Read at Boston Psa Soc, 24 Feb 1965)
        Abs Stone, A. A. Bull Phila Ass Psa 1965, 15:116-119

78220 (& Wapner, S.) (Eds) Perspectives in Psychological Theory. Essays in Honor of Heinz Werner. NY: IUP 1960, 384 p
        Rv Berezin, M. A. Q 1964, 33:278-279

See Werner, Heinz

KAPLAN, BERT

78221 (& Lawless, R.) Culture and visual imagery; a comparison of Rorschach responses in eleven societies. In Spiro, M. E. *Context and Meaning in Cultural Anthropology*, Glencoe, Ill: Free Pr 1965, 295-311

78222 (Ed) The Inner World of Mental Illness. A Series of First Person Accounts of What it Was Like. NY/Evanston/London: Harper & Row 1964, xii + 467 p

78223 The method of the study of persons. In Norbeck, E. et al: *The Study of Personality*, NY: Holt, Rinehart & Winston 1968, 121-133

78224 On "reason in madness" in *King Lear*. In Bugental, J. F. T. *Challenges of Humanistic Psychology*, NY: McGraw-Hill 1967, 313-318

78225 Psychological themes in Zuni mythology and Zuni TAT's. Psa St Soc 1962, 2:255-262

78226 (& Johnson, D.) The social meaning of Navaho psychopathology and psychotherapy. In Kiev, A. *Magic, Faith, and Healing*, Glencoe, Ill: Free Pr 1964, 203-229

78227 (Ed) Studying Personality Cross-Culturally. NY/Evanston/London: Harper & Row 1961, ix + 687 p

KAPLAN, DAVID M.

78228 (& Mason, E. A.) Maternal reactions to premature birth viewed as an acute emotional disorder. Ops 1960, 30:539-552
    Abs JMa RFPsa 1962, 26:317

78229 Observations on crisis theory and practice. Soc Casewk 1968, 49:151-155

78230 Study and treatment of an acute emotional disorder. Ops 1965, 35:69-77
    Abs JMa RFPsa 1966, 30:522

See Caplan, Gerald; Langsley, Donald G.

KAPLAN, DONALD M.

78231 Character and theatre: psychoanalytic notes on modern realism. Tulane Drama Rev 1966, 10:93-108

78232 Classical psychoanalysis: policies, values and the future. (Read at 3rd Scientific Conf on Psa, Council of Psychoanalytic Psychotherapists, 14 Feb 1965) R 1966, 53:99-111
    Abs SRS Q 1967, 36:139-140

78233 (& Goodrich, W.) Developing systematic descriptions of aggressive behavior in children. Wisc Welfare 1955, 14:4-13

78234 The emergence of projection in a series of dreams. PPR 1962, 49:37-52
    Abs LDr RFPsa 1962, 27:354. RLG Q 1963, 32:135

78235 (& Goodrich, W.) A formulation for interpersonal anger. Ops 1957, 27:387-395

78236 Homosexuality and American theatre: a psychoanalytic comment. Tulane Drama Rev 1965, 9:25-55

78237 Introduction: language and communication. R 1964, 51(1):3-4

78238 (Ed) Language and Communication, A Special Issue of The Psychoanalytic Review 1964, Vol. 51(1), 168 p

78239 On the dialogue in classical psychoanalysis. In Hammer, E. F. *Use of Interpretation in Treatment: Technique and Art*, NY: Grune & Stratton 1968, 129-140

78240 Theatre architecture: a derivation of the primal cavity. Tulane Drama Rev 1968, 12:105-116

78241 Theodor Reik. A student's memoir. Am Im 1968, 25:52-58
    Abs JWS Q 1969, 38:339

REVIEWS OF:

78242 Abt, L. E. & Weissman, S. L. (Eds) Acting Out: Theoretical and Clinical Aspects. R 1967, 54:710-712

78243 Andreas-Salomé, L. The Freud Journal of Lou Andreas-Salomé. R 1965, 52:488-491

78244 Bernays, E. L. Biography of an Idea: Memoirs of Public Relations Counsel Edward L. Bernays. R 1966, 53(1):134-135

78245 Deutsch, F. Body, Mind and the Sensory Gateways. R 1963, 50:686-687

78246 Erikson, E. H. Insight and Responsibility: Lectures on the Ethical Implications of Psychoanalytic Insight. R 1965, 52(1):133-136

78247 Ernst, M. L. & Schwartz, A. U. Censorship: The Search for the Obscene. R 1964, 51:683-685
78248 Flescher, J. Dual Therapy and Genetic Psychoanalysis. R 1969, 56:483-485
78249 Grotjahn, M. Psychoanalysis and the Family Neurosis. PPR 1961, 48 (1):117-122
78250 Seeley, J. R. The Americanization of the Unconscious. Am Im 1969, 26:89-92
78251 Shakow, D. & Rapaport, D. The Influence of Freud on American Psychology. R 1964, 51:674-675
78252 Shapiro, D. Neurotic Styles. R 1967, 54(1):188-189
78253 Sherman, H. M. (Ed) A Rorschach Reader. PPR 1962, 49(3):125-127
78254 Stein, M. R. The Eclipse of Community. An Interpretation of American Studies. PPR 1961, 48(1):117-122
78255 Westwood, G. A Minority. A Report on the Life of the Male Homosexual in Great Britain. PPR 1962, 49(4):126-127

KAPLAN, ELIZABETH BREMNER

78256 (Contributor to) Pearson, G. H. J. *A Handbook of Child Psychoanalysis,* NY/London: Basic Books 1968
78257 (Reporter) Panel on classical forms of neurosis in infancy and early childhood. (Am Psa Ass, Dec 1961) J Am Psa Ass 1962, 10:571-578
       Abs CG RFPsa 1964, 28:458
78258 Reflections regarding psychomotor activities during the latency period. Psa St C 1965, 20:220-238

KAPLAN, EUGENE A.

78259 Homosexuality. A search for the ego-ideal. Arch gen Psychiat 1967, 16:355-358

See Hollender, Marc H.; Malev, Jonathan S.

KAPLAN, EUGENE H.

78260 Attitudes toward automobiles: an aid to psychiatric evaluation and treatment of adolescents. J Hillside Hosp 1961, 10:3-13
       Abs JA Q 1962, 31:136
78261 Congenital absence of vagina. Psychiatric aspects of diagnosis and management. NYSJM 1968, 68:1937-1941
78262 (Reporter) The female orgasm. (Panel: Long Island Psa Soc, Mar 1967) J Hillside Hosp 1968, 17:44-50
78263 Organic visual defects in a case of obsessional neurosis. J Hillside Hosp 1962, 11:80-85
       Abs JA Q 1963, 32:290

See Esman, Aaron; Glenn, Jules; Wieder, Herbert

KAPLAN, F.

78264 Effects of anxiety and defense in a therapy-like situation. JAbP 1966, 71:449-458

KAPLAN, GERSON H.

78265 (& Chessick, R. D.) Liaison psychiatry in a Veterans Administration hospital. Psychosomatics 1962, 3:397-403

KAPLAN, HAROLD IRWIN

78266 (& Freedman, A. M.; Nagler, S. H.) Combined psychiatric residency and psychoanalytic training. P 1966, 122:806-809
    Abs Loeb, L. Q 1968, 37:628-629
78267 History of psychosomatic medicine. Compreh Txbk Psychiat 1036-1037
78268 (& Kaplan, H. S.; Freedman, A. M.) Residency training in psychiatry for physician mothers. JAMA 1964, 189:11-14

See Freedman, Alfred M.; Kaplan, Helen S.

KAPLAN, HAROLD J.

78269 Hemingway and the passive hero. In author's The Passive Voice, Columbus, Ohio: Ohio State Univ Pr 1966, 93-110

KAPLAN, HELEN SINGER

78270 The concept of psychogenicity in medicine. Compreh Txbk Psychiat 1120-1124
78271 (& Kaplan, H. I.) Current concepts of psychosomatic medicine. Compreh Txbk Psychiat 1039-1044
78272 Treatment of psychophysiological disorders. Compreh Txbk Psychiat 1113-1119

See Kaplan, Harold I.

KAPLAN, HOWARD M.

See Burton, Genevieve

KAPLAN, JUSTIN

78273 On Mark Twain: "never quite sane in the night." R 1969, 56:113-127

KAPLAN, LEAH

See Heinicke, Christoph M.

KAPLAN, LOUIS S.

78274 Foundations of Human Behavior. NY: Harper & Row 1965, ix + 368 p
78275 Ruth Stephenson—a tribute. Bull Phila Ass Psa 1966, 16:1-3
78276 Snow White: a study in psychosexual development. (Read at Phila Ass Psa, 15 Mar 1963) Bull Phila Ass Psa 1963, 13:49-65
    Abs Cowitz, B. Bull Phila Ass Psa 1963, 13:94-95. EFA Q 1964, 33:300. PLe RFPsa 1967, 31:305

KAPLAN, LOUISE J.

REVIEW OF:
78277 Ekstein, R. Children of Time and Space, of Action and Impulse. R 1969, 56:344-345

KAPLAN, MARTIN F.

78278   (& Singer, E.) Dogmatism and sensory alienation: an empirical investigation. J consult Psychol 1963, 27:486-491. In Lindzey, G. & Hall, C. S. *Theories of Personality*, NY: Wiley 1965, 1966, 1968, 125-130

78279   Elicitation of information and response biases of repressors, sensitizers, and neutrals in behavior prediction. J Pers 1968, 36:84-91

78280   Repression—descriptive behavior: response versus situational cue variables. JAbP 1967, 72:354-361

KAPLAN, MARVIN L.

78281   Ego impairment and ego adaptation in schizophrenia. J proj Tech 1967, 31:7-17

KAPLAN, MAURICE

78282   Problems between a referring source and a child guidance clinic. Q J Behav 1952. In Szurek, S. A. & Berlin, I. N. *The Antisocial Child: His Family and His Community*, Palo Alto, Calif: Sci & Behav Books 1969, 116-131

KAPLAN, MORTON A.

78283   *The American Imago* in retrospect. An article-review. Lit & Psych 1963, 13:112-116

78284   Article-review of Morris Philipson's "Outline of a Jungian Aesthetics." Lit & Psych 1965, 15:57-64

78285   Dream at Thebes. Lit & Psych 1961, 11:12-19

78286   Psychoanalyst looks at politics: a retrospective tribute to Robert Waelder. World Politics 1968, 20:694-704

KAPLAN, SAMUEL

78287   A clinical contribution to the study of a narcissism in infancy. (Read at Boston Psa Soc & Inst, 22 Apr 1962) Psa St C 1964, 19:398-420

78288   Discussion of Malone, C. A. "Some observations on children of disorganized families and problems of acting out. In Rexford, E. N. *A Developmental Approach to Problems of Acting Out*, NY: IUP 1966, 41-46

S-49978 (Reporter) Panel: the latency period.
        Abs AL An Surv Psa 1957, 8:206-209

KAPLAN, SEYMOUR ROBERT

78289   Therapy groups and training groups: similarities and differences. Int J grp PT 1967, 17:473-504

        See Peck, Harris B.

KAPLAN, STANLEY M.

78290   (& Gottschalk, L. A.; Magliocco, E. B.; Rohovit, D. D.; Ross, W. D.) Hostility in verbal productions and hypnotic dreams of hypertensive patients: studies of groups and individuals. PSM 1961, 23:311-322
        Abs Luchina, I. Rev Psicoanál 1961, 18:408

78291 (& Whitman, R. M.) The negative ego-ideal. (Read at Am Psa Ass, 3 May 1963) J 1965, 46:183-187
Abs Cueli, J. Cuad Psa 1965, 1:313. EVN Q 1967, 36:317
78292 Psychiatry and medicine. Compreh Txbk Psychiat 1124-1130

See Gottschalk, Louis A.; Parens, Henri; Whitman, Roy M.

KAPLAN-DE-NOUR, ATARA
See Noy, Pinchas

KAPLOWITZ, DANIEL

78293 Teaching empathic responsiveness in the supervisory process of psychotherapy. PT 1967, 21:774-781
78294 Techniques effecting change in analytically oriented psychotherapy. P 1960, 14:677-690

KAPP, F. I.
See Friedman, Jacob H.

KAPP, FREDERIC T.

78295 The bases of conflictual styles in academic life. Institute for Research and Training in Higher Education Bulletin 1968, 1:4-5
78296 Discussion of Boyer, L. B. "Pioneers in the psychoanalysis of schizophrenia." Psa Forum 1969, 3:232-233
78297 (& Gottschalk, L. A.) Drug therapy. Prog Neurol Psychiat 1962, 17: 536-558
78298 Ezra Pound's creativity and treason: clues from his life and work. Comprehen Psychiat 1968, 9:414-427
78299 Freud's dream discoveries—an example of the creative process. In Kramer, M. *Dream Psychology and the New Biology of Dreaming*, Springfield, Ill: Thomas 1969
78300 (& Gleser, G.; Brissenden, A.) Group participation and self-perceived personality change. JNMD 1964, 139:255-265
78301 Psychogenic pain. Compreh Txbk Psychiat 1105-1107
S-17776 (& Rosenbaum, M.; Romano, J.) Psychological factors in men with peptic ulcers. In Palmer, J. O. & Goldstein, M. J. *Perspectives in Psychopathology*, NY: Oxford Univ Pr 1966, 63-69
78302 Report of talk to Cincinnati Psychoanalytic Seminar by E. Rexford on "Child analysis in our institutes today." Bull Chicago Soc 1965, 1:25-26
78303 School desegregation: comment on the Garrett Pamphlet. In *Classroom Desegregation—More to the Story*, Cincinnati Public Schools (Pamphlet) 1966, 1-3
78304 Some psychologic factors in prolonged labor due to inefficient uterine action. Comprehen Psychiat 1963, 4:9-18
78305 Student Motivation. Cincinnati, Ohio: Cincinnati School Foundation (Pamphlet) 1966, 14 p

See Ross, Donald W.

KAPPUS, HAROLD C.

See Masserman, Jules H.

KAPULER, WILLIAM P.

ABSTRACTS OF:

78306 Balkányi, C. Psycho-analysis of a stammering girl. Q 1962, 31:283

78307 Bellak, L. Free association: conceptual and clinical aspects. Q 1962, 31:281

78308 Bowlby, J. Processes of mourning. Q 1962, 31:576

78309 Boyer, L. B. Provisional evaluation of psycho-analysis with few parameters employed in the treatment of schizophrenia. Q 1962, 31:557

78310 Bradley, N. The doll: some clinical, biological and linguistic notes on the toy-baby and its mother. Q 1962, 31:581

78311 Bychowski, G. The ego and the object of the homosexual. Q 1962, 31:285

78312 Cameron, N. Introjection, reprojection, and hallucination in the interaction between schizophrenic patient and therapist. Q 1962, 31:283

78313 Carlson, H. B. The relationship of the acute confusional state to the ego development. Q 1962, 31:581

78314 Chertok, L. On the discovery of the cathartic method. Q 1962, 31:286

78315 Edel, L. The biographer and psycho-analysis. Q 1962, 31:579

78316 Eissler, K. R. A hitherto unnoticed letter by Sigmund Freud. Q 1962, 31:283

78317 Garma, A. Colour in dreams. Q 1962, 31:581-582

78318 Giovacchini, P. L. Resistance and external object relations. Q 1962, 31:285

78319 Hollender, M. H. Prostitution, the body, and human relatedness. Q 1962, 31:578

78320 Koff, R. H. A definition of identification: a review of the literature. Q 1962, 31:576-577

78321 Krapf, E. E. The concepts of normality and mental health in psychoanalysis. Q 1962, 31:579

78322 Leveton, A. F. The night residue. Q 1962, 31:580

78323 Levin, S. & Michaels, J. J. The participation of psychoanalysis in the Medical Institutions of Boston. Q 1962, 31:286

78324 Lewy, E. Responsibility, free will, and ego psychology. Q 1962, 31:285-286

78325 Löfgren, L. B. A case of bronchial asthma with unusual dynamic factors, treated by psychotherapy and psycho-analysis. Q 1962, 31:578

78326 Lomas, P. Family role and identity formation. Q 1962, 31:557

78327 Novey, S. Further considerations on affect theory in psychoanalysis. Q 1962, 31:281

78328 Ostow, M. The clinical estimation of ego libido content. Q 1962, 31:580

78329 Pedersen, S. Personality formation in adolescence and its impact upon the psychoanalytic treatment of adults. Q 1962, 31:557

78330 Peto, A. The fragmentizing function of the ego in the transference neurosis. Q 1962. 31:285

78331 Pleune, F. G. Aggression and the concept of aim in psychoanalytic drive theory, Q 1962, 31:579-580
78332 Pollock, G. H. Mourning and adaptation. Q 1962, 31:576
78333 Racker, G. T. De On the formulation of the interpretation. Q 1962, 31:282
78334 Ramzy, I. The range and spirit of psycho-analytic technique. Q 1962, 31:580
78335 Rose, G. J. Pregenital aspects of pregnancy fantasies. Q 1962, 31:581
78336 Rosen, V. H. The relevance of "style" to certain aspects of defence and the synthetic function of the ego. Q 1962, 31:579
78337 Ruddick, B. Agoraphobia. Q 1962, 31:581
78338 Saul, L. J. & Beck, A. T. Psychodynamics of male homosexuality. Q 1962, 31:282
78339 Searles, H. F. Anxiety concerning change, as seen in the psychotherapy of schizophrenic patients—particular reference to the sense of personal identity. Q 1962, 31:283
78340 Shengold, L. Chekov and Schreber: vicissitudes of a certain kind of father-son relationship. Q 1962, 31:578
78341 Sperling, O. E. Variety and analyzability of hypnagogic hallucinations and dreams. Q 1962, 31:284
78342 Stern, M. M. Blank hallucinations: remarks about trauma and perceptual disturbances. Q 1962, 31:284
78343 Stewart, H. Jocasta's crimes. Q 1962, 31:578
78344 Veszy-Wagner, L. The analytic screen: an instrument or an impediment in the psycho-analytic technique. Q 1962, 31:281-282
78345 White, R. B. The mother-conflict in Schreber's psychosis. Q 1962, 31:282
78346 Wisdom, J. O. A methodological approach to the problem of hysteria. Q 1962, 31:284

KARACAN, ISMET

78347 (& Goodenough, D. R.; Shapiro, A.; Starker, S.) Erection cycle during sleep in relation to dream anxiety. Arch gen Psychiat 1966, 15:183-189

KARASIC, JEROME

78348 Symptoms, transference, and the past. (Read at Phila Ass Psa, 7 Jan 1966) Bull Phila Ass Psa 1967, 17:75-85
Abs Dalsimer, W. Bull Phila Ass Psa 1966, 16:104-106

KARDENER, S. H.

78349 The family—structure, patterns, and therapy. MH 1968, 52:524-531

KARDINER, ABRAM

S-49991 Adaptational theory: the cross cultural point of view.
Abs JA An Surv Psa 1956, 7:66
S-49997 Freud: the man I knew, the scientist, and his influence.
Abs AEC An Surv Psa 1956, 7:33

S-49998 (& Karush, A.; Ovesey, L.) A methodological study of Freudian theory.
        I. Basic concepts. Int J Psychiat 1966, 2:489-544; 576-587
78350   Pyschoanalysis and anthropology. Sci Psa 1961, 4:21-27
78351   A psychoanalytic understanding of monogamy. Marriage Relat 21-29
78352   Reflections on the integrative processes. In Daniels, G. E. et al: *New
        Perspectives in Psychoanalysis*, NY: Grune & Stratton 1965
78353   The relation between frame of reference and nosology. In Daniels,
        G. E. et al: *New Perspectives in Psychoanalysis*, NY: Grune & Stratton
        1965
78354   (& Preble, E.) Sigmund Freud: chimney sweeping. In authors' *They
        Studied Man* 224-239
78355   (& Preble, E.) They Studied Man. Cleveland: World Publ Co 1961;
        London: Secker & Warburg 1962, 287 p
            Rv Carstairs, G. M. J 1964, 45:588-590

KARDOS, ELIZABETH

S-50006 (& Peto, A.) Contributions to the theory of play.
            Abs AJE An Surv Psa 1956, 7:127-128

KARIER, CLARENCE J.

78357   Rebel and the revolutionary: Sigmund Freud and John Dewey.
        Teachers Coll Rec 1963, 64:605-613

KARKALAS, YANI

78358   (et al) The capgras syndrome: a rare psychiatric condition. Love-hate
        conflict resolved by directing ambivalent feelings to an imagined
        double. Rhode Island Med J 1969, 52:452-454

KAROL, CECILIA K.

        ABSTRACTS OF:
78359   Neubauer, P. B. (Chm) Panel discussion on adult and child analysis:
        mutual influences. Q 1968, 37:168-171
78360   Weich, M. The terms "mother" and "father" as a defense against
        incest. Q 1969, 38:519-520
78361   Wilson, C. P. The "boy friend," the "girl friend": psychoanalytic in-
        vestigation of a mannerism of speech. Q 1969, 38:519

KARON, B.

        See Sheppard, Edith

KARON, BERTRAM P.

78362   A clinical note on the specific nature of an "oral" trauma. ASP 1960,
        61:480-481
78363   An experimental study of parental castration phantasies in schizo-
        phrenia. Brit J Psychiat 1964, 110:67-73

S-50007 (& Rosberg, J.) The homosexual urges in schizophrenia.
　　　　Abs Kawi, A. An Surv Psa 1958, 9:188-189
78364　(& O'Grady, P.) Intellectual test changes in schizophrenic patients in
　　　　the first six months of treatment. Psychotherapy 1969, 6:88-96
78365　The resolution of acute schizophrenic reactions: a contribution to the
　　　　development of non-classical psychotherapeutic techniques. Psycho-
　　　　therapy 1963, 1:27-43

　　　　See Karon, Edward S.

KARON, EDWARD S.

78366　(& Karon, B. P.) Techniques of primitive witchcraft in modern psy-
　　　　chotherapy. Acta psychother psychosom 1962, 9:393-400

KARP, S. A.

　　　　See Wikin, Herman A.

KARPE, MARIETTA

S-50009 (& Karpe, R.) The meaning of Barrie's Mary Rose.
　　　　Abs JAL An Surv Psa 1957, 8:328

KARPE, RICHARD

S-50013 Freud's reaction to his father's death.
　　　　Abs AS An Surv Psa 1956, 7:36
78367　My recent trip to Israel. Ops 1962, 32:193-194
78368　The rescue complex in Anna O's final identity. (Read at Western New
　　　　England Psa Soc, Feb 1959; at Am Psa Ass, Apr 1959) Q 1961,
　　　　30:1-27

　　　　See Karpe, Marietta

KARPF, FAY B.

78369　Remembered experiences relating to Dr. Rank. J Otto Rank Ass 1969,
　　　　4(2):74-87

KARPMAN, BENJAMIN

78370　Criminality in the service of civilization. Arch crim Psychodyn 1961,
　　　　4:231-242
S-50023 Dream life in a case of pyromania.
　　　　Abs An Surv Psa 1955, 6:242
S-17861 Dream life in a case of transvestism. PT Pervers 300-357
78371　From the dream life of a voyeur: a study in the psychodynamics of
　　　　antisocial paraphilias. Conclusion. Arch crim Psychodyn 1961, 4:317-
　　　　365
78372　From the emotional and dream life of a transvestite. Arch crim Psy-
　　　　chodyn 1961, 4:815-879
78373　The structure of neurosis: with special differentials between neurosis,
　　　　psychosis, homosexuality, alcoholism, psychopathy and criminality
　　　　(editorial). Arch crim Psychodyn 1961, 4:599-646

78374 (& Cruvant, B.; Diamond, B. L.; Gilbert, M.; Mueller, G. O. W.;
       Overholser, W.) Symposium: What is insanity? Its relation to psycho-
       sis, neurosis, sociopathy, mental deficiency: the problem of responsi-
       bility, partial insanity, temporary insanity. Arch crim Psychodyn 1961,
       4:285-316
78375 Towards the psychodynamics of voyeurism: a case study. Arch crim
       Psychodyn 1960, 4:95-142

       See Diamond, Bernard L.

KARS, PIETER C.

78376 The existential moment in psychotherapy. Ps 1961, 24:153-163
       Abs HRB Q 1962, 31:428-429

KARUSH, AARON

78377 An adaptational approach to psychic representation, perception, and
       the psychic apparatus. In Goldman, G. S. & Shapiro, D. *Developments
       in Psychoanalysis at Columbia University*, NY: Hafner Publ Co 1966,
       3-31
78378 Adaptational psychodynamics. Contempo PT 305-318
78379 Ego strength: an unsolved problem in ego psychology. Sci Psa 1967,
       11:103-133
78380 (& Easser, B. R.; Cooper, A.; Swerdloff, B.) The evaluation of ego
       strength. I. A profile of adaptive balance. JNMD 1964, 139:332-349
       Abs BFM Q 1966, 35:159-160
78381 Reparative psychotherapy and adaptational theory. Contempo PT 319-
       337
78382 (& Daniels, G. E.; O'Connor, J. F.; Stern, L. O.) The response to
       psychotherapy in chronic ulcerative colitis, I: Pretreatment factors.
       II: Factors arising from the treatment situation. PSM 1968, 30:255-276;
       1969, 31:201-226
78383 (& Ovesey, L.) Unconscious mechanisms of magical repair. Arch gen
       Psychiat 1961, 5:55-69
       Abs KR Q 1962, 31:589
78384 Working through. (Read at Ass Psa Med, Oct 1966) Bull Ass Psa Med
       1966, 6(2):23-28. Q 1967, 36:497-531
       Abs Cuad Psa 1968, 4:41-42

       See Blos, Peter; Cooper, Arnold M.; Daniels, George E.; Kardiner,
       Abram; O'Connor, John F.

REVIEW OF:
78385 Cattell, R. B. & Scheier, I. H. The Meaning and Measurement of
       Neuroticism and Anxiety. Q 1964, 33:124-127

KARUSH, NATHANIEL
       See Jacobs, Martin A.

KARWIN, LOUIS

78386 "I was thinking to myself": an analysis of a defense. J Hillside Hosp
       1968, 17:183-185

KASAHARA, YOSHIMI

78387 [Hitomishiri—on fear of eyeball-to-eyeball confrontation: symposium on "Hitomishiri."] (Jap) Jap J Psa 1969, 15(2):30-33

KASANIN, JACOB S.

S-17935 (Ed) Language and Thought in Schizophrenia.
Linguaje y pensamiento en la esquizofrenia. Buenos Aires: Horme 1958
Rv Smolensky, G. Rev Psicoanál 1963, 20:285

KASATKIN, V. NIKOLAI

78388 [On diagnostic significance of dreams.] (Rus) Zh Nevropat Psikhiat Korsakov 1959, 59:1100-1105

KASIN, EDWIN

78389 Interpretation as active nurture: an interpersonal perspective. In Hammer, E. F. *Use of Interpretation in Treatment: Technique and Art,* NY: Grune & Stratton 1968, 197-207

KASPER, AUGUST M.

78390 The narcissistic self in a masochistic character. J 1965, 46:474-486

See Tabachnick, Norman

KASPER, JOSEPH C.

See Schulman, Jerome L.

KASS, WALTER

78391 (& Ekstein, R.) Thematic Appreciation Test diagnosis of a Nazi war criminal. Trans Kansas Acad Sci 1948, 51:344-350

See Hirschberg, J. Cotter

KASSEN, JULIAN

ABSTRACT OF:
78392 Tarachow, S. Definitions of psychotherapy. Q 1962, 31:601-603

KASTEIN, S.

See Michal-Smith, Harold

KASTENBAUM, ROBERT

78393 Developmental-field theory and the aged person's inner experience. Gerontologist 1966, 6:10-13
78394 (Ed) New Thoughts on Old Age. NY: Springer 1964, xii + 333 p

See Shere, Eugenia

KASTL, ALBERT J.

78395 Changes in ego functioning under alcohol. Quart J Stud Alcohol 1969, 30:371-383

KASWAN, JAQUES

78396 (& Wasman, M.; Freedman, L. Z.) Aggression and the picture-frustration study. J consult Psychol 1960, 24:446-452

KATAN, ANNY

S-50057 The nursery school as a diagnostic help to the child guidance clinic. In Weinreb, J. *Recent Developments in Psychoanalytic Child Therapy*, NY:IUP 1960, 93-107
    Abs RTh J 1961, 42:473
78397 Preface. Ther Nurs Schl 1-3
78398 Some thoughts about the role of verbalization in early childhood. Psa St C 1961, 16:184-188

See Furman, Robert A.

KATAN, MAURITS

78399 A causerie on Henry James's "The Turn of the Screw." Psa St C 1962, 17:473-493
S-50060 Contribution to the panel on ego-distortion. ("as-if" and "pseudo as-if").
    Abs JLS An Surv Psa 1958, 9:156-158
S-50064 Dream and psychosis: their relationship to hallucinatory process. (Read at NY Psa Soc, 12 Apr 1960)
    Rêve et psychose: leur rapport avec les processus hallucinatoires. RFPsa 1961, 25:681-700
    Traum und Psychose. Psyche 1961, 14:589-607
    Abs Malev, M. Q 1961, 30:157-160. JBi Q 1962, 31:118
78400 Fetishism, splitting of the ego, and denial. (Read at Int Psa Cong, July-Aug 1963) J 1964, 45:237-245
    Fétichisme, dissociation du moi et dénégation. RFPsa 1967, 31:447-464
    Abs Cowitz, B. Bull Phila Ass Psa 1964, 14:40-42. EVN Q 1966, 35:458-459
78401 The link between Freud's works and aphasia, fetishism and constructions in analysis. J 1969, 50:547-553
78402 The origin of "The Turn of the Screw" (by Henry James). Psa St C 1966, 21:583-635
78403 Precursors of the concept of the death instinct. Psa—Gen Psychol 86-103
78404 A psychoanalytic approach to the diagnosis of paranoia. Psa St C 1969, 24:328-357
78405 Schnitzler's *Das Schicksal des Freiherrn von Leisenbohg*. J Am Psa Ass 1969, 17:904-926
S-50070 Schreber's hereafter. Its building-up (Aufbau) and its downfall.
    Abs RTh J 1961, 42:473-474

KATAYAMA, TOWAKO

78406 [Some technical principles for adolescent girls.] (Jap) Abs (Eng) (Read at Jap Psa Ass, Oct 1968) Jap J Psa 1969, 15(5):1-6; 26

See Kitami, Yoshio

KATCHER, NAOMI

78407 (Ed) The Catalogue of the Freud Centenary Exhibit. NY: IUP 1956 Abs An Surv Psa 1956, 7:8

KATICIC, N.

See Betlheim, Stjepan

KATO, C.

78408 [Patients with sex problems.] (Jap) Jap J Publ Health Nurse 1967, 23:75-79

KATO, MASAHIDE

78409 [Psychiatry for the aged.] (Jap) J Nutr, Tokyo 1961, 19:44-45

KATOVSKY, W.

See Rafferty, Janet E.

KATWAN, J.

See Jorswieck, Eduard

KATZ, ALAN S.

See Bolman, William M.

KATZ, ALFRED HYMAN

78410 (& Felton, J. S.) (Eds) Health and the Community: Readings in the Philosophy and Sciences of Public Health. NY: Free Pr 1965, xviii + 877 p

78411 The role of parent groups in services to the mentally retarded. 2nd Int Cong Ment Retard Vienna, 14-19 Aug 1961

78412 Some psychological themes in a novel by Christina Stead. Lit & Psych 1965, 15:210-215

KATZ, ARNOLD

78413 (& Webb, L.; Stotland, E.) Cognitive regulation of autonomic responses. (Read at Seattle Psa Soc) Abs Goforth, E. Psa Forum 1967, 2:88-89

KATZ, BARNEY

See Thorpe, Louis P.

KATZ, DANIEL

See Janis, Irving L.

KATZ, EVELYN W.

78414 A content-analytic method for studying themes of interpersonal behavior. Psychol Bull 1966, 66:419-422

KATZ, HARRIET

See Brown, Fred

KATZ, IRWIN

See Deutsch, Martin

KATZ, JAY

78415 (& Goldstein, J.) Abolish the insanity defense—why not? JNMD 1964, 138:57-69
        Abs BFM Q 1965, 34:138-139
78416 Family law and psychoanalysis—some observations on interdisciplinary collaboration. Family Law Q 1967, 1:69-77
78417 Non-directive psychotherapy: a little girl talks to herself. 2. Med J Aust 1967, (1):1166-1168
78418 On primary gain and secondary gain. (Read at Western New England Psa Soc, 22 Feb 1963) Psa St C 1963, 18:9-50
78419 (& Goldstein, J.; Dershowitz, A. M.) Psychoanalysis, Psychiatry and the Law. NY: Free Pr; London: Collier-Macmillan 1967, xxiii + 822 p
        Abs J Am Psa Ass 1967, 15:732. Rv Slovenko, R. R 1968-69, 55:702-703

        See Goldstein, Joseph; Newman, Richard

KATZ, JOSEPH

78420 Dreams of flying: omnipotency variances in ego development. Israel Ann Psychiat 1968, 6:162-172
78421 The Joseph dreams anew. R 1963, 50:252-278
78422 On the death of the president: President Kennedy's assassination. R 1964-65, 51:661-664
78423 Reply [to Ansbacher, H. L. (et al): "Lee Harvey Oswald: an Adlerian interpretation."] R 1966, 53:390-392

REVIEWS OF:
78424 Gottwald, A. The Third Reich of Dreams. R 1969, 56:351-353
78425 Sacerdote, P. Induced Dreams. R 1969, 56:351-353
78426 Waldhorn, H. F. The Place of the Dream in Clinical Psychoanalysis. R 1969, 56:351-353

KATZ, LAWRENCE

See Boesky, Dale

KATZ, MARTIN M.

78427 (& Cole, J. O.; Barton, W. E.) (Eds) The Role and Methodology of Classification in Psychiatry and Psychopathology. Chevy Chase, Md: NIMH, U.S. Dept of Health, Education, and Welfare 1968, ix + 590 p

KATZ, MELVYN

78428 Obesity, race, body-cathexis, and self-confrontation on closed circuit television. Diss Abstr Int 1969, 30(4-B):1899

KATZ, P.

78429 The diagnosis and treatment of borderline schizophrenia in adolescence. Canad Psychiat Ass J 1967, 12:247-251

78430 Dynamics and treatment of foster children. Canad Psychiat Ass J 1968, 13:295-300

KATZ, PHYLLIS A.

See Deutsch, Martin

KATZ, ROBERT L.

78431 Empathy: Its Nature and Uses. NY/London: Free Pr of Glencoe 1963, xii + 210 p
Abs J Am Psa Ass 1966, 14:229

KATZENSTEIN, BETTI

78432 Psychology is a nuisance. Crianca Port 1956-57, 15-16(1)

78433 Two cases of writing and reading difficulties. Crianca Port 1956-57, 15-16(1)

KAUFER, GEORGE

See Riess, Bernard F.

KAUFMAN, FREDA

78434 Myopia seen psychoanalytically. R 1963, 50(1):24-39
Abs Ekboir, J. G. de Rev Psicoanál 1964, 21:187

KAUFMAN, I. CHARLES

78435 (& Rosenblum, L. A.) Depression in infant monkeys separated from their mothers. Science 1967, 155:1030-1031

78436 (& Rosenblum, L. A.) Effects of separation from mother on the emotional behavior of infant monkeys. Ann NY Acad Sci 1969, 159:681-695

78437 Panel discussion: Symposium on research in infancy and early childhood. J Amer Acad child Psychiat 1962, 1:92-107

78438 (& Rosenblum, L. A.) The reaction to separation in infant monkeys: anaclitic depression and conservation-withdrawal. PSM 1967, 29:648-675

S-50104 Some ethological studies of social relationships and conflict situations. Abs JTM Q 1962, 31:131-132

S-50105 Some theoretical implications from animal behavior studies for the
         psychoanalytic concepts of instinct, drive, and energy.
         Quelques implications théoriques tirées de l'étude du comportement
         des animaux et pouvant faciliter la conception de l'instinct de l'energie
         et de la pulsion. RFPsa 1961, 25:633-649
         Instinkt, Energie und Trieb—einige Folgerungen aus der Verhaltens-
         forschung bei Tieren für die psychoanalytische Theorie. Psyche 1961,
         15:494-507
         Abs JBi Q 1962, 31:117
78439   (& Rosenblum, L. A.) The waning of the mother-infant bond in two
         species of macaque. In Foss, B. M. Determinants of Infant Behavior IV,
         London: Methuen 1969, 41-59

         See Bandler, Bernard

         REVIEW OF:
78440   Hendrick, I. Psychiatry Education Today. Q 1966, 35:444-448

KAUFMAN, IRVING

78441   (& Frank, T.; Friend, J.; Heims, L.; Weiss, R.) Adaptation of treatment
         techniques to a new classification of schizophrenic children. J Amer
         Acad Child Psychiat 1963, 2:460-483
78442   Conversion hysteria in latency. J Amer Acad Child Psychiat 1962,
         1:385-396
78443   Crimes of violence and delinquency in schizophrenic children. J Amer
         Acad Child Psychiat 1962, 1:269-283
78444   The defensive aspects of impulsivity. BMC 1963, 27:24-32
         Abs HD Q 1964, 33:603-604
78445   (& Durkin, H., Jr.; Frank, T.; Heims, L.; Jones, D.; Ryter, Z.; Stone, E.;
         Zilbach, J.) Delineation of two diagnostic groups among juvenile de-
         linquents: the schizophrenic and the impulse-ridden character disorder.
         J Amer Acad Child Psychiat 1963, 2:292-318
78446   Differential methods in treating persons with character disorders. Smith
         Coll Stud soc Wk 1962, 33
78447   (& Peck, A. L.; Tagiuri, C. K.) The family constellation and overt
         incestuous relations between father and daughter. In Bell, N. W. &
         Vogel, E. F. A Modern Introduction to the Family, NY: Free Pr;
         London: Collier-Macmillan 1968, 599-609
78448   Helping people who cannot manage their lives. Children 1966, 13:93-
         98
78449   (& Kelly, F. J.; Maloney, F. H.; Prentice, N. M.; Tessman, L. H.)
         Issues in the implementation of mental health services in correctional
         institutions. (Digest) Ops 1964, 34:251-252
78450   Maximizing the strengths of adults with severe ego defects. Soc
         Casewk 1962, 43
78451   The psychiatrist in the institution. Crime Delinq 1966, 12:17-21
78452   Psychodynamics of protective casework. In Parad, H. J. & Miller, R. R.
         Ego-Oriented Casework, NY: Fam Serv Ass Amer 1963, 191-205
78453   Psychotherapy of children with conduct and acting out disorders. In
         Hammer, M. & Kaplan, A. M. The Practice of Psychotherapy with
         Children, Homewood, Ill: Dorsey 1967

78454 (& Heims, L. W.; Reiser, D. E.) A re-evaluation of the psychodynamics of firesetting. Ops 1961, 31:123-136
Abs JMa RFPsa 1962, 26:324
S-50097 Relationship between therapy of children and superego development.
Abs JTM Q 1961, 30:595-596
78455 Stages in the Treatment of the Juvenile Delinquent. Proceedings of the Third World Congress of Psychiatry. Montreal, Canada: McGill Univ Pr 1962
78456 (& Frank, T.; Friend, J.; Heims, L.; Weiss, R.) Success and failure in the treatment of childhood schizophrenia. P 1962, 118:909-915
S-50100 Superego development and pathology in childhood. (Panel)
Abs JFr An Surv Psa 1958, 9:254-266
78457 (& Frank, T.; Heims, L.; Herrick, J.; Reiser, D. E.; Willer, L.) Treatment implications of a new classification of parents of schizophrenic children. P 1960, 116:920-924
Abs Leavitt, M. Q 1961, 30:455

See Snyder, Benson, R.; Tessman, Lora H.; Zinberg, Norman E.

ABSTRACTS OF:
78458 Feldman, S. S. Alarm-dreams. An Surv Psa 1957, 8:176-177
78459 Flumerfelt, J. M. A problem of technique in the analysis of a transference. An Surv Psa 1957, 8:261-262
78460 Hamburger, W. Legal guilt and the unconscious. An Surv Psa 1957, 8:131-132
78461 Jaffe, D. S. Analysis of a repetitive dream with painful content. An Surv Psa 1957, 8:177-178
78462 Johnson, D. E. The neurotic character of a gentleman. An Surv Psa 1957, 8:115-116
78463 Musta, W. A technical problem of acting out. An Surv Psa 1956, 7:327
78464 Orens, M. H. The shift of object in regression. An Surv Psa 1957, 8:104-105
78465 Waelder, R. Critical discussion of the concept of an instinct of destruction. An Surv Psa 1956, 7:55

KAUFMAN, JOSEPH J.

78466 Organic and psychological factors in the genesis of impotence and premature ejaculation. In Wahl, C. W. *Sexual Problems,* NY: Free Pr 1967, 133-148

KAUFMAN, MELVIN E.

78467 The effects of institutionalization on development of stereotyped and social behaviors in mental defectives. Amer J ment Defic 1967, 71:581-585

KAUFMAN, MOSES RALPH

78468 Brief psychotherapy. Proc IV World Cong Psychiat 1966, 461-462
78469 Discussant: "Physicians in the community." Teach Dyn Psychiat 185-187

78470   (& Heiman, M.) Discussion and summary of "On pituitary anterior lobe insufficiency" by M. Schur and C. V. Medvei. In authors' *Evolution of Psychosomatic Concepts* 198-201

78471   Discussion of da Silva, G. "The loneliness and death of an old man." J geriat Psychiat 1967, 1:28-44

78472   Discussion of Saul, L. J. "Sudden death at impasse." Psa Forum 1966, 1:91

78473   Education for psychiatry. The role of the general hospital in the education and training of the resident in psychiatry. Psychiat Q 1964, 38:329-340

78474   (& Heiman, M.) (Eds) Evolution of Psychosomatic Concepts. Anorexia Nervosa: A Paradigm. NY: IUP 1964; London: Hogarth 1965, xii + 399 p
        Rv Am Im 1965, 22:217. VC Q 1965, 34:451-453

78475   Factors contributing to causes of mental illness and health: the viewpoint of psychiatry and psychoanalysis. J Mount Sinai Hosp 1961, 28:450-460

78476   Functional and organic mental disorders in the elderly. J Mount Sinai Hosp 1965, 32(6)

78477   The Greeks had some words for it. Early Greek concepts on mind and "insanity." Psychiat Q 1966, 40:1-33

78478   Hypnosis in psychotherapy today. Anachronism, fixation, regression or valid modality? Arch gen Psychiat 1961, 4:30-39
        Abs KR Q 1962, 31:296

78479   Incidence of psychiatric conditions in patients of non-psychiatric departments in a general hospital. Med Rec Ann 1966, 59(1)

78480   A network of clinics for out-patients. Hospitals 1964, 38

78481   Obituary: Felix Deutsch 1884-1964. J Am Psa Ass 1964, 12:439-441

78482   The problems of the psychoanalyst as a teacher in general psychiatry. (Read at Boston Psa Soc, 28 Mar 1962) Psychiat Q 1963, 37:340-354
        Abs Stalvey, H. D. Bull Phila Ass Psa 1962, 12:120-122. Engle, B. Q 1964, 33:456

78483   Psychiatric aspects of medical practice. Psychiatry in medicine: sibling or stepchild? Maryland State med J 1961, 10:245-248

78484   (& Lehrman, S.; Franzblau, A. N.; Tabbat, S.; Weinroth, L.; Friedman, S.) Psychiatric findings in admissions to a medical service in a general hospital. J Mount Sinai Hosp 1959, 26:160-170

78485   (Ed) The Psychiatric Unit in a General Hospital. Its Current and Future Role. NY: IUP 1965, xvi + 482 p
        Rv Lehrman, S. R. Q 1967, 36:308-309

78486   The psychiatrist's dilemma. J Mount Sinai Hosp 1967, 34(4)

78487   Psychiatry in medical education. Canad Psychiat Ass J 1968, 13:399-409

78488   (Ed) Psychiatry of the non-psychiatrist. Med Clin N Amer 1967, 51(6)

78489   Psychiatry: why "medical" or "social" model? Arch gen Psychiat 1967, 17:347-360

78490   Psychoanalysis and American psychiatry. Psychiat Q 1969, 43:301-318

78491   The role of psychoanalysis in psychiatric residency training. The Bulletin 1964, 7(4)

78492 The role of the general hospital in community psychiatry. Comprehen Psychiat 1963, 4:426-432

78493 Schilder's application of psychoanalytic psychiatry. The Schilder Memorial Address. Arch gen Psychiat 1962, 7:311-320
   Abs KR Q 1964, 33:140

See Bernstein, Stanley; Brown, Fred; Kleinschmidt, Hans J.; Mannucci, Mannuccio; Safirstein, Samuel L.; Stafford-Clark, David; Stein, Aaron; Waller, John V.; Zucker, H. D.

KAUFMANN, L.

78494 (& Muller, C.) [Family research and therapy in schizophrenics.] (Ger) Nervenarzt 1969, 40:302-308

78495 L'oedipe dans la famille des schizophrènes. [Oedipus in the family of schizophrenics.] RFPsa 1967, 31:1145-1150

78496 Psychotherapie psychoanalytique d'une psychose avec composante épileptique. [Psychoanalytic psychotherapy of a psychosis with an epileptic component.] Psychother Psychosom 1967, 15:339-350

78497 Zum Problem der Katamnesen nach psychotherapeutischen Behandlungen. [The problem of follow-up studies after psychotherapy.] Nervenarzt 1964, 35:436-443

See Müller, Christian

KAUFMANN, WALTER ARNOLD

78498 Freud and the tragic virtues. Amer Scholar 1960, 29:469-481

78499 (Ed) Religion from Tolstoy to Camus. NY: Harper 1961, 450 p

KAUL, R. N.

78500 Freud and Gita. Res J Philos soc Sci 1964, 1:34-40

78501 Freud's contribution to ethical theory. R 1964-65, 51:612-618
   Abs SRS Q 1966, 35:162

KAUNITZ, PAUL E.

78502 (& Tec, L.) Unsuccessful initiation rites among adolescent boys. JNMD 1965, 140:175-179

KAUSCH, DONALD FREDERICK

78503 Manifestation of aggression in children as a function of parent behavior. Diss Abstr 1963, 24:834-835

KAUSEN, RUDOLF

78504 Kompensation, Überkompensation und Fehlkompensation im psychischen Bereich. [Compensation, overcompensation and wrong compensation in the psychic sphere.] Med Klin 1967, 62:1213-1215

78505 "Selbsterhaltungstrieb" und Neurose. ["Instinct of self-preservation" and neurosis.] Z Psychother med Psychol 1961, 11:66-70

KAVANAU, J. L.

78506 Behavior: confinement, adaptation, and compulsory regimes in laboratory studies. Science 1964, 143(3605):490

KAVKA, JEROME

78507 Ego synthesis of a life-threatening illness in childhood. Psa St C 1962, 17:344-362
         Abs SLe RFPsa 1964, 28:814-815
78508 The fractionated dream narratives as transference communication. (Read at Chicago Psa Soc, 23 Jan 1968)
         Abs Beigler, J. S. Bull Phila Ass Psa 1968, 18:205-209
78509 Pregnancy during the Oedipal phase: a female identity crisis. (Read at Chicago Psa Soc, 26 Feb 1963)
         Abs Auth Bull Phila Ass Psa 1964, 14:157-162
78510 The referring physician and psychoanalytic treatment. Chicago Med 1961, 64:7-10
78511 The theme of patricide in a female chess player. (Read at Am Psa Ass, 5 May 1962) Am Im 1963, 20:149-159

         See Sklansky, Morris A.

ABSTRACTS OF:
78512 Bonnard, A. Impediments of speech: a special psychosomatic instance. Bull Phila Ass Psa 1962, 12:174-176
78513 Dewald, P. A. Reactions to the forced termination of analysis. Bull Phila Ass Psa 1964, 14:231-234
78514 Frankl, L. Self preservation and accident proneness in children and adolescents. Bull Phila Ass Psa 1964, 14:162-166
78515 Gitelson, M. et al: Analyzability: a panel discussion. Bull Phila Ass Psa 1963, 13:36-39
78516 Seitz, P. F. D. Representations of structures in the concrete imagery of dreams: a clinical method for investigating the structural theory. Bull Phila Ass Psa 1963, 13:89-94
78517 Sklansky, M. et al: Identity: three short papers. Bull Phila Ass Psa 1964, 14:157-162

KAWAI, HAYAO

         See Boyer, L. Bryce

KAWAI, HIROSHI

78518 [A dynamic psychopathology of borderline cases—psychotherapeutic observations and technical considerations.] (Jap) Abs (Eng) Jap J Psa 1965, 12(1):19-37; 40-41
78519 [The locus of "Little Hans" case: Symposium on "Little Hans" case.] (Jap) Jap J Psa 1969, 15(3):12-14
78520 [Psychoanalytical study of puberty.] (Jap) Jap J Child Psychiat 1969, 10(3):147-150

KAWENOKA, MARIA

         See Sandler, Joseph; Thomas, Ruth

KAWI, ALI A.

78521 On anxiety: relationship between methods of evaluation. Dis nerv Sys 1961, 22:565-568

ABSTRACT OF:
78522 Karon, B. P. & Rosberg, J. The homosexual urges in schizophrenia. An Surv Psa 1958, 9:188-189

KAWIN, MARJORIE R.

78523 Defense choice and identification. Diss Abstr 1966, 27:304-305

KAY, M.

78524 The libido and the NYX. Am Im 1964, 21:37-51

KAY, PAUL

78525 The acting out child. Acting Out 48-67
78526 A boy's wish to give his analyst a gift. J Amer Acad Child Psychiat 1967, 6:38-50
78527 Can physical disease be a way of life? Why Rep 153-166
78528 The phenomenology of schizophrenia in childhood: a review of the literature and clinical material. J Hillside Hosp 1962, 11:206-216
          Abs JA Q 1963, 32:291

See Schneer, Henry I.

ABSTRACT OF:
78529 Orgel, S. On time and timelessness. Q 1962, 31:444-446

KAYE, HARVEY EARLE

78530 (& Berl, S.; Clare, J.; Eleston, M. R.; Gershwin, B. S.; Gershwin, P.; Kogan, L. S.; Torda, C.; Wilbur, C. B.) Homosexuality in women. Arch gen Psychiat 1967, 17:626-634

KAYSER, H.

See Wieser, S.

KAYWIN, LOUIS

78531 Discussion of Walsh, M. N. "A possible cryptomnesic influence in the development of Freud's psychoanalytic thought." Psa Forum 1967, 2: 363-364
S-50143 An epigenetic approach to the psychoanalytic theory of instincts and affects.
          Abs JTM Q 1962, 31:129-130
78532 The evocation of a genie: a study of an "as if" character type. Q 1968, 37:22-41
S-50144 Notes on the concept of self-representation.
          Abs KOS An Surv Psa 1957, 8:85-86
78533 Notes on the psychoanalytic theory of affect. R 1966, 53:275-282
          Abs SRS Q 1967, 36:471. CG RFPsa 1968, 32:369

78534   Orientation and conviction in the psychotherapist. J Hillside Hosp 1961, 10:203-218
        Abs JA Q 1962, 31:585-586
78535   Problems of sublimation. J Am Psa Ass 1966, 14:313-334
        Abs Cuad Psa 1966, 2:121. JLSt Q 1969, 38:336

REVIEWS OF:
78536   Gill, M. M. Topography and Systems in Psychoanalytic Theory. R 1963, 50:688-689
78537   Jones, R. M. Ego Synthesis in Dreams. Q 1963, 32:257-258

KAZAN, AVRAAM T.

78538   (& Browning, T. B.; Cohen, A. D.) Emotional implication of child care practices on pediatric units of general hospitals in Westchester County, survey and recommendations. NYSJM 1965, 65:2568-2573

KAZANJIAN, VARD

78539   (& Stein, S.; Weinberg, W. L.) An Introduction to Mental Health Consultation. U. S. Dept of Health, Education & Welfare 1961, 13 p

KAZIN, ALFRED

78540   The conquistador: or Freud in his letters. In author's *Contemporaries*, Boston: Little, Brown 1962, 377-382
S-50146 The Freudian revolution analyzed.
        Abs AEC An Surv Psa 1956, 7:18
78541   The language of pundits; an American view. Cornhill 1961, 172:153-164. In Rolo, C. J. *Psychiatry in American Life*, Boston: Little, Brown 1963, 193-207. In Manheim, L. & Manheim, E. *Hidden Patterns*, NY: Macmillan 1966, 37-49
78542   Lesson of the master. Reporter 1959, 20(16 Apr):39-41. In author's *Contemporaries*, Boston: Little, Brown 1962, 373-377
78543   Psychoanalysis and literary culture today. In *The Partisan Review Anthology*, Holt 1962, 238-245. In author's *Contemporaries*, Boston: Little, Brown 1962, 362-373. In Ruitenbeek, H. M. *Psychoanalysis and Literature*, NY: Dutton 1964, 3-13
78544   Sigmund Freud, 1856-1956: portrait of a hero. In author's *Contemporaries*, Boston: Little, Brown 1962, 353-362

KAZIWARA, TATUSKAN

REVIEW OF:
78545   Aichhorn, A. Verwahrloste Jugend. (Japanese translation) Jap J Psa 1965, 11(5):29

KEARNEY, J.

See Renneker, Richard E.

KEARNEY, T. R.

78546   Emotionally disturbed adolescents with alcoholic parents. Acta Paedopsychiat, Basel 1969, 36:215-221

KECAKEMETI, PAUL

78547 Punishment as conflict resolution: toward the clarification of the problem of punishment and psychotherapy. Symposium on psychotherapy. Arch crim Psychodyn 1961, 4:700-723

KEEHN, JACK DENNIS

78548 Behaviorism and the unconscious. Acta Psychol 1967, 26:75-78
78549 Experimental studies of "the unconscious": operant conditioning of unconscious eyeblinking. Behav Res Ther 1967, 5:95-102
78550 The Prediction and Control of Behavior. A Shorter Introduction to Psychology. London: Constable 1963, 268 p

KEELY, H.

See Eisenbud, Jule

KEISER, SYLVAN

78551 The adolescent exhibitionist. Adolescents 113-131
78552 Discussion of Sherfey's paper on female sexuality. J Am Psa Ass 1968, 16:449-456
78553 Disturbance of ego functions of speech and abstract thinking. (Read at Psa Ass NY, 20 Mar 1967) J Am Psa Ass 1962, 10:50-73
         Abs Hurwitz, M. H. Q 1961, 30:622-623. Stanton, J. Q 1961, 30: 623-624. JBi Q 1963, 32:130-131. IBa RFPsa 1964, 28:454
S-50157 Disturbances in abstract thinking and body-image formation.
         Abs Solomon, R. G. An Surv Psa 1958, 9:159-160
S-18071 The fear of sexual passivity in the masochist. PT Pervers 158-179
78554 Freud's concept of trauma and a specific ego function. J Am Psa Ass 1967, 15:781-794
78555 (& Console, W. A.) Obituary: Sidney Tarachow, M.D. 1908-1965. J Am Psa Ass 1966, 14:858-859
78556 An observation concerning the somatic manifestations of anxiety. J Hillside Hosp 1961, 10:219-223
         Abs JA Q 1962, 31:586
78557 Psychoanalysis—taught, learned, and experienced. J Am Psa Ass 1969, 17:238-267
78558 Superior intelligence. Its contribution to neurogenesis. J Am Psa Ass 1969, 17:452-473
S-50161 (Reporter) The technique of supervised analysis. (Panel: Am Psa Ass, Dec 1955)
         Abs BEM An Surv Psa 1956, 7:370-372

See Blos, Peter

REVIEWS OF:
78559 Fliess, R. Ego and Body Ego: Contributions to Their Psychoanalytic Psychology. J 1963, 44:242-245
78560 Schilder, P. Contributions to Developmental Neuropsychiatry. Q 1966, 35:146-149

KEISMAN, IRA B.

REVIEWS OF:

78561   Hillman, J. Emotion: A Comprehensive Phenomenology of Theories and
and Their Meanings for Therapy. PPR 1962, 49(4):135-136

78562   Whyte, L. L. The Unconscious Before Freud. R 1964, 51(1):162-163

KEITEL, NORMA B.

See Akutagawa, Donald

KEITH, CHARLES R.

78563   Multiple transfers of psychotherapy patients: a report of problems and
management. Arch gen Psychiat 1966, 14:185-189
Abs PB Q 1969, 38:166-167

78564   Some aspects of transference in dream search. BMC 1962, 26:248-257
Abs HD Q 1964, 33:602

78565   The therapeutic alliance in child psychotherapy. J Amer Acad Child
Psychiat 1968, 7:31-43

78566   (& Stamm, R. A.) The use of the prison code as a defense. BMC 1964,
28:251-259

KELLAM, SHEPPARD G.

78567   (& Schiff, S. K.) Adaptation and mental illness in the first-grade class-
rooms of an urban community. Psychiat Res Rep 1967, (21):79-91

78568   (& Schiff, S. K.) The origins and evolution of an urban community
mental health center in Woodlawn. In Duhl, L. L. R. *Mental Health
and Urban Social Policy*, San Francisco: Jossey-Bass 1968, Ch 6

78569   Science and psychoanalysis. JNMD 1961, 132:449-451

78570   (& Schiff, S. K.; Branch, J. B.) The Woodlawn community-wide mental
health program of assessment, prevention, and early treatment. Proceedings of the Midwest Regional School Social Work Conference, 30 Sept
1968

78571   (& Schiff, S. K.) The Woodlawn Mental Health Center: a community
mental health center model. Soc S R 1966, 40: 255-263

KELLER, ADOLF

78572   Wie Man Angst und Sorgen überwindet; die Angst, das grösste Lebens-
gift. [How Man Overcomes Fear and Anxiety; Fear, the Greatest Poison
of Life.] Gelnhausen: H. Schwab 1966, 118 p

KELLER, MARY JANE

See Haworth, Mary R.

KELLER, W.

78573   Freiheit, Wille und Schuld. [Freedom, will and guilt.] Nervenarzt 1962,
33:97-111

KELLEY, B.

See Janowsky, D. S.

KELLEY, HAROLD O.

See Hovland, Carl I.

KELLNER, ERICH

78574 Freud und Mendelssohn. [Freud and Mendelssohn: prehistory of psychoanalytic thinking.] Bull Leo Baeck Inst 1962, 5:171-178

KELLNER, HAROLD

78575 (& Butters, N.; Wiener, M.) Mechanisms of defense: an alternative response. J Pers 1964, 32:601-621

See Gamble, Kenneth R.

KELLNER, ROBERT

78576 The evidence in favour of psychotherapy. M 1967, 40:341-358
78577 Family Ill Health: An Investigation in General Practice. Springfield, Ill: Thomas 1964, xi + 112 p
78578 (& Sheffield, B. F.) Symptom rating test scores in neurotics and normals. Brit J Psychiat 1967, 113:525-526

KELLY, E. LOWELL

See Dennis, Wayne

KELLY, FRANCIS J.

See Kaufman, Irving; Prentice, Norman M.

KELLY, GEORGE A.

78579 Non-parametric factor analysis of personality theories. J ind Psych 1963, 19:115-147
78580 A Theory of Personality. NY: Norton 1963, 190 p

KELLY, H. T.

78581 The total man: some guidelines in the holistic approach of prosthodontics. J Prosth Dent 1965, 15:360-366

KELLY, J. F.

See Vandenbergh, Richard L.

KELLY, M.

78582 Some medical myths. World med J 1964, 11:205-207

KELLY, WILLIAM E.

78583 Regression of the superego. Bull Phila Ass Psa 1965, 15:224-235
       Abs EFA Q 1967, 36:629. PLe RFPsa 1967, 31:311

REVIEW OF:
78584 Robitcher, J. B. Pursuit of Agreement: Psychiatry and the Law. Bull Phila Ass Psa 1967, 17:33-37

KELMAN, HAROLD

78585 (Ed) Advances in Psychoanalysis. Contributions to Karen Horney's Holistic Approach. NY: Norton 1964, 255 p
       Rv Brody, M. W. Q 1964, 33:586. Levine, J. M. J Am Psa Ass 1967, 15:166-212

78586 Alienation: its historical and therapeutic context. Psa 1961, 21:198-206

78588 (& Weiss, F. A.; Wenkart, A.) The changing image of psychoanalysis. Psa 1966, 26:169-192

78589 Communing and relating. PT 1960, 14:70-96

78590 Communion et la conscience temoin. [Communing as witness consciousness.] In Nacht, S. Roger Godel—de l'Humanisme a l'Humain, Paris: Belles Lettres Ass Guillaume Beidé 1963, 205-225

78591 Creative talent and creative passion as therapy. Psa 1963, 23:133-143

78592 Current approaches to psychoanalysis. In Hoch, P. & Zubin, J. Theoretical Approaches, NY: Grune & Stratton 1960, 63-78

78593 A definition of terms. In Merin, J. H. The Etiology of the Neuroses, Palo Alto: Sci & Behav Books 1966, 141-148

78594 Discussion of Bennis, W. G. "A psychoanalytic inquiry into the two cultures dilemma." Psa Forum 1969, 3:177-179

78595 Discussion of psycho-physiological papers [by N. Kleitman & E. A. Weinstein]. Dreams Contempo Psa 116-127

78596 Discussion of Salzman, L. "Sociopsychological theories in psychoanalysis." Sci Psa 1964, 7:90-92

78597 Discussion of Will, O. A., Jr. "Processes in psychoanalytic education." Sci Psa 1962, 5:100-102

° ° °   Editor of Horney, K. Feminine Psychology.

78598 Existentialism: a phenomenon of the West. Int J soc Psychiat 1960, 5:299-302

78599 Free association. Comprehen Psychiat 1960, 1:273-280

78600 Free associating: its phenomenology and inherent paradoxes. Psa 1962 22:176-200

78601 (& Weiss, F. A.; Tillich, P.; Horney, K.) Human nature can change. In Doniger, S. The Nature of Man, NY: Harper & Brothers 1962, 171-182

78602 (Moderator) Intervention in psychotherapy. Psa 1962, 22:43-83

78603 Introduction. Existentialism and psychiatry: a round table discussion. Psa 1963, 23:20

° ° °   Introduction to Horney, K. Feminine Psychology, NY: Norton 1967, 7-31

78604 "Kairos" and the therapeutic process. J existent Psychiat 1960, 1:233-269

78605 Kairos: the auspicious moment. Psa 1969, 29:59-83

78606 Karen Horney on feminine psychology. Psa 1967, 27:163-183

78607 Kurt Goldstein—and psychoanalysis. PT 1959, 13:698-708

78608 (Ed) New Perspectives in Psychoanalysis: Contributions to Karen Horney's Holistic Approach. NY: Norton 1965, 249 p
       Abs J Am Psa Ass 1966, 14:228. Rv Holt, H. R 1966, 53(1):154-158. Brauer, P. H. Q 1968, 37:291-293

78609 (& Vollmerhausen, J. W.) On Horney's psychoanalytic techniques: developments and perspectives. Psa Tech 379-423

78610 Oriental psychological processes and creativity. Psa 1963, 23:67-84

78611 Our youth: apathy, rebellion and growth. A symposium. Psa 1968, 28:35-36

78612 Perspectives on psychoanalysis. J existent Psychiat 1962, 3:1-26

78613 A phenomenologic approach to dream interpretation. I. Phenomenology —an historical perspective. II. Clinical examples. Discussion. Psa 1965, 25:188-202; 1967, 75-94; 184-187

78614 The Process in Psychoanalysis; a Manual. NY: Am Inst Psa 1963, 159 p

78615 Prognosis in psychotherapy. Psychiat Neurol Neurochir 1960, 63:81-94

78616 Psychoanalysis and existentialism. Mod Con Psa 115-126

78617 Psychoanalysis and the study of etiology: a definition of terms. In Merin, J. H. & Nagler, S. H. *The Etiology of the Neuroses*, Palo Alto, Calif: Sci & Behav Books 1966, 141-148

78618 Psychoanalysis in cosmology. Comprehen Psychiat 1968, 9:581-607

78619 Psychoanalysis: some philosophical and international concerns. Mod Psa 114-122

78620 The psychoanalyst and the welfare state. A round table discussion. Psa 1968, 28:120-128

78621 The psychoanalytic approach to the psychoses. Psa 1966, 26:63-80

78622 Psychotherapy in Scandinavia: an American viewpoint. Int J soc Psychiat 1964, 10:64-72

78623 The role of psychoanalysis in psychiatry, present and future. Bull NY State District Branches, Am Psychiat Ass 1968, 10:5

78624 Techniques in dream interpretation. Psa 1965, 25:3-26

78625 Tension is not stress. Fortschr PSM 1963, 3:21-27

78626 Therapy of esssential hypertension. In Burton, A. *Modern Psychotherapeutic Practice*, Palo Alto, Calif: Sci & Behav Books 1965, 307-335

78627 Toward a definition of mind. In Scher, J. M. *Theories of the Mind*, NY: Free Pr of Glencoe 1962, 243-270

78628 Training analysis: past, present and future. Psa 1963, 23:205-222. Fortschr Psa 1966, 2:152-170

78629 A unitary theory of anxiety. In author's *Advances in Psychoanalysis* 88-132

78630 The use of the analytic couch. In author's *New Perspectives in Psychoanalysis* 160-190

78631 What is technique? Psa 1969, 29:157-169

KELMAN, NORMAN

78632 Man: creator, discoverer, instrument. Psa 1963, 23:175-184

78633 Social and psychoanalytical reflections on the father. In Ruitenbeek, H. M. *Psychoanalysis and Social Science*, NY: Dutton 1962
    Abs Knobel, M. Rev Psicoanál 1967, 24:954-957

KELMAN, NORMAN JOSEPH

78634 Psychoanalysis and morality. Amer Scholar Reader 1960, 351-362

KEMME, MARY L.
See Arthur, Bettie

KEMMI, KAZUO

78635 (& Nozawa, E.) [Some observations in the psychotherapy of a borderline patient—considerations from the viewpoint of ego psychology on
depersonalization.] (Jap) Abs (Eng) Jap J Psa 1969, 15(1):14:20; 27

KEMP, C. GRATTON

78636 Another note on counseling and the nature of man. J counsel Psychol
1961, 8:186-188

KEMPER, KATTRIN A.

78637 L'interprétation per allusion. Ses rapports avec les relations et les perceptions préverbales. [Interpretation by allusion. Its connection with
preverbal relations and perceptions.] RFPsa 1965, 29:85-104
78638 El significado del contacto epidérmico en relacion con el premer objeto.
[The significance of skin contact in relation to the primary object.] Rev
urug Psa 1966, 8:289-302

KEMPER, WERNER WALTER

S-50252 Die "Abstinenzregel" in der Psychoanalyse.
Abs An Surv Psa 1955, 6:333
78639 [Critical comparison of the results of psychiatric and psychoanalytic
therapy.] (Por) Rev bras Med 1966, 23:17-22; 332-336
78640 Die Doppelgesichtigkeit von Tatbeständen. Zur Begutachtung von
Entschädigungs ansprüchen Wegen nationalsozialistischer Verfolgung.
[The double aspect of facts. Toward assessment of compensation for
national socialist persecution.] Psyche 1964, 18:546-562
78641 [Introduction to the following contribution.] (Ger) Z PSM 1969, 15:
204-205
S-50268 The manifold possibilities of therapeutic evaluation of dreams.
Abs GLG An Surv Psa 1958, 9:214-215
78642 [A meeting with E. Kretschmer.] (Por) J bras Psiquiat 1964, 13:53-61
78643 Nuevas contribuciones filogenéticas a la psicología de la mujer. [New
phylogenetic contributions to the psychology of women.] Rev Psicoanál
1964, 21:108-113
Neue Beiträge aus der Phylogenese zur Bio-Psychologie der Frau. Z
PSM 1965, 11:77-82
Abs Vega Q 1965, 34:625. Rv Baranger, M. Rev urug Psa 1964,
6:509-514
78644 Obituary: In memoriam. J. F. Rittmeister zum Gedächtnis. [In memoriam John F. Rittmeister.] Z PSM 1968, 14:147-149
78645 Das Problem der Gleichzeitigkeit von Individual—und Gruppenanalyse.
[The problem of simultaneous individual and group analysis.] Psyche
1964, 18:314-320
S-50276 Über das Prospektive im Traum.
Abs HA An Surv Psa 1956, 7:236-238

78646   Sociedad psicoanalítica de Rio de Janeiro. [The Rio de Janeiro Psychoanalytic Society.] Rev Psicoanál 1961, 18:65-70
78647   Die spezifischen Schwierigkeiten und Möglichkeiten einer Ausbildung
in der psychosomatischen Medizin unter besonderer Berücksichtigung
der Situation in Brasilien. [The specific difficulties and possibilities of
training in psychosomatic medicine, with special reference to the situation in Brazil.] In Deutsch, F. et al: *Advances in Psychosomatic Medicine. IV. Training in Psychosomatic Medicine,* Acta Psychother Psychosom, Basel: S. Karger AG 1964
S-50284 Subjektsufen- und Kategoriale Interpretation des Traumes.
Abs HA An Surv Psa 1957, 8:173-174
78648   Synchrone Verzahnung von Interpretation und Agieren. Zugleich krit-
ischer Beitrag zum Auftreten parapsychologischer Phänomene in der
analytischen Situation. [Synchronous dovetailing of interpretation and
acting-out.] Psyche 1969, 23:862-866
S-50286 Die Übertragung in Lichte der Gegenübertragung.
Abs An Surv Psa 1955, 6:149
78649   Übertragung und Gegenübertragung als funktionale Einheit. [Trans-
ference and countertransference as functional unit.] J Psa 1969, 6:35-68
78650   Zum Problem der Ausbildung von Gruppenpsychotherapeuten. [On
the problem of the development of group psychotherapy.] Z PSM
1964, 10:191-198

KEMPF, EDWARD J.

78651   Abraham Lincoln's Philosophy of Common Sense: An Analytical
Biography of a Great Mind. NY: New York Acad Sci 1965, xxiv +
1443 p

KEMPH, JOHN P.

78652   Communicating with the psychotic child. Int Psychiat Clin 1964, 1:53-
72
78653   (& Cain, A. C.; Finch, S. M.) New directions in the inpatient treatment of psychotic children in a training center. P 1963, 119:934-939
78654   (& Harrison, S. I.; Finch, S. M.) Promoting the development of ego
functions in the middle phase of treatment of psychotic children. J
Amer Acad Child Psychiat 1965, 4:401-412
78655   Psychotherapy with patients receiving kidney transplant. P 1967, 124:
623-629
78656   Renal failure, artificial kidney and kidney transplant. P 1966, 122:
1270-1274
78657   The treatment of psychotic children. Curr psychiat Ther 1964, 4:74-
78

See Yorukoglu, Atalay

KEMPLER, WALTER

78658   Family therapy of the future. Int Psychiat Clin 1969, 6(3):135-138

KEMPSTER, STEPHEN W.

78659 (& Savitsky, E.) Training family therapists through "live" supervision. In Ackerman, N. W. et al: *Expanding Theory and Practice in Family Therapy*, NY: Fam Serv Ass Amer 1967, 125-134

See Ackerman, Nathan W.; Gralnick, Alexander

KENDEL, K.

78660 Zum Übertragungsproblem in der Gruppenpsychotherapie. Ein Traum ohne Kontext. [Contribution to the problem of transference in group psychotherapy. (A dream without a context.)] Prax PT 1967, 12:105-110

KENDLER, HOWARD HARVARD

78661 Basic Psychology. NY: Appleton-Century-Crofts 1963, xiii + 750 p
78662 Motivation and behavior. In *Nebraska Symposium on Motivation* 1965, 1-23

See Dennis, Wayne

KENDRICK, CURTIS

ABSTRACTS OF:
78663 Adatto, C. P. On pouting. An Surv Psa 1957, 8:121
78664 Anthony, J. Symposium on the contribution of current theories to an understanding of child development. Part IV: The system makers: Piaget and Freud. An Surv Psa 1957, 8:185-186
78665 Bergler, E. Fear of heights. An Surv Psa 1957, 8:100-101
78666 Bergler, E. Further contributions to the problem of blushing. An Surv Psa 1957, 8:158-159
78667 Bernstein, I. (Reporter) Panel: indications and goals of child analysis as compared with child psychotherapy. An Surv Psa 1957, 8:227-228
78668 Brody, E. B. Superego, introjected mother, and energy discharge in schizophrenia: contribution from the study of anterior lobotomy. An Surv Psa 1958, 9:189-190
78669 Elkisch, P. The psychological significance of the mirror. An Surv Psa 1957, 8:106-107
78670 Freeman, T. et al: The state of the ego in chronic schizophrenia. An Surv Psa 1957, 8:146
78671 Glover, E. The future of "dynamics" psychology. An Surv Psa 1957, 8:23-24
78672 Grauer, D. How autonomous is the ego? An Surv Psa 1958, 9:114
78673 Heiman, M. The problem of family diagnosis. An Surv Psa 1956, 7:155-156
78674 Hoffman, F. H. & Brody, M. W. The symptom, fear of death. An Surv Psa 1957, 8:101
78675 Kanzer, M. (Reporter) Panel: acting out and its relation to impulse disorders. An Surv Psa 1957, 8:128-140
78676 Kraemer, W. P. Transference and counter-transference. An Surv Psa 1957, 8:265-266

78677 Menninger, K. Theory of Psychoanalytic Technique. An Surv Psa 1958, 9:380-382

78678 Reider, N. Problems in the prediction of marital adjustment. An Surv Psa 1956, 7:155

78679 Rosen, V. H. (Reporter) Panel: preoedipal factors in neurosogenesis. An Surv Psa 1957, 8:27-29

78680 Schmideberg, M. Hypocrisy, detachment and adaptation. An Surv Psa 1957, 8:123-124

78681 Sperling, M. Pavor Nocturnus. An Surv Psa 1958, 9:297-298

78682 Sperling, S. J. The symbolic meaning of the corner. An Surv Psa 1957, 8:110-111

78683 Teplitz, Z. The ego and motility in sleepwalking. An Surv Psa 1958, 9:146

KENDRICK, DONALD CLIVE

78684 Effects of drive and effort on inhibition with reinforcment. M 1960, 51:211-219

KENISTON, KENNETH

78685 Psychological issues in the development of young radicals. Sci Psa 1968, 13:82-97

78686 Social change and youth in America. Youth 161-187

78687 The Uncommitted: Alienated Youth in American Society. NY: Dell Publ 1967, viii + 500 p

KENNA, J. C.

See Sedman, G.

KENNEDY, HANNA ENGEL

See Sandler, Joseph; Thomas, Ruth

KENNEDY, JANET A.

78688 (& Bakst, H.) The influence of emotions on the outcome of cardiac surgery: a predictive study. Bull Ass Psa Med 1966, 6:8-10

KENNEDY, MIRIAM

See Cormier, Bruno M.

KENNEDY, STEPHEN C.

See Eng, Erling

KENNELL, JOHN H.

78689 (& Bergen, M. E.) Early childhood separations. Pediatrics 1966, 37: 291-298

78690 (& Boaz, W. D.) Infancy and early childhood. In Green, M. & Haggerty, R. J. *Ambulatory Pediatrics*, Phila/London/Toronto: Saunders 1968, 334-388

78691   (& Boaz, W. D.) The physician's children as patients. Pediatrics 1962,
        30:100-108

KENNEY, BLAIR G.

78692   Nelly Dean's witchcraft. Lit & Psych 1968, 18:225-232

KENNEY, H. J.

See Bruner, Jerome S.

KENNY, W. F., JR.

78693   The effects of maternal deprivation. McGill med J 1960, 29:141-144

KENT, CAROLYN A.

See Buskirk, Martha

KENT, CARON

78694   Interdependence of psyche and soma in psychotherapeutic processes.
        (Read at Nat Pychol Ass Psa, 23 May 1963) R 1964, 51:438-450
78695   Man's Hidden Resources. On Healing and Maturing of Mind and Body.
        Melbourne, Australia: The Hawthorn Pr, n. d.
            Les ressources cachées de l'homme. RFPsa 1962, 26:87-134; 267-
        295
            Abs Tagliacozzo, R. Riv Psa 1965, 11:78
78696   Roots of violence in modern man. R 1966, 53-555-575

KENT, DONALD P.

78697   Aging within the American social structure. J geriat Psychiat 1968, 2:
        19-32

KENWARD, JOHN F.

78698   Psychiatric consultation in high schools; a panel. Bull Chicago Soc
        Adol Psychiat 1968, 2:20-22

KENWORTHY, MARION E.

78699   The need for constructive planning for children. Bull NY Acad Med
        1960, 36:596-603
78700   Obituary: Albert Deutsch (1905-1961). P 1962, 118:1064-1068
78701   Obituary: Edward Liss, M.D. 1891-1967. Q 1967, 36:589
78702   The prenatal and early postnatal phenomena of consciousness. In Child,
        C. M. The Unconscious, Freeport, NY: Books for Libraries Pr 1966
78703   (Ed) William C. Menninger Memorial Volume. NY: Clarke & Way,
        Inc. 1967

KENYON, ALLAN T.

See Carmichael, Hugh T.

KENYON, MARK

See Lenzner, Abraham S.

KEPECS, JOSEPH G.

78704 Observations on the microdevelopment of certain defenses. (Read at Chicago Psa Soc, 27 Mar 1962)
Abs Miller, A. A. Bull Phila Ass Psa 1962, 12:125-127

S-50299 The oral triad applied to psychosomatic disorders.
Abs SO An Surv Psa 1957, 8:155-156

78705 Psychoanalysis today; a rather lonely island. Arch gen Psychiat 1968, 18:161-167

78706 Theories of transference neurosis. Q 1966, 35:497-521
Teorías sobre la neurosis de transferencia. Rev Psicoanál 1967, 24: 597-622
Abs Cuad Psa 1967, 3:57

78707 (& Robin, M.; Munro, C.) Tickle in atopic dermatitis. Interference with the organization of a patterned response. Arch gen Psychiat 1960, 3:243-251

78708 (& Robin, M.; Munro, C.) Tickle. The organization of a patterned response. Arch gen Psychiat 1961, 5:237-245
Abs KR Q 1962, 31:589

See Rice, Gunther

KEPINSKI, A. I. T.

78709 [Considerations on the psychopathology of anxiety: basic emotional traits.] (Pol) Pol Tyg Lek 1966, 21:366-368

78710 (& Gatarski, J.) [Principal analytical trends in modern psychotherapy.] (Pol) Pol Tyg Lek 1960, 15:605-609

79711 (& Winid, B. F.) Psychotherapy in Poland. Prog PT 1960, 5:207-211

KEPPE, N. R.

78712 [Schools of clinical psychology. Sigmund Freud—psychoanalysis.] (Por) Arqu Cir Clin Exp 1964, 27:198-206

78713 [Schools of clinical psychology. 3. Carl Gustav Jung's analytical psychology.] (Por) Arqu Cir Clin Exp 1964, 27:210-212

KERCKHOFF, ALAN C.

78714 (& Back, K. W.) The June Bug; A Study of Hysterical Contagion. NY: Appleton-Century-Crofts 1968

KERÉKJÁRTÓ, MARGIT VON

78715 [Possibilities and limitations in the application of psychological testing procedures.] (Ger) Verh Dtsch Ges inn Med 1967, 73:36-42

See Jores, Arthur

KÉRI, HEDVIG

S-50310 Ancient games and popular games.
Abs SL An Surv Psa 1958, 9:242-243

KERMAN, JULIE

TRANSLATION OF:
Jeanniere, A. [77745]

KERN, HOWARD M., JR.

78716 (& Chandler, C. A.) The cultivation of community mental hygiene leadership ability as part of a psychiatric resident's training. P 1960, 117:346-347

78717 (& Spiro, H. R.; Kolmer, M. B.) Preparing psychiatric residents for community psychiatry. Hosp Comm Psychiat 1966, 17:360-363

78718 (& Hess, J. B.) Preparing the psychiatrist for leadership in a changing society. Ops 1965, 35:795-798

78719 Training in community psychiatry. Folia psychiat neurol Jap 1963, (Suppl 7): 119-121

KERN, S.

See Selzer, Melvin L.

KERNBERG, OTTO FRIEDMANN

78720 Borderline personality organization. (Read at Am Psa Ass, 17 Dec 1966) J Am Psa Ass 1967, 15:641-685

78721 A contribution to the ego-psychological critique of the Kleinian school. (Read at Pan-Amer Cong Psa, Feb 1969) J 1969, 50:317-333

78722 Discussion of J. D. Sutherland's paper "Object-relations theory and the conceptual model of psychoanalysis." M 1963, 36:121-124

78723 Notes on countertransference. (Read at Am Psa Ass, 7 Dec 1963) J Am Psa Ass 1965, 13:38-56
        Abs CG RFPsa 1968, 32:337. JLSt Q 1968, 37:466-467

78724 Prognostic factors in the psychoanalytic treatment of narcissistic personalities. (Read at Chicago Psa Soc, 24 Oct 1967)
        Abs Beigler, J. S. Bull Phila Ass Psa 1968, 18:143-148

78725 Some effects of social pressures on the psychiatrist as a clinician. BMC 1968, 32:144-159

78726 Structural derivatives of object relationships. (Read at Int Psa Cong, July 1965) J 1966, 47:236-253
        Abs EVN Q 1968, 37:311

78727 Three methods of research on psychoanalytic treatment. (Read at Int Cong Psa, July 1965) Int MH Res Newsletter 1965, 7(4):11-13

78728 The treatment of patients with borderline personality organization. (Read at Am Psa Ass, 6 May 1967) J 1968, 49:600-619

KESLER, D. J.

See Yulis, S.

KESSEL, PAUL

78729 (& McBrearty, J. F.) Values and psychotherapy: a review of the literature. Percept mot Skills 1967, 25:669-690

KESSLER, EVA
TRANSLATION OF:
Jacobson, E. [15661]

KESSLER, JANE W.
78730 Psychopathology of Childhood, Englewood Cliffs, N.J.: Prentice-Hall 1966, ix + 533 p

KESSLER, MORRIS M.
78731 (Contributor to) Anderson, R. S. (Ed) *Neuropsychiatry in World War II*, Washington Office of Surgeon General, Dept of the Army 1966
S-50320 The double manner by which an appendage organ like the penis presents itself sensorially to the ego and its importance in the production of castration anxiety.
Abs AaSt An Surv Psa 1956, 7:104-105
78732 Use of familiar dynamic consideration to explain the schizophrenic process. Dyn Psychiat 1969, 2:40-46. Abs (Ger) 47-49

KESSLER, ROBERT A.
78733 The psychological effects of the judicial robe. Am Im 1962, 19:35-66

KESTEMBERG, EVELYNE
78734 L'anorexie mentale (Table ronde). Approche psychanalytique. [Mental anorexia (round table): psychoanalytic approach.] Rev Méd psychosom 1968, 10:452-460
78735 (& Kestemberg, J.) Contribution à la perspective génétique en psychanalyse. [Contribution to the genetic viewpoint in psychoanalysis.] RFPsa 1966, 30:569-774
78736 Discussion of Diatkine, R. "Aggressivité et fantasmes d'aggression." RFPsa 1966, 30(Spec. No.):121-127
78737 Discussion of Lebovici, S. "Colloque sur les interprétations en thérapeutique psychanalytique." RFPsa 1962, 26:32
78738 L'identité et l'identification chez les adolescents. Problèmes théoriques et techniques. [Identity and identification in adolescents. Problems in theory and techniques.] Psychiat Enfant 1962, 5(2):441-552. (Summary) Perspectives psychiat 1964, (3):725
78739 Problèmes posés par la fin de traitements psychanalytiques dans les névroses de caractère. RFPsa 1966, 30:271-286
Problems regarding the termination of analysis in character neuroses. (Read at Int Psa Cong, July-Aug 1963) J 1964, 45:350-357
Abs EVN Q 1966, 35:463
78740 La psychanalyse des adolescents. [Psychoanalysis of adolescents.] Psychiat Enfant 1960, 3(10):291-309
78741 Psychologie de l'adolescence. [Psychology of adolescence.] Rev Med 1967, 385-391
78742 Puberté et adolescence—6e congrès International de Psychiatrie de l'Enfant. Edinbourg 24-26 Juin 1966. [Puberty and adolescence—Summary of the 6th International Child Psychiatry Congress.] Psychiat Enfant 1967, 10(4):256-273

S-50322 Quelques considérations à propos de la fin du traitement des malades
à structure psychotique.
Abs JLL An Surv Psa 1958, 9:425-427

See Braunschweig, Denise

KESTEMBERG, JEAN

78743 A propos de la relation érotomanique. [On erotomanic relationship.]
RFPsa 1962, 26:533-604
Abs Auth Rev Psicoanál 1963, 20:96. Perrotti, R. Riv Psa 1965,
11:81. Rosenfeld, D. Rev Psicoanál 1964, 21:386
78744 (& Decobert, S.) Approche psychanalytique pour la compréhension de
la dynamique des groupes thérapeutiques. (Variantes dynamiques dans
les groupes dits stables ou instables.) [A psychoanalytical approach
towards understanding the dynamics of group treatment. (Dynamic
variants in the so-called stable and unstable groups.)] RFPsa 1964,
28:393-418
78745 (Round table discussion) En relisant en 1966 "Analyse terminable et
analyse interminable." Colloque de la Société Psychanalytique de Paris
1966. [On rereading in 1966 "Analysis terminable and interminable."]
RFPsa 1968, 32:191-193, 301-317
78746 (& Decobert, S.) Étude differentielle des phénomènes de transfert au
travers de variantes dynamiques dans les groupes dits stables ou instables. [Differential study of transference phenomena through dynamic
variables in so-called stable and unstable groups.] In Moreno, J. L.
et al: The International Handbook of Group Psychotherapy, NY: Philos
Libr 1966, 274-278
78747 Notes sur le traitement par le psychodrame analytique des malades
psychotique hospitalisés. [Notes on the treatment by analytic psychodrama of hospitalized psychotic patients.] RFPsa 1968, 32:555-567
78748 (& Decobert, S.) Qu'est-ce que le psychodrame analytique? [What is
the psychoanalytical psychodrama?] Gaz med Fran 1966, 73:3091-3101
78749 (& Decobert, S). Le psychodrame analytique. [Psychoanalytic psychodrama.] Inform psychiat 1964, 40:231-252

See Kestemberg, Evelyne

REVIEWS OF:
78750 Garma, A. Les Maux de Tête. RFPsa 1964, 28:441-442
78751 Koehler, W. Dynamische Zusammenhänge in der Psychologie. RFPsa
1963, 27:326
78752 Saada, D. L'Heritage de Freud. RFPsa 1968, 32:151

KESTENBAUM, CLARICE J.

78753 (& Horowitz, W. A.; Jarvik, L.; Person, E.) Identical twin—"idiot sa-
vants." Calendar calculators. P 1965, 121:1075-1079

KESTENBERG, JUDITH S.

78754 Acting out in the analysis of children and adults. (Read at Int Psa
Cong, July 1967) J 1968, 49:341-346

78755 Childhood and adult pathology. J Hillside Hosp 1968, 17:186-199
78756 Discussion of Sanford, B. "Cinderella." Psa Forum 1967, 2:138-139
78757 Discussion of Sherfey's paper on female sexuality. J Am Psa Ass 1968, 16:417-423
78758 Menarche. Adolescents 19-50
S-50324 On the development of maternal feelings in early childhood. Observations and reflexions.
    Abs SGo An Surv Psa 1956, 7:103-104
78759 Outside and inside, male and female. J Am Psa Ass 1968, 16:457-520
78760 Phases of adolescence with suggestions for a correlation of psychic and hormonal organizations. I. Antecedents of adolescent organizations in childhood. II. Prepuberty diffusion and reintegrations. III. Puberty growth, differentiation and consolidation. J Amer Acad Child Psychiat 1967, 6:426-463; 577-614; 1968, 7:108-151
78761 Problems of technique of child analysis in relation to the various developmental stages: prelatency. (Read at Am Ass Child Analysis, 1969) Psa St C 1969, 24:358-383
78762 Rhythm and organization in obsessive-compulsive development (Read at Int Psa Cong, July 1965) J 1966, 47:151-159
    Rythme et organization dans le développement obsessionel compulsif. RFPsa 1967, 31:573-588
    Ritmo e organizzazione nello sviluppo ossessivo-coatto. Psiche 1965, 2(4):201-222
    Abs Cuad Psa 1967, 3:161-162. EVN Q 1968, 37:309
78763 The role of movement patterns in development. I. Rhythms of movement. II. Flow of tension and effort. III. The control of shape. Q 1965, 34:1-36; 517-563; 1967, 36:356-409
    Abs LDr RFPsa 1966, 30(Spec. No.):325. Cuad Psa 1967, 3:319-321
S-50327 Vicissitudes of female sexuality.
    Abs CFH An Surv Psa 1956, 7:100-103

REVIEWS OF:
78764 Bosselman, B. C. et al: Introduction to Developmental Psychiatry. Q 1966, 35:292-294
78765 Brackbill, Y. (Ed) Infancy and Early Childhood. Q 1969, 38:647-650
78766 Freud, A. Normality and Pathology in Childhood. Assessments of Development. Q 1967, 36:98-100

KETTNER, MELVIN G.

78767 Patterns of masculine identity. In Wheelwright, J. B. *The Reality of the Psyche: Proceedings of the 3rd International Congress of Analytical Psychology*, NY: Putnam 1968, 165-178

KETY, SEYMOUR S.

78768 (& Evarts, E. V.; Williams, H. L.) (Eds) Sleep and Altered States of Consciousness. Baltimore: Williams & Wilkins 1967, xii + 591 p

See Appel, Kenneth E.; Rosenthal, David; Wender, Paul H.

KEW, CLIFTON E.

78769 Counter-transference and the group therapist. Pastoral Counselor 1963, 1:9-18
78770 The nature, etiology and treatment of stuttering. Pastoral Counselor 1966, 4:28-36
78771 (& Kew, C. J.) Writing was an aid in pastoral counseling and psychotherapy. Pastoral Psychol 1963, 14:37-43

See Aull, Gertrude J.

KEW, CLINTON J.

See Kew, Clifton E.

KHALETSKII, A. M.

78772 Freudianism, microsociology, and existentialism. Soviet R 1965-66, 6(Winter):35-43
       Russian: Zh Nevropat Psikhiat Korsakov 1965, 65:624-630

KHAN, A. U.

78773 (& Zarsadias, R.) Effects of hypnosis on the psychiatric interview. Dis nerv Sys 1966, 27:665-669
78774 A therapeutic technique based on the interpersonal theory of psychiatry and the family dynamics. Psychother Psychosom 1969, 17:226-240

KHAN, M. MASUD R.

S-50339 Clinical aspects of the schizoid personality: affects and techniques.
       Aspects cliniques de la personalité schizoide: affects et technique. RFPsa 1961, 25:825-839
       Abs JBi Q 1962, 31:119-120
78775 Comment on Dr. Naiman's paper, "The role of the superego in certain forms of acting out." (Read at Int Psa Cong, July 1965) J 1966, 47:293-294
78776 The concept of cumulative trauma. (Read at Hampstead Child-Therapy Clinic, 6 Jan 1963; at Inst of Psa, London, 6 Feb 1963; at Topeka Psa Soc, 12 Apr 1963) Psa St C 1963, 18:286-306
78777 Discussion of Greenacre, P. & Winnicott, D. W. "The theory of the parent-infant relationship. Further remarks." Contributions to discussion (xii). J 1962, 43:253-254
78778 Dream psychology and the evolution of the psycho-analytic situation. (Read at Int Psa Cong, Aug 1961) J 1962, 43:21-31
       La psychologie du rêve et l'évolution de la situation psychanalytique. RFPsa 1964, 28:113-132
       Abs FTL Q 1963, 32:283. PCR RFPsa 1964, 28:307
78779 Ego distortion, cumulative trauma, and the role of reconstruction in the analytic situation. (Read at Int Psa Cong, July-Aug 1963) J 1964, 45:272-279
       Abs EVN Q 1966, 35:460

78780   Ego ideal, excitement and the threat of annihilation. (Read at Psa Ass NY, 15 Apr 1963) J Hillside Hosp 1963, 12:195-217
        Abs SO Q 1964, 33:317-320. JA Q 1967, 36:136-137

78781   Foreskin fetishism and its relation to ego pathology in a male homosexual. (Read at Phila Ass Psa, 15 Apr 1964; at Los Angeles Psa Soc, 1964; at Brit Psa Soc, 20 Jan 1965) J 1965, 46:64-80
        Abs Freedman, A. Bull Phila Ass Psa 1965, 15:50-53. EVN Q 1967, 36:314

78782   The function of intimacy and acting out in perversions. In Slovenko, R. *Sexual Behavior and the Law*, Springfield, Ill: Thomas 1965, 397-412

78783   (& Sutherland, J. D.) Introduction to Rycroft, C. *Imagination and Reality*, London: Hogarth; NY: IUP 1968

78784   Notes additionelles. [Additional notes.] Bull Ass psa Fran 1969, (5): 103-106

78785   On symbiotic omnipotence. (Read at Am Psa Ass, 1965) Psa Forum 1969, 3:137-147; 157-158

78786   On the clinical provisions of frustrations, recognitions, and failures in the analytic situation; an essay on Dr. Michael Balint's researches on the theory of psychoanalytic technique. (Read at Brit Psa Soc, 6 Nov 1968) J 1969, 50:237-248

S-50340 Regression and integration in the analytic setting.
        Abs Bianchedi, E. T. de Rev Psicoanál 1961, 18:178

78787   Reparation to the self as an idolised internal object: a contribution to the theory of perversion formation. Dyn Psychiat 1968, 1(2):92-98.
        Abs (Ger) 97-98

78788   The role of infantile sexuality and early object relations in female homosexuality. In Rosen, I. *The Pathology and Treatment of Sexual Deviation*, London: Oxford Univ Pr 1964, 221-292

78789   Role of phobic and counterphobic mechanisms and separation anxiety in schizoid character formation. (Read at Int Psa Cong, July 1965) J 1966, 47:306-313
        Abs EVN Q 1968, 37:312-313

78790   The role of polymorph-perverse body-experiences and object-relations in ego-integration. M 1962, 35:245-261
        Abs Greenberg, R. M. Q 1963, 32:456-457. JCS RFPsa 1964, 28: 312-313

78791   Role of the "collated internal object" in perversion-formations. J 1969, 50:555-565

78792   Silence as communications. BMC 1963, 27:300-313

78793   Vicissitudes of being, knowing and experiencing in the therapeutic situation. M 1969, 42:383-393
        Les vicissitudes de l'être, du connaître et de l'éprouver dans la situation analytique. Bull Ass psa Fran 1969 (5):132-144

REVIEWS OF:

78794   Lacan, J. Écrits. (Le Champ Freudien—Collection Dirigée par Jacques Lacan) J 1967, 48:611

78795   Levitt, M. (Ed) Readings in Psychoanalytic Psychology. J 1961, 42:292

78796   Stein, M. R. et al (Eds) Identity and Anxiety. Survival of the Person in Mass Society. J 1961, 42:292

KHAN, TASWIR A.

78797 Continuous association and the attitude type. J Psychol 1966, 3:34-42

KHANTZIAN, EDWARD J.

78798 On hatred, violence and assassinations: a clinician's view. Psychiat
Opin 1968, 5(5):32-35
78799 (& Dalsimer, J. S.; Semrad, E. V.) The use of interpretation in the
psychotherapy of schizophrenia. PT 1969, 23:182-197

KHLENTZOS, M. T.

78800 (& Pagliaro, M. A.) Observations from psychotherapy with unwed
mothers. Ops 1965, 35:779-786
Abs JMa RFPsa 1967, 31:188

KIĆOVIĆ, P.

78801 [Uterine bleeding of psychogenic origin.] (Bulg) Srpski Arkh Tselop
Lek 1966, 94:15-20

KIDD, ALINE H.

78802 (& Rivoire, J. L.) (Eds) Perceptual Development in Children. NY:
IUP 1966, xix + 548 p
Abs J Am Psa Ass 1967, 15:733. Rv Fries, M. E. Q 1968, 37:139-140
78803 (& Beere, D. B.) Relationship between kinaesthetic figural aftereffect
and certain personality variables. Percept mot Skills 1968, 26:577-578

KIDSON, MARY C.

See Soddy, Kenneth

KIELHOLZ, PAUL

78804 Diagnose und Therapie der Depression für den Praktiker. [Diagnosis
and Therapy of Depression for the Practitioner.] Munich: J. F. Lehmann 1966, 140 p
78805 (& Beck, D.) Diagnosis, automatic tests, treatment and prognosis of
exhaustion depressions. Comprehen Psychiat 1962, 3:8-14
78806 Diagnostik und Therapie der sogenannten klimakterischen Depressionen. [Diagnosis and treatment of so-called climacteric depressions.]
Geburtsch U Frauenheilk 1960, 20:614-618

KIELL, NORMAN

78807 (Ed) Psychoanalysis, Psychology and Literature: A Bibliography. Madison, Wisconsin: Univ Wisconsin Pr 1963, 225 p
Abs J Am Psa Ass 1964, 12:260. Rv JCS RFPsa 1964, 28:310
78808 The Universal Experience of Adolescence. London: Bailey Bros; NY:
IUP 1964, 942 p
Abs J Am Psa Ass 1966, 14:623. Rv Strean, H. S. R 1964, 51:679-
681. PB Q 1965, 34:296-298

KIENER, HÉLÈNE

78809 Le Problème Religieux dans l'Oeuvre de C. G. Jung. [The Problem of Religion in the Work of C. G. Jung.] Fontainebleau: Association Ferrière 1968, 58 p

KIENZLE, RICHARD

78810 Symbolbildung als schopferischer Prozess. [Symbol formation as a creative process.] Psychologische Beitrage 1969, 11(2):182-190

KIERMAN, THOMAS

See Roback, Abraham A.

KIERNAN, IRENE R.

78811 The clinician as a college teacher. Personn Guid J 1964, 42:970-976
78812 Mental health in children. The Harvest 1960, 4:5-9
78813 Psychiatric evaluation and reporting in admissions. J Ass Coll Admission Counselors 1968, 13:16-17, 25
78814 (& Porter, M. E.) A study of behavior-disorder correlations between parents and children. Ops 1963, 33:539-541

KIESLER, CHARLES A.

78815 (& Singer, R. D.) The effects of similarity and guilt on the projection of hostility. Clin Psych 1963, 19:157-162

KIESLER, DONALD J.

See Rogers, Carl R.

KIESLER, FRANK

78816 Factors in professional staff morale. Out-Patient Schiz 187-194

KIETZMAN, MITCHELL L.

See Zubin, Joseph

KIEV, ARI

78817 Beliefs and delusions of West Indian immigrants to London. Brit J Psychiat 1963, 109:356-363
78818 Curanderismo, Mexican-American Folk Psychiatry. NY: Free Pr 1968, 207 p
       Abs J Am Psa Ass 1969, 17:275-276. Rv Boyer, L. B. Q 1969, 38: 329-332. Ehrenwald, J. Am Im 1969, 26:84-85. Marshall, S. Contempo Psa 1969, 5(2):188-190
78819 Impressions on English psychiatric training—with special reference to postgraduate training. Comprehen Psychiat 1964, 5:67-73
78820 (Ed) Magic, Faith, and Healing: Studies in Primitive Psychiatry Today. (Foreword: Frank, J. D.) Glencoe, Ill: Free Pr; London: Collier-Macmillan 1964, xvii + 475 p
       Rv Boyer, L. B. Q 1965, 34:606-610

78821   Patterns of social performance. Int J Psychiat 1967, 3:239-240
78822   Primitive religious rites and behavior: clinical considerations. Int Psychiat Clin 1969, 5(4):119-131
78823   (Ed) Psychiatry in the Communist World. NY: Science House 1968, x + 276 p
78824   Ritual goat sacrifice in Haiti. Am Im 1962, 19:349-359
78825   Some background factors in recent English psychiatric progress. P 1963, 119:851-856
78826   The study of folk psychiatry. Int J Psychiat 1965, 1:524-549
78827   The theory and practice of psychiatry in Haitian voodoo. Proc 3rd Int Cong Psychiat, Montreal, June 1961

See Gruenberg, Ernest M.; Pollack, Irwin W.

KIKUCHI, M.

See Okonogi, Keigo

KILIAN, HANS

S-50384 Psychoanalyse und Anthropologie.
Abs HK An Surv Psa 1956, 7:391-392

KILLINS, ELIZABETH

See McDermott, John F., Jr.

KILMAN, GILBERT

See Wolfenstein, Martha

KIMELDORF, CAROL

78828   (& Geiwitz, P. J.) Smoking and the Blacky orality factors. J proj Tech 1966, 30:166-168

KIMURA, B.

78829   [Guilt experience and climate (FUHDO).] (Ger) Nervenarzt 1966, 37:394-400
78830   (& Saka, K.; Yamamura, O.) [On a familial denial syndrome.] (Jap) Psychiat Neurol jap 1968, 70:1085-1109
78831   [Phenomenology of the guilt complex from a comparative psychiatric viewpoint.] (Ger) Bibl Psychiat Neurol 1967, 133:54-65
78832   Zur Phänomenologie der Depersonalisation. [On the phenomenology of depersonalisation.] Nervenarzt 1963, 34:391-397

KIND, HANS

78833   Prognosis. In Bellak, L. & Loeb, L. The Schizophrenic Syndrome, NY/London: Grune & Stratton 1969, 714-734
78834   The psychogenesis of schizophrenia. A review of the literature. Int J Psychiat 1967, 3:383-403

78835 Welche Fakten stützen heute eine psychogenetische Theorie der Schizophrenie? Eine kritische Übersucht über die Literatur der Letzten 30
Jahre. [What facts today corroborate a psychogenetic theory of schizophrenia? A critical survey of the literature of the last 30 years.] Psyche
1965, 19:188-218

See Benedetti, Gaetano; Ernst, Klaus

KINDER, M. I.

See Goldstein, Michael J.

KING, C. DALY

78836 The States of Human Consciousness. (Foreword: Finch, R.) New
Hyde Park, NY: Univ Books 1963, xiii + 176 p
Rv MK Q 1964, 33:597

KING, CHARLES H.

See Minuchin, Salvador; Scheidlinger, Saul

KING, DOROTHY C.

See King, Francis W.

KING, FRANCIS W.

78837 (& King, D. C.) Projective assessment of the female's sexual identification, with special reference to the Blacky Pictures. J proj Tech pers
Assess 1964, 28:293-299

KING, GERALD F.

78838 (& Schiller, M.) Ego strength and type of defensive behavior. J consult
Psychol 1960, 24:215-217
78839 (& Armitage, S. G.; Tilton, J. R.) A therapeutic approach to schizophrenics of extreme pathology: an operant-interpersonal method. ASP
1960, 61:276-286. In Goldstein, A. P. & Dean, S. J. *The Investigation
of Psychotherapy*, NY: Wiley 1966, 179-190

KING, H. E.

78840 Some explorations in psychomotility. Psychiat Res Rep 1961, No. 14:
62-90

KING, J. M.

78841 Denial. Amer J Nurs 1966, 66:1010-1013
78842 A nurse's communication patterns and a patient's use of denial. Nurs
Res 1967, 16:137-140

KING, LUCY JANE

See O'Neal, Patricia

KING, PEARL

78843 Alienation and the individual. Brit J soc clin Psychol 1968, 7:81-92
78844 The curative factors in psycho-analysis. Symposium. Contributions to discussion (iii) J 1962, 43:225-227
           Abs RLG Q 1963, 32:598-599
78845 Discussion of Gitelson, M. "La première phase de la psychanalyse." RFPsa 1963, 27:461-467

KING, PETER D.

78846 Controlled study of group psychotherapy in schizophrenics receiving chlorpromazine. Psychiat Dig 1963, 24:21-26
78847 Nature and nurture. Science 1961, 133:1642-1643
78848 The Principle of Truth. NY: Philos Libr 1960, 110 p
78849 Schizophrenic reactions. Med Trial Tech Q 1967, 14(1):63-70; (2): 51-59
78850 (& Ekstein, R.) The search for ego controls: progression of play activity in psychotherapy with a schizophrenic child. (Read at Am Psa Ass, Dec 1962) R 1967, 54:639-648
           Abs SRS Q 1969, 38:163
78851 Short-term psychiatric treatment. (Letter) JAMA 1967, 202:172-173
78852 Theoretical considerations of psychotherapy with a schizophrenic child. J Amer Acad Child Psychiat 1964, 3:638-649

See Ekstein, Rudolf

KINGSLEY, LEONARD

78853 Process analysis of a leaderless countertransference group. Psychol Rep 1967, 20:555-562

KINGSTON, A. J.

See White, William F.

KINROSS-WRIGHT, JOHN

See Knight, James A.

KINZIE, WAYNE

78854 (& Zimmer, H.) On the measurement of hostility, aggression anxiety, projection and dependency. J proj Tech 1968, 32:388-391

KIPMAN, D.

See Haim, A.

KIRBY, JOYCE

78855 A psychoanalytic clinic reaches out to the community. Comm ment Hlth J 1967, 3:245-249

KIRK, WILLIAM E.

See Kahn, Marvin W.

KIRKENDALL, LESTER A.

78856 (& Rubin, I.) Sexuality and the Life Cycle. NY: Sex Information & Education Council of the U.S., Inc. (SIECUS) 1968, 32 p

KIRSCH, JAMES

78857 Affinities between Zen and analytic psychology. Psychologia 1960, 3:85-91
78858 Shakespeare's Royal Self. (Foreword: Adler, G.) NY: G. P. Putnam's Sons 1966, xix + 422 p
Rv HS Am Im 1966, 23:283

KIRSCH, THOMAS B.

78859 The relationship of the REM state to analytical psychology. P 1968, 124:1459-1463

KIRSCHBAUM, ROBERTA A.

See Jensen, Joseph S.

KIRSCHENBAUM, MARTIN

See Blinder, Martin G.

KIRSCHNER, DAVID

78860 The death of a president: reactions of psychoanalytic patients. Behav Sci 1965, 10:1-6
78861 Some reactions of patients in psychotherapy to the death of the president. R 1964, 51:665-669

KIRSTE, H.

78862 [The 4 faces of Eros in antiquity. A contribution to ancient psychology.] (Ger) Ann Inst Pasteur 1966, 111:2241-2243

KISHIDA, SHU

78863 A psychoanalytic theory of child development. J child Develpm 1967, 3:21-30

KISHIMOTO, K.

78864 A preliminary theory about psychotherapy based on Oriental thought. Acta psychother psychosom 1962, 10:428-438

KISHNER, IRA A.

78865 (& Muensterberger, W.) Hazards of culture clash: a report on the history and dynamics of a psychotic episode in a West-African exchange student. Psa St Soc 1967, 4:99-123
Interkultureller Konflikt und Psychose: Ein Bericht über die Vorgeschichte und Dynamik einer psychotischen Episode bei einem westafrikanischen Austauschstudenten. Z Psa 1968, 22:247-270

78866   (& Gross, M. M.; Sirota, M.) Sleep disturbances and hallucinations in
        the acute alcoholic psychoses. JNMD 1966, 142:493-514

See Muensterberger, Warner

KISIELEWSKI, J.
See Shore, Milton F.

KISKER, GEORGE W.
78867   The Disorganized Personality. NY: McGraw-Hill 1964, 631 p

KISKER, K. P.
78868   Sprache und Situation eines Schizophrenen. [Speech and situation of a
        schizophrenic.] In Kranz, H. *Psychopathologie Heute,* Stuttgart: Georg
        Thieme 1962, 123-138

KISLEY, ANTHONY J.
See Finzer, William F.

KISSEL, P.
78869   (& Barrucand, D.) L'hypnose selon Pierre Janet: décadence et actualité.
        [Hypnosis according to Pierre Janet: decline and present state.] Ann
        méd-psychol 1967, 125(1):505-520
78870   (& Barrucand, D.) Le sommeil hypnotique, d'après l' "École de Nancy"
        (A. Liébeault, 1823-1904; H. Bernheim, 1837-1919). [Hypnotic sleep
        according to the "School of Nancy" (A. Liébeault, 1823-1904; H. Bern-
        heim, 1837-1919).] Encéph 1964, 53:572-588

KISSEL, STANLEY
78871   Anxiety, affiliation and juvenile delinquency. Clin Psych 1967, 23:173-
        175
78872   The "paradoxical" response of schizophrenics to sensory deprivation:
        a psychoanalytic interpretation. Psychol Rec 1965, 15:245-248
78873   The positive spiral in parent-child relationships. MH 1967, 51:21-23

KISSEN, DAVID MORRIS
78874   (& LeShan, L. L.) (Eds) Psychosomatic Aspects of Neoplastic Disease.
        (Proc of 3rd Int Conf of International Psychosomatic Cancer Study
        Group, 22-26 July 1963) London: Pitman Med Publ; Phila/Montreal:
        Lippincott 1964, xii + 231 p

See Freeman, Thomas

KISSEN, M.
See Voth, Harold M.

KISSIN, BENJAMIN
78875   (& Gross, M. M.) Drug therapy in alcoholism. P 1968, 125:31-41

KISSINGER, R. D.

See Toler, Alexander

KITADA, JONOSUKE

78876 [Psychotherapy and family dynamics of a hebephrenic—a trial to estab-
lish the relationship between case study and all around family study.]
(Jap) Abstr (Eng) (Read at Jap Psa Ass, Oct 1965) Jap J Psa 1967,
13(5):2-8; 26-27

78877 [Psychotherapy of hebephrenics and family dynamics (No. 3)—on the
omnipotent image projected to the therapist and its vicissitude.] (Jap)
Abstr (Eng) Jap J Psa 1969, 15(1):1-9; 25

KITAMI, YOSHIO

78878 [A consideration on ego ideal-super ego conflict in mid-adolescence
—parent-child relationship in school maladjustment.] (Jap) Jap J Psa
1964, 11(1):18-21

78879 [The defense mechanism against separation anxiety and the process of
their resolution in a mid-adolescent case.] (Jap) Jap J Psa 1966, 12(3):
27-30

78880 (& Takeda, M.; Suzuki, T.; Sato, N.) [Family traits of manic-depres-
sives—especially on their parents' patterns.] (Jap) Jap J Psa 1967,
13(3):20-26

78881 (& Shimoda, S.; Shinozaki, T.) [Group Psychoanalysis.] (Jap) Tokyo:
Seishin Shobo Publ Co 1963, 303 p

78882 [On the variation of dreams with the process of psychoanalytic treatment.] (Jap) Jap J Psa 1960, 7(3):71-76

78883 [Psychoanalysis and education—a chronological study based on
works of four psychoanalysts.] (Jap) Jap J Psa 1962, 9(1):5-9

78884 (& Sato, N.) [Psychoanalysis in Everyday Life.] (Jap) Tokyo: Seishin
Shobo Publ Co 1964, 294 p

78885 (& Takeda, M.; Okonogi, K.; Suzuki, T.; Iwasaki, T.; Sato, N.; Tsuji, S.;
Katayama, T.) [Some therapeutic problems in a psychoanalytically
oriented private hospital (Part II & III).] (Jap) Jap J Psa 1967, 13(6):
1-9

See Takeda, Makoto

KITAY, PHILIP M.

78886 Symposium on "reinterpretations of the Schreber case: Freud's theory
of paranoia." Introduction. A note on Dr. Niederland's paper; summary.
J 1963, 44:191-194; 207; 222-223
Italian: Riv Psa 1965, 11:183-184
Abs EVN Q 1965, 34:615; 616-617

KITCHENER, HOWARD

78887 (& Sweet, B.; Citrin, E.) Problems in the treatment of impulse disorder
in children in a residential setting. Ps 1961, 24:347-356

KITS VAN HEIJNINGEN, H.

78888 Psychodynamic factors in acute myocardial infarction. J 1966, 47:370-
374

78889 Some notes on the psychiatric aspects of patients with coronary occlu-
sion. Adv Psm Med 294-298

KLAF, FRANKLIN S.

78890 Evidence of paranoid ideation in overt homosexuals. J soc Ther 1961,
7:48-51

78891 Female homosexuality and paranoid schizophrenia. A survey of seventy-
five cases and controls. Arch gen Psychiat 1961, 4:84-86

78892 (& Davis, C. A.) Homosexuality and paranoid schizophrenia: a survey
of 150 cases and controls. P 1960, 116:1070-1075
Abs Leavitt, M. Q 1961, 30:456. Loeb, L. Q 1961, 30:146

78893 The power of the group leader: a contribution to the understanding of
group psychology. PPR 1961, 48(2):41-51

78894 (& Pisetsky, J. E.) A son is rendered impotent by his father. Psychiat
Q 1962, 36:519-529

KLAGES, I.

See Klages, W.

KLAGES, W.

78895 (& Czernik, A.) [Identification experiences and their preconditions.]
(Ger) Psychiat Clin, Basel 1968, 1:129-142

78896 (& Klages, I.) [Isolation and development.] (Ger) Intern Prax 1965,
5:455-457

KLAGSBRUN, FRANCINE

78897 Sigmund Freud. NY: Franklin Watts 1967, ix + 150 p
Abs J Am Psa Ass 1967, 15:732

KLAIN, E.

78898 [The psychiatrist in the manifest dreams of his patients.] (Cro) Neuro-
psihijatrija 1969, 17:1-13

See Cividini, E.

KLAJN, V.

78899 (& Jerotic, V.; Bogicevic, D.) [Current medical and social aspects of
impotence.] (Serb) Med Glas 1966, 20:373-379

KLAPAHOUK, F.

See Amado-Haguenauer, G.

KLAPAHOUK, M. F.

78900   Le rêve de Franz Schubert: des relations entre le rêve et la création artistique: la fonction esthétique du moi. [The dream of Franz Schubert: relations between the dreams and artistic creativity: the esthetic function of the ego.] Encéph 1968, 57:51-97; 143-180

KLAPMAN, H. J.

See Harrison, Saul I.

KLAPMAN, JACOB W.

S-50412 Group Psychotherapy—Theory and Practice. (2nd ed)
        Abs J 1964, 45:609

KLARE, V.

78901   Rehabilitation und Poliomyelitis. [Rehabilitation and poliomyelitis.] In Hoff, H. *Therapeutische Fortschritte in der Neurologie und Psychiatrie,* Vienna: Verlag Urban & Schwarzenberg 1960, 166-199

KLATSKIN, ETHELYN H.

See Lewis, Melvin

KLAUBER, JOHN

78902   An attempt to differentiate a typical form of transference in neurotic depression. A description of three stages. (Read at Brit Psa Soc, at Toronto Group of the Canadian Soc; at Chicago, Los Angeles, San Francisco, & Mexican Societies) J 1966, 47:539-545
        Drei Typische Stadien der Übertragung in der Analyse neurotischer Depressionen. Jb Psa 1967, 4:202-216
        Abs Shane, M. Bull Phila Ass Psa 1967, 17:58-60. EVN Q 1968, 37:465
78903   History-taking in the light of knowledge of unconscious mental processes. Lancet 1961, July 22
78904   On the dual use of historical and scientific method in psychoanalysis. J 1968, 49:80-88
        Über die Verwendung Geisteswissenschaftlicher und Naturwissenschaftlicher Methoden in der Psychoanalyse. Psyche 1968, 22
78905   On the significance of reporting dreams in psycho-analysis. (Read at Brit Psa Soc; at Chicago Inst of Psa; at NY Psa Soc) J 1967, 48:424-432
        Über die Bedeutung des Berichtens von Traümen in der Psychoanalyse. Psyche 1969, 23:280-294
        Abs LHR Q 1969, 38:506
78906   The present status of Freud's views on religion. Synagogue Rev 1960, 34(9 May)
        Freuds Ansichten zur Religion aus der heutigen Sicht. Psyche 1962, 16:50-57

78907   Der Psychiater in der internistischen Abteilung. Ein Versuch, anhand
        von Erstinterview psychodynamische Prinzipen darzustellen. [The psy-
        chiatrist in the department of internal medicine. An attempt to demon-
        strate psychodynamic principles on the basis of first interviews.] Psyche
        1961, 15:363-381
78908   Psycho-analysis in human history. Middx Hosp J 1962, 63
78909   Der Psychoanalytiker als Person. Psyche 1967, 21:745-757
        The psychoanalyst as a person. M 1968, 41:315-322
78910   Psychoanalytische Beiträge zur psychosomatischen Medizin mit Be-
        sonderer Berücksichtigung der Konversionstheorie. [Psychoanalytical
        contributions to psychosomatic medicine with special reference to the
        conversion theory.] Psyche 1966, 20:294-304
78911   (Reporter) Report of discussions of acting out—English language sec-
        tion I. [Symposium: Acting out.] J 1968, 49:224-225
        Abs LHR Q 1969, 38:668
78912   Die Struktur der psychoanalytischen Sitzung als Leitlinie für die
        Deutungsarbeit. [The structure of the psychoanalytical session as a
        guide line for analysis.] Psyche 1966, 20:29-39
78913   Symposium on old age and capacity introduction. Geront Clin, Basel
        1968, 10:129-133

        REVIEW OF:
78914   Lampl-de Groot, J. The Development of the Mind. J 1967, 48:122

KLAUSBERGER, E. M.

See Gloning, K.

KLAUSNER, SAMUEL Z.

78915   (Ed) The Quest for Self-Control. NY: Free Pr 1965, xiv + 400 p
        Rv Daly, R. W. R 1966, 53:680-683
78916   Sacred and profane meanings of blood and alcohol. Soc Psych 1964,
        64:27-43

KLEE, GERALD D.

78917   (& Bertino, J. R.; Callaway, E.; Weintraub, W.) Clinical studies with
        LSD-25 and two substances related to serotonin. JMS 1960, 106:301-
        308
78918   (& Bertino, J. R.; Weintraub, W.; Callaway, E.) The influence of vary-
        ing dosage on the effects of lysergic acid diethylamide (LSD-25) in
        humans. JNMD 1961, 132:404-409
78919   Lysergic acid diethylamide (LSD-25) and ego functions. Arch gen
        Psychiat 1963, 8:461-474

        See Bertino, Joseph R.; Monroe, Russell R.; Silverstein, Arthur B.;
        Weintraub, Walter

KLEEGMAN, S. J.

See Heiman, Marcel

KLEEMAN, JAMES A.

78920 A boy discovers his penis. Psa St C 1965, 20:239-266

78921 Dreaming for a dream course. (Read at Israel Psa Soc, Dec 1960)
Q 1962, 31:203-231
  Abs LDr RFPsa 1963, 27:357

78922 Genital self-discovery during a boy's second year. Psa St C 1966, 21: 358-392

78923 The peek-a-boo game: Part I: Its origins, meanings, and related phenomena in the first year. Psa St C 1967, 22:239-273

KLEEMAN, SUSAN THURMAN

78924 Psychiatric contributions in the treatment of asthma. Ann Allerg 1967, 25:611-619

KLEIN, ANNETTE

See Grinker, Roy R., Sr.

KLEIN, D. B.

78925 Psychopathology. In Seward, G. H. & Seward, J. P. *Current Psychological Issues,* NY: Henry Holt 1958, 303-328

KLEIN, DONALD C.

78926 (& Lindemann, E.) Preventive intervention in individual and family crisis situations. In Caplan, G. *Prevention of Mental Disorders in Children,* NY: Basic Books 1961, 283-306

See Ferneau, Ernest W., Jr.

KLEIN, DONALD F.

78927 (& Blank, H. R.) Psychopathological treatment of bereavement and its complications. In Kutscher, A. H. *Death and Bereavement,* Springfield, Ill: Thomas 1969, 299-305

KLEIN, F.

See Lebovici, Serge

KLEIN, GEORGE S.

78928 Blindness and isolation. (Read at Western New England Psa Soc, 4 Nov 1961) Psa St C 1962, 17:82-93

78929 Credo for a "clinical psychologist": a personal reflection. BMC 1963, 27:61-73
  Abs HD Q 1964, 33:604

78930 The ego in psychoanalysis: a concept in search of identity. (The emergency of ego psychology: a symposium.) R 1969-70, 56:511-525

78931 Freud's two theories of sexuality. In Breger, L. *Clinical-Cognitive Psychology: Models and Integrations,* Englewood Cliffs, N.J.; Prentice Hall 1969, 136-181

78932 On hearing one's own voice: an aspect of cognitive control in spoken

thought. (Read at Phila Ass Psa, 12 Feb, 1964) Dr Af Beh 2:87-117.
Psa Curr Biol Thought 245-273
  Abs Cowitz, B. Bull Phila Ass Psa 1964, 14:241-244
78933 On inhibition, disinhibition, and "primary process" in thinking. In
  Nielson, G. *Proceedings of the XIV International Congress of Applied
  Psychology, Vol. 4. Clinical Psychology,* Copenhagen, Denmark: Munksgaard 1962, 179-198
78934 Peremptory ideation: structure and force in motivated ideas. Psychol
  Issues 1967, 5:80-128. In Holt, R. R. *Motives and Thought,* NY: IUP
  1967, 78-128. In Jessor, R. & Feshbach, S. *Cognition, Personality &
  Clinical Psychology; A Symposium Held at the University of Colorado,*
  San Francisco: Jossey-Bass 1967, 1-61
78935 (& Barr, H. L.; Wolitzky, D. L.) Personality. Ann Rev Psychol 1967,
  18:467-560
78936 Semantic power measured through the interference of words with color-
  naming. AJP 1964, 77:576-588
78937 The several grades of memory. Psa—Gen Psychol 377-389

  See Fiss, Harry; Gill, Merton M.; Schlesinger, Herbert J.

KLEIN, H.

78938 Psychological effects of dental treatment on children of different ages.
  J Dent Child 1967, 34:30-36

KLEIN, H. SYDNEY

78939 Notes on a case of ulcerative colitis. (Read at Brit Psa Soc, Apr 1962)
  J 1965, 46:342-351
  Abs EVN Q 1967, 36:623
78940 The use of analysis in a child psychiatric clinic. J child Psychol Psychiat
  1961, 1:288-297

KLEIN, HENRIETTE R.

78941 Brief psychotherapy. Proc IV World Cong Psychiat 1966, 456-457
S-50572 The Columbia Psychoanalytic Clinic: a development in psychoanalytic
  training.
  Abs JA An Surv Psa 1956, 7:365-366
78942 Discussion of Dorn, R. M. "Psychoanalysis and psychoanalytic education." Psa Forum 1969, 3:255-256
78943 Myths of psychiatric training. Int J Psychiat 1967, 4:448-450
78944 Obstetrical and gynecological disorders. Compreh Txbk Psychiat 1076-
  1085
78945 Psychoanalysts in Training: Selection and Evaluation. (Foreword:
  Kolb, L. C.) (Pref: Lewin, B. D.) NY: Columbia Univ Pr 1965, 131 p
  Abs J Am Psa Ass 1967, 15:221-222. Rv Fleming, J. Q 1967, 36:
  435-436. Keiser, S. J Am Psa Ass 1969, 17:238-267
78946 What are the differences between Freudian psychoanalytic treatment
  and other methods of psychological treatment? Why Rep 513-525
78947 What is mental health? Why Rep 492-493

  See Bennett, Stephen L.; Jameson, Jean; Potter, Howard W.

ABSTRACT OF:
78948 Ovesey, L. et al: A psychodynamic formulation for psychotherapy of male homosexuality. Q 1963, 32:622-623

KLEIN, HILEL

78949 Contributor to Krystal, H. *Massive Psychic Trauma*

KLEIN, MARJORIE H.

78950 (& Dittman, A. T.; Parloff, M. B.; Gill, M. M.) Behavior therapy: observations and reflections. J consult clin Psychol 1969, 33:259-266

See Alper, Thelma G.; Gendlin, Eugene T.

KLEIN, MELANIE

78951 Bibliography. J 1961, 42:7-8
S-18466 A contribution to the psychogenesis of manic-depressive states.
Zur Psychogenese der manisch-depressiven Zustände. Psyche 1960, 14:256-283
S-18472 On the criteria for the termination of a psycho-analysis.
Sobre los criterions para la terminación de un psicoanálisis. (Tr: Baranger, M.) Rev urug Psa 1961-62, 4:280-285
S-50577 On the development of mental functioning.
Abs JAL An Surv Psa 1958, 9:233
S-18473 The early development of conscience in the child. Heirs Freud 253-270
78952 Las Emociones Básicas del Hombre. (Foreword: Grinberg, L.) Includes [50578, 50580]. Buenos Aires: Ed. Paidós
S-50578 Envy and Gratitude.
Spanish: In author's *Las Emociones Básicas del Hombre*
78953 Essais de Psychanalyse. [Essays on Psychoanalysis.] (Pref: Abraham, N.; Torok, M.) Paris: Payot 1967
Rv Schmitz, B. RFPsa 1968, 32:319-321
S-18483 The importance of symbol-formation in the development of the ego.
Die Bedeutung der Symbolbildung für die Ichentwicklung. Psyche 1960, 14:242-255
78954 Infantile anxiety situations reflected in a work of art and in the creative impulse. In Ruitenbeek, H. M. *The Creative Imagination*, Chicago: Quadrangle Books 1965, 55-66
S-50580 Love, Hate and Reparation.
Spanish: In author's *Las Emociones Básicas del Hombre*
78955 On mental health. M 1960, 33:237-241
Abs RDT Q 1961, 30:459
S-18487 Mourning and its relation to manic-depressive states. In Ruitenbeek, H. M. *Death: Interpretations*, NY: Dell Publ 1969, 237-267
78956 Narrative of a Child Analysis. NY: Basic Books; London: HPI 1961, 496 p
Rv Lax, R. F. PPR 1962, 49(4):136-137. Geleerd, E. R. J 1963, 44:493-506; J Am Psa Ass 1964, 12:242-258. Lowenfeld, Y. Q 1963, 32:409-415. Segal, H. & Meltzer, D. J 1963, 44:507-513

78957 Narrative of a child analysis. JNMD 1962, 134:383-387
78958 Note sur la dépression chez le schizophrène. [A note on depression in schizophrenia.] RFPsa 1961, 25:937-940
S-18495 The origins of transference.
Los origenes de la transferencia. Rev urug Psa 1961-62, 4:116-128
78959 Our adult world and its roots in infancy. Hum Relat 1959, 12:291-303
Il mondo di noi adulti e le sue radici nell'infanzia. (Tr: Forti, L. di) Riv Psa 1966, 12:283-297. Arch Psicol Neurol Psichiat 1967, 28:41-59
78960 Our Adult World and Other Essays. London: Heinemann Medical Books; NY: Basic Books 1963, vi + 121 p
Rv Green, A. RFPsa 1964, 28:816-819. Lowenfeld, Y. Q 1964, 33: 582-584. PLe RFPsa 1964, 28:819-821. Stokes, A. J 1964, 45:131-134
S-50582 The psychoanalytic play technique. In Haworth, M. R. *Child Psychotherapy*, NY/London: Basic Books 1964, 119-121; 277-286
Abs An Surv Psa 1955, 6:249-251
S-18499 The psychotherapy of the psychoses. In *Contributions to Psychoanalysis*, London: Hogarth Pr 1930, 1960
Abs Goldberg, L. Cuad Psa 1965, 1:387
78961 Das Seelenleben des Kleinkindes und andere Beiträge zur Psychoanalyse. [The Emotional Life of the Infant and Other Contributions to Psychoanalysis.] Stuttgart: Ernst Klett 1962, 203 p
S-18506 Some theoretical conclusions regarding the emotional life of the infant.
Über das Seelenleben des Kleinkindes. Einige theoretische Betrachtungen. Psyche 1960, 14:284-316
S-50585 Symposium on "depressive illness."
Abs JBi Q 1962, 31:121-122

KLEIN, MILTON

78962 Freud and Hypnosis: The Interaction of Psycho-Dynamics and Hypnosis. NY: Matrix House 1966, xii + 207 p

KLEIN, R. F.

See Bogdonoff, M. D.; Tinling, D. C.

KLEINBERGER, ELIZABETH

78963 (Participant) Depression in infancy and childhood. Panel discussion: the management of depression in children and adults. Contempo Psa 1965, 2(1):36-41; 54-61

KLEINER, HENRY T.

78964 Vicissitudes of the superego in the adult. (Read at Phila Ass Psa, 15 Apr 1966) Bull Phila Ass Psa 1966, 16:122-135
Abs EFA Q 1968, 37:158-159

KLEINER, JACK

78965 Management of anxiety related to beginning school. J Albert Einstein Med Center 1960, 8:224-227

78966   A meaning of persistence in a young child. Bull Phila Ass Psa 1961, 11:76-79
        Abs PLe RFPsa 1963, 27:336
78967   On a lullaby. Bull Phila Ass Psa 1961, 11:183-189
        Abs PLe RFPsa 1963, 27:339

KLEINER, ROBERT J.

78968   (& Tuckman, J.; Lavell, M.) Mental disorder and status based on race. Ps 1960, 23:271-274
        Abs HRB Q 1961, 30:300

See Parker, Seymour

KLEINMUNTZ, BENJAMIN

78969   Personality Measurement: An Introduction. Homewood, Ill: Dorsey 1967, xiii + 463 p

KLEINSCHMIDT, HANS J.

78970   The angry act: the role of aggression in creativity. Am Im 1967, 24:98-128
78971   Beyond Philip Rieff: the triumph of Sigmund Freud. Am Im 1966, 23:244-256
78972   Critique. An Surv Psa 1956, 7:44-79; 1957, 8:14-21; 1958, 9:17-35
78973   (& Kaufman, M. R.; Diener, H.) Experience in teaching basic psychiatry to medical practitioners at the Mount Sinai Hospital, N.Y. J Mount Sinai Hosp 1963, 30(5)
78974   Letter to the editor [re G. Heilbrunn's "How 'cool' is the beatnik?"]. Psa Forum 1967, 2:380
78975   On the psychology of medical observation. J Mount Sinai Hosp 1964, 31:348-357

See Hulse, Wilfred C.

ABSTRACTS OF:
78976   Binswanger, H. Freuds Psychosentherapie. An Surv Psa 1956, 7:35-36
78977   Colby, K. M. A Skeptical Psychoanalyst. An Surv Psa 1958, 9:26-28
78978   Cremerius, J. Freuds Bedeutung für die psychosomatische Medizin. An Surv Psa 1956, 7:17
78979   Eissler, K. R. Julius Wagner-Jaurregs Gutachten über Sigmund Freud und seine Studien zur Psychoanalyse. An Surv Psa 1958, 9:33-34
78980   Eissler, K. R. Kritische Bemerkungen zu Renée Gicklhorns Beitrag "Eine mysteriöse Bildaffäre." An Surv Psa 1958, 9:34
78981   Elhardt, S. Freuds Bedeutung für Beziehung zwischen Arzt und Patient. An Surv Psa 1956, 7:16
78982   Hoffman, G. Die Beziehungen zwischen Aktualneurosen, Psychoneurosen und Realitätsprinzip. An Surv Psa 1958, 9:52-53
78983   Kilian, H. Psychoanalyse und Anthropologie. An Surv Psa 1956, 7:391-392
78984   Klüwer, K. Zum neuen Verständnis der psychischen Entwicklung des Kinds durch Freud. An Surv Psa 1956, 7:16-17

78985   Klüwer, R. Psychoanalyse und religiöser Glaube. An Surv Psa 1956, 7:402
78986   Krapf, E. E. Entwicklungslinien der psychoanalytischen Technik. An Surv Psa 1957, 8:10-13
78987   Langhans, S. Das Strukturmodell des menschlichen Psyche, ein wesentlicher Beitrag Freuds zur Psychologie. An Surv Psa 1956, 7:16
78988   Matussek, P. Die allgemeine Bedeutung Freuds für die Psychiatrie. An Surv Psa 1956, 7:16
78989   Riemann, F. Freud als Begründer der Psychotherapie. An Surv Psa 1956, 7:14-15
78990   Rosenfeld, H. A. Bemerkungen zur Psychopathologie der Schizophenie. An Surv Psa 1956, 7:177-178
78991   Schiefele, H. Freuds Bedeutung für die Kunstbetrachtung (Marcel Proust, James Joyce, Thomas Mann). An Surv Psa 1956, 7:17
78992   Seitz, W. Freud und seine Gegner. An Surv Psa 1956, 7:15-16
78993   Székely, L. Deckerinnerung als erfüllte "Vorahnung." An Surv Psa 1957, 8:112-114

KLEINSORGE, H.

78994   [Allergy—a psychosomatic disease.] (Ger) Med Klin 1964, 59:1193-1195

KLEITMAN, NATHANIEL

78995   The physiology of dreaming. Dreams Contempo Psa 37-54
78996   Sleep and Wakefulness. (Rev & enl) Chicago: Univ Chicago Pr 1963, 550 p
        Rv Lewin, B. D. Q 1964, 33:430-432

KLEMME, HERBERT L.

See Murphy, Gardner

KLEMPERER, EDITH

78997   Dissociation and projection in hypnotic states. Amer J Hyp 1966, 9:114-117
78998   Past ego states emerging in hypnoanalysis. Int J clin exp Hyp 1965, 13:132-143
78999   Past Ego States Emerging in Hypnoanalysis. Springfield, Ill: Thomas 1968, xvii + 270 p
79000   Primary object-relationships as revealed in hypnoanalysis. Int J clin exp Hyp 1961, 9:3-11
79001   "Shortest distance" therapy in hypnoanalysis. Int J clin exp Hyp 1961, 9:63-77
79002   Symptom removal by revivification. Amer J clin Hyp 1963, 5:277-280

KLEMPERER, PAUL

79003   Pathologic anatomy in modern medicine. In Kaufman, M. R. & Heiman, M. Evolution of Psychosomatic Concepts, NY: IUP 1964, 36-46

KLERMAN, GERALD L.

See Gershon, Elliot S.; Greenblatt, Milton; Grunebaum, Henry U.;
Lazare, Aaron

KLIBANSKY, RAYMOND

79004 (& Panofsky, E.; Saxl, F.) Saturn and Melancholy. Studies in the
History of Natural Philosophy, Religion, and Art. NY: Basic Books
1964, 429 p
Rv Simon, B. Q 1968, 37:145-149

KLIGERMAN, CHARLES

79005 A psychoanalytic study of Pirandello's "Six Characters in Search of an
Author." J Am Psa Ass 1962, 10:731-744
Abs JBi Q 1963, 32:449
S-50599 A psychoanalytic study of the confessions of St. Augustine.
Abs CFH An Surv Psa 1957, 8:301-303

KLIJNHOUT, A. E.

79006 Ethos and eros. Crianca Port 1956-57, 15-16, (1)
79007 Two papers on the psychopathology of sexuality. Crianca Port 1956-57,
(1):15-16

KLIMAN, GILBERT

79008 (& Goldberg, E. L.) Improved visual recognition during hypnosis. Arch
gen Psychiat 1962, 7:155-162
Abs KR Q 1963, 32:454
79009 Oedipal themes in children's reactions to the assassination. Chld Dth
Pres 107-134; 234-248
79010 Psychological Emergencies of Childhood. NY/London: Grune & Stratton 1968, 160 p

See Wolfenstein, Martha

KLIMMER, R.

79011 Urolagnie: eine form des fetischismus? [Urolagnia: a form of fetishism?] Psychiat Neurol med Psychol 1968, 20:219-222

KLIMO, Z.

79012 K otazkevedomia, podvedomia, vevedomia.[To the problem of consciousness, subconsciousness, and non-consciousness.] Ceskoslov Psychiat 1969, 65(2):99-103

KLINE, FRANK M.

79013 (Participant) On regression: a workshop. (West Coast Psa Soc, 14-16
Oct 1966) Psa Forum 1967, 2:293-316

KLINE, LAWRENCE Y.

See Koegler, Ronald R.

KLINE, LINDA VIKAN
See Heller, Kenneth

KLINE, MILTON V.

79014   (Ed) Clinical Correlations of Experimental Hypnosis. Springfield, Ill: Thomas 1963, xv + 524 p
         Rv Am Im 1964, 21:187-188
79015   Clinical interpretation in hypnoanalysis. In Hammer, E. F. *Use of Interpretation in Treatment: Technique and Art,* NY: Grune & Stratton 1968, 344-350
79016   Hypnosis and clinical psychology. Prog clin Psych 1960, 4:65-84
79017   (& Arther, R. O.) Hypnosis and hypnotic dreaming: a polygraph investigation. In Lassner, J. *Hypnosis and Psychosomatic Medicine,* Berlin/Heidelberg/NY: Springer 1967, 186-193
79018   Hypnotherapy. In Wolman, B. B. *Handbook of Clinical Psychology,* NY: McGraw-Hill 1965, 1275-1295
79019   Hypnotic age regression. Dis nerv Sys 1961, 22(4, Suppl):118-120
79020   Hypnotic age regression and psychotherapy; clinical and theoretical observations. Int J clin exp Hyp 1960, 8:17-35
79021   Hypnotic amnesia in psychotherapy. Int J clin exp Hyp 1966, 14:112-120
79022   The nature of hypnotically induced behavior. Psychol Rep 1960, 6:332
79023   (& Linder, M.) Psychodynamic factors in the experimental investigation of hypnotically induced emotions with particular reference to blood glucose measurements. J Psychol 1969, 71:21-25
79024   (Ed) Psychodynamics and Hypnosis: New Contributions to the Practice and Theory of Hypnotherapy. Springfield, Ill: Thomas 1967, xi + 194 p
79025   The reinforcement of hypnotically induced responses through age regression and age regression dreams. J Amer Soc Psychosom Dent Med 1965, 12:92-104
79026   Sensory hypnoanalysis. Int J clin exp Hyp 1968, 16:85-100
79027   (Ed) Transactions of 1961 International Congress on Hypnosis. NY 1961

KLINE, NATHAN

79028   Discussion of Wedge, B. "Psychiatry and international affairs." Int J Psychiat 1968, 5:330-344

KLINE, PAUL

79029   The anal character: a cross-cultural study in Ghana. Brit J soc clin Psychol 1969, 8:201-210
79030   Obsessional traits and emotional instability in a normal population. M 1967, 40:153-158
79031   Obsessional traits, obsessional symptoms and anal erotism. M 1968, 41:299-305
79032   A study of the Oedipus complex and neurotic symptoms in a non-psychiatric population. M 1969, 42:291-292
79033   The validity of the dynamic personality inventory. M 1968, 41:307-313

KLINGSPORN, M. J.

79034 (& Peters, C. R.; Enns, M. P.; Iles, R.) Near optimal processing of information during concept identification. Psychonomic Science 1967, 9:537-538

KLOEK, J.

79035 De psychiater op een dwaalspoor? Overpeinzingen omtrent waarheid en waarde van het Bowlby-rapport. [The psychiatrist on a wrong track? Reflections on the truth and value of the Bowlby report.] Maandbl geest Volksgezondh 1960, 15(4):117-136

KLOES, K. B.

79036 (& Weinberg, A.) Countertransference: a bilateral phenomenon in the learning model. Perspect psychiat Care 1968, 6:152-162

KLOPFER, BRUNO

79037 Bibliography. J proj Tech 1960, 24:238-239
79038 (& Meyer, M.) (Eds) Developments in the Rorschach, Vol. III. NY: Harcourt, Brace & World 1967, 2 Vols.
79039 Foreword to Harrower, M. R. et al: *Creative Variations in the Projective Techniques,* Springfield, Ill: Thomas 1960
79040 (& Boyer, L. B.) Notes on the personality structure of a North American Indian shaman: Rorschach interpretation. J proj Tech 1961, 25: 170-178
79041 Obituary: C. G. Jung—1875-1961. J proj Tech 1961, 25:250-251
79042 Suicide: the Jungian point of view. In Farberow, N. L. & Schneidman, E. S. *The Cry for Help,* NY: McGraw-Hill 1961, 193-203

See Boyer, L. Bryce

KLOPFER, WALTER G.

79043 Clinical patterns of aging. In Wolman, B. B. *Handbook of Clinical Psychology,* NY: McGraw-Hill 1965, 826-837
79044 The metamorphosis of projective methods. J proj Tech 1968, 32:402-404
79045 The Psychological Report: Use and Communication of Psychological Findings. (Foreword: Bellak, L.) NY: Grune & Stratton 1960, 146 p
    Rv Schlesinger, H. J. Q 1961, 30:293-295

KLORMAN, RAFAEL

79046 (& Chapman, L. J.) Regression in schizophrenic thought disorder. JAbP 1969, 74:199-204

KLOSS, ROBERT J.

79047 Review-article: "The Subconscious Language" by Theodore Thass-Thienemann. Lit & Psych 1968, 18:233-238

KLOTZ, H.-P.

79048 (Ed) La Médecine Psychosomatique. [Psychosomatic Medicine.] Paris: Expansion Scientifique 1965
       Rv Auth RFPsa 1966, 30:511. J. S. RFPsa 1968, 32:631-632
79049 (& Balier, C.; Javal, I.) [Presentation of a case of mental anorexia which required hospitalization in a female identical twin.] (Fr) Rev Méd psychosom 1961, 3(2):37-52
       Abs RJA Q 1962, 31:436

See Aubry, J.

KLOTZ, R.

See Jarreau, R.

KLUCKHOHN, CLYDE K.

S-50654 The impact of Freud on anthropology.
       Abs Segel, N. P. An Surv Psa 1956, 7:26-27

KLUGER, JULES M.

79050 Childhood asthma and the social milieu. J Amer Acad Child Psychiat 1969, 8:353-366

KLUGER, RIVKAH S.

79051 Flood dreams. In Wheelwright, J. B. *The Reality of the Psyche: Proceedings of the Third International Congress for Analytical Psychology,* NY:Putnam 1968, 45-53

KLUGMAN, DAVID J.

79052 (& Litman, R. E; Wold, C. I.) Suicide: answering the cry for help. Soc Wk 1965, 10:43-50

KLÜWER, KARL

79053 Stationäre Psychotherapie bei jugendlichen Dissozialen. [Residential psychotherapy in juvenile dissocials.] Z Psychother med Psychol 1968, 18:82-90. Hbh Kinderpsychother 808-817
S-50661 Zum neuen Verständnis der psychischen Entwicklung des Kindes durch Freud.
       Abs HK An Surv Psa 1956, 7:16-17
79054 Zur Frage der Deutung und Interpretation in der psychoanalytischen Therapie. [On the problem of the importance and interpretation in psychoanalytical therapy.] Z PSM 1962, 8:36-45

KLÜWER, ROLF

79055 Probleme und Aufgaben der Katamnese. [Problems and aims of follow-up examinations.] Psyche 1968, 22:786-791
       Abs J 1969, 50:399

S-50662 Psychoanalyse und religiöser Glaube.
Abs HK An Surv Psa 1956, 7:402

See Cremerius, J.

KNAPP, PETER HOBART

79056 (& Nemetz, S. J.) Acute bronchial asthma: I. Concomitant depression and excitement and various antecedent patterns in 406 attacks. PSM 1960, 22:42-55
Abs Powelson, H. Q 1961, 30:304. M'Uzan, M. de RFPsa 1962, 26: 337

79057 Acute bronchial asthma: II. Psychoanalytic observations on fantasy, emotional arousal, and partial discharge. PSM 1960, 22:88-105
Abs EMW Q 1961, 30:305

79058 (& Bliss, C. M.; Wells, H.) Addictive aspects in heavy cigarette smoking. P 1963, 11:245-280

79059 (& Mushatt, C.; Nemetz, S. J.) Asthma, melancholia, and death. I. Psychoanalytic considerations. PSM 1966, 28:114-133

79060 (& Carr, H. E., Jr.; Mushatt, C.; Nemetz, S. J.) Asthma, melancholia, and death. II. Psychosomatic considerations. PSM 1966, 28:134-154

79061 The asthmatic child and the psychosomatic problem of asthma. In Schneer, H. I. The Asthmatic Child, NY: Harper & Row 1963, 234-255

79062 (& Mushatt, C.; Nemetz, S. J.) Collection and utilization of data in a psychoanalytic psychosomatic study. Meth Res PT 401-422

79063 Discussion of Swartz, J. "The erotized transference and other transference problems." Psa Forum 1969, 3:329-332

79064 (& Mushatt, C.; Nemetz, S. J.) Emotion, instinctive arousal, and defense—a method of psychoanalytic psychosomatic investigation. (Read at joint meeting of Boston Psa Soc & Inst and Western New England Psa Soc, 22 Oct 1966)
Abs Reich, P. Bull Phila Ass Psa 1967, 17:247-250

79065 (& Bahnson, C. B.) The emotional field: a sequential study of mood and fantasy in 2 asthmatic patients. PSM 1963, 25:460-483

79066 (Ed) Expression of the Emotions in Man. NY: IUP; London: Bailey Bros 1963, 351 p
Abs J Am Ass 1964, 12:261. Rv Brody, M. W. Q 1964, 33:435-436

79067 Image, symbol, and person. The strategy of psychological defense. Arch gen Psychiat 1969, 21:392-406

79068 Libido: a latter-day look. JNMD 1966, 142:395-417

79069 Models and methods: a psychodynamic predictive approach to bronchial asthma. JNMD 1962, 135:440-454

79070 Psychiatric research in the general hospital: a case history. Int Psychiat Clin 1966, 3(3):113-122

79071 Purging and curbing: an inquiry into disgust, satiety and shame. JNMD 1967, 144:514-534

S-50669 Sensory impressions in dreams.
Abs SO An Surv Psa 1956, 7:226

79072 Short-term psychoanalytic and psychosomatic predictions. (Read at Montreal Psa Soc; at Boston Psa Soc, 17 May 1961; at Southern Calif Soc for Psa; at Am Psa Ass) J Am Psa Ass 1963, 11:245-280

      Abs Fineman, J. A. B. Bull Phila Ass Psa 1961, 11:192-194. JBi Q
1964, 33:136-137
79073 Some riddles of riddance. Relationships between liminative processes
and emotion. Arch gen Psychiat 1967, 16:586-602
S-50671 (& Levin, S.; McCarter, R. H.; Wermer, H.; Zetzel, E.) Suitability for
psychoanalysis: a review of 100 supervised analytic cases.
      Abs LDr RFPsa 1962, 26:334

See Heim, Edgar; Jacobs, Martin A.

KNAPP, ROBERT H.

79074 (& McElroy, L. R.; Vaughn, J.) On blithe and melancholic aestheticism.
J gen Psychol 1962, 67:3-10

See Holzberg, J. D.

KNIGHT, EDWARD HENRY

79075 Overt male homosexuality. In Slovenko, R. *Sexual Behavior and the
Law,* Springfield, Ill: Thomas 1965, 434-461
79076 Some considerations regarding the concept "autism." Dis nerv Sys 1963,
24:224-229

KNIGHT, J.

See De Reuck, A. V. S.

KNIGHT, JAMES A.

79077 Acting out through the child. Ops 1960, 30:422-423
79078 The adolescent as the builder of the future. Tulane St soc Welfare
1965, 8:76-88
79079 Adolescent development and religious values. Voices 1969, 4:68-72
79080 (& McGovern, J. P.) Allergy and Human Emotions. Springfield, Ill:
Thomas 1967
79081 Calvinism and psychoanalysis: a comparative study. Pastoral Psychol
1963, 14:10-17
79082 Church phobia. Pastoral Psychol 1967, 18:33-38
79083 Community psychiatry in psychiatric education. Bull Tulane Univ
Med Fac 1963, 22:169-174
79084 Conscience. Union Seminary Quart R 1964, 19:131-139. J pastoral
Care 1964, 18:132-139
79085 Conscience and Guilt. NY: Appleton-Century-Crofts 1969, 189 p
79086 Drug-induced hepatic injury: Marplan hepatitis. P 1961, 118:73-74
79087 (& Baird, V. C.) Early detection of emotional disorder. J occup Med
1961, 3:412-416
79088 (& Friedman, T. I.; Sulianti, J.) Epidemic hysteria: a field study. Amer
J Publ Hlth 1965, 55:858-865
79089 The executioner becomes the executed. Psychiat Q 1960, 34:92-102
79090 False pregnancy in a male. PSM 1960, 22:260-266
      Abs JPG Q 1961, 30:452

79091 For the Love of Money: Human Behavior and Money. Phila/NY/ Toronto: J. B. Lippincott 1968, 184 p
Rv Barron, J. R 1968-69, 55:713-714

79092 From conflict to cooperation between religion and psychiatry. Psychiat Q Suppl 1960, 34:326-337

79093 (& McGovern, J. P.; Haywood, T. J.; Chao, D. H.) Headache in children—Part I: Classification. Part II: The psychological implications of headache in children. Part III: Headache due to systemic disease. Part IV: The migraine syndrome. Headache 1961, (3):11-16; 1962, (1): 30-37; (11):41-45; 1963, (3):13-20

79094 The impact of confrontation in learning. J med Educ 1966, 41:670-678

79095 (& Kinross-Wright, J.; Cohen, I. M.) The management of neurotic and psychotic states with RO 5-0690 (Librium). Dis nerv Sys 1960, 21:23-26

79096 (& Davis, W. E.) A Manual for the Comprehensive Community Mental Health Clinic. Springfield, Ill: Thomas 1964

79097 (& Baird, V. C.) Mental hygiene among employees. J occup Med 1961, 3:365-368

79098 Metaphysical concerns and mental health. MH 1962, 46:249-255

79099 Motivation in skiing. West J Surg Obs Gyn 1961, 69:395-398

79100 Partners in healing. Pulpit Dig 1964, Oct: 11-18

79101 (& Baird, V. C.) Part-time psychiatrist in industry. J occup Med 1961, 3:463-466

79102 Philosophical implications of terminal illness. N. C. Med J 1961, 22: 493-495

79103 A portrait of Sigmund Freud. Texas State J Med 1960, 56:314-315

79104 The profile of the normal adolescent. Ann Allerg 1967, 25:129-136

79105 The psychiatrist in the life and work of the church. Pastoral Psychol 1964, 15:27-36

79106 A Psychiatrist Looks at Religion and Health. NY/Ashville: Abingdon Pr 1964, 207 p

79107 Psychodynamics of the allergic eczemas. Ann Allerg 1967, 25:392-396

79108 The psychological care of the allergic patient. Psychosomatics 1968, 9:160-165

79109 Psychological factors in industrial medicine. In Lief, H. I. et al: *The Psychological Basis of Medical Practice,* NY: Harper & Row 1963, 469-481

79110 Religious-psychological conflicts of the adolescent. In Usdin, G. L. *Adolescence,* Phila: Lippincott 1967, 31-50

79111 Sex in today's culture—a concern of religion and medicine. Med Ann DC 1965, 34:161-165

79112 Some significant perspectives in the work of Carl Gustav Jung. J existent Psychiat 1962, 3:179-196

79113 A study of religious beliefs and attitudes of senior medical students. J med Educ 1961, 36:1557-1564

79114 Suicide among students. In Resnik, H. L. P. *Suicidal Behaviors: Diagnosis and Management,* Boston: Little, Brown 1968, 228-240

79115 The use and misuse of religion by the emotionally disturbed. Pastoral Psychol 1962, 13:10-18

See Bowers, Margaretta K.; Slovenko, Ralph

KNIGHT, JOHN (pseud)

79116 An old world mother; excerpt from "The story of my psychoanalysis."
In Eisenberg, A. L. *The Golden Land*, Cranbury, NJ: Yoseloff 1964,
190-196

KNIGHT, P. R.

See Cramond, W. A.

KNIGHT, ROBERT P.

79117 Obituary: David Rapaport 1911-1960. Q 1961, 30:262-264
79118 Preface. In Searles, H. R. *Collected Papers on Schizophrenia and Related Subjects*, NY: IUP 1965
S-55683 (& Friedman, C. R.) (Eds) Psychoanalytical Psychiatry and Psychology: Clinical and Theoretical Papers.
Psiquiatría Psicoanalítica Psicoterapia y Psicología Clinica. (Foreword: Grinberg, L.) Buenos Aires: Ed. Hormé 1960
Rv Resnikoff, B. Rev Psicoanál 1963, 20:389

KNIGHT, ROBERT T.

* * * Foreword to Shapiro, D. *Neurotic Styles*

KNIGHTS, L. C.

79119 (& Cottle, B.) (Eds) Metaphor and Symbol. Proceedings of the
Twelfth Symposium of the Colston Research Society. London: Butterworths Sci Publ 1960, 150 p

KNITTLE, JEROME L.

See Glucksman, Myron L.

KNOBEL, MAURICIO

79120 Child psychiatry social action in underdeveloped countries. Acta paedopsychiat 1964, 31:19-23
79121 On psychotherapy of adolescence. Acta paedopsychiat 1966, 33:168-
175

See Aberastury, Arminda; Szpilka, Jaime I.

ABSTRACTS OF:
79122 Friedman, D. B. Toward a unitary theory on the passing of the Oedipal
conflict. Rev Psicoanál 1967, 24:691
79123 Kelman, N. Social and psychoanalytical reflections on the father. Rev
Psicoanál 1967, 24:954-957
79124 Mussen, P. H. et al: The influence of father-son relationships on adolescent personality and attitudes. Rev Psicoanál 1964, 21:387-388

KNOBLOCH, FERDINAND

79125 [About fundamental questions in the theory of neuroses.] (Cz) Acta
Univ Carol [Med], Praha 1960, 6:59-86

79126 Die Familienstruktur als Modell psychotherapeutischer Methoden. [The family structure as the model for psychotherapeutic methods.] Prax PT 1967, 12:257-264
79127 Family psychotherapy. Psychother Psychosom 1965, 13:155-163
79128 [Ideological struggle and forms of critique.] (Cz) Ceskoslov Psychiat 1959, 55:337-339
79129 Marxists reject libido theory. Int J Psychiat 1966, 2:558-560
79130 The system of group-centered psychotherapy for neurotics in Czechoslovakia. P 1968, 124:1227-1231

KNOEPFEL, H. K.

79131 [Example of a brief psychotherapy.] (Ger) Praxis 1966, 55:583-590
79132 Zum Widerstand in der analytischen Psychotherapie. [Resistance in analytical psychotherapy.] Schweiz med Wschr 1963, 93:61-64

KNÖLL, HARRY

79133 Psychagogik: Gedanken zur Begriffbestimmung. [Psychology: thoughts about definition.] Prax Kinderpsychol 1968, 17:155-157
79134 Störungen der Libidoentwicklung im Bereich der genitalen Entwicklungsstrufe und der Objektliebe bei Heimkindern. [Developmental disturbances of the libido within the framework of the genital stage and object love in institutionalized children.] Prax Kinderpsychol 1967, 16:133-143

KNOPP, WALTER

See Wolpe, Joseph

KNORR, W.

79135 (& Rennert, H.) [The Wartegg-sign-test in schizophrenics.] (Ger) Fortschr Neurol 1966, 34:276-296

KNOWLES, LOIS

See Granlund, Elnore

KNOWLES, MARION C.

79136 The explanatory role of unconscious determinants in psychoanalytic theory. Austral Psychol 1966, 1:87-88

KNOX, R. S.

See Giel, R.

KNUDSON, ALFRED G., JR.

79137 (& Natterson, J. M.) Participation of parents in the hospital care of fatally ill children. Pediatrics 1960, 26:482-490

See Natterson, Joseph M.

KOBAYASHI, YOSHINARI
See Tsuji, Satoru

KOBLER, ARTHUR L.
See Ekstein, Rudolf

KOBLER, FRANZ
79138 Die Mutter Sigmund Freuds. [Sigmund Freud's mother.] Bull Leo Baeck Inst 1962, 5:149-170

KOCH, ADELHEID L.
79139 Discussion of Aull, G. & Strean, H. S. "The analyst's silence." Psa Forum 1967, 2:81-82

KOCH, ADRIENNE
79140 (Ed) Philosophy for a Time of Crisis; an Interpretation with Key Writings by Fifteen Great Modern Thinkers. NY: Dutton 1959, 382 p

KOCH, SIGMUND
79141 (Ed) Biologically Oriented Fields: Their Place in Psychology and in Biological Science. (Vol. 4 of Psychology: A Study of a Science, Study II: Empirical Substructure and Relations with Other Sciences.) NY/Toronto/London: McGraw-Hill 1962, xxxix + 731 p
79142 (Ed) Formulations of the Person and the Social Context. (Vol. 3 of Psychology: A Study of a Science, Study I: Conceptual and Systematic.) NY/Toronto/London: McGraw-Hill 1959, x + 837 p
79143 (Ed) General Systematic Formulations, Learning, and Special Processes. (Vol. 2 of Psychology: A Study of a Science, Study I: Conceptual and Systematic.) NY/Toronto/London: McGraw-Hill 1959, x + 706 p
79144 (Ed) Investigations of Man as Socius: Their Place in Psychology and the Social Sciences. (Vol. 6 of Psychology: A Study of a Science, Study II: Empirical Substructure and Relations with Other Sciences.) NY/Toronto/London: McGraw-Hill 1963, ix + 791 p
79145 (Ed) The Process Areas, the Person, and Some Applied Fields: Their Place in Psychology and in Science. (Vol. 5 of Psychology: A Study of a Science, Study II: Empirical Substructure and Relations with Other Sciences.) NY/Toronto/London: McGraw-Hill 1963, xii + 967 p
79146 (Ed) Sensory, Perceptual, and Physiological Formulations. (Vol. 1 of Psychology: A Study of a Science, Study I: Conceptual and Systematic.) NY/Toronto/London: McGraw-Hill 1959, v + 710 p

KOCKELMANS, JOSEPH J.
79147 Merleau-Ponty on sexuality. J existent Psychiat 1965-66, 6:9-29
79148 On suicide: reflections upon Camus' view of the problem. R 1967, 54: 31-48

KODMAN, FRANK, JR.
79149 (& Blanton, R. L.) Perceptual defense mechanisms and psychogenic deafness in children. Percept mot Skills 1960, 10:211-214

KOEBNER, L.

79150   The quintessence of the dream in modern biology. Int J Np 1966, 2: 562-571

KOEGLER, RONALD R.

79151   Brief contact therapy and drugs in outpatient treatment. Int Psychiat Clin 1966, 3(4):139-154
79152   Brief therapy with children. Int Psychiat Clin 1966, 3(4):155-175
79153   Psychotherapy of schizophrenia. PT 1960, 14:648-665
79154   (& Kline, L. Y.) Psychotherapy research: an approach utilizing autonomic response measurements. PT 1965, 19:268-279
79155   (& Cannon, J. A.) Treamtent for the many. Int Psychiat Clin 1966, 3(4):93-105
79156   (& Brill, N. Q.) Treatment of Psychiatric Outpatients. NY: Appleton-Century-Crofts 1967, xvii + 223 p
79157   (& Brill, N. Q.; Epstein, L. J.; Jordan, S. J.) The vanishing American. Int J soc Psychiat 1964, 10:14-18

See Wayne, George J.

KOEHLER, W.

79158   Dynamische Zusammenhänge in der Psychologie. [Dynamic Relationships in Psychology.] Bern/Stuttgart: Huber 1958
        Rv Kestenberg, J. RFPsa 1963, 27:326

KOELLE, GEORGE

See Appel, Kenneth E.

KOENIG, HAROLD

See Seitz, Philip F. D.

KOENIG, K. P.

See Sarason, Irwin G.

KOENIG, RUTH

See Seitz, Philip F. D.

KOENIG, WERNER

79159   Chronic or persisting identity diffusion. P 1964, 120:1081-1084

KOENIGSBERG, RICHARD A.

79160   Culture and unconscious fantasy: observations on courtly love. R 1967, 54:36-50
        Abs SRS Q 1968, 37:471
79161   Culture and unconscious phantasy: observations on Nazi Germany. R 1968, 55:681-696

79162   F. Scott Fitzgerald: literature and the work of mourning. Am Im 1967,
         24:248-270
             Abs JWS Q 1969, 38:165

KOESTENBAUM, PETER

79163   Existential psychiatry, logical positivism, and phenomenology. J exist-
         ent Psychiat 1960-61, 1:399-425
79164   Outlines of an existential theory of neuroses. J Amer Med Wom Ass
         1964, 19:472-488
79165   Phenomenological foundations for the behavioral sciences: the nature
         of facts. J existent Psychiat 1965-66, 6:305-341
79166   The vitality of death. J existent Psychiat 1964-65, 5:139-166

KOESTLER, ARTHUR

79167   The act of creation. In *Brain Function, Vol. 4: UCLA Forum Medical
         Science*, Berkeley: Univ Calif Pr 1963
79168   The Act of Creation. A Study of the Conscious and Unconscious Process
         of Humor, Scientific Discovery and Art. NY: Macmillan 1964, 751 p
             Rv JC J Am Psa Ass 1965, 13:634-703
79169   Evolution and revolution in the history of science. Encounter 1965,
         25(6):32-38
79170   The Ghost and the Machine. The Urge to Self-Destruction. A Psycho-
         logical and Evolutionary Study of Modern Man's Predicament. NY:
         Macmillan 1967, 384 p
79171   Insight and Outlook. Lincoln, Nebraska: Univ Nebraska Pr 1965, xiv
         + 442 p
79172   Neither lotus nor robot. Encounter 1961, 16(2):58-59
79173   The pressure of the past. PPR 1961, 48(3):25-40
79174   The Sleep Walkers; A History of Man's Changing Vision of the Uni-
         verse. NY: Macmillan 1959.
79175   A stink of Zen. The lotus and the robot (II). Encounter 1960, 15(4):
         13-32
79176   The three domains of creativity. In Bugental, J. F. T. *Challenge of
         Humanistic Psychology*, NY: McGraw-Hill 1967, 31-40
79177   Yoga unexpurgated. The lotus and the robot (1). Encounter 1960,
         15(2):7-26

KOFF, C.

See Sobel, Raymond

KOFF, ROBERT H.

79178   A definition of identification: a review of the literature. J 1961, 42:362-
         370
             Abs WPK Q 1962, 31:576-577. PCR RFPsa 1964, 28:302
S-50779 The therapeutic man Friday.
             Abs EDJ An Surv Psa 1957, 8:335-336
79179   (& Anthony, E. J.; Haug, E.; Littner, N.) Transference in children; a
         panel discussion. (Read at Chicago Psa Soc, 22 May 1962)
             Abs Miller, A. A. Bull Phila Ass Psa 1962, 12:127-129

KOGAN, LEONARD S.

See Kaye, Harvey E.

KOGAN, NATHAN

79180 (& Wallach, M. A.) Risk Taking: A Study in Cognition and Personality. NY: Holt, Rinehart & Winston 1964, x + 278 p

See Mandler, George; Wallach, Michael A.

KOGAN, W. S.

79181 (& Dorpat, T. L.; Holmes, T. H.) Semantic problems in evaluating a specificity hypothesis in psychophysiologic relations. PSM 1965, 27:1-8

KOHATA, N.

79182 [Studies on psychogenesis in selecting somatic syndromes. I. The aspect of hysterical syndrome-selections through cases reported on this subject.] (Jap) Med J Hiroshima Univ 1962, 10(5-7):133-138

KOHEN-RAEZ, REUVEN

79183 [On the problem of prolonged adolescence.] (Heb) Urim 1962-63, 20:193-198

KOHL, RICHARD NIEMES

79184 Premature termination of treatment. Prog Pt 1960, 5:99-104

KOHLBERG, LAWRENCE

79185 Cognitive stages and preschool education. Hum Develpm 1966, 9:5-17
79186 Early education: a cognitive-developmental view. Child Develpm 1968, 39:1013-1062. Ann Prog child Psychiat 1969, 72-124

KÖHLER, ALFRED

79187 Homosexualität und Strafrecht. [Homosexuality and penal law.] Z PSM 1965, 11:200-206
79188 "Statistische" Untersuchung einiger prognostischer Merkmale. ["Statistical" examination of some prognostic signs.] Z PSM 1965, 11:137-146

KOHLER, IVO

79189 The Formation and Transformation of the Perceptual World. (Psychol Issues Monogr No. 12) NY: IUP 1964, 166 p

KOHLER, MARIANE

79190 Connaître Freud. [To Know Freud.] Paris: P. Waleffe 1968, 175 p

KOHLER-HOPPE, C.

79191 Über den Behandlungseffekt komplexer Psychotherapie auf vegetative Störungen bei Neurosen. [On the effect of the treatment of vegetative

disorders caused by neurosis by means of complex psychotherapy.]
Psychiat Neurol med Psychol 1963, 15:52-60

KOHLSAAT, BARBARA

See Kolb, Lawrence C.

KOHN, MARTIN

79192 (& Levenson, E. A.) Differences between accepted and rejected patients in a treatment project of college dropouts. J Psychol 1966, 63:
143-156
79193 (& Rudnick, M.) Individualized teaching with therapeutic aims: a
methodological study. Genet Psychol Monogr 1965, 72:91-137
79194 (& Levenson, E. A.) Some characteristics of a group of bright, emotionally disturbed college dropouts. J Amer Coll Hlth Ass 1965, Dec

See Levenson, Edgar A.

KOHRMAN, JANET

See Grinker, Roy R., Sr.

KOHRMAN, ROBERT

79195 (Reporter) Problems of termination in childhood analysis. (Panel: Am
Psa Ass, 10 May 1968) J Am Psa Ass 1969, 17:191-205

See Lichtenberg, Philip; Weiss, Samuel

KOHUT, HEINZ

79196 Autonomy and integration. (Read at Am Psa Ass, 2 May 1965). J Am
Psa Ass 1965, 13:851-856
S-50787 (Reporter) Clinical and theoretical aspects of resistance. (Panel)
Abs AL An Surv Psa 1957, 8:242-244
79197 (& Seitz, P. F. D.) Concepts and theories of psychoanalysis. In Wepman,
J. M. & Heine, R. W. *Concepts of Personality*, Chicago: Aldine 1963,
113-141
S-50788 *Death in Venice* by Thomas Mann: a story about the disintegration of
artistic sublimation. In Ruitenbeek, H. M. *Psychoanalysis and Literature: An Anthology*, NY: Dutton 1964, 282-302
Abs AHM An Surv Psa 1957, 8:327
79198 Discussion of Alvarez de Toledo, L. G. et al: "Termination of training analysis." Psa Amer 193-204
Discussion of Alvarez de Toledo, L. G. et al: Terminacion del análisis didáctico. Rev Psicoanál 1967, 24:308-310
79199 The evaluation of applicants for psychoanalytic training. J 1968, 49:
548-554
79200 Forms and transformations of narcissism. (Read at Am Psa Ass, 5 Dec
1965) J Am Psa Ass 1966, 14:243-272
Formen und Umformungen des Narzissmus. Psyche 1966, 20:561-
587
Abs JLSt Q 1969, 38:335

79201   Franz Alexander, M.D., 1891-1964. In *Chicago Institute for Psycho-analysis*, Chicago: The Institute 1964, 44 p

S-50789 Introspection, empathy, and psychoanalysis. An examination of the relationship between mode of observation and theory.
        Abs JTM Q 1961, 30:138-139

S-50790 Observations on the psychological functions of music.
        Abs EDJ An Surv Psa 1957, 8:336-337

79202   Phyllis Greenacre—a tribute. J Am Psa Ass 1964, 12:3-5
        Abs JLSt Q 1966, 35:152

79203   La position du fantasme dans la psychologie psychanalytique. [The place of fantasy in psychoanalytic psychology.] RFPsa 1964, 28:471-472

79204   The psychoanalytic curriculum. (Read at Am Psa Ass, May 1961) J Am Psa Ass 1962, 10:153-163

79205   The psychoanalytic treatment of narcissistic personality disorders: outline of a systematic approach. (Read at Pan-American Psa Cong, 2 Aug 1966; at Psa Soc NY, 20 May 1968) Psa St C 1968, 23:86-113
        Die psychoanalytische Behandlung narzissistischer Persönlichkeitsstörungen. Psyche 1969, 23:321-348
        Abs Weich, M. J. Q 1969, 38: 679-680

79206   (& Anderson, A. R.; Moore, B. E.) A statement on the use of psychiatric opinions in the political realm by the American Psychoanalytic Association. J Am Psa Ass 1965, 13:450-451

79207   Symposium on fantasy. Some problems of a metapsychological formulation of fantasy. (Read at Int Psa Cong, July-Aug 1963) J 1964, 45: 199-202
        Quelques problèmes de formulation métapsychologique du fantasme. RFPsa 1964, 28:575-579
        Abs EVN Q 1966, 35:455-456

79208   Transferencia y contratransferencia en el análisis de personalidades narcisistas. [Transference and countertransference in the analysis of narcissistic personalities.] In Grinberg, L. et al: *Psicoanálisis en Las Américas: El Proceso Analítico, Transferencia y Contratransferencia*, Buenos Aires: Ed Paidos 1968, 174-185

79209   Values and objectives. (Read at Am Psa Ass, 3 May 1964) J Am Psa Ass 1964, 12:842-845

KOILE, EARL A.

See Sutherland, Robert L.

KOLANSKY, HAROLD

S-50802 Castration anxiety following recovery from the rash of measles during the oedipal period.
        Abs DJM An Surv Psa 1957, 8:214

79210   A child's reflections in her last analytic hour. Bull Phila Ass Psa 1962, 12:112-115

79211   Contributor to Pearson, G. H. J. *A Handbook of Child Psychoanalysis*, NY/London: Basic Books 1968

79212 (& Stennis, W.) Focus of training in child psychiatry. J Albert Einstein Med Center 1968, 16(Spring):19-24
79213 A note on disease anxiety at puberty. Bull Phila Ass Psa 1961, 11:190-191
         Abs PLe RFPsa 1963, 27:339
79214 An overview of child psychiatry. J Albert Einstein Med Center 1968, 16
79215 Prevention of severe anxiety states in the pre-school child. J Albert Einstein Med Center 1960, 8
79216 (& Colarusso, C. A.) Psychiatry for law students in a department of psychiatry. J. Albert Einstein Med Center 1969, 17(Summer):60-62
79217 (& Moore, W. T.) Some comments on the simultaneous analysis of a father and his adolescent son. (Read at Baltimore, Cleveland, Phila Psa Cong, 11 June 1966) Psa St C 1966, 21:237-268
79218 Some psychoanalytic considerations on speech in normal development and psychopathology. Psa St C 1967, 22:274-295
S-50805 Treatment of a three-year-old girl's severe infantile neurosis: stammering and insect phobia.
         Abs EFA Q 1961, 30:601

KOLB, LAWRENCE COLEMAN

79219 Academic and community psychiatry. Ment Hosp 1963, 14:61-71
79220 (& Daniels, G. E.) The Columbia University Psychoanalytic Clinic: an experiment in university training in psychoanalysis. J med Educ 1960, 35(2)
79221 The concept of the community mental health center. In author's Urban Challenges to Psychiatry 3-16
79222 Consultation and psychotherapy. Curr psychiat Ther 1968, 8:1-10
79223 (& Rainer, J. D.; Mesnikoff, A. M.; Carr, A. C.) Divergent sexual development in identical twins. Proc III World Cong Psychiat 1961, 530-534
S-50809 (& Johnson, A. M.) Etiology and therapy of overt homosexuality.
         Abs An Surv Psa 1955, 6:222-223
S-50810 (& Montgomery, J.) An explanation for transference cure: its occurrence in psychoanalysis and psychotherapy.
         Abs SO An Surv Psa 1958, 9:398-399
79224 Failure in bureaucratic organization and hope from local action. In author's Urban Challenges to Psychiatry 235-248
79225 Forces affecting family: commentaries. NYSJM 1968, 68:2535-2539
79226 Foreword to Klein, H. R. Psychoanalysts in Training: Selection and Evaluation, NY: Columbia Univ Pr 1965, 131 p
79227 (& Bernard, V. W.; Trussell, R. E.; Barnard, M. W.; Dohrenwend, B. P.; Kohlsaat, B.; Weiss, R.) Limitations of medical traditions on community mental health programs. P 1961, 117:972-979
79228 The matter of bias in the American Board of Psychiatry and Neurology. P 1969, 126:888-891
79229 Medical and psychiatric services. In author's Urban Challenges to Psychiatry 175-191
79230 Mental health research and training. (Interviewer: Perkins, M. E.) In Ziskind, R. Viewpoint on Mental Health, NY: NYC Comm Ment Hlth Board 1967, 335-340

79231 (& Masland, R. L.; Cooke, R. E.) (Eds) Mental Retardation. (Proceedings of the Association for Research in Nervous and Mental Disease.) Baltimore: Williams & Wilkins 1962, vii + 331 p

79232 The metropolis and social psychiatry. Int J soc Psychiat 1962, 8:245-249

79233 Obituary: Adelaide Johnson 1905-1960. J Am Psa Ass 1961, 9:364-366

79234 Phantom sensation, hallucinations and the body image. In West, L. J. *Hallucinations,* NY: Grune & Stratton 1962, 239-248

79235 The Presidential address: American psychiatry 1944-1969 and beyond. P 1969, 126:1-20

79236 Programs for other disciplines in the hospital. In Kaufman, M. R. *The Psychiatric Unit in a General Hospital,* NY: IUP 1965, 332-341; 384-401

79237 Psychiatric aspects of the treatment of headache. Neurology 1963, 13(3)Pt 2:34-37

S-50819 Psychotherapeutic evolution and its implications.
        Abs AaSt An Surv Psa 1956, 7:350-351

79238 Psychotherapy in general practice. Texas State J Med 1961, 57:558-562

79239 Response to the Presidential Address. P 1968, 125:16-18

79240 The role of identification in the achievement of goals in medical education. In Earley, L. W. et al: *Teaching Psychiatry in Medical School,* Wash, DC: Am Psychiat Ass 1969, 31-34

79241 (& Kallmann, F. J.; Polatin, P.) (Eds) Schizophrenia. (Int Psychiat Clin 1964, Vol. 1, No. 4) Boston: Little, Brown 1964, xii + 699-999

79242 Search and research. In author's *Urban Challenges to Psychiatry* 475-496

79243 Soviet psychiatric organization and the community mental health center concept. P 1966, 123:433-440

79244 Summary report of the preparatory commission on philosophy and goals. In Earley, L. W. et al: *Teaching Psychiatry in Medical School,* Wash, DC: Am Psychiat Ass 1969, 36-39

79245 Therapy of homosexuality. Curr psychiat Ther 1963, 3:131-137

79246 (& Bernard, V. W.; Dohrenwend, B. P.) Urban Challenges to Psychiatry: The Case History of a Response. Boston: Little, Brown 1969, xxiii + 512 p

79247 The Washington Heights Community Mental Health Project. In author's *Urban Challenges to Psychiatry* 17-38

79248 Who should administer psychiatric facilities? Hosp Comm Psychiat 1969, 20:170-173

See Carluccio, Charles; Daniels, George E.; Dohrenwend, Bruce P.; Gruenberg, Ernest M.; Horowitz, William A.; Kornfeld, Donald S.; Mesnikoff, Alvin M.; Noyes, Arthur P.; Rainer, John D.; Singer, Paul

KOLEV, NICOLAÏ

See Dimitrov, Christo T.

KOLKART, LYDIA

See Thomas, Ruth

KOLKER, JOSEPH
ABSTRACT OF:
79249   Kanzer, M. Verbal and nonverbal aspects of free association. Q 1961,
30:167-169

KOLKO, SEYMOUR
79250   The acute psychosis—the pathogenic community. Psychiat Res Rep
1963, 16:95-104

KOLLE, KURT
79251   Einführung in die Psychiatrie. Stuttgart: G. Thieme 1964, 1966, 93 p
An Introduction to Psychiatry. (Tr: Baskin, W.) NY: Philos Libr
1963, 71 p

KOLLER, K. M.
79252   (& Castanos, J. N.) The influence of childhood parental deprivation in
attempted suicide. Med J Aust 1968, (1):396-399

KOLMER, M. B.
See Kern, Howard M., Jr.

KOLODNY, RALPH L.
See Garland, James A.

KOLOSKI, EMILY
See Mandell, W.

KOLSCAR, SHELOMO
79253   [Data on distortion of the face-body pattern.] (Heb) Ofakim 1959,
13:196-201

KOLTES, JOHN ALBERT
79254   A psychiatric unit in a general hospital. Penn med J 1959, 62:1671-
1674
79255   The psychoneuroses. Delaware med J 1968, 40:213-217

KONDÁŠ ONDREJ
79256   Podiel Učenia v Psychoterapii. [Role of Learning in Psychotherapy.]
Bratislava: Publishing House of the Slovak Academy of Sciences 1964,
234 p

KONDO, AKIHISA
79257   Morita therapy and its development in relation to contemporary psychiatry in Japan. Prog Pt 1960, 5:221-224

KONOPKA, GISELA

79258 "A chi la responsabilita?" [To whom the responsibility?] From author's *Group Work in the Institution.* Il Tralcio 1957, 2:16-19

79259 Adolescent delinquent girls. Children 1964, 2:21-26. Child and Family 1965, 4(4):41-50

79260 Adolescent Girl in Conflict. Englewood Cliffs, N.J.: Prentice-Hall 1966

79261 The application of social work principles to international relations. In *The Social Welfare Forum,* NY: Columbia Univ Pr 1953, 279-288

79262 Attention must be paid. Ops 1964, 34:805-817

79263 Changes in the group living situation. Ops 1961, 31:32-39

79264 Changing definitions and areas of social work research. Soc Wk J 1955, 36(2):55-59, 62

79265 The constructive and destructive forces in today's society: their effect on the individual. Lutheran soc Welfare Q 1968, 1(4):43-54

79266 Differential use of groups in social work practice. In *Social Work with Groups,* Canad Ass Soc Workers 1962

79267 Discipline in youth groups. Amer J Cath Youth Wk 1960, 1(1):21-28

79268 Effective Communication with Adolescents in Institutions. NY: Child Welfare League of America 1965, 13 p. In Tod, R. J. N. *Children in Care,* London: Longmans, Green 1968, 86-102

79269 (& Harlow, M.) (Eds) Group Methods in Therapeutic Settings. Proceedings of an Institute conducted at the Graduate School of Social Work, Univ of Pittsburgh, 13-14 May 1960

79270 Group treatment of the mentally ill: education for life. Canad ment Hlth 1967, Suppl 54

79271 Group work: a heritage and a challenge. In *Social Work with Groups,* NY: N.A.S.W. 1960, 7-21

79272 Group work in psychiatric settings. In author's *Group Methods in Therapeutic Settings* 1-9. Canad ment Hlth 1960, (Sept):1-11

79273 Group work in residential treatment: an historical review. In Maier, H. W. *Group Work as Part of Residential Treatment,* NY: N.A.S.W. 1965, 13-25

S-50866 Group Work in the Institutions: A Modern Challenge.

Arbejdet med Grupper pa Institutioner. Ved H. C. Rasmussen, Jaegerspris Serien: 1 (Borneforsorgsskolen Jaegerspris 03 331 36) 1965

Gruppenarbeit in einem Heim. Wiesbaden, Germany: Verlag Haus Schwalback 1964

Japanese: Tokyo: Prentice-Hall, International Division 1967

Müesseselerde Grup Çalismasi. Bir Alan, Akin Matbassi, Ankara 1964

79274 Group work with adolescents. Ment Hlth in Virginia 1966, 16(4):5-12

79275 A healthy group life—social group work's contribution to mental health. MH 1961, 45:327-335

79276 Herje's implications of Freudianism stirs interesting points of view. Minnesota Welfare 1961, 13(3):35-42

79277 Institutional life—no stigma but help. Minnesota Welfare 1961, 13(4): 33-45

79278 Institutional treatment of emotionally disturbed children—what is and what must be. Crime Delinq 1962, 8:52-57

79279 L'instituto moderno di rieducazione. [The modern correctional institution.] Il Tralcio 1958, 3(1):12-14
79280 Method of social group work. In Friedlander, W. A. *Concepts and Methods of Social Work*, Englewood Cliffs, N.J.: Prentice-Hall 1958, 116-200

Soziale Gruppenarbeit. In Friedlander, W. A. *Grundbegriffe und Methoden der Sozialarbeit*, Neuwied/Berlin: Herman Luchterhand Verlag 1966

Il metodo del servizio sociale di gruppo. In Friedlander, W. A. *Principio e Metodo del Servizio Sociale*, Bologna: Societa Editrice il Mulino 1962

Grup sosoyal calisma metodu. In Friedlander, W. A. *Sosoyal Hizmentin Kazram ze Metodlari*, Ankara, Turkey: Kardes Malbaasi 1965, 109-195
79281 Needed—a generic social work method. The Social Worker (Le Travailleur Social) 1962, 30(2):18-30
79282 Reaching disadvantaged youth. Minnesota Welfare 1965, 17(1):4-15, 43
79283 Rehabilitation of the delinquent girl. Adolescence 1967, 2(5):69-82
S-50867 Resistance and hostility in group members. In Trecker, H. B. *Group Work—Foundations and Frontiers*, NY: Whiteside, Inc. 1955, 130-142
79284 Review of social work with groups, 1958: selected paper from the National Conference on Social Welfare. Ops 1960, 30:214-216
79285 Self respect—a necessity in prison. The Menard Times 1964, 15(9):10
79286 Self-respect: the basis of treatment. In *Chapel Hill Workshops 1966, Part II*, Chapel Hill, North Carolina, 24-29 July 1966, 68-79
79287 Social Group Work: A Helping Process. Englewood Cliffs, N.J.: Prentice-Hall 1963, 308 p

Groepswerk. Arnhem, Holland: Van Loghum Slaterus 1964

Soziale Gruppenarbeit, ein helfender Prozess. Weinheim/Berlin: Verlag Julius Beltz 1968

Japanese: Tokyo: Prentice-Hall, International Division 1967
79288 Social group work: a social work method. Soc Wk 1960, 5(4):53-61
S-50870 The social group work method: its use in the correctional field.

Il metodo del servizio sociale di gruppo: suo uso nel campo della rieducazione. Amministrazione per la Attivita Assistenziali Italiane e Internazionali
79289 Social work as an active cultural change agent. Proc Minnesota Acad Sci 1960, 28:146-152
79290 Social work philosophy in historical perspective. Lutheran soc Welfare Q 1962, 2(4):1-13
79291 Sozialarbeit in der Welt von heute. [Social work in the world of today.] Neues Beginnen 1960, (11):168-170
79292 Straffallige Mädchen. [Young woman deserving punishment.] In Hardesty, F. & Eyferth, K. *Forderungen an die Psychologie*, Bern/Stuttgart: Verlag Hans Huber 1965, 189-199
79293 (& Wallinga, J. V.) Stress as a social problem. Symposium: Best interest of the child. Ops 1963, 33:381-382; 1964, 34:536-542
79294 The teenage girl. (Pamphlet) NY: New York State Division for Youth 1967

S-50873 Therapeutic Group Work with Children.
Gruppenarbeit mit 11-17 jahrigen Jungen in einem amerikanischen
Auffangheim. Munich/Dusseldorf: Verlag Wilhelm Steinebach 1954,
84 p
Japanese: (Tr: Hayasaka, T. & Ushikuho, H.) 1959

79295 Traitement en groupe des malades mentaux. [Group treatment of the
mentally ill: education for life.] Canad Ment Hlth 1967, Suppl 54
(Jan-April)

79296 Über die Grundlagen der Sozialarbeit. [On the foundation of social
work.] Neues Beginnen 1961, No. 9, Sept:134-136
English: In author's *Eduard C. Lindeman and Social Work Philosophy*, Minneapolis: Univ Minn Pr 1958, Ch.9

79297 Über Ziel- und Wertvorstellungen in der Sozialarbeit, besonders in
der sozialen Gruppenarbeit. [On the concepts of goal and value in
social work, especially in social group work.] Unsere Jugend 1962,
14:339-345

79298 Understanding the delinquent girl. In *The Role of Agencies Serving
Low-Income Girls*, 1966, 1-17. In *Techniques of Probation*, Law-
Medicine Institute, Training Center in Youth Development, Boston
Univ 1967, 18-41

79299 The unwed mother: let her have her baby with dignity. Sexology 1967,
33(11):738-741; (12):809-811; (13):65-68

79300 L'utilisation des groupes dans la pratique du service social. [Group
work in social work.] Service Social 1966, 15(1-2-3)

79301 Values in conflict in social work practice. J Jewish comm Serv 1963,
39:343-357

79302 What houseparents should know. Children 1956, 3(2):49-54. In
Keith-Lucas, A. *Reading for House Parents of Children's Institutions*,
Chicago: Materials Center for Children's Institutions (A Department
of Workman's Book House) 1956, 3-15. Soc Wk Rev (Korea) 1964,
80-89. In Tod, R. J. N. *Children in Care*, London: Longmans, Green
1968, 28-39

79303 (Chairman) Workshop, 1960, Implications of a changing residential
treatment. Ops 1961, 31:17-39

See Little, Harry M.

KOOLHAAS, GILBERTO

79304 La angustia laberintica. [The labyrinthine anxiety.] Rev urug Psa 1960,
3:41-69

79305 El espacio onirico. [The dream space.] Rev urug Psa 1960, 3

79306 Las fantasías inconscientes de los processos mentales conscientes. [Un-
conscious fantasies of conscious mental processes.] Rev urug Psa 1964,
6:64-82

79307 La figura parental combinada. [The combined parental figure.] Rev
urug Psa 1966, 8:331-338

79308 La humanización del esquema corporal. [The human development of
the body image.] Rev urug Psa 1960, 3:276-364

79309 Melancolia no es depresión. [Melancholia is not depression.] Rev
Psicoanál 1962, 19:92-99

79310   Las raices de la conciencia. [The roots of consciousness.] Rev urug
        Psa 1962, 4:666-725
79311   Sueño diurno, memoria pantalla, recuerdo imaginativo. [Daydream,
        screen memory, imaginative remembrance.] Rev urug Psa 1964,
        6:46-63
S-50881 (& Baranger, W.) Un sueño típico: el ascensor.
        Abs Vega An Surv Psa 1956, 7:229

        ABSTRACT OF:
79312   Yazmajian, R. V. The testes and body-image formation in tranvestitism.
        Rev urug Psa 1967, 9:243

KOPORCIC, P.

See Betlheim, Stjepan

KORANYI, ERWIN K.

79313   Psychodynamic theories of the "survivor syndrome." Canad Psychiat
        Ass J 1969, 14:165-174

        See Sarwer-Foner, Gerald J.

KORCHIN, SHELDON J.

79314   (& Herz, M. I.) Differential effects of "shame" and "disintegrative"
        threats on emotional and adrenocortical functioning. Arch gen Psychiat
        1960, 2:640-651
79315   Discussion of Levitt, M. & Rubenstein, B. "Some observations on the
        relationship between cultural variants and emotional disorders." Ops
        1964, 34:432-435
79316   Form perception and ego functioning. In Rickers-Ovsiankina, M. A.
        Rorschach Psychology, NY: John Wiley 1960, 109-129
79317   Stress. Ency Ment Hlth 1975-1982

        See Heath, Helen A.; Oken, Donald

KORIN, HYMAN

See Tarachow, Sidney

KORIN, SANTIAGO

        ABSTRACT OF:
79318   Balint, M. Psycho-analysis and medical practice. Rev Psicoanál 1967,
        24:952-954

KORMAN, MAURICE

79319   Ego strength and conflict discrimination: an experimental construct
        validation of the ego strength scale. J consult Psychol 1960, 24:294-298

KORN, SAM

See Thomas, Alexander

KORNER, ANNELIESE F.

79320 (& Opsvig, P.) Developmental considerations in diagnosis and treatment. A case illustration. J Amer Acad Child Psychiat 1966, 5:594-616
79321 Some hypotheses regarding the significance of individual differences at birth for later development. Psa St C 1964, 19:58-72
79322 (& Grobstein, R.) Visual alertness as related to soothing in neonates: implications for maternal stimulation and early deprivation. Child Develpm 1966, 37:867-876

See Heinicke, Christoph M.

KORNER, IJA N.

79323 (& Allison, R. B., Jr.) Comparative study of metaphoric thinking. J Psychol 1965, 60:67-70
79324 The mechanics of suppression: an experimental investigation. J consult Psychol 1966, 30:269-272
79325 (& Allison, R. B., Jr.; Beier, E.) The patient as a constant in psychotherapy. Clin Psych 1964, 20:403-406

KORNFELD, DONALD S.

79326 (& Kolb, L. C.) The use of closed-circuit television in the teaching of psychiatry. JNMD 1964, 138:452-459

See Druss, Richard G.

KORNGOLD, MURRAY

79327 L.S.D. and the creative experience. R 1963, 50:682-685
       Abs SRS Q 1964, 33:609

KORNHUBER, H. H.

79328 Zur Situationsabhängigkeit von Bedürfnissen und Neurosen nach Erfahrungen in Gefangenenlagern. [The dependence of needs and neuroses on environment: studies on prison populations.] In Kranz, H. *Psychopathologie Heute,* Stuttgart: Georg Thieme 1962, 252-257

KORNRICH, MILTON

79329 A view of acting-out. Voices 1968, 4(2):24-25

KOROB, ABRAHAM

79330 [Technic of psychotherapy of a group of psychotics centered on analysis of the constraints.] (Sp) Rev Arg Neurol Psiquiat 1964, 1:316-318

KOROTKIN, I. I.

79331 (& Suslova, M. M.) [Physiological study of unconscious motivations of higher nervous activity in man.] (Rus) Zh vyssh nervn Deiatel 1963, 13(1):3-10

KORS, PIETER C.

79332 The existential moment in psychotherapy. Ps 1961, 24:153-162
79333 The fear and/or wish toward penetration. J existent Psychiat 1962, 3:263-276
79334 The organo-dynamism theory of Henry Ey. JNMD 1962, 134:566-571

KORSTVEDT, ARNE J.

See Berger, Ellen T.

KORZEWNIKOW, IZABELLA

79335 [Personality analysis performed on juvenile delinquents placed in groups under semi-liberty conditions.] (Pol) Neurol Neurochir Psychiat Pol 1966, 16:1407-1413

KOS, M.

See Spiel, Walter

KOSKOFF, YALE DAVID

79336 (& Shoemaker, R. J.) (Eds) Vistas in Neuropsychiatry. Pittsburgh (Neuropsychiatric Society): Univ Pitt Pr 1964, xiv + 242 p

KOS-ROBES (SRAMOTA), MARTA

79337 Die Beendigung der Kinderpsychotherapie. [The termination of child psychotherapy.] Prax Kinderpsychol 1964, 13:7. Hbh Kinderpsychother 371-378
79338 [The family tradition and the ultimate individuality in child psychotherapy.] (Fr) Rv Np inf 1965, 13:175-180
79339 (& Biermann, G.) Ökonomische Probleme der Kinderpsychotherapie. [Economic problems of child psychotherapy.] Hbh Kinderpsychother 590-598
79340 Die Rolle der sexuellen Aufklärung in der Kinderpsychotherapie. [The role of sexual explanation in child psychotherapy.] Mschr Kinderheilk 1965, 113:209. Hbh Kinderpsychother 347-353
       Le rôle des éclaircissements sur les faits sexuels en psychothérapie infantile. Rv Np inf 1965, 13:859-865
79341 Der "unerreichbare" Vater. [The "unapproachable" father.] Acta paedopsychiat 1964, 31:254-257

KOSTRUBALA, THADDEUS

See Masserman, Jules H.

KOTHARI, UJAMLAL

79342 The animals and their symbolic meanings. Am Im 1962, 19:157-162
79343 On the bullfight. PPR 1962, 49(1):123-128

KOTIS, JOHN P.

79344 Initial sessions of group counseling with alcoholics and their spouses. Soc Casewk 1968, 49:228-232

KOTKIN, MICHAEL S.

79345   The effects of various modeling conditions upon aggression and catharsis behavior. Diss Abstr 1968, 29(1-B):372-373

KOTKOV, BENJAMIN

79346   Disposition of the school leaver. Dis nerv Sys 1966, 27:178-182
79347   Emotional syndromes associated with learning failure. Dis nerv Sys
1965, 26:48-55
79348   Power factors in psychotherapy groups. PPR 1961, 48(2):68-77
79349   Psychotherapy of the six-year-old boy. Dis nerv Sys 1963, 24:669-674

KOTLER, PHILIP

79350   Behavioral models for analyzing buyers. J Marketing 1965, 29:37-45

KOULACK, DAVID

79351   The effects of somatosensory stimulation on the content of dreams. Diss
Abstr 1967, 28:2643

KOUPERNIK, CYRILLE

79352   [Depression.] (Fr) Concours Méd 1964, 86:3037-3048
79353   Epileptic paroxysms of a vegetative and anxious nature in children:
two case histories. J child Psychol Psychiat 1960, 1:146-155
79354   [Lasting psychotic regression in a 4-year-old girl, victim of a rape.]
(Fr) Rv Np inf 1967, Suppl:63-66
79355   "Maturation"—a report on the first European Congress of Paedopsychi-
atry. J child Psychol Psychiat 1961, 2:216-223
79356   Notion de stades de developpement dans l'oeuvre de H. Wallon. [No-
tion of stages of development in the work of H. Wallon.] Évolut psychiat 1962, 27:101
          Abs Auth Rev Psicoanál 1963, 20:82
79357   [Psychoanalysis as seen by a psychiatrist.] (Fr) Cah Coll Med Hop
Paris 1969, 10:399-402
79358   [Psychoanalysis in contemporary French psychiatry.] (Rus) Zh Nervpat
Psikhiat Korsakov 1961, 61:1255-1259
79359   [The subjective syndrome of head and neck injuries. Introduction.]
(Fr) Councours Méd 1964, 86:7097-7100; 7139-7146
79360   [The wages of anxiety.] (Fr) Councours Méd 1964, 86:6399-6403

KOURETAS, DEMETRIOS

79361   Aspects modernes des cures psychothérapiques pratiquées dans le sanc-
tuaire de la Grèce antique. [Modern aspects of psychotherapeutic cures
practiced at the sanctuaries of ancient Greece.] XVIIe Congrès International d'Histoire de la Médecine, Athènes-Cos 1960, 11-92. RFPsa
1962, 26:299-309. In La Route Divine, 85-96
          Spanish: Prensa Med Mex 1963, 28:166-170
79362   [A bid of psychoanalysis to linguistics.] (Gr) Nea Estia 1959, Nov:
776-1432

79363   [Brainwashing and its ancient Greek prototype.] (Gr) Am Med, Athens
        1966, (11)
        The oracle of Trophonius: a kind of shock treatment associated with
        sensory deprivation in ancient Greece. Brit J Psychiat 1967, 113:1441-
        1446
        Provozierte Persönalichkeitz-veräncherung im Griechischen Altertum
        und heutige gehirn wäsche. Wien Z Nervenheilk 1967, 25(2-4)
79364   La catharsis d'après Hippocrate, Aristote et Breuer-Freud. [Catharsis
        according to Hippocrates, Aristotle, and Breuer-Freud.] Ann Med,
        Athens 1962, Sept-Oct
79365   [Clearing up the Oedipus complex.] (Gr) Ann Med, Athens 1962,
        (3):737
79366   Early symptoms of schizophrenia. Postgraduate courses for internists.
        Annual report of Athens University Department of Psychiatry 1966
79367   [First steps in psychoanalysis.] (Gr) Ann Med, Athens 1963, (4)
79368   [The foundation of psychosomatic medicine.] (Gr) (Lecture) Annals
        of Evangelismos Hospital. Nosokomiaka Chronika 1965, (6)
79369   [The heart as the seat of psychic phenomenon in ancient Greece.] (Gr)
        In The Origins of Medicine in Greece, Athens 1968
79370   (et al) L'homosexualité du père d'Oedipe et ses conséquences. [The
        homosexuality of the father of Oedipus and its consequences.] Ann
        Med, Athens 1963, 2(5-6)
79371   [Interpretation of Aesculapius treatments in Epidaurus.] (Gr) Pelopo-
        nesian Rev 1961
79372   (& Papathomopoulos, E.) Marriage by arrangement in Greece and its
        psychiatric implications: a sociocultural study. Proc IV World Psychiat
        Cong 1966, 2526-2529
79373   [Nietzscheism and Freudianism.] (Gr) Hellenike Iatrike 1960, 29:437-
        456. Nea Estia 1960, 790:730-739
79374   [The Oedipus myth. How and why Sophocles constructed the myth
        for the stage and how and why it was interpreted by Freud.] (Gr)
        Akadimaiki Iatriki 1961, 257 (Jan)
        Abs Papathomopoulos, E. & Seidenberg, R. Q 1963, 32:142-143
79375   Paraboles and anecdotes. In Freud, S. The Interpretation of Dreams.
        Volume in commemoration of Dr. Kyriakos, Athens 1968
79376   Peculiar forms of neurosis. (Psychogenic anorexia, boulimia, tics, en-
        uresis, stammering, professional spasm, etc.) Medical Chronicles 1968,
        June
S-50920 Psychanalyse et mythologie: la névrose sexuelle des Danaïdes.
        Abs JBa An Surv Psa 1957, 8:310
79377   [A psychiatrist looks at Shakespeare's King Lear.] (Gr) Paraskenia
        Journal 1938, Nov
79378   [Psychoanalysis of parapraxias (slips of the tongue etc.) in dreams.]
        (Gr) Proc Hellenic Med Ass 1951, March
79379   [Psychocathartic Action of Ancient Greek Tragedy.] (Gr) (12 lectures
        organized by the Hellenic National Theater.) 1963
79380   (& Sakellaropoulos, P.) [The psychodynamics of anxiety neurosis. Intro-
        ductory paper.] (Gr) Proc III Cong Greek Neuropsychiatrists, Athens
        1966

79381 [The psychogenesis of depressions.] (Gr) Ann Med, Athens 1962:182. Enkefalos 1962:73

79382 [The psychology of propaganda for political war-like purposes.] (Gr) Annual Report of Department of Psychiatry of the Athens University 1966:101

79383 [Psychosomatic medicine and its benefit upon general medicine. Postgraduate courses for internists, Athens 1965.] (Gr) Annual Report of Athens University Psychiatry Department 1965, 80-98

79384 [Recent advances in the Etiopathogenesis of Schizophrenia.] (Gr) Athens: Ciba 1967

79385 [The scientific value of Carl Jung's work: a critique from a psychoanalytic angle.] (Gr) Nea Estia 1961, 816-902

79386 Sur la fréquence et la valeur sémiologique des rêves précédant l'éclosion de la psychose. [On the frequency and the semiological value of dreams preceding the appearance of psychosis.] Proc IV World Cong Psychiat 1966, 201-206

79387 [The therapeutic practices in the temple of Amphiaros.] (Fr) Rev Med psychosom 1965, 7:7-15
  Greek: Ann Med, Athens 1966, Aug

79388 Trois cas de nécrophilie dans l'antiquité. [Three cases of necrophilia in antiquity.] LVIe Congrès de Psychiatrie et de Neurologie de Langue Française, Strasbourg 1958, 705-711

79389 [The Trophonius temple in Lebadea and the Neptune's sanctuary in Mantinea.] (Gr) Peloponesian Rev 1963

79390 [The unconscious significance of "Letter to Father" by Kafka.] (Gr) Educ Hyg 1963, 211. Epoches 1963, 5. Ann Med, Athens 1967, March

KOURILSKY, R.

79391 (& Gendrot, J. A.; Raimbault, E.) La formation psychologique des médecins par les "Groupes Balint." [The psychological education of physicians by the "Balint Groups."] Rev Méd psychosom 1964, 6:51-55

79392 Psychophysiologie de l'allergie. [Psychophysiology of allergy.] Rev Méd psychosom 1965, 7:229-252

KOVACS, V.

79393 Analyse didactique et analyse de contrôle. [Didactic analysis and control analysis.] Bull Ass psa Fran 1966, (2)

KOVAR, LEO

79394 A reconsideration of paranoia. Ps 1966, 29:289-305

See Hanfmann, Eugenia

KOVEL, JOEL S.

See Barchilon, José

KOYAMA, HIROSHI

See Nozawa, Eiji

KRACKE, WAUD H.

79395 The maintenance of the ego: implications of sensory deprivation research for psychoanalytic ego psychology. M 1967, 40:17-28

KRADER, LAWRENCE

79396 Person, ego, human spirit in Marcel Mauss: comments. R 1968, 55:482-490
       Abs SRS Q 1969, 38:675

KRAEMER, R.

79397 [Moral aspects of social psychiatry.] (Ger) Bibl Psychiat Neurol 1969, 141:49-57

KRAEMER, W. P.

79398 Transference and counter-transference. M 1957, 30:63-74
       Abs CK An Surv Psa 1957, 8:265-266

KRAFT, IRVIN A.

79399 (& Austin, V.) Art therapy in the educational use of multiple impact therapy. In *Psychiatry and Art*, NY/Basel: S. Karger 1968, 106-115.
79400 Group therapy. Compreh Txbk Psychiat 1463-1468
79401 (& Marcus, I. M.; Wilson, W.; Swander, D. V.; Rumage, N. S.; Schulhoffer, E.) Methodological problems in studying the effect of tranquilizers in children with specific reference to Meprobamate. Southern med J 1959, 52:179-185
79402 Multiple impact therapy as a teaching device. Psychiat Res Rep 1966, (20): 218-223
79403 The nature of sociodynamics and psychodynamics in a therapy group of adolescents. Int J grp PT 1960, 10:313-320
79404 Outpatient child psychopharmacotherapy. Curr psychiat Ther 1969, 9:19-25
79405 (& Ardali, C.) An overview of child psychopharmacotherapy. Med Rec Ann 1968, 61:354-357
79406 An overview of group therapy with adolescents. Int J grp PT 1968, 18:461-480
79407 Pseudo-homosexuality as studied in group psychotherapy. Psa 1960, 20:207-211
79408 (& Ardali, C.) Psychiatric study of children with diagnosis of regional ileitis. Southern med J 1964, 57:799-802
79409 Psychoactive drugs in the care of adolescents. In Usdin, G. L. *Adolescence Care and Counseling*, II, Phila: Lippincott 1967, 160-175
79410 (& Bedford, Z.) Psychologic preparation of a five-year-old pseudohermaphrodite for surgical sexual charge. Pediat Clin N Amer 1963, 10
79411 The role of fantasy in adolescent medicine. Southern med J 1961, 54: 1111-1114
79412 Special considerations in adolescent group therapy. Int J grp PT 1961, 11:196-203
79413 To the id: onward and sideways. Worm Runners Dig 1967, 9:101-103

79414 Use of dreams in adolescent psychotherapy. Psychotherapy 1969, 6: 128-130

79415 The use of psychoactive drugs in the outpatient treatment of psychiatric disorders of children. P 1968, 124:95-101. Ann Prog child Psychiat 1969, 651-661

79416 (et al) Use of volunteers as social work technicians in a child psychiatry clinic. MH 1966, 50:460-462

See Duffy, James H.; Hart, Juanita

KRAFT, TOM

79417 Erotisierte Übertragung in der Verhaltenstherapie. [Erotized transference in behavior therapy.] Z PSM 1969, 15:126-130

79418 Psychoanalysis and behaviorism: a false antithesis. PT 1969, 23:482-487

KRAGH, ULF

79419 (& Kroon, T.) An analysis of aggression and identification in young offenders by the study of perceptual development. Hum Develpm 1966, 9:209-221

79420 A case of infantile animal phobia in adult precognitive organization. Vita hum 1962, 5:111-124

79421 Pathogenesis in dipsomania. An illustration of the actual-genetic model of perception-personality. I. Theoretical frame. Anamnesis. II. Presentation and analysis of the actual-genetic series. III. The retest series. The pathogenic transformations. Repression and regression. Acta Psychiat Scand 1960, 35:207-222; 261-288; 480-497

KRALL, VITA

See Murphy, Lois B.

KRAMER, CHARLES H.

79422 (& Kramer, J. R.) Afraid to go to bed. Geriat Nurs 1967, 3(2):11-17

79423 Aphorisms for understanding the aged. Prof nurs Home 1966, April

79424 Are MDs wary of treating aged, chronically ill? *Crosscurrents of Controversy*, Medical Tribune, Weekend Edition 1965, 27 March

79425 (& Johnston, G. F.) Community attitudes toward nursing homes. Prof nurs Home 1965, July

79426 Conflicts between adults and aged parents. Nursing Homes 1964, Jan

79427 (& Johnston, G. F.) Correcting confusion in the brain-damaged. Prof nurs Home 1965, May

79428 (& Jones, W. E.) Creating a therapeutic language atmosphere. Prof nurs Home 1967, Sept

79429 (& Dunlop, H. E.) Crisis in a nursing home. Prof nurs Home 1967, June

79430 (& Johnston, G. F.) Doctor's standing orders for the nursing home. Nursing Homes 1964, Nov

79431 (& Dunlop, H. E.) The dying patient. Geriat Nurs 1966, Sept-Oct

79432 (& Kramer, J. R.) Establishing a therapeutic community in a nursing home. Prof nurs Home 1966, Sept-Oct-Nov; 1967, Jan-Feb-March
79433 Extra-marital affairs. The Phil Lind Interview 1967, 27 July
79434 (& Johnston, G. F.) Got a personnel problem? Maybe it's you. Nursing Home Administrator 1965, March-April
79435 (& Johnston, G. F.) How to involve your doctors. Prof nurs Home 1965, Sept
79436 (& Dunlop, H. E.) If wishing could make it so. Geriat Nurs 1967, 3(5):8-13
79437 Institutional barrier to changes in nursing homes. Nursing Homes 1965, Nov
79438 (& Kramer, D. R.) Is medical care improving? Prof nurs Home 1968, Jan
79439 Man with a message. Psychiat Reporter 1965, Jan-Feb
79440 (& Kramer, J. R.) Managing the hostile patient. Geriatric Nursing 1966, May-June
79441 Maxwell Gitelson: analytic aphorisms. Q 1967, 36:260-270
79442 (& Lessing, J. C.) Medical care in Illinois nursing homes. J Amer Geriat Soc 1962, 10:983-994
79443 (& Sondag, R. F.) Medical care of nursing home patients. Gerontologist 1964, 4:89-91
79444 Mental health in nursing homes. Nursing Home Administrator 1963, June
79445 More aphorisms for understanding the aged. Prof nurs Home 1966, July
79446 (& Kramer, J. R.) A new approach to staff training. Prof nurs Home 1963, June
79447 (& Dunlop, H. E.) Nurses accept failure. Geriat Nurs 1967, 3(8):8-10
79448 (& Dunlop, H. E.) Optimal frustration aids recovery. Geriat Nurs 1967, 3(3):14-18
79449 (& Dunlop, H. E.) The paranoid patient. Geriat Nurs 1966, Nov-Dec
79450 (& Johnston, G. F.) The problem of physician responsibility. Prof nurs Home 1965, Aug
79451 Psychiatric knowledge can help you do a better job. Prof nurs Home 1964, Feb
79452 Psychoanalytically oriented family therapy: ten year evolution in a private child psychiatry practice. (Multilitho) 40 p
79453 Reflections of a psychiatrist. Prof nurs Home 1967, Aug
79454 The relationships between child and family psychopathology: a suggested extension of psychoanalytic theory and technique. (Multilitho) 55 p
79455 (& Dunlop, H. E.; Kramer, J. R.) Resolving grief. Geriat Nurs 1966, July-Aug
79456 (& Kramer, J. R.) Safety vs rehabilitation—a liability risk. Prof nurs Home 1965, Oct
79457 Staff involvement can be overdone. Ment Hosp 1964, 15:406-407
79458 Ten ways to improve staff relationships. Geriat Nurs 1967, Nov
79459 (& Johnston, G. F.; Joadwine, M. M.) Therapeutic care of the blind. Prof nurs Home 1966, Jan-Feb-March
79460 (& Johnston, G. F.) Too much T. L. C. can backfire. Prof nurs Home 1965, June

79461 Total therapeutic situation for the aged. Geriat Focus 1966, 15 May
79462 (& Peterson, L. S.) Volunteer's discussion group. Prof nurs Home 1967, May

See Sondag, Roger F.

KRAMER, DANIEL R.

See Kramer, Charles H.

KRAMER, EDITH

79463 The fables test. J proj Tech 1968, 32:530-532
79464 Kunst-Therapie mit Kindern. [Art therapy with children.] Hbh Kinder-psychother 477-487

KRAMER, JAN

See Farberow, Norman L.; Litman, Robert E.

KRAMER, JEANNETTE R.

See Kramer, Charles H.

KRAMER, JOHANNA

79465 A study of an aspect of transference as a factor in interpersonal perception. Diss Abstr 1967, 28:965-966

KRAMER, MARIA K.

S-50948 On the continuation of the analytic process after psycho-analysis (a self-observation).
Abs PCR RFPsa 1961, 25:284

KRAMER, MILTON

79466 (& Ornstein, P. H.; Whitman, R. M.; Baldridge, B. J.) The contribution of early memories and dreams to the diagnostic process. Comprehen Psychiat 1967, 8:344-374
79467 (& Whitman, R. M.; Baldridge, B.; Lansky, L.) Depression: dreams and defenses. P 1965, 122:411-419
Abs Loeb, L. Q 1967, 36:473
79468 (Ed) Dream Psychology and the New Biology of Dreaming. Springfield, Ill: Thomas 1969, xxvi + 459 p
79469 (& Whitman, R. M.; Baldridge, W.; Lansky, L. M.) Dreaming in the depressed. Canad Psychiat Ass J 1966, 11(Suppl):S178-S192
79470 (& Ornstein, P. H.; Whitman, R. M.) Drug therapy. Prog Neurol Psychiat 1965, 20:723-753
79471 (& Whitman, R. M.; Baldridge, B.; Ornstein, P. H.) Drugs and dreams III: The effects of imipramine on the dreams of depressed patients. P 1968, 124:1385-1392
79472 Drugs, depression, and dream sequences. An exploration of dream content changes induced by medication, by psychopathologic conditions, and by variations in the ego's adaptability. Ohio State med J 1966, 62:1277-1280

79473   (& Baldridge, B. J.; Whitman, R. M.; Ornstein, P. H.; Smith, P. C.)
        An exploration of the manifest dream in schizophrenic and depressed
        patients. Psychophysiology 1968, 5:221. Dis nerv Sys 1969, 30(Suppl):
        126-130
79474   More on depression and dreams. P 1966, 123:232-233
79475   (& Whitman, R. M.; Baldridge, B. J.; Lansky, L. M.) Patterns of
        dreaming. The interrelationship of the dreams of a night. JNMD 1964,
        139:426-439
            Abs BFM Q 1967, 36:140
79476   Psychiatric transactions and the use of the experimental dream. J Nat
        Med Ass 1966, 58:185-190

        See Baldridge, Bill J.; Gottlieb, Anthony A.; Ornstein, Paul H.; Whit-
        man, Roy M.

KRAMER, PAUL

S-50949 On discovering one's identity. A case report.
            Abs An Surv Psa 1955, 6:206-208
79477   Discussion on Dr. Anthony's paper "A study of 'screen sensations.'"
        Psa St C 1961, 16:246-250
S-50951 Note on one of the preoedipal roots of the superego.
            Abs EDJ An Surv Psa 1958, 9:269-270
79478   Obituary: Maxwell Gitelson 1902-1965. Q 1965, 34:441-444

        See Fleischmann, Otto; Gitelson, Maxwell

KRAMER, SELMA

79479   (& Settlage, C. F.) On the concepts and technique of child analysis.
        J Amer Acad Child Psychiat 1962, 1:509-535

REVIEW OF:
79480   Freud, A. The Psycho-Analytical Treatment of Children. Technical
        Lectures and Essays. Q 1961, 30:271-275

KRAMER, SOL

79481   Ethology and human character formation. Int Psychiat Clin 1965, 2:
        303-350
79482   Fixed motor patterns in ethologic psychoanalytic theory. Sci Psa 1968,
        12:124-155

KRANTZLER, BARBARA

        See Cooper, Shirley

KRANZ, HEINRICH

79483   Der Begriff des Autismus und die endogenen Psychosen. [The concept
        of autism and endogenous psychoses.] In author's *Psychopathologie
        Heute* 61-71
79484   (Ed) Psychopathologie Heute. [Psychopathology Today.] Stuttgart:
        Georg Thieme 1962, xi + 378 p

KRAPF, E. EDUARDO

79485 L'activité de l'Organization mondiale de la Santé dans le domaine de la santé mentale. Hyg ment 1960, 49:215-232; 433-436
The work of the World Health Organization in the field of mental health. MH 1960, 44:315-338

79486 The Bleulerian concept of schizophrenia and the comparative approach. JNMD 1964, 138:332-339

79487 (& Moser, J.) Changes of emphasis and accomplishments in mental health work, 1948-1960. MH 1962, 46:163-191

S-50966 Cold and warmth in the transference experience.
Abs SLP An Surv Psa 1956, 7:340-341

79488 The concept of social psychiatry. Int J soc Psychiat 1960, 6:6-8

79489 The concepts of normality and mental health in psycho-analysis. J 1961, 42:439-446
Abs WPK Q 1962, 31:579

S-50963 Entwicklungslinien der psychoanalytischen Technik.
Abs HK An Surv Psa 1957, 8:10-13

79490 El grupo de las esquizofrénias y la psiquiatria comparada. [The group of schizophrenias and comparative psychiatry.] Acta psiquiat psicol Arg 1963, 9(1):1-7

79491 The international approach to the problems of mental health. Int soc sci J 1959, 11:63-71

S-50973 Sur les phénomènes moteurs dans le transfert.
Abs An Surv Psa 1955, 6:326-329

79492 The relationship of psychiatry and mental health care to clinical medicine and the sciences of man. WHO Publ Hlth Pap 1961, 9:9-13

79493 Psiquitría, Volume I. Buenos Aires: Editorial Paidós 1959
Psychiatry, Volume I. Principles. NY/London: Grune & Stratton 1961, 244 p
Rv Usandivaras, R. J. Rev Psicoanál 1961, 18:174. MG Q 1963, 32:597. ESt J 1963, 44:115-116

S-50981 Shylock and Antonio. A psychoanalytic study of Shakespeare and anti-semitism.
Abs An Surv Psa 1955, 6:450-451

S-50960 Über die Sprachwahl in der Psychoanalyse von Polyglotten.
Abs An Surv Psa 1955, 6:346-347

S-50986 Transference and motility.
Abs SO An Surv Psa 1957, 8:264-265

79494 Zum Begriff der psychischen Normalität. [The concept of psychic normality.] Schweiz ANP 1963, 91:65-69

KRAPF, EVA

TRANSLATION OF:
Caruso, I. A. [43488]

KRASNER, JACK D.

79495 (& Feldman, B.; Liff, Z.; Mermelstein, I.; Aronson, M. L.; Guttman, O.) Observing the observers. Int J grp PT 1964, 14:214-217

See Aronson, Marvin L.; Kadis, Asya L.

KRASNER, LEONARD

79496 Behavior control and social responsibility. Am Psych 1962, 17:199-204. In Goldstein, A. P. & Dean, S. J. *The Investigation of Psychotherapy,* NY: Wiley 1966, 57-62

79497 Behavior modification research and the role of the therapist. Meth Res PT 292-311

* * * The reinforcement machine. See [79500]

79498 Reinforcement, verbal behavior, and psychotherapy. Ops 1963, 33:601-613. In Goldstein, A. P. & Dean, S. J. *The Investigation of Psychotherapy,* NY: Wiley 1966, 26-35

79499 (& Ullmann, L. P.; Weiss, R. L.) Studies in role perception. J gen Psychol 1964, 71:367-371

79500 The therapist as a social reinforcement machine. In Strupp, H. A. & Luborsky, L. *Research in Psychotherapy,* Wash DC: APA 1962, 61-94. With title: The reinforcement machine. In Berenson, B. G. & Carkhuff, R. R. *Sources of Gain in Counseling and Psychotherapy,* NY/Chicago/ San Francisco: Holt, Rinehart & Winston 1967, 193-240

KRATOCHVÍL, STANISLAV

79501 Úzkostná neuróza: príspevek k etiopatogeneze. [Anxiety neurosis: contribution to etiopathogenesis.] Ceskoslov Psychol 1965, 9:395-402

KRAUDE, W.

See May, Philip R. A.

KRAULAND-STEINBEREITHNER, F.

79502 (& Ringel, E.) Die Therapie der psychosomatischen Erkrankungen. [Treatment of psychosomatic diseases.] In Hoff, H. *Therapeutische Fortschritte in der Neurologie und Psychiatrie,* Vienna: Verlag Urban & Schwarzenberg 1960, 414-424

KRAUPP, O.

79503 (& Pateisky, K.) Therapeutische Probleme der neuromuskulären Erkrankungen. [Therapeutic problems with neuromuscular diseases.] In Hoff, H. *Therapeutische Fortschritte in der Neurologie und Psychiatrie,* Vienna: Verlag Urban & Schwarzenberg 1960, 21-32

KRAUS, H.

See Hoff, Hans; Schindler, Raoul

KRAUS, ROBERT F.

79504 Cross-cultural validation of psychoanalytic theories of depression. Penn psychiat Q 1968, 8(3):24-33

79505 Psychiatric concepts from the perspective of historical process. Penn psychiat Q 1969, 9:36-40

KRAUSE, MERTON S.

79506 An analysis of Carl R. Rogers' theory of personality. Genet Psychol Monogr 1964, 69:49-99

79507 Defensive and nondefensive resistance. Q 1961, 30:221-231

KRAUSS, HELMUTH

79508 Kasuistischer Beitrag aus der nervenärztlichen Praxis: ein Fall von "Schizophrenie." [Casuistic contribution from the medically nervous patient: a case of schizophrenia.] Praxis PT 1964, 9:106-108

KRAUSS, ROBERT M.

See Deutsch, Morton

KRAUSS, RUDOLF

79509 Sigmund Freud und die pädagogische Psychologie. [Sigmund Freud and pedagogical psychology.] Westdeutsche Schulzeitung 1964, 73: 253-257

KRAUT, ARTHUR P.

See Malev, Jonathan S.

KRAVITZ, ARTHUR R.

79510 (& Thomas, D. P.) Emotional reactions to long-term anticoagulant therapy. Arch intern Med 1964, 114:663-668

ABSTRACTS OF:

79511 Aarons, Z. A. Notes on a case of *maladie des tics.* An Surv Psa 1958, 9:140-141

79512 Bellak, L. Creativity: some random notes to a systematic consideration. An Surv 1958, 9:489-490

79513 Bibring, G. L. Old age: its liabilities and its assets. A psychological discourse. Bull Phila Ass Psa 1967, 17:43-47

79514 Buchenholz, B. Models for pleasure. An Surv Psa 1958, 8:83-84

79515 Carlisky, M. The Oedipus legend and "Oedipus Rex." An Surv Psa 1958, 9:446

79516 Feldman, S. S. Blanket interpretations. An Surv Psa 1958, 9:357-358

79517 Heilbrunn, G. Comments on a common form of acting out. An Surv Psa 1958, 9:408-409

79518 Langer, W. L. The next assignment. An Surv Psa 1958, 9:453-454

79519 McPeek, J. A. S. Richard and his shadow world. An Surv Psa 1958, 9:497

79520 Racker, H. Psychoanalytic technique and the analyst's unconscious masochism. An Surv Psa 1958, 9:404-405

79521 Rowley, B. A. Psychology and literary criticism. An Surv Psa 1958, 9:499-500

79522 Veszy-Wagner, L. Serf Balázs: a "boy without the dike;" a stage before the solution of the oedipal conflict. An Surv Psa 1958, 9:446-447

KRAVITZ, HENRY

79523 Disordered mind. (film) CBC 1965
79524 Emotional factors in general practice. (film) Geigy Film 1966
79525 Management of adolescents in general hospital setting. Canad fam
Physician 1968, Oct
79526 Management of Adolescents in General Hospital Setting. Schering
Corp 1968
79527 Psychological mechanism in pregnancy and childbirth. Canad J Physio-
ther 1965, July
79528 The scapegoat mechanism. Canad Jewish Rev 1962, Feb
79529 Unwed mothers—condensed. Dig Obs Gyn 1967, Spring
79530 (& Trossman, B.; Feldman, R. B.) Unwed mothers. Practical and theoretical considerations. Canad Psychiat Ass J 1966, 11:456-464

KRECH, DAVID

See Dennis, Wayne

KREICI, ERIKA

79531 Die Entwicklung der Mutter-Kind Bezeihung in der Bildserie eines 5-
jährigen asthmatischen Knaben. [Development of the mother-child relationship in a series of drawings by a 5-year-old asthmatic boy.] Prax
Kinderpsychol 1969, 18:161-168

KREISLER, LÉON

79532 (& Fain, M.; Soulé, M.) La clinique psychosomatique de l'enfant. A
propos des troubles fonctionnels du nourrisson: coliques idiopathiques
du premier trimestre, insomnie, mérycisme, anorexie, vomissements.
[Psychosomatic conditions in pediatrics. Functional disorders of infancy: idiopathic colics of the first trimester, insomnia, rumination, anorexia, vomiting.] Psychiat Enfant 1966, 9:89-222
79533 (& Fain, M.; Soulé, M.) La clinique psychosomatique de l'enfant. Les
états frontières dans la nosologie. [Psychosomatic medicine in childhood. The nosology of the borderline states.] Psychiat Enfant 1967,
10:157-198
79534 Reflexions d'un pédiatrie. [A pediatrician's reflections.] RFPsa 1966,
30:762-765

See Lebovici, Serge

KREITLER, HANS

79535 (& Kreitler, S.) Children's concepts of sexuality and birth. Child Develpm 1966, 37:363-378
79536 (& Kreitler, S.) Die Dimension der kognitiven Orientierung und ihre
Bedeutung für die Kinderpsychotherapie. [The dimension of cognitive
orientation and its significance for child psychotherapy.] Hbh Kinderpsychother 53-63
79537 (& Elblinger, S.) Individual psychotherapy, group psychotherapy, psychodrama; a report from Israel. Prog Pt 1960, 5:212-217

79538   (& Elblinger, S.) Psychiatrische und kulturelle Aspekte des Wider-
        standes gegen das Psychodrama. [Psychiatric and cultural aspects of re-
        sistances to psychodrama.] Psyche 1961, 15:155-161
79539   (& Kreitler, S.) Unhappy memories of "the happy past": studies in cog-
        nitive dissonance. Brit J Psychol 1968, 59:157-166
79540   (& Kreitler, S.) Validation of psychodramatic behaviour against be-
        haviour in life. M 1968, 41:185-192

KREITLER, SHULAMITH

79541   Symbolschöpfung und Symbolerfassung. Eine experimentalpsycho-
        logische Untersuchung. [The Creation and Understanding of Symbols.
        An Inquiry in Experimental Psychology.] Munich/Basel: E. Reinhardt
        1965, 215 p

        See Kreitler, Hans

KREITZER, SHELDON FRED

79542   The effects of frustration and permissiveness on young children's fan-
        tasy aggression. Diss Abstr 1964, 24:4781-4782

KRÉKJÁRTÓ, M. VON

        See Jores, Arthur

KREMER, MALVINA, W.

79543   (& Rifkin, A. H.) The early development of homosexuality: a study of
        adolescent lesbians. P 1969, 126:91-96
79544   Identity formation in male and female adolescent homosexuals. Sci Psa
        1969, 15:51-59

        See Bieber, Irving; Sager, Clifford J.

KRESH, N. K.

79545   Partial resolution of an obsession. Psychiat Comm 1960, 3:115-118

KRESTNIKOV, ANGEL N.

        See Dimitrov, Christo T.

KREVELEN, D. A. VAN

79546   Analysis of a prostitute. Acta paedopsychiat 1966, 33:109-117
79547   [Children who don't want to go to school.] (Dut) NTvG 1967, 111:
        1281-1286
79548   [Children who refuse to go to school.] (Dut) T Ziekenverpl 1968, 21:
        405-408
79549   On the relationship between early infantile autism and autistic psycho-
        pathy. Acta paedopsychiat 1963, 30:303-323
79550   The problem of communicating the diagnosis to the parents. Acta
        paedopsychiat 1965, 32:33-34

79551 Prognosis of childhood neuroses and psychoses. Proc IV World Cong Psychiat 1966, 85-90
79552 [Rejection by the father.] (Dut) NTvG 1965, 109:737-741

KRICH, ARON

79553 Before Kinsey: continuity in American sex research. R 1966, 53:233-254
       Abs SRS Q 1967, 36:471
79554 (Ed) The Sexual Revolution. NY: Delta 1963, 352 p; Dell 1965, xxviii + 225 p

See Greenwald, Harold

REVIEWS OF:
79555 Lowen, A. Love and Orgasm. R 1966, 53:310-312
79556 Reik, T. The Many Faces of Sex. R 1967, 54(1):190-191
79557 Slovenko, R. (Ed) Sexual Behavior and the Law. R 1966, 53(1):149-154

KRICHHAUFF, GISELA

S-51026 Der Asthmatiker und seine Innenwelt.
       Abs Spiegel, N. An Surv Psa 1956, 7:204-205

KRIEG, P.

See Schneider, Pierre-Bernard

KRIEGER, JUDITH A.

79558 Psychoanalytic theory: a science? Conn Coll Psychol J 1964, 1:69-78

KRIEGER, MARGERY H.

79559 (& Worchel, P.) A quantitative study of the psychoanalytic hypotheses of identification. Psychol Rep 1959, 5:448
79560 (& Worchel, P.) A test of the psychoanalytic theory of identification. J ind Psych 1960, 16:56-63

KRIEGMAN, GEORGE

79561 Anxiety and learning in children with special problems. Proc IX Nemours Foundation Conf on Crippled Children. Virginia J Educ 1962, 55(Apr):12-15
79562 A systematic approach to the evaluation and treatment of marital problems. MCV Q 1966, 1(4)
79563 Totem poles and space perception. Torch Mag 1964, July

See Kriegman, Lois

KRIEGMAN, LOIS S.

79564 (& Kriegman, G.) The PaTE Report: a new psychodynamic and therapeutic evaluation procedure. Psychiat Q 1965, 39:646-674

KRIEKEMANS, ALBERT JAN JOSEF

79565 Genetische Psychologie Systematisch und Historisch: 7. De Geschiedenis van de Kinderpsychologie tot en met Sigmund Freud, Anna Freud en Melanie Klein. [A Systematic and Historical Account of Genetic Psychology. Child Psychology According to Sigmund Freud, Anna Freud, and Melanie Klein.] Belgium: Lennoo 1965, 212 p

KRIES, DIETRICH V.

79566 Zur Kritik der Aggressionstrieb-Hypothese. [On the criticism of aggression drive hypothesis.] Dyn Psychiat 1969, 2:144-146. Abs (Eng) 146-147

KRIES, ILSE VON

S-51031 Zur Differentialdiagnose der Angstneurose und Angsthysterie. Ein Beitrag zur Entwicklungsgeschichte der psychoanalytischen Theorie. Abs HA An Surv Psa 1957, 8:111-112

KRIETMAN, N.

79567 Psychiatric training. A transatlantic viewpoint. Int J Psychiat 1967, 4: 451-452

KRIJGERS JANZEN, E.

79568 ["Déjà vu" and "depersonalisatie." 2 poems by Achterberg. A confrontation with clinical phenomenology.] (Dut) Ned Tijdschr Psychol 1966, 21:136-147

KRILL, D. F.

79569 Loosening the oedipal bind through family therapy. Soc Casewk 1967, 48:563-569

KRIM, MURRAY

ABSTRACTS OF:
79570 Schachtel, E. G. Notes on Freud's personality and style of thought. Discussion of Holt, R. R. "Freud's cognitive style." Contempo Psa 1965, 1(2):149-150

KRIMS, MARVIN B.

79571 Observations on children who suffer from dwarfism. Psychiat Q 1968, 42:430-443
79572 Psychiatric observations on children with precocious physical development. J Amer Acad Child Psychiat 1962, 1:397-413

ABSTRACT OF:
79573 Kris, M. & Solnit, A. J. Trauma and infantile experiences—a longitudinal perspective. Bull Phila Ass Psa 1966, 16:95-99

KRIMSLEY, JOSEPH M.

ABSTRACT OF:

79574 Van der Leeuw, P. J. A clinical contribution to the problem of early neglect. Q 1961, 30:618-620

KRINGLEN, EINAR

79575 [The Eysenck school. A survey and criticism.] (Nor) Nord Psyk Tiksskr 1964, 18:256-271

79576 Heredity and Environment in the Functional Psychoses. An Epidemiological-Clinical Twin Study. Oslo: Universitetsforlagt 1967

79577 Heredity and Environment in the Functional Psychoses. Case Histories. Oslo: Universitetsforlagt 1967

79578 Obsessional neurotics: a long-term follow-up. Brit J Psychiat 1965, 111: 709-722

79579 The prognosis in obsessional illness. A follow-up study. Acta Psychiat Scand 1964, 40:180:155-157

79580 [Sigmund Freud and the dream research of today.] (Nor) Nord Psyk Tidsskr 1968, 22:295-307

KRINSKY, A.

See Bowers, Margaretta K.

KRINSKY, L. W.

79581 (& Jennings, R. M.) The management and treatment of acting-out adolescents in a separate unit. Hosp Comm Psychiat 1968, 19:72-75

See Rolo, A.

KRIPPNER, STANLEY

79582 Investigations of "extrasensory" phenomena in dreams and other altered states of consciousness. J Amer Soc Psychosom Dent Med 1969, 16: 7-14

79583 The paranormal dream and man's pliable future. R 1969, 56:28-43

KRIS, ANTON O.

TRANSLATION OF:

Hug-Hellmuth, H. von: [77362]

KRIS, ERNST

79584 Decline and recovery in the life of a three-year-old; or: Data in psychoanalytic perspective on the mother-child relationship. Psa St C 1962, 17:175-215
Abs SLe RFPsa 1964, 28:812

S-18907 Ego psychology and interpretation in psychoanalytic therapy.
Ich-Psychologie und Deutung in der psychoanalytischen Therapie. Psyche 1968, 22:173-186

S-18923A Neutralization and sublimation. Observations on young children.
Abs An Surv Psa 1955, 6:124-127

S-18928A The personal myth: a problem in psychoanalytic technique.
　　　　Abs CFH An Surv Psa 1956, 7:316-319
S-18929 On preconscious mental processes.
　　　　Considerazioni sui processi psichici del preconscio. Riv Psa 1961,
　　　　7:83-100
S-18933A Psychoanalysis and the study of creative imagination. In Ruitenbeek,
　　　　H. M. *The Creative Imagination,* Chicago: Quadrangle Books 1965,
　　　　23-45
S-18934 Psychoanalytic Explorations in Art. NY: Schocken 1964, 384 p
　　　　Ricerche Psicoanalitische sull'Arte. (Tr: Fachinelli, E.) Turin:
　　　　Einaudi 1967
S-18937B The recovery of childhood memories in psychoanalysis.
　　　　Abs SGo An Surv Psa 1956, 7:304-307
S-18943AA On some vicissitudes of insight in psycho-analysis.
　　　　Acerca de algunas vicisitudes del "insight" en psicoanálisis. Rev urug
　　　　Psa 1961-62, 4:287-309
　　　　Abs SG An Surv Psa 1956, 7:303-304

　　　　See Hartmann, Heinz H.

KRIS, MARIANNE

79585 Problems of early childhood and latency. In Neubauer, P. B. *Children
　　　　in Collectives. Child-Rearing Aims and Practices in the Kibbutz,* Spring-
　　　　field, Ill: Thomas 1965, 69-127
79586 (& Solnit, A. J.) Trauma and infantile experiences—a longitudinal per-
　　　　spective. (Read at joint meeting of Western New England Psa Soc &
　　　　Boston Psa Soc, 9 Oct 1965)
　　　　Abs Krims, M. B. Bull Phila Ass Psa 1966, 16:95-99
S-51037 The use of prediction in a longitudinal study. In Weinreb, J. *Recent
　　　　Developments in Psychoanalytic Child Therapy,* NY: IUP 1960, 108-
　　　　123
　　　　Abs EMW An Surv Psa 1957, 8:183-185

　　　　See Solnit, Albert J.; Solomon, Alfred P.

KRITZER, HERBERT

79587 (& Phillips, C. A.) Observing group psychotherapy—an affective learning
　　　　experience. PT 1966, 20:471-476

KROGER, WILLIAM S.

79588 An analysis of valid and invalid objections to hypnotherapy. Amer J
　　　　clin Hyp 1963, 6:120-131

KROJANKER, ROLF J.

79589 Leuner's symbolic drama. Amer J Hyp 1966, 9:56-61

KRONENBERGER, EARL J.

79590 (& Heck, E. M.) Child-parent identification between reading ability
　　　　groups. Psychology 1964, 1:2-4

KRONFELD, GERDA

79591 Inwiefern kann die Psychoanalyse die "progressive Personalisation" fördern? [To what extent can psychoanalysis benefit "progressive personalization?"] In Edelweiss, M. L. et al: *Personalisation,* Vienna: Herder 1964, 50-61

KRONHAUSEN, EBERHARD

See Kronhausen, Phyllis

KRONHAUSEN, PHYLLIS

79592 (& Kronhausen, E.) The Sexually Responsive Woman. NY: Grove Pr 1964, 255 p
Rv Heiman, M. Q 1966, 35:305-307. Woltmann, A. G. R 1966, 53: 303-308

KRONHOLM, JEAN

See Chessick, Richard D.

KRONOLD, EDWARD

79593 Obituary: Robert Waelder: 1900-1967. Q 1968, 37:282

KROON, T.

See Kragh, Ulf

KROSS, ANNA M.

79594 Woman's role. The educated woman and modern society: a panel. Sci Psa 1966, 10:123-126

KROTH, J. A.

79595 (& Forrest, M. S.) Effects of posture and anxiety level on effectiveness of free association. Psychol Rep 1969, 25:725-726

KRUG, C. M.

See Victor, R. G.

KRUG, OTHILDA

79596 (& Gardner, G. E.; Hirschberg, J. C.; Lourie, R. S.; Rexford, E. N.; Robinson, J. F.) (Eds) Career Training in Child Psychiatry. Wash: Am Psychiat Ass 1964, 260 p
79597 (& Dember, C. F.) The diagnostic and therapeutic utilization of children's reactions to the president's death. Chld Dth Pres 80-98

KRÜGER, H.

79598 Zur Psychodynamik der Gestationspsychosen. [The psychodynamics of gestational psychoses.] Z Psychother med Psychol 1965, 15:230-252

KRUGER, STANLEY I.

See Kanter, Stanley S.

KRUGMAN, DOROTHY C.

79599   Differences in the relation of parents and children to adoption. Child Welfare 1967, 46:267-270
79600   A new home for Liz. Behavioral changes in a deviant child. J Amer Acad Child Psychiat 1968, 7:398-420
79601   Reality in adoption. Child Welfare 1964, 43:349-358

KRUPP, GEORGE R.

79602   The bereavement reaction—a cross cultural evaluation. J Relig Hlth 1962, 1
79603   The bereavement reaction: a special case of separation anxiety. Socio-cultural considerations. Psa St Soc 1962, 2:42-74
79604   Identification as a defence against anxiety in coping with loss. J 1965, 46:303-314
          Abs EVN Q 1967, 36:622

KRUPP, NEAL E.

79605   Psychiatric implications of chronic and crippling illness. Psychosomatics 1968, 9:109-113

KRUSE, F.

S-51069 Grundsätzliche Unterschiede in der Übertragung männerlicher und weiblicher Patienten.
          Abs An Surv Psa 1955, 6:367

KRUSH, T. P.

79606   The search for the golden key. BMC 1964, 28:77-82

KRUTCH, JOSEPH W.

79607   Genius and neuroticism. In Nunokawa, W. D. *Readings in Abnormal Psychology: Human Values and Abnormal Behavior,* Chicago: Scott, Foresman 1965, 116-120

KRYSPIN-EXNER, K.

See Berner, P.

KRYSTAL, HENRY

79608   (& Moore, R. A.; Dorsey, J. M.) Alcoholism and the force of education. Personn Guid J 1966, 45:134-139
79609   The current status of postgraduate psychiatric education. P 1962, 119:483-484
79610   Discussion of Hoppe, K. D. "The emotional reactions of psychiatrists when confronting survivors of persecution." Psa Forum 1969, 3:205-207

79611 (& Petty, T. A.) Dynamics of adjustment to migration. Proc III World Cong Psychiat. Psychiat Q Suppl 1963, 37:119-133

79612 Giorgio de Chirico. Ego states and artistic production. (Read at Am Psa Ass, May 1961) Am Im 1966, 23:210-226
       Abs Cuad Psa 1967, 3:244-245. JWS Q 1967, 36:629-630

79613 (Ed) Massive Psychic Trauma. NY: IUP 1969, xvii + 369 p

79614 The opiate-withdrawal syndrome as a state of stress. Psychiat Q Suppl 1962, 36:53-65

79615 The phenomena of transference in the practice of medicine. Mich Med 1960, 59:1369-1373

79616 Postgraduate teaching in psychiatry combining television and FM-radio with seminars (a report of a demonstration project and survey). Psychosomatics 1962, 3:188-192

79617 The problem of abstinence by the patient as a requisite for the psychotherapy of alcoholism. II. The evaluation of the meaning of drinking in determining the requirement of abstinence by alcoholics during treatment. Quart J Stud Alcohol 1962, 23:112-121

79618 Psychic sequelae of massive psychic trauma. Discussion. Proc IV World Cong Psychiat 1966, 931-936

79619 A psychoanalytic contribution to the theory of cyclicity of the financial economy. (Read at Am Psa Ass, Dec 1963) Psa Forum 1966, 1:358-365; 372-376
       Abs Cuad Psa 1967, 3:247

79620 (& Petty, T. A.) The psychological processes of normal convalescence. Psychosomatics 1961, 2:366-372

79621 Therapeutic assistants in psychotherapy with regressed patients. Curr psychiat Ther 1964, 4:230-232

79622 (& Moore, R. A.) Who is qualified to treat the alcoholic? A discussion. I: Introduction. II: Advantages of the professional psychotherapist. III: Advantages of nonpsychotherapists. IV: Summary of general discussion. Quart J Stud Alcohol 1963, 24:705-720

79623 Withdrawal from drugs. Psychosomatics 1966, 7:299-302

       See Chodorkoff, Bernard; Margolis, Marvin O.; Moore, Robert A.; Niederland, William G.

REVIEWS OF:
79624 Lifton, R. J. Death in Life. Survivors of Hiroshima. Q 1969, 38:488-491

79625 Nagera, H. Vincent Van Gogh: A Psychological Study. Q 1968, 37:606-608

KUBIE, LAWRENCE SCHLESINGER

79626 Die Auflösung der Übertragung; ein offenes Probleme der psychoanalytischen Behandlung. Psyche 1967, 21:84-96
       Unsolved problems in the resolution of the transference. Q 1968, 37:331-352

79627 Bailey on the man, Freud; an editorial book review. JNMD 1966, 142:393-394

79628   Die Beziehung der Psychose zum neurotischen Prozess. [The relationship of psychoanalysis to the neurotic process.] Dyn Psychiat 1968, 1: 35-45

79629   The biological basis of psychiatry; viewpoint of the psychoanalyst. Recent Adv biol Psychiat 1965, 7:135-141

79630   Blocks to creativity. Int Sci Technol 1965, June:69-78. In Mooney, R. L. & Razik, T. A. *Explorations in Creativity*, NY: Harper & Row 1967, 33-42

79631   The central affective potential and its trigger mechanisms. In Gaskill, H. S. *Counterpoint: Libidinal Object and Subject*, NY: IUP 1963, 106-120

79632   The challenge of divorce: editorial. JNMD 1964, 138:511-512

79633   The changing economics of psychotherapeutic practice. JNMD 1964, 139:311-312
        Abs BFM Q 1966, 35:159

79634   Chronic schizophrenics. JNMD 1963, 136:421

79635   A complex process. In Schneidman, E. S. *On the Nature of Suicide*, San Francisco: Jossey-Bass 1969, 81-86; 87-99

79636   The concept of change in psychology. (Read at Boston Psa Soc, 27 Jan 1965)
        Abs Mogul, S. L. Bull Phila Ass Psa 1965, 15:43-47

79637   The concept of dream deprivation: a critical analysis. PSM 1962, 24: 62-65

79638   The concepts of medicine and psychotherapy. JNMD 1968, 147:103-104

79639   (& Mackie, J. B.) Critical issues raised by operations for gender transmutation. JNMD 1968, 147:431-443

79640   The cultural significance of psychiatry: the potential contribution of psychiatry to the struggles of the human spirit. Publication Office, Friends Hospital, May 1965

79641   Discussant: "Medical students." Teach Dyn Psychiat 71-73

79642   Discussant: "Psychiatric residents." Teach Dyn Psychiat 118-122

79643   Discussion of Eysenck, H. J. "The effects of psychotherapy." Int J Psychiat 1965, 1:175-178

79644   The disintegrating impact of "modern" life on the family in America and its explosive repercussions. In Liebman, S. *Emotional Forces in the Family*, Phila/Montreal: Lippincott 1959, 135-149

79645   The eagle and the ostrich. Arch gen Psychiat 1961, 5:109-119

79646   Editorial. JNMD 1961, 132:1-2; 1968, 147:103-104

79647   (& Robinson, H. A.) Editorial: Introduction, JNMD 1963, 136:339; 421

79648   Edward Glover. Abstracted from a biographical sketch of Edward Glover. Q 1969, 38:521-531

79649   An example of psychotic disorganization arising in early childhood out of a prepsychotic neurosis. PT 1966, 20:615-626

79650   Faith, culture and the American university. Harvard Alumni Bulletin 1961, 64:113-116

79651   The fallacious misuse of the concept of sublimation. (Read at Am Psa Ass, May 1961) Q 1962, 31:73-79
        Abs LDr RFPsa 1963, 27:355

79652 Florence Rena Sabin. Perspectives 1961, 4:306-315

79654 Foreword to Harrower, M. R. *Psychodiagnostic Testing*, Springfield, Ill: Thomas 1965

79655 The fostering of creative scientific productivity. Daedalus 1962, 91: 294-309

79656 Frontiers of research in psychiatry. In Redlich, F. C. et al: *The University and Community Mental Health*, New Haven: Yale Univ Pr 1968, 71-80

79657 The future of the private psychiatric hospital. Int J Psychiat 1968, 6:419-432; 449-450. Crosscurrents in Ps & Psa 179-199; 241-242

79658 Guilt by loose analogy: an editorial. JNMD 1961, 133:281-282

79659 How can the educational process become a behavioral science? Reiss-Davis Clin Bull 1968, 5:11-28. Learn Love 245-260

79660 Hypnotism: a focus for psychophysiological and psychoanalytic investigations. Arch gen Psychiat 1961, 4:40-54
  Abs KR Q 1962, 31:296

79661 The impact of uncontrolled birth on our democratic process. Humanist 1961, 21:3-13

S-51101 Influence of symbolic processes on the role of instincts in human behavior.
  Abs RZ An Surv Psa 1956, 7:88-90

S-51103 Introduction to Jones, R. M. *An Application of Psychoanalysis to Education*. In Rosenblith, J. F. & Allinsmith, W. *The Causes of Behavior*, Boston: Allyn & Bacon 1966, 225

79662 Is preventive psychiatry possible? Daedalus 1959, 88:646-668

79663 A look into the future of psychiatry. MH 1966, 50:611-617

79664 The maturation of psychiatrists or the time that changes take. JNMD 1962, 135:286-288

79665 Medicine as a spiritual challenge. J Relig Hlth 1964, 3:39-55

79666 Missing and wanted: heterodoxy in psychiatry and psychoanalysis. JNMD 1963, 137:311

79667 The modern massacre of the innocents. JNMD 1962, 135:1-4

79668 Multiple determinants of suicidal efforts. JNMD 1964, 138:3-8
  Abs BFM Q 1965, 34:138

79669 The nature of psychological change and its relation to cultural change. In Rothblatt, B. *Changing Perspectives on Man*, Chicago: Univ Chicago Pr 1968, 135-148
  Seelische Wandlung und deren Bezeihung zur sich wandelnden Kultur. Psyche 1969, 23:700-711

79670 Neurosis and normality. Ency Ment Hlth 1346-1353

S-51111 Neurotic Distortion of the Creative Process.
  German: Hamburg: Rowohlts Deutsche Enzyklopadie 1966, 118 p
  El Proceso Creativo. Su Distorsión Neurótica. Editorial Pax Mexico
  Abs EMD An Surv Psa 1958, 9:490-496

79671 New forces constraining the American family. 39th Annual Conference of Child Study Association of America, 4 Mar 1963. Publ by Better Homes & Gardens and distributed by the Association in April 1964, C1-C5

79672 Obituary: In memoriam, Jacob Finesinger, M.D., 1903-1959. Trans Neur Ass, NY: Springer 1960, 249-250

79673 Obituary: Sir David Henderson, 1884-1965. JNMD 1965, 141:263-264

79674 Obituary: Dr. William C. Menninger (1899-1966) "The Bill Treatment." JNMD 1967, 144:1

79675 The ontogeny of racial prejudice. JNMD 1965, 141:265-273

79676 The overall manpower problem and the creation of a new discipline: the nonmedical psychotherapist. In Klutch, M. *Mental Health Manpower, Vol. II,* California Medical Education and Research Foundation 1967, 112-120

79677 The overall manpower problem in mental health personnel. JNMD 1967, 144:466-470

79678 Pitfalls of community psychiatry. Arch gen Psychia 1968, 18:257-266

79679 Practical and Theoretical Aspects of Psychoanalysis. NY: Frederick A. Praeger 1961, xvii + 258 p

79680 Preface to Erickson, M. H. *Advanced Techniques of Hypnosis and Therapy;* (ed: Haley, J.) NY: Grune & Stratton 1967, vii-viii

79681 Preface to Scheflen, A. E. *A Psychotherapy of Schizophrenia: Direct Analysis,* Springfield, Ill: Thomas 1961, ix-xiv

79682 Provisions for the care of children of divorced parents: a new legal instrument. Yale Law J 1964, 73:1197-1200

S-51128 Psychoanalysis and marriage: practical and theoretical issues.
           Abs AHM An Surv Psa 1956, 7:395-397

S-51130 Psychoanalysis and scientific methods. JNMD 1960, 131:495-512

79683 Psychoanalysis and the American scene. 50 Yrs Psa 62-76

79684 A psychoanalytic approach to the pharmacology of psychological processes. In Uhr, L. M. & Miller, J. G. *Drugs and Behavior,* NY: Wiley 1960, 209-224

79685 The psychotherapeutic ingredient in the learning process. Int Psychiat Clin 1969, 6:224-242

79686 A reconsideration of thinking, the dream process, and "the dream." (Read at Am Psa Ass, Dec 1964) Q 1966, 35:191-198

79687 Reflections on training. Psa Forum 1966, 1:96-100; 110-112; 238-239

79688 The relation of psychotic disorganization to the neurotic process. (Read at Am Psa Ass, 3 Dec 1965) J Am Psa Ass 1967, 15:626-640

79689 Research in protecting preconscious functions in education. Transactions of the ASDC 7th Curriculum Research Institute, Washington, D.C., 2 Dec 1961 (Publ Apr 1964) 28-42

79690 Research in psychiatry: problems in training, experience and strategy. In Brosin, H. W. *Lecture on Experimental Psychiatry,* Univ Pittsburgh Pr 1961, 213-225

S-51134 Research into the process of supervision in psychoanalysis.
           Abs EMD An Surv Psa 1958, 9:433-435

S-51136 The Riggs Story: The Development of the Austin Riggs Center for the Study and Treatment of the Neuroses.
           Rv Bookhammer, R. S. Q 1961, 30:286-288

S-51137 (& Israel, H. A.) "Say you're sorry."
           Abs An Surv Psa 1955, 6:295-296

79691 (& Israel, H. A.) "Say you're sorry" [with a ten-year follow-up]. PT 1966, 20:616-623

79692   A school of psychological medicine within the framework of a medical school and university. J med Educ 1964, 39(5)

79693   The scientific problems of psychoanalysis. In Wolman, B. B. & Nagel, E. *Scientific Psychology*, NY: Basic Books 1965, 316-340

79694   Some aspects of the significance to psychoanalysis of the exposure of a patient to the televised audio-visual reproduction of his activities. JNMD 1969, 148:301-309

S-51142 Some unsolved problems of psychoanalytic psychotherapy.
        Abs AS An Surv Psa 1956, 7:351-352

S-51143 Some unsolved problems of the scientific career. In Stein, M. R. et al: *Identity and Anxiety*, Glencoe, Ill: Free Pr 1960, 241-268

79695   Stanley Cobb: a tribute. JNMD 1960, 131:465-467

79696   The struggle between preconscious insights and psychonoxious rewards in psychotherapy. PT 1965, 19:365-371

79697   The teleological fallacy in dynamic psychology: editorial. JNMD 1964, 138:103-104
        Abs Sluzki, C. Rev Psicoanál 1964, 21:262

79698   Theoretical aspects of sensory deprivation. In Solomon, P. & Kubzansky, P. E. *Sensory Deprivation*, Cambridge, Mass: Harvard Univ Pr 1961, 208-220

79699   Traditionalism in psychiatry. JNMD 1964, 139:6-19
        Abs BFM Q 1966, 35:156-157

79700   Unresolved problems of resolution of the transference: who can and cannot resolve it? (Read at So Calif Psa Soc)
        Abs Schrut, A. H. Psa Forum 1967, 2:96-97

79701   The unsolved problem in education. (Maryland Conference on Elementary Education, Baltimore, 11 April, 1962) Baltimore, Md: Maryland State Dept of Education 1962, 36-44

79702   Unsolved problems of scientific education. Daedalus 1965, 94:564-587

79703   The utilization of preconscious functions in education. In Bower, E. M. & Hollister, W. G. *Behavioral Science Frontiers in Education*, NY: Wiley 1967, 90-109

79704   Various aspects of the drop-out problem. Editorial. JNMD 1965, 141: 395-402

See Erickson, Milton H.

REVIEW OF:
79705   Ashby, W. R. Design for a Brain. Q 1962, 31:277-279

KUBIS, J. F.

See Howard, S. M.

KUBZANSKY, PHILIP E.

See Leiderman, P. Herbert; Mendelson, Jack H.; Solomon, Philip

KUČERA, OTAKAR

79706   On being acted on. (Read at Int Psa Cong, July 1967) J 1968, 49:495-497

79707 [On the problem of the so-called active psychotherapy.] (Cz) Ceskoslov Psychiat 1968, 64:223-229
79708 [On the 70th anniversary of Anna Freud.] (Cz) Ceskoslov Psychiat 1966, 62:280-281
79709 [Report on the state of pediatric and juvenile psychiatry in Norway and the 25th Psychoanalytic Congress in Copenhagen.] (Cz) Cesk Psychiat 1969, 65:346-349
79710 (& Matejcek, Z.; Langmeier, J.) Some observations of dyslexia in children in Czechoslovakia. Ops 1963, 33:448-456
         Abs JMa RFPsa 1964, 28:451

KUEHN, JOHN L.

79711 Encounter at Leyden: Gustav Mahler consults Sigmund Freud. R 1965-66, 52:345-365
         Abs SRS Q 1966, 35:627-628
79712 The practice of medicine. Transference, dialectic and human encounter. Postgrad Med 1966, 40:A113-A118

KUHLEN, RAYMOND G.

79713 Aging and life-adjustment. In Birren, J. E. *Handbook of Aging and the Individual,* Chicago: Univ Chicago Pr 1959, 852-897
79714 (& Thompson, G. G.) (Eds) Psychological Studies of Human Development. NY: Appleon-Century-Crofts 1963, (2nd ed) xii + 638 p

KUHN, R.

79715 Daseinsanalytische Psychotherapie. [Dasein-analytic psychotherapy.] Proc IV World Cong Psychiat 1966, 1339-1340
79716 Obituary: [Ludwig Binswanger (1881-1966).] (Ger) Schweiz ANP 1967, 99:113-117
79717 On existential analysis. Comprehen Psychiat 1960, 1:62-68

KÜHNEL, G.

S-51164 Tiefenpsychologische Erkenntnisse über depressive Symptomenbilder.
         Abs EW An Surv Psa 1957, 8:151
S-51165 Die Übertragung in der Gruppenanalyse.
         Abs An Surv Psa 1955, 6:378

KUHNS, RICHARD F.

79718 Modernity and death: *The Leopard* by Giuseppe di Lampedusa. Contempo Psa 1969, 5(2):95-119

KUIPER, PIETER C.

79719 Aanpassing in theorie en praktijk. [Adaptations in theory and practice.] Utrecht: J. Bijleveld 1968
79720 Abwehrformen (neurotischer Schulgefühle in der Gegenwart. [Currently used defences against neurotic guilt feelings.] Psyche 1968, 22:689-700
         Abs J 1969, 50:397

79721 Betrachtungen über die psychoanalytische Technik bei der Behandlung neurotischer Patientinnen. [Observations on psychoanalytic technique in the treatment of neurotic female patients.] Psyche 1962, 15:651-668
Abs IBa RFPsa 1964, 28:461
79722 Comment on the papers by Drs. Orgel and Shengold. "The fatal gifts of Medea." (Read at Int Psa Cong, July 1967) J 1968, 49:383-385
79723 Controversen. [Controversies.] Arnhem: Van Loghum 1965
79724 The curative factors in psycho-analysis. [Symposium] Contributions to discussion. (Read at Int Psa Cong, July-Aug 1961) J 1962, 43:218-220
Abs RLG Q 1963, 32:598-599
79725 Diltheys Psychologie und ihre Beziehung zur Psychoanalyse. [Dilthey's psychology and its relationship to psychoanalysis.] Psyche 1965, 19:241-249
79726 Discussion of Gitelson, M. "La première phase de la psychanalyse." RFPsa 1963, 27:449-453
79727 The future of clinical-nosological psychiatry. Psychiat Neurol Neurochir 1963, 66:381-386
79728 Hysterische Neurosen beim Mann. [Hysterical neuroses in men.] Psyche 1968, 22:215-232
79729 Indications and contraindications for psychoanalytic treatment. (Read at Int Psa Cong, July 1967) J 1968, 49:261-264
Abs LHR Q 1969, 38:669
79730 Der negative Ödipuskomplex beim Mann. [The negative Oedipus complex in men.] Jb Psa 1961-62, 2:63-79
Over het negative Oedipuscomplex. In Hart de Ruyter, T. *Capita Selecta uit de Kinderen Jeugdpsychiatrie*, Zeist: de Haan 1963
79731 Neurosenleer. [On Neuroses.] Arnhem: Von Laghum Slaterus 1966
Die seelischen Krankheiten des Menschen, psychoanalytische Neurosenlehre. Bern: Hans Huber; Stuttgart: Ernst Klett 1966, 278 p
79732 On Being Genuine and Other Essays. (Foreword: Murphy, G.) NY/London: Basic Books 1967, 176 p
Rv Chalfen, L. R 1969, 56:350-351
79733 Overdracht en tegenoverdracht beschouwd vanuit de metapsychologische gezichtspunten. Een bijdrage tot de theorie der techniek. [Transference and countertransference considered from a metapsychological point of view. A contribution to the theory of technique.] In Van der Leeuw, P. J. et al: *Hoofdstukken uit de Henendaagse Psychoanalyse*, Arnhem: Van Loghum Slaterus 1967
Zur Metapsychologie von Übertragung und Gegenübertragung. Psyche 1969, 23:95-120
Abs J 1969, 50:402-403
79734 Perversionen. [Perversions.] Psyche 1962, 16:497-511
79735 Probleme der psychoanalytischen Technik in bezug auf die passiv-feminine Gefühlseinstellung des Mannes, das Verhältnis der beiden Ödepuskomplexe und die aggression. [Problems of psychoanalytic technique relative to the male passive-feminine attitude, the relation of the two Oedipus complexes, and aggression.] Psyche 1962, 16:321-344

79736 Die psychoanalytische Biographie der schöpferischen Persönlichkeit. [Psychoanalytic biography of the creative personality.] Psyche 1966, 20:104-127

79737 Psychoanalytische gruppentherapie. [Psychoanalytic group therapy.] Soc Psychiat 1969, 4:120-125

79738 Soziale Implikationen des Ödipuskomplexes. [Social implications of Oedipus complex.] Psyche 1969, 23:796-802

79739 Tiefenpsychologische Betrachtungen über Wahnformung. [Depth psychological considerations about paranoid conditions.] Stud Gen 1967, 20:660-668

79740 Über eine Untersuchung der Struktur der psychoanalytischen Theorie. [On a study of the structure of psychoanalytic theory.] Psyche 1962, 16:814-819. In Rapaport, D. *Zur Struktur der psychoanalytischen Theorie*, Stuttgart: Klett 1962

79741 Verstehende Psychologie und Psychoanalyse. [Understanding psychology and psychoanalysis.] Psyche 1964, 18:15-32

See Leeuw, P. J. van der

KULENKAMPFF, CASPAR

79742 Über das Syndrom der Herzphobie. [A syndrome of heart phobia.] Nervenarzt 1960, 31:443-454

KULKA, ANNA M.

79743 (& Fry, C. P.; Goldstein, F. J.) Kinesthetic needs in infancy. Ops 1960, 30:562-571

79744 (& Walter, R. D.; Fry, C. P.) Mother-infant interaction as measured by simultaneous recording of physiological processes. J Amer Acad Child Psychiat 1966, 5:496-503

79745 Psychosomatic diseases in childhood. Fortschr PSM 1963, 3:187-195

KUMAR, SANTOSH

79746 (& Rege, V. L.) Trichotillomania: a case report. Indian J med Sci 1967, 21:263-264

KUMMER, JEROME M.

79747 Abortions and emotions. In Wahl, C. W. *Sexual Problems*, NY: Free Pr; London: Collier-Macmillan 1967, 79-88

KUNDU, RAMANATH

79748 A review of psychoneurotic studies. Samiksa 1966, 20(2): 135-150

KUNKEL, ROBERT L.

79749 (& Gottschalk, L. A.) Hope and denial in metastatic carcinoma—a preliminary report. US Med 1966, 2:31

See Gottschalk, Louis A.

KUNZ, EDITH

79750   Persönlicher Rückblick einer praktischen Ärztin auf die Teilnahme an
einer Ärztegruppe. [Personal review by a female general practitioner of
her participation in a group of physicians.] Psyche 1966, 20:952-954

KUNZ, HANS

79751   Die eine Welt und die Weisen des In-der-Welt-Seins. Bemerkungen zu
den Voraussetzungen der daseinanalytisch-anthropologischen Interpretation psychologischer Phänomene. [One world and the manner of be-
ing-in-the-world. Remarks in presuppositions of existential analytic-
anthropological interpretations of psychopathological phenomena.]
Psyche 1962-63, 16:59-80; 142-159; 221-239; 378-400; 464-480; 544-
560; 705-720

79752   Zur Frage nach der Natur des Menschen. [On the question on the
nature of men.] Psyche 1964, 17:685-720

KÜNZEL, E.

79753   Familiensituation und neurotische Verwarhlosung. [Family situation
and neurotic neglect.] Prax Kinderpsychol 1966, 15:284-289

79754   [Juvenile delinquency and neglect. Their origin and treatment from
the viewpoint of depth psychology.] (Ger) Prax Kinderpsychol 1965,
(Suppl):1-136

KÜNZLER, ERHARD

79755   Angst und Angstabwehr in der menschlichen Gemeinschaft. [Anxiety
and its defense in human society.] In Wiesbrock, H. *Die politische und
gesellschaftliche Rolle der Angst. Politische Psychologie, Vol. 6*, Frankfurt am Main: Europäische Verlagsanstalt 1967, 231-245

79756   Erfahrungsberichte psychoanalytischer Institute. Zur Methodik und
Praxis ärztlicher Dokumentation. [Reports on experiences at psycho-
analytic institutes. On method and practice of medical documentation.]
Psyche 1964, 18:204-240

79757   Gefühlsbestimmte Haltungen und Reaktionen in der Patient-Arzt-
Beziehung. [Patient-doctor-interactions determined by emotions.] Med
Klin 1968, 63:433-437

79758   Die gestörte menschliche Seele. Zum 25. Todestag Sigmund Freuds.
[The disturbed human mind. In commemoration of the 25th anniversary of Sigmund Freud's death.] Frankfurter Rundschau 1964, 23(9)

79759   Psychosomatische Erkrankungen in psychoanalytischer Auffassung.
[Psychoanalytic concepts of psychosomatic diseases.] Landarzt 1967,
43:269-275

79760   (& de Boor, C.) Die psychosomatische Klinik und ihre Patienten.
Erfahrungsbericht der psychosomatischen Universitätsklinik Heidel-
berg. [The psychosomatic clinic and its patients (in- and outpatients).
Report on experiences gathered at the Psychosomatic Clinic of the
University of Heidelberg.] Bern/Stuttgart: Huber-Klett 1964, 274 p

79761   Pubertätskonflikte eines männlichen Patienten mit einer Anorexia
nervosa. [Puberty conflicts of a male patient suffering from anorexia

nervosa.] In Meyer, J.-E. & Feldmann, H. *Anorexia Nervosa*, Stuttgart: Georg Thieme 1965, 161-166

79762 Statistischer Beitrag zur Frage der Grenzfälle in der klinischen Praxis. [Statistical contribution to the problem of borderline-cases in clinical practice.] Psyche 1964, 18:52-58

79763 Das Tierexperiment in der Psychosomatik. [Experiments with animals in psychosomatic medicine.] Verh Dtsch Ges inn Med 1967, 73:70-78

79764 Über die Möglichkeit einer Zusammenarbeit von Ethologie und Psychoanalyse. [On the possibility of cooperation between ethology and psychoanalysis.] Psyche 1967, 21:166-192

79765 Wer legt die Therapie fest? [Who determines the therapy?] Med Klin 1966, 61:1349-1352

79766 (& Zimmermann, I.) Zur Eröffnung des Erstinterviews. [On opening the initial interview.] Psyche 1965, 19:68-79

79767 Zur Früherkennung psychosomatischer Erkrankungen. [On the early recognition of psychosomatic diseases.] Hippokrates 1968, 39:447-453

79768 Zur Genese der Potenzstörungen. [On the genesis of disorders of potency.] Med Welt 1966, (17):2821-2825

79769 Zwei Hypothesen über die Natur der frühkindlichen Sozialbeziehungen. [Two hypotheses concerning the nature of early infantile social relations.] Psyche 1969, 23:25-27
Abs J 1969, 50:401-402

See Boor, Clemens de

KUPPER, HERBERT I.

79770 Contributor to Anderson, R. S. *Neuropsychiatry in World War II*, Washington: Office of Surgeon General, Dept of the Army 1966

KURIAN, MILTON

79771 (& Hand, M. H.) (Eds) Lectures in Dynamic Psychiatry. NY: IUP; London: Bailey Bros 1963, 137 p
Rv JTM Q 1964, 33:589-592

KURLAND, ALBERT A.

See Unger, Sanford

KURLAND, MORTON L.

79772 Giles de la Tourettes syndrome—the psychotherapy of 2 cases. Comprehen Psychiat 1963, 4

79773 Pedophilia erotica. JNMD 1961, 131:394-403

KURLANDER, LE ROY FRANK

79774 (& Colodny, D.) "Pseudoneurosis" in the neurologically handicapped child. Ops 1965, 35:733-738
Abs JMa RFPsa 1967, 31:187

KUROMARU, SEISHIRO

79775 [Child development from the psychoanalytic point of view.] (Jap)
Jap J Psa 1969, 15(2):1-11

79776 Prognosis of infantile neuroses and psychoses. Proc IV World Cong
Psychiat 1966, 106-113

KURSH, CHARLOTTE OLMSTED

79777 Heracles and the Centaur. R 1968, 55:387-399
Abs SRS Q 1969, 38:673

KURTH, FREDERICK

79778 (& Patterson, A.) Structuring aspects of the penis. (Read at Los
Angeles Psa Soc, 21 Nov 1968) J 1968, 49:620-628
Abs Wallace, L. Bull Phila Ass Psa 1969, 19:236-238. Wallace, L.
Bull Los Angeles Psa Soc & Inst 1969, 6:1

KURTH, GERTRUD M.

REVIEWS OF:
79779 Beck, S. J. The Rorschach Experiment. Ventures in Blind Diagnosis.
Q 1962, 31:411-413
79780 Harrower, M. et al: Creative Variations in the Projective Techniques.
Q 1962, 31:570-573

KURTZ, PAUL

See Handy, Rollo

KURTZ, RICHARD

79781 (& Hirt, M.; Ross, W. D.; Gleser, G.; Hertz, M. A.) Investigation of
affective meaning of body products. J exp Res Pers 1968, 3:9-14

See Hirt, Michael; Ross, W. Donald

KURTZBERG, RICHARD L.

79782 (& Cavior, N.; Lipton, D. S.) Sex drawn first and sex drawn larger by
opiate addict and non-addict inmates on the draw-a-person test. J
proj Tech 1966, 30:55-58

KURZWEIL, TSEVI A.

79783 [Progressive education, its role, proponents and ways of development.]
(Heb) Hahinukh 1965-66, 37:1-10

KURZWEIL, Z. E.

79784 Anxiety and Education. NY: Thomas Yoseloff (Barnes) 1968, 201 p

KUSHNER, MARTIN D.

79785 Freud, a Man Obsessed. Phila: Dorrance 1967, 151 p

KUTASH, SAMUEL B.

79786　Group psychotherapy and the educative process. J grp Psa Proc 1968, 1(1):83-88

79787　Psychoneuroses. In Wolman, B. B. *Handbook of Clinical Psychology*, NY: McGraw-Hill 1965, 948-975

KUTEN, J.

79788　An ego-analytic approach to administration. (The application of psychotherapeutic principles in the organization and development of child guidance for U.S. Air Forces in Europe.) Psychother Psychosom 1968, 16:64-73

KUTNER, BERNARD

79789　Physician-patient relationships: a theoretical framework. In Peatman, J. G. & Hartley, E. L. *Festschrift for Gardner Murphy*, NY: Harper 1960, 259-273

KUTSCHER, AUSTIN H.

79790　(Ed) But Not to Lose: A Book of Comfort for Those Bereaved. NY: Simon & Schuster 1969

79791　(Ed) Death and Bereavement. Springfield, Ill: Thomas 1969, xxviii + 364 p

79792　(& Zegarelli, E. V.; Hyman, G. A.) (Eds) Pharmacotherapeutics of Oral Disease. NY: McGraw-Hill 1964, 690 p

KVALE, STEINER

79793　The significance of Husserl, Heidegger and Marx for psychology. Nord Psykol 1964, 16:186-198

79794　"Unconscious processes" in concept formation: an empirical fact or a theoretical construction? Acta psychol 1968, 28: 344-362

KWALWASSER, SIMON

79795　(& Green, S. L.) Institutional treatment. Adolescents 282-300

KYSAR, JOHN EDWIN

79796　The two camps in child psychiatry: a report from a psychiatrist-father of an autistic and retarded child. P 1968, 125:103-109. Ann Prog child Psychiat 1969, 456-467

L

LAB, P.

79797 Prévention du suicide chez les jeunes atteints de maladies mentales. [Prevention of suicide in young people afflicted with mental illness.] Z Praventimed 1965, 485-486

See Danon-Boileau, Henri; Douady, D.

LA BARBA, RICHARD C.

79798 The psychopath and anxiety: a reformulation. J ind Psych 1965, 21: 167-170

LA BARRE, MAURINE BOIE

79799 Dynamic factors in psychiatric team collaboration. M 1960, 33:53-60
79800 (& Jessner, L.; Ussery, L.) The significance of grandmothers in the psychopathology of children. Ops 1960, 30:175-185
79801 The strengths of the self-supporting poor. Soc Casewk 1968, 48:459-466
79802 (& La Barre, W.) "The worm in the honeysuckle": a case study of a child's hysterical blindness. Soc Casewk 1965, 36:399-413

LA BARRE, WESTON

79803 Géza Róheim 1891-1953. Psychoanalysis and anthropology. Psa Pioneers 272-281
S-51209 The influence of Freud on anthropology.
   Abs SL An Surv Psa 1958, 9:451-453
79804 Personality from a psychoanalytic viewpoint. In Norbeck, E. et al: *The Study of Personality: An Interdisciplinary Appraisal*, NY: Holt, Rinehart & Winston 1968, 65-85
79805 Psychoanalysis in anthropology. Sci Psa 1961, 4:10-20
79806 They Shall Take up Serpents: Psychology of the Southern Snake-Handling Cult. Minneapolis: Univ Minneapolis Pr 1962; NY: Schocken Books 1969, ix + 208 p

See Devereux, George; LaBarre, Maurine B.

REVIEW OF:
79807 Muensterberger, W. & Axelrad, S. (Eds) The Psychoanalytic Study of Society, Vol. 1. Q 1962, 31:385-386

LABHARDT, F.

79807A Der psychosomatische Aspekt der Angst. [The psychosomatic aspect of anxiety.] In Kielholz, P. *Angst:Psychische und Somatische Aspekte,* 149-156

LABORDE, V.

See Chiozza, L.

LABORIT, H.

See Danon-Boileau, Henri

LABOUCARIÉ, J.

See Riser, M.

LACAMERA, R. G.

See Wessel, M. A.

LACAN, JACQUES

79808 (Ed) Écrits. [Writings.] Paris: Editions du Seuil 1967, 912 p
        Rv Kahn, M. M. R. J 1967, 48:611
S-51229 Fonction et champ de la parole et du langage en psychanalyse.
        The Language of the Self: The Function of Language in Psycho-analysis. (Tr: Wilden, A.) Baltimore, Md: Johns Hopkins Pr 1968, 336 p
79809 Freud: semantics not sex? Réalités 1967, (202)Sept

See Aubry, J.

LACASSIH, A.

See Bastie, J.

LACASSIN, P.

See Riser, M.

LACAVA, MARTA DE

See Agorio, Rodolfo; Prego, Vida M. de

LACHENBRUCH, PETER A.

See Wilson, Arnold W.

LACHENBRUCH, RUTH

See Brunswick, David

LACHMANN, FRANK M.

79810 Perceptual-motor development in children retarded in reading ability. J consult Psychol 1960, 24:427-431
79811 (& Lapkin, B.; Handelman, N. S.) The recall of dreams: its relation to repression and cognitive control. ASP 1962, 64:160-162

79812 (& Bailey, M. A.; Berrick, M. E.) The relationship between manifest anxiety and clinicians' evaluations of projective test responses. Clin Psych 1961, 17:11-13

See Bailey, Mattox A.

LACOMBE, PIERRE

S-51237 Réactions inconscientes au conflit international du Canal de Suez.
 Abs JBa An Surv Psa 1957, 8:319-320
S-51239 A special mechanism of pathological weeping.
 Un mécanisme de pleurer pathologique. RFPsa 1965, 29:79-84
 Abs DJM An Surv Psa 1958, 9:146-147. Ferretti, E. Riv Psa 1966, 12:328
79813 Why war? Were there unconscious causes underlying the Suez conflict and the "Summit" breakdown? MH 1963, 47:205-215

LACOUR, M.

79814 [Prelude to the psychopathology of implantation.] (Fr) Rev Odonto-implant 1967, 8:39-40

LACY, ELIZABETH

See Chafetz, Morris E.

LADEE, G. A.

79815 Automutilatie. [Self-mutilation syndrome.] Voordrachtenreeks van de Nederlandse Vereniging van Psychiaters in Dienstverband 1967, 9: 37-48
79816 Hypochondrische Syndromen. (Thesis) Amsterdam: Naarden 1961, 517 p
 Hypochondriacal Syndromes. Amsterdam: Elsevier 1966, viii + 424 p
79817 [The steps falter . . .] (Dut) T Ziekenverpl 1968, 21:628-630

LADERMAN, PETER

79818 Is there such a thing as an "ideal" relationship between a man and a woman? Why Rep 17-26

ABSTRACTS OF:
79819 Adelson, J. The mystique of adolescence. Q 1965, 34:623-624
79820 Sharaf, M. R. & Levinson, D. J. The quest for omnipotence in professional training. Q 1965, 34:624

LA DOU, J.

See Mendelson, Jack H.

LAERE, J. VAN

79821 [Laus Stultitiae.] (Dut) Verh Kon Vlaam Acad Geneesk Belg 1969, 31:241-263

79821A [On psychopathological painting.] (Dut) Verh Kon Vlaan Acad Geneesk Belg 1967, 29:377-437

LA FARGA CORONA, JUAN

TRANSLATION OF:
Bosselman, B. C. [3733]

LA FAVE, LAWRENCE

79822 (& Teeley, P.) Involuntary nonconformity as a function of habit lag. Percept mot Skills 1967, 24:227-234

LAFFAL, JULIUS

79823 An approach to the total content analysis of speech in psychotherapy. In Shlien, J. M. et al: *Research in Psychotherapy, Vol. III*, Wash DC: APA 1968, 277-294
79824 The contextual associates of sun and God in Schreber's autobiography. ASP 1960, 61:474-479
79825 Freud's theory of language. Q 1964, 33:157-175
79826 Language, consciousness, and experience. Q 1967, 36:61-66
      Abs Cuad Psa 1967, 3:242
79827 Pathological and Normal Language. NY: Atherton Pr 1965, xxi + 249 p
      Abs J Am Psa Ass 1966, 14:237. Rv Niederland, W. G. Q 1967, 36:108-112
79828 The use of contextual associates in the analysis of free speech. J gen Psychol 1963, 69:51-64. In Vetter, H. J. *Language Behavior in Schizophrenia*, Springfield, Ill: Thomas 1968, 108-122

See Ameen, Lane

LAFONTAINE, C.

See Gratton, L.

LAFORGUE, RENÉ

79829 A propos du rôle joué par le chirurgien au service de la névrose de ses malades. [Apropos of the part played by the surgeon in furthering the neuroses of his patients.] Maroc Med 1960, 39:1306-1308. Acta psychother psychosom 1961, 9:163-168
S-51250 Baudelaire et sa pensée.
      Abs An Surv Psa 1955, 6:451-452
79830 De la névrose familiale. [Family neuroses.] Évolut psychiat 1962, 27:313-325
79831 Erlebnis, Struktur und Bildgestaltung. [Experience, structure, and picture form.] Prax PT 1960, 5:260-265
79832 Familienneurosen in psychoanalytischer Sicht. [Family neuroses according to the psychoanalytic view.] Z PSM 1960, 7:1-9
79833 Psychopathologie de la souffrance. [The psychopathology of suffering.] Psyché, Paris 1963, 18 (Sp issue), 61 p

79834   Psychopathologie de l'Échec. [Psychopathology of Failure.] Paris: Payot 1969, 240 p

79835   Réflexions Psychanalytiques. [Reflections on Psychoanalysis.] (Preface: Bourguignon, A.) Geneva: Ed du Mont-Blanc 1965

79836   Über den Beginn einer psychoanalytischen Behandlung. [The beginning of a psychoanalytical treatment.] Z PSM 1960, 6:265-275

79837   Über Persönlichkeitsstruktur und Krankheitssymptome. [On personality structure and disease symptoms.] Z PSM 1967, 13:2-12
        Estructura de la personalidad y síntomas patológicos. Rev Psicoanal Psiquiat Psicol 1968, 8:90-102

S-51263 Über Psyche und Konstitution in analytischer Sicht. Fortschr PSM 1960, 1:128-143

LA FRANCHI, STEVEN

See Ritvo, Edward R.

LAGACHE, DANIEL

79838   (& Lévy-Valensi, J.; Borel, A.) Accès maniaque consécutif à une perte de sang. [An attack of mania following loss of blood.] Sem Hop 1935, 11:65-66

79839   [Acting out and action: terminological problems.] RFPsa 1968, 32: 1055-1066

79840   Aporte para un estudio sobre el cambio individual durante el proceso analítico. [Contribution to a study on individual change during the analytic process.] Rev Psicoanál 1969, 26:97-122

79841   Le complexe d'Oedipe. [The Oedipus complex.] Bull Psychol, Paris 1955-56, 9:176-178, 229-239, 296-303, 522-532; 1956-57, 10:152-158, 211-223

79842   La condition humaine dans l'expérience psychanalytique. [Human condition in psychoanalytic experience.] In Actes du IIIe Congrès de Psychiatrie 1962

79843   Conduites criminelles de l'adulte. [Criminal behavior of adults.] Bull Psychol, Paris 1960-61, 14:272-283, 415-418, 501-508, 598-601, 639-649

79844   Conscience et structures. [Consciousness and structures.] Évolut psychiat 1960, 25:491-513

79845   Discussion of Greenacre, P. and Winnicott, D.W. "The theory of the parent-infant relationship. Further remarks." Contributions to discussion (viii). J 1962, 43: 250-251

79846   Discussion of Segal, H. "Melanie Klein's technique." Psa Forum 1967, 2:223-225

79847   Eléments de psychopathologie clinique. [Elements of clinical psychopathology.] Bull Psychol, Paris 1955-56, 9:179-183; 402-407; 463-468; 592-594

79848   Étude de cas. [Case study.] Bull Psychol, Paris 1957-59, 12:589-593; 708-714

79849   Fantaisie, réalité, vérité. Bull Psychol, Paris 1963, 16:1013-1021; 17:10-29. Psychanalyse 1964, 8:1-9. RFPsa 1964, 28:515-538
        Fantasy, reality and truth. (Read at Int Psa Cong, July-Aug 1963) J 1964, 45:180-189

Fantasia, realidad y verdad. (Tr: Driscoll, P. M. de) Rev urug Psa 1965, 7:233-254

Abs EVN Q 1966, 35:455-456

79850 Henri Wallon. In *Association Amicale des Anciens Élèves de l'École Normale Supérieure* 1965, 42-46

79851 Histoire de jaloux. [History of jealousy.] In *La Vie du Couple*, Paris: Denoël 1969, 246-291

79852 Initiation à la psycho-pathologie. [Introduction to psychopathology.] Bull Psychol, Paris 1959-60, 13:136-147; 279-284; 350-352

79853 Les insuffisances corticales. [Cortical insufficiencies.] In *Encyclo-pédie Française*, Paris: Larousse 1938, Vol. 8, Fasc. 38, 1-6

79854 Introduction à la psychologie pathologique. [Introduction to patho-logical psychology.] Bull Psychol, Paris 1957-58, 11:244-263, 402-408; 1958-59, 12:282-293

79855 Leçons pratiques d'introduction à la psychanalyse. [Practical lessons on introduction to psychoanalysis.] Bull Psychol, Paris 1957-58, 11:408-418; 598-603

79856 Un ménage de toicomanes (document médico-légal). [A home for drug addicts (medico-legal document).] Évolut psychiat 1951, 16:429-456

79857 La méthode clinique en psychologie humaine. [Clinical method in human psychology.] In *Mélanges 1945, No. 4, Études Philosophiques*, Faculté des Lettres de Strasbourg

79858 La méthode psychanalytique. [The psychoanalytic method.] In Michaux, L. *Psychiatrie*, Editions Médicales Flammarion 1965, 1036-1066

79859 Le modèle psychanalytique de la personnalité. [The psychoanalytic model of personality.] In *Le Modèle Scientifique des Personnalités*, Paris: PUF 1965, 91-117

79860 Nomenclature et classification des jeunes inadaptés. [Nomenclature and classification of maladjusted youth.] Bull Psychol, Paris 1947-48, 1:5-8; 10-14

79861 Obituary: Elsa Breuer (1888-1967). Bull Ass psa Fran 1967, 2:309-311

79862 La personne en psychanalyse. [The self in psychoanalysis.] Bull Psy-chol, Paris 1957-58, 11:603-614; 806-832; 884-908

79863 Le point de vie diachronique en métapsychologie. [The diachronic viewpoint in metapsychology.] RFPsa 1966, 30:811-818

S-51282 Sur le polyglottisme dans l'analyse.

Abs Baranger, W. Rev urug Psa 1961-62, 4:369

79864 Pour une étude sur le changement individuel au cours du processus analytique. [For a study on individual change in the course of the analytic process.] Bull Ass psa Fran 1967, 2(3):7-43

79865 Pouvoir et personne. [Power and personality.] Évolut psychiat 1962, 27:111-119

Abs Bleger, J. Rev Psicoanál 1963, 20:82

79866 Preface to Anzieu, D. *L'Auto-Analyse.*

79867 Preface to Hesnard, A. L. M. *Les Phobies et la Névrose Phobique*, Paris: Payot 1961

79868 Preface to Levy-Schoen, A. *L'Image d'Autrui chez l'Enfant. Recherche Expérimentale sur la Perception des Mimiques.*
79869 Preface to Moscovici, S. *La Psychanalyse, son Image et son Public.*
79870 Preface to Rocheblave-Spenle, A.-M. *Les Rôles Masculins et Féminins.*
79871 La psicoanalisi come sublimazione. [Psychoanalysis as sublimation.] Psiche 1965, 2(2-3):85-125
       Abs Gaburri, G. Riv Psa 1966, 12:325-327
S-51283 La psychanalyse. Bull Psychol, Paris 1959-60, 13: 520-524, 569-573, 624-630, 693-699, 773-775, 781-782, 812-813, 915-917, 957-958; 1960-61, 14:673-683, 791-798, 849-852, 966-973
       Psychoanalysis. (Tr: Scott, B.) NY: Walker 1963, 151 p
       Hebrew: Tel-Aviv, Israel: M. Mizrahi 1963, 123 p
79872 La psychanalyse et la structure de la personnalité. [Psychoanalysis and personality structure.] Psychanalyse 1961, 6:5-54
79873 La psychanalyse et l'idée de nature humaine. [Psychoanalysis and the idea of human nature.] In *Existence et Nature*, Paris: PUF 1962
79874 Psychoanalysis as an exact science. Psa—Gen Psychol 400-434
79875 La psychologie et les sciences humaines. [Psychology and human sciences.] Rev Enseignement Supérieur 1960, 1:51-57
79876 La psychologie et les sciences psychologiques. [Psychology and psychological sciences.] Rev Enseignement Supérieur 1966, 3-10
79877 (& Rouard, J.) La "Psychopathologie Générale" de Karl Jaspers. ["General Psychopathology" of Karl Jaspers.] J psychol norm pathol 1935, 32:776-797
79878 Le siècle de l'enfant et l'enfant du siècle. [The century of the child and the child of the century.] Acta paedopsychiat 1964, 31:185-195; 225-234
79879 Situation de l'agressivité. [The situation of aggressiveness.] Bull Psychol, Paris 1960, 14:99-112
79880 La structure en psychologie. La structure en psycho-pathologie. La structure en psychanalyse. [Structure in psychology. Structure in psychopathology. Structure in psychoanalysis.] In Bastide, R. *Sens et Usages du Terme de Structure dans les Sciences Humaines et Sociales,* La Haye: Mouton 1962, 81-88
79881 Les techniques de psychologie humaine: leur application à l'étude des enfants et des adolescents inadaptés. [The techniques of human psychology: their application to the study of children and maladjusted adolescents.] Sauvegarde Enfan 1948, 3(21):3-21
79882 Théorie du transfert. [Theory of transference.] Bull Psychol, Paris 1956-57, 10:728-733, 792-797
79883 Les théories psychanalytiques. [Psychoanalytic theories.] Bull Psychol, Paris 1957-58, 11:76-91
79884 L'Unité de la Psychologie: Psychologie Expérimentale et Psychologie Clinique. [The Unity of Psychology: Experimental Psychology and Clinical Psychology.] Paris: PUF 1969, 74 p
79885 Vues psychanalytiques sur le bonheur. [Psychoanalytic views on happiness.] In *Les Conditions du Bonheur*, Neuchatel: Éd de la Baconnière 1961, 59-75

       See Laplanche, Jean

TRANSLATIONS OF:

Bornstein, B. [3595]. (& Lagache, M.) Freud, A. [73550]. Leeuw, J. P. van der [80333]

LAGACHE, MARIANNE

79886   L'homme aux rats et le petit eyolf. [The Rat Man and Little Hans.] Bull Ass psa Fran 1968, (4):109-121

See Lagache, Daniel

LA GAIPA, JOHN JAMES

79887   Stress, authoritarianism, and the enjoyment of different kinds of hostile humor. J Psychol 1968, 70:3-8

LAGRAVINESE, N.

79888   [With Carl Gustav Jung disappeared the collective unconscious.] (It) Rass Clin Ter 1961, 60:313-319

LA GRONE, CYRUS WILSON

79889   Sex and personality differences in relation to fantasy. J consult Psychol 1963, 27:270-272

LA GUARDIA, ERIC

S-51298 Sire de Maletroit's door.
Abs DJM An Surv Psa 1958, 9:496

LAI, G.

79890   Le complexe d'Oedipe dans les relations malade-milieu hospitalier. Colloque sur la psychanalyse des psychoses. [The Oedipus complex in patient-hospital relations. Round table on the psychoanalysis of the psychoses.] RFPsa 1967, 31:1151-1156

79891   [Egocentric language and intermediate area of experience.] (It) Arch Psicol Neurol Psichiatr 1969, 30:309-325

79892   L'évolution psychodynamique des patients déprimés dans la sénescence. [Psychodynamic development of depressed patients in senescence.] Évolut psychiat 1968, 33:113-137

79893   (& Lavanchy, P.) Le langage du schizophrène: ses relations avec le développement et la psychothérapie. [The language of the schizophrenic patient: its relations with the development and of the psychotherapy.] Schweiz ANP 1967, 99:391-405

79894   Quelques considérations sur la psychothérapie de groupe de psychotiques. [Observations on group therapy for psychotics.] Acta psychother psychosom 1964, 12:354-368

79895   Le rôle du psychanalyste dans la situation psychiatrique italienne actuelle. [The role of the psychoanalyst in the present-day Italian psychiatric situation.] Soc Psychiat 1967, 2:127-129

79896 Rôle du sexe des cotherapeutes dans la structuration dynamique des groupes. [Role of the sex of cotherapists in the dynamic structure of groups.] Ann méd-psychol 1968, 126(2):1-23

79897 [Training of a psychiatrist—various considerations on training in the relational aspect of professional activity of social operators according to the method of human sciences.] (Fr) Évolut Psychiat 1969, 34:775-788

See Perrot, E. de

LAIDLAW, ROBERT W.

79898 The "constellation approach" to marriage counseling. Psa 1967, 27:131-134

79899 The psychiatric unit in the general hospital [interviewed by Perkins, M. E.]. In Ziskind, R. Viewpoint on Mental Health, NY: NYC Comm Ment Hlth Board 1967, 53-59

79900 The psychotherapy of marital problems. Prog PT 1960, 5:140-147

See Crowley, Ralph M.

LAING, RONALD DAVID

79901 (& Esterson, A.) The abbotts. In authors' Sanity, Madness, and the Family, London: Tavistock Publ 1964, 15-34. In Scheff, T. J. Mental Illness and Social Processes, NY: Harper & Row 1967, 130-148

79902 The Divided Self. A Study of Sanity and Madness. (Studies in Existential Analysis and Phenomenology) London: Tavistock 1960, 240 p; Baltimore, Md: Penguin Books 1965, 218 p
       Rv MBr J 1961, 42:288-291

79903 (& Esterson, A.) Families and schizophrenia. Int J Psychiat 1967, 4:65-71

79904 Family and individual structure. In Lomas, P. The Predicament of the Family, London: HIP 1967, 107-125

79905 (& Phillipson, H.; Lee, A. R.) Interpersonal Perception: A Theory and a Method of Research. NY: Springer; London: Tavistock 1966, x + 179 p

79906 Mystification, confusion, and conflict. In Boszormenyi-Nagy, I. & Framo, J. L. Intensive Family Therapy, NY: Harper & Row 1965, 343-363

79907 The Politics of Experience. NY: Pantheon Books 1967, xv + 138 p
       Phänomenologie der Erfahrung. (Tr: Figge, K. & Stein, W.) Frankfurt: Suhrkamp 1969, 152 p

79908 Practice and theory. The present situation. Psychother Psychosom 1965, 13:58-67

79909 (& Cooper, D. G.) Reason and Violence. A Decade of Sartre's Philosophy 1950-1960. London: Tavistock 1964, 184 p
       Rv Coltart, N. E. C. J 1965, 46:394-395

79910 (& Esterson, A.) Sanity, Madness and the Family, Vol. 1: Families of Schizophrenics. London: Tavistock 1964, 272 p; NY: Basic Books 1965, viii + 262 p
       Rv Lomas, P. J 1965, 46:390-392

79911 The Self and Others. Further Studies in Sanity and Madness. (Studies

in Existential Analysis and Phenomenology) London: Tavistock 1961, 186 p; 1969, 169 p. Chicago: Quadrangle Books 1962, 186 p
Rv Lowenfeld, H. J 1963, 44:116-118. Litman, R. E. Q 1964, 33: 283-284

79912   The study of family and social contexts in relation to the origin of schizophrenia. In Romano, J. *The Origins of Schizophrenia,* Amsterdam/NY: Excerpta Medica Found 1967, 139-146

79913   Violence and love. J existent Psychiat 1965, 5:416-422

REVIEWS OF:

79914   Auerbach, A. (Ed) Schizophrenia: An Integrated Approach. J 1961, 42:478

79915   Jaspers, K. General Psychopathology. J 1964, 45:590-593

79916   Pittenger, R. E. et al: The First Five Minutes. J 1961, 42:477-478

79917   Sullivan, H. S. Schizophrenia as a Human Process. J 1963, 44:376-378

LAKIN, MARTIN

79918   (& Lieberman, M. A.) Diagnostic information and psychotherapists' conceptualization. Clin Psych 1965, 21:385-388

LA MAR, NORVELLE C.

79920   Gerald H. J. Pearson—a tribute. Bull Phila Ass Psa 1964, 14:53-54

LAMASSON, FRANÇOIS

79921   Point du vue d'un médecin praticien sur la psychanalyse. [A practicing physician's viewpoint on psychoanalysis.] Aquinas 1962, 5:365-403; 1963, 6:34-108

LAMB, W.

See Tempone, Vincent J.

LAMBERT, ANNE

79922   (& Mahler, M. S. et al) A settlement house approach to community mental health. Publ Hlth Rep 1959, 74:957-964

LAMBERT, H.

See Shaskan, Donald A.

LAMBERT, KENNETH

79923   Can theologians and analytical psychologists collaborate? J anal Psych 1960, 5:129-146

79924   Memorial meeting to C. G. Jung. Jung's later work. Historical studies. M 1962, 35:191-197

LAMBERT, P. A.

79925   (Ed) La Relation Médecin-Malade au Cours des Chimiothérapies Psychiatriques. [Physician-Patient Relationship in the Course of Psychiatric Chemotherapies.] Paris: Masson Ed 1965

LAMBLIN, B.

79926 Esthétique: fonction du cinema: la poétique de l'espace. [Esthetics: function of the cinema: poetic space.] Bull Psychol, Paris 1965, 18: 1249-1257

LAMONT, JOHN H.

79927 Hawthorne's last novels: a study in creative failure. (Read at Boston Psa Soc, 29 Nov 1961)
          Abs Carter, G. H. Bull Phila Ass Psa 1962, 12:38-39
79928 Which children outgrow asthma and which do not? In Schneer, H. I. *The Asthmatic Child*, NY: Harper & Row 1963, 16-26

See Jessner, Lucie

LAMOULEN, J.

79929 La Médecine Française et la Psychanalyse de 1895 à 1926. [French Medicine and Psychoanalysis.] Paris: Thèse de Médecine 1966, 102 p

LAMPL, E. ESTHER

See Tennes, Katherine T.

LAMPL, HANS

S-51316A On determinism.
          Abs An Surv Psa 1955, 6:58

LAMPL-DE GROOT, JEANNE

S-51318 On adolescence. Dev Mind 308-316
S-51326 Anmerkungen zur psychoanalytischen Triebtheorie.
          Abs BB An Surv Psa 1956, 7:91-92
79930 Die Behandlungstechnik bei neurotischen Patientinnen. [Treatment technique with neurotic female patients.] Psyche 1962, 15:681-683
          Abs IBa RFPsa 1964, 28:462
S-19522 Considerations of methodology in relation to the psychology of children. Dev Mind 93-103
S-51319 On defense and development: normal and pathological. Dev Mind 273-285
          Abs EMW An Surv Psa 1957, 8:91-92
79931 Depression und Aggression. [Depression and aggression.] Jb Psa 1960, 1:145-160
S-51320 Depression and aggression: a contribution to the theory of the instinctual drives. Dev Mind 213-230
S-19524 On the development of ego and superego. Dev Mind 114-125

79932 The Development of the Mind. Psychoanalytic Papers on Clinical and Theoretical Problems. (Foreword: Freud, A.) NY: IUP 1965, x + 391 p; London: HIP 1966, 373 p
    Abs J Am Psa Ass 1966, 14:235. Rv JKl J 1967, 48:122. Niederland, W. G. Q 1967, 36:287-290

S-19525 Discussion on evolution and present trends in psychoanalysis. Dev Mind 166-171

79933 Ego ideal and superego. (Read at Int Psa Cong, Aug 1961) Psa St C 1962, 17:94-106. Dev Mind 317-328
    Idéal du moi et surmoi. RFPsa 1963, 27:529-541
    Ich-Ideal und Über-Ich. Psyche 1963, 17:321-322

79934 Die Entwicklung der Psychoanalyse in Deutschland bis 1933. [The development of psychoanalysis in Germany up to 1933.] In *Ausprachen und Forträge zur Einweihung des Institutsneubaues am 14 Oktober 1964, Sigmund Freud Institut, Frankfurt am Main*

S-19523 Zur Entwicklungsgeschichte des Ödipuskomplexes der Frau.
    The evolution of the Oedipus complex in women. Dev Mind 3-18

79935 Gedanken über Vorteil und Gefahren der "Einseitigkeit" in der wissenschaftlischer Forschung. [Thoughts on advantages and dangers of "onesidedness" in scientific research.] Psyche 1968, 22:672-678

S-51321 Groepsbesprekingen met stiefmoeders.
    Group discussions with stepmothers. Dev Mind 238-246

79936 Heinz Hartmanns Beiträge zur Psychoanalyse. [Heinz Hartmann's contributions to psychoanalysis.] Psyche 1964, 18:321-329

S-19526 Hemmung und Narzissmus.
    Inhibition and narcissism. Dev Mind 58-81

79937 Introduction. Dev Mind ix-x

S-19527 Masochismus und narzissmus.
    Masochism and narcissism. Dev Mind 82-92

S-19528 On masturbation and its influence on general development. Dev Mind 172-197

S-19529 Neurotics, delinquents, and ideal formation. Dev Mind 138-148

79938 An obstacle to cure in psychoanalysis: a discussion of Freud's "Analysis terminable and interminable." (Read at NY Psa Soc, 16 May 1967)
    Abs Grossman, W. I. Q 1968, 37:479-481

79939 Obstacles standing in the way of psychoanalytic cure. Psa St C 1967, 22:20-35

79940 The origin and development of guilt feelings. Dev Mind 126-137

S-19530 The preoedipal phase in the development of the male child. Dev Mind 104-113

S-19531 Zu den Problemen der Weiblichkeit.
    Problems of femininity. Dev Mind 19-46

S-51322 Problems of psychoanalytic training. Dev Mind 231-238

S-51323 Psychoanalysis and its relation to other fields of natural science. Dev Mind 286-307

S-51324 Psychoanalytische Ich-Psychologie und ihre Bedeutung für die Fehlentwicklung bei Kindern.
    Psychoanalytic ego psychology and its significance for maldevelopment in children. Dev Mind 258-265
    Abs HA An Surv Psa 1956, 7:249-251

S-19533 Re-evaluation of the role of the Oedipus complex. Dev Mind 198-212
79941   Reflections on the development of psychoanalysis: technical implications
         in analytic treatment. J 1969, 50:567-572
79942   Remarks on genesis, structuralization, and functioning of the mind.
         Psa St C 1964, 19:48-57. Dev Mind 364-373
S-19534 Some remarks on the development of psychoanalysis during the last
         decades. Dev Mind 149-165
S-19536 Review of "Die Kastrationsangst des Weibes," by Sandor Rado.
         Review of "Fear of Castration in Women," by Sandor Rado. Dev
         Mind 47-57
S-51325 The role of identification in psycho-analytic procedure. Dev Mind 266-
         272
         Abs SG An Surv Psa 1956, 7:302-303
79943   Some thoughts on adaptation and conformism. Psa—Gen Psychol 338-
         348
79944   Superego, ego ideal, and masochistic fantasies. Dev Mind 351-363
79945   Symptom formation and character formation. (Read at Int Psa Cong,
         July-Aug 1963) J 1963, 44:1-11. Dev Mind 329-350
         Formation de symptômes et formation du caractère. RFPsa 1963,
         27:7-29
         Symptombildung und Charakterbildung. Psyche 1963-64, 17:1-22
         Formazione del sintomo e formazione del carattere. Riv Psa 1963, 9:
         23-62
         Formación de síntomas y formación del carácter. Rev Psicoanál 1963,
         20:20-37
         Abs Vega Q 1964, 33:311. EVN Q 1965, 34:463
S-51326 The theory of instinctual drives. Dev Mind 247-257
         Abs JAL An Surv Psa 1956, 7:88
79946   Die Zusammenarbeit von Patient und Analytiker in der psychoanaly-
         tischen Behandlung. [The cooperation of patient and analyst in psycho-
         analytic therapy.] Psyche 1967, 21:73-83

         See Arlow, Jacob A.; Frijling-Schreuder, Bets

LANCASTER, ROBERT C.

See Lief, Harold I.

LAND, ARCHIE

See Hoppe, Klaus D.

LAND, MELVIN

See Weiner, Myron F.

LANDA, LUIS

See Palacios López, Agustin; Villalobos, J. Jesus

LANDAU, FELICIA LYDIA

See Fine, Bernard D.

ABSTRACT OF:
79947   Psyche 1966, Vol. 20,(1). Q 1968, 37:160

LANDAU, R.

See Wijsenbeek, Henricus

LANDAUER, EVA

79948   A description of some aspects of the clinical work at the Child Develop-
        ment Center, New York. J child PT 1966, 1(4)

LANDAUER, KARL

S-19579 Die Zurückweisung der Aufklärung durch das Kind. In Bittner, G. &
        Rehm, W. *Psychoanalyse und Erziehung*, Bern/Stuttgart: Goldmann
        1964

LANDER, JOSEPH

79949   Clinical studies. An Surv Psa 1956, 7:140-221
79950   History. An Surv Psa 1957, 8:3-13; 1958, 9:3-16
79951   (& Schulman, R.) Homicide, acting out and impulse. Ops 1963, 33: 928-
        930

ABSTRACTS OF:
79952   Brosin, H. W. The primary processes and psychoses. An Surv Psa 1957,
        8:31-32
79953   Burchard, E. M. L. Psychoanalysis, cultural history and art. An Surv
        Psa 1958, 9:467-468
79954   Bychowski, G. Art, magic and the creative ego. An Surv Psa 1957, 8:
        332
79955   Devereux, G. Dream learning and individual ritual differences in
        Mohave shamanism. An Surv Psa 1957, 8:323
79956   Devereux, G. A primitive slip of the tongue. An Surv Psa 1957, 8:111
79957   Diether, J. Mahler and psychoanalysis. An Surv Psa 1958, 9:476
79958   Feldman, A. B. Dostoevsky and father-love. Exemplified by *Crime and
        Punishment*. An Surv Psa 1958, 9:475
79959   Feldman, A. B. A moral reformer damaged in the making. From fiction
        case-histories of Anton Chekhov. An Surv Psa 1957, 8:336
79960   Fortes, M. Malinowski and Freud. An Surv Psa 1958, 9:15-16
79961   Hilgard, E. R. Freud and experimental psychology. An Surv Psa 1957,
        8:7
79962   Taubes, J. Religion and the future of psychoanalysis. An Surv Psa
        1957, 8:304-305
79963   Viet, I. Freud's place in the history of medicine. An Surv Psa 1957,
        8:7-8
79964   Weisskopf, W. A. The "socialization" of psychoanalysis in contempo-
        rary America. An Surv Psa 1957, 8:18-19
79965   Witzleben, H. D. von: Symposium on Freud—history, psychiatry, and
        the behavioral sciences. An Surv Psa 1957, 8:6-7

REVIEW OF:
79966 Jonas, A. D. Ictal and Subictal Neurosis. Diagnosis and Treatment. Q 1967, 36:619-620

LANDER, P.

See Maccoby, Michael

LANDERS, JUDAH

See McReynolds, Paul

LANDESMAN, C.

79967 Reply [to Friedenberg, E. Z. "Neo-Freudianism & Erich Fromm."] Commentary 1963, 35:78

LANDIS, BERNARD

79968 A study of ego boundaries. Diss Abstr 1964, 24:3381-3382

LANDIS, CARNEY

79969 Contributor to: Mettler, F. A. *Varieties of Psychopathological Experience.* NY: Holt, Rinehart & Winston 1964
79970 Psychoanalysis and experimental psychology. Mod Con Psa 58-73

LANDMAN, L.

See Agoston, Tibor

LANDSMAN, ELIOT

ABSTRACT OF:
79971 Schur, M. Metapsychological aspects of phobias in adults. Bull Phila Ass Psa 1963, 13:86-89

LANDUCCI-RUBINI, L.

79972 [Effects of affective maternal deprivation in the infant.] (It) Lattante 1965, 36:8-20
79973 (& Faienza, C.; Bassanetti, F.) [Study of effects of maternal deprivation in infancy: investigations conducted in institutionalized children (Foundling Hospital of Parma).] (It) Lattante 1965, 36:250-258

LANDY, EUGENE E.

79974 Sex differences in some aspects of smoking behavior. Psychol Rep 1967, 20:575-580

LANE, RONALD W.

79975 The effect of preoperative stress on dreams. Diss Abstr 1967, 27:4126-4127

LANES, SAMUEL

REVIEW OF:
79976   Lawson, R. Frustration. The Development of a Scientific Concept.
        Q 1967, 36:458-459

LANFRANCHI, G.

79977   Psychoanalyse de la nature humaine. [Psychoanalysis of human nature.]
        Études philos 1961, 16(3):18-26

LANFSLEY, DONALD G.

See Barter, James T.

LANG, JEAN-LOUIS

S-51717 L'abord psychanalytique des psychoses chez l'enfant.
        Abs TC An Surv Psa 1958, 9:309-310
79978   [Backwardness and psychosis.] (Fr) Laval Méd 1967, 38:3-15
79979   Caractère et névrose de caractère: prospections introductives. [Char-
        acter and character neurosis: introductory prospectus.] Cah Publ Soc
        Fran Psychanal 1964
79980   Commentaires techniques à propos des discussions sur le cas "Frankie,"
        la névrose obsessionnelle et la psychanalyse d'enfants. [Technical re-
        marks apropos of the discussions of the case of "Frankie," obsessional
        neurosis and child psychoanalysis.] (Read at Int Psa Cong, July 1965)
        Bull Ass psa Fran 1966, 1:5
79981   Commentaires techniques sur "Analyse d'un enfant phobique" de B.
        Bornstein. [Technical remarks on "Analysis of a phobic child" by B.
        Bornstein.] Entretien de Psychanalyse 1965, Dec. Cah Publ Soc Fran
        Psychanal 1965
79982   (& Duche, J.-D.) Introduction: psychanalyse et assistance. [Introduc-
        tion: psychoanalysis and guidance.] Rv Np inf 1967, 15:811-814
79983   Notes on early psychotic states. [Symposium: child analysis and pedi-
        atrics.] (Read at Int Psa Cong, July 1967) J 1968, 49:286-289
        Abs LHR Q 1969, 38:669
79984   Notes sur le masochisme chez Melanie Klein. [Notes on masochism
        according to Melanie Klein.] Bull Ass psa Fran 1968, 4:58-59
79985   La psychanalyse des enfants. [Child psychoanalysis.] (Read at Int Psa
        Cong, July 1967) Bull Ass psa Fran 1967, 3:295-306
79986   Psychothérapie—psychanalyse—assistance. [Psychotherapy—psychoanaly-
        sis—guidance.] Rv Np inf 1967, 15:901-915
79987   Sémiologie des mécanismes de défense dans les psychoses de l'enfant:
        à propos du champ psychanalytique dans les psychoses infantiles.
        [Semiology of defense mechanisms in child psychoses. Apropos of the
        psychoanalytic scope in child psychoses.] Ann méd-psychol 1967,
        125(2):807. Rv Np inf 1967(Suppl):15-18
79988   Le sens d'un symptôme: le retrait d'agressivité. [The meaning of a
        symptom: shrinking of aggression.] In Compte Rendu de Congrès Euro-
        péen Pédopsychiatrie, Rome, May-June 1963, Vol. 2:599, 605

LANGE, ERIKA

79989   Selbstentmannung als Selbstbestrafung. [Self-castration as a form of self-punishment.] Psychiat Neurol med Psychol 1960, 12:106-109

LANGE, G.

See Fontan, M.

LANGE, J.

See Fleck, Lili

LANGEN, D.

79990   Die Entwicklung zur modernen Psychotherapie. [The development of modern psychotherapy.] Dtsch med Wschr 1967, 92:1293-1298

79991   Die gezielte Analyse als Form einer Kurzpsychotherapie. [Selective analysis as a form of brief psychotherapy.] MMW 1967, 109:1645-1649

79992   Indikation und Prognose in der klinischen Psychotherapie. [Indication and prognosis in the clinical psychotherapy.] Z PSM 1966, 12:128-131

79993   [Pain and influencing pain.] (Ger) Psychother Psychosom 1968, 14(Suppl):137-140

79994   Die Steuerung der Übertragungsdynamik bei einer aktiv analytischen Therapie. [Direction of transference dynamics in active analytic therapy.] Psychother Psychosom 1966, 14:313-322

79995   Zur Problematik der "Kurzpsychotherapie." [On the problems of "brief psychotherapy."] Proc IV World Cong Psychiat 1966, 438-441

LANGER, J.

See Rosenberg, Benjamin G.

LANGER, MARIE

79996   (& Puget, J.; Teper, E.) Algunos problemas en relación con la enseñanza de la teoría de la técnica. [Some problems in relation to the teaching of the theory of the technique.] Rev Psicoanál 1962, 19:99-102

79997   El aporte de Melanie Klein al análisis didáctico. [Melanie Klein's contribution to training analysis.] Rev Psicoanál 1962, 19:323-330

S-51723 Barrabás o la persecusión por un ideal.
        Abs Vega An Surv Psa 1956, 7:412

79998   Dificultades psicológicas del psicoanalista principiante. [Psychological difficulties of the beginning psychoanalyst.] Rev Psicoanál 1963, 20:333-345
        Abs Vega Q 1965, 34:142

79999   Discussion of Balint, E. "Training as an impetus to ego development." Psa Forum 1967, 2:63-65

80000   Discussion of Liberman, D. "Entropia e information en el proceso terapéutico." Rev Psicoanál 1967, 24:68-70

80001   (& Puget, J.; Teper, E.) Un enfoque methodológico para la enseñanza del psicoanálisis. [Focus on the teaching methods of psychoanalysis.] Rev Psicoanál 1967, 24:579-595

80002   Fantasías Eternas. [Eternal Fantasies.] Buenos Aires: Paidós 1964
S-51726 Freud y la sociología.
         Abs Rodrigue, E. An Surv Psa 1965, 7:20-21
S-51728 La interpretación basada en la vivencia contratransferencial de co-
         nexión o desconexión con el analizado.
         Abs RHB An Surv Psa 1957, 8:255-256
80003   Maternidad y Sexo: Enfoque Psicoanalítico y Psicosomático. [Mater-
         nity and Sex, Psychoanalytic and Psychosomatic Approach.] Buenos
         Aires: Paidós 1964
80004   (& Puget, J.; Teper, E.) Mesa redonda sobre teoría de la técnica.
         [Round table on the theory of technique.] Rev Psicoanál 1963, 20:38-
         62
         Abs Vega Q 1964, 33:311
80005   (& Puget, J.; Teper, E.) A methodological approach to the teaching of
         psycho-analysis. J 1964, 45:567-574
         Abs EVN Q 1966, 35:622-623
80006   El Miedo a la Muerte. Capítulo de Psicología y Cáncer Escrito en
         Colaboración. [The Fear of Death. Chapter of Psychology and Cancer
         Written in Collaboration.] Buenos Aires: Hormé 1965
80007   Obituary: Heinrich Racker. Rev Psicoanál 1961, 18:295-298. J 1962,
         43:80-81
80008   Psicoanálisis y ética. [Psychoanalysis and ethics.] Rev Psicoanál 1961,
         18:268-276
80009   Selection criteria for the training of psycho-analytic students, I. (Read
         at Int Psa Cong, July-Aug 1961) J 1962, 43:272-276
         Critères de sélection applicables à la formation des étudeants en
         psychanalyse. RFPsa 1964, 28:7-27
         Abs RLG Q 1963, 32:601-602. Soifer Rev Psicoanál 1963, 20:196-
         198
S-51731 Sterility and envy.
         Abs JAL An Surv Psa 1958, 9:208-209
80010   Symposium on the formation of symptoms and the formation of char-
         acter. Contribution to the discussion. J 1964, 45:158-160
         French: RFPsa 1966, 30:248-253
         Abs EVN Q 1966, 35:454-455
80011   (& Puget, J.) Wissenschaftstheoretischer Bezugsrahmen der Gruppen-
         therapie. [Scientific theoretical framework of group therapy.] Z Psy-
         chother med Psychol 1961, 11:1-10

         See Aberastury, Arminda; Alvarez de Toledo, Luisa G. de; Grinberg,
         Léon; Schavelzon, Jese

         ABSTRACTS OF:
80012   Racker, E. Algunas consideraciones sobre la personalidad de Freud.
         Rev Psicoanál 1961, 18:250
80013   Racker, E. Técnica analítica y el masoquismo inconsciente del analista.
         Rev Psicoanál 1961, 18:260

         REVIEW OF:
80014   Racker, H. Estudios sobre Técnica Psicoanalítica. Rev Psicoanál 1961,
         18:260

LANGER, WILLIAM L.

80015 Discussion of Grotjahn, M. "The new technology and our ageless unconscious." Psa Forum 1966, 1:14

S-51745 The next assignment.
Abs ARK An Surv Psa 1958, 9:453-454

LANGEVELD, M. J.

80016 Zum Problem des Vaters in der Entwicklung des mannlichen Kindes. [On the father problem in the development of the male child.] Vita hum 1964, 7:33-48

LANGFELDT, GABRIEL

80017 The Erotic Jealousy Syndrome: A Clinical Study. Copenhagen: Muksgaard 1961, 66 p

80018 La portée d'une dichotomie du groupe des schizophrènes. [The range of a dichotomy in a group of schizophrenics.] Évolut psychiat 1966, 31:321-327

LANGHANS, SIEGFRIED

S-51750 Das Strukturmodell des menschlichen Psyche, ein wesentlicher Beitrag Freuds zur Psychologie.
Abs HK An Surv Psa 1956, 7:16

LANGLOIS, JEAN-LOUIS

ABSTRACTS OF:

80019 Bénassy, M. Évolution de la psychanalyse. An Surv Psa 1956, 7:39-40

80020 Berge, A. Psychanalyse et prophylaxie mentale. An Surv Psa 1956, 7:292-293

80021 Viderman, S. Aperçu sur l'historie de la littérature psychanalytique. An Surv Psa 1956, 7:40

LANGLOIS, JEAN-PAUL

ABSTRACTS OF:

80022 Grumberger, B. Préliminaires à une étude topique du narcissisme. An Surv Psa 1958, 9:70-71

80023 Kestemberg, E. Quelques considérations à propos de la fin du traitement des malades à structure psychotique. An Surv Psa 1958, 9:425-427

80024 Muller, A. Petite incursion dans la mythologie grecque. An Surv Psa 1957, 8:307-308

80025 Racamier, P. C. Sur les conditions techniques d'application de la psychanalyse aux schizophrènes. An Surv Psa 1957, 8:280-281

80026 Sechehaye, M. A. La réalisation symbolique, un catalyseur de la structuration du moi schizophrènique. An Surv Psa 1957, 8:281-283

LANGMAN, LAUREN

80027 The estrangement from being: an existential analysis of Otto Rank's psychology. J existent Psychiat 1961, 1:455-477

LANGMEIER, JOSEF
See Kučera, Otakar

LANGS, ROBERT J.

80028 Earliest memories and personality: a predictive study. Arch gen Psychiat 1965, 12:379-390
80029 First memories and characterologic diagnosis. JNMD 1965, 141:318-320
80030 Manifest dreams from three clinical groups. Arch gen Psychiat 1966, 14:634-643
  Abs PB Q 1969, 38:343
80031 Manifest dreams in adolescents: a controlled pilot study. JNMD 1967, 145:43-52
80032 Stability of earliest memories under LSD-25 and placebo. JNMD 1967, 144:171-184

See Linton, Harriet B.

LANGSLEY, DONALD G.

80033 (& Fairbairn, R. H.; Deyoung, C. D.) Adolescence and family crises. Canad Psychiat Ass J 1968, 13:125-133
80034 (& Schwartz, M. N.; Fairbairn, R. H.) Father-son incest. Comprehen Psychiat 1968, 9:218-226
80035 (& Kaplan, D. M.) The Treatment of Families in Crisis. (Foreword: Felix, R. H.) NY: Grune & Stratton 1968, xxiv + 184 p

See Barter, James T.; Pittman, Frank S.

LANGSTON, ROBERT DORN

80036 Children's overt and fantasy aggression toward peers as a function of perceived severity of parental punishment. Diss Abstr 1961, 21:2367

LANHAM, RICHARD A.

80037 Chaucer's *Clerk's Tale:* the poem not the myth. Lit & Psych 1966, 16:157-165

LANSING, CORNELIUS

80038 Sexual symptoms as presenting complaints. In Nash, E. M. et al. *Marriage Counseling in Medical Practice,* Chapel Hill: Univ of North Carolina Pr 1964, 25-40

See Speers, Rex W.

LANSKY, LEONARD M.
See Kramer, Milton

LANTER, R.

80039 (& Heinrich, J.-P.) Délire mélancolique à thème de négation. [Melancholic delusion with a negation pattern.] Cah Psychiat 1960, 14:1-11

LANTERI-LAURA, G.

80040 Imaginaire et psychiatrie. [The imaginary and psychiatry.] Évolut psychiat 1968, 33:19-52

80041 La notion de processus dans la pensée psychopathologique de K. Jaspers. [The idea of process in the psychopathological thought of K. Jaspers.] Évolut psychiat 1962, 27:459-499

80042 (& Philippi, J. D.) [Structural analysis of a lapse.] (Fr) Enceph 1969, 58:193-238

LANTOS, BARBARA

80043 Discussion of Greenacre and Winnicott, "The theory of the parent-infant relationship. Further remarks." Contributions to discussion (vi). J 1962, 43:249

80044 Kate Friedländer 1903-1949. Prevention of juvenile delinquency. Psa Pioneers 508-518

S-51754 On the motivation of human relationships. A preliminary study based on the concept of sublimation.
Abs An Surv Psa 1955, 6:127-129

S-51756 The two genetic derivations of aggression with reference to sublimation and neutralization.
Abs SLP An Surv Psa 1958, 9:77-78

LA PERRIERE, KITTY

See Mahler, Margaret S.

LA PIERE, RICHARD TRACY

S-51757 The Freudian Ethic.
Rv Waelder, R. J Am Psa Ass 1963, 11:628-651

LAPINSKI, M.

80045 (& Malewski, J.; Strzelecka, H.) [Problems connected with the utilization of dreams in psychotherapy.] (Pol) Psychiat Pol 1969, 3:193-198

LAPKIN, BENJAMIN

80046 The relation of primary-process thinking to the recovery of subliminal material. JNMD 1962, 135:10-25

See Lachmann, Frank M.; Silverman, Lloyd H.

LAPLANCHE, JEAN

80047 (& Pontalis, J.-B.) Connaître Freud avant de la traduire. [Knowing Freud before translating his work.] Le Monde 1967, Suppl

80048 La défense et l'interdit. [Defense and prohibition.] La Nef 1967, (31):43-55

80049 (& Pontalis, J.-B.) Délimitation du concept freudien de projection. [Delimitation of the Freudian concept of projection.] Bull Psychol, Paris 1963, 17:62-66

80050 (& Pontalis, J.-B.) Fantasme originaire, fantasmes des origines, origine du fantasme. Temps mod 1964, 19(215):1833-1868
Fantasy and the origins of sexuality. J 1968, 49:1-18

80051 Hölderlin et la Question du Père. [Hölderlin and the Father Question.] Paris: PUF 1961, 144 p
Rv Boons-Grafé, M. C. RFPsa 1964, 28:280-283

80052 (& Leclaire, S.) L'inconscient une étude psychanalytique. [The unconscious, a psychoanalytic study.] Temps mod 1961, 17(183):81-129. Inconscient 1966, 95-177

80053 Interpréter (avec) Freud. [Interpreting (with) Freud.] L'Arc 1968, (34):37-46

80054 (et al) Le langage. [The language.] Entretiens télévisés de philosophie. In *Dossiers Pédagogiques de la Radio Télévision Française*, Paris 1966-67

80055 Notes sur Marcuse et la psychanalyse. [Notes about Marcuse and psychoanalysis.] La Nef 1969, (36)

80056 La position originaire du masochisme dans le champ de la pulsion sexuelle. [Original position of masochism in the field of sexual drive.] Bull Ass psa Fran 1968, (4):35-53

° ° ° Preface to Pankow, G. *L'Homme et Sa Psychose.*

80057 Les principes du fonctionnement psychique. [The principles of psychic functioning.] RFPsa 1969, 33:185-200

80058 La Réalité dans la Névrose et la Psychose. [Reality in Neurosis and Psychosis.] Paris: S.F. P. 1961, 53 p

80059 La recherche psychanalytique. [Psychoanalytic research.] Rev Enseignement Supérieur 1966 (2-3):147-153

80060 (Reporter) Report of discussions of acting out—French language section. [Symposium: acting out.] J 1968, 49:228-230
Abs LHR Q 1969, 38:668

80061 (& Pontalis, J.-B.; Lagache, D.) Vocabulaire de la Psychanalyse. [Vocabulary of Psychoanalysis.] Paris: PUF 1967, xx + 520 p; 1968, xx + 527 p

See Kamouh, M. C.

TRANSLATIONS OF:
Freud, S. [10391, 10409, 10434, 10484]. (& Pontalis, J-B.) Freud, S. [10534, 10551, 10609, 10616, 10620, 10623, 10710A]

LAPLANTE, J.

80062 [The pyromaniac.] (Fr) Laval Med 1969, 40:1062-1072

LAPOINTE, J. L.

80063 [Depression and delinquency.] (Fr) Laval Med 1969, 40:936-938

LA PORTA, ERNESTO

80064 (& Nunes, E. P.; Schneider, G.) [Group psychotherapy with psychotics.] (Por) J Bras Psiquiat 1964, 13:317-329
Abs Vega Q 1966, 35:475

See Oliveira, Walderedo Ismael de

LAQUEUR, H. PETER

80065 Comparison of the dynamics of individual therapy and multiple family therapy. J Psa in Groups 1966-67, 2(1):11-17
80066 General systems theory and multiple family therapy. In Gray, W. et al: *General Systems Theory and Psychiatry*, Boston: Little, Brown 1969, 409-434

LAQUEUER, WALTER

S-51760 Psychoanalyse in sowjetischer Perspektive.
Abs BB An Surv Psa 1956, 7:77-79

LAROCHE, J.

REVIEW OF:
80067 Mueller, F. L. Histoire de la Psychologie de l'Antiquité à Nos Jours. RFPsa 1963, 27:326

LARSON, JAMES D.

See Foulkes, David

LARSON, LAWERENCE W.

80068 Self-knowledge and the unconscious. Diss Abstr 1968, 29(2-A):636-637

LARSON, W. R.

See Palola, E. G.

LASCAULT, G.

80069 [Monsters in the artistic works of mental patients.] (Fr) Confin psychiat 1965, 8:102-114

LASHINSKY, BERTHA KAHN

REVIEW OF:
80070 Freeman, L. & Greenwald, H. Emotional Maturity in Love and Marriage. PPR 1961, 48(4):141

LASKI, L.

See Bernstein, Stanley

LASKOWITZ, DAVID

80071 Personality characteristics of adolescent addicts: manifest rigidity. Corrective Psychiat 1963, 9:215-218

LASSWELL, HAROLD DWIGHT

S-51765 Approaches to human personality: William James and Sigmund Freud.
Abs EMW Q 1961, 30:307-308

80072	The changing image of human nature. The sociocultural aspect. Future-oriented man. Psa 1966, 26:157-168
80073	Psychoanalytic conceptions in political science. Sci Psa 1961, 4:60-76

See Freedman, Lawrence Z.; Rubenstein, Robert

LATHBURY, VINCENT T.

S-51783 An interesting screen memory.
	Abs DJM An Surv Psa 1957, 8:114
80074	Limitations of psychoanalysis may be more apparent than real. Bull Phila Ass Psa 1961, 11:32-35
	Abs PLe RFPsa 1963, 27:335

LATHROP, DONALD D.

80075	Acting out in supportive group therapy. Voices 1958, 4(2):42-43

LAUBACH, FRANK CHARLES

80076	Symbology vs. illiteracy. In Whitney, E. *Symbology: The Use of Symbols in Visual Communication,* NY: Hastings House 1960, 87-102

LAUBER, H. L.

80077	(& Lewin, B.) Über das Phänomen der Verdrängung beim sensitiven Beziehungswahn. [On the phenomenon of repression in sensitive delusion of reference.] Z Psychother med Psychol 1961, 11:46-50

LAUDRY, HARALD

TRANSLATION OF:
Menninger, K. A. et al [83595]

LAUER, RACHEL M.

80078	Relationship between value orientation and primary process thinking. Diss Abstr 1964, 25:1338

LAUFER, MAURICE W.

80079	(& Gair, D. S.) Childhood schizophrenia. In Bellak, L. & Loeb, L. *The Schizophrenic Syndrome,* NY/London: Grune & Stratton 1969, 378-461

LAUFER, MOSES

80080	Assessment of adolescent disturbances. The application of Anna Freud's diagnostic profile. (Read at Int Psa Cong. July 1965) Psa St C 1965, 20:99-123
80081	The body image, the function of masturbation, and adolescence: problems of the ownership of the body. (Read at Brit Psa Soc, July 1968) Psa St C 1968, 23:114-137
80082	Comment on Dr. Kestenberg's paper, "Acting out in the analysis of children and adults." (Read at Int Psa Cong, July 1967) J 1968, 49:344-346

80083 Defensive use of identification in adolescence. Acta paedopsychiat 1966, 33:215

80084 Ego ideal and pseudo ego ideal and adolescence. Psa St C 1964, 19:196-221

80085 Object loss and mourning during adolescence. (Read at Chicago Inst Psa, April 1966; at Canad Psa Soc, April 1966) Psa St C 1966, 21:269-293

80086 A psycho-analytic approach to work with adolescents. A description of the Young People's Consultation Centre, London. J child Psychol Psychiat 1964, 5:217-229

80087 A psychoanalytical approach to work with adolescents. The work of the Young People's Consultation Centre (London) with remarks on diagnosis and technique. In *Proceedings of the 6th International Congress of Psychotherapy,* Basel: Karger 1965, Part 2, 44-50. Psychother Psychosom 1965, 13:292-298

LAUGHLIN, HENRY P.

80088 The age of anxiety. In *Panhellenic Union for Mental Hygiene,* Parnossos Aud, Athens, Greece, 1966, 10 p

80089 Anxiety, its nature and origins: an introductory essay to a series on psychoneuroses. Med Ann DC 1953, 22:401-412

80090 The anxiety reactions: the acute anxiety attack or panic, anxiety and tension states and anxiety neuroses. Med Ann DC 1953, 22:463-473

80091 (& Ruffin, M.) A biographical review of the history of psychiatry. In *University of California Syllabus ZM,* mimeo, Berkeley/Los Angeles: Univ Calif Pr 1954, 107-114

80092 Conversion reaction. In *Annual Report of the Department of Psychiatry, Athens University School of Medicine* (Athens, Greece) 1966, 12-17

80093 The conversion reactions. Med Ann DC 1953, 22:581-594

80094 Counseling and psychotherapy by non-medical personnel—editorial. Med Ann DC 1958, 27(7):357-359; 27(8):4-5

80095 The current status of psychiatry in the United Kingdom. P 1961, 118:308-310

80096 Denial. Med Bull Mont Co Med Soc 1960, 4(9):18-24

80097 Denial: a primitive dynamism of disavowal and disclaiming. Med Bull Mont Co Med Soc 1960, 4(3):19-24

80098 Denial in alcoholism, depression and psychic pain. Med Bull Mont Co Med Soc 1960, 4(4):20-24

80099 Denial in one's self picture, and a cultural dilemma. Med Bull Mont Co Med Soc 1960, 4(5):19-23

80100 Depression and the suicidal attempt. State of Mind, Ciba 1957, 1(6)

80101 The dissociative reactions. Dissociation, double personality, depersonalization, amnesia, fugue states, somnambulism and hypnosis. Med Ann DC 1953, 22(10):541-552

80102 The Ego Defenses. NY: Appleton-Century-Crofts 1969, 800 p

80103 The Emotional Reactions to Trauma. Wash DC/London: Butterworths 1967, 86 p

80104   European psychiatry: England, Denmark, Italy, Greece, Spain, and Turkey. P 1960, 116:769-776
80105   Fear and phobias. Med Ann DC 1954, 23:379-391; 439-448
80106   (et al) (Eds) Handbook. Wash DC: Wash Med Surg Soc 1962, 28 p; 1963, 28 p
80107   Historical sketch: "The Washington Medical and Surgical Society." Med Ann DC 1964, 33:633
S-51810 King David's anger. J Pastoral Care 1954, 8:147-153
80108   The mental mechanisms. Med Bull Mont Co Med Soc 1959, 3(9):12-26
80109   Mental Mechanisms. London: Butterworths; NY: Appleton-Century-Crofts 1963, 262 p
80110   The mental mechanisms. Compensation. Med Bull Mont Co Med Soc 1959, 3(10):12-26
80111   The mental mechanisms. Inversion. Med Bull Mont Co Med Soc 1959, 3(11):17-34
80112   The mental mechanisms. Sublimation. Med Bull Mont Co Med Soc 1960, 4(1):15-39
80113   The mental mechanisms. Undoing. Med Bull Mont Co Med Soc 1959, 3(12):21-39
80114   The Neuroses. London: Butterworts; NY: Appleton-Century-Crofts 1967, xii + 1076 p
80115   The neuroses following trauma. Med Ann DC 1954, 23:492-502, 567-580. In Cantor, P. D. *Traumatic Medicine and Surgery for the Attorney, Vol. 6*, Wash DC/London: Butterworths 1962, 76-125
S-51811 The Neuroses in Clinical Practice.
        Le Nevrosi Nella Practica Clinica. (Tr: Farne, M.)
        Florence: Barbera Universitaria 1967, 800 p
80116   Neurosis, conditioning, and the rule of impression priority. J Med Sch New Jersey 1961, 58:454-461
80117   The obsessive personality: the clinical and dynamic features of the obsessive character defenses. Med Ann DC 1954, 23(4):202-214
80118   The operation of denial in physical illness, and the denial of death. Med Bull Mont Co Med Soc 1960, 4(6):23-28
80119   (& Ruffin, M.) An Outline of Dynamic Psychiatry. Wash DC: George Wash Univ Med Sch 1949-54, 257 p
80120   Overconcern-with-health. Somatic and physiologic preoccupation: hypochondriasis. Med Ann DC 1954, 23:96-105, 147-152
80121   The psychiatric aspects of fatigue: emotional fatigue, fatigue states and neurasthenia. Med Ann DC 1954, 23:22-37
80122   A Psychiatric Contribution to the Development of Executives: The Development of a Psychoanalytically Oriented Approach to Training in Human Relations. Bethesda, Md: NIMH 1953, 30 p
80123   A psychiatric glossary. Amer Psychiat Ass 1952-53, 19 p; 1953, 25 p. In author's *An Outline of Dynamic Psychiatry* 219-232. In *University of California Syllabus ZM* 1954, 81-107. In author's *The Neuroses in Clinical Practice* 693-745. In author's *The Neuroses* 950-1029
80124   (Ed) Psychiatry. In Cantor, P. D. *Traumatic Medicine and Surgery for the Attorney*, Wash DC/London: Butterworths 1962, 387-474

80125 (& Hall, M.) Psychiatry for executives: an experiment in the use of group analysis to improve relationships in an organization. P 1951, 107:493-497

80126 Psychiatry in Asia and the Middle East. P 1958, 115:193-202

80127 The Psychoneuroses. Wash DC: George Wash Univ Med Sch 1955, 116 p

80128 Research in sleep deprivation and exhaustion: an invitation to further observation and study. Int Rec Med 1953, 166:305-310

80129 The role of sleep in emotional health. State of Mind, Ciba 1958, 2(4). Child-Family Dig 1958, 17(4):24-27. Courier of the George Washington University Medical Center 1958, Dec:20-24. Med Bull Mont Co Med Soc 1959, 3(4):12

80130 Suicide: impulse and remorse. Quart Rev Psychiat Neurol 1953, 8:19-26

80131 Unraveling the phobic defense. P 1967, 123:1081-1086

LAUGHLIN, WILLIAM S.

80132 Primitive theory of medicine: empirical knowledge. In Galdston, I. *Man's Image in Medicine and Anthropology*, NY: IUP 1963, 116-140

LAUNAY, C.

80133 Réflexions sur l'hôpitalisme. [Comments on the subject of hospitalism.] Évolut psychiat 1956, 21:267-271
       Abs HFM An Surv Psa 1956, 7:265

80134 [Rehabilitation and psychotherapy in 2 cases of encopresis.] (Fr) Concours Méd 1963, 85:4637-4640

80135 (& Trelat, J.; Daymas, S.) [The role of the father in the development of juvenile anorexia.] (Fr) Rv Np inf 1965, 13:740-743

80136 (& Col, C.; Girard, J. Y.) [Treatment of anxiety in the child and adolescent.] (Fr) Rev Prat 1964, 14(Suppl):142-145

LAUREN, M.

80137 Psychological approaches to literary criticism. Cath Sch J 1968, 68(2):57-59

LAURENZI, G. B.

See Felici, F.

LAURIAT, KARIN

See Bonstedt, Theodor

LAURY, GABRIEL VERNET

80138 (& Meerloo, J. A. M.) Mental cruelty and child abuse. Psychiat Q Suppl 1967, 41:203-254

LAUTERBACH, CARL G.

See Vogel, William

LAUX, GÜNTER

80139 Über eine Ursache chronischen (Ver-)Schweigens. [On reasons for chronic concealment.] Z PSM 1968, 14:274-281

See Heigl-Evers, Annelise

LAUX, W.

80140 Zur Genese der Angst nach Hirntraumen bei Kindern. [On the origin of anxiety following brain traumas in children.] Z Psychother med Psychol 1965, 15:31-38

LAUZEL, J. P.

80141 [Why kidnapping?] (Fr) In Ey, H. *Entretiens Psychiatriques, No. 10*, Toulouse, France: Edouard Privat 1964

LAUZUN, GÉRARD

80142 Sigmund Freud et la Psychanalyse. Paris: Seghers 1962, 254 p.
Sigmund Freud, the Man and his Theories. (Tr: Evans, P.) NY: P. S. Eriksson 1962, 1965, 224 p

LAVALEE, C.

See Mailloux, N.

LAVANCHY, P.

See Lai, G.

LAVELL, MARTHA

See Kleiner, Robert J.

LAVERS, N.

80143 Freud. The clerkes tale, and literary criticism. College English 1964, 26:180-187

LAVI, ZVI

80144 [Freud's contribution to education: on the occasion of the 25th anniversary of his death.] (Heb) Urim 1965, 22:251-257

LAVIE, J.-C.

80145 Discussion [changement individuel et processus analytique.] [Individual change and the analytic process.] Bull Ass psa Fran 1967, (3)
80146 Le souvenir dans la cure. [Memory in treatment.] Bull Ass psa Fran 1966, (2)

LA VIETES, RUTH L.

80147 Day treatment. Compreh Txbk Psychiat 1478-1479
80148 (& Cohen, R. S.; Reens, R.; Ronall, R.) Day treatment center and school: seven years experience. Ops 1965, 35:160-169
Abs JMa RFPsa 1966, 30:523

80149   (& Hulse, W. C.; Blau, A.) A psychiatric day treatment center and school for young children and their parents. Ops 1960, 30:468-482
         Abs JMa RFPsa 1962, 26:317
80150   Psychiatry and the school. Compreh Txbk Psychiat 1479-1487
80151   Psychotic disorders, II: Treatment. Compreh Txbk Psychiat 1438-1442
80152   The teacher's role in the education of the emotionally disturbed child. Ops 1962, 32:854-862
         Abs JMa RFPsa 1964, 28:445

        See Cohen, Rosalyn S.

LAVITOLA, G.

80153   [Psychotherapy in the psychiatric hospitals.] (It) Arch Neurobiol 1965, 28:677-713

LAVITRY, S.
        See Danon-Boileau, Henri

LAVONDÈS, V.
        See Lebovici, Serge

LAWLESS, RICHARD
        See Kaplan, Bert

LAWLOR, W. G.
        See Shakow, David

LAWRENCE, D.
        See Warnecke, R.

LAWRENCE, DAVID HERBERT

80154   The two principles. In author's The Symbolic Meaning, NY: Viking 1964, 159-173

LAWRENCE, J. R.
        See Cramond, W. A.

LAWRENCE, MARGARET MORGAN

80155   (& Spanier, I. J.; Dubowy, M. W.) An analysis of the work of the school mental health unit of a community mental health board. Ops 1962, 32:99-108. In Clark, D. H. & Lesser, G. S. Emotional Disturbance and School Learning, Chicago: Sci Res Ass 1965, 261-273
80156   Behavior disorders in children. J Nat Med Ass 1960, 52(2)
80157   Discussion of Galdston, I. "The psychopathology of paternal deprivation." Sci Psa 1969, 14:45-46
80158   Discussion of Heath, R. G. & Shelton, W. H. "The psychoanalyst's role in community mental health centers." Sci Psa 1968, 12:265-266

80159   Introduction. The educated woman and modern society: a panel. Sci Psa 1966, 10:121-122

80160   Minimal brain injury in child psychiatry. Comprehen Psychiat 1960, 1(6)

80161   Organization and techniques of public school consultation. Current psychiat Ther 1968, 8

LAWREY, LAWSON G.

80162   Introduction. Therapeutic play techniques: symposium, 1954. Ops 1955, 25:574-575

80163   (& Conn, J. H.) Therapeutic play techniques. Ops 1955, 25:747-787

LAWSON, D. F.

80164   The R. H. Fetherston memorial lecture: the anxieties of pregnancy. Med J Aust 1960, (2):161-166

LAWSON, ELENA PADILLA

See Wolberg, Arlene

LAWSON, LEWIS A.

80165   The grotesque-comic in the Snopes Trilogy. Lit & Psych 1965, 15:107-119. In Manheim, L. F. & Manheim, E. B. *Hidden Patterns*, NY: Macmillan 1966, 243-258

80166   Wilkie Collins and *The Moonstone*. Am Im 1963, 20:61-79

LAWSON, R. H.

80167   Schnitzler's *Das Tagebuch der Redegonda*. Germ Rev 1960, 35:202-213

LAWSON, REED

80168   Frustration. The Development of a Scientific Concept. NY: Macmillan 1965, x + 192 p
        Rv Lanes, S. Q 1967, 36:458-459

LAWTON, JAMES J., JR.

80169   (& Sisko, F. J.) Mental health aspects of pregnancy. Psychiat Q Suppl 1961, 35

LAWTON, MARCIA J.

See Davids, Anthony

LAX, RUTH F.

80170   An experimental investigation of children's size estimation under neutral and fear-arousing conditions. Diss Abs 1962, 22:11

S-51841 Infantile deprivation and arrested ego development.
        Abs EMD An Surv Psa 1958, 9:317-318

80171 Some considerations about transference and countertransference manifestations evoked by the analyst's pregnancy. J 1969, 50:363-372

REVIEWS OF:
80172 Klein, M. Narrative of a Child Analysis. PPR 1962, 49(4):136-137
80173 Madison, P. Freud's Concept of Repression and Defense: Its Theoretical and Observational Language. R 1963, 50:692-693

LAXER, ROBERT MENDEL

80174 Relation of real self-rating to mood and blame and their interaction in depression. J consult Psychol 1964, 28:538-546
80175 Schizophrenia and parental rejection or ambivalence. Psychol Rep 1967, 20:987-993

LAYARD, JOHN

80176 In pursuit of first principles. The third uniting factor. J anal Psych 1966, 11:41-48

LAYMAN, EMMA M.

See Lourie, Reginald S.; Millican, Frances K.

LAZARE, AARON

80177 (& Klerman, G. L.: Armor, D. J.) Oral, obsessive, and hysterical personality patterns. An investigation of psychoanalytic concepts by means of factor analysis. Arch gen Psychiat 1966, 14:624-630

LAZAROFF, PHILIP

See Wylie, Harold W., Jr.

LAZARUS, ARNOLD A.

80178 Behavior therapy and graded structure. Int Psychiat Clin 1969, 6:134-154
80179 (& Davidson, G. C.; Polefka, D. A.) Classical and operant factors in the treatment of a school phobia. Case report. JAbP 1965, 70:225-229
80180 The converging paths of behavior therapy and psychotherapy. Significant differences and insignificant similarities. Int J Psychiat 1969, 7:511-513
80131 New methods in psychotherapy: a case study. In Eysenck, H. J. *Behaviour Therapy and the Neuroses*, NY: Pergamon Pr 1960, 144-152
80132 (& Abramovitz, A.) The use of "emotive imagery" in the treatment of children's phobias. JMS 1962, 108:191-195

LAZARUS, RICHARD S.

80183 (& Riess, W. F.) Clinical psychology and the research problems of stress and adaptation. Prog clin Psych 1960, 4:32-45
80184 A program of research in psychological stress. In Peatman, J. G. & Hartley, E. L. *Festschrift for Gardner Murphy*, NY: Harper 1960, 313-329

80185 Psychological Stress and the Coping Process. NY: McGraw-Hill 1966
80186 (& Opton, E. M., Jr.) The study of psychological stress: a summary of
       theoretical formulations and experimental findings. In Spielberger, C.
       D. *Anxiety and Behavior,* NY/London: Academic Pr 1966, 225-262

See Speisman, Joseph C.

LAZURE, DENIS

80187 Psychotherapy of adolescents: some considerations on technique.
       Canad Psychiat Ass J 1961, 6:286-290

LEACH, DAVID

S-51853 (Reporter) Panel: technical aspects of transference.
       Abs JFr An Surv Psa 1958, 9:387-393

ABSTRACTS OF:
80188 Fedotov, D. The Soviet view of psychoanalysis. An Surv Psa 1957,
       8:17
80189 Reider, N. A psychoanalyst replies. An Surv Psa 1957, 8:17

LEACH, EDMUND R.

80190 Frazer and Malinowski on the "founding fathers." Encounter 1965,
       25(5):24-36
80191 Pulleyar and the Lord Buddha: an aspect of religious syncretism in
       Ceylon. PPR 1962, 49(2):81-102
80192 (Ed) The Structural Study of Myth and Totemism. London: Tavistock
       1967, 185 p

LEACH, P. J.

80193 A critical study of the literature concerning rigidity. Brit J soc clin
       Psychol 1967, 6:11-22

LEACHMAN, R. D.

See Abram, Harry S.

LEAKEY, L. S.

80194 Development of aggression as a factor in early human and pre-human
       evolution. UCLA Forum med Sci 1967, 7:1-33

LEAL, M. R.

80195 Group-analytic play therapy with pre-adolescent girls. Int J grp PT
       1966, 16:58-64

LEAVITT, A.

80196 Treatment of an adolescent with school phobia. J Amer Acad Child
       Psychiat 1965, 4:655-669

LEAVITT, MAIMON

ABSTRACTS OF:

80197 Bartemeier, L. H. Structure and function of the predominating symptom in some borderline cases. Q 1961, 30:144

80198 Chapman, A. H. Psychiatrogenic illness. Q 1961, 30:145

80199 Davis, J. M. et al: The effect of visual stimulation on hallucinations and other mental experiences during sensory deprivation. Q 1961, 30:146

80200 Fisher, C. Subliminal and supraliminal influences on dreams. Q 1961, 30:455-456

80201 Grunebaum, H. U. et al: Sensory deprivation and personality. Q 1961, 30:145

80202 Hollender, M. H. The psychiatrist and the release of patient information. Q 1961, 30:145

80203 Hunt, R. G. Social class and mental illness. Q 1961, 30:456

80204 Kaufman, I. et al: Treatment implications of a new classification of parents of schizophrenic children. Q 1961, 30:455

80205 Klaf, F. S. & Davis, C. A. Homosexuality and paranoid schizophrenia. Q 1961, 30:456

80206 Lehrman, N. S. Precision in psychoanalysis. Q 1961, 30:456-457

80207 Mendelson, J. H. et al: Psychiatric observations on congenital and acquired deafness: symbolic and perceptual processes in dream. Q 1961, 30:145-146

80208 Miller, J. G. Information input overload and psychopathology. Q 1961, 30:144

80209 Walter, W. G. Where vital things happen. Q 1961, 30:143-144

80210 Ziegler, F. J. et al: Contemporary conversion reactions: a clinical study. Q 1961, 30:454-455

LEAVY, STANLEY A.

80211 Clinical observations on the development of religion in later childhood. (Read at Western New Engl Psa Soc, 23 May 1959; at Am Psa Ass, 7 May 1960) Bull Phila Ass Psa 1961, 11:61-75
    Abs PLe RFPsa 1963, 27:336

80213 A footnote to Jung's "Memories." Q 1964, 33:567-574

80214 Introduction to Andreas-Salomé, L. "The dual orientation of narcissism." Q 1962, 31:1-3

80215 Introduction to Andreas-Salomé, L. The Freud Journal.

80216 Lou Andreas-Salomés Freud-Tagbuch. [Lou Andreas-Salomé's The Freud Journal.] Psyche 1965, 19:219-240

80217 Psychiatry in its relations with religion. Conn State Med J 1950, 14 (11):1014.

80218 The psychic function of religion in mental illness and health. GAP Rep 1968, 67:647-730

80219 Psychoanalysis and moral change. Psychiat Opin 1966, 3(5):33-38

S-51887 A religious conversion in a four-year-old girl, a historical note.
    Abs DJM An Surv Psa 1957, 8:303

TRANSLATIONS OF:
Andreas-Salomé, L. [65818, 65819]

REVIEWS OF:
80220 Goodenough, E. R. The Psychology of Religious Experiences. Q 1967, 36:292-293
80221 Peters, H. F. My Sister, My Spouse: A Biography of Lou Andreas-Salomé. Q 1963, 32:578-581

LEBCEUF, G.

See Gauthier, Yvon

LEBEDINSKI, M. S.

80222 Psychotherapy in the Soviet Union. Prog PT 1960, 5:225-230

LE BEUF, JACQUES

80223 (& Lefebvre, P.) Contribution à la l'étude de la sado-nécrophilie. [Contribution to the study of sado-necrophilia.] Canad Psychiat Ass J 1966, 11:123-131

LEBLANC, J.

80224 [Anna O. and Emmy von M. Contribution to the history of psychoanalysis.] (Fr) Laval Med 1968, 39:232-239

LEBO, DELL

80225 The present status of research on nondirective play therapy. In Haworth, M. R. *Child Psychotherapy*, NY/London: Basic Books 1964, 421-430

See Begley, Carl; Ginott, Haim G.

LE BON, GUSTAV

S-19827 Psychologie der Massen.
The Crowd: A Study of the Popular Mind. NY: Viking Pr 1960, 207 p

LEBOVICI, C.

80226 Discussion of Fain, M. "Contribution à l'étude des variations de la symptomatologie." RFPsa 1962, 26:378, 381

LEBOVICI, SERGE

80227 L'abord écologique en psychiatrie infantile. [The ecological approach in child psychiatry.] Psychiat Enfant 1964, 7:197-268
80228 (& Roumajon, Y.) L'adolescent et les bandes. [The adolescent and gangs.] Hyg ment 1960, 49:259-277
S-51894 Die Aspekte der frühen Objekt-Beziehungen: die analytische Beziehung.
Abs BB An Surv Psa 1956, 7:99-100

80229 L'avenir psycho-pathologique des enfants surdoués. [The psycho-pathologic future of exceptionally gifted children.] Rv Np inf 1960, 8:214-216

S-51899 (& Diatkine, R.) Die Bilanz der Kinder-Psychoanalyse in Frankreich. Abs An Surv Psa 1955, 6:247-249

S-51901 (& McDougall, J.) Un Cas de Psychose Infantile: Étude Psychanalytique.
Dialogue with Sammy: A Psycho-Analytical Contribution to the Understanding of Child Psychosis. (Ed: James, M.) (Tr: McDougall, J.) London: HIP 1969, x + 274 p
Rv Bychowski, G. Q 1962, 31:262-264. Diatkine, R. RFPsa 1963, 27:320. Geleerd, E. R. J Am Psa Ass 1964, 12:242-258

80230 A child psychiatrist on children in day-care centres. WHO Publ Hlth Pap 1964, 24:76-92

80231 The clinical study of object relations in appreciating the mental health of the child. M 1960, 33:259-262

80232 Colloque sur les interprétations en thérapeutique psychanalytique. Introduction. [Conference on interpretations in psychoanalytic therapy. Introduction.] RFPsa 1962, 26:5-22, 37-42
Abs Donadeo, J. Q 1964, 33:612-613

80233 Community therapy. In Miller, E. *Foundations of Child Psychiatry*, Oxford/NY: Pergamon Pr 1968, 609-623

80234 Compte rendu de colloque sur la psychanalyse d'enfants. [Report of the conference on the psychoanalysis of children.] RFPsa 1967, 31:1105-1111

80235 The concept of maternal deprivation: a review of research. In *Deprivation of Maternal Care: A Reassessment of Its Effects,* WHO Publ Hlth Pap 1962, No. 14

80236 Le contre-transfert dans le traitement des psychoses par le psycho-drame psychanalytique. [Countertransference in the treatment of psychoses by psychoanalytic psychodrama.] In Benedetti, G. & Müller, C. *Psychotherapy of Schizophrenia (2nd Int Symp 1959),* Basel/NY: Karger 1960, 47-69

80237 (& Diatkine, R.) The contribution to the theory of the technique of child analysis to the understanding of character neuroses. (Read at Int Psa Cong, July 1963) J 1964, 45:344-349
Contribution de la théorie de la technique en psychanalyse infantile à la comprehension des névroses de caractère. RFPsa 1966, 30:287-293
Abs EVN Q 1966, 35:463

80238 Contribution to the symposium on acting out. (Read at Int Psa Cong, July 1967) J 1968, 49:202-205
Abs LHR Q 1969, 38:668

80239 Discussion of Dunham, H. W. "Community psychiatry: the newest therapeutic bandwagon." Int J Psychiat 1965, 1:567-568

80240 Discussion of Greenacre and Winnicott. "The theory of the parent-infant relationship. Further remarks." Contributions to discussion (iii) J 1962, 43:246-247

80241 Discussion of Grunberger, B. "De l'image phallique." RFPsa 1964, 28:233-234

80242 Discussion of Grunberger, B. "Considèrations sur le clivage entre le narcissisme et la maturation pulsionelle." RFPsa 1967, 26:201

80243 Discussion of Held, R. "Contribution à l'étude psychanalytique du phénomène religieux." RFPsa 1962, 26:259

80244 Discussion of Kestemberg, E. & Kestemberg, J. "Contributions à la perspective génétique en psychanalyse." RFPsa 1966, 30:755-759

80245 Discussion of Kestemberg, J. "A propos de la relation érotomanique." RFPsa 1962, 26:590

80246 Discussion of Pasche, F. "On depression." RFPsa 1963, 27:221

80247 Discussion of Racamier, P. C. "Propos sur la realité dans la théorie psychanalytique." RFPsa 1962, 26:708-709

80248 Discussion of Ritvo, S. "Correlation between a childhood and an adult neurosis." RFPsa 1967, 31:569-572

80249 Discussion of Rouart, J. "La temporisation comme maîtrise et comme défense." RFPsa 1962, 26:416-417

80250 (& Diatkine, R.) La dynamique de groupe. [The group dynamic.] Psychiat Enfant 1962

80251 (& Diatkine, R.; Lavondès, V.; Debray, R.; Shentoub, V.) Elements d'une recherche concernant l'avenir eloigne des psychoses de l'enfant. [Elements of a study on distant outcome of childhood psychoses.] Rv Np inf 1967, 15:13-18

80252 En relisant en 1966 "Analyse terminable et analyse interminable." [On rereading in 1966 "analysis terminable and interminable": introduction.] RFPsa 1968, 32:231-234

80253 (& Diatkine, R.) Essai d'approache de la notion de prepsychose en psychiatrie infantile. [Essay on the approach to the idea of prepsychosis in child psychiatry.] Bull Psychol, Paris 1963, 17:20-23

80254 (& Paumelle, P.) Une expérience de travail de secteur en psychiatrie infantile. [An experiment with sector work in child psychiatry.] Acta psychother psychosom 1962, 10:1-12

80255 (& Diatkine, R.) Fonction et signification du jeu chez l'enfant. [Function and significance of play for the child.] Psychiat Enfant 1962, 5:207-253

80256 Freud et Jung. [Freud and Jung.] Psychiat Enfant 1966, 9:223-249
    Abs Abels, M. E. RFPsa 1968, 32:334

80257 (& Kreisler, L.) L'homosexualité chez l'enfant et l'adolescent. [Homosexuality in children and adolescents.] Psychiat Enfant 1965, 8:57-133

80258 [Indications of psychotherapy in homosexuality.] (Fr) Therapeutique 1960, 36:629-632

80259 Milestones in psychoanalytic theorizing. Int J Psychiat 1967, 3:314-316

80260 (& Diatkine, R.; Klein, F.; Diatkine-Kalmanson, D.) Le mutisme et les silences de l'enfant. [Mutism and silences of children.] Psychiat Enfant 1963, 6:79-138

80261 Obituary. Melanie Klein 1881-1960. RFPsa 1961, 25:431

S-51926 Sur l'observation directe d'enfant par le psychanalyste. Notes sur l'observation directe de l'enfant.
    Abs HFM An Surv Psa 1958, 9:234-235

S-51929 Une observation de psychose infantile: étude des mécanismes de défense.
    Abs HFM An Surv Psa 1956, 7:286-287

S-51930 (& Diatkine, R.) Les obsessions chez l'enfant.
  Abs Noble, D. An Surv Psa 1957, 8:214-217
S-51931 Der Platz der Psychoanalyse in der Psychotherapie des Kindes.
  Abs Wolff, P. H. An Surv Psa 1957, 8:225-226
80262 Problèmes cliniques et techniques du contre-transfert. [Clinical and
  technical problems of countertransference.] RFPsa 1963, 27(Suppl):
  217-221
80263 Problems of a community psychiatric center. Int J Psychiat 1968, 5:
  483-485
80264 Le pronostic des névroses et des psychoses de l'enfant. [The prognosis
  of neuroses and psychoses in the child.] Proc IV World Cong Psychiat
  1966, 101-105
80265 (& Braunschweig, D.) A propos de la névrose infantile. [About child
  neurosis.] Psychiat Enfant 1967, 10:43-122
S-51934 A propos des indications et des techniques psychanalytiques dans les
  états prépsychotiques de l'enfance.
  Abs HFM An Surv Psa 1956, 7:287-288
80266 (& Benoît, G.; Poncin, C.; Poncin, M.; Talan, I.; Rozenhold, M.) A
  propos des observations de calculateurs de calendrier. [The cases of
  calendar calculators.] Psychiat Enfant 1966, 9:341-396
  Abs Abels, E. RFPsa 1968, 32:335
80267 A propos de la lecture des textes freudiens sur le narcissisme. [Apropos
  of reading Freudian texts on narcissism.] RFPsa 1965, 29:485-493
S-51938 (& Diatkine, R.; Favreau, J.-A.; Luquet-Parat, P.) La psychanalyse des
  enfants.
  Abs WAF An Surv Psa 1956, 7:240-241
S-51941 Die psychoanalytischen Auffassungen über die affektive Entwicklung
  des Kindes und ihre Integration in neurobiologische und kulturelle
  Gegebenheiten.
  Abs Wolff, P. H. An Surv Psa 1957, 8:200-201
80268 Psychodrama as applied to adolescents. J child Psychol Psychiat 1961,
  1:298-305
80269 Das Psychodrama mit Kindern und Jugendlichen. [Psychodrama with
  children and adolescents.] Hbh Kinderpsychother 771-777
80270 (& Klein, F.) La psychotherapie de l'enfant dans certains milieux socio-
  culturels sous-privilegiés. [Psychotherapy of children in various under-
  privileged sociocultural environments.] Rv Np inf 1968, 16:435-446
80271 La relation objectale chez l'enfant. [Object relation in the child.] Psychiat Enfant 1960, 3:147-226
S-51950 Symposium on psychotic object relationships.
  Abs JBi Q 1962, 31:123
80272 The teaching of medical psychology and sociology. WHO Publ Hlth
  Pap, 1961, 9:94-105

  See Ajuriaguerra, J. de; Braunschweig, Denise; Buckle, Donald F.;
  Caplan, Gerald; Nacht, Sacha

ABSTRACTS OF:
80273 Coolidge, J. C. et al: Patterns of aggression in school phobia. RFPsa
  1964, 28:814

80274 Deutsch, F. Correlations of verbal and nonverbal communication in interviews elicited by the associative anamnesis. RFPsa 1961, 25:156

80275 Deutsch, F. Principles of sector therapy. RFPsa 1961, 25:156

80276 Eissler, K. R. On the metapsychology of preconsciousness: a tentative contribution to psychoanalytic morphology. RFPsa 1964, 28:810

80277 Esman, E. H. Visual hallucinoses in young children. RFPsa 1964, 28: 814

80278 Frankl, V. E. Existenzanalyse und Logotherapie. RFPsa 1961, 25:156

80279 Freud, A. Assessment of childhood disturbances. RFPsa 1964, 28:811

80280 Hellman, I. Hampton Nursery follow-up studies. Sudden separation and its effect followed after 20 years. RFPsa 1964, 28:812

80281 Kavka, J. Ego synthesis of a life-threatening illness in childhood. RFPsa 1964, 28:814-815

80282 Kris, E. Decline and recovery in the life of a 3-year-old, or Data in psychoanalytic perspective on the mother-child relationship. RFPsa 1964, 28:812

80283 Lipton, S. D. On the psychology of childhood tonsillectomy. RFPsa 1964, 28:815

80284 Lustman, S. L. Defense, symptom and character. RFPsa 1964, 28:813

80285 Robertson, J. Mothering as an influence on early development. RFPsa 1964, 28:813

80286 Rubinfine, D. L. Maternal stimulation, psychic structure and early object relations. RFPsa 1964, 28:814

80287 Sandler, J. et al: The classification of superego material in the Hampstead Index. RFPsa 1964, 28:810

80288 Sandler, J. & Rosenblatt, B. The concept of the representational world. RFPsa 1964, 28:810

80289 Sechehaye, M. A. Techniques de gratification en psychothérapie analytique. RFPsa 1962, 26:145

80290 Spitz, R. A. Autoeroticism re-examined: the role of early sexual behavior patterns in personality formation. RFPsa 1964, 28:814

80291 Sprince, M. P. The development of a pre-oedipal partnership between an adolescent girl and her mother. RFPsa 1964, 28:815

REVIEWS OF:

80292 Berge, A. Les Maladies de la Vertu. RFPsa 1962, 26:311

80293 Boss, M. Psychanalyse et Analyse du "Dasein." RFPsa 1961, 25:156

80294 David, C. L'Attitude Conceptuelle en Médecine Psychosomatique. RFPsa 1961, 25:405

80295 Marty, P. et al: L'Investigation Psychosomatique. RFPsa 1964, 28: 285-289

80296 Robert, M. La Révolution Psychanalytique. RFPsa 1964, 28:623-625

80297 Rosen, J. N. Direct Analysis. RFPsa 1962, 26:142

80298 Spitz, R. A. A Genetic Field Theory of Ego Formation. RFPsa 1961, 25:281

LEBZELTERN, G.

80299 Aspekte der Suggestionstheorie. [Aspects of suggestion theory.] Z Psychother med Psychol 1967, 17:220-231

LECHAT, FERNAND

S-52052 Notes sur les premières relations objectales et sur leurs conséquences
à l'age adulte.
Abs Noble, D. An Surv Psa 1957, 8:81-85
S-52053 Autour du principe du plaisir.
Abs JBa An Surv Psa 1957, 8:30-31
S-52054 Du principe de sécurité.
Abs An Surv Psa 1955, 6:24; 81-86

LECHEVALIER, B.

See Delay, Jean Paul Louis

LECKIE, E. V.

80300 (& Withers, R. F. J.) A test of liability to depressive illness. M 1967,
40:273-282

LECLAIRE, F.

See Gauthier, Yvon

LECLAIRE, SERGE

80301 The economic standpoint—recent views. (Tr: Palin, D.) (Read at Int
Psa Cong, July-Aug 1963) J 1964, 45:324-330
Abs EVN Q 1966, 35:462
S-52062 Les grands rythmes de la cure psychanalytique.
The major rhythms of the psychoanalytic treatment. Problems in
Psa 43-56
80302 Le point de vue économique en psychanalyse. [The economic aspect of
psychoanalysis.] Évolut psychiat 1965, 30:189-213
S-52067 A propos de l'épisode psychotique que présenta "l'homme aux loups."
Abs TC An Surv Psa 1958, 9:190-191
80303 Psychanalyse. Essai sur l'Ordre de l'Inconscient et la Pratique de la
Lettre. [Psychoanalysis. Essay on the Regulation of the Unconscious.]
Paris: Ed Seuil 1968, 189 p
S-52069 Réflexions sur l'étude clinique d'une manifestation de transfert.
Abs An Surv Psa 1955, 6:322-324

See Laplanche, Jean; Raclot, Marcel

LE COULTRE, RITSKE

S-52071 Some special aspects of the transference-phenomenon.
Abs An Surv Psa 1955, 6:324
S-52072 Eine häufig vorkommende Lösung des Oedipuskonfliktes
Abs Wolff, P. H. An Surv Psa 1956, 7:150
80304 [Splitting of the ego as a neurotic manifestation.] (Dut) NTvG 1967,
111:1501-1508

LE CRON, LESLIE M.

80305 The uncovering of early memories by ideomotor responses to questioning. Int J clin exp Hyp 1963, 11:137-142

See Cheek, David B.

LEDDY, KEVIN

REVIEW OF:
80306 Guntrip, H. Healing the Sick Mind. J 1967, 48:471-472

LEDER, ALFRED

80307 Zur Psychopathologie der Schlaf- und Aufwachepilepsie. (Ein psychodiagnostische Untersuchung). [On the psychopathology of sleeping and wakening epilepsy. (A psychodiagnostic investigation).] Nervenarzt 1967, 38:434-442

LEDER, RUTH

80308 (& Schwartz, E. K.) The development stages of a therapy group and their implications for social living. Inter-Amer Soc Psychol, 1967, Dec

See Schwartz, Emanuel K.

LEDER, S.

80309 [Some comments on recent trends in the theory and practice of psychotherapy.] (Rus) Zh Nevropat Psikhiat 1963, 63:1245-1248

LEDERER, WILLIAM J.

80310 (& Jackson, D. D. Q.) The Mirages of Marriage. (Introd: Menninger, K. A.) NY: Norton 1968, 473 p

LEDERER, WOLFGANG

80311 Dragons, Delinquents, and Destiny. An Essay on Positive Superego Functions. NY: IUP 1964 (Psychol Issues, Monogr 15), 83 p
        Rv Am Im 1965, 22:216. Curry, A. E. R 1966, 53(1):143-144
80312 The Fear of Women. NY/London: Grune & Stratton 1968, viii + 260 p
80313 Historical consequences of father-son hostility. R 1967, 54:248-276
        Abs SRS Q 1968, 37:472-473
80314 Oedipus and the serpent. R 1964-65, 51:619-644
        Abs SRS Q 1966, 35:162

LEDERMAN, DONALD GEORGE

80315 Delinquency and the concept of identification. Diss Abstr 1961, 22(4):1254

LEE, A. R.

See Laing, Ronald D.

LEE, GILBERT

80316 The controversy in retrospect. Psychiat Opin 1968, 5(4):35-36

LEE, HAROLD

See Burke, Joan L.

LEE, JOAN COOK

80317 (& Griffith, R. M.) Forgetting of jokes: a function of repression. J ind Psych 1963, 19:213-215

LEE, LESTER C.

80318 An investigation of Erich Fromm's theory of authoritarianism. Diss Abstr 1963, 24(6):2558

LEE, MARY LIL

See Berkovitz, Irving H.

LEE, RITA E.

See Robey, Ames

LEE, ROBERT S.

See Chein, Isidor

LEE, S. G.

See Poser, E. G.

LEEDS, ANTHONY

80319 The functions of war. Sci Psa 1963, 6:69-82

LEEDY, JACK J.

80320 (Ed) Poetry Therapy: The Use of Poetry in the Treatment of Emotional Disorders. Phila/Toronto: Lippincott 1969, 288 p

LEEKS, S. R.

80321 The maintenance of the mother and child relationship in a psychiatric unit. New Zeal med J 1967, 66:95-98

LEEPER, ROBERT WARD

80322 Learning and the fields of perception, motivation, and personality. In Koch, S. *Psychology: A Study of a Science, Vol. 5*, NY: McGraw-Hill 1963, 365-487
80323 Some needed developments in the motivational theory of emotions. In *Nebraska Symposium on Motivation*, 1965, 25-122

LEESE, S.

80324 Psychotherapy in combination with antidepressant drugs. PT 1962, 16:407-423

LEEUW, PIETER J. VAN DER

80325 Allocution. [Address.] (Read at Cong Romance Language Psa, 1966) RFPsa 1967, 31:736-737

80326 A clinical contribution to the problem of early neglect. (Read at NY Psa Soc, 23 May 1961)

Abs Krimsley, J. M. Q 1961, 30:618-620

80327 Comment on Dr. Ritvo's paper, "Correlation of a childhood and adult neurosis: based on the adult analysis of a reported childhood case (summary)." (Read at Int Psa Cong, July 1965) J 1966, 47:132-135

Discussion: Ritvo, S. "Corrélation entre une névrose infantile at une névrose à l'âge adulte." RFPsa 1967, 31:549-553

80328 Comment on Drs. Lebovici and Diatkine's paper, "The contribution of the theory of the technique of child analysis to the understanding of character neuroses." J 1964, 45:347-349

Abs EVN Q 1966, 35:463

80329 Concernant le concept de défense. [Concerning the concept of defense.] RFPsa 1969, 33:5-24

80330 (& Frijling-Schreuder, E. C. M.; Kuiper, P. C.) (Eds) Hoofdstukken uit de Hedendaagse Psychoanalyse. [Chapters of Present-Day Psychoanalysis.] Arnhem: van Loghum Slaterus 1967, 311 p

Rv Sandler, J. J 1968, 49:113. Weyl, S. Q 1969, 38:318-326

80331 Obituary: Willi Hoffer: 1897-1967. (Read at Brit Psa Soc, 16 Oct 1968) J 1969, 50:262-263

80332 On Freud's theory formation. J 1969, 50:573-581

S-52084 On the pre-oedipal phase of the male.

La fase pre-edípica del varón. Rev Psicoanál 1966, 23:1-21

Abs GLG An Surv Psa 1958, 9:253-254

80333 The psycho-analytic society. (Read at Int Psa Cong, July 1967) J 1958, 49:161-164

Sur la vie des sociétés de psychanalyse. (Tr: Lagache, D.) Bull Ass psa Fran 1969, (5):197-205

80334 Symposium: selection criteria for the training of psycho-analytic students, II. (Read at Int Psa Cong, July-Aug 1961) J 1962, 43:277-282

Symposium: Critères de sélection applicables à la formation des étudiants en psychanalyse. RFPsa 1964, 28:17-27

Über Auswahlkriterien für die Zulassung zur Ausbildung zum Psychoanalytiker. Jb Psa 1964, 3:227-239

Simposio: criterios de seleccion para la formacion de estudiantes de psicoanalisis. Rev Psicoanál 1965, 22:253-262

Abs RLG Q 1963, 32:601-602. Soifer, R. Rev Psicoanál 1963, 20:198-199. Barriguete C., A. Cuad Psa 1967, 3:61-62. Vega Q 1967, 36:322

80335 Über die Entwicklung des Metapsychologiebegriffs. [On the development of the concept of metapsychology.] Psyche 1967, 21:125-137

80336 Über die metapsychologische Betrachtungsweise. [Concerning the metapsychological approach.] Psyche 1963, 16:653-669

80337   Zur Entwicklung des Begriffs der Abwehr. [On the development of the concept of defense.] Psyche 1965, 19:161-171

See Musaph, Herman

LEEUWEN, KATO VAN

80338   Pregnancy envy in the male. (Read at Int Psa Cong, July 1965) J 1966, 47:319-324
        Abs Cuad Psa 1967, 3:163
80339   (& Pomer, S. L.) The separation-adaptation response to temporary object loss. J Amer Acad Child Psychiat 1969, 8:711-733

LEFCOURT, HERBERT MICHAEL

80340   (& Barnes, K.; Parke, R.) Anticipated social censure and aggression-conflict as mediators of response to aggression induction. Soc Psych 1966, 70:251-263
80341   Belief in personal control: research and implications. J ind Psych 1966, 22:185-195

LEFCOWITZ, BARBARA F.

80342   The inviolate grove. (Metamorphosis of a symbol in *Oedipus at Colonus*.) Lit & Psych 1967, 17:78-86

LEFEBRE, LUDWIG B.

TRANSLATION OF:
Boss, M. [68345]

LEFEBVRE, PAUL

See Croco, Louis; Le Beuf, Jacques

LEFER, JAY

80343   Counter-resistance in family therapy. J Hillside Hosp 1966, 15:205-210
80344   Psychosis, somatic disease and the perceived body. J Hillside Hosp 1964, 13:18-31
        Abs JA Q 1967, 36:319

LEFER, LEON

80345   A psychoanalytic view of a dental phenomenon. Psychosomatics of the temporomandibular joint pain dysfunction syndrome. (Read at Int Forum Psa, July 1965) Contempo Psa 1966, 2(2):135-150

LEFERENZ, H.

80346   Zur Problematik der Psychopathie im Kindes- und Jugendalter. [The problems of psychotherapy in childhood and adolescence.] In Kranz, H. *Psychopathologie Heute,* Stuttgart: Georg Thieme 1962, 355-362

LEFF, J.

80347   Trauma and predictive memories. M 1969, 42:290-291

LEFKOWITZ, J.
See Lefkowitz, M.

LEFKOWITZ, M.
80348 (& Lefkowitz, J.) The serpent of Asclepios as a symbol of healing. Hebrew med J 1963, 2:232-241

LEFKOWITZ, MONROE M.
See Eron, Leonard D.

LEFRANÇOIS, J.-J.
See Delay, Jean Paul Louis

LEFTON, MARK
See Dinitz, Simon; Pasamanick, Benjamin

LE GALL, ANNE-MARIE
TRANSLATION OF:
Jones, E. [16594]

LEGEAY, C.
80349 "A failure to thrive": a nursing problem. Nurs Forum 1965, 4:56-71

LEGER, J. M.
80350 (& Ranty, Y.) [Psychopathologic aspects of the tic in Gilles de la Tourette's disease.] (Fr) Ann Medicopsychol 1969, 2:689-695

LEGERSKI, A. T.
See Rychlak, Joseph F.

LEGMAN, G.
80351 Rationale of the Dirty Joke. NY: Grove Pr 1968, 811 p

LEGRAND, DAVID D.
80352 Psychoanalytic principles applied to pediatric surgery. Maryland State med J 1964, 13:113-117

LEGRAND, J.-P.
80353 Réflexions à propos de la loi Belge de défense sociale. [Reflections on the Belgian law of social defense.] In Kranz, H. *Psychopathologie Heute,* Stuttgart: Georg Thieme 1962, 274-277

LE GUEN, C.
80354 A propos de Goya: sur l'art et l'alienation. [Goya, art, and mental illness.] Évolut psychiat 1961, 26:33-67

LEHAMBRE, J.

80355 ["Paradoxal intention," a psychotherapeutic procedure.] (Fr) Acta neurol psychiat Belg 1964, 64:725-735

LEHMAN, EDWARD

80356 The monster test. Arch gen Psychiat 1960, 3:535-544

LEHMANN, G.

80357 [Experiences with extemporaneous fairy play within the framework of clinical psychotherapy.] (Ger) Psychiat Neurol med Psychol 1968, 20:374-380

LEHMANN, HEINZ EDGAR

80358 On the phenomenology of the depressive illness. Canad Psychiat Ass J 1966, 11(Suppl):S3-S6
80359 Pharmacotherapy of schizophrenia. Proc Amer Psychopath Ass 1966, 54:388-412
80360 Phenomenology and pathology of addiction. Comprehen Psychiat 1963, 4:168-180
80361 The placebo response and the double-blind study. Proc Amer Psychopathy Ass 1964, 52:75-93
80362 Psychodynamic aspects of psychopharmacology. Proc IV World Cong Psychiat 1966, 296-304
80363 Psychopharmacology. A discussion of current problems. Ohio State med J 1963, 59:1091-1097
80364 (& Ban, T.) (Eds) The Thioxanthenes. (Modern Problems of Pharmacopsychiatry, Vol. 2) Basel/NY: Karger 1969, 116 p

LEHMANN, HERBERT

80365 A conversation between Freud and Rilke. Q 1966, 35:423-427
80366 Freud, Zweig, and biography. Q 1963, 32:94-97
80367 The lion in Freud's dreams. Psa Forum 1967, 2:230-236, 241-243
80368 Two dreams and a childhood memory of Freud. (Read at San Francisco Psa Soc, Oct 1964; at Am Psa Ass, Dec 1964) J Am Psa Ass 1966, 14:388-405
    Abs Cuad Psa 1966, 2:123. JLSt Q 1969, 38:337

ABSTRACTS OF:
80369 Burton, A. Death as a countertransference. Q 1963, 32:610-611
80370 Eisenbud, J. Discussion of Strean and Nelson's "A further clinical illustration of the paranormal triangle hypothesis." Q 1963, 32:452
80371 Friedman, D. B. On the phrase, "beautiful but dumb." Q 1963, 32:611
80372 Hall, C. S. Out of a dream came the faucet. Q 1963, 32:612
80373 Joseph, F. Transference and countertransference in the case of a dying patient. Q 1963, 32:611
80374 Meerloo, J. A. M. The dual meaning of human regression. Q 1963, 32:452
80375 Meyerson, B. G. & Stollar, L. A psychoanalytical interpretation of the crucifixion. Q 1963, 32:612

80376 Rosenbaum, J. B. Holiday, symptom and dream. Q 1963, 32:452
80377 Schneck, J. M. The psychodynamics of "déjà vu." Q 1963, 32:611
80378 Searles, H. F. Scorn, disillusionment and adoration in the psycho-therapy of schizophrenia. Q 1963, 32:451
80379 Shugart, G. The unique self. Q 1963, 32:611
80380 Spotnitz, H. The need for insulation in the schizophrenic personality. Q 1963, 32:451
80381 Strean, H. S. & Nelson, M. C. A further clinical illustration of the paranormal triangle hypothesis. Q 1963, 32:452
80382 Wolf, R. Castration symbolism in patristic thought: preliminary studies in the development of Christianity. Q 1963, 32:451
80383 Wolstein, B. On the psychological absurdity of existential analysis. Q 1963, 32:452

LEHRBURGER, H.

See Eisenbud, Jule

LEHRMAN, NATHANIEL S.

80384 Anarchy, dictatorship and democracy within the family, a bio-social hierarchy. Psychiat Q 1962, 36:455-474
80385 Anti-therapeutic and anti-democratic aspects of Freudian dynamic psy-chiatry. J ind Psych 1963, 19:167-181
80386 Creativity, consciousness and revelation. Dis nerv Sys 1960, 21:431-439, 499-504
80387 Do our hospitals help make acute schizophrenia chronic? Dis nerv Sys 1961, 22:489-493
80388 Follow-up of brief and prolonged psychiatric hospitalization. Com-prehen Psychiat 1961, 2:227-240
80389 The joint interview: an aid to psychotherapy and family stability. PT 1963, 17:83-93
80390 Pleasure, pain and human relations. Dis nerv Sys 1961, 22:201-207
80391 Precision in psychoanalysis. P 1960, 116:1097-1103
    Abs Leavitt, M. Q 1961, 30:456-457
80392 The unconscious wish: an operational examination. Psa 1961, 21:85-91

LEHRMAN, SAMUEL R.

80393 Ego, superego and id—or life, liberty and the pursuit of happiness. Some thoughts on psychoanalysis and the current scene. Psychiat Q 1968, 42:381-390
80394 On the linkage between neurosis and schizophrenia. J Hillside Hosp 1968, 17:200-208
80395 Psychopathology in mixed marriages. (Read at Long Island Psa Soc, 1965) Q 1967, 36:67-82
    Abs Cuad Psa 1967, 3:242
S-52111 Reactions to untimely death. In Ruitenbeek, H. M. *Death and Mourn-ing,* NY: Dell Publ 1967
    Abs AaSt An Surv Psa 1956, 7:166-167

See Kaufman, M. Ralph

REVIEW OF:
80396 Kaufman, M. R. (Ed) The Psychiatric Unit in a General Hospital.
Q 1967, 36:308-309

LEIBBRAND, WERNER

80397 [Relations between psychology and psychopathology from the middle
of the 18th century up to 1900.] (Ger) Bibl Psychiat Neurol 1964
(1):1-35

LEIBERMAN, HARVEY

See Galbraith, Gary G.

LEIBOVICI, MIGUEL

80398 (& Sifneos, P. E.) Educating psychiatrists to become teachers: an important dimension of post-graduate training. Proc IV World Cong
Psychiat 1966, 3121-3122

See Caquot, A.

LEIBY, ROBERT

See Unger, Sanford

LEICHTY, MARY M.

80399 The effect of father-absence during early childhood upon the Oedipal
situation as reflected in young adults. Merrill-Palmer Q 1960, 6:212-
217
80400 Family attitudes and self concept in Vietnamese and U. S. children.
Ops 1963, 33:38-50
Abs JMa RFPsa 1964, 28:447

LEIDER, ROBERT J.

80401 Silence in psychoanalysis. n. p. 1967 (Multilithographed), 26 p

LEIDERMAN, P. HERBERT

80402 (& Kubzansky, P. E.; Mendelson, J. H.; Wexler, D.; Solomon, P.)
Contributions of sensory deprivation to the study of human behavior.
Proc Int Cong Psychiat 1959. Neurosis 1961
80403 Loneliness: a psychodynamic interpretation. Int Psychiat Clin 1969,
6(2):155-174
80404 (& Shapiro, D.) (Eds) Psychobiological Approaches to Social Behaviour. Stanford: Stanford Univ Pr 1964; London: Tavistock 1965,
203 p
80405 (& Mendelson, J. H.; Wexler, D.; Solomon, P.) Sensory deprivation:
clinical aspects. Arch intern Med 1958, 101:389-396

See Greenberg, Ramon; Mendelson, Jack H.; Solomon, Philip

LEIFER, RONALD

80406 Avoidance and mastery: an interactional view of phobias. J ind Psych 1966, 22:80-93

See Hollender, Marc H.; Malev, Jonathan S.

LEIGH, DENIS

80407 The contributions of psychoanalysis and psychiatry to psychosomatic medicine. Psychother Psychosom 1967, 15:153-161. In Philippopoulos, G. S. *Dynamics in Psychiatry*, Basel/NY: Karger 1968, 69-77

80408 The form complete. The present states of psychosomatic medicine. Proc RSM 1968, 61:375-384

80409 (& Marley, E.) Genetic aspects of asthma and allergy. Proc IV World Cong Psychiat 1966, 570-572

80410 The Historical Development of British Psychiatry, Volume I. Oxford: Pergamon 1961, 277 p

80411 The psychology of the pet owner. J Small Anim Pract 1966, 7:517-521

LEIGHTON, ALEXANDER H.

80412 The etiology of diagnosis. P 1969, 125:1426-1427

80413 Social psychiatry: socioeconomic factors in mental health and disease. In Galdston, I. *Historic Derivations of Modern Psychiatry*, NY: Mc-Graw-Hill 1967, 219-232

LEININGER, MADELEINE M.

See Hofling, Charles K.

LEISCHNER, A.

80414 Über Träume in fremden Sprachen bei Gesunden und Aphasischen. [Dreaming in foreign languages in normal subjects and in patients with aphasia.] Neuropsychologia 1965, 3:191-204

LEITCH, A.

80415 Male homosexuality as a medico-legal and sociological problem in the United Kingdom. Int J soc Psychiat 1959, 5:98-106

LEITE, DANTE MOREIRA

80416 Psicologia e Literatura. [Psychology and Literature.] São Paulo: Editôra Nacional 1967, 256 p

LEITO LOBO, FABIO

80417 Invenção do en reestruturação de unego feminino acompanhada na produção poetica de una paciente. [Imagination in the restructuring of a feminine ego accompanying a patient's poetic production.] Rev Psicoanál 1961, 18:71-84

LEITES, NATHAN

S-52127 Panic and defenses against panic in the Bolshevik view of politics. Abs An Surv Psa 1955, 6:433-435

LEITH, JENNIFER
TRANSLATION OF:
Fraisse, P. [73266]

LELAND, THOMAS W.
80418 The faint smile syndrome. Ops 1961, 31:420-421
       Abs JMa RFPsa 1962, 26:327

See Bowers, Margaretta K.

LÉLY, GILBERT
80419 The Marquis de Sade. A Biography. (Tr: Brown, A.) London: Elek
       Books 1961, 464 p.

LEMAINE, J. M.
80420 [Birth order and social behavior (1959-1967).] (Fr) Ann Psychol
       1968, 68:593-610

LEMBKE, PERNILLA
See Cohen, Richard L.

LEME, WANDA P.
80421 (& Caminha, M. E.) Simpósio sobre psicopatia e neurose: o ponto de
       vista clínico: experiéncia no ambulatório. [Symposium on psycho-
       therapy and neurosis: the clinical point of view: experience of ambu-
       latory patients.] J Bras Psiquiat 1963, 12:9-21

LE MEN, J.
See Fau, R. B.

LEMERCIER, GREGORY
80422 A Benedictine monastery in psychoanalysis. Bull Guild Cath Psychia-
       trists 1966, 13(1)
80423 Freud in the cloister: interview. Atlas 1967, 13:33-37

LEMERE, FREDERICK
80424 Brief psychotherapy. Psychosomatics 1968, 9:81-83

LEMERT, E. M.
80425 Dependency in married alcoholics. Quart J Stud Alcohol 1962, 23:590-
       609

LEMIUX, M.
See Azima, Hassan

LEMKAU, PAUL V.

80426 The anatomy of a group of illness and states. Int J Psychiat 1969, 7:412-413

S-52129 Freud and prophylaxis.
Abs Shevin, F. F. An Surv Psa 1956, 7:28

LEMPÉRIÈRE, T.

See Delay, Jean Paul Louis

LENNARD, HENRY L.

80427 (& Bernstein, A.; Hendin, H. C.; Palmore, E. B.) The Anatomy of Psychotherapy: Systems of Communication and Expectation. NY: Columbia Univ Pr 1960, 209 p
Rv Pfeffer, A. Z. Q 1962, 31:407-408

LENNOX, K.

See Beckett, Peter G. S.

LENNY, M. R.

80428 Acting-out behavior of psychiatric nurses. Perspect psychiat Care 1966, 4:10-13

LENOX, JOHN

See Hilgard, Ernest R.

LENZ, H.

80429 [Interpretation of modern delusions.] (Ger) Nervenarzt 1969, 40:547-549

LENZ, ROSA

See Sager, Clifford J.

LENZNER, ABRAHAM S.

80430 Freud, Jung & Adler. Mendentian 1939, Dec; 1940, Jan
80431 The liaison psychiatric service. Psychosomatics 1968, 9:326-330
80432 Mental health problems of the aging. J Jewish Comm Serv 1956, 33:147-152
80433 Practice and perspectives in geriatric psychiatry. J Hillside Hosp 1958, 7(3-4)
80434 (& Kenyon, M.) Psychiatric education. Nassau med News 1968, 11(8):14-15
80435 Symposium on drugs: abuse, dependence, and addiction. Glen Oaks, New York, The Society of Hillside Hospital, 1967, Vol. XVI, No. 2, 76 p

See Blau, Abram

LEÓN, CARLOS A.

80436 Modalidades depresivas en las reacciones psiconeuroticas y psicóticas. [Depressive modalities in psychoneurotic and psychotic reactions.] Act Np Arg 1960, 6:189-198

LEONARD, CALISTA V.

80437 Understanding and Preventing Suicide. Springfield, Ill: Thomas 1967, xii + 351 p

See Farberow, Norman L.

LEONARD, JAMES R.

80438 Hypnotic age regression: a test of the functional ablation hypothesis. JAbP 1965, 70:266-269

LEONARD, MARJORIE R.

80439 Fathers and daughters: the significance of "fathering" in the psychosexual development of the girl. (Read at Am Psa Ass, May 1965; at Int Psa Cong, July 1965) J 1966, 47:325-334
    Abs EVN Q 1968, 37:313
80440 Problems in identification and ego development in twins. (Read at Los Angeles Psa Soc, March 1959; at Am Psa Ass, April 1959) Psa St C 1961, 16:300-320
80441 Twins. In *The Encyclopedia of Child Care and Guidance*, Garden City, New Jersey: Doubleday 1954, 570-572
80442 Twins: the myth and the reality. Child Study 1953, 30(2):9-13, 38-41

TRANSLATION OF:
Goja, H. [12075]

REVIEWS OF:
80443 Ekstein, R. et al: Children of Time and Space, of Action and Impulse. Q 1968, 37:132-135
80444 Silverman, H. L. Psychology and Education. Q 1962, 31:402-404

LEONARD, MARTHA F.

80445 (& Rhymes, J. P.; Solnit, A. J.) Failure to thrive in infants—a family problem. Amer J Dis Childr 1966, 111:600-612

LEONARDI, PIERO

80446 Difese anali e nevrosi. [Anal and neurotic defence.] Riv Psa 1967, 13:163-174

See Cazzullo, Carlo L.

LEONELLI, L.

80447 [The position of the critic in presence of the psychopathological figurative expression.] (It) Riv Sper Freniat 1968, 92 (Suppl 1):273-275

LEONHARD, KARL

80448 Akzentuierte Persönlichkeiten. [Personalities under Stress.] Berlin: Verlag Volk & Gesundheit 1968, 287 p

80449 (& Briewig, E.-M.) Ätiologische Differenzierung von Depressionen jenseits des 60. Lebensjahres. [Etiological differentiation of depressions in patients over 60 years of age.] Arch Psychiat Nervenkr 1964, 205:358-374

80450 Gewöhnung und Neurose. [Habituation and neurosis.] Z Psychol 1967, 173:269-273

80451 Individualtherapie schwerer Zwangsneurosen. [Individual therapy of severe obsession neuroses.] Psychiat Neurol med Psychol 1967, 19:2-10

80452 Schizophrene mit typischen Defektzuständen nach ihren eigenen Schriftstücken. (Mit Bemerkungen über die Briefe und die Psychose van Goghs.) [Typical residual states of schizophrenics illustrated by their own writings. (With comments on the letters and psychosis of van Gogh.)] Arch Psychiat Nervenkr 1968, 211:7-22

80453 Was ist eine Sexualstörung? [What is a sexual disturbance?] Psychiat Neurol med Psychol 1968, 20:1-3

80454 Der weibliche Körper in der Kunst und in der Mode in Beziehung zur gesellschaftlichen Stellung der Frau. [The female body in art and in fashion in relation to the social position of women.] Psychiat Neurol med Psychol 1966, 18:82-86

LEOPOLD, EDITH A.

See Leopold, Robert L.

LEOPOLD, J. V.

See Carroll, Edward J.

LEOPOLD, K.

See Marson, E.

LEOPOLD, ROBERT L.

80455 (& Friedman, J.; Lindemann, E.; Dillon, H.) The Kennedy assassination. Penn Med 1966, 69(7):55-56

80456 (& Dillon, H.) Psycho-anatomy of a disaster: a long term study of post-traumatic neuroses in survivors of a marine explosion. P 1963, 119:913-921

80457 (& Leopold, E. A.) Rapprochement between social psychiatrist and community organizer: a blending of two disciplines. Proc IV World Cong Psychiat 1966, 2498-2500

80458 (& Duhl, L. J.) Relationship with social agencies: community implications. In Marmor, J. *Modern Psychoanalysis—New Directions and Perspectives*, NY: Basic Books 1968, 557-597

See Duhl, Leonard J.

LEPORE, MICHAEL

See Daniels, George E.; O'Connor, John F.

LEPP, IGNACE

80459 Clartés et Ténebrès de l'Âme.
The Depths of the Soul: A Christian Approach to Psychoanalysis.
Staten Island, NY: Alba House 1966, 280 p; Garden City, NY: Image
Books 1967, 274 p

80460 Liebe, Neurose und christliche Moral. Fünf Aufsätze zum Verhältnis
von Tiefenpsychologie und Glaube. [Love, Neurosis and Christian
Morality. Five Essays on the Relation of Depth Psychology and Belief.] Würzburg: Arena Verlag 1960, 123 p

80461 La Mort et ses Mystères, Approches Psychanalytiques.
Death and Its Mysteries. (Tr: Murchland, B.) London: Burns &
Oates 1969, xxv + 194 p

80462 Psychanalyse de l'Amour.
The Psychology of Loving. (Tr: Gilligan, B. B.) Baltimore: Helicon
1963, ix + 223 p

LEPPMANN, PETER K.

See Evans, Richard I.

LEPPO, LUCIANO V.

80463 Analisi di una condotta masochistica. [Analysis of masochistic behavior.] Riv Psa 1966, 12:175-198

80464 Aspetti psicodinamici delle nevrosi motorie. [Psychodynamic aspects
of tics.] Lav Np 1963, 33:1-5

80465 Diagnosi differenziale tra psicosi anfetaminiche e schizofrenia. [Dif-
ferences in the diagnosis of schizophrenia and amphetaminic psychosis.]
Lav Np 1967, 127:248-255

80466 Discussion of Fajrajzen, S. "Alcune considerazione sull'aggressività
controtransferenziale nel trattamento di pazienti psicotici." Riv Psa
1966, 12:105

80467 Discussion of Fajrajzen, S. "Reazioni depressive del paziente e dell'-
analista nella situazione analitica, e natura del processo terapeutico."
Riv Psa 1967, 18:318

80468 Discussion of Limentani, A. "Problemi di ambivalenza, riparazione e
le situazioni edipiche." Riv Psa 1967, 13:301

80469 Discussion of Muratori, A. M. "Vicissitudini della relazione simbiotica
e angosce d'identità." Riv Psa 1967, 13:323

80470 Discussion of Turillazzi, M. S. M. "Evoluzione di alcuni condotte sessuali nel corso di un trattamento psicoanalitico." Riv Psa 1967, 13:305

80471 (& Donini, G.) Il fattore "isolamento nella genesi delle psicosi indotte."
Considerazioni su di un caso di "folie à deux." [Isolation as a factor
in the genesis of the "folie à deux."] Riv sper Freniat 1961, 85:836-843

80472 Fenomenologia del sogno nella schizofrenia. [Phenomenology of the
dream in schizophrenia.] Riv Psichiat 1966, 1:222-240

80473 La malinconia involutiva. [Involutional depression.] (Monogr) Rome:
Arte della Stampa 1966, 96 p

80474 Sensory deprivation. Lav Np 1962, 31(Suppl 3):1-27

80475 Studio psicopatologico e genetico di una coppia di gemelli monozigoti schizofrenici. [Psychopathological and genetic study of a couple of male schizophrenic monozygotic twins.] Lav Np 1965, 36:442-457

80476 Sui rapporti tra omosessualita e "identità di genere." [Homosexuality and gender identity.] Sessuologia 1965, 6:184-186

80477 Le tossicomanie. [Drug addiction.] (Monogr) Rome: Arte della Stampa 1966, 177 p

80478 Trattamento dell' "ejaculatio praecox" con tioridazina. [Treatment of "ejaculatio praecox" with thioridazine.] Riv Psichiat 1966, 1:165-175

LEPSON, DAVID S.

See Jones, Austin

LERNER, ARTHUR

80479 Psychoanalytically-oriented criticism of three American poets: Poe, Whitman, and Aiken. Diss Abstr 1968, 28(4-A):1229

LERNER, BARBARA

80480 Dream function reconsidered. JAbP 1967, 7:85-100

80481 Rorschach movement and dreams. A validation study using drug-induced dream deprivation. JAbP 1966, 71:75-86

LERNER, BENJAMIN

80482 Auditory and visual thresholds for the perception of words of anal connotation: an evaluation of the "sublimation hypothesis" on philatelists. Diss Abstr 1966, 27:2122

LERNER, BURTON

80483 (& Raskin, R.; Davis, E. B.) On the need to be pregnant. J 1967, 48:288-297

Abs Bull Ass psa Med 1966, 5:3,31-34. EVN Q 1969, 38:160-161

LERNER, J.

80484 Disability evaluation in psychiatric illness and the concept of hysteria. Canad Psychiat Ass J 1966, 11:350-355

80485 Evaluation of psychiatric disability and the concept of regression. JAMA 1964, 188:369-370

LERNER, J. J.

See Rychlak, Joseph F.

LERNER, MARCELO

80486 Hipoanálisis de los mecanismos inconcientes de resistencia a la curación. [Hypnoanalysis of unconscious mechanisms or resistance to cure.] Acta psiquiat psicol Arg 1962, 8:127-134

80487 Hipoanálisis del fenómeno de desdoblamiento en una psicosis alucinatoria. [Hypnoanalysis of the phenomenon of splitting in an hallucinatory psychosis.] Act Np Arg 1960, 6:72-78

80488   Psicoanálisis e hipnoanálisis: breve estudio comparativo. [Psychoanalysis and hypnoanalysis: a brief comparative study.] Act Np Arg 1961, 7:283-289

LERNER, MAX

80489   Letter to the editor [re the Beatnik-Hippie]. Psa Forum 1967, 2:381-382

LERNER, MELVIN J.

See Baxter, James C.; Becker, James C.

LERNER, MILDRED S.

80490   Obituary: Jule Nydes: 1911-1967. (Read at Nat Psychol Ass Psa, 2 April 1967) R 1967, 54:373-377

LESCHE, CARL

80491   A Metascientific Study of Psychosomatic Theories and Their Application in Medicine. Copenhagen: Munksgaard; NY: Humanities Pr 1962, 64 p
80492   Psykosomatiska problem. [Psychosomatic problems.] In Valpola, V. *Människan som Forskiningsobjekt,* Oslo: Nordiska Sommaruniv 1960, 13-37
80493   Teknikens världsåskådning och datamaskinmusik. [The world picture of technology and computer music.] Fylkingen Bull 1968, 1:14
80494   Världsåskådning, vetenskap, teknik och konst. Fylkingen Bull 1967, 1:36-44
          Weltanschaung, science, technology and art. Fylkingen Int Bull 1967, 1:42-51

LESER, LOUIS S.

80495   (& Bry, T.) The role of death fears in the etiology of phobic anxiety as revealed in group psychotherapy. Int J grp PT 1960, 10:287-297
          Abs GPK Q 1961, 30:605

LESHAN, EDA

See LeShan, Lawrence L.

LE SHAN, LAWRENCE L.

80496   Changing trends in psychoanalytically oriented psychotherapy. MH 1962, 46:454-463
80497   (& LeShan, E.) Psychotherapy and the patient with a limited life span. Ps 1961, 24:318-323. In Ruitenbeek, H. M. *Death: Interpretations,* NY: Dell Publ 1969, 105-115
          Abs HRB Q 1962, 31:429. Soifer, R. Rev Psicoanál 1962, 19:269
80498   Some observations on the problem of mobilizing the patient's will to live. In Kissen, D. M. & LeShan, L. L. *Psychosomatic Aspects of Neoplastic Disease,* London: Pitman Med Publ; Phila/Montreal: Lippincott 1964, 109-120

80499   Untersuchungen zur Persönlichkeit der Krebskranken. [Examination on the personality of person with ulcer.] Z PSM 1963, 9:246-256

See Bowers, Margaretta K.; Kissen, David M.

LESKY, ERNA

80500   Die Wiener Medizinische Schule im 19. Jahrhundert. [The Vienna Medical School in the 19th Century.] Grazköln: Hermann Böhlaus Nachfolger 1965, 660 p
Rv Eissler, K. R. Q 1966, 35:127-130

LESSE, HENRY

80503   Research in psychiatric training programs. Bull Los Angeles Neurol Soc 1963, 28(3):167-169

LESSE, STANLEY

80504   Anti-depressant drugs in combination with psychotherapy: indications and results. Proc IV World Cong Psychiat 1966, 1847-1849

80505   Automation and psychiatry—current realities and challenges. PT 1966, 20:561-563

80506   Combined drug and psychotherapy of severely depressed ambulatory patients. Canad Psychiat Ass J 1966, 11(Suppl):123-130

80507   A dance macabre—psychiatry and the law. PT 1964, 18:183-187

80508   Decompression of anxiety by various techniques. Psychodynamic relationships between anxiety and other clinical psychiatric symptoms. J Neuropsychiat 1959, 1:28-31

80509   (& Mathers, J.) Depression sine depression (masked depression). NYSJM 1968, 68:535-543

80510   (& Adler, A.; Arieti, S.; Hoch, P. H.; Pacella, B.; Sager, C.) An eclectic approach to psychotherapy—is it desirable or necessary? PT 1963, 17:107-125

80511   Evaluation and process: the road to the future. PT 1966, 20:1-2

80512   (Ed) An Evaluation of the Results of the Psychotherapies. Springfield, Ill: Thomas 1968, xiv + 351 p
Rv Share, I. A. Bull Phila Ass Psa 1969, 19:169-170

80513   Hypochondriasis and psychosomatic disorders masking depression. PT 1967, 21:607-620

80514   Indications for the use of psychotherapy in combination with psychotropic drugs in ambulatory patients. Psychosomatics 1968, 9:84-88

80515   Individualism—a dying anachronism. PT 1964, 18:373-376

80516   The influence of socioeconomic and sociotechnologic systems on emotional illness. PT 1968, 22:569-576

80517   The intensity of anxiety: its relationship to the process of treatment. In author's An Evaluation of the Results of the Psychotherapies 18-37

80518   Management of apparent remissions in suicidal patients. Curr psychiat Ther 1967, 7:73-76

80519   Management of suicidal patients. Curr psychiat Ther 1968, 8:56-59

80520   Masked depression—a diagnostic and therapeutic problem. Dis nerv Sys 1968, 29:169-173

80521   The multivariant masks of depression. P 1968, 124(Suppl):35-40
80522   Obsolescence in psychotherapy. PT 1969, 23:381-395
80523   Patients, therapists, and socioeconomics. In author's *An Evaluation of the Results of the Psychotherapies* 239-253
80524   Placebo reactions and spontaneous rhythms in psychotherapy. Arch gen Psychiat 1964, 10:497-505
80525   Psychiatry and psychotherapy—their role in futurology. PT 1967, 21:719-722
80526   Psychodynamic consideration in current psychopharmacologic practices. Psychosomatics 1963, 4:353-358
80527   Psychodynamic mechanisms of emotional illness in executives. Int J soc Psychiat 1966, 12:24-28
80528   (& Wolf, W.) Psychotherapie im 21. Jarhundert. Eine Untersuchung über die Hauptdeterminanten und -strömungen der Psychotherapie in unserer künftigen Gesellschaft. Prax PT 1968, 13:49-57
        Psychotherapy in the twenty-first century. An exploration of the basic determinants and trends of psychotherapy in our future society. Psychother Psychosom 1968, 16:47-54
80529   The psychotherapist and apparent remissions in depressed suicidal patients. PT 1965, 19:436-444
80530   Psychotherapy—an apocalyptic view. PT 1967, 21:561-564
80531   Psychotherapy in combination with anti-depressant drugs. J Neuropsychiat 1962, 3:154-158
80532   Psychotherapy plus drugs in severe depressions—technique. Comprehen Psychiat 1966, 7:224-231
80533   Psychotherapy training institutes and current realities. PT 1966, 20:203-205
80534   The relationships between socioeconomic and sociopolitical practices and psychotherapeutic techniques. PT 1964, 18:574-583
80535   Revolution, vintage 1968: a psychosocial view. PT 1969, 23:584-598
80536   Studies of anxiety in schizophrenia. Dis nerv Sys 1960, 21:158-160

LESSER, GERALD

80537   (& Kandel, D.) Cross-cultural research: advantages and problems. Les recherches transculturelles: avantages et problèmes. Hum Context 1969, 1:347-376; 377-397

        See Kagan, Jerome

LESSER, SIMON O.

S-52185 Fiction and the Unconscious.
        Abs WAF An Surv Psa 1957, 8:337-342
S-52186 Freud and *Hamlet* again.
        Abs An Surv Psa 1955, 6:451
80538   Hawthorne and Anderson: conscious and unconscious perception; excerpt from "Fiction and the Unconscious." In Malin, I. *Psychoanalysis and American Fiction*, NY: Dutton 1965, 87-110
80539   The nature of psychoanalytic criticism. Lit & Psych 1962, 12:5-9

80540 Oedipus the king: the two dramas, the two conflicts. College English 1967, 29:175-197
80541 Our feelings about man-made creatures, imaginary and "real." Comments on "The golem and the robot" by Robert Plank. Lit & Psych 1965, 15:28-31
80542 The role of unconscious understanding in Flaubert and Dostoevsky. Daedalus 1963, 92:363-382
80543 Saint and sinner—Dostoevsky's *Idiot*. In Manheim, L. & Manheim, E. *Hidden Patterns,* NY: Macmillan 1966, 132-150

LESSER, STANLEY ROBERT
See Easser, Barbara R.

REVIEW OF:
80544 Shaw, C. R. The Psychiatric Disorders of Childhood. Q 1969, 38:327-329

LESSER, WALTER
80545 Clinical social work in a therapeutic community: the day treatment center. Int J soc Psychiat 1965, 11(1)
80546 The developing role of social work in a neuropsychiatric day center. Soc Casewk 1960, 41

LESSING, ELISE E.
80547 Prognostic value of the Rorschach in a child guidance clinic. J proj Tech 1960, 24:310-321
80548 Racial differences in indices of ego functioning relevant to academic achievement. J genet Psychol 1969, 115:153-167

See Pieper, William J.

LESSING, JOHN C.
See Kramer, Charles H.

LESSLER, KEN
80549 Cultural and Freudian dimensions of sexual symbols. J consult Psychol 1964, 28:46-53
80550 (& Erickson, M. T.) Response to sexual symbols by elementary school children. J consult Psychol 1968, 32:473-478
80551 Sexual symbols, structured and unstructured. J consult Psychol 1962, 26:44-49

See Fox, Ronald E.

LESSOW, HERBERT
See Daniels, Robert S.

LESTER, B. K.
See West, Louis Jolyon

LESTER, DAVID

80552 Antecedents of the fear of the dead. Psychol Rep 1966, 19:741-742
80553 Attempted suicide and body image. J Psychol 1967, 66:287-290
80554 Attempted suicide as a hostile act. J Psychol 1968, 68:243-248
80555 The effect of fear and anxiety on exploration and curiosity: toward a theory of exploration. J gen Psychol 1968, 79:105-120
80556 The fear of death of those who have nightmares. J Psychol 1968, 69:245-247
80557 A new method for the determination of the effectiveness of sleep-inducing agents in humans. Comprehen Psychiat 1960, 1(5)
           Abs Saucier, J. L. RFPsa 1962, 26:606
80558 Relation between discipline experiences and the expression of aggression. Amer Anthropologist 1967, 69:734-737
80559 Suicide as an aggressive act. J Psychol 1967, 66:47-50

LESTER, EVA P.

80560 Brief psychotherapies in child psychiatry. Canad Psychiat Ass J 1968, 13:301-309

See Dudek, Stephanie Z.; Wittkower, Eric D.

LESTER, MARIANNE WEIL

80561 Counterpoint in psychoanalytic thinking. Prog clin Psych 1964, 6:79-112

LESTER, MILTON

S-52191 The analysis of an unconscious beating fantasy in a woman.
           Abs SLP An Surv Psa 1957, 8:120-121

LEUNER, B.

80562 [Emotional intelligence and emancipation. A psychodynamic study on women.] (Ger) Prax Kinderpsychol 1966, 15:196-203

LEUNER, HANSCARL

80563 [Association psychology and psychiatry.] (Ger) Bibl Psychiat Neurol 1964, 1:154-175
80564 Das assoziative Vorgehen im Symboldrama. (Ergebnisse VIII des experimentellen katathymen Bilderlebens (EkB).) [The associative procedure in symbolic drama. (Result 8 of the experimental catathymic picture life.)] Z Psychother med Psychol 1964, 14:196-211
80565 Basic functions involved in the psychotherapeutic effect of psychotomimetics. In Shlien, J. M. et al: Research in Psychotherapy, Vol. III, Wash DC: APA 1968, 466-470
80566 Einige Bemerkungen zum Thema "Kurzpsychotherapie." [Some remarks on the theme "brief psychotherapy."] Proc IV World Cong Psychiat 1966, 450-455
80567 The Interpretation of Visual Hallucinations. Basel/NY: Karger 1964, Series 3

80568 Das katathyme Bilderleben (Symboldrama) in der Psychotherapie von Kindern und Jugendlichen. [Catathymic picture imagination (symbolic drama) in the psychotherapy of children and adolescents.] Hbh Kinderpsychother 393-406

80569 "Kurzpsychotherapie," ihre Problematik und ihre Notwendigkeit. ["Brief psychotherapy," its problems and its necessity.] Z PSM 1967, 17:125-131

80570 Obituary: [On the death of Carl Gustav Jung.] (Ger) Z Psychother med Psychol 1961, 11:157-158

80571 Die psycholytische Therapie im Dienste der Rehabilitation: Ergebnisse und Kasuistik. [Psychotic therapy in rehabilitation: results and case studies.] Psychother Psychosom 1967, 15:40

80572 [Psychotherapy with the aid of hallucinogenic drugs.] (Ger) Arzneimittelforschung 1966, 16:253-255

80573 Über einige Grundprinzipien der Kurztherapie. [On some basic principles of brief therapy.] Z PSM 1969, 15:199-202

See Ferandez-Cerdeño, A.; Holfeld, H.

LEVALLOIS, M.

See Truc, E.

LEVENSON, EDGAR A.

80574 Counseling the college dropout. J Ass Coll Admissions Counselors 1967, 12(1)

80575 (& Kohn, M.) A demonstration clinic for college dropouts. Coll Hlth 1964, 12(4)

80576 Discussion of Galdston, I. "Psychiatry and the maverick." Sci Psa 1968, 13:18-19

80577 The family album as a therapeutic tool. Ps 1960, 23:219-223

80578 (& Stockhamer, N.; Feiner, A. H.) Family transaction in the etiology of dropping out of college. Contempo Psa 1967, 3:134-157

80579 Some socio-cultural issues in the etiology and treatment of college dropouts. In Pervin, L. A. et al: The College Dropout and the Utilization of Talent, Princeton Univ Pr 1966, 189-206

80580 (& Kohn, M.) A treatment facility for college dropouts. MH 1965, 49(3)

80581 The treatment of school phobias in the young adults. PT 1961, 15:539-552

80582 Why do they drop out? In author's Teaching and Learning, (J of the Ethical Culture Schools of NYC) 1965, 8:25-32

See Feiner, Arthur H.; Kohn, Martin

LEVENSTEIN, A.

80583 Work incentives in the age of automation. Ops 1968, 38:893-899

LEVENTHAL, DONALD S.

80584 The significance of ego psychology for the concept of minimal brain dysfunction in children. J Amer Acad Child Psychiat 1968, 7:242-251

LEVENTHAL, HOWARD

See Janis, Irving L.

LEVENTHAL, THEODORE

80585 Control problems in runaway children. Arch gen Psychiat 1963, 9:122-128

80586 Inner control deficiencies in runaway children. Arch gen Psychiat 1964, 11:170-176

80587 (& Sills, M. R.) The issue of control in therapy with character problem adolescents. Ps 1963, 26:149-167

80588 (& Sills, M. R.) Self-image in school phobia. Ops 1964, 34:685-695

80589 (& Weinberger, G.; Stander, R. J.; Stearns, R. P.) Therapeutic strategies with school phobics. Ops 1967, 37:64-70

LEVETON, ALAN F.

80590 The night residue. J 1961, 42:506-516
       Abs WPK Q 1962, 31:580

80591 Reproach: the art of shamemanship. M 1962, 35:101-111
       Abs ICFH Q 1963, 32:142

80592 Time, death and the ego-chill. J existent Psychiat 1965, 6:69-80

LEVEY, HARRY B.

80593 A theory concerning free creation in the inventive arts. In Ruitenbeek, H. M. *The Creative Imagination,* Chicago: Quadrangle Books 1965, 245-250

LEVI, AURELIA LEFFLER

80594 Parent treatment and outcome of child's therapy. Diss Abstr 1961, 22(4):1255

LEVI, GUGLIELMO

80595 Brevità subìta e brevità voluta nei trattamenti psicoterapici su base analitica. [Short-term therapy prematurely terminated and extended short-term analytic psychotherapy.] Riv Psichiat 1967, 2:507-515

LEVI, JOSEPH

80596 Acting out indicators on the Rorschach Test. Acting Out 252-256

LEVICK, MYRA F.

80597 The goals of the art therapist as compared to those of the art teacher. J Albert Einstein Med Center 1967, 15:157-170

80598 (& Goldman, M. J.; Fink, P. J.) Training for art therapists: community mental health center and college of art join forces. Bull Art Ther 1967, 6:121-124

See Fink, Paul Jay

LEVIE, HERMAN DE

80599 Medische geschiktheid tot het besturen van motorrijtuigen. Kantteke-
ningen van een oud-gediende bij het desbetreffende rapport van de
Gezondheidsraad. [Physical ability to drive a motor vehicle. Notes on
a report by a veteran of the National Institute of Health.] NTvG 1968,
112:214-220

LEVIN, A. J.

80600 The Geriatric Revolution. NY: Pageant Pr 1968, 243 p
S-52217 Oedipus and Samson: the rejected hero-child.
Abs AEC An Surv Psa 1957, 8:308-309

LEVIN, D. C.

80601 The self: a contribution to its place in theory and technique. (Read
at Int Psa Cong, 1969) J 1969, 50:41-51
80602 A systematic theory and nosology for psychiatry. Canad Psychiat Ass
J 1963, 8:374-384

LEVIN, GID'ON

80603 [Activity and passivity in human behavior.] (Heb) Ofakim 1960,
14:240-243

LEVIN, JOAN

See Fried, Marc

LEVIN, LEON A.

80604 A sexual preoccupation in a little girl. BMC 1961, 25:129-137
Abs HD Q 1962, 31:295

LEVIN, MAX

80605 Monism and dualism in the study of behavior: is there a conflict between the psychodynamic and the organic points of view? P 1961,
118:53-57
80606 The nature of psychiatric research with reflections on the research of
Freud and Hughlings Jackson and on the limitations of statistics. P
1962, 119:404-409
80607 Pornography and its effects. Psychiat Opin 1969, 6(1):6-8

See Prelinger, Ernst

LEVIN, RACHEL RABIN

80608 An empirical test of the female castration complex. JAbP 1966, 71:181-
188
80609 The psychology of women: an empirical test of a psychoanalytic construct. Diss Abstr 1963, 24(2):837

LEVIN, REVELLA

80610   Truth versus illusion in relation to death. R 1964, 51:190-200
          Abs SRS Q 1965, 34:469

REVIEWS OF:
80611   Bowers, M. K. et al. Counseling the Dying. R 1965, 52:136-137
80612   Brand, M. Savage Sleep. Am Im 1969, 26:194-196
80613   Rosen, J. N. Direct Analysis II. Am Im 1969, 26:194-196

LEVIN, RICHARD

80614   Sexual equations in the Elizabethan double plot. Lit & Psych 1966,
          16:2-14

LEVIN, SAMUEL J.

80615   (& Scherer, R. A.) Are emotional factors of importance in allergic dis-
          eases in children? Ann Allerg 1965, 23:192-198

LEVIN, SIDNEY

80616   A common type of marital incompatibility. (Read at Am Psa Ass, Dec
          1966; at Boston Psa Soc & Inst, Jan 1967) J Am Psa Ass 1969, 17:421-
          436
80617   (Reporter) Depression and object loss. (Panel: Am Psa Ass, April
          1965) J Am Psa Ass 1966, 14:142-153
80618   Depression in the aged: a study of the salient external factors. Geri-
          atrics 1963, 18:302-307. In Kastenbaum, R. *New Thoughts on Old
          Age*, NY: Springer 1964, 179-185. In Berezin, M. A. & Cath, S. H.
          Geriatric Psychiatry, NY: IUP 1965, 203-205
80619   Discussion of Guy da Silva. "The loneliness and death of an old man."
          J geriat Psychiat 1967, 1:41-42
80620   Further comments on a common type of marital incompatibility. (Read
          at Boston Psa Soc, 29 Nov 1967) J Am Psa Ass 1969, 17:1097-1113
          Abs Altman, H. G. Bull Phila Ass Psa 1968, 18:100-102
80621   (& Michaels, J. J.) Incomplete psychoanalytic training. J Am Psa Ass
          1965, 13:793-818
          Abs JLSt Q 1968, 37:628
80622   (& Kahana, R. J.) Introduction. Psychodyn St Aging 13-19
80623   Libido equilibrium. In Zinberg, N. E. & Kaufman, I. *Normal Psychol-
          ogy of the Aging Process*, NY: IUP 1963, 160-168
80624   Mastery of fear in psychoanalysis. (Read at Am Psa Ass 1962) Q
          1964, 33:375-387
80625   The occurrence of phobias in states of depression. (Read at Am Psa
          Ass, 6 May 1966) Bull Phila Ass Psa 1969, 19:65-75
80626   (& Michaels, J. J.) The participation of psycho-analysis in the Medical
          Institutions of Boston. J 1961, 42:271-283
          Abs WPK Q 1962, 31:286
S-52226 Problems in the evaluation of patients for psychoanalysis.
          Abs EFA Q 1961, 30:601
80627   (& Kahana, R. J.) (Eds) Psychodynamic Studies on Aging: Creativity,
          Reminiscing, and Dying. NY: IUP 1967, 345 p

Abs J Am Psa Ass 1969, 17:269. Rv McIntyre, W. M. J 1968, 49:742-743

80628 A review of Freud's contributions to the topic of masturbation. Bull Phila Ass Psa 1963, 13:15-24
Abs PLe RFPsa 1967, 31:304

80629 Saul's illness. Cent Afr J Med 1965, 11:301-302

80630 (& Wermer, H.) The significance of giving gifts to children in therapy. J Amer Acad Child Psychiat 1966, 5:630-652

80631 Some comments on learning problems in the medical student. The Pharos of Alpha Omega Alpha 1967, 30:21-25. The Scalpel of Alpha Epsilon Delta 1967, 37:111-115. Plexus 1967, 3

80632 Some comments on the distribution of narcissistic and object libido in the aged. (Read at Am Psa Ass, 3 May 1963) J 1965, 46:200-208
Abs EVN Q 1967, 36:318

80633 Some comparative observations of psychoanalytically oriented group and individual psychotherapy. (Read at Boston Psa Soc & Inst, Oct 1959) Ops 1963, 33:148-160
Abs JMa RFPsa 1964, 28:447. PS Q 1964, 33:307

80634 Some economic factors in the etiology of depression. (Read at Am Psa Ass, Dec 1965) Bull Phila Ass Psa 1968, 18:65-75

80635 (& Kanter, S. S.) Some general considerations in the supervision of beginning group psychotherapists. Int J grp PT 1964, 14:318-331

80636 Some group observations on reactions to separation from home in first year college students. J Amer Acad Child Psychiat 1967, 6

80637 Some metapsychological considerations on the differentiation between shame and guilt. (Read at Am Psa Ass, Dec 1964; at Boston Psa Soc & Inst, 9 June 1965) J 1967, 48:267-276
Abs Shambaugh, B. Bull Phila Ass Psa 1965, 15:241-244. EVN Q 1969, 38:160

80638 Some suggestions for treating the depressed patient. Q 1965, 34:37-65. In Gaylin, W. The Meaning of Despair, NY: Sci House 1968
Einige Vorschlage zur Behandlung depressiver Patienten. Psyche 1967, 21:393-418

S-52227 A study of fees for control analysis.
Abs Cowitz, B. An Surv Psa 1958, 9:435

80639 Therapeutic and educational effects of psychoanalytically oriented seminars for teachers of nursing. J Hillside Hosp 1966, 15

80640 Toward a classification of external factors capable of inducing psychological stress. J 1966, 47:546-551
Abs EVN Q 1968, 37:465

See Cooke, Robert E.; Knapp, Peter H.; Wermer, Henry

ABSTRACTS OF:

80641 Almansi, R. J. A hypnagogic phenomenon. An Surv Psa 1958, 9:141-143

80642 Blank, H. R. Dreams of the blind. An Surv Psa 1958, 9:224-226

80643 Kéri, H. Ancient games and popular games. An Surv Psa 1958, 9:242-243

80644 La Barre, W. The influence of Freud on anthropology. An Surv Psa 1958, 9:451-453

80645 Naftalin, M. Footnote to the genesis of Moses. An Surv Psa 1958, 9:34
80646 Ostow, M. The illusory reduplication of body parts in cerebral disease.
       An Surv Psa 1958, 9:124
80647 Posinsky, S. H. Instincts, culture and science. An Surv Psa 1958,
       9:40-42
80648 Sheppard, E. & Saul, L. J. An approach to a systematic study of ego
       function. An Surv Psa 1958, 9:224
80649 Slap, J. W. The genesis of Moses. An Surv Psa 1958, 9:444-445
80650 Weissman, P. Why Booth killed Lincoln: a psychoanalytic study of a
       historical tragedy. An Surv Psa 1958, 9:471-472
80651 Wiebe, G. D. Social values and ego ideal: recollections of the Army-
       McCarthy hearings. An Surv Psa 1958, 9:461-464

LEVIN, TOM

80652 Psychoanalysis and social change. R 1967, 54:458-468

LEVIN, VICTORIA S.

See Alper, Thelma G.

LEVINE, ABRAHAM

80653 Appraising ego strength from the projective test battery. J Hillside
       Hosp 1960, 9:228-240
80654 A comparative evaluation of latent and overt schizophrenic patients
       with respect to the concept of ego strength. J Hillside Hosp 1959,
       8:243-265

See Franco, Daisy; Graubert, David N.

LEVINE, CONALEE

80655 A comparison of the conscious and unconscious identifications with
       both parental figures among addicted and non-addicted male ado-
       lescent character disorders. Diss Abstr 1960, 20:3380-3381

LEVINE, DAVID

80656 (Ed) Nebraska Symposium on Motivation. Lincoln, Nebraska: Univ
       Nebraska Pr 1964, x + 284 p; 1965, xi + 344 p; 1966, ix + 209 p;
       1967; 1968, ix + 335 p
80657 Rorschach genetic-level and mental disorder. J proj Tech 1959, 23:436-
       439
80658 Rorschach genetic level and psychotic symptomatology. Clin Psych
       1960, 16:164-167

LEVINE, EDNA SIMON

80659 The Psychology of Deafness. Techniques of Appraisal for Rehabilita-
       tion. NY: Columbia Univ Pr 1960, 383 p
       Rv HRB Q 1961, 30:115-116

LEVINE, EDWARD M.

80660 The twist: a symposium of identity problems as social pathology. Israel Ann Psychiat 1966, 4:198-210

LEVINE, JACOB

S-52232 (& Redlich, F. C.) Failure to understand humor.
   Abs An Surv Psa 1955, 6:138; 209-211
80661 (& Redlich, F. C.) Intellectual and emotional factors in the appreciation of humor. J gen Psychol 1960, 62:25-35
80662 Regression in primitive clowning. Q 1961, 30:72-83

See Gollob, Henry F.

LEVINE, JEROME

See Ludwig, Arnold M.

LEVINE, JEROME MERRILL

80663 Through the looking glass: an examination of some critiques of Freudian psychoanalysis. J Am Psa Ass 1967, 15:166-212

ABSTRACT OF:
80664 Sperling, O. E. The romantic irony. Q 1961, 30:321-324

LEVINE, M.

See Ross, W. Donald

LEVINE, MARK D.

REVIEWS OF:
80665 Bettelheim, B. Dialogues with Mothers. R 1967, 54:714
80666 Braun, J. R. (Ed) Clinical Psychology in Transition. A Selection of Articles from the American Psychologist. PPR 1962, 49(1):141-142
80667 Reik, T. Jewish Wit. PPR 1962, 49(4):122-123

LEVINE, MATTHEW E.

80668 Psychotherapy of borderline patients. P 1968, 125:704-705

LEVINE, MAURICE

80669 Escape and dedication. In Titchener, J. Surgery as a Human Experience, NY: Oxford Univ Pr 1960
80670 Foreword to Hofling, C. K. & Leininger, M. M. Basic Psychiatric Concepts in Nursing, Phila: Lippincott 1960
S-20148 Psychotherapy in Medical Practice.
   Psicoterapie en la Practica Medica. (Tr: Gonzales, A.) Buenos Aires: Libreria y Edit "El Ateneo" 1951, 302 p
80671 Self-scrutiny in the discussion of medical education. In Earley, L. W. et al: Teaching Psychiatry in Medical School, Wash DC: Am Psychiatr Ass 1969, 25-31

S-20152 Trends in psychoanalysis in America.
Le tendenze della psicanalisi in America. Cervello 1951, 27(2):126-127
80672 Unconscious motivations in big-brother work. MH 1938, 22:99-108

See Stewart, Robert L.; Titchener, James L.

LEVINE, MILTON I.
See Bell, Anita I.

LEVINE, MURRAY
80673 (& Spivack, G.) Adaptation to repeated exposure to the spiral visual aftereffect in brain-damaged, emotionally disturbed and normal individuals. Percept mot Skills 1962, 14:425-426
80674 (& Chorost, S.; Spivack, G.) Bender Gestalt rotations and EEG abnormalities in children. J consult Psychol 1959, 23:559
80675 (& Meltzoff, J.) Cognitive inhibition and Rorschach responses. J consult Psychol 1956, 20:119-122
80676 (& Gelfand, D.; Lewis, D.; Monheit, R.; Shapiro, S.; Thomson, H.; Hagen, J.) Factors relating to unsuccessful vocational adjustment of cardiac patients. J occup Med 1960, 2:62-70
80677 (& Spivack, G.) Human movement responses and verbal expression in the Rorschach test. J proj Tech 1962, 26:229-304
80678 Incentive, time conception and self-control in a group of emotionally disturbed adolescents. Clin Psych 1959, 15:110-113
80679 (& Meltzoff, J.; Glass, H.) The inhibition process, Rorschach human movement responses and intelligence. J consult Psychol 1957, 21:43-45
80680 (& Spivack, G.; Wight, B.) The inhibition process, Rorschach human movement responses and intelligence: some further data. J consult Psychol 1959, 23:306-312
80681 (& Spivack, G.; Fuschillo, J.; Tavernier, A.) Intelligence and measures of inhibition and time sense. Clin Psych 1959, 15:224-226
80682 (& Spivack, G.; Sprigle, H.) Intelligence test performance and the delay function of the ego. J consult Psychol 1959, 23:429-431
80683 "Not alike" response in Wechsler's Similarities subtest. J consult Psychol 1959, 22:480
80684 (& Spivack, G.) Note on the relationship between figural aftereffects and intelligence in diffusely brain-damaged individuals. J percept mot Skills 1961, 13:342
80685 (& Galanter, E. H.) A note on the "tree and trauma" interpretation in the HTP. J consult Psychol 1953, 17:74-75
80686 Psychological test of children. In Hoffman, M. & Hoffman, L. *Review of Child Development Research*, NY: Russel Sage Found 1966
80687 (& Spivack, G.) Rate of reversal of the Necker cube in diffuse brain injury. Clin Psych 1962, 18:122-124
80688 Residential change and school adjustment. Comm ment Hlth J 1966, 2:61-69
80689 (& Spivack, G.) The Rorschach Index of Ideational Repression: application to quantitative sequence analysis. J proj Tech 1963, 27:73-78

80690 (& Spivack, G.) Rorschach Index of Repression. Manual and Case Study. Devereux Found, Devon 1958; 1960 (Rev)

80691 (& Spivack, G.) The Rorschach Index of Repressive Style. Springfield, Ill: Thomas 1964, xvi + 164 p
   Rv Hammer, E. F. Am Im 1965, 22:158-159

See Goldman, Alfred E.; Herskovitz, Herbert H.; Meltzoff, Julian; Thompson, David C.

LE VINE, RACHEL A.

80692 A school therapy project for aggressive acting-out children under age ten excluded from the public school. Ops 1962, 32:246-247

80693 Toward a psychology of populations: the cross-cultural study of personality. Hum Develpm 1966, 30:30-46

LEVINE, SEYMOUR

80694 The effects of infantile experience on adult behavior. In Bachrach, A. J. *Experimental Foundations of Clinical Psychology*, NY: Basic Books 1962, 139-169

See Newton, Grant

LEVINE, SOL

80695 (& Scotch, N. A.) The impact of psychoanalysis on sociology and anthropology. Mod Psa 598-625

LEVINSON, ALMA

See Deutsch, Martin

LEVINSON, B. M.

80696 The pet and the child's bereavement. MH 1967, 51:197-200

LEVINSON, DANIEL J.

80697 (& Gallagher, E. B.) Patienthood in the Mental Hospital. An Analysis of Role, Personality and Social Structure. Boston: Houghton Mifflin 1964, xvii + 265 p
   Rv Linn, L. Q 1965, 34:460-461

See Greenblatt, Milton; Hartmann, Ernest L.; Levinson, M. H.; Sharaf, Myron R.

LEVINSON, HARRY

80698 Emotional Health: In the World of Work. NY: Harper & Row 1964, xii + 300 p

80699 The future of health in industry. Industr Med Surg 1965, 34:321-334

80700 (& Price, C. R.; Munden, K. J.; Mandl, H. J.; Solley, C. M.) Men, Management, and Mental Health. Cambridge, Mass: Harvard Univ Pr 1962, xv + 205 p

80701 What killed Bob Lyons? Executive's emotional problems. Harv bus
       Rev 1963, 41:127-142
80702 What work means to a man. Menn Q 1964, 18:1-11

LEVINSON, M. H.

80703 (& Levinson, D. J.) Jews who intermarry: sociopsychological bases of
       ethnic identity and change. Yivo Annual of Jewish Social Science 1959

LEVITA, D. J. DE

80704 On the psycho-analytic concept of identity. (Read at Int Psa Cong,
       July 1965) J 1966, 47:299-305

LEVITAN, HAROLD L.

80705 Depersonalization and the dream. Q 1967, 36:157-171
          Abs Cuad Psa 1967, 3:242
80706 The depersonalizing process. Q 1969, 38:97-109
80707 An exhibitionist. Q 1963, 32:246-248
80708 A traumatic dream. Q 1965, 34:265-267
80709 The turn to mania. Q 1968, 37:56-62

LEVITAS, GLORIA B.

80710 (Ed) The World of Psychoanalysis. NY: Braziller 1965, xxi + 1113 p
          Rv Akmakjian, H. R 1966, 53:495
80711 (Ed) The World of Psychology. 2 volumes. NY: Braziller 1963, 563 p,
       583 p
          Abs Am Im 1964, 21(1-2):187

LEVITOV, E. S.

See Sklansky, Morris A.

LEVITT, ESTHER G.

See Heiman, Marcel

LEVITT, EUGENE E.

80712 (& Persky, H.; Brady, J. P.; Fitzgerald, J.; Breeijen, A. den) Evidence
       for hypnotically induced amnesia as an analogue of repression. JNMD
       1961, 133:218-221
          Abs Powelson, H. Q 1963, 32:293
80713 The Psychology of Anxiety. NY: Bobbs-Merrill 1967, xiv + 223 p
          Rv Engel, G. L. Q 1969, 38:667
80714 The results of psychotherapy with children. J consult Psychol 1957,
       21:189-196. In Clark, D. H. & Lesser, G. S. *Emotional Disturbance
       and School Learning*, Chicago: Sci Res Ass 1965, 182-193. With title:
       The undemonstrated effectiveness of therapeutic processes with chil-
       dren. In Berenson, B. G. & Carkhuff, R. R. *Sources of Gain in Counsel-
       ing and Psychotherapy*, NY: Holt, Rinehart & Winston 1967, 33-45

* * * The undemonstrated effectiveness of therapeutic processes with children. See [80714]

See Beck, Samuel J.

LEVITT, LOUIS

80715 Rehabilitation of narcotics addicts among lower class teenagers. Ops 1968, 38:56-62

LEVITT, MORTON

80716 (& Rubenstein, B. O.) The American dream: culture and personality. J Pan-Hellenic Union MH 1964
80717 (& Rubenstein, B. O.) The children's crusade. Ops 1968, 38:591-598
80718 Countertransference. In Haworth, M. R. *Child Psychotherapy*, NY: Basic Books 1964
80719 Discussion of Sandford, B. "Cinderella." Psa Forum 1967, 2:135-137
80720 (& Meyer, R.; Falick, M. L.; Rubenstein, B. O.) Essentials of Pediatric Psychiatry. NY: Appleton-Century-Crofts 1962, 208 p
S-52311 Freud and Dewey on the Nature of Man.
Rv Niederland, W. G. Q 1961, 30:109-110
80721 Introduction. Ops Law 7-18
80722 (& Rubenstein, B. O.) Medical school faculty attitudes toward applicants and students with emotional problems. J med Educ 1967, 42:742-751
80723 (& Rubenstein, B. O.) (Eds) Orthopsychiatry and the Law. A Symposium. Detroit: Wayne Univ Pr 1968, 255 p
S-52315 (Ed) Readings in Psychoanalytic Psychology.
Rv Khan, M. M. R. J 1961, 42:292
80724 (& Rubenstein, B. O.) Some observations on the relationship between cultural variants and emotional disorders. Ops 1964, 34:423-435
Abs JMa RFPsa 1966, 30:518

See Meyer, Ruben; Rubenstein, Ben O.

LÉVY, ARNAUD

80725 Le désir du psychanalyste et son insertion oedipienne. [The desire of the psychoanalyst and his oedipal insertion.] Bull Ass psa Fran 1966, (2)
80726 Quelques remarques à propos de l'interprétation. [Some remarks on interpretation.] Bull Ass psa Fran 1969, (5):59-64

LEVY, DAVID M.

80727 The act as a unit. Ps 1962, 25:295-314
80728 The "act" as an operational concept in psychodynamics. PSM 1962, 24:49-57
80729 Beginnings of the child guidance movement. Ops 1968, 38:799-803
80730 Child psychiatry. In *International Encyclopedia of the Social Sciences*, NY: Macmillan & the Free Pr 1968

S-52323 Development and psychodynamic aspects of oppositional behavior. Abs AaSt An Surv Psa 1956, 7:252-254

80731 The dynamics of hostility. In Johnson, F. E. *World Order: Its Intellectual and Cultural Foundations,* NY/London: Harper & Row 1945, 66-73

80732 The early development of independent and oppositional behavior. In *Mid-Century Psychiatry,* Springfield, Ill: Thomas 1953, 113-121

80733 Early infantile deprivation. Mental Retardation 1962, 39:243-255

80734 Hostility patterns. In Howells, J. G. *Theory and Practice of Family Psychiatry,* Edinburgh/London: Oliver & Boyd 1968

80735 The infants' earliest memory of inoculation: a contribution to public health procedure. J genet Psych 1960, 96:3-46

80736 Looking ahead in the fields of orthopsychiatric research (Symposium 1949). Ops 1950, 20:97-103

80737 Maternal Overprotection. NY: Norton 1966, ix + 417 p

80738 Modification of the psychiatric interview. PT 1964, 18:435-451

80739 (& Goldfarb, W.; Meyers, D. I). Relational behavior of schizophrenic children and their mothers: a methodologic study. Ops 1962, 32:337

S-20209 Release therapy. Ops 1939, 9:713-736

80740 (& Tulchin, S.) Rorschach Test differences in a group of Spanish and English refugee children. Ops 1945, 15:361-368

80741 Studies of reaction to genital differences. Ops 1940, 10:755-762

80742 The use of projective techniques in the interpretation of hostility patterns. In Anderson, H. H. & Anderson, G. L. *An Introduction to Projective Techniques,* NY: Prentice-Hall 1951

See Goldfarb, William

LEVY, E.

See Danon-Boileau, Henri; Douady, D.

LEVY, EDWIN Z

80743 The importance of the children's needs in residential treatment. BMC 1967, 31:18-31

80744 The subject's approach: important factor in experimental isolation? BMC 1962, 26:30-42
Abs HD Q 1963, 32:133-134

LEVY, FLORENCE J.

80745 On the significance of Christmas for the "Wolf Man." R 1968, 55:615-622

LEVY, JACQUES M.

80746 Regression in the service of the ego, cognitive control, and sexual identification. Diss Abstr 1962, 23(1):309-310

LEVY, JOSHUA

80747 Early memories: theoretical aspects and application. J proj Tech 1965, 29:281-291

80748 (& Grigg, K. A.) Early memories. Thematic-configurational analysis. Arch gen Psychiat 1962, 7:57-69
80749 (& McNickle, R. K.) (Eds) Meeting the Treatment Needs of Children. Boulder, Colorado: Western Interstate Commission for Higher Education 1963.

LEVY, KATA

S-52333 Silence in the analytic session.
       Abs JAL An Surv Psa 1958, 9:409
80750 Unconscious interaction between mother and child. BMC 1960, 24:250-257
80751 Zehn Jahre Erziehungs- und Jugendberatung in einer Mädchenschule. [Ten years of educational and youth guidance in a school for girls.] In Bolterauer, L. *Aus der Werkstatt des Erziehungsberaters,* Vienna: Verlag für Jugend und Volk 1960, 52-75

LEVY, LEON H.

80752 Psychological Interpretation. NY: Holt, Rinehart & Winston 1963, 368 p
       Rv Am Im 1964, 21:190

LEVY, LEONARD

See Cameron, D. Ewen

LEVY, MILTON H.

See Stein, Aaron

LEVY, N.

See MacLennan, Beryce W.

LEVY, NORMAN A.

80753 Discussion of Alexander, R. P. "Omnipotence and the avoidance of pleasure." Psa Forum 1966, 1:284-285
80754 Discussion of Lowinger, P. & Dobie, S. "An evaluation of the role of the psychiatrist's personality in the interview." Sci Psa 1964, 7:226-229
80755 An investigation into the nature of psychoanalytic process: a preliminary report. Sci Psa 1961, 4:125-140

LEVY, NORMAN J.

80756 Conforming and differing, healthy and neurotic. PT 1961, 15:561-573
80757 Evolution of Horney's theory of neurosis. Ind J Psychiat 1960, 2:21-25
80758 Karen Horney's concept of human motivation. Psychologia 1960, 3:113-118
80759 Metodos parahacer mas efectiva la terapía psicoanalítica. [Methods for making psychoanalytic therapy more effective.] Orientacion Medica (Argentina) 1962, 11:540. Arch Crimin Neuropsiq 1963, 11:527-530

80760 Notes on the creative process and the creative person. Psychiat Q 1961, 35:68-77. Tokyo J Psa 1962, 20
    Abs Engle, B. Q 1962, 31:135
80761 Therapy of psychotic patients in office practice. Psa 1969, 29:23-33
80762 The use of drugs by teenagers for sanctuary and illusion. Psa 1968, 28:48-58

LÉVY, PIERRE

80763 Production artistique et action psychotherapeutique. [Artistic production and psychotherapeutic action.] Encéph 1968, 57(Suppl):1-11

ABSTRACTS OF:
80764 Aarons, Z. A. On negativism and the character trait of obstinacy. RFPsa 1967, 31:307
80765 Aarons, Z. A. On the genesis of an asthmatic attack. RFPsa 1963, 27:340
80766 Badal, D. W. Transitional and pre-psychotic symptoms in depression. RFPsa 1967, 31:309
80767 Bergler, E. The "aristocracy" among homosexuals: lovers of "trade." RFPsa 1963, 27:340
80768 Bettelheim, B. Early ego development in a mute, autistic child. RFPsa 1967, 31:310
80769 Bromberg, N. On polygamous women. RFPsa 1963, 27:338
80770 Cath, S. H. & Fischberg, B. Some psychological implications of comic strips. RFPsa 1967, 31:307
80771 Conrad, S. W. On phantasies and their functions. RFPsa 1967, 31:311
80772 Conrad, S. W. Phallic aspects of obesity. RFPsa 1967, 31:311
80773 Conrad, S. W. Physiologic determinants in phantasm formation. RFPsa 1967, 31:310
80774 Dratman, M. D. Affects and consciousness. RFPsa 1967, 31:309
80775 Galinsky, M. D. & Pressman, M. D. Intellectualization and intellectual resistance. RFPsa 1967, 31:306
80776 Gardiner, M. M. The seven years of dearth. RFPsa 1967, 31:303
80777 Greenspan, J. The original persecution: a case study. RFPsa 1967, 31:307
80778 Haag, E. van der: Psychoanalysis and utopia. RFPsa 1967, 31:310
80779 Horn, E. N. Surgery, a child and a toy gun. RFPsa 1963, 27:338
80780 Kaplan, A. Maturity in religion. RFPsa 1967, 31:305
80781 Kaplan, L. S. Snow White: a study in psychosexual development. RFPsa 1967, 31:305
80782 Kelly, W. E. Regression of the superego. RFPsa 1967, 31:311
80783 Kleiner, J. On a lullaby. RFPsa 1963, 27:339
80784 Kleiner, J. A meaning of persistence in a young child. RFPsa 1963, 27:336
80785 Kolansky, H. A note on disease anxiety at puberty. RFPsa 1963, 27:339
80786 Lathbury, V. T. Limitations of psychoanalysis may be more apparent than real. RFPsa 1963, 27:335
80787 Leavy, S. A. Clinical observations on the development of religion in later childhood. RFPsa 1963, 27:336

80788 Levin, S. A review of Freud's contributions to the topic of masturbation. RFPsa 1967, 31:304
80789 Lilly, J. C. The biological versus psychoanalytic dichotomy. RFPsa 1963, 27:337
80790 Luborsky, L. & Shevrin, H. Artificial induction of day-residues: an illusion and examination. RFPsa 1967, 31:303
80791 Luborsky, L. A psychoanalytic research on momentary forgetting during free association. RFPsa 1967, 31:308
80792 Menninger, K. A. The cause of illness. RFPsa 1963, 27:336
80793 Pearson, G. H. J. The psychological significance of the omen by which dreams were interpreted. RFPsa 1967, 31:306
80794 Pearson, G. H. J. A young girl and her horse. RFPsa 1967, 31:311
80795 Peller, L. E. About "telling the child" of his adoption. RFPsa 1963, 27:338
80796 Peller, L. E. Language and its pre-stages. RFPsa 1967, 31:307
80797 Pressman, M. D. On the analytic situation: the analyst is silent. RFPsa 1963, 27:339
80798 Pressman, M. D. Silence in analysis. RFPsa 1963, 27:336
80799 Schlezinger, N. Psychoanalysis of a gastric neurosis. RFPsa 1963, 27:340
80800 Silberstein, R. M. The problem of enuresis. RFPsa 1967, 31:303

REVIEWS OF:
80801 Balint, M. & Balint, E. Psychotherapeutic Techniques in Medicine. RFPsa 1964, 28:289-290
80802 Cosnier, J. Experimental Neuroses from Animal to Human Psychology. RFPsa 1967, 31:491
80803 Dubouchet, J. An Attempt at a Formulation of Psychology. RFPsa 1967, 31:299-301
80804 Hjelmslev, L. Le Langage. RFPsa 1968, 32:328
80805 Klein, M. Our Adult World and Other Essays. RFPsa 1964, 28:819-821
80806 Toman, W. Family Constellation. RFPsa 1964, 28:284-285
80807 Lupasco, S. Qu'est-ce qu'une Structure? RFPsa 1968, 32:326-328
80808 Uexkull, T. von: La Médecine Psychosomatique. RFPsa 1968, 32:321-326
80809 Wolberg, L. R. (Ed) Short Term Psychotherapy. RFPsa 1967, 31:491

LEVY, ROBERT I.

80810 Child management structure and its implications in a Tahitian family. In Vogel, E. & Bell, N. A Modern Introduction to the Family, NY: Free Pr 1968, 590-598
80811 Ma'ohi drinking patterns in the Society Islands. J Polynesian Soc 1966, 75:304-320
80812 On getting angry in the Society Islands. In Caudill, W. & Lin, T.-Y. Mental Health Research in Asia and the Pacific, Honolulu: East-West Center Pr 1969
80813 Personal forms and meanings in Tahitian Protestantism. J Société des Océanistes 1969, 25:125-136
80814 Personality studies in Polynesia and Micronesia: Stability and Change. Social Science Research Institute, Honolulu: Univ Hawaii 1969

80815   The psychodynamic functions of alcohol. Quart J Stud Alcohol 1958, 19(4)
80816   Tahiti observed: early European impressions of Tahitian personal style. J Polynesian Soc 1968, 77:33-42
80817   Tahitian adoption as a psychological message. In Carroll, V. *Adoption in Easter Oceania,* Honolulu: Univ Hawaii Pr 1969
80818   Tahitian folk psychotherapy. Int ment Hlth Newsletter 1967, 9

LEVY, SIDNEY J.

See Glick, Ira D.

LEVY, SOL

80819   Current trend in the treatment of depressive reactions. Amer Practit 1960, 11:757-762

LEVY-SCHOEN, ARIANE

80820   L'Image d'Autrui chez l'Enfant. Recherche Expérimentale sur la Perception des Mimiques. [The Child's Image of Others. Experimental Study on the Perception of Mimics.] (Preface: Lagache, D.) Paris: PUF 1964, 127 p

LÉVY-VALENSI, E. AMADO

80821   Psychanalyse et psychothérapie. Psychoanalysis and psychotherapy. Psicoanálisis y psicoterapia (resumen). Hum Context 1969, 1:191-199, 200-208, 209-212

LÉVY-VALENSI, J.

See Lagache, Daniel

LEWIN, B.

See Lauber, H. L.

LEWIN, BERTRAM D.

80822   American psychoanalytic education: historical comments. (Read at Am Psa Ass, May 1961) J Am Psa Ass 1962, 10:119-126
S-52347 The analytic situation: topographical considerations.
            Abs Baranger, W. Rev urug Psa 1961-62, 4:369
80823   Bibliography of Bertram D. Lewin (1926-1966). Q 1966, 35:488-496
S-52349 Clinical hints from dream studies.
            Abs An Surv Psa 1955, 6:242-244
80824   The consultation service. (Read at Am Psa Ass, May 1961) J Am Psa Ass 1962, 10:139-144
S-52352 Dream psychology and the analytic situation.
            Psicologia del sueño y la situación analitica. Rev urug Psa 1961-62, 4:86-115
            Abs An Surv Psa 1955, 6:241, 314
° ° °   Editor of Abraham, K. *On Character and Libido Development: Six Essays.*

S-52354 Education or the quest for omniscience.
      Abs HW An Surv Psa 1958, 8:431-432
80825 Foreword to Novey, S. *The Second Look,* Baltimore: Johns Hopkins
      Pr 1968, iii – v
80826 The Image and the Past. NY: IUP 1968, 128 p
* * * Introduction to Garma, A. *The Psychoanalysis of Dreams.*
80827 Knowledge and dreams. (Read at Phila Ass Psa, 4 June 1962; at NY
      Psa Soc, 14 May 1963) Bull Phila Ass Psa 1962, 12:97-111
      Abs Jucovy, M. E. Q 1964, 33:148-151

OBITUARIES:
80828 John D. Benjamin 1901-1965. Q 1966, 35:125-126
80829 Robert Waelder. Bull Phila Ass Psa 1968, 18:8-9

80830 The organization of psychoanalytic education. Historical and current.
      In Hendrick, I. *The Birth of an Institute,* Freeport, Maine: Bond
      Wheelwright 1961, 95-118
80831 The past and future of psychiatry. Psychiat Comm 1967, 9:1-12
80832 Phobias. In *International Encyclopedia of the Social Sciences, Vol. 12,*
      1968, 81-85
* * * Preface to Klein, H. R. *Psychoanalysts in Training: Selection and
      Evaluation.*
80833 Psychoanalytic education and research. In Koskoff, Y. D. & Shoemaker,
      R. J. *Vistas in Neuropsychiatry,* Pittsburgh: Univ Pittsburgh Pr 1964,
      83-94
S-52361 (& Ross, H.) Psychoanalytic Education in the United States.
      Abs J Am Psa Ass 1962, 10:222. Rv Keiser, S. J Am Psa Ass 1969,
      17:238-267
80834 Reflections on affect. (Read at Los Angeles & South Calif Psa Soc, 16
      April 1964) Dr Af Beh 2:23-37
      Abs RZ Bull Phila Ass Psa 1965, 15:47-49
80835 Reflections on depression. Psa St C 1961, 16:321-331
80836 Remarks on creativity, imagery, and the dream. JNMD 1969, 149:115-
      121
80837 Reminiscence and retrospect. 50 Yrs Psa 35-42
80838 (& Ross, H.) Supervision: A Report Based on the Responses of 192
      Supervisors to a Questionnaire. NY: Am Psa Ass 1962
80839 Teaching and the beginnings of theory. J 1965, 46:137-139
      Abs EVN Q 1967, 36:316

      See Eidelberg, Ludwig; Hendrick, Ives

REVIEWS OF:
80840 Guillain, G. J.-M. Charcot, 1825-1893. His Life—His Work. Q 1961,
      30:111-113
80841 Kleitman, N. Sleep and Wakefulness. Q 1964, 33:430-432

LEWIN, KARL KAY

80842 A method of brief psychotherapy. Psychiat Q 1966, 40:482-489
80843 Nonverbal cues and transference. Psychiat Comm 1963, 6:45-50. Arch
      gen Psychiat 1965, 12:391-394

80844 Psychiatric supervision by direct observation. J med Educ 1966, 41:860-864
80845 The value of psychoanalytic literary criticism. Psychiat Comm 1962, 5:103-106

LEWIN, KURT

80846 Formalization and progress in psychology. In author's *Studies in Topological and Vector Psychology, I.*, ACC 942. In Lindzey G. & Hall, C. S. *Theories of Personality*, NY: Wiley 1965, 1966, 1968
80847 (et al) El Niño y su Ambiente. [The Child and his Environment.] Buenos Aires: Paidós, n. d.
       Rv Rosarios, H. Rev Psicoanál 1966, 23:68

LEWINSKY, HILDE

S-20352A The closed circle. An early image of sexual intercourse.
       Abs SLP An Surv Psa 1956, 7:141-142

LEWIS, ALFRED B., JR.

80848 Perception of self in borderline states. P 1968, 124:1491-1498

LEWIS, AUBREY

80849 Inquiries in Psychiatry. London: Routledge & Kegan Paul; NY: Sci House 1967, 326 p
80850 A note on personality and obsessional illness. Psychiat Neurol, Basel 1965, 150:299-305
80851 Problems presented by the ambiguous word "anxiety" as used in psychopathology. Israel Ann Psychiat 1967, 5:105-121
80852 The State of Psychiatry, Vol. 1. London: Routledge & Kegan Paul; NY: Sci House 1967, 298 p
80853 [Survival of hysteria.] (Fr) Évolut psychiat 1966, 31:159-165

LEWIS, CLAUDELINE P.

See Boswell, John J., Jr.

LEWIS, D.

See Levine, Murray

LEWIS, D. C.

See Zinberg, Norman E.

LEWIS, DAVID JAMES

80854 Lilliputian hallucinations in the functional psychoses. Canad Psychiat Ass J 1961, 6:177-201

LEWIS, EVE

80855 Initiation of an obsessional adolescence boy. In Moustakas, C. *Existentialism Child Therapy*, NY: Basic Books 1966, 152-176

See Champernowne, H. Irene

LEWIS, HARVEY

S-52373 The effect of shedding the first deciduous tooth upon the passing of the Oedipus complex of the male.
Abs EDJ An Surv Psa 1958, 9:249-251

LEWIS, HELEN BLOCK

80856 A case of watching as defense against an oral incorporation fantasy. R 1963, 50:68-80
Abs Ekboir, J. G. de Rev Psicoanál 1964, 21:187
80857 (& Goodenough, D. R.; Shapiro, A.; Sleser, I.) Individual differences in dream recall. JAbP 1966, 71:52-59
S-52375 Organization of the self as reflected in manifest dreams.
Abs Vilar, J. Rev Psicoanál 1961, 18:180
S-52376 Over-differentiation and under-individuation of the self.
Abs Wolfman, C. An Surv Psa 1958, 9:117-120
80858 Pre-sleep experience and dreams: an experimental approach to dream content and dream recall. Sci Psa 1966, 9:164-169
80859 Some clinical implications of recent dream research. Prog clin Psych 1969, 8:91-113

See Bertini, Mario; Witkin, Herman A.

LEWIS, I. M.

80860 Some strategies of non-physical aggression in other cultures. J psychosom Res 1969, 13:221-227

LEWIS, MELVIN

80861 (& Solnit, A. J.) The adolescent in a suicidal crisis. In Solnit, A. J. & Provence, S. A. *Modern Perspectives in Child Development*, NY: IUP 1963, 229-245
80862 The "brain damage" syndrome in children. Cerebral Palsy Bull 1961, 3:75-76
80863 Child development in the problem family. J Amer Wom Med Ass 1968, 23:44-53
80864 (& Codling, L.) Child psychiatry in relation to the community and its facilities. Conn Med 1966, 30:637-644
80865 Confidentiality and the community mental health center. Ops 1967, 37:946-955
80866 Considerations regarding the theory of aggressive drive development and aggressive behavior in childhood. Conn Med 1968, 32:579-583
80867 (& Solnit, A. J.; Stark, M. H.; Gabrielson, I. W.; Klatskin, E. H.) An exploration study of accidental ingestion of poison in young children. J Amer Acad Child Psychiat 1966, 5:255-271
80868 (& Stark, M. H.) Family-centered diagnosis and treatment in a pediatric clinic. Soc Casewk 1966, 42:13-18
80869 The management of parents of acutely ill children in the hospital. Ops 1962, 32:60
80870 (& Sarrel, P. M.) The management of sexual assault upon children. In

Green, M. & Haggerty, R. J. *Ambulatory Pediatrics*, Phila: Saunders 1968, 790-799

80871 The nursery school and democracy. Young Children 1966, 22:107-122

80872 Privacy, behavioral research and social values. Int J Psychiat 1968, 5:506-509

80873 Psychosexual development and sexual behavior in children. Conn Med 1968, 32:437-443

80874 (& Sarrel, P. M.) Some psychological aspects of seduction, incest, and rape in childhood. J Amer Acad Child Psychiat 1969, 8:606-619

80875 (Editor) Symposium on the clinical aspects of the psychological development of the child, June 1968. Conn Med 1968, 32:430

LEWIS, MURRAY D.

80876 A case of transvestism with multiple body-phallus identification. (Read at Am Psa Ass, 8 Dec 1961) J 1963, 44:345-351
　　　Abs EVN Q 1965, 34:619

LEWIS, NOLAN D. C.

80877 (& Hoch, P. H.) Clinical psychiatry and psychotherapy. P 1960, 116:590-595; 1961, 117:591-594; 1962, 118:591-595; 1963, 119:616-621; 1964, 120:637-643; 1965, 121:643-648

80878 (& Strahl, M. O.) (Eds) The Complete Psychiatrist—The Achievements of Paul H. Hoch, M. D. Albany: State Univ NY Pr 1968, xvii + 723 p

80879 The future of psychotherapy. PT 1961, 15:184-192

80880 History of the nosology and the evolution of the concepts of schizophrenia. Proc Amer Psychopath Ass 1966, 54:1-18

80881 Identification, description and selection of the chronic schizophrenic patient. Dis nerv Sys 1961, 22 (Suppl, 2):30-36

80882 Pathological firesetting and sexual motivation. In Slovenko, R. *Sexual Behavior and the Law*, Springfield, Ill: Thomas 1965, 627-642

80883 Preface to Kasanin, J. S. (Ed) *Language and Thought in Schizophrenia*, NY: Norton 1964

80884 (& Cheek, F. E.) Psychoanalysis and social science. Mod Con Psa 98-114

80885 Reflections on the past, present, and future of psychiatry. In Hoch, P. H. & Zubin, J. *The Future of Psychiatry*, NY/London: Grune & Stratton 1962, 147-181

80886 Some possible basic determinants of depersonalization phenomena. Proc Amer Psychopath Ass 1965, 53:193-202

80887 Some theriomorphic symbolisms and mechanisms in ancient literature and dreams, I: Cat, dog and horse dreams. R 1963, 50:536-556

80888 Smith Ely Jelliffe 1866-1945. Psychosomatic medicine in America. Psa Pioneers 224-234

See Tobin, James M.

REVIEWS OF:

80889 Polatin, P. A Guide to Treatment in Psychiatry. R 1968, 55:324-325

80890 Rushing, W. A. The Psychiatric Professions. R 1964, 51:686-687

LEWIS, ROBERT T.

See Thorpe, Louis P.

LEWIS, SELMA A.

80891 Experimental induction of castration anxiety and anxiety over loss of love. Diss Abstr Int 1969, 30(6-B):2910-2911

LEWIS, WILLIAM C.

80892 Coital movements in the first year of life: earliest anlage of genital love. (Read at Am Psa Ass, May 1962) J 1965, 46:372-374
    Abs Aberastury, A. Rev Psicoanál 1966, 23:204. EVN Q 1967, 36:624
80893 The importance of the gelding. Q 1965, 34:438-440
80894 Some observations relevant to early defences and precursors. J 1963, 44:132-142
    Abs Gaddini, E. Riv Psa 1965, 11:73. EVN Q 1965, 34:614
80895 Structural aspects of the psychoanalytic theory of instinctual drives, affects, and time. Psa Curr Biol Thought 151-180
80896 (& Berman, M.) Studies on conversion hysteria, I: Operational study of diagnosis. Arch gen Psychiat 1965, 13:275-282

See Calden, George; Greenfield, Norman S.

LEWY, ERNST

80897 Responsibility, free will, and ego psychology. J 1961, 42:260-270
    Abs WPK Q 1962, 31:285-286. Auth Rev Psicoanál 1963, 20:88
80898 The transformation of Frederick the Great: a psychoanalytic study. Psa St Soc 1967, 4:252-311

LEYENS, J. P.

80899 [Identification as a learning process.] (Fr) Ann Psychol 1968, 68:251-267

LEYT, SAMUEL

TRANSLATION:
Schwarz, B. E. & Rugieri, B. A. [58986]

LHOTSKY, JAROMÍR

80900 Präventive und adaptive Wirkungen der axiotischen Psychotherapie im Lichte der Futurologie. [Preventive and adaptive applications of axiologic psychotherapy in the light of futurology.] Psychother Psychosom 1967, 15:40

LIBERMAN, DAVID

S-52416 Acerca de la percepción del tiempo.
    Abs An Surv Psa 1955, 6:99

80901   Comment on Dr Waldhorn's paper, "Indications and contraindications: lessons from the second analysis." (Read at Int Psa Cong, July 1967) J 1968, 49:362-363

80902   La Comunicación en Terapéutica Psicoanalítica. [Communication in Psychoanalytic Therapy.] Buenos Aires: Eudeba 1962
Rv Zac, J. Rev Psicoanál 1964, 21:374-377

80903   (& Ferschtut, G.; Sor, D.) El contrato analitico. [The analytic contract.] Rev Psicoanál 1961, 18:85-98

80904   Criteria for interpretation in patients with obsessive traits. (Read at Int Psa Cong, July 1965) J 1966, 47:212-217
Critères d'interprétation pour des patients à traits obsessionnels. RFPsa 1967, 31:707-716
Abs EVN Q 1968, 37:311

80905   (& Lumerman, S.) Criterio de adecuación de la interpretación y el nivel de regresión transferencial. [Criterion for adequacy of the interpretation and level of transferential regression.] Rev Psicoanál 1964, 21:114-128

80906   Discussion of Giovacchini, P. L. "Characterological aspects of marital interaction." Psa Forum 1967, 2:23-25

80907   Discussion of Toledo, L. G. de A. de "Terminación del análisis didáctico." Rev Psicoanál 1967, 24:291-305

80908   Discussion of Wisdom, J. O. "A methodological approach to the problem of hysteria." Rev Psicoanál 1967, 24:528-544

S-52420 Los efectos del conflicto matrimonial en el desarrollo del niño, inferiods de la situación analítica.
Abs JO An Surv Psa 1958, 9:293-294

80909   Entropía e información en el proceso terapéutico. [Entropy and information in the course of therapy.] Rev Psicoanál 1967, 24:23-78

80910   (et al) El ideal del yo. [The ideal in ego.] Rev Psicoanál 1968, 25:277-296

S-52423 Identificación proyectiva y conflicto matrimonial.
Abs AN An Surv Psa 1956, 7:341-342

S-52424 Interpretación correlativa entre relato y repetición: su aplicación en una paciente con personalidad esquizoide.
Abs RHB An Surv Psa 1957, 8:254-255

80911   (et al) Modos de reparación y desenlaces de processos terapeúticos psicoanalíticos. [Modes of reparation and the outcomes of psychoanalytic therapeutic processes.] Rev Psicoanál 1969, 26:123-139

80912   Una nota acerca de la aplicación de la teoría de la comunicación a la comprensión y explicación de la situación analítica. [A note on the application of the theory of communication in the understanding and explanation of the analytical situation.] Rev Psicoanál 1961, 18:338-343

80913   Obituary: Heinrich Racker. Rev Psicoanál 1961, 18:285-286

80914   Psicoanálisis del alcoholismo y de la adicción a las grogas. [Psychoanalysis of alcoholism and drug addiction.] Act Np Arg 1959, 5:161-171

80915   (& Avenburg, R.; Carpinacci, J. A.) Ruptura del bloqueo emocional e incremento de información en la situación analítica. [Breaking the

emotional block and increasing information in the analytic situation.]
Rev Psicoanál 1964, 21:214-219

80916 (Round table on) [Theory of the instincts.] (Sp) Rev Psicoanál 1963,
20:155-161, 176-177

See Aberastury, Arminda; Carpinacci, Jorge A.; Grinberg, León;
Rascovsky, Arnaldo

LIBERTY, PAUL G., JR.
See Moulton, Robert W.

LICHTENBERG, CHARLOTTE
See Lichtenberg, Joseph D.

LICHTENBERG, JOSEPH D.

80917 (& Cader, G.) The interrelationship between physical and psychic stress
in a case of Sheehans' disease: postpartum necrosis of the anterior
pituitary. Southern med J 1959, 52:594-604

80918 On giving up smoking. (Read at Am Psa Ass, Dec 1964) Dyn Psychiat
1968, Suppl:23-25

80919 Passivity, awe, and narcissism: a pathological response to a charismatic
parent. (Read at Am Psa Ass, 11 May 1968) Bull Phila Ass Psa 1969,
19:1-15

80920 (& Lichtenberg, C.) Prince Hal's conflict, adolescent idealism, and buf-
foonery. (Read at Am Psa Ass 1967) J Am Psa Ass 1969, 17:873-887

80921 (& Pao, P.-N.) The prognostic and therapeutic significance of the hus-
band-wife relationship for hospitalized schizophrenic women. Ps 1960,
23:209-213

80922 Prognostic implications of the inability to tolerate failure in schizophrenic patients. Ps 1957, 20:365-371

80923 The return to reality as a critical phase in the treatment of schizophrenic patients. Ps 1963, 26:26-38

80924 Theoretical and practical considerations of the management of the
manic phase of the manic-depressive psychosis. JNMD 1959, 129(3)

80925 Untreating—its necessity in the therapy of certain schizophrenic patients. M 1963, 36:311-317
     Abs Hirsh, H. Q 1964, 33:612

See Cohen, Irvin H.; Pao, Ping-Nie; Wolbarsht, Myron L.

ABSTRACT OF:
80926 Ferber, L. & Gray, P. Beating fantasies—clinical and theoretical considerations. Bull Phila Ass Psa 1966, 16:216-222

LICHTENBERG, PHILIP

S-52435 (& Kohrman, R.; MacGregor, H.) Motivation for Child Psychiatry
Treatment.
     Rv Rexford, E. N. Q 1962, 31:388-392

80927 Psychoanalysis: Radical and Conservative. NY: Springer 1969, 127 p

LICHTENSTEIN, E.

80928 Cognitive controls and free-association behavior. J gen Psychol 1965, 73:117-123

LICHTENSTEIN, HEINZ

80929 The dilemma of human identity: notes on self-transformation, self-objectivation, and metamorphosis. J Am Psa Ass 1963, 11:173-223
        Abs Guiard, F. Rev Psicoanál 1966, 23:278
80930 Identity and sexuality: a study of their interrelationship in man. (Read at Western NY Psa Group, 21 Sept 1957) J Am Psa Ass 1961, 9:179-260
        Abs FB Q 1962, 31:291-292. SAS RFPsa 1962, 26:616
80931 The role of narcissism in the emergence and maintenance of a primary identity. (Read at Boston Psa Soc & Inst, 21 April 1962) J 1964, 45:49-56
        Abs Auth Rev urug Psa 1965, 7:103. EVN Q 1966, 35:311
80932 Towards a metapsychological definition of the concept of self. J 1965, 46:117-128
        Abs EVN Q 1967, 36:315

LICHTER, SOLOMON O.

See Sklansky, Morris A.

LICHTMAN, HARRY S.

See Brody, Matthew

LICKORISH, JOHN R.

80933 The casket scenes from "The Merchant of Venice": symbolism or life style. J ind Psych 1969, 25:202-212

LIDDON, S. C.

See Eisenbud, Jule

LIDE, P. D.

80934 Dynamic mental representation: an analysis of the emphatic process. Soc Casewk 1966, 47:146-151

LIDZ, RUTH WILMANNS

80935 (& Lidz, T.) Discussion of Searles, H. F. "Positive feelings on the relationship between the schizophrenic and his mother." [Letter to the editor.] J 1961, 42:129-130
80936 Emotional factors in the success of contraception. Fertil Steril 1969, 20:761-771
80937 (& Lidz, T.) Homosexual tendencies in mothers of schizophrenic women. JNMD 1969, 149:229-235

LIDZ, THEODORE

80938 The adolescent and his family. In Caplan, G. & Lebovici, S. *Adolescence,* NY: Basic Books 1969, 105-112

80939 Adolf Meyer. In *International Encyclopedia of the Social Sciences,* Vol. 10, NY: Macmillan & Free Pr 1968

80940 Adolf Meyer and the development of American psychiatry. P 1966, 123:320-321. (Summary) Psychiat Spectator 1966, 3(7)

80941 August Strindberg: a study of the relationship between his creativity and schizophrenia. (Read at Int Psa Cong, July-Aug 1963) Bonniers Litteraire Magasin 1963, 32:548-556. J 1964, 45:399-410. Ezra Stiles Coll Mag 1964

August Strindberg: eine Untersuchung über die Beziehung zwischen seiner Schöpferkraft und seiner Schizophrenie. Psyche 1965, 18:591-605

Abs EVN Q 1966, 35:465

80942 Causalgia. In Cecil & Loeb *Textbook of Medicine,* Phila: Saunders 1963

80943 Comment on Evert Sprinchorn's "Strindberg and the Psychiatrists." Lit & Psych 1965, 15:41-44

80944 (& Fleck, S.; Cornelison, A.) Comparison of parent-child relationships of male and female schizophrenic patients. Arch gen Psychiat 1963, 8:1-7

80945 The development of American psychiatry. P 1967, 123:320-332

Abs Loeb, L. Q 1969, 38:510

80946 The effects of children on marriage. Marriage Relat 121-131

80947 (& Schafer, S.; Fleck, S.; Cornelison, A.; Terry, D.) Ego differentiation and schizophrenic symptom formation in identical twins. (Read at Am Psa Ass, Dec 1959) J Am Psa Ass 1962, 10:74-90

Abs JBi Q 1963, 32:131

80948 Familie, Sprache und Schizophrenie. [Family, speech and schizophrenia.] Psyche 1968, 22:701-719

Abs J 1969, 50:397

80949 The Family and Human Adaptation: Three Lectures. London: Hogarth Pr 1964, 120 p

Abs J Am Psa Ass 1966, 14:621-622. Rv GPK Q 1964, 33:442-444. Smirnoff, V. N. J 1964, 45:602-606

80950 The family, personality development, and schizophrenia. In Romano, J. *The Origins of Schizophrenia,* Amsterdam/NY: Excerpta Medica Found 1967, 131-138

80951 (& Fleck, S.) Family studies and a theory of schizophrenia. Forest Hosp Publ 1965, 3

80952 Following clinical leads. Int J Psychiat 1966, 2:417

° ° ° Foreword to Parker, B. *My Language Is Me.*

° ° ° Foreword to Werkman, S. L. *The Role of Psychiatry in Medical Education.*

80953 Hysteria. Ency Ment Hlth 818-826

80954 The influence of family studies on the treatment of schizophrenia. Ps 1969, 32:237-251

80955 (& Smith, D. C.) Interrelated schizophrenic psychoses in fraternal twins. Arch gen Psychiat 1964, 10:423-430

S-52455 (& Cornelison, A. R.; Fleck, S.; Terry, D.) The intrafamiliar environment of the schizophrenic patient, I: The father.
Abs JA An Surv Psa 1957, 8:149-150

S-52459 Intrafamilial environment of the schizophrenic patient: the transmis-
sion of irrationality. In Handel, G. *The Psychosocial Interior of the
Family: A Sourcebook for the Study of Whole Families*, Chicago:
Aldine 1967

80956 Juan Ramon Jimenez—a remembrance. Yale Rev 1962, Winter:342-344

80957 The marital relationship, family structure and personality development. Proc III World Cong Psychiat 1961, 3:117-120

80958 The Person, His Development Through the Life Cycle. NY: Basic
Books 1968, 558 p
Rv Freedman, A. Am Im 1969, 19:223-225

80959 Prediction of family interaction from a battery of projective techniques.
In Handel, G. *Psychosocial Interior of the Family: A Sourcebook for
the Study of Whole Families*, Chicago: Aldine 1967

80960 (& Rothenberg, A.) Psychedelism: Dionysius reborn. Ps 1968, 31:116-
125

80961 Psychoanalytic theories of development and maldevelopment: some
recapitulations. Psa 1967, 27:115-126

80962 The relevance of family studies to psychoanalytic theory. JNMD 1962,
135:105-112

80963 Schizophrenia. In *International Encyclopedia of the Social Sciences*,
Vol. 14, NY: Macmillan & Free Pr 1968

S-52470 Schizophrenia and the family.
Abs WCW An Surv Psa 1958, 9:182

80964 (& Fleck, S.; Cornelison, A. R.) Schizophrenia and the Family. NY:
IUP 1966, 477 p
Abs J Am Psa Ass 1967, 15:730-731. Rv Robbins, L. L. Q 1967,
36:604-605

80965 (& Fleck, S.; Alanen, Y. O.; Cornelison, A. R.) Schizophrenic patients
and their siblings. Ps 1963, 26:1-18. In Palmer, J. O. & Goldstein, M.
J. *Perspectives in Psychopathology*, NY: Oxford Univ Pr 1966, 21-41.
In Howells, J. G. *Theory and Practice of Family Psychiatry*, Edin-
burgh/London: Oliver & Boyd 1968, 782-806
Abs HRB Q 1964, 33:143

80966 (& Fleck, S.) Some explored and partially explored sources of psychopathology. In Zuk, G. H. & Boszormenyi-Nagy, I. *Family Therapy and
Disturbed Families*, Palo Alto, Calif: Sci & Behav Books 1967, 41-46

80967 (& Fleck, S.; Wild, C.; Schafer, S.) The thought disorders of parents
of schizophrenic patients. Proc III World Cong Psychiat 1961, 1:169-
173

80968 (& Rosman, B.; Wild, C.; Ricci, J.; Fleck, S.) Thought disorders in the
parents of schizophrenic patients: a further study utilizing the object
sorting test. J psychiat Res 1964, 2:211-221

80969 (& Wild, C.; Schafer, S.; Rosman, B.; Fleck, S.) Thought disorders in
the parents of schizophrenic patients: a study utilizing the object sorting test. J psychiat Res 1963, 1:193-200

80970 The value of specificity concepts in psychosomatic disorders. In Bulletin of Joint Meeting of American Psychiatric Association and Sociedad Mexicana de Neurologia y Psiquiatria 1964, 40 p

See Ciarlo, Dorothy D.; Fleck, Stephen; Lidz, Ruth W.; Smith, Daniel C.

LIEBERMAN, FLORENCE

80971 (& Taylor, S. S.) Combined group and individual treatment of a schizophrenic child. Soc Casewk 1965, 46:80-85
80972 Transition from latency to prepuberty in girls: an activity group becomes an interview group. Int J grp PT 1964, 14:455-464

LIEBERMAN, MORTON A.

80973 Comments on W. E. Henry's "Some observations on the lives of healers." Hum Develpm 1966, 9:57-60
80974 (& Daniels, R. S.; McFarland, R. I.) Group psychotherapy. Prog Neurol Psychiat 1964, 19:599-605
80975 (& Meyer, G. G.; McFarland, R. L.) Group psychotherapy. Prog Neurol Psychiat 1966, 21:579-585
80976 (& Whitaker, D. S.) Problems and potential of psychoanalytic and group-dynamic theories for group psychotherapy. Int J grp PT 1969, 19:131-141

See Daniels, Robert S.; Lakin, Martin; McFarland, Robert L.; Meyer, George G.; Perlmutter, Jerry; Whitaker, Dorothy S.; Whitman, Roy M.

LIEBERMANN, LUCY P.

80977 Case history of a borderline personality. M 1964, 37:301-312
Abs Hirsh, H. Q 1966, 35:316

LIEBERT, ROBERT S.

80978 History and psychoanalysis. Int J Psychiat 1969, 7:484-487

LIEBMAN, SAMUEL

80979 (Ed) Emotional Forces in the Family. Phila/Montreal: Lippincott 1959, viii + 157 p

LIEBOWITZ, JOEL

See Ekstein, Rudolf

LIEF, HAROLD I.

80980 Adaptation and maladaptation of medical students. In Proceedings of the Conference of the Midwestern Professors of Psychiatry, Univ of Mich 1966, 68-108
80981 Alice or Little Hans in wonderland. Int J Psychiat 1967, 4:49-50
80982 Anxiety reaction. Compreh Txbk Psychiat 857-870
80983 An atypical stereotype of the Negroes' social worlds. Ops 1962, 32:86-88

80984 Changing sexual patterns and their impact on clinical practice. Med Opin Rev 1965, 1:10-14
80985 Comments on Dr. Clark's view of mental illness and racism. Roche Rep: Frontiers of Clinical Psychiatry 1966, 3(14):2
80986 Contemporary forms of violence. Sci Psa 1963, 6:56-68. In Endleman, S. *Violence in the Streets*, Chicago: Quadrangle Books 1968, 49-62
80987 Correspondence on psychiatric illness in medical students. P 1962, 118:1053-1055
80988 Discussion—clinical studies. In Heath, R. G. *Serological Factors in Schizophrenia*, NY: Harper & Row 1963, 235-239
80989 Discussion of Davidman, H. "Contributions of Sandor Rado to psychodynamic science." Sci Psa 1964, 7:35-38
80990 Discussion of Shainess, N. "The problem of sex today." P 1968, 124:99-102
80991 Family planning and undergraduate medical education. Fertility Control 1967, 2(2):16-19
80992 Generic and specific aspects of phobic behavior. Int J Psychiat 1968, 6:470-473
80993 (& Lancaster, R. C.; Spruiell, V.) Is "self-kick" the answer? J med Educ 1963, 38:971-973
80994 (& Lief, V. F.; Warren, C. O.; Heath, R. G.) Low dropout rate in a psychiatric clinic. Special reference to psychotherapy and social class. Arch gen Psychiat 1961, 5:200-211
80995 The Masters-Johnson Research—an evaluation. SIECUS Newsletter 1966, 2(1) & 2(2). Bull NY State District Branches, Am Psychiat Ass 1966, 9(3)
80996 Mental illness among medical students. Psychiat Spectator 1966, 3(6):1
80997 Needed: sex education for physicians. Physician's Panorama 1965, 3(3):23
80998 (& Reed, D. M.) Normal psychosexual functioning. Compreh Txbk Psychiat 258-265
80999 Orientation of future physicians in psychosexual attitudes. In Calderone, M. S. *Manual of Contraceptive Practice*, Baltimore: Williams & Wilkins 1964, 109-119
81000 Panel discussion on contraceptive practice. Pacif Med Surg 1965, 73(1-A):86-95
81001 The physician and family planning. JAMA 1966, 197:646-650
81002 (& Thompson, W. C.) The prediction of behavior from adolescence to adulthood. Ps 1961, 24:32-38
81003 Psychiatric aspects of the prevention of nuclear war. Formulated by the committee on social issues, Group for the Advancement of Psychiatry. Int J Psychiat 1965, 1:341-408
81004 Psychoanalysis and psychiatric training. Sci Psa 1969, 14:1-13
81005 (& Young, K.; Spruiell, V.; Lancaster, R. C.; Lief, V. F.) A psychodynamic study of medical students and their adaptational problems: preliminary report. J med Educ 1960, 35:696-704
81006 (& Dingman, J. F.; Bishop, M. P.) Psychoendocrinologic studies in a male with cyclic changes in sexuality. PSM 1962, 24:357-369
     Abs ELG Q 1963, 32:608-609

81007 (& Filler, W.) A psychological approach to the gynecologic patient. In author's *The Psychological Basis of Medical Practice* 449-460

81008 (& Lief, V. F.; Lief, N. R.) (Eds) The Psychological Basis of Medical Practice. Evanston/NY: Harper & Row, 1963, xvi + 572 p

81009 (& Mayerson, P.) Psychotherapy of homosexuals: a follow-up study of nineteen cases. In Marmor, J. *Sexual Inversion*, NY: Basic Books 1965, 302-344

81010 Psychotherapy of medical students. Curr psychiat Ther 1967, 7:50-60

81011 (Moderator) Roundtable: sex after 50. Panel discussion. J Med Asp hum Sexual 1968, 2(1):41-47

81012 Sex and the medical educator. J Amer Med Wom Ass 1968, 23:195-196

81013 Sex education of medical students and doctors. Pacif Med Surg 1965, 73(1-A):52-58

81014 Sexual attitudes and behavior of medical students: implications for medical practice. In Nash, E. et al; *Marriage Counseling in Medical Practice,* Chapel Hill: Univ of North Carolina Pr 1964, 301-318

81015 Silence as intervention in psychotherapy. Psa 1962, 22:80-83

81016 Subprofessional training in mental health. Arch gen Psychiat 1966, 15:660-664

81017 Teaching doctors about sex. In Brecher, R. & Brecher, E. *An Analysis of Human Sexual Response,* Boston: Little, Brown 1966, 275-279

81018 (& Fox, R. C.) Training for "detached concern" in medical students. In author's *Psychological Basis of Medical Practice* 12-35

81019 Training in broad-spectrum psychotherapy. In Dellis, N. P. & Stone, H. K. *Training in Psychotherapy,* Baton Rouge: Louisiana State Univ Pr 1961, 68-81

81020 What medical schools teach about sex. Bull Tulane Univ Med Fac 1963, 22(3):161-168. Southern med Bull 1964, 52(4):36-42

See Heath, Robert G.; Lief, Victor F.; Savitz, Leonard D.

LIEF, NINA R.

See Lief, Harold I.; Lief, Victor F.

LIEF, VICTOR F.

81021 (& Lief, H. I.; Young, K. M.) Academic success: intelligence and personality. J med Educ 1965, 40:114-124

81022 (& Lief, N. R.) The general practitioner and psychiatric problems. In Lief, H. I. et al: *The Psychological Basis of Medical Practice,* NY: Harper & Row 1963, 485-500

81023 The medical examination in psychiatric assessment. Compreh Txbk Psychiat 542-545

See Adriani, John; Lief, Harold I.

LIEM, S. T.

See Stokvis, Berthold

LIENDO, ERNESTO CÉSAR

81024   Las relaciones objetals y la symbolización de la angustia. [Object relations and symbolization of anguish.] Rev Psicoanál 1967, 24:839-897

LIÉVANO, JAMES

81025   Observations about payment of psychotherapy fees. Psychiat Q 1967, 41:324-338

LIFF, ZANVEL A.

81026   The psychoanalytic roots of political impasse: implications for the United Nations. Int ment Hlth Res Newsletter 1968, 10:3

See Aronson, Marvin L.; Krasner, Jack; Markowitz, Max

LIFSCHUTZ, JOSEPH EMANUEL

81027   Brief review of psychoanalytic ego psychology. Soc Casewk 1964, 45:3-9
81028   (& Stewart, T. B.; Harrison, A. M.) Psychiatric consultation in the public assistance agency. Soc Casewk 1958, 39:3-9
81029   (Participant in round table) A psychoanalytic view of the family: a study of family member interactions. Psa Forum 1969, 3:11-65

LIFTON, NORMAN

81030   (& Smolen, E. M.) Group psychotherapy with schizophrenic children. Int J grp PT 1966, 16:23-41

LIFTON, ROBERT JAY

81031   Contributor to Krystal, H. *Massive Psychic Trauma.*
81032   Death in Life. Survivors of Hiroshima. NY: Random House 1967, 594 p
            Rv Krystal, H. Q 1969, 38:488-491
81033   On death and death symbolism: the Hiroshima disaster. Ps 1964, 27:191-210. In Bugental, J. F. T. *Challenges of Humanistic Psychology,* NY: McGraw-Hill 1967, 195-206
81034   Methods of forceful indoctrination: psychiatric aspects of Chinese Communist thought reform. GAP Symp 1957 (4):234-249. In Stein, M. R. et al: *Identity and Anxiety,* Glencoe, Ill: Free Pr 1960, 480-492
81035   Psychological effects of the atomic bomb in Hiroshima: the theme of death. Daedalus 1963, 92:462-497. Death & Identity 8-42
81036   Revolutionary Immortality. Mao Tse-tung and the Chinese Cultural Revolution. NY: Vintage Books 1968
81037   Thought Reform and the Psychology of Totalism. A Study of "Brainwashing" in China. NY: Norton 1961, 1963, xiv + 510 p
            Rv Bond, D. D. Q 1962, 31:279-280
81038   (Eds) The Woman in America. Boston, Mass: Houghton Mifflin 1965, ix + 293 p
81039   Youth and history: individual change in postwar Japan. Youth 217-242

LIGHTHALL, FREDERICK F.

See Ruebush, Britton K.; Sarason, Seymour B.

LILIENFELD, ABRAHAM M.
See Oleinick, Martha S.

LILIENFELD, ALFRED

ABSTRACTS OF:

81040 Barchilon, J. On countertransference "cures." An Surv Psa 1958, 9:400-401

81041 Bird, B. A consideration of the etiology of prejudice. An Surv Psa 1957, 8:127-129

81042 Devereux, G. The significance of the external female genitalia and of female orgasm for the male. An Surv Psa 1958, 9:469

81043 Eissler, K. R. Some comments on psychoanalysis and dynamic psychiatry. An Surv Psa 1956, 7:56-57

81044 Engel, G. L. & Reichsman, F. Spontaneous and experimentally induced depression in an infant with a gastric fistula: a contribution to the problem of depression. An Surv Psa 1956, 7:267-271

81045 French, T. M. The art and science of psychoanalysis. An Surv Psa 1958, 9:325-327

81046 Kaplan, S. (Reporter) Panel: the latency period. An Surv Psa 1957, 8:206-209

81047 Kohut, H. (Reporter) Panel: clinical and theoretical aspects of resistance. An Surv Psa 1957, 8:242-244

81048 Lipton, S. D. A note on the connection between preliminary communications and subsequently reported dreams. An Surv Psa 1958, 9:216-217

81049 Loewenstein, R. M. A contribution to the psychoanalytic theory of masochism. An Surv Psa 1957, 8:116-118

81050 Munroe, R. L. Schools of Psychoanalytic Thought: An Exposition, Critique, and Attempt at Integration. An Surv Psa 1955, 6:15-16, 519-558

81051 Ostow, M. (Reporter) Panel: theory of aggression. An Surv Psa 1957, 8:66-68

81052 Racker, H. Counterresistance and interpretation. An Surv Psa 1958, 9:405-406

81053 Rubinfine, D. L. (Reporter) Panel: problems of identity. An Surv Psa 1958, 9:114-117

81054 Saul, L. & Sheppard, E. An attempt to qualify emotional forces using manifest dreams: a preliminary study. An Surv Psa 1956, 7:226-227

81055 Sloane, P. (Reporter) Panel: the technique of supervised analysis. An Surv Psa 1957, 8:290-292

81056 Spitz, R. A. Countertransference: comments on its varying role in the analytic situation. An Surv Psa 1956, 7:345-346

81057 Tower, L. E. Countertransference. An Surv Psa 1956, 7:346-347

81058 Wangh, M. (Reporter) Panel: the scope of the contribution of psychoanalysis to the biography of the artist. An Surv Psa 1957, 8:324-326

REVIEW OF:

81059 Frank, I. & Powell, M. (Eds) Psychosomatic Ailments in Childhood and Adolescence. R 1968-69, 55:712-713

LILIENTHAL, JESSE
See Peck, Robert F.

LILLESKOV, ROY
ABSTRACTS OF:
81060 Balkanyi, C. Language, verbalization, and superego: some thoughts on the development of the sense of rules. Q 1968, 37:484-485
81061 Lorand, S. Biographical notes on Sandor Ferenczi (1875-1933). Q 1964, 33:468-470

LILLY, JOHN C.
S-52510 An anxiety dream of an 8-year-old boy and its resolution.
   Abs An Surv Psa 1955, 6:241, 277-278
81062 The biological versus psychoanalytic dichotomy. Bull Phila Ass Psa 1961, 11:116-119
   Abs PLe RFPsa 1963, 27:337
81063 (& Shurley, J. T.) Experiments in solitude in maximum achievable physical isolation with water suspension in intact, healthy persons. In Flaherty, B. J. *Psychophysiological Aspects of Space Flight*, NY: Columbia Univ Pr 1961, 238-247
S-52513 The psychophysiological basis for two kinds of instincts. Implications for psychoanalytic theory.
   Abs JTM Q 1962, 31:130-131

LIMA, HEITOR DE ANDRADE
See Chebabi, Wilson de Lyra; Oliveira, Walderedo Ismael de

LIMENTANI, AMADEO
81064 Discussion of Flarsheim, A. "The psychological meaning of the use of marijuana and LSD in one case." Psa Forum 1969, 3:122-124
81065 On drug dependence: clinical appraisals of the predicaments of habituation and addiction to drugs. J 1968, 49:578-590
81066 Problemi di ambivalenza, reparazione e situazione edipiche. [Problems of ambivalence, reparation, and the oedipal situation.] Riv Psa 1966, 12:253-267; 1967, 13:296-301
81067 A re-evaluation of acting out in relation to working through. (Read at Int Psa Cong, July 1965) J 1966, 47:274-282
   Abs EVN Q 1968, 37:312

LIN, TSUNG-YI
81068 A brief outline of the WHO standardization program. Int J Psychiat 1969, 7:404-406
81069 Some epidemiological findings on suicides in youth. In Caplan, G. & Lebovici, S. *Adolescence*, NY/London: Basic Books 1969, 233-243

LINANE, J.
See McConaghy, N.

LINCKE, HAROLD

81070 Aggression und Selbsterhaltung. [Aggression and self-preservation.] In Mitscherlich, A. *Aggression und Anpassung,* Munich: Piper 1969

S-52520 Einige Bemerkungen zur Triebentwicklung.
Abs EW An Surv Psa 1957, 8:198-200

81071 Die frühesten Formen der Identifikation und die Überichbildung. [The earliest forms of identification and the superego development.] Schweiz Z Psychol 1963, 22:338-348

81072 Zur Traumbildung. [On dream development.] Jb Psa 1960, 1:161-179

LINCOLN, C. ERIC

81073 Discussion of Pinderhughes, C. A. "The psychodynamics of dissent." Sci Psa 1968, 13:79-81

LINCOLN, GERALDINE

See Friedman, Alfred S.

LIND, ALICE

81074 (& Gralnick, A.) Integration of the social group worker and psychiatrist in the psychiatric hospital. In Gralnick, A. *The Psychiatric Hospital as a Therapeutic Instrument,* NY: Brunner/Mazel 1969, 259-268

LIND, DETLEV L.

See Brady, John P.

LINDE, E.

81075 Analytical psychotherapy: case report and discussion. New Zeal med J 1966, 65:239-242

LINDAUER, M. S.

81076 Quantitative analyses of psychoanalytic studies of Shakespeare. J Psychol 1969, 72:3-9

LINDEMANN, ERICH

81077 Adolescent behavior as a community concern. PT 1964, 18:405-417

81078 Discussant: "Physicians in the community." Tech Dyn Psychiat 188-189

81079 Feldstudien in der vorbeugenden Psychiatrie. [Field studies in preventive psychiatry.] Prax PT 1960, 5:22-33

81080 Grief. Ency Ment Hlth 703-706

81081 Group Studies and Social Psychiatry. (Film, 22 minutes) (Excerpt from the Lindemann Lectures) Available through Harvard Medical School

81082 Guilt. Ency Ment Hlth 716-718

81083 The Psychiatrist in the Community. (Film, 22 minutes) (Excerpt from the Lindemann Lectures) Available through Harvard Medical School

81146 Pichon-Rivière, A. A. de: Dentition, walking and speech in relation to the depressive position. An Surv Psa 1958, 9:251

81147 Pichon-Rivière, A. A. de: House construction play: its interpretation and diagnostic value. An Surv Psa 1958, 9:315

81148 Rascovsky, A. Beyond the oral stage. An Surv Psa 1956, 7:96-97

81149 Rodrigue, E. Notes on symbolism. An Surv Psa 1956, 7:85-87

81150 Rosenfeld, H. A. Contribution to the discussion on variations in classical technique. An Surv Psa 1958, 9:349

81151 Rosenfeld, H. A. Discussion on ego distortion. An Surv Psa 1958, 9:159

81152 Rosenfeld, H. A. Some observations on the psychopathology of hypochondriacal states. An Surv Psa 1958, 9:192

81153 Segal, H. Depression in the schizophrenic. An Surv Psa 1956, 7:175-176

81154 Segal, H. Notes on symbol formation. An Surv Psa 1957, 8:32-33

81155 Servadio, E. Transference and thought transference. An Surv Psa 1956, 7:344

81156 Silbermann, I. Two types of pre-oedipal character disorders. An Surv Psa 1957, 8:218-219

81157 Sperling, M. The psycho-analytical treatment of ulcerative colitis. An Surv Psa 1957, 8:160-161

81158 Sterba, R. F. & Sterba, E. The anxieties of Michelangelo Buonarroti. An Surv Psa 1956, 7:414-416

81159 Székely, L. On the origin of man and the latency period. An Surv Psa 1957, 8:206

81160 Toman, W. Repetition and repetition compulsion. An Surv Psa 1956, 7:93-94

81161 Veszy-Wagner, L. An Irish legend as proof of Freud's theory of joint parricide. An Surv Psa 1957, 8:306

81162 Waelder, R. Introduction to the discussion on problems of transference. An Surv Psa 1956, 7:330-331

81163 Wheelis, A. B. The vocational hazards of psychoanalysis. An Surv Psa 1956, 7:64-66

81164 Winnicott, D. W. The capacity to be alone. An Surv Psa 1958, 9:111

81165 Winnicott, D. W. On transference. An Surv Psa 1956, 7:334-335

81166 Winterstein, A. On the oral basis of a case of male homosexuality. An Surv Psa 1956, 7:215

81167 Zetzel, E. R. Ernest Jones: his contribution to psychoanalytic theory. An Surv Psa 1958, 9:5-6

REVIEW OF:

81168 Boyer, L. B. & Giovacchini, P. L. Psychoanalytic Treatment of Characterological and Schizophrenic Disorders. Psa Forum 1967, 2:375-377

LINDSLEY, OGDEN R.

81169 Discussion of Homme, L. E. "Human motivation and environment." Kansas Stud Educ 1966, 16(2):30-47

81170 Experimental analysis of social reinforcement: terms and methods. Ops 1963, 33:612-633

81084 Psycho-social factors as stressor agents. In Tanner, J. M. *Stress and Psychiatric Disorder*, Oxford: Blackwell Sci Publ 1960, 13-16

81085 The relation of drug-induced mental changes to psychoanalytic theory. Bull WHO 1959, 21:517-526

81086 Some Beginnings of Social Psychiatry. (Film, 14 minutes) (Excerpt from the Lindemann Lectures) Available through Harvard Medical School

S-20718 Symptomatology and management of acute grief. Death & Identity 186-201

81087 The timing of psychotherapy. In *Proceedings of the VIth International Congress of Psychotherapy*, Basel: Karger 1965, Part IV

See Barry, Herbert, Jr.; Fried, Marc; Klein, Donald C.; Leopold, Robert L.

LINDEN, JAMES I.

81088 On expressing physical affection to a patient. Voices 1968, 4(2):34-38

LINDEN, MAURICE E.

81089 The emotional problem of aging. In Brill, N. Q. *Psychiatry in Medicine*, Berkeley/Los Angeles: Univ Calif Pr 1962, 100-119

81090 (& Goodwin, H. M.; Resnick, H.) Group psychotherapy of couples in marriage counseling. Int J grp PT 1968, 18

LINDENAUER, GEOFFREY G.

81091 Emotional awareness of children. J emot Educ 1967, 7:8-14

81092 Freud-Jung-Adler-Ferenczi-List: emotional education. J emot Educ 1967, 7:18-21

LINDER, M.

See Kline, M. V.

LINDGREN, DONN BYRNE

See Lindgren, Henry C.

LINDGREN, HENRY CLAY

81093 Pedagogy and group leadership. MH 1960, 44:83-86

81094 (& Lindgren, D. B.) Psychology: An Introduction to the Study of Human Behavior. NY: Wiley 1961, xi + 429 p

81095 (Ed) Readings in Educational Psychology. NY: Wiley 1968

LINDINGER, HELGE

81096 [Basic principles of psychoanalysis (Sigmund Freud).] (Ger) Landarzt 1967, 43:1337-1345

81097 Einige Bemerkungen zur Theorie und Therapie der Psychopathie. [Remarks on the theory and therapy of psychotherapy.] Z Psychother med Psychol 1964, 14:153-157

81098 Psychische Faktoren der Puerperalpsychose in einem Falle akuter Verwirrtheit beim Manne. [Psychic factors of puerperal psychosis in a case of acute confusion in a man.] Ärztl Forsch 1964, 18:258-262

81099 Rationalisierung einer Psychose als "Folge von Perversion." [Rationalization of a psychosis as a "consequence of perversion."] Nervenarzt 1962, 33:161-165

81100 Eine Selbstdeutung in der Gruppe. [Self-interpretation in group therapy.] Psyche 1965, 19:398-402

81101 Über den "spiegelbildlich wechselnden" Ablauf einiger Widerstandphänomene in der Gruppe. [On the changing "mirror-image-like" termination of a resistance phenomenon in the group.] Z PSM 1968, 14:200-204

81102 Zur Frage der neurotischen Fixierungen in der Vorentwicklung schizophrener Psychosen. [On the problem of neurotic fixations in the premorbid schizophrenic psychosis.] Psyche 1963, 17:333-356

81103 Zur Frage der Prinzipien einer Psychotherapie schizophrener Psychosen. [On the problem of the principles of a psychotherapy of schizophrenic psychoses.] Nervenarzt 1966, 37:168-173

LINDNER, HAROLD

81104 (& Stevens, H.) Hypnotherapy and psychodynamics in the syndrome of Gilles de la Tourette. Int J clin exp Hyp 1967, 15:151-155

81105 The shared neurosis: hypnotist and subject. Int J clin exp Hyp 1960, 8:61-70

81106 Spontaneity in the analytic interpretation. In Hammer, E. F. *Use of Interpretation in Treatment: Technique and Art*, NY: Grune & Stratton 1968, 71-73

LINDO, TREVOR

See Butts, Hugh F.

LINDON, JOHN ARNOLD

81107 Discussion of Bion, W. R. "Notes on memory and desire." Psa Forum 1967, 2:274-275

81108 Grow or . . . . Psa Forum 1967, 2(1):4

81109 Introduction. Psa Forum 1969, 3:5-6

81110 Melanie Klein 1882-1960. Her view of the unconscious. Psa Pioneers 360-372

81111 Nonsense. Psa Forum 1967, 2(3):194

81112 On Freud's concept of dream-action. Psa Forum 1966, 1:32-37, 43, 142

81113 (Ed & participant) On regression: a workshop. (West Coast Psa Soc, 14-16 Oct 1966) Psa Forum 1967, 2:293-316

    Sobre la regresion: un grupo de discusion. Rev Psicoanál 1968, 25(2)

81114 (Ed) The Psychoanalytic Forum, Vol. 3, NY: Sci House 1969, 348 p

81115 (Ed) A psychoanalytic view of the family: a study of family member interactions. (Round table, 30 April 1967) Psa Forum 1969, 3:11-65

81116 A student's bench is good for the head. Psa Forum 1967, 2(4):290

81117 The twentieth century. Psa Forum 1967, 2(2):104

81118 Two birthdays. Psa Forum 1966, 1(4):334

81119 Who can be analyzed. Psychiat soc Sci Rev 1966, 1(1):3-6

81120 You are invited. Psa Forum 1966, 1(3):240

See Grotjahn, Martin

ABSTRACTS OF:

81121 Balint, M. The three areas of the mind. Theoretical considerati Surv Psa 1958, 9:69-70

81122 Baumeyer, F. Schreber case. An Surv Psa 1956, 7:29, 178-179

81123 Bowlby, J. The nature of the child's tie to his mother. An S 1958, 9:240-241

81124 Bychowski, G. Struggle against the introjects. An Surv Ps 9:123-124

81125 Devereux, G. The awarding of a penis as compensation for r Surv Psa 1957, 8:309-310

81126 Eissler, K. R. Remarks on some variations in psychoanalytic tec An Surv Psa 1958, 9:327

81127 Fraiberg, L. B. Freud's writings on art. An Surv Psa 1956, 7:

81128 Freud, S. Memorandum on the electrical treatment of war n An Surv Psa 1956, 7:29, 296-297

81129 Freud, S. & Breuer, J. On the psychical mechanism of hysteri nomena. An Surv Psa 1956, 7:29

81130 Garma, A. Peptic ulcer and pseudo peptic ulcer. An Surv Ps 9:200

81131 Glauber, I. P. The rebirth motif in homosexuality and its tele significance. An Surv Psa 1956, 7:215-216

81132 Glover, E. Psycho-analysis and criminology: a political sur Surv Psa 1956, 7:404-406

81133 Grinker, R. R. On identification. An Surv Psa 1957, 8:81

81134 Hitschmann, E. Some psycho-analytic aspects of biography. Psa 1956, 7:411

81135 Hoffer, W. Transference and transference neurosis. An Surv Ps 7:332-333

81136 Karpe, M. & Karpe, R. The meaning of Barrie's Mary Rose. Psa 1957, 8:328

81137 Klein, M. On the development of mental functioning. An S 1958, 9:233

81138 Lampl-de Groot, J. The theory of instinctual drives. An Surv Ps 7:88

81139 Langer, M. Sterility and envy. An Surv Psa 1958, 9:208-209

81140 Levy, K. Silence in the analytic session. An Surv Psa 1958, 9:

81141 Lorand, S. Dream interpretation in the Talmud. An Surv Ps 8:179-180

81142 Mann, T. Freud and the future. An Surv Psa 1956, 7:29

81143 Mead, M. Changing patterns of parent-child relations in ar culture. An Surv Psa 1957, 8:212-213

81144 Milner, M. The communication of primary sensual experien yell of joy). An Surv Psa 1956, 7:165

81145 Nunberg, H. Character and neurosis. An Surv Psa 1956, 7:18

81171 Free-operant conditioning and psychotherapy. Curr psychiat Ther 1963, 3:47-56
81172 (& Nathan, P. E.; Marland, J.) Receptive communi ation in psychiatric nurse supervision. J counsel Psychol 1965, 12:259-267

See Azrin, Nathan H.; Barrett, Beatrice H.; Mednick, Martha T.

LINDY, JANET

See McDermott, John F., Jr.

LINDZEY, GARDNER

81173 (& Lykken, D. T.; Winston, H. D.) Infantile trauma, genetic factors, and adult temperament. ASP 1960, 61:7-14. In author's *Theories of Personality* 49-56
81174 Projective Techniques and Cross-Cultural Research. NY: Appleton-Century-Crofts 1961, ix + 339 p
81175 Psychoanalytic theory: paths of change. J 1968, 49:656-661
81176 Some remarks concerning incest, the incest taboo, and psychoanalytic theory. Am Psych 1967, 22:1051-1059
81177 (& Hall, C. S.) (Eds) Theories of Personality: Primary Sources and Research. NY/London/Sydney: Wiley 1965, 1966, 1968, xiii + 549 p

See Boring, Edwin G.; Hall, Calvin S.

LINK, WILLIAM E.

81178 Psychotherapy outcome in the treatment of hyperaggressive boys: a comparison of behavioristic and traditional therapy techniques. Diss Abstr 1968, 29(6-B):2205

LINN, LAWRENCE S.

81179 The mental hospital from the patient perspective. Ps 1968, 31:213-223
81180 Social identification and the seeking of psychiatric care. Ops 1968, 38:83-88

LINN, LOUIS

81181 (& Stein, M.) Acute alcoholic furor. Med Bull NATO 1944, 2:81-82
81182 Clinical manifestations of psychiatric disorders. Compreh Txbk Psychiat 546-577
81183 (& Chaplik, M.) Les dépressions: vers un élargissement des points de vue théoriques et practiques. In *Extraits des Comptes rendus du Congrès de Psychiatrie et de Neurologie,* Anvers, 9-14 July 1962
       Depression: broadening concepts in theory and practice. Psychiat Q Suppl 1962, 36:1-13
81184 Discussion of Weinstein, E. A. "The relationship to dreams of symbolic patterns following brain injury." Dreams Contempo Psa 96-101
81185 (& Weinroth, L. A.; Shamah, R.) The four-phase concept of hospital care: a theoretical and practical approach to inpatient psychiatry. Proc III World Cong Psychiat 1961, 2:606
81186 The fourth psychiatric revolution. P 1968, 124:1043-1048

81187   (Ed) Frontiers in General Hospital Psychiatry. NY: IUP 1961, xxvi +
        483 p
            Rv Robbins, L. L. Q 1963, 32:426-427
81188   (& Bernstein, M. H.; Meyerson, A. T.) Hospitalisation élective à temps
        partiel. [Elective part-time hospitalization.] Inform psychol 1965,
        June:483-499
81189   (& Tureen, L.) Intensive electro-convulsive therapy of the acute ex-
        cited states. Med Bull NATO 1944, 2:80-81
81190   Jackson and Freud: the relation of dissolution to regression. Bull NY
        Acad Med 1960, 36:277-284
81191   A note on "manner of approach" in the Rorschach Test as a measure
        of psychic energy. Psychiat Q 1948, 22:634-637
81192   (& Weinroth, L. A.; Shamah, R.) Occupational Therapy in Dynamic
        Psychiatry: An Introduction to the Four-Phase Concept in Hospital
        Psychiatry. Wash DC: Am Psychiat Ass 1962, 78 p
81193   On the difference between psychiatry and religion. In Noveck, S. Juda-
        ism and Psychiatry, NY: Basic Books 1956
81194   A philosophy of psychiatric research. Ment Hosp 1963, 14:21-24
81195   Progress in health planning: the role of community psychiatry. Curr
        psychiat Ther 1969, 9:284-291
81196   (& Goldman, I. B.) Psychiatric observations concerning rhinoplasty.
        PSM 1949, 11:307-314
81197   Psychiatric reactions complicating cataract surgery. In Thedore, F. H.
        Complications after Cataract Surgery, Boston: Little, Brown 1964.
        Int Ophthal Clin 1965, 5:143-154
81198   (& Stein, M.) A psychiatric study of blast injuries of the ear. Med Bull
        NATO 1944, 1:6-7. War Med 1945, 8:32-33
81199   The psychiatric unit in the general hospital [interviewed by Perkins,
        M. E.]. In Ziskind, E. Viewpoint on Mental Health, NY: NYC Comm
        Ment Hlth Board 1967, 60-65
81200   The psychiatric ward administrator: a discussion. J ment Hosp 1959,
        10:20
81201   Psychoanalysis and community psychiatry: a new challenge and re-
        sponsibility. J Hillside Hosp 1967, 16:234-254
81202   The psychoses of pregnancy. Dis nerv Sys 1941, 1:390-395
81203   Psychosomatic medicine. JAMA 1941, 116:70
81204   (& Cohen, S.; Zimmerman, J.) The role of hyperhydrosis in trench foot:
        psychiatric considerations. Med Bull Office of the Chief Surgeon, ETO
        1945, 1:27-29
81205   The Rorschach Test in the evaluation of military personnel. Rorschach
        Exchange 1946, 10:20-27
81206   Some aspects of a psychiatric program in a voluntary general hospital.
        In Bellak, L. Handbook of Community Psychiatry and Community
        Mental Health, NY: Grune & Stratton 1964, 126-143
S-52632 Some comments on the origin of the influencing machine.
            Abs Margolis, N. M. An Surv Psa 1958, 9:191-192
S-52633 Some developmental aspects of the body image.
            Abs An Surv Psa 1955, 6:105-106, 258
81207   Some psychoanalytic notes concerning music appreciation. J Hillside
        Hosp 1968, 17:209-222

81208   (& Tureen, L.; Bernstein, B. L.) A study of neurotic tendencies in groups of overseas soldiers. Trans Amer Neurol Ass 1946, June
81209   Towards a philosophy of psychiatric research. Ment Hosp 1963, 14
81210   The use of drugs in psychotherapy. Psychiat Q 1964, 38:138-148
81211   What do we look for in a church building? Psychological considerations. J Amer Inst Architects 1964, Sept:49-64

See Polatin, Phillip; Spiegel, Herbert; Zussman, Leon

REVIEWS OF:
81212   Bühler, C. Values in Psychotherapy. Q 1964, 33:119-120
81213   Cofer, C. N. & Appley, M. H. Motivation: Theory and Research. Q 1965, 34:610-611
81214   Engel, G. L. Psychological Development in Health and Disease. Q 1964, 33:120-122
81215   Levinson, D. J. & Gallagher, E. B. Patienthood in the Mental Hospital. An Analysis of Role, Personality and Social Structure. Q 1965, 34:460-461
81216   The Psychic Function of Religion in Mental Illness and Health. GAP Rep No. 67. Q 1969, 38:498-501

LINNEMANN, EBBE J.

81217   Comment on Dr. Wood's paper, "Acting out viewed in the context of the psychotherapeutic hospital." (Read at Int Psa Cong, July 1967) J 1968, 49:442-444
81218   (& Zahle, V.) The concept of iatrogenic neurosis. Acta Psychiat Scand 1959, 34(Suppl):172-178
81219   On anxiety states. Acta Psychiat Scand 1959, 34(Suppl):153-164

LINNÉR, BRIGITTA

81220   (& Westholm, B.) Familj och Samlevnad. [Family life and Relationship.] Stockholm: Liber 1967, 215 p
81221   Sex and Society in Sweden. NY: Pantheon Books 1967, xvii + 204 p; London: Jonathan Cape 1968
            Sexualité et Vie Sociale en Suède. Paris: Gonthier 1968
            German: Güttersloh: Bertelsmann Verlag
            Sexo y Sociedad en Suecia. Mexico: Editorial Diana 1968
            Sex i Samhället. Stockholm: Rabén & Sjögren 1968
81222   Sexual morality and sexual reality—the Scandinavian approach. Ops 1966, 36:683-693
            Abs JMa RFPsa 1968, 32:380
81223   (& Westholm, B.) Sexualliv och Samlevnad. [Sexual Life and Relationship.] Stockholm: Liber 1968, 64 p

LINTON, HARRIET B.

81224   (& Langs, R. J.; Paul, I. H.) Retrospective alterations of the LSD-25 experience. JNMD 1964, 138:409-423
            Abs BFM Q 1966, 35:155

LINTON, JOHN

TRANSLATION OF:
(& Vaughan, R.) Adler, A. [440]

LIPIN, THEODORE

81225 The repetition compulsion and maturational drive representatives.
(Read at NY Psa Soc, 15 Oct 1963) J 1963, 44:389-406
Abs HW Q 1964, 33:312-314. EVN Q 1966, 35:308
81226 Sensory irruptions and mental organization. J Am Psa Ass 1969,
17:1055-1073

LIPKOWITZ, MARVIN H.

81227 Homosexuality as a defense against feminine strivings: a case report.
JNMD 1964, 138:394-398
Abs BFM Q 1965, 34:312

See Green, Sidney L.

ABSTRACTS OF:
81228 Orchinik, C. W. On tickling and stuttering. An Surv Psa 1958, 9:135-
136
81229 Riese, W. The pre-Freudian origins of psychoanalysis. An Surv Psa
1958, 9:37-38
81230 Sperling, M. Trichotillomania, trichophagy, and cyclic vomiting: a
contribution to the psychopathology of female sexuality. Q 1969,
38:171-172

LIPMAN, RONALD S.

81231 (& Griffith, B. C.) Effects of anxiety level on concept formation: a test
of drive theory. Amer J ment Defic 1960, 65:342-348

LIPOWSKI, ZBIGNIEW JERZY

81232 Psychopathology as a science: its scope and tasks. Comprehen Psychiat
1966, 7:175-182
81233 (& Wittkower, E. D.) Research possibilities in psychosomatic medicine.
Méd Hyg 1967, 25:141-142
81234 Review of consultation psychiatry and psychosomatic medicine. 3.
Theoretical issues. PSM 1968, 30:395-422

LIPPITT, RONALD

See Redl, Fritz

LIPPMAN, HYMAN S.

81235 Certain behavior responses in early infancy. Pedag Sem & J genet
Psych 1927, 34(3):424
81236 A child psychiatrist's thoughts on delinquency. Int ment Hlth Res
Newsletter 1959, 1(2-3)

81237 Contribution to the diagnosis and treatment of psychiatric problems of children by group services. In *Workbook for NSAW Workshop Conference*, June 1958, 1

81238 Emotional aspects of juvenile delinquency. Minn Med 1960, 43:84

81239 Emotional factors in juvenile delinquency. In *Proceedings of 68th Annual Congress of American Prison Association*, Oct 1938, 271

81240 Emotional problems of children. In Farnsworth, D. L. & Braceland, F. J. *Psychiatry, the Clergy, and Pastoral Counseling*, Collegeville, Minn: Inst for Mental Health, St. John's Univ Pr 1969, 71-85

81241 Emotional problems presented by the child in the school setting. Bull Nat Ass Sch Soc Workers 1952, 28(2)

81242 Highlights personal and educational in the training and clinical experience of a child psychiatrist. J Amer Acad Child Psychiat 1963, 2(2)

81243 Impulsive behavior in childhood delinquency. Lancet 1932, 52(2):27

81244 Kindliche Depressionen. [Depression in children.] In Bolterauer, L. *Aus der Werkstatt des Erziehungsberaters*, Vienna: Verlag Jugend & Volk 1960, 214-229

81245 Mental hygiene work with children—direct treatment. In *Proceedings of the National Conference of Social Work*, Philadelphia 1932, 353

81246 Play therapy. Ops 1938, 8:518

81247 The phobic child and other related anxiety states. In Hammer, M. M. & Kaplan, A. *The Practice of Psychotherapy with Children*, Homewood, Ill: Dorsey Pr 1968, 73

81248 Preventing delinquency. Fed Probation 1953, 17:24

81249 Psychiatric therapy for the neurotic delinquent. Osteopathic Profession 1958, 25(9):36

81250 The psychoanalytic orientation in family case work. Ops 1943, 13:27

81251 Restlessness in infancy. JAMA 1928, 91:1849

81252 Role of the individual, family and community in the prevention of crime. In *Crimes of Violence*, Univ Colorado Pr 1950, 85

81253 The role of the probation officer in the treatment of delinquency in children. Fed Probation 1948, 12(2):36. In Vedder, C. V. *The Juvenile Offender*, Garden City, NY: Doubleday 1954, 360

81254 The suitability of the child for adoption. Ops 1937, 7:270

81255 The thorny youngster. Minn Med 1958, 41:813

81256 Treatment of behavior problems, particularly delinquency, in European clinics visited during summer of 1935. Minn Med 1936, 19:421

81257 Treatment of juvenile delinquents. In *Proceedings of National Conference of Social Work*, May-June 1945

S-52657 Treatment of the Child in Emotional Conflict. NY/Toronto/London: McGraw-Hill 1962 (2nd ed), xii + 367 p
          Abs J Am Psa Ass 1963, 11:665. Rv Gilder, R., Jr. Q 1963, 32:123

81258 Understanding the offender through understanding ourselves. Fed Probation 1940, 4(3):14

81259 The use of case work in the treatment of delinquency. In *Papers in Honor of Everett Kimball*, Smith Coll School of Soc Work, 1943, 173

81260 Vandalism as an outlet for aggression. Fed Probation 1954, 18(1):5

LIPPSITT, LEWIS PAEFF

81261 (& Spiker, C. C.) (Eds) Advances in Child Development and Behavior. NY/London: Academic Pr 1963, Vol. 1, xiii + 387 p; 1965,
Vol. 2, x + 269 p; 1967, Vol. 3, xii + 272 p

81262 (& Reese, H. W.) (Eds) Advances in Child Development and Behavior, Vol. 4. NY/London: Academic Pr 1969, xii + 333 p

LIPSHER, DAVID H.

See Bandura, Albert

LIPSHUTZ, DANIEL M.

81263 Combined group psychotherapy. Top Probl PT 1960, 2:79-85
81264 Some dynamic factors in the problem of aggression. Psychiat Q 1961,
35:78-87
    Abs Engle, B. Q 1962, 31:136
S-52663 Transference in borderline cases.
    Abs An Surv Psa 1955, 6:329

LIPSITT, DON R.

81265 "Hypochondriasis": whose responsibility? Psychiat Opin 1969, 6(4):26-
34
81266 Integration clinic: an approach to the teaching and practice of medical
psychology in an outpatient setting. In Zinberg, N. E. *Psychiatry and
Medical Practice in a General Hospital*, NY: IUP 1964, 231-249
81267 The "rotating" patient: a challenge to psychiatrists. J geriat Psychiat
1968, 2:51-61

LIPSON, CHANNING T.

81268 Denial and mourning. J 1963, 44:104-107. In Ruitenbeek, H. M.
Death: Interpretations, NY: Dell Publ 1969, 268-275
    Abs EVN Q 1965, 34:465

LIPTON, DOUGLAS S.

See Kurtzberg, Richard L.

LIPTON, EARLE L.

81269 (& Steinschneider, A.; Richmond, J. B.) Autonomic function in the
neonate. PSM 1960, 22:57-64

See Caldwell, Bettye M.

LIPTON, EDGAR L.

81270 The cross-eyed bear—the cross I bear: a study of the psychological
effects of strabismus. (Read at NY Psa Soc, 31 Jan 1967)
    Abs Sternschein, I. Q 1968, 37:165-168
81271 Some psychological aspects of strabismus. Amer Orthopt J 1969, 19:48-
54

81272 (& Gilkeson, E. C.) Utilizing a school for children to supplement the training of medical personnel: a report of an experimental program. J Amer Acad Child Psychiat 1966, 5:393-430

See Fine, Bernard D.

LIPTON, H. R.

81273 (& Bryan, L. L.) The significance of hostile acting-out in confinement. Dis nerv Sys 1966, 27:61-64

LIPTON, ROSE C.

See Provence, Sally A.

LIPTON, SAMUEL D.

81274 (Reporter) Aggression and symptom formation. (Panel: Am Psa Ass, 10 Dec 1960) J Am Psa Ass 1961, 9:585-592
S-52665 A clinical note on the occurrence of malingering in a case of paranoia.
       Abs DJM An Surv Psa 1957, 8:149
81275 Discussion of Alger, I. "The clinical handling of the analyst's responses." Psa Forum 1966, 1:297-298, 427-428
81276 Freud's position on problem solving in dreams. M 1967, 40:147-149
81277 The last hour. (Read at Am Psa Ass, 4 Dec 1959) J Am Psa Ass 1961, 9:325-330
       Abs FB Q 1962, 31:293. Auth Rev Psicoanál 1963, 20:92
81278 Later developments in Freud's technique (1920-1939). Psa Tech 51-92
S-52666 A note on the compatibility of psychic determinism and freedom of will.
       Abs An Surv Psa 1955, 6:58
S-52667 A note on the connection between preliminary communications and subsequently reported dreams.
       Abs AL An Surv Psa 1958, 9:216-217
81279 Observations on rapid manifestations of drives and defenses. (Read at Chicago Psa Soc, 23 May 1967)
       Abs Beigler, J. S. Bull Phila Ass Psa 1967, 17:176-177
81280 On the psychology of childhood tonsillectomy. (Read at Chicago Psa Soc, 28 March 1961) Psa St C 1962, 17:363-417
       Abs Seitz, P. F. D. Bull Phila Ass Psa 1961, 11:135-136. SLe RFPsa 1964, 28:815

LISS, EDWARD

S-52670 Motivations in learning.
       Abs An Surv Psa 1955, 6:110-113, 263

LISTON, EDWARD H., JR.

See Brill, Norman Q.; Wahl, Charles W.

LITIN, EDWARD M.

81281 The chronically ill and their impact on the family. J Amer Med Wom Ass 1963, 18:223-226

S-52674 (& Giffin, M. E.; Johnson, A. M.) Parental influence in unusual sexual behavior in children.
  Abs AHM An Surv Psa 1956, 7:273-274

81282 The psychologic management of the patient with carcinoma. J Int Coll Surg 1961, 36:588-595

See Aronson, Arnold E.; Beckett, Peter G. S.; Taylor, B. W.

LITKEI, ANDREA FODOR

81283 Precognition—or telepathy from the past? R 1969, 56:138-141

LITMAN, ROBERT E.

81284 Acutely suicidal patients. Management in general medical practice. Calif Med 1966, 104:168-174

81285 Community action in the prevention of suicide: Suicide Prevention Center, Los Angeles, California. In Yochelson, L. *Symposium on Suicide,* Wash DC: George Wash Univ Pr 1967, 142-150

81286 Discussion of Dr. Lindon's article, "On Freud's concept of dream-action." Psa Forum 1966, 1:141-142

81287 Discussion of Shneidman, E. S. "Orientations toward death: a vital aspect of the study of lives." Int J Psychiat 1966, 2:197-198

81288 (& Farberow, N. L.) Emergency evaluation of self-destructive potentiality. In Farberow, N. L. & Shneidman, E. S. *The Cry for Help,* NY: McGraw-Hill 1961, 48-59

81289 (& Tabachnick, N.) Fatal one-car accidents. Q 1967, 36:248-259
  Abs Cuad Psa 1967, 3:243-244

81290 (& Farberow, N. L.) The hospital's obligation toward suicide-prone patients. Hospitals 1966, 40(16 Dec):64-68, 124

81291 Immobilization response to suicidal behavior. Arch gen Psychiat 1964, 11:282-285
  Abs KR Q 1965, 34:470-471

81292 Interpersonal reactions involving one homosexual male in a heterosexual group. Int J grp PT 1961, 4:440-448

81293 (& Curphey, T.; Shneidman, E. S.; Farberow, N. L.; Tabachnick, N.) Investigation of equivocal suicides. JAMA 1963, 184:924-929

81294 (& Shneidman, E. S.; Farberow, N. L.) Los Angeles Suicide Prevention Center. P 1961, 117:1084-1087

81295 Medical-legal aspects of suicide. Washburn Law Rev 1967, 6:395-401

81296 Preface. Psa Amer vii

81297 The prevention of suicide. Curr psychiat Ther 1966, 6:268-276

81298 Psychiatric hospitals and suicide prevention centers. Comprehen Psychiat 1965, 6:119-127

81299 (Ed) Psychoanalysis in the Americas: Original Contributions from the First Pan-American Congress for Psychoanalysis. NY: IUP; London: Bailey Bros 1966, xi + 315 p
  Abs J Am Psa Ass 1968, 16:180-181. Rv Grinstein, A. Q 1968, 37:126-128

81300 (& Tabachnick, N. D.) Psychoanalytic theories of suicide. In Resnik, H. L. P. *Suicidal Behaviors: Diagnosis and Management,* Boston: Little, Brown 1968, 73-81

81301 Psychotherapists' orientations toward suicide. In Resnik, H. L. P. *Suicidal Behaviors: Diagnosis and Management,* Boston: Little, Brown 1968, 357-363

81302 Sigmund Freud on suicide. (Read at South Calif Psa Soc, 15 Nov 1965) Psa Forum 1966, 1:206-214, 220-221, 323-324. In Shneidman, E. S. *Essays in Self-Destruction,* NY: Science Pr 1967. Bull Suicidology 1968, July:11-23
       Abs JLS Psa Forum 1966, 1:139-140

81303 Suicide: a clinical manifestation of acting out. Acting Out 76-86

81304 (& Shneidman, E. S.; Farberow, N. L.) A suicide prevention center. Curr psychiat Ther 1961, 1:8-16

81305 (& Farberow, N. L.; Shneidman, E. S.; Heilig, S. M.; Kramer, J.) Suicide prevention telephone service. JAMA 1965, 192:21-25

81306 When patients commit suicide. PT 1965, 19:570-576

       See Farberow, Norman L.; Klugman, David J.; Shneidman, Edwin S.; Tabachnick, Norman D.

       REVIEW OF:
81307 Laing, R. D. The Self and Others. Further Studies in Sanity and Madness. Q 1964, 33:283-284

LITOWITZ, NORMAN S.

81308 (& Newman, K. M.) Borderline personality and the theatre of the absurd. Arch gen Psychiat 1967, 16:268-280

LITT, SHELDON

See Margoshes, Adam

LITTLE, HARRY M.

81309 (& Konopka, G.) Group therapy in a child guidance center. Ops 1947, 17:303-311

LITTLE, KENNETH B.

81310 (& Adams, D. K.) The catharsis value of aggression fantasy. J proj Tech 1965, 29:336-340

LITTLE, MARGARET

81311 Alkolikler kimlerdir? [Who is an alcoholic?] Tipta Yeniliker 1961, 6:8-11

81312 Comment on Dr Sperling's paper, "The balancing function of the ego —with special emphasis on learning." J 1964, 45:261-262
       Abs EVN Q 1966, 35:459

81313 Countertransference. M 1960, 33:29-31
       Abs IH Q 1961, 30:152

S-20829 Counter-transference and the patient's response to it.
       Abs Baranger, M. Rev urug Psa 1961-62, 4:194

81314 Obituary: Willi Hoffer 1897-1967. (Read at Brit Psa Soc, 16 Oct 1968) J 1969, 50:268

S-52677 On basic unity.
     Sur l'unité de base. RFPsa 1961, 25:749-764
     Abs JBi Q 1962, 31:118-119
S-52678 On delusional transference (transference psychosis).
     Abs SLP An Surv Psa 1958, 9:395-396.
     Baranger, M. Rev urug Psa 1961-62, 4:191
S-52680 "R"—the analyst's total response to his patient's needs.
     Abs SLP An Surv Psa 1957, 8:270-271
81315 Transference in borderline states. (Read at Austin Riggs Center, 15
     Oct 1965; at Los Angeles Psa Soc, 20 Oct 1964; at Chestnut Lodge,
     9, Nov 1964; at Brit Psa Soc, 2 June 1965) J 1966, 47:476-485
     Abs EVN Q 1968, 37:463

REVIEW OF:
81316 Searles, H. F. Collected Papers on Schizophrenia and Related Subjects.
     J 1967, 48:112-117

LITTLE, RALPH B.

81317 (& Pearson, M. M.) The management of pathologic interdependency
     in drug addiction. P 1966, 123:554-560
81318 Oral aggression in spider legends. Am Im 1966, 23:169-179
     Abs Cuad Psa 1967, 3:59-60. JWS Q 1967, 36:472-473
81319 The resolution of oral conflicts in spider phobia. (Read at Int Psa
     Cong, July 1967) J 1968, 49:492-494
81320 Spider phobias. Q 1967, 36:51-60
     Abs Cuad Psa 1967, 3:242
81321 Transference, countertransference and survival reactions following an
     analyst's heart attack. (Read at Phila Psa Soc, 20 Jan 1964) Psa Forum
     1967, 2:108-113, 124-126
     Abs Cuad Psa 1968, 4:44
81322 Umbilical cord symbolism of the spider's dropline. Q 1966, 35:587-590
     Abs Cuad Psa 1967, 3:59

See Pearson, Manuel M.

LITTLE, S.

81323 Psychotherapeutic aspects of chronic illness in children. GP 1965,
     31:132-135

LITTMAN, RICHARD A.

81324 (& Nidorf, L. A.; Sundberg, N. D.) Characteristics of a psychosexual
     scale: the Krout personal preference scale. J genet Psych 1961, 98:19-
     27

LITTNER, NER

81325 Adult fairy tales. New City 1968, 15 June
81326 The child's need to repeat his past—some implications for placement.
     Soc S R 1960, 34:128-148. In *Changing Needs and Practices in Child
     Welfare*, Child Welfare League of America 1960

81327   Discussion. In *Dentistry and the Social Sciences*, Tel Aviv: Federation Dentaire Internationale 1966, 83

81328   Discussion. Smith Coll Stud soc Wk 1967, Feb:119-126

81329   Effect on child welfare of recent trends in mental health theory and practice. Child Welfare 1967, 46

81330   Emotional development and learning in the preschool child. Ill Schools J 1967, 47:163-170

81331   A guaranteed minimum income for all Americans. Public Welfare 1966

81332   Helping and dealing with the disturbed child and his parents. Bull, AMA Assistants 1964, 8(1)

81333   Is social work education keeping pace with our deepening knowledge of children. In *Proceedings of the 10th Anniversary Annual Program Meeting*, Council on Social Work Education 1962

81334   Montessori today: a psychoanalyst's view. Ill Schools J 1968, 48:83-88

81335   Personality factors and emotional barriers. J dent Educ 1960, 24(4)

81336   The present position of psychoanalytically oriented psychotherapy. Reiss-Davis Clin Bull 1968, 5(2):62-67

81337   The social worker and the psychiatrist—their respective roles. Child Welfare 1961, 40

81338   The unmarried mother . . . a point of view. In *Florence Crittenton Association of America*, Chicago, May 1967.

See Josselyn, Irene M.; Koff, Robert H.; Schour, Esther

LITZOW, T. J.

See Taylor, B. W.

LIVERMORE, JEAN

81339   Letter to the editors [re "Conjoint therapy."] Psa Forum 1966, 1:326-327

LIVINGSTON, GOODHUE

81340   The role of activity in the treatment of schizoid or schizophrenic patients. Psychotherapy 1964, 1:184-189

LIVINGSTON, MARTIN

See Vogel, William

LIVINGSTON, P. B.

81341   (& Zimet, C. N.) Death anxiety, authoritarianism and choice of specialty in medical students. JNMD 1965, 140:222-230

LIVSON, FLORINE

See Reichard, Suzanne

LIVSON, NORMAN

81342   Parental behavior and children's involvement with their parents. J genet Psych 1966, 109:173-194

81343 (& Peskin, H.) Prediction of adult psychological health in a longitudinal study. JAbP 1967, 72:509-518

LIZARAZO, A.

81344 (& Martinez, A.; Rosselli, H.; Villar, A.; Angel, G.; Zubiría, R. de; García, H.; González, M.; Márquez, J. A.) Indicaciones y limitaciones del psicoanálisis. [Indications and limitations of psychoanalysis.] Acta psiquiát psicol Amér Latina 1964, 10:283-295

LLEWELLYN, CHARLES E., JR.

81345 Psychotherapy with marriage partners. In Nash, E. M. et al: *Marriage Counseling in Medical Practice*, Chapel Hill: Univ North Carolina Pr 1964, 283-297

See Smith, Robert E.

LLORENS, LELA A.

81346 (& Rubin, E. Z.) Developing Ego Functions in Disturbed Children: Occupational Therapy in Milieu. Detroit: Wayne State Univ Pr 1967, 146 p

LLORENS ROZAS, JORGE R.

81347 Relato de la primera hora de analisis de un niño de cuatro anos. [An account of the first hour of analysis of a four-year-old child.] Rev arg Psicol 1966, (1):19-20

LOBB, L. G.

See Gericke, O. L.

LOBECK, ROBIN

See Bieri, James

LOBO, FABIO LEITE

81348 (& Domingues de Moraes, O.) Identidade de sexo e seus disturbios— aspectos teoricos e clinicos. [Sex identity and its disturbances—clinical and theoretical aspects.] Rev bras Psa 1969, 3(1-2):31-48

LOCH, WOLFGANG

81349 Aggression und Liebesobjekt: eine Beitrag zur Frage der Partnerwahl. [Aggression and love-object: a contribution to the problem of partner-choice.] In *Gesellschaft und Neurose, Almanach*, Stuttgart: Klett 1965, 99-121

81350 Amenorrhoische Phasen: Ödipale Abwehr und narzisstische Regression. [Amenorrhoic phases: oedipal defense and narcissistic regression.] In *Das Lebensproblem und die Krankheit*, Stuttgart: Klett 1968

81351 Anmerkungen zur Pathogenese und Metapsychologie einer schizophrenen Psychose. [Notes on the pathogenesis and metapsychology of a schizophrenic psychosis.] Psyche 1962, 15:684-720

402 Klaf, F. S. & Davis, C. A. Homosexuality and paranoid schizophrenia: a survey of 150 cases and controls. Q 1961, 30:146

403 Kramer, M. et al: Depression: dreams and defenses. Q 1967, 36:473

404 Lidz, T. The development of American psychiatry. Q 1969, 38:510

405 Mandell, A. J. & Mandell, M. P. The biochemical aspects of rapid eye movement sleep. Q 1967, 36:473

406 Masterson, J. F., Jr. & Washburn, A. The symptomatic adolescent: psychiatric illness or adolescent turmoil? Q 1968, 37:629

407 Meerloo, J. A. M. Spinoza: a look at his psychological concepts. Q 1966, 35:314

408 Mesnikoff, A. M. et al: Intrafamilial determinants of divergent sexual behavior in twins. Q 1964, 33:609

409 Miller, T. P. The child who refuses to attend school. Q 1963, 32:291-292

410 O'Neal, P. et al: Parental deviance and the genesis of sociopathic personality. Q 1963, 32:607

411 Ornitz, E. M. et al: Dreaming sleep in autistic and schizophrenic children. Q 1967, 36:473

412 Pierce, C. M. et al: Dream patterns in narcoleptic and hydroencephalic patients. Q 1967, 36:473

413 Selesnick, S. T.: C. G. Jung's contributions to psychoanalysis. Q 1965, 34:140

414 Snyder, F. Progress in the new biology of dreaming. Q 1967, 36:473

415 Snyder, F. Toward an evolutionary theory of dreaming. Q 1969, 38:510

416 Thomas, A. et al: Individuality in responses of children to similar environmental situations. Q 1962, 31:134

417 Toolan, J. M. Suicide and suicidal attempts in children and adolescents. Q 1963, 32:607

418 Wangh, M. Psychoanalytic thought on phobia: its relevance for therapy. Q 1969, 38:510

LOESCH, JOHN G.

419 (& Greenberg, N. H.) Some specific areas of conflict observed in pregnancy: a comparative study of married and unmarried pregnant women. Ops 1962, 32:624-636
    Abs RLG Q 1963, 32:138

LOESSER, LEWIS H.

420 (& Bry, T.) The role of death fears in the etiology of phobic anxiety as revealed in group psychotherapy. Int J grp PT 1960, 10:287-297

LOEVINGER, JANE

421 (& Sweet, B.) Construction of a test of mothers' attitudes. In Glidewell, J. C. Parental Attitudes and Child Behavior, Springfield, Ill: Thomas 1961, 110-123

422 The meaning and measurement of ego development. Am Psych 1966, 21:195-206

423 Measurement in clinical research. In Wolman, B. B. Handbook of Clinical Psychology, NY: McGraw-Hill 1965, 78-94

81352 Balint-Seminare: Instrumente zur Diagnostik und Therapie pathogener zwischenmenschlicher Verhaltensmuster. [Balint seminars: instruments for diagnosis and treatment of pathogenic social behavior patterns.] Jb Psa 1969, 6:141-156

81353 Bemerkungen zur Rolle des Sexualtabus. [Notes on the role of the taboos of sexuality.] Psyche 1968, 22:720-727
    Abs J 1969, 50:397-398

81354 Biologische und gesellschaftliche Faktoren der Gewissensbildung. [Biological and social factors of conscience-formation.] Wege zum Menschen 1962, 15:10

81355 Grundriss der psychoanalytischen Theorie. [Fundamentals of psychoanalytic theory.] In author's Die Krankheitslehre der Psychoanalyse

81356 Heilung als Ich-Integration. [Cure as ego-integration.] Wege zum Menschen 1961, 13(6-7)

81357 Identifikation—Introjektion. Definitionen und genetische Determinanten. [Definitions and genetic determinants of identification and introjection.] Psyche 1968, 22:271-286

81358 (Ed) Die Krankeitslehre der Psychoanalyse. [Psychoanalytic Psychopathology.] Stuttgart: Hirzel 1967, xii + 290 p
    Rev Veszy-Wagner, L. J 1967, 48:607-608

81359 Mord—Selbstmord oder die Bildung des Selbstbewusstseins. [Murder—suicide or the formation of self-awareness.] Wege zum Menschen 1967, 19:262

81360 Psychoanalyse und Kausalitätsprinzip. [Psychoanalysis and causality principle.] Psyche 1962, 16:401-419

81361 Psychoanalytische Aspekte zur Pathogenese und Struktur depressiv-psychotischer Zustandsbilder. [Psychoanalytic aspects of the pathogenesis and structure of depressive-psychotic conditions.] Psyche 1967, 21:758-779

81362 Psychoanalytischer Beitrag zum Verständnis der Perversion, insbesondere der Homosexualität. [Psychoanalytic contribution to the understanding of perversions, particularity of homosexuality.] Dtsch Zbl Krankenpfl 1963, 7:93-95

81363 Psychotherapeutische Behandlung psychosomatischer Krankheiten in der ärztlichen Sprechstunde. [Psychotherapeutic treatment of psychosomatic diseases in the surgery.] Ärztliche Mitteilungen 1964, 2:73

81364 Regression: über den Begriff und seine Bedeutung in einer allgemeinen psychoanalytischen Neurosentheorie. [Regression: on the concept and its significance in a general psychoanalytic theory of neuroses.] Psyche 1963, 17:516-545

81365 Schulpsychiatrie—Psychoanalyse in Konvergenz? [Academic psychiatry—psychoanalysis in convergence?] Psyche 1960, 14:801-810
    Abs IBa RFPsa 1962, 26:620

81366 Über einige allgemeine Strukturmerkmale und Funktionen psychoanalytischer Deutungen. [On some general structural features and functions of psychoanalytic interpretations.] Psyche 1966, 20:377-397

81367 Über theoretische Voraussetzungen einer psychoanalytischen Kurztherapie Anmerkungen zur Begründung der Fokaltherapie nach Michael Balint. [On theoretical presuppositions of a psychoanalytical brief therapy. Notes on the *raison-d'etre* of Michael Balint's focal therapy.] Jb Psa 1967, 4:82-101

81368 Über die Zusammenhänge zwischen Partnerschaft, Struktur und Mythos. [On the relationships of partnership, structure, and mythos.] Psyche 1969, 24:481-506

81369 Übertragung—Gegenübertragung. Anmerkungen zur Theorie und Praxis. [Transference—countertransference. Remarks on theory and practice.] Psyche 1965, 19:1-23

81370 Voraussetzungen, Mechanismen und Grenzen des psychoanalytischen Prozesses. [Hypotheses, Mechanisms and Limitations of the Psychoanalytical Process.] Bern/Stuttgatt: Huber 1965, 78 p
    Rv Veszy-Wagner, L. J 1967, 48:121-123

81371 Zur Problematik des Seelenbegriffs in der Psychoanalyse. [On the problems connected with the concept of the soul in psychoanalysis.] Psyche 1961, 15:88-97
    Abs IBa RFPsa 1962, 26:624

81372 Zur Problematik tiefenpsychologisch fundierter Psychotherapie als Pflichtleistung der RVO-Kassen. [On the problems of psychoanalytically oriented psychotherapy as a duty of compulsory insurance.] In *Das Lebensproblem und die Krankheit*, Stuttgart: Klett 1968

81373 Zur Struktur und Therapie schizophrener Psychosen aus psychoanalytischer Perspektive. [On the structure and therapy of schizophrenic psychoses from the psychoanalytic point of view.] Psyche 1965, 19:172-187

REVIEW OF:

81374 Malan, D. H. A Study of Brief Psychotherapy. J 1965, 46:261-265

LO CICERO, VICTOR J.

81375 Group therapy. Int Psychiat Clin 1964, 1:417-430

LOCKE, NORMAN MALCOLM

81376 A Decade of Group Psychotherapy: The Bibliography for 1950-1959. NY: Group Psychotherapy Center 1960, 48 p

81377 The early Maya: a repressed society. Am Im 1963, 20:49-60

81378 Emotional factors in the analyst's attitude to group psychoanalysis. PT 1961, 15:436-441

81379 Group Psychoanalysis: Theory and Technique. NY: NY Univ Pr 1961, ii + 253 p
    Rv Semrad, E. V. & Day, M. J Am Psa Ass 1966, 14:591-618

81380 A myth of ancient Egypt. Am Im 1961, 18:105-128

LOCKEY, ANN

See Carter, Pauline

LOCKHART, J.

81381 The emotional reactions to acute illness. Lahey Clin Found Bull 1969, 18:175-180

LOEB, DOROTHY G.

See Chapman, Arthur T.; Perlmutter, Morton S.

LOEB, FELIX F., JR.

81382 (& Carroll, E. J.) General systems theory and psych plication to psychoanalytic case material (Little 25:388-398

81383 The microscopic film analysis of the function of a rec pattern in a psychotherapeutic session. JNMD 1968,

LOEB, LAURENCE

81384 Adolescent schizophrenia. In Bellak, L. & Loeb, L. T *Syndrome*, NY/London: Grune & Stratton 1969, 462-

See Bellak, Leopold

ABSTRACTS OF:

81385 Alexander, F. The dynamics of psychiatry in the theory. Q 1965, 34:140-141

81386 Bowlby, J. Childhood mourning and its implication: Q 1963, 32:292

81387 Brickman, H. R. et al: The psychoanalyst as commu Q 1968, 37:629

81388 Dement, W. C. Recent studies of the biological role of ment sleep. Q 1967, 36:473

81389 Eissler, K. R. Perverted psychiatry? Q 1969, 38:511

81390 Erikson, E. H. Psychoanalysis and on-going history: p tity, hatred, and non-violence. Q 1967, 36:473

81391 Fier, M. Contact lens phobia. Q 1966, 35:313

81392 Finch, S. M. & Hans, J. H. Ulcerative colitis in children.

81393 Fish, B. et al: The prediction of schizophrenia in infa year follow-up report of neurological and psychologic Q 1966, 35:313-314

81394 Fisher, C. & Dement, W. C. Studies on the psychopa and dreams. Q 1964, 33:609-610

81395 Fisher, C. Subliminal and supraliminal influences on c 30:146

81396 Gillman, R. D. Brief psychotherapy: a psychoanalytic 36:474

81397 Hammett, Van B. O. A consideration of psychoanalys to psychiatry generally, circa 1965. Q 1967, 36:473

81398 Hoch, P. H. et al: The course and outcome of pseudo phrenia. Q 1963, 32:608

81399 Jacobs, E. G. & Mesnikoff, A. M. Alternating psychos port of four cases. Q 1962, 31:134

81400 Kane, R. P. & Chambers, G. S. Improvement—real or ap 31:134

81401 Kaplan, H. I. et al: Combined psychiatric residency and training. Q 1968, 37:628-629

81424   Patterns of parenthood as theories of learning. ASP 1959, 59:148-150. In Rosenblith, J. F. & Allinsmith, W. *The Causes of Behavior*, Boston: Allyn & Bacon 1966, 119-121

81425   Theories of ego development. In Berger, L. *Clinical-Cognitive Psychology: Models and Integrations*, Englewood Cliffs, N.J.: Prentice-Hall 1969, 83-135

81426   Three principles for a psychoanalytic psychology. JAbP 1966, 71:432-443

LOEW, F.

See Tönnis, W.

LOEW, LOIS HENDRICKSON

See Tilton, James R.

LOEWALD, HANS W.

81427   Comments on some instinctual manifestations of superego formation. (Read at Chicago Psa Soc, 28 Nov 1961)
        Abs Miller, A. A. Bull Phila Ass Psa 1962, 12:43-45

S-52727 Hypnoid state, repression, abreaction and recollection.
        Abs An Surv Psa 1955, 6:117-118, 311

81428   Internalization, separation, mourning, and the superego. (Read at Topeka Psa Soc 1959; at Western New Engl Psa Soc 1960; at Am Psa Ass, Dec 1960) Q 1962, 31:483-504

81429   Obituary: Samuel Novey, M. D. 1911-1967. Q 1967, 36:590

S-52728 (Reporter) Psychoanalytic curricula—principles and structure. (Panel: Am Psa Ass, May 1955)
        Abs IS An Surv Psa 1956, 7:367-370

81430   The superego and the ego-ideal. Symposium II: Superego and time. (Read at Int Psa Cong, July-Aug 1961) J 1962, 43:264-268
        Le surmoi et le temps. RFPsa 1963, 27:555-564
        Abs RLG Q 1963, 32:599-601

S-52729 On the therapeutic action of psychoanalysis.
        Abs JBi Q 1961, 30:296. PCR RFPsa 1964, 28:292-293

REVIEWS OF:

81431   Arlow, J.A. & Brenner, C. Psychoanalytic Concepts and the Structural Theory. Q 1966, 35:430-436

81432   Thomä, H. Anorexia Nervosa. J 1963, 44:110-113

LOEWENBERG, PETER

81433   Emotional problems of graduate education. J higher Educ 1969, 40:610-623

81434   An interdisciplinary psychoanalytic study group on political leadership in Los Angeles. J Hist behav Sci 1969, 5:271-272

LOEWENSTEIN, RUDOLPH MAURICE

81435   Comment on Dr. Naiman's paper, "Short term effects as indicators of the role of interpretations in psychoanalysis." (Read at Int Psa Cong, July 1967) J 1968, 49:356-357

S-52734 A contribution to the psychoanalytic theory of masochism.
Abs AL An Surv Psa 1957, 8:116-118

81436 (Chm) Contribution to the study of the manifest dream. (Panel: NY Psa Soc, 28 June 1960)
Abs WAS Q 1961, 30:464-466

81437 Defensive organization and autonomous ego functions. (Read at Am Psa Ass, 7 May 1966) J Am Psa Ass 1967, 15:795-809

81438 Developments in the theory of transference in the last fifty years. J 1969, 50:583-588

81439 Europe comes to America. 50 Yrs Psa 44-45

81440 Heinz Hartmann b. 1894. Psychology of the ego. Psa Pioneers 469-483

81441 An historical review of the theory of psychoanalytic technique. (Read at Chicago Psa Soc, 25 March 1968) In *Traditional Subjects Reconsidered* (Proceedings of the 2nd Regional Conference, Chicago Psychoanalytic Society) 1968
Abs Beigler, J. S. Bull Phila Ass Psa 1969, 19:58-60

81442 Introduction to panel, "The silent patient." (Am Psa Ass, 6 Dec 1958) J Am Psa Ass 1961, 9:2-6
Abs Soifer, R. Rev Psicoanál 1961, 18:398. FB Q 1962, 31:286-287. SAS RFPsa 1962, 26:614

81443 Obituary: Marie Bonaparte 1882-1962. (Read at Int Psa Cong, 29 July 1963) J Am Psa Ass 1963, 11:861-863
Hommage à la mémoire de Marie Bonaparte. RFPsa 1965, 29:7-10

81444 Observational data and theory in psychoanalysis. Dr Af Beh 2:38-59

81445 On the theory of the superego: a discussion. Psa—Gen Psychol 298-314

81446 (& Newman, L. M.; Schur, M.; Solnit, A. J.) Preface. Psa—Gen Psychol ix-xi

S-20850 The problem of interpretation.
Das Problem der Deutung. Psyche 1968, 22:187-198

S-20852 Psychanalyse de l'Antisémitisme.
Christians and Jews: A Psychoanalytic Study. NY: Dell Publ 1963, 226 p
Christenen en Joden. Amsterdam: Polak & Van Genep 1966, 180 p
Psychoanalyse des Antisemitismus. Frankfurt am Main: Suhrkamp Verlag 1968, 175 p
Estudio Psicoanalítico del Antisemitismo. Buenos Aires: Ed Hormé 1966, 239 p

81447 (& Newman, L. M.; Schur, M.; Solnit, A. J.) (Eds) Psychoanalysis—A General Psychology. Essays in Honor of Heinz Hartmann. NY: IUP; London: Bailey Bros 1966, xii + 684 p
Abs J Am Psa Ass 1967, 15:729. Rv Friedman, P. Q 1968, 37:596-597. Radomisli, M. R 1969, 56:147-150

81448 Psychoanalysis: therapeutic methods. In *International Encyclopedia of the Social Sciences,* NY: Macmillan & Free Pr 1968, 13:31-37

81449 Psychoanalytic theory and the teaching of dynamic psychiatry. Teach Dyn Psychiat 104-114, 137-138

81450 Rapport sur la psychologie psychanalytique de H. Hartmann, E. Kris et R. Loewenstein. Contribution à la théorie psychanalytique. [Report on the psychoanalytic psychology of H. Hartmann, E. Kris and R.

Loewenstein, presented by R. Loewenstein. Contribution to psycho-analytic theory.] RFPsa 1966, 30:775-820

81451 (Chm) Reconstruction in psychoanalysis. (Panel: NY Psa Soc, 27 June 1961)
Abs Fine, B. D. Q 1962, 31:142-144

S-52741 Réflexions sur le traitement d'un cas de névrose compulsionnelle.
Abs JBi An Surv Psa 1956, 7:322-324

S-52742 Remarks on some variations in psychoanalytic technique.
Bemerkungen über einige Variation der psychoanalytischen Technik. Psyche 1959-60, 13:594-608, 635-640
Abs SLP An Surv Psa 1958, 9:344-345. JLS An Surv Psa 1958, 9:349-350. Agorio, R. Rev urug Psa 1965, 7:380

81452 Some considerations on free association. (Read at Western New Engl Psa Soc, 20 Oct 1962; at Am Psa Ass, 9 Dec 1962) J Am Psa Ass 1963, 11:451-473
Abs Dubcovsky, S. Rev Psicoanál 1963, 20:393. Ennis, J. Q 1964, 33:454

81453 Some problems of ego psychology. (Read at NY Psa Soc, 26 Feb 1963)
Abs Margolis, N. M. Q 1963, 32:468-470

S-52745 Some remarks on the role of speech in psychoanalytic technique.
Abs SG An Surv Psa 1956, 7:319-321. Baranger, W. Rev urug Psa 1961-62, 4:370

S-52746 Some thoughts on interpretation in the theory and practice of psycho-analysis. Psa Clin Inter 162-188
Abs EMW An Surv Psa 1957, 8:251-252

81454 Symptom formation and character formation. Contribution to discus-sion of prepublished papers by Lampl-de Groot and Arlow (iii). J 1964, 45:155-157
French: RFPsa 1966, 30:243-247
Abs EVN Q 1966, 35:454-455

See Hartmann, Heinz

REVIEW OF:
81455 Ariès, P. L'Enfant et la Vie Familiale sous l'Ancien Régime. Q 1962, 31:559-560

LÖFGREN, L. BÖRJE

81456 A case of bronchial asthma with unusual dynamic factors, treated by psychotherapy and psycho-analysis. (Read at Swedish Psa Soc, Sept 1960) J 1961, 42:414-423
Abs WPK Q 1962, 31:578

81457 Castration anxiety and the body ego. (Read at Int Psa Cong, July 1967) J 1968, 49:408-412

81458 Comments on "Swedish psychiatry." P 1959, 116:83

81459 Contributor to Snellman, A. Proctology, Copenhagen 1958

81460 Difficulties and ambiguities in using "results" as an evaluating norm in psychiatry. M 1960, 33:95-103

81461 Excitation, anxiety, affect, some tentative reformulations. (Read at Int Psa Cong, July-Aug 1963) J 1964, 45:280-285
Abs EVN Q 1966, 35:460

81462 Medicinske masseundersögelser. Teoretiska synpunkter. [Mass screening examination. Theoretical views.] Nord Med 1959
81463 Nagelbitning—gummilappar, paladonskenor eller psykoterapi? [Nail-biting—rubber protection, paladon covers or psychotherapy?] Sv Läkartidning 1950, 47:1729
81464 Några psykoterapeutiska metoder utanför psykoanalysens ram. [Some psychotherapeutic methods outside the framework of psychoanalysis.] Nord psyk Medl 1959, 13:7-17
81465 Några teoretiska reflexioner om förhållandet mellan nykterister och alkoholister. [Some theoretical notes on the relation between alcoholics and total abstainers.] Soc med Tidskr 1958, 35:401-404
81466 On weeping. (Read at Int Psa Cong, July 1965) J 1966, 47:375-383 Abs Cuad Psa 1967, 3:164. EVN Q 1968, 37:314
81467 (Reporter) Psychoanalytic theory of affects. (Panel: Am Psa Ass, Dec 1967) J Am Psa Ass 1968, 16:638-650
81468 Psykoanalys. [Psychoanalysis.] Sv Tandläkare-Tidskr 1963, 56:663-675, 735-742
81469 Recent publications on parapsychology. J Am Psa Ass 1968, 16:146-178
81470 Sedativa och hypnotika. [Sedative and hypnotic drugs.] Nord Med 1954, 53:220
81471 Synpunkter på jagstrukturen hos patienter på psykiatrisk klinik. [Notes on the ego structure of patients in an open hospital setting.] Nord psyk Medl 1959, 13:1-7
81472 Testing the foreign doctor. Resident Physician 1960, 6(11):66-70
81473 Två körkortsärenden. [On the psychiatric prediction of the ability to drive safely.] Sv Läkartidning 1958, 55:3300-3305
81474 Varför köper folk pornografi? [Why do people buy pornography?] Hörde NI 1953, 12:881
81475 Vem var Freud? [Who was Freud?] Psykisk Hälsa 1964, 5:66-75
81476 Vetenskap, statistik och psykiatri. [Science, statistics and psychiatry.] Nord Med 1958, 60:1379

TRANSLATION OF:
Thompson, C. & Mullahy, P. [33274]

LÖFGREN, ULLA

81477 Child psychodiagnosis. Nord Psykol 1965, 17:177-283

LOFTUS, THOMAS A.

81478 Behavioral and psychoanalytic aspects of anovulatory amenorrhea. Fertility & Sterility 1962, 13:20-28
81479 Meaning and Methods of Diagnosis in Clinical Psychiatry. Phila: Lea & Febiger 1960, 160 p
81480 (& Crouse, F. R.; Pandelidis, P. K.) Mental health. Prog Neurol Psychiat 1962, 17:412-420
81481 (& Whitcomb, D. T.; Plutzky, M.) Mental health. Prog Neurol Psychiat 1963, 18:505-515
81482 (& Mashikian, H. S.) Mental health. Prog Neurol Psychiat 1964, 19:505-512

81483 (& Preble, E.; Bradlow, P. A.; McLeod, S. W.) Mental health. Prog
       Neurol Psychiat 1965, 20:600-607
81484 Mental hygiene. Prog Neurol Psychiat 1961, 16:416-424

LOGGEM, MANUEL VAN

See Musaph, Herman

LOGSDON, F. M.

81485 Age-regression in diagnosis and treatment of acrophobia. Amer J clin
       Hyp 1960, 3:108-109

LOHMANN, R.

81486 [Pictures from the subconscious as a methodical aid to psychodiag-
       nosis and therapy of anorexia nervosa.] (Ger) Verh Dtsch Ges inn
       Med 1967, 73:725-729

LOHRENZ, J. G.

See Hunter, Robin C. A.

LOHRENZ, LEANDER J.

See Gardner, Riley W.

LOMAS, PETER

81487 The concept of maternal love. Ps 1962, 25:256-262
81488 Defensive organization and puerperal breakdown. M 1960, 33:61-66
81489 Dread of envy as an aetiological factor in puerperal breakdown. M
       1960, 33:105-112
81490 Family interaction and the sick role. In Wisdom, J. O. & Wolff, H. H.
       The Role of Psychosomatic Disorder in Adult Life, London: Pergamon
       1965
81491 Family role and identity formation. J 1961, 42:371-380
       Abs WPK Q 1962, 31:557
81492 Observations on the psychotherapy of puerperal breakdown. M 1961,
       34:245-253
81493 The origin of the need to be special. M 1962, 35:339-346
       Abs Greenberg, R. M. Q 1963, 32:458
81494 Passivity and failure of identity development. J 1965, 46:438-454
       Abs EVN Q 1967, 36:625
81495 (Ed) The Predicament of the Family: A Psycho-Analytical Symposium.
       London: HIP; NY: IUP 1967, 219 p
       Abs J Am Psa Ass 1969, 17:268-269
81496 Psychoanalysis: Freudian or existential? In Rycroft, C. *Psychoanalysis
       Observed.* London: Constable; NY: Coward-McCann 1966
81497 Ritualistic elements in the management of childbirth. M 1966, 39:207-
       213
81498 The significance of post-partum breakdown. In author's *The Predica-
       ment of the Family* 126-139

81499 The study of family relationships in contemporary society—introduction. In author's *The Predicament of the Family* 9-25

81500 Taboo and illness. M 1969, 42:33-39

REVIEWS OF:

81501 Brody, S. Passivity: A Study of Its Development and Expression in Boys. J 1965, 46:394

81502 Ehrenwald, J. Neurosis in the Family and Patterns of Psychosocial Defense: A Study of Psychiatric Epidemiology. J 1965, 46:268-270

81503 Laing, R. D. & Esterson, A. Sanity, Madness and the Family, Vol. I: Families of Schizophrenics. J 1965, 46:390-392

81504 Levita, D. J. de: The Concept of Identity. J 1967, 48:124

LOMBARD, EVERETT E.

81505 (& St. Clair, W. F.) Transference in a one-team mental hygiene clinic. Dis nerv Sys 1962, 23:93-94

LOMONACO, S.

See Witkin, Herman A.

LONDON, LOUIS S.

81506 Homosexual panic with hallucinations—a case study. Med Times 1964, 92:175-189

LONDON, PERRY

81507 (& Rosenhan, D.) (Eds) Foundations of Abnormal Psychology. NY: Holt, Rinehart & Winston 1968, x + 644 p

81508 The Modes and Morals of Psychotherapy. NY: Holt, Rinehart & Winston 1964, x + 278 p
Rv Haley, J. R 1965, 52:489-492

81509 (& Schulman, R. E.; Black, M. S.) Religion, guilt, and ethical standards. Soc Psych 1964, 63:145-159

See Black, Michael S.

LONG, B. H.

See Ziller, Robert C.

LONG, ROBERT T.

See Jessner, Lucie

ABSTRACT OF:

81510 Erikson, E. H. The psychosexual and psychosocial dimension in the interpretation of dreams. Bull Phila Ass Psa 1961, 11:38-39

LONGABAUCH, RICHARD

See Eldred, Stanley H.

LONGHI, S.
See Agresti, Enzo

LONGSTRETH, LANGDON EWERT
81511 Psychological Development of the Child. NY: Ronald Pr 1968, 571 p

LÔO, P.
81512 Les Névroses. [The Neuroses.] Paris: Vigot Frères 1960, 216 p

LOOMIE, LEO S.
S-52779 (& Rosen, V. H.; Stein, M. H.) Ernst Kris and the gifted adolescent project.
       Abs Steinberg, S. An Surv Psa 1958, 9:289-291
81513 Some ego considerations in the silent patient. J Am Psa Ass 1961, 9:56-78
       Abs Soifer, R. Rev Psicoanál 1961, 18:400. FB Q 1962, 31:288-289. SAS RFPsa 1962, 26:615

LOOMIS, EARL A., JR.
S-52786 The concurrent presentation of a rare detail in the dreams of two patients.
       Abs IS An Surv Psa 1956, 7:229-230
81514 Pastoral counseling. Ency Ment Hlth 1449-1457
81515 (& Shugart, G.) Play, fantasy, and symptoms in psychotic children and their families. Penn Psychiat Q 1961, 1:29-35
81516 Religion and psychiatry. Ency Ment Hlth 1748-1759
81517 The Self in Pilgrimage. NY: Harper 1960, xvii + 109 p
S-52798 The symbolic meaning of the elbow.
       Abs An Surv Psa 1955, 6:173
S-52800 The use of checkers in handling certain resistances in child therapy and child analysis. In Haworth, M. R. *Child Psychotherapy*, NY/London: Basic Books 1964, 407-411
       Abs BEM An Surv Psa 1957, 8:235

REVIEW OF:
81518 Hammond, G. B. Man in Estrangement: A Comparison of the Thought of Paul Tillich and Erich Fromm. Q 1968, 37:455-456

LOPES, L.
81519 [Psychosomatic aspects of glaucoma.] (Por) J bras Psiquiat 1966, 15:5-13

LOPEZ, DAVIDE
81520 Alcune perplessità sulla psicoterapia dei gruppo. [Some problems in psychotherapy in groups.] Riv Psa 1965, 11:57-65
81521 Discussion of Muratori, A. M. "Sogni di progresso et sogni di regresso nella pratica psicoanalitica." Riv Psa 1963, 9:126
81522 Discussion of Roch, M. "Du surmoi, heritier du complexe d'oedipe." RFPsa 1967, 31:1089-1090

81523 Rileggendo Freud: il caso Dora. [Rereading Freud: the case of Dora.] Riv Psa 1967, 13:215-262

LÓPEZ, R. E.

81524 La psicoterapia dinámica breve. [Brief dynamic psychotherapy.] Acta psiquiát psicol Amér Latina 1967, 13:260-262

LÓPEZ, SHEILLA L. DE

See Rolla, Edgardo H.

LÓPEZ-IBOR, JUAN JOSÉ

81525 [Anxiety as a basic disorder in neuroses and its treatment.] (Ger) Dtsch Med J 1961, 12:572-577
81526 Basic anxiety as the core of neurosis. Acta Psychiat Scand 1965, 41:329-332
81527 Der Einfluss der Psychotherapie auf die klinische Nosologie. [The influence of psychotherapy on clinical nosology.] Acta psychother psychosom 1962, 10:409-418
81528 (Ed) Proceedings of the Fourth World Congress of Psychiatry. Amsterdam/NY/London: Excerpta Medica Found 1967-68, 3203 p
81529 Psychiatry, II: Symposia. Amsterdam: Excerpta Medica Found 1968, 675 p
81530 Sobre la psicopatologica de las depresiones. [Psychopathology of depressions.] In Kranz, H. *Psychopathologie Heute*, Stuttgart: Thieme 1962, 139-144

LÓPEZ PIÑERO, JOSÉ MARÍA

81531 Orígenes Históricos del Concepto de Neurosis. [Historical Origins of the Concept of Neurosis.] Valencia: Cátedra e Instituto de Historia de la Medicina 1963, 206 + vii p

LORAND, RHODA L.

81532 How important are the first feeding experiences in the life of the child? Why Rep 281-295
81533 Love, Sex and the Teenager. NY: Macmillan 1963, 288 p
Rv Geleerd, E. R. Q 1966, 35:608-609. Woltmann, A. G. R 1966, 53:303-308
81534 Therapy of learning problems. Adolescents 251-272
81535 What forces mold the sex life of the teenager? Why Rep 305-323

REVIEW OF:
81536 Donahue, G. T. & Nichtern, S. Teaching the Troubled Child. Q 1967, 36:304

LORAND, SANDOR

81537 Adolescent depression. (Read at Am Psa Ass, Dec 1965) J 1967, 48:53-60
Abs EVN Q 1969, 38:157

81538 (& Schneer, H. I.) (Eds) Adolescents: Psychoanalytic Approach to Problems and Therapy. (Foreword: Englehardt, D. M.) NY: Harper & Row 1961, xvi + 378 p; NY: Dell 1961, 378 p; NY: Dell 1965, xiv + 378 p
       Rv Hellman, I. J 1963, 44:514. Wermer, H. Q 1963, 32:114-115
S-20938 Anorexia nervosa: report of a case. In Kaufman, M. R. & Heiman, M. *Evolution of Psychosomatic Concepts*, NY: IUP 1964, 298-319
81539 Biographical notes on Sandor Ferenczi (1875-1933). (Read at Psa Ass NY, 16 Dec 1963)
       Abs Lilleskov, R. Q 1964, 33:468-470
81540 The body image and the psychiatric evaluation of patients for plastic surgery. J Hillside Hosp 1961, 10:224-232
       Abs JA Q 1962, 31:586
81541 Clinical and theoretical aspects of resistance. Psychother Psychosom 1967, 15:162-178. In Philippopoulos, G. S. *Dynamics in Psychiatry*, Basel/NY: Karger 1968, 78-94
81542 Discussion of Lindon, J. A. "On Freud's concept of dream-action." Psa Forum 1966, 1:38-39
S-52822 Dream interpretation in the Talmud.
       Abs JAL An Surv Psa 1957, 8:179-180
S-20955 Fetishism in statu nascendi. PT Pervers 211-221
81543 Fragments of psychoanalytic therapy in a case of spastic colitis. J Hillside Hosp 1968, 17:223-229
81544 Introduction to Kurian, M. & Hand, M. H. *Lectures in Dynamic Psychiatry*, NY: IUP 1963, 4-5
81545 Modifications in classical psychoanalysis. (Read at Am Psa Ass, Dec 1961) Q 1963, 32:192-204
81546 Preface. Adolescents xiii-xiv
81547 Present trends in psychoanalytic therapy. Curr psychiat Ther 1963, 3:68-73
81548 Psycho-analytic therapy of religious devotees. (A theoretical and technical contribution). (Read at NY Psa Soc, 15 Nov 1960; at Am Psa Ass, 10 Dec 1961) J 1962, 43:50-56
       Abs Donadeo, J. Q 1961, 30:316-318. FTL Q 1963, 32:284
81549 Reflections on the development of psychoanalysis in New York from 1925 to the present. (Read at Psa Ass NY, 19 April 1965) J 1969, 50:589-595
       Abs Wilson, C. P. Q 1966, 35:171-172
81550 Regression. Technical and theoretical problems. J Hillside Hosp 1963, 12:67-79
       Abs JA Q 1967, 36:135
81551 The role of the psychoanalyst in marital crisis. Marriage Relat 225-236
81552 Sándor Ferenczi 1873-1933. Pioneer of pioneers. Psa Pioneers 14-35
81553 (& Schneer, H. I.) Sexual deviations, III: Fetishism, transvestitism, masochism, sadism, exhibitionism, voyeurism, incest, pedophilia, and bestiality. Compreh Txbk Psychiat 977-988
81554 Should a parent appear nude before his children? Why Rep 343-350
81555 Some basic concepts of the dynamics of therapy. In Kurian, M. & Hand, M. H. *Lectures in Dynamic Psychiatry*, NY: IUP 1963, 6-56

S-52828 (& Feldman, S.) The symbolism of teeth in dreams.
Abs An Surv Psa 1955, 6:239-241
S-52830 (& Console, W. A.) Therapeutic results in psychoanalytic treatment
without fee (observation on therapeutic results).
Abs GLG An Surv Psa 1958, 9:411-412
S-52831 The therapy of perversions. PT Pervers 41-55
81556 Treatment of adolescents. Adolescents 235-250

LORAS, O.

81557 L'angoisse obsessionnelle du mot chez un schizophrène. [A schizophrenic's obsessional anxiety over words.] Évolut psychiat 1960,
25:585-616
81558 La psychoanalyse dans le mouvement psychanalytique contemporain.
[Psychoanalysis in the current psychoanalytic movement.] Concours
Méd 1963, 85:5767-5770
81559 [Various time-space-language aspects in psychopathology. Records of
analysis and psychotherapy.] (Fr) Évolut Psychiat 1969, 34:65-106

LORCH, S.

See McGuire, Michael T.

LORDI, WILLIAM MICHAEL

81560 (& Silverberg, J.) Infantile autism: a family approach. Int J grp PT
1964, 14:360-365

LORENZ, KONRAD

81561 On Aggression. (Tr: Wilson, M. K.) NY: Harcourt, Brace & World
1963, 1966, xiv + 306 p
Rv Blum, H. P. Q 1967, 36:609-612. Radomisli, M. R 1968, 55:57-61
81562 On aggression. Fish, birds, rats and men(I). Encounter 1966, 27(2):29-
40
81563 Discussion of Devereux, G. "The cannibalistic impulses of parents."
Psa Forum 1966, 1:128-129
81564 Ecce homo! Fish, birds, rats and men(II). From author's On Aggression. Encounter 1966, 27(3):25-39. Insight 1968, 6(4):2-19
81565 A scientist's credo. In Gaskill, H. S. Counterpoint: Libidinal Object
and Subject, NY: IUP 1963, 6-26
81566 Das sogenannte Böse (zur Naturgeschichte der Aggression). [The So-
Called Evil (On the Natural History of Aggression).] Vienna: Borotha-
Scheoler 1963, 391 p

LORENZER, ALFRED

81567 Ein Abwehrsyndrom bei traumatischen Verläufen. (Read at Frankfurter
Psa Cong, Oct 1964) Psyche 1965, 18:685-700
81568 Form und Funktion. [Form and function.] Bauwelt Bd 1968, 59:961
81569 Methodologische Probleme der Untersuchung traumatischer Neurosen.
[Methodological problems of the examination of traumatic neuroses.]
Psyche 1968, 22:861-874
Abs J 1969, 50:400

81570 Planung—wofür: [Planning—for what?] In *Sozialpsychologische Überlegungen zu Stadtplanung und Raumordnung*, Bundesbaublatt 1964,
296

81571 Some observations on the latency symptoms in patients suffering from
persecution. Sequelae. (Read at Int Psa Cong, July 1967) J 1968,
49:316-318
      Abs LHR Q 1969, 38:669

81572 Städtebau: Funktionalismus und Sozialmontage? Zur sozialpsycholog-
ischen Funktion der Architektur. [Town planning: functionalism and
social display. On the social-psychological function of architecture.]
In Berndt, H. et al: *Architektur als Ideologie*, Frankfurt: Suhrkamp
1968, 51

81573 (& Thomä, H.) Über die zweiphasige Symptomentwicklung bei traumatischen Neurosen. [On the two-phase symptom development in
traumatic neuroses.] Psyche 1965, 18:674-684

81574 Zum Begriff der traumatischen Neurose. [On the concept of traumatic
neurosis.] Psyche 1966, 20:481-492

See Berndt, Heide; Mitscherlich, Alexander

LORENZINI, GIACOMO

81575 Freud e la Psicanalisi. [Freud and Psychoanalysis.] Turin: Libereria
Dottrina Cristiana 1960, 60 p

LORGI, I.

See Goldfarb, William

LORIOD, J.

81576 Observation clinique d'un malade psychosomatique. [Clinical observation of a psychosomatic patient.] RFPsa 1969, 33:255-272

LORMEAU, Y.

See Marchais, P.

LORR, MAURICE

81577 (& McNair, D. M.) An analysis of professed psychotherapeutic techniques. J consult Psychol 1964, 28:265-271

81578 (& McNair, D. M.; Russell, S. B.) Characteristics of psychiatric out-
patients receiving tranquilizers. Clin Psych 1960, 16:442-446

81579 (& McNair, D. M.) Correlates of length of psychotherapy. Clin Psych
1964, 20:497-504

81580 (& McNair, D. M.; Michaux, W. M.; Raskin, A.) Frequency of treatment and change in psychotherapy. ASP 1962, 64:281-292. In Goldstein, A. P. & Dean, S. J. *The Investigation of Psychotherapy*, NY:
Wiley 1966, 238-249

81581 (& McNair, D. M.) Methods relating to evaluation of therapeutic outcome. Meth Res PT 573-594

See McNair, Douglas M.; Michaux, William W.

LORTON, WILLIAM L.

See Beckett, Peter G. S.

LOSSERAND, JEAN

81582 Psychopathologie des transports. [Psychopathology of transportation.]
Évolut psychiat 1964, 29:621-646

LOSSY, FRANK T.

81583 The charge of suggestion as a resistance in psycho-analysis. (Read at
San Francisco Psa Soc, Oct 1961) J 1962, 43:448-467
    Abs EVN Q 1965, 34:308

ABSTRACTS OF:

81584 Astley, M. R. C. Comment on Dr Lorand's paper, "Psycho-analytic
therapy of religious devotees." Q 1963, 32:284

81585 Badal, D. W. The repetitive cycle in depression. Q 1963, 32:287

81586 Elles, G. The mute sad-eyed child: collateral analysis in a disturbed
family. Q 1963, 32:284

81587 Engel, G. L. Anxiety and depression-withdrawal: the primary affects
of unpleasure. Q 1963, 32:285-286

81588 Gottschalk, L. A. & Whitman, R. M. Some typical complications mobilized by the psycho-analytic procedure. Q 1963, 32:287

81589 Guntrip, H. The manic-depressive problem in the light of the schizoid
process. Q 1963, 32:286

81590 Hampshire, S. Disposition and memory. Q 1963, 32:284-285

81591 Harris, I. D. Dreams about the analyst. Q 1963, 32:287-288

81592 James, M. Infantile narcissistic trauma. Observations on Winnicott's
work in *Infant Care and Child Development*. Q 1963, 32:285

81593 Khan, M. M. R. Dream psychology and the evolution of the psychoanalytic situation. Q 1963, 32:283

81594 Lorand, S. Psycho-analytic therapy of religious devotees. Q 1963,
32:284

81595 Miller, S. C. Ego-autonomy in sensory deprivation, isolation and stress.
Q 1963, 32:283

81596 Rycroft, C. An observation on the defensive function of schizophrenic
thinking and delusion-formation. Q 1963, 32:283-284

81597 Schiffer, I. The psycho-analytic study of the development of a conversion symptom. Q 1963, 32:288

81598 Stokes, A. On resignation. Q 1963, 32:288-289

81599 Weissman, P. Structural considerations in overt male bisexuality. Q
1963, 32:288

81600 Wisdom, J. O. Comparison and development of the psycho-analytical
theories of melancholia. Q 1963, 32:286-287

LOSTIA, MARCELLO

81601 Valore diagnostico dello Z-test individuale. [Diagnostic value of the
individual Z test.] Boll Psicol appl 1967, (79):81-82; (80):121-138

LOUIS, V.

81602 [On the so-called compensation neurosis.] (Ger) Praxis 1967, 56:1125-1127

LOUISELL, D.

See Diamond, Bernard L.

LOURIE, REGINALD S.

81603 The adolescent's crisis today (reactor). NYSJM 1967, 67:2011-2013
81604 Alcoholism in children. Ops 1943, 13:322
81605 Anorexia nervosa. Clin Proc Child Hosp DC 1940, 4:91
81606 (& Cole, M.; Straight, B.; Robinson, M.) Anorexia nervosa. Clin Proc Child Hosp DC 1958, 14:49
81607 (& Meers, D. R.) Assessment of childhood development: review of *Normality and Pathology in Childhood: Assessments of Development*, by A. Freud. Children 1966, 13:3-32
81608 Basic problems involved in the use of the newer neuropharmacological drugs in childhood. Child Res Psychopharmacol 1961
81609 Basic science and the future of orthopsychiatry. Ops 1958, 28:445
81610 Beyond anatomy. Pediatrics 1967, 39(4)
81611 Child psychiatry. Ency Ment Hlth 313-320
81612 Child psychiatry in the USSR. J Amer Acad Child Psychiat 1963, 2:569
81613 Child suicides seen related to infants' concepts of death. Pediat Herald 1966, 7(2)
81614 Clinical studies of attempted suicide in childhood. Clin Proc Child Hosp DC 1966, 22(June):163
81615 Commentary on "A history of the care and study of the mentally retarded" by Leo Kanner. P 1964, 121:620
81616 Comments on psychotherapy of character disorders. In *I Disturbi Del Carattere Nell'Eta Evolutiva: U.E.P. II Congresso Europeo di Pedopsichiatria*, Tipografia Porziuncola, Assisi 1963, 1:206
81617 (& Rioch, M. J.; Schwartz, S.) The concept of a training program for child development counselors. Amer J Publ Hlth 1967, 57:1754-1758
81618 The contributions of child psychiatry to the pathogenesis of hyperactivity in children. Clin Proc Child Hosp DC 1963, 19:247
81619 (& Layman, E. M.; Millican, F. K.; Takahashi, L.) Cultural influences and symptom choice: clay eating customs in relation to the etiology of pica. Psychol Rec 1963, 13:249
81620 (& Meers, D. R.) "Culturally determined" retardation: clinical exploration of variability and etiology. n.p., n.d. (Multilithographed) 35 p
81621 Delinquency prevention and the health worker. Children 1955, 2:168
81622 Diagnosis in adolescent problems. Clin Proc Child Hosp DC 1967, 23:33-40
81623 (& Chandler, C. A.; Peters, A. D.) Early Child Care. The New Perspectives. NY: Atherton Pr 1968, 385 p
81624 Emotional difficulties encountered in children with poliomyelitis. Clin Proc Child Hosp DC 1953, 9:130
81625 Emotional factors encountered during the treatment of eczema in infants. Clin Proc Child Hosp DC 1957, 13:41

81626 The emotionally disturbed child. In *Proceedings of Allenbury Conference*, Penna Dept Publ Welfare & NIMH 1963, p 13

81627 Familial dysautonomia, psychological aspects. Ops 1957, 27

81628 Foreword to Meers, D. R. "A diagnostic profile of psychopathology in a latency child." Psa St C 1966, 21:483-484

81629 (& Marans, A. E.) Hypotheses regarding the effects of child-rearing patterns of the disadvantaged child. In Deutsch, M. et al: *The Disadvantaged Child*, Seattle, Wash: Special Child Publ 1967

81630 The impact of the mentally defective child on the family unit. Clin Proc Child Hosp DC 1953, 9:25

81631 (& Silber, E.) Juvenile schizophrenia. Clin Proc Child Hosp DC 1957, 13(8):159

81632 (& Ozer, M. N.; Fishman, M.) Learning problems in children, II: Emotional aspects. Clin Proc Child Hosp DC 1966, 22(July-Aug):193

81633 Mental health aspects of venereal disease in adolescents. Arch environ Hlth 1966, 12:684

81634 Mental health in school age children. Proc Nemours Found Conf 1963, 12:44

81635 The mental health role of the health services in the problem of juvenile delinquency. Clin Proc Child Hosp DC 1955, 11:191

81636 New mental health services for children. George Wash Univ Mag 1966, Fall

81637 Mental retardation in the USSR. In *Proceedings of the Conference on Mental Retardation*, DC Dept of Public Welfare 1962, 3:10

81638 (& Werkman, S. L.) Normal psychologic development and psychiatric problems of adolescence. In Cooke, R. & Levin, S. *The Biologic Basis of Pediatric Practice*, NY/Toronto/Sydney: McGraw-Hill 1968, 1662-1670

81639 Pediatric psychiatric aspects of obesity in children. Pediatrics 1957, 20:553

81640 The pediatrician and the handling of terminal illness. Pediatrics 1962, 32:447

81641 Pediatrics and society (comment). Pediatrics 1958, 21

81642 Personality development and the genesis of neurosis. Clin Proc Child Hosp DC 1967, 23(6):167

81643 The physician and the prevention of juvenile delinquency. Med Ann DC 1961, 28:274

81644 Pica in Children as a Pattern of Early Addiction in Psychopathology of Addiction. NY: Grune & Stratton 1958

81645 (Ed) Planning Psychiatric Service for Children in the Community Mental Health Program. Wash DC: Am Psychiat Ass 1964, 47 p

81646 (& Millican, F. K.; Layman, E. M.; Takahashi, L.; Dublin, C.) The prevalence of ingestion and mouthing of non-edible substances by children. Clin Proc Child Hosp DC 1962, 18(3):207

81647 Problems of diagnosis and treatment: communication between pediatrician and psychiatrist; retrospect and prospect. Pediatrics 1966, 37:1000-1004

81648 Psychopathic behavior in infants and children: critical survey of existing concepts (pediatric-psychiatric viewpoint). Ops 1951, 21:237

81649   The psychopathic delinquent child, some basic mental factors. Ops 1950, 20:229

81650   The role of individual constitutional differences ﾠin early personality development. Clin Proc Child Hosp DC 1966, 22:282-284

81651   Role of rhythmic patterns in childhood. P 1949, 105:653

81652   Rumination in infancy. Clin Proc Child Hosp DC 1950, 6:337

81653   Schizophrenic-like psychoses in children. Clin Proc Child Hosp DC 1954, 10:6

81654   Social and psychological aspects, President's Panel on Mental Retardation. Amer J Dis Childr 1964, 108:324

81655   Studies of head banging, bed rocking and related rhythmic patterns. Clin Proc Child Hosp DC 1949, 5(11):295

81656   Studies on the prognosis in schizophrenic-like psychoses in childhood. P 1943, 99:542

81657   Suicide and attempted suicide in children and adolescents. Texas Med 1967, 63(11):58-63. In Yochelson, L. *Symposium on Suicide,* Wash DC: George Wash Univ Pr 1967, 93-105

81658   (& Walsh, B. J.) Sydenham's chorea. Clin Proc Child Hosp DC 1958, 14:16

81659   The teaching of child psychiatry in pediatrics. J Amer Acad Child Psychiat 1962, 1:477

81660   (& Rioch, M. J.; Schwartz, S.) Training program for child development counsellors. Child Care Publ 1967

81661   Treatment of psychosomatic problems in infants (with emphasis on rumination). Clin Proc Child Hosp DC 1955, 11:142

81662   (& Layman, E. H.) Waiting room observation as a technique of analysis of communication behavior in children and their parents. In *Psychopathology of Communication,* NY: Grune & Stratton 1957

81663   What to tell the parents of the child with cancer. Clin Proc Child Hosp DC 1961, 17:91

81664   (& Layman, E. M.; Millican, F. K.) Why children eat things that are not food. Children 1963, 10:143-146

See Chandler, Caroline; Cytryn, Leon; Krug, Othilda; Millican, Frances K.; Werkman, Sidney L.

LÖVAAS, O. IVAR

81665   Effect of exposure to symbolic aggression on aggressive behavior. Child Develpm 1961, 32:37-44

81666   Some studies on the treatment of childhood schizophrenia. In Shlien, J. M. et al: *Research in Psychotherapy, Vol. III,* Wash DC: APA 1968, 103-121

LOVE, J. G.

81667   (& Emmett, J. L.) "Asymptomatic" protruded lumbar disk as a cause of urinary retention: preliminary report. Mayo Clin Proc 1967, 42:249-257

LOVE, SIDNEY

81668 (& Feldman, Y.) The disguised cry for help: narcissistic mothers and their children. PPR 1961, 48(2):52-67

LOVELAND, NATHENE

81669 The relation Rorschach: a technique for studying interaction. JNMD 1967, 145:93-105

LOVELL, L. L.

See Horowitz, Frances D.

LOVSHIN, L. L.

81670 Anorectal symptoms of emotional origin. Dis Colon Rectum 1961, 4:399-402

LOW-BEER, MARIANNE

TRANSLATION OF:
Hartmann, H. [13658]

LOWEN, ALEXANDER

81671 The Betrayal of the Body. NY: Macmillan 1967, 307 p
81672 Love and Orgasm. NY: Macmillan 1965; London: Staples 1966, 303 p
   Rv Krich, A. R 1966, 53:310-312. Woltmann, A. G. R 1966, 53:303-308

REVIEWS OF:
81673 Fried, E. The Ego in Love and Sexuality. PPR 1961, 48(3):126-129
81674 Higgins, M. & Raphael, C. M. (Eds) Reich Speaks of Freud: Wilhelm Reich Discusses His Work and His Relationship with Sigmund Freud. R 1969, 56:355-357

LOWENFELD, HENRY

81675 Betrachtungen zu einem Fall von Zwangsneurose im Wandel der Zivilisation. [Observations on a case of compulsion neurosis in a changing civilization.] Psyche 1964, 18:191-203
81676 Comment on Dr. Grunberger's and Dr. Wangh's papers, "The antisemite and the oedipal conflict" and "National socialism and the genocide of the Jews. A psycho-analytic study of historical event." J 1964, 45:396-398
   Abs EVN Q 1966, 35:464-465
81677 Obituary: Ludwig Binswanger 1881-1966. J Am Psa Ass 1967, 15:459-460
81678 Über den Niedergang des Teufelsglaubens und seine Folgen für die Massenpsychologie. Psyche 1967, 21:513-519
   The decline in belief in the devil. The consequence for group psychology. Q 1969, 38:455-462

REVIEWS OF:
81679 Freud, S. & Bullitt, W. C. Thomas Woodrow Wilson. A Psychological
       Study. Q 1967, 36:271-279
81680 Laing, R. D. The Self and Others. Further Studies in Sanity and Mad-
       ness. J 1963, 44:116-118
81681 Mitscherlich, A. Auf dem Weg zur vaterlosen Gesellschaft. Ideen zur
       Sozialpsychologie. Q 1964, 33:427-430
81682 Storr, A. Human Aggression. Q 1969, 38:491-494
81683 Veith, I. Hysteria: The History of a Disease. J 1968, 49:101-103

LOWENFELD, JOHN

81684 Negative affect as a causal factor in the occurrence of repression, sub-
       ception, and perceptual defense. J Pers 1961, 29:54-63

LOWENFELD, YELA

REVIEWS OF:
81685 Klein, M. Narrative of a Child Analysis. Q 1963, 32:409-415
81686 Klein, M. Our Adult World and Other Essays. Q 1964, 33:582-584

LOWENHAUPT, ELIZABETH

S-52881 Two cases of chicken phobia.
        Abs An Surv Psa 1955, 6:146-147

LOWER, RICHARD B.

81687 On Raskolnikov's dreams in Dostoyevsky's Crime and Punishment.
       (Read at Am Psa Ass, 10-13 May 1968) J Am Psa Ass 1969, 17:728-742
81688 Psychotherapy of neurotic dependency. P 1967, 124:514-519

LOWINGER, PAUL

81689 (& Dobie, S.; Mood, D.) Does the race, religion or social class of the
       psychiatric patient affect his treatment? Sci Psa 1966, 9:129-147
81690 Evaluation of mephenoxalone in a single and double-blind design.
       P 1963, 120:66-67
81691 (& Dobie, S.) An evaluation of the role of the psychiatrist's personality
       in the interview. Sci Psa 1964, 7:211-226
81692 Psychiatrists against psychiatry. P 1966, 123:490-494
81693 Sex, Selma and segregation: a psychiatrist's reaction. Int J soc Psychiat
       1968, 14:119-124
81694 (& Dobie, S.) Studies of the therapist in psychotherapy. Proc IV World
       Cong Psychiat 1966, 2818-2820

       See Darrow, Charlotte

LOWNAU, H.

81695 [The adolescent and sexuality from the neurotic and psychological
       viewpoint.] (Ger) Prax Kinderpsychol 1968, 17:242-250

LOWNAU, H. W.

81696 [Disorders of intentionality exemplified by suicide in childhood and adolescence.] (Ger) Acta paedopsychiat 1964, 31:12-19

LOWREY, O. W.

See Abram, Harry S.

LOWRY, RICHARD

81697 Galilean and Newtonian influences on psychological thought. AJP 1969, 82:391-400
81698 Psychoanalysis and the philosophy of physicalism. J Hist behav Sci 1967, 3:156-167

LOWTZKY, FANNY

S-52889 Das Problem des Masochismus und des Strafbedürfnisses im Lichte klinischer Erfahrung.
Abs EW An Surv Psa 1956, 7:220-221

LOWY, FREDERICK

See Wylie, Harold W., Jr.

LOWY, SAMUEL

S-52890 (& Gutheil, E. A.) Active analytic therapy (Stekel).
Abs AS An Surv Psa 1956, 7:352-353
81699 New research results in practical dream interpretation. R 1967, 54: 510-526
Abs SRS Q 1969, 38:162
81700 Principles of Rational Dreamanalysis. NY: Privately printed 1960
81701 Should You Be Psychoanalyzed? NY: Philos Libr 1963; NY: Citadel Pr 1967, 308 p
S-52892 Transference in modified analytical theories; supplementary communication.
Abs An Surv Psa 1955, 6:361-362

LOYO, MIGUEL

See Villalobos, J. Jesus

LU, YI-CHUANG

81702 Mother-child role relations in schizophrenia. A comparison of schizophrenic patients with nonschizophrenic siblings. Ps 1961, 24:133-142
Abs HRB Q 1962, 31:428

LUBIN, ALBERT J.

S-52893 A boy's view of Jesus.
Abs RTh J 1961, 42:471
81703 Discussion of Berliner, B. "Psychodynamics of the depressive character." Psa Forum 1966, 1:254-256

81704 The influence of the Russian Orthodox Church on Freud's Wolf-Man:
a hypothesis (with an epilogue based on visits with the Wolf-Man).
Psa Forum 1967, 2:146-162, 170-174, 284-285
81705 A psychoanalytic view of religion. Int Psychiat Clin 1969, 5(4):49-60
81706 Vincent Van Gogh's ear. Q 1961, 30:351-384

REVIEWS OF:
81707 Muensterberger, W. & Axelrad, S. (Eds) The Psychoanalytic Study of
Society, Vol. III. Q 1966, 35:284-289
81708 Waldhorn, H. F. Indications for Psychoanalysis: The Place of the
Dream in Clinical Psychoanalysis. Q 1969, 38:138-141

LUBIN, ALICE W.

See Lubin, Bernard

LUBIN, ARDIE

See Morris, Gary O.; Williams, Harold L.

LUBIN, BERNARD

81709 (& Lubin, A. W.) Bibliography of group psychotherapy 1956-1963.
Group PT 1964, 17:177-230
81710 (& Lubin, A. W.) Group Psychotherapy: A Bibliography of the Literature from 1956 through 1964. East Lansing, Mich: Mich State Univ
Pr 1966, 186 p

LUBIN, MARC

81711 Study of the high rate of male Jewish membership in the profession of
psychoanalysis. Proc Ann Conv APA 1969, 4(2):527-528

LUBITZ, IRIS A.

See Eiduson, Bernice T.

LUBORSKY, LESTER B.

81712 (& Shevrin, H.) Artificial induction of day-residues: an illustration and
examination. (Read at Topeka Psa Soc. 26 Feb 1959; at Phila Ass
Psa, 27 April 1962) Bull Phila Ass Psa 1962, 12:149-167
Abs Silverman, D. Bull Phila Ass Psa 1962, 12:131-134. PLe RFPsa
1967, 31:303
S-52896 (& Shevrin, H.) Dream and day residues: a study of the Poetzl observation.
Abs AaSt An Surv Psa 1956, 7:224-225
81713 (& Shevrin, H.) Forgetting of tachistoscopic exposures as a function of
repression. Percept mot Skills 1962, 14:189-190
81714 (& Blinder, B.) Looking, recalling, and GSR as a function of defense.
JAbP 1965, 70:270-280
81715 Momentary forgetting during psychotherapy and psychoanalysis: a
theory and research method. Psychol Issues 1967, 5:177-217.

81716 A psychoanalytic research on momentary forgetting during free association. Bull Phila Ass Psa 1964, 14:119-137
       Abs PLe RFPsa 1967, 31:308
81717 (& Schimek, J.) Psychoanalytic theories of therapeutic and developmental change: implications for assessment. In Worchel, P. & Byrne, D. *Personality Change,* NY: Wiley 1964
81718 (& Auerbach, A. H.) The symptom-context method: quantitative studies of symptom formation in psychotherapy. J Am Psa Ass 1969, 17:68-99

       See Auerbach, Arthur H.; Hollender, Marc H.; Holt, Robert R.; Shevrin, Howard; Silverman, Lloyd H.; Strupp, Hans H.

LUCA, P. L. DE

81719 (& Sacchettini, B.) Painting as a Means of Psychodiagnostic Research: Relationship with the Rorschach Test. (Psychopathology and Pictorial Expression, Series 2) Basel/NY: Karger 1964, 4 p + 12 plates (in portfolio)

LUCAS, ALEXANDER RALPH

81720 Anorexia nervosa. In Shaw, C. R. *The Psychiatric Disorders of Childhood,* NY: Appleton-Century-Crofts 1966, 287-293
81721 The imagery of Hieronymus Bosch. P 1968, 124:1515-1525

LUCAS, WINAFRED B.

       See Eiduson, Bernice T.; Meyer, Mortimer M.

LUCE, GAY GAER

81722 Current Research on Sleep and Dreams. Bethesda, Md., US Dept of Health, Education, and Welfare, Public Health Service, National Institutes of Health, National Institute of Mental Health, Research Grants Branch; Wash DC: US GPO 1965, vii + 125 p

LUCE, RALPH A., JR.

81723 From hero to robot: masculinity in America—stereotype and reality. R 1967, 54:609-630
       Abs SRS Q 1969, 38:163

LUCHINA, A.

       See Grinberg, León

LUCHINA, ISAAC L.

81724 (& Aizenberg, S.) Una aguda amenaza de muerte: "el infarto de miocardio" (a la lez de las ideas Kleiniana). [An acute premonition of of death—myocardial infarction, in the light of Kleinian ideas.] Rev Psicoanál 1962, 19:103-106
81725 (& Wender, L.) Yo motor, aprendizaje u duelo. El "núcleo paralítico

temprano." [Motor ego, learning and mourning. The early paralytic nucleus.] Rev Psicoanál 1964, 21:227-238

   Abs Vega Q 1965, 34:626

See Schavelzon, Jese

ABSTRACTS OF:

81726 Kaplan, S. M. et al: Hostility in verbal productions and hypnotic dreams of hypertensive patients: studies of groups and individuals. Rev Psicoanál 1961, 18:408

81727 Ruesch, J. Medícina psicosomática y las ciencias de la conducta. Rev Psicoanál 1961, 18:408

81728 Spersman, J. C. et al: Análisis de las resistencias catáneas y de la frecuencia cardiáca en reposo y en circunstancias que producen stress. Rev Psiconanál 1961, 18:408

LUCHINS, ABRAHAM SAMUEL

81729 Group Therapy: A Guide. NY: Random House 1964, x + 170 p

LUCKEY, ELEANORE BRAUN

81730 Marital satisfaction and parent concepts. J consult Psychol 1960, 24: 195-204

LUCKY, ARTHUR WELLINGTON

81731 (& Grigg, A. E.) Repression-sensitization as a variable in deviant responding. Clin Psych 1964, 20:92-93

LÜDERS, WOLFRAM

81732 Bericht über die II. Arbeitstagung der Mitteleuropäischen Psychoanalytischen Vereinigungen, September 1960. [Report on the 2nd workshop of the Middle European Psychoanalytic meeting, September 1960.] Jb Psa 1961-62, 2:294-302

81733 Lern- und Leistungsstörungen. Ein Beitrag zur Psychoanalyse der Arbeitsstörungen. [Learning and achievement disorders. A contribution to psychoanalysis of performance disorders.] Psyche 1967, 21:915-938

LUDWIG, ALFRED O.

81734 (& Murawski, B. J.; Sturgis, S. H.) Psychosomatic Aspects of Gynecological Disorders: Seven Psychoanalytic Case Studies. Cambridge, Mass: Harvard Univ Pr 1969, 119 p

LUDWIG, ARNOLD MYRON

81735 (& Levine, J.) Alterations in consciousness produced by hypnosis. JNMD 1965, 140:146-153

81736 Altered states of consciousness. Arch gen Psychiat 1966, 15:225-234

81737 (& Levine, J.) Hypnodelic therapy. Curr psychiat Ther 1967, 7:130-141

81738 The Importance of Lying. Springfield, Ill: Thomas 1965, xi + 238 p
81739 Relationship of attitude to behavior: preliminary results and implica-
       tions for treatment evaluation studies. In Shlien, J. M. et al: *Research
       in Psychotherapy, Vol. III,* Wash DC: APA 1968, 471-487
81740 (& Lyle, W. H., Jr.) Tension induction and the hyperalert trance. ASP
       1964, 69:70-76
81741 The trance. Comprehen Psychiat 1967, 8:7-15
81742 The weapons of insanity. PT 1967, 21:737-749
81743 Witchcraft today. Dis nerv Sys 1965, 26:288-291

       See Galvin, James A.

LUFT, H.

81744 [Transference psychoses. On delusional-hallucinatory crises in the
       course of psychotherapeutic treatments.] (Ger) Nervenarzt 1961, 32:
       199-210

LUIS GONZALEZ, JOSE

81745 (& Remus Araico, J.) Discussion of Zetzel, E. R. "The analytic situa-
       tion." Psa Amer 107-111

LUKENS, JOHN J.

81746 Selected comparisons of the use of denial in normal and mentally ill
       children. Diss Abstr 1967, 28(5-B):2143-2144

LUKIANOWICZ, N.

81747 "Body image" disturbances in psychiatric disorders. Brit J Psychiat
       1967, 113:31-47
81748 Case report: a rudimentary form of transvestism. PT 1962, 16:665-675
81749 Imaginary sexual partner. Visual masturbatory fantasies. Arch gen
       Psychiat 1960, 3:429-449
81750 Sexual drive and its gratification in schizophrenia. Int J soc Psychiat
       1963, 9:250-258
81751 Symbolical self-strangulation in a transvestite schizophrenic. Psychiat
       Q 1965, 39:244-257
81752 Transvestite episodes in acute schizophrenia. Psychiat Q 1962, 36:44-
       54

LUKOMSKII, I. I.

81753 [On psychoanalysis as a psychotherapeutic method.] (Rus) Zh Nevro-
       pat Psikhiat Korsakov 1966, 66:469-471

LUMBYE, J.

       See Spanheimer, L.

LUMERMANN, SILVIO

       See Granel, Julio A.; Liberman, David

LUMINET, DANIEL

81754 De la métapsychologie à la relation d'objet—essai de clinique psycho-somatique. [From metapsychology to object relations. Essay on psycho-somatic clinical medicine.] Évolut psychiat 1967, 32:657-701

81755 [On the psychophysiology of respiration.] (Fr) Acta Neurol Belg 1969, 69:123-172

See Goldfarb, S.

LUND, CURTIS J.

See Friederich, M. A.

LUNDE, DONALD T.

See Yalom, Irvin D.

LUNDSTEDT, S.

See Hallenbeck, Phyllis N.

LUNZER, E. A.

TRANSLATION OF:
(& Rapert, D.) Inhelder, B. & Piaget, J. [77491]

LUPTON, MARY JANE

81756 The dark dream of "dejection." Lit & Psych 1968, 18:39-47

LUQUET, PIERRE

81757 A propos de contre-transfert de l'integration secondaire de l'auto-analyse et de l'attention flottante. [Apropos of counter-transference in the secondary integration of auto-analysis and floating attention.] RFPsa 1963, 27(Suppl):177-184

S-52965 A propos des facteurs de guérison non verbalizables de la cure ana-lytique.
Abs HFM An Surv Psa 1957, 8:274-275

81758 [Analytic process and integrative impetus of the ego.] (Fr) RFPsa 1969, 33:973-980

81759 Art et fantasmes. [Art and fantasy.] RFPsa 1964, 28:581-589

81760 Compte rendu de XXIIe Congres de Psychanalystes de Langues Ro-manes. [Report of 22nd Congress of Romance-Language Psychoana-lysts.] RFPsa 1962, 26(Suppl): 3-4

81761 Discussion of Grunberger, B. "Considérations sur le clivage entre le narcissisme et la maturation pulsionelle." RFPsa 1962, 26:202

81762 Discussion of Hellman, I. et al "Analyse simultanée de la mére et de son enfant." RFPsa 1963, 27:638

81763 Discussion of Kestemberg, J. "A propos de la relation érotomanique." RFPsa 1962, 26:601

81764 Discussion of Mendel, G. "La sublimation artistique." RFPsa 1964, 28:781, 789-794

81765 Discussion of Viderman, S. "De l'instinct de mort." RFPsa 1961, 25:124-127

81766 Les identifications précoces dans la structuration et la restructuration du moi. RFPsa 1962, 26(Suppl):117-247, 304-315
Early identifications and structuration of the ego. (Read at Int Psa Cong, July-Aug 1963) J 1964, 45:263-271
Abs EVN Q 1966, 35:459-460

81767 Intégration et répression. [Integration and repression.] RFPsa 1966, 30:467-472

81768 Introduction sur le narcissisme secondaire. [Introduction to the discussion on secondary narcissism.] RFPsa 1965, 29:519-528

81769 Le mouvement oedipien du moi. [The oedipal movement of the ego.] RFPsa 1967, 31:841-852

81770 [On the newborn aggressive investment in the object relationship or organization of aggressiveness.] (Fr) RFPsa 1966, 30(Suppl):105-110

81771 Ouvertures sur l'artiste et le psychanalyste: la fonction esthétique du moi. [Approaches to the artist and the psychoanalyst: the esthetic function of the ego.] RFPsa 1963, 27:585-618

81772 [Preliminary remarks on metapsychology and thought structure.] (Fr) RFPsa 1969, 33:869-873

81773 Processus primaire et fonction onirique. [Primary process and dream function.] RFPsa 1963, 27(Suppl):365-371

LUQUET-PARAT, C.-J.

81775 A propos de quelques psychothérapies de névroses de caractère. [Apropos of various psychotherapies of character neuroses.] RFPsa 1968, 32:610-614

81776 Le changement à objet. [Changing the object.] In Chasseguet-Smirgel, J. Recherches Psychanalytiques Nouvelles sur la Sexualité Féminine, Paris: Payot 1964, 115-127
Rv Baranger, M. Rev urug Psa 1964, 6:514-517

81777 Discussion of Barande, R. "Essai métapsychologique sur le silence: de l'objet total phallique dans la clinique du silence." RFPsa 1963, 27: 103-106

81778 Discussion of Stein, C. "La castration comme négation de la fémininité." RFPsa 1961, 25:241

81779 Discussion of Viderman, S. "Le rapport sujet-objet et la problématique du désir." RFPsa 1968, 32:759-780

81780 Les identifications de l'analyste. [The analyst's identifications.] RFPsa 1962, 26(Suppl):289-292

81781 L'organisation oedipienne du stade génital. [Oedipal organization at the genital state.] RFPsa 1967, 31:743-911

81782 Réflexions sur le transfert homosexuel dans le cas particulier d'un homme analysé par une femme. [Reflections on homosexual transference in the case of a man analyzed by a woman.] RFPsa 1962, 26: 501-532
Abs Auth Rev Psicoanál 1963, 20:95. Perrotti, R. Riv Psa 1965, 11:80

81783 La structure obsessionelle. Problèmes techniques. [The obsessional structure. Technical problems.] RFPsa 1961, 25:309-317
Abs Auth Rev Psicoanál 1962, 19:283. RJA Q 1962, 31:432

LUQUET-PARAT, P.
See Lebovici, Serge

LURIA, ALEXANDER ROM

81784 The directive function of speech in development and dissolution, I:
Development of the directive function of speech in early childhood.
II: Dissolution of the regulative function of speech in pathology of the
brain. Word 1959, 15:341-352; 453-464. In Miller, E. *Foundations of
Child Psychiatry*, Oxford/NY: Pergamon Pr 1968, 273-282; 282-284
81785 An objective approach to the study of the abnormal child. Ops 1961,
31(1)
   Abs JMa RFPsa 1962, 26:322

LURIE, ABRAHAM

81786 The adolescent in the family. Soc Wk 1967, 12:104. In Nichtern, S.
Mental Health Services for Adolescents, Proceedings of the 2nd Hillside Hosp Conf, Frederick A. Praeger 1968, 197-208
81787 (et al) Alternate use of individual and group counseling with husbands
of psychiatric patients. J grp Psa Proc 1968-69, 1
81788 (& Pinsky, L.) Collaboration between psychiatric hospital and community agencies in the rehabilitation of mental patients. In Greenblatt,
M. et al: *Mental Patients in Transition*, Springfield, Ill: Thomas 1964,
163-174
81789 A critical review of principles of interdisciplinary practice. Canad ment
Hlth 1966, 14(5-6):3-9
81790 (et al) Resocialization of former psychiatric patients in a community
center. MH 1965, 49(2)
81791 (et al) Socialization of the ex-mental patient. J Jewish comm Serv 1964,
41(2)
81792 Summation. Ego-Psychology 1963, June 10-11:80-84

   See Berkowitz, Louis; Chwast, Jacob; Eisen, Arnold; Glasgow, Douglas

LÜSCHER, MAX

81793 Die Methode der strukurellen Funktionpsychologie. [The method of
structural functional psychology.] Heilpadag Werkbl 1962, 31(2):65-
69

LUSSHEIMER, PAUL

81794 The diagnosis of marital conflicts. Psa 1967, 27:127-131
81795 The growth of artistic creativity through the psychoanalytic process.
Psa 1963, 23:185-194. In Ruitenbeek, H. M. *The Creative Imagination*,
Chicago: Quadrangle Books 1965, 325-335
81796 Horney's heritage. Psa 1963, 23:3-4

LUSSIER, ANDRÉ
See Burlingham, Dorothy T.

LUSTER, HENRY H.

81797 (Participant) On regression: a workshop. (Held at West Coast Psa Soc, 14-16 Oct 1966) Psa Forum 1967, 2:293-316

LUSTIG, B.

81798 [On the peculiarities of psychiatric diagnosis and psychiatric patients in the Soviet Union.] (Ger) Bibl Psychiat Neurol 1967, 133:11-21

LUSTIG, NOEL

81799 (& Dresser, J. W.; Spellman, S. W.; Murray, T. B.) Incest: a family group survival pattern. Arch gen Psychiat 1966, 14:31-40
Abs PB Q 1968, 37:629-630

See Greenberg, Harvey R.; Greene, Bernard L.

LUSTIG, S.

See Rascovsky, Arnaldo

LUSTMAN, SEYMOUR L.

81800 Behavior disorders in childhood and adolescence. In Redlich, F. C. & Freedman, D. X. *The Theory and Practice of Psychiatry*, NY: Basic Books 1966, 676-704
81801 Defense, symptom, and character. Psa St C 1962, 17:216-224
Abs SLe RFPsa 1964, 28:813
81802 The economic point of view and defense. Psa St C 1968, 23:189-203
81803 Emotional problems of children as they relate to orthodontics. Amer J Orthodontics 1960, 46:358-362
81804 Impulse control, structure and the synthetic function. Psa—Gen Psychol 190-221
81805 Introduction to panel on the use of the economic viewpoint in clinical psychoanalysis. The economic point of view and defence. (Read at Int Psa Cong 1969) J 1969, 50:95-102
81806 The meaning and purpose of curriculum planning. (Read at Am Psa Ass, 6 Dec 1966) J Am Psa Ass 1967, 15:862-875
81807 Mental health research and the university: a position paper to the joint commission on mental health of children. Arch gen Psychiat 1969, 21:291-301
81808 (& Richmond, J.) On the acceptance of realistic goals in medicine. In Provence, S. A. et al: *Modern Perspectives in Child Development*, NY: IUP 1963, 558-574
S-52984 Psychic energy and mechanisms of defense.
Psychische Energie und Abwehrmechanismen. Psyche 1969, 23:170-183
Abs EMW An Surv Psa 1957, 8:203-205
S-52985 Rudiments of the ego.
Abs SGo An Surv Psa 1956, 7:98-99
81809 The scientific leadership of Anna Freud. J Am Psa Ass 1967, 15:810-827

81810   Some issues in contemporary psychoanalytic research. Psa St C 1963, 18:51-74
81811   Split custody, a clinical evaluation. In Goldstein, J. & Katz, J. *The Family and the Law,* NY: Free Pr 1965
81812   Structuralized delay and the synthetic function. (Read at Chicago Psa Soc, 15 Feb 1966)
        Abs Sadow, L. Bull Phila Ass Psa 1966, 16:226-229

LUTHE, R.

81813   ["Reactive experience in personality changes" as an idea of a given opinion on the right of indemnity.] (Ger) Nervenarzt 1968, 39:465-467

LUTHE, W.

81814   Autogenic neutralization: methods, theory and clinical application. Proc IV World Cong Psychiat 1966, 862
81815   Autogenic training: method, research and application in psychiatry. Dis nerv Sys 1962, 23:383-392
81816   Method, research and applications of autogenic training. Amer J clin Hyp 1962, 5:17-23

LUTHIER, J.

81817   [Paternal deprivation and delinquency in boys.] (Fr) Ann Med Leg, Paris 1967, 47:646-648

LUTZ, J.

81818   [Symbiotic infantile psychosis.] (Ger) Acta Paedopsychiatr, Basel 1969, 36:262-268
81819   Towards a better understanding of infantile autism as a disturbance of ego-consciousness, ego-activity and ego-imprint. Acta paedopsychiat 1968, 35:160-177

LUZA, SEGISFREDO

81820   Contribucion al estudio de la delusion y la conciencia del yo. [A study of delusions and consciousness of the ego.] Rev Psicopatol, Psicol med y Psicoter 1962, 1:137-145

LUZES, PEDRO

81821   Discussion of Roch, M. "Du surmoi, heritier du complexe d'oedipe." RFPsa 1967, 31:1076-1078
81822   (& Cabbabé, G.) L'hospitalisme psychiatrique vu à travers la psycho-thérapie pavillonnaire. [Psychiatric hospitalism as seen through "Pavillon" psychotherapy.] Hyg ment 1962, 51:273-282
81823   O inconsciente na criação artistica. [Unconscious factors in artistic creation.] J Med (Port) 1962, 48:751-758
81824   Neurose e normalidade na creança. [Neurosis and normality in the child.] Rev port Pediat Puericultura 1964, 27(11)
81825   Psicanálise das psicoses. [Psychoanalysis of psychoses.] J Med (Port) 1960, 43:811-816

81826 Psicanálise e psicoterapia das psicoses ditas endogenas. [Psychoanalysis and psychotherapy of so-called endogenous psychoses.] J Med (Port) 1966, 60:501-508

81827 Psicofármacos e psicoterapia no tratamento das neuroses. [Drugs and psychotherapy in the treatment of neuroses.] Bol Ordem Méd 1966

81828 Psicopatologia da homosexualidade masulina. [Psychopathology of masculine homosexuality.] J Med (Port) 1963, 50:693-697

81829 Les Troubles de la Pensée en Clinique Psychanalytique. [Difficulties of Thought in Clinical Psychoanalysis.] Paris: PUF 1968, 101 p

81830 Les troubles de la pensée en clinique psychanalytique. [Difficulties of thought in clinical psychoanalysis.] RFPsa 1969, 33:727-844

LUZURIAGA, ISABEL

81831 Función y disfunción de la inteligencia. [Function and dysfunction of intelligence.] Rev Psicoanál 1964, 21:38-57, 138-162
    Abs Vega Q 1965, 34:314

LWOFF, S.

See Ferdière, G.

LYDENBERG, JOHN

81832 Comment on Mr. Spilka's paper, "The Turn of the Screw." Lit & Psych 1964, 14:6-8

LYERLY, O. G.

See Weinstein, Edwin A.

LYKKEN, DAVID T.

See Lindzey, Gardner

LYLE, WILLIAM HENRY, JR.

See Ludwig, Arnold M.

LYMAN, MARGARET S.

See Chess, Stella

LYMAN, STANFORD M.

See Scott, Marvin B.

LYND, HELEN MERRELL

S-52994 On Shame and the Search for Identity.
    Rv Coltrera, J. T. J Am Psa Ass 1962, 10:166-215. Lichtenstein, H. J Am Psa Ass 1963, 11:173-223

LYNDON, BENJAMIN H.

81833 Social work: the contribution of a related profession to medical education. In Earley, L. W. et al: *Teaching Psychiatry in Medical School,* Wash DC: Am Psychiat Ass 1969, 416-424

LYNN, DAVID BRANDON

81834 Parental and Sex-Role Identification: A Theoretical Formulation. Berkeley, Calif: McCutchan 1969, vii + 131 p

LYNN, ROSALIE

81835 Personality characteristics of the mothers of aggressive and unaggressive children. J genet Psychol 1961, 99:159-164

LYON, WALDO B.

See Molish, H. B.

LYONS, IRWIN

See Fink, Paul Jay

LYONS, JOSEPH

81836 Existential psychotherapy: fact, hope, fiction. ASP 1961, 62:242-249
81837 The problem of existential inquiry. J existent Psychiat 1963-64, 4:141-150

LYRA, ALBERTO

81838 [Psychiatry and mysticism.] (Por) Arquivos do Departmento de Assistencia a Psicopatas do Estado de São Paulo 1962, 28:15-41
    Abs Vega Q 1965, 34:628

LYRA CHEBABI, WILSON DE

See CHEBABI, WILSON DE LYRA